Communications
in Computer and Information Science 346

Fu Lee Wang Jingsheng Lei
Rynson W.H. Lau Jingxin Zhang (Eds.)

Multimedia and Signal Processing

Second International Conference, CMSP 2012
Shanghai, China, December 7-9, 2012
Proceedings

 Springer

Volume Editors

Fu Lee Wang
Caritas Institute of Higher Education
18 Chui Ling Road, Tseung Kwan O, Hong Kong, China
E-mail: pwang@cihe.edu.hk

Jingsheng Lei
Shanghai University of Electric Power
School of Computer and Information Engineering
Shanghai 200090, China
E-mail: jshlei@shiep.edu.cn

Rynson W.H. Lau
City University of Hong Kong
Department of Computer Science
Tat Chee Avenue, Kowloon, Hong Kong, China
E-mail: rynson.lau@cityu.edu.hk

Jingxin Zhang
Monash University
Department of Electrical and Computer Systems Engineering
P.O. Box 35, Clayton, VIC 3800, Australia
E-mail: jingxin.zhang@eng.monash.edu.au

ISSN 1865-0929   e-ISSN 1865-0937
ISBN 978-3-642-35285-0   e-ISBN 978-3-642-35286-7
DOI 10.1007/978-3-642-35286-7
Springer Heidelberg Dordrecht London New York

Library of Congress Control Number: 2012952469

CR Subject Classification (1998): I.2.10, I.4, I.5, H.3.3, H.5.1, H.5.5

Typesetting: Camera-ready by author, data conversion by Scientific Publishing Services, Chennai, India

Printed on acid-free paper

Springer is part of Springer Science+Business Media (www.springer.com)

Preface

The 2012 International Conference on Multimedia and Signal Processing (CMSP 2012) was held in Shanghai, China during December 7–9, 2012. CMSP 2012 received 328 submissions from 10 countries and regions. After rigorous reviews, 79 high-quality papers were selected for publication in the CMSP 2012 proceedings. The acceptance rate was 24.08%.

The aim of CMSP 2012 was to bring together researchers working in many different areas of multimedia, image, video and signal processing to foster the exchange of new ideas and promote international collaboration. In addition to the large number of submitted papers, there were several internationally well-known keynote speakers.

On behalf of the Organizing Committee, we thank Shanghai University of Electric Power for its sponsorship and logistics support. We also thank the members of the Organizing Committee and the Program Committee for their hard work. We are very grateful to the keynote speakers, session chairs, reviewers, and student helpers. Last but not least, we thank all the authors and participants for the great contributions that made this conference possible.

December 2012

Jingsheng Lei
Fu Lee Wang
Rynson W. H. Lau
Jingxin Zhang

Organization

Organizing Committee

General Co-chairs

Hao Zhang   Shanghai University of Electric Power, China
Yunhao Liu   Tsinghua University, China

Program Committee Co-chairs

Rynson W. H. Lau   City University of Hong Kong, Hong Kong
Jingxin Zhang   Monash University, Australia

Steering Committee Chair

Jingsheng Lei   Shanghai University of Electric Power, China

Local Arrangement Co-chairs

Junjie Yang   Shanghai University of Electric Power, China
Haizhou Du   Shanghai University of Electric Power, China

Proceedings Co-chairs

Fu Lee Wang   Caritas Institute of Higher Education,
     Hong Kong
Ting Jin   Fudan University, China

Sponsorship Chair

Zhiyu Zhou   Zhejiang Sci-Tech University, China

Program Committee

George Baciu   Hong Kong Polytechnic University, Hong Kong
Jinannong Cao   Hong Kong Polytechnic University, Hong Kong
Li Chai   Central Queensland University, Australia
Antoni Chan   City University of Hong Kong, Hong Kong
Gary Chan   Hong Kong University of Science and
     Technology, Hong Kong
Min Chen   Swansea University, UK
Shu-Ching Chen   Florida International University, USA
Qi Cheng   Western Sydney University, Australia
Arjan Egges   University of Utrecht, The Netherlands

Jidong Wang	RMIT University, Australia
Song Wang	LaTrobe University, Australia
Raymond Wong	City University of Hong Kong, Hong Kong
Enhua Wu	University of Macau, Macau
Henry Wu	RMIT University, Australia
Yong Xiang	Deakin University, Australia
Nanfeng Xiao	Southeast University of Science and Technology, China
Ran Yan	Sun Yat Sen University, China
Xiaomei Yang	Sichuan University, China
Cha Zhang	Microsoft Research, USA
Cishen Zhang	Nanyang Technological University, Singapore
Jingxin Zhang	Monash University, Australia
Jiang Yu Zheng	IUPUI, USA

Table of Contents

Computer and Machine Vision

Feature Extraction

Image Enhancement and Noise Filtering

Image Retrieval

Image Segmentation

Imaging Techniques and 3D Imaging

Pattern Recognition

Multimedia Systems, Architecture, and Applications

Visualization

Signal Modeling, Identification and Prediction

Speech and Language Processing

Time-Frequency Signal Analysis

The Improved Partition Entropy Coefficient

Jian Mei Chen

School of Mechanical Engineering,
Hunan University of International Economics,
Changsha China, 410205
jianmeich@163.com

Abstract. This paper proposed an improved partition entropy coefficient (IPE) index by making using of the trend of partition entropy coefficient (PE) index to increase as the cluster number increases. Comparisons between IPE index and PE index and two existed cluster validity indexes are conducted on four real data sets. Experimental results show that IPE is able to identify the cluster number underlying the data set in the case that PE index is unable to do and outperforms the two existed cluster validity indexes.

Keywords: partition entropy coefficient, fuzzy c-means, cluster number.

1   Introduction

Bezdek proposed the partition entropy coefficient (PE) that measures the amount of overlap among clusters [1]. The range of values for PE is [0, logac], where c is the cluster number and a is the base of logarithm. The closer the value of PE, the harder the clustering is. On the other hand, the closer the value of PE to logac, the fuzzier the clustering is. Values close to logac indicate the absence of any clustering structure in X or the adopted clustering algorithm failed to unravel it [2].

A disadvantage of PE index is that it exhibits a dependence on c with a trend to increase, as c increases. Thus, when it is employed to identify the number of clusters, one has to seek significant knees for PE in the plot of the index PE versus c. Moreover, it is also sensitive to the fuzzifier m of fuzzy c-means clustering algorithm. It can be shown that as $m \rightarrow 1+$, PE tends to 0 for all c's, that is, it is unable to discriminate between different values of c. On the other hand, as $m \rightarrow +\infty$, PE tends to logac and exhibit the most significant knee at c=2 [3].

The above disadvantages of PE may result in multiple significant knees in the plot of PE versus c when PE does not increase strictly as c increases, and no significant knee in the plot of PE versus c when PE increases strictly as c increases. Thus, users are hard to determine the number of clusters in these cases. PE index is simple and easy to compute. If its disadvantages can be avoided, it may be a good cluster validity index for identifying the cluster number.

This paper devotes to overcoming PE's disadvantages by turning them into advantages. Experiments show that PE increase sharply as c increases when the base a of

F.L. Wang et al. (Eds.): CMSP 2012, CCIS 346, pp. 1–7, 2012.

logarithm grows bigger. Thus, the sensitivity of PE to the base a of logarithm can be utilized to turn PE index into a strict increasing function of c. when the cluster number grows from c to c+1 and c+1 to c+2, respectively, the differences PE(c)- PE(c+1) and PE(c+1)- PE(c+2) may be different. The differences may be an indicator of optimal number of clusters underlying a data set.

This paper is organized as follows. In the next section an improved PE index is proposed. Numerical experiments are given in section 3. Conclusions and discussions are given in section 4.

2   An Improved Partition Coefficient Index

Let $X = \{x_1, x_2, \cdots, x_N\}$ be a set of data in l-dimensional space. $U = (u_{ij})_{c \times N}$ represents the fuzzy partition matrix of X, where u_{ij} is the membership degree of data x_j in cluster I, c is the cluster number. The partition entropy coefficient is defined as

$$PE(c) = -\frac{1}{N}\sum_{i=1}^{c}\sum_{j=1}^{N}u_{ij}\log_a u_{ij} . \tag{1}$$

Supposing that $PE(c)$ is a increasing function respective to c. we define the difference of PE respective to c as

$$diff(c \to c-1) = \frac{PE(c) - PE(c-1)}{c - (c-1)} = PE(c) - PE(c-1) \tag{2}$$

The big value of $diff(c \to c-1)$ means that dividing X into c clusters is very different from dividing X into c-1 clusters, and it is more possible to divide X into c clusters than to divide X into c-1 clusters. Comparison between $diff(c+1 \to c)$ and $diff(c \to c-1)$ may give a hint of the optimal cluster number underlying X. If $diff(c \to c-1)$ is big and $diff(c+1 \to c)$ is small, dividing X into c clusters is very different from dividing X into c-1 clusters while dividing X into c+1 clusters is not different from dividing X into c clusters. That is, it is more possible to divide X into c clusters than to divide X into c-1 and c+1 clusters Thus, the difference between $diff(c \to c-1)$ and $diff(c+1 \to c)$ relative to the sum of $diff(c \to c-1)$ and $diff(c+1 \to c)$ may be an indicator of the optimal cluster number underlying X. Based on the above analysis, the improved PE index is defined as

$$IPE(c) = \frac{diff\left(c \to c-1\right) - diff\left(c+1 \to c\right)}{diff\left(c \to c-1\right) + diff\left(c+1 \to c\right)}$$

$$= \frac{2PE(c) - PE(c-1) - PE(c+1)}{PE(c+1) - PE(c-1)}$$

(3)

The big value of $IPE(c)$ may be resulted from big $diff\left(c \to c-1\right)$ and small $diff\left(c+1 \to c\right)$, so it is more possible to divide X into c clusters than to divide X into $c-1$ and c clusters. The optimal cluster number c_{opt} underlying X is obtained from

$$c_{opt} = \arg\max_{2 \leq c \leq c_{max}} \{IPE(c)\}$$

(4)

Where c_{max} is the maximum of cluster number.

The definition of $IPE(c)$ index is based on the assumption that $PE(c)$ index is the increasing function of c. In fact, $PE(c)$ index only exhibit a dependence on c with a trend to increase, as c increases. This does not ensure that $PE(c_1) \leq PE(c_2), c_1 < c_2$ always holds for any data set. The sensitivity of PE to the base a of logarithm implies that the adjustment of a may result in $PE(c_1) \leq PE(c_2), c_1 < c_2$ for a given data set. So we devise a scheme that automatically selects a's value so that PE becomes the increasing function respective to c. In the sequel, we describe an algorithm that employs $IPE(c)$ index and FCM [4] to determine the number of clusters underlying X.

Algorithm 1. The pseudo of the algorithm determining the optimal cluster number underlying X

```
a=1;
termination termℰ =1;
whileℰ ≠0
   a= a +1;
   for c=2:c_max
      FCM generates a fuzzy clusteringU(c)=(u_ij)_cxN of X;
      Compute the value of PE(c) index using U(c);
   End for
   Examine whether PE(c) is a increasing function of c. if
   it is true, ℰ =0;
End while
Compute IPE(c) using PE(1)=0, PE(2), ..., PE(c_max) for c=2,
3, ..., c_max-1;
The optimal cluster number is obtained from formula (4);
```

3   Experiments

In the following experiments FCM [4] is employed to partition the data set. The *Computational Protocols* for FCM is: convergence term $\varepsilon=0.0001$, maximum number of iterations=100, fuzzifier $m=2$. The initial cluster center of FCM is derived from the cluster center initialization method using k-d-tree [5]. Four real data sets, monks_1[6], splice[7], sonar [7], heart disease (cleverland) [6], are employed to test IPE. Algorithm 1 automatically determine $a=2$ for four data sets. The comparison between PE and IPE is conducted over four data sets. The comparative results are pictured in Fig.1-4, in which the red circle corresponds to the optimal cluster number identified by IPE. These figures show that for four data sets, IPE index correctly identifies the cluster number, while PE is unable to do. Because PE increases strictly as c increases when $a=2$ and no significant knee indicates the optimal cluster number. We also compare IPE with other two indexes, fpbm [8] and xb [9] over the real data sets whose attributes are listed in Table 1. Comparative results in Table 1 show that IPE outperforms fpbm [8] and xb [9] in the experiments, for both fpbm [8] and xb [9] fail to identify the cluster number for four data sets while IPE succeeds to do.

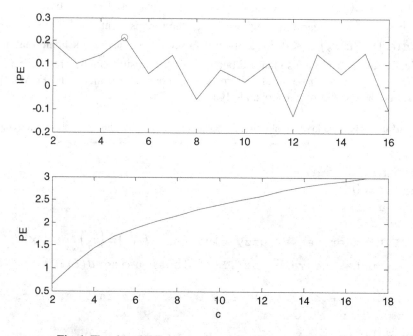

Fig. 1. The plot of IPE versus c over heart disease (cleverland)

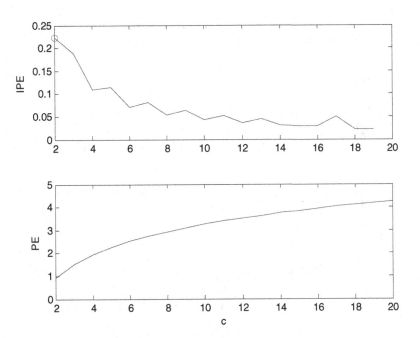

Fig. 2. The plot of IPE versus c over monks_1

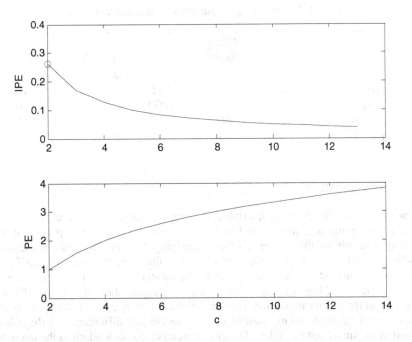

Fig. 3. The plot of IPE versus c over sonar

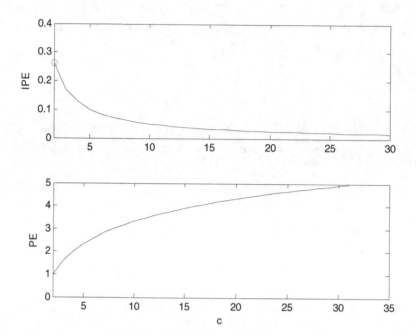

Fig. 4. The plot of IPE versus c over splice

Table 1. The attributes of data sets and comparative results

Data set	c	attributes dimension	size	IPE a=2	fpbm	xb
monks_1	2	6	432	2	3	17
splice	2	60	1000	2	2	30
sonar	2	60	208	2	10	9
heart disease	5	13	303	5	11	15

4   Conclusions

PE index has two disadvantages, exhibiting a trend to increase as the cluster number increases and being sensitive to the base a of logarithm function, that prevent it from correctly determining the cluster number underlying the data set. Making use of the sensitivity of PE index to the base a of logarithm function, PE index is transformed into a strictly increasing function respect to the cluster number by automatically adjusting the base a of logarithm function. Then we compute the difference of PE index respective to the cluster number c. The ratio of the difference between two successive differences of PE index to the sum of the two successive differences of PE index is defined as the improved PE index. The cluster number corresponding to the maximum value of IPE indicates the optimal cluster number. Experiments on four real data sets show that IPE is preferable to PE index and two existed cluster validity indexes.

Acknowledgement. This work is supported by the programs granted by 2010-9115 and 2011-76.

References

1. Bezdek, J.C.: Mathematical models for systematics and taxonomy. In: Proceedings 8th International Conference in Numerical Taxonomy, pp. 143–166. Freeman, San Francisco (1975)
2. Pal, N.R., Bezdek, J.C.: on cluster validity for the fuzzy c-means model. IEEE Transactions on Fuzzy Systems 3(3), 370–379 (1995)
3. Theodoridis, S., Koutroumbas, K.: Pattern recognition, 4th edn., p. 888. China Machine Press, Beijing
4. Bezdek, C.: Pattern Recognition with Fuzzy Objective Function Algorithms. Plenum Press, New York (1981)
5. Redmond, S.J., Heneghan, C.: A method for initializing the K-means clustering algorithm using kd-trees. Recognition Letters 28, 965–973 (2007)
6. The UCI Machine Learning Repository (1993),
   http://www.ics.uci.edu/~mlearn/MLRepository.html
7. Chang, C.-C., Lin, C.-J.: LIBSVM: a library for support vector machines (2001),
   http://www.csie.ntu.edu.tw/~cjlin/libsvm
8. Pakhira, M., Bandyopadhyay, S., Maulik, U.: Validity index for crisp and fuzzy clusters. Pattern Recognit. 37(3), 487–501 (2004)
9. Xie, X.L., Beni, G.: A validity measure for fuzzy partition. IEEE Trans. Pattern Anal. Mach. Intell. 13, 841–847 (1991)

A Multi-features Based Particle Filtering Algorithm for Robust and Efficient Object Tracking

Shuang Ye[1,3], Yanguo Zhao[1], Feng Zheng[1], and Zhan Song[1,2]

[1] Shenzhen Institutes of Advanced Technology,
Chinese Academy of Sciences, China
[2] The Chinese University of Hong Kong, Hong Kong, China
[3] Wuhan University of Technology, Wuhan, China
{shuang.ye,yg.zhao,feng.zheng,zhan.song}@siat.ac.cn

Abstract. This works presents a novel approach for robust and efficient object tracking. To make the feature representation more robust, color and the local binary pattern features are fused via a proposed scheme. The partial filter is used for the feature tracking. To improve its efficiency, a mean shift based method is introduced to decrease the required partials so as to decrease the computation cost. With the robust multi-features description and boosted partial filter algorithm, satisfied tracking results can be obtained via the experiments with different datasets, and showed distinct improvements in both tracking robustness and efficiency.

Keywords: object tracking, multi-features, mean-shift, particle filter.

1   Introduction

Object tracking has been an important research issue in computer vision domain. Current tracking algorithms can be generally divided into two categories according to Ref. 1: the certainty method and the random method. The former tracks the target by looking for the optimal matching target, such as the mean-shift (MS) algorithm [2] .The later tracks the target via state estimation, such as the particle filter (PF) algorithm [3]

Various image features have been used for the target representation and tracking. However, the tracking via sole feature is usually lack of robustness subject the complicate background and scenarios. Much of recent methods have focused on the fusion of multiple image features. [4-12] In Ref. 4, a PF-based method combined with multiple image cues is proposed for the object tracking, but its efficiency still needs improvement for real-time application. In Ref. 7, a geometric particle filter algorithm is presented based on the affine group with optimal importance functions. In Ref. 12, a new approach combined with MS of regional color distribution and the PF algorithms is introduced for the efficient object tracking.

In this paper, a multi-features based approach for the efficient and robust object tracking is presented. The color and local binary pattern (LBP) features are adopted

F.L. Wang et al. (Eds.): CMSP 2012, CCIS 346, pp. 8–15, 2012.
© Springer-Verlag Berlin Heidelberg 2012

and fused for the robust feature representation. And then, the traditional partial filter method is improved by the introduction of mean shift method to boost its efficiency. The combined tracking algorithm utilizes advantages of the two algorithms and shows distinct improvements in both robustness and efficiency via extensive experiments and comparisons.

The paper is organized as follows. Section 2 presents the fusing scheme of color and LBP features. Section 3 introduces how the mean shift method is used to improve the efficiency of the traditional partial filter method. Experiments are given in Section 4 and the conclusion is offered in Section 5.

2 The Fusion of Color and LBP Features

Let $\{x_i\ i=1,...,n\}$ be the normalized pixel location in the target region centered at 0, n is the pixel number, $b(x_i)$ associates the pixel x_i to the histogram bin. By diving the feature space into m subspace, the target model and the probability of the feature $u=1,...,m$ in the target area can be expressed as:

$$q = \{q_u\}_{u=1,...,m} \quad q_u = C\sum_{i=1}^{n} k\left(\|x_i\|^2\right)\delta[b(x_i)-u] \tag{1}$$

where $k(.)$ is the kernel profile, δ is the Kronecker delta function. C is norm-aliz ed coefficient defined as $C = 1/\sum_{i=1}^{n} k(\|x_i\|^2)$.

Similarly, let $\{x_i,\ i=1,...,n_h\}$ denote the pixel positions in the candidate region centered at y in the current frame, the target candidate model $p(y)$ can be defined as:

$$p(y) = \{p_u(y)\}_{u=1...m} \quad p_u(y) = C_h\sum_{i=1}^{n_h} k(\|(y-x_i)/h\|^2)\delta\left[b(x_i)-u\right] \tag{2}$$

Where $p_u(y)$ is the feature $u=1,...,m$ in the target candidate area, C_h is a normalized coefficient defined as $C_h = 1/\sum_{i=1}^{n_h} k(\|(y-x_i)/h\|^2)$, h is the bandwidth defines the scales of the target candidate.

The image is firstly transformed from the RGB space to HSV space. The $b(x_i)$ is represented as $C(x_i)$ in HSV space, and the histograms of HSV channels are divided into 8×8×4 bins according to Eqn.(2), then we obtain the color model.

To ensure the model to be adaptive to illumination changes, the feature of texture is represented via the well-known LBP operator, which is defined as follows:

$$LBP_{P,R}(y) = \sum_{i=1}^{P-1} s(g_p - g_c)2^i \tag{3}$$

where R is the distance between the central pixel x_i and its neighbors, P is the number of neighboring pixels, g_c is the intensity of centeral point y, g_p is the intensity of P which distributed equally on the circle with radius of R. $s(x)$ is a two-valued function, which is equal to 1 if $x>0$. Since $s(.)$ is only related to the relative pixel intensity, LBP is robust to illumination changes.

By varying P and R, we have LBP operators under different quantization of the angular space and spatial resolution and multi-resolution analysis can be accomplished by using multiple $LBP_{P,\ R}$ operators. In this work, as shown in Fig. 1, we choose the $LBP_{8,\ 1}$. $b(x_i)$ is represented as $LBP\ (x_i)$ in LBP, we obtain the LBP model according to Eqn. (2), the LBP histograms in target area are divided into $2^7=128$ bins. The LBP image is obtained by $LBP_{8,\ 1}$ as shown in Fig.2.

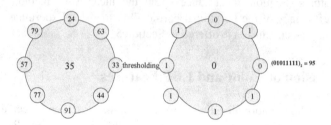

Fig. 1. Illustration of LBP8, 1

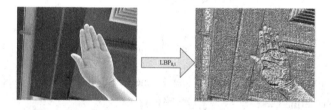

Fig. 2. The LBP image processed with $LBP_{8,\ 1}$.

The tracking procedure is performed via two stages. Fuse the color and LBP features to get the weights in the PF and MS algorithm, and integration of MS and PF to prevent degeneracy problem and reduce the required number of particles. With respect to the two stages, how to fuse the two image features are depicted as follows.

Treated as the observation information, the Bhattacharyya distance between target and candidate region histograms d_c^i and d_l^i can be calculated by $d = \sqrt{1 - \rho(y)}$ with the Bhattacharyya coefficient $\rho(y) \equiv \rho[p(y), q] = \sum_{i=1}^{m} \sqrt{p_u(y) q_u}$. Given the variance of Gaussian distribution σ, define $w_c^i = \exp(-(d_c^i)^2 / 2\sigma^2) / \sigma\sqrt{2\pi}$ as the weights extracted from color information, and $w_l^i = \exp(-(d_l^i)^2 / 2\sigma^2) / \sigma\sqrt{2\pi}$ as the weights extracted from LBP. And denote the likelihood measurement $p(Z_k \mid X_k^i)$ as the weights of particles in PF. In the PF algorithm, we fuse the color and LBP information to get the particle weights by multiplying the weights:

$$w^i = w_c^i w_l^i = \exp\{-\frac{(d_l^i)^2 + (d_c^i)^2}{2\sigma^2}\} / 2\pi\sigma^2 \qquad (5)$$

Further iterative optimization by MS is necessary to prevent degeneracy problem and reduce the required number of particles, we compute the weights of pixels in target area λ_i by additive fusion in MS stage.

$$\lambda_i = \alpha\lambda_c^i + (1-\alpha)\lambda_l^i \tag{6}$$

Where λ_c^i is the weights extracted from color information, λ_l^i is the weights extracted from LBP according to following equation, λ^i is obtained by Taylor expansion around the values $p_u(y_0)$. For more information about MS, please refer to Ref. 2.

$$\lambda^i = \sum_{i=1}^{m} \delta[b(x_i) - u]\sqrt{q_u/p_u(y_0)} \tag{7}$$

α is a balancing variable, which can be set to 0.5 empirically. The feature fusion procedure can be depicted as Fig. 3.

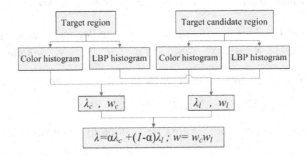

Fig. 3. Fusion procedure of color and LBP features

3 Tracking Algorithm Based on the Multi-features

The main idea of the PF is an infinite approximation of the *pdf*(posterior probability density function)of the system state with a set of weighted particles that sampled from the importance density function q (.).The major limit of PF is the limited capability of the weighted particles which describe the *pdf* when the state space is not densely sampled. To overcome this problem, a large number of particles is required thus increasing the computational load. For more information about PF, please refer to Ref. 3. MS algorithm can find the most similar region to the target in the new frame, but if the center of the object shifts more than the kernel size in two consecutive frames or there is an occlusion, the tracking is likely failed. How to overcome the defects of MS and PF and inherit their advantages is a key problem.

Based on the fused image features, a combined tracking algorithm is also introduced in this work. Firstly N_p particles are sampled from q (.) by PF algorithm. Secondly, N_m particles near the possible position that calibrated by MS are randomly sampled. They effectively utilize the observation information of the target, keep the diversity of particles thus reduce the required number of particles, in addition, the N_p

particles restrain the defects that MS is easy to fall into local optimum. Thirdly, both the N_p particles and N_m particles are updated by PF and we obtain the state output of the N_p particles and N_m particles. And then, likelihood in the state output of N_m and N_p particles are calculated. If the likelihood in the state output of N_m particles is larger than the N_p particles, remove N_m particles in the N_p particles and add the N_m optimized particles by MS method and we obtain new N_p particles. Otherwise, remain the primary N_p particles. Finally, the final position of target with new N_p particles can be computed. Details about the tracking procedure can be depicted as follows.

1) *Initialization*
   a) *Extract the color and LBP template at frame $k=0$, and calculate the LBP and color histograms of the target model;*
   b) *Set N_p as the particles number that sampled from $q(.)$ in PF stage, N_m as the particles number that sampled in MS stage, N_{thr} as the resample threshold;*
   c) *Sample the initial particles $S=\{ X_0^i, i=1.... N_p \}$ from the prior probability density function. Particles weights are set as $1/N_p$, let $k=1$.*

2) *Sampling*
   In PF stage: Load the next frame, transfer particles of last time by target State transition model $X_k = f(X_{k-1}) + u_{k-1}$. For $i = 1,..., N_p$, sample the particles $\{ X_k^i, i=1...N_p \}$ at time k from $q(.) = p(X_k^i \mid X_{k-1}^i)$, then the particles set is updated to be $S_p = \{ X_{0:k}^i \} = \{ X_k^i, X_{0:k-1}^i \mid i = 1,..., N_p \}$.

   In MS stage: Search the target possible position by MS and calibrate it by back projection to a new position $y_1 = \sum_{i=1}^{n_h} g(\|(y - x_i)/h\|^2)\lambda_i x_i / \sum_{i=1}^{n_h} g(\|(y - x_i)/h\|^2)\lambda_i$

   according to Ref. 2, the weights λ_i is calculated by additive fusion according to Eqn. (6). Randomly sample N_m particles near the new position as the PF stage do, the particles set is $S_m = \{ X_{0:k}^i \} = \{ X_k^i, X_{0:k-1}^i \mid i = 1,..., N_m \}$.

3) *Weight update*
   While a measurement Z_k is available, extract color and LBP features, calculate observation likelihood function w_c^i and w_l^i. w_k^i is obtained by multiplying the weights extracted in color and LBP according to Eqn. (5). The weights of N_m particles S_m and N_p particles S_p are updated to:
   $$w_k^i \propto w_{k-1}^i p(Z_k \mid X_k^i) \quad i \in N_m \text{ or } N_p \tag{8}$$
   After normalization, the weights of particle set S_m and S_p can be calculated as:
   $$\tilde{w}_k^i = w_k^i / \sum_{i=1}^{N_m} w_k^i, \quad \tilde{w}_k^i = w_k^i / \sum_{i=1}^{N_p} w_k^i \tag{9}$$

4) *State output*
   State estimation of two particle set S_p and S_m can be calculated as:

$$\tilde{X}_p \approx \sum_{i=1}^{N_p} \tilde{w}_k^i X_k^i, \quad \tilde{X}_m \approx \sum_{i=1}^{N_m} \tilde{w}_k^i X_k^i \tag{10}$$

The Bhattacharyya likelihood between target candidate position $\tilde{X}_p$, $\tilde{X}_m$ and the target position can be calculated. If the likelihood in $\tilde{X}_m$ is larger than $\tilde{X}_p$, randomly remove the low-ranking N_m particles in the N_p particles and add the N_m particles to the N_p particles. Otherwise remain the primary N_p particles.

5) *Resample*

Compute an estimate of the effective number of particles as N_{eff}

$$N_{eff} = 1/\sum_{i=1}^{N_p} (w_k^i)^2 \tag{11}$$

If $N_{eff} < N_{thr}$, copy the particles with large weight and remove the particles with small weight.

Let $w_k^i = 1/N_p$, $i=1... N_p$, we can obtain the new particles set { $X_k^{j^*}$, w_k^i, $j=1....N_p$} as the initial particles at time $k+1$, and then go back to step 2).

4   Experiment Results

The experiments are conducted on three video clips, *face.avi*, *hand.avi*, and *soccer.avi*. The former two videos are captured via a normal USB webcam at 25fps with the resolution of 240×320 pixels. The last one is downloaded from public database with the resolution of 480×360 pixels. The algorithms are implemented with OpenCv2.0 and vs. 2008 on a desktop with 2G RAM and Core2 2.4GHz CPU. The MS algorithm from Ref. 2, and the PF algorithm from Ref. 3 are used for the comparison.

To compare the efficiency, the traditional PF method can achieve a running speed of 75fps on the face and hand datasets. In comparison, the proposed method is more efficient with a speed of 125fps. Since the particle number of 100 is required by PF, only 70 particles are needed in the proposed method.

Fig. 4(a) shows the tracking results under illumination changing. The 1st row shows the results by our method, the 2nd and 3rd rows are the results by MS and PF algorithms respectively. As the result shows, when illumination suddenly changed from bright to dim, the proposed algorithm can still locate the eyes precisely. But the MS and PF algorithms are seriously affected. It strong robustness to illumination change mainly comes from the use of LBP feature in the proposed algorithm.

Fig. 4(b) evaluates the performance of different algorithms with occlusions. The 1st row shows the result by the proposed algorithm, and the 2nd and 3rd rows show the results by PF and MS algorithms respectively. When a partial of the hand is occluded, the PF and our method still work but the MS algorithm failed. When occlusion is seriously, both PF and MS algorithms loss the tracking target.

The dataset of *soccer.avi* is used to evaluate the performance of different algorithms under the target with continuous and huge appearance change. The tracking results on the frame 23, 96, 120, 132, 165, 235, 278 are given for comparison. As time going on, the degradation of particles is seriously by PF method. As shown in Fig. 5, the 1st row shows the tracking result by the proposed method in different frames, and the results by MS and PF algorithms are displayed in the 2nd and 3rd rows. When it goes to 835th frame, there is serious deviation by the method of PF. However, the proposed tracking method still works well, since it can effectively utilize the observation information of the target in current frame. And thus, it can keep the diversity of particles and treat well with the degeneracy problem.

(a)   (b)

Fig. 4. Tracking results by the proposed algorithm (1st row), MS (2nd row) and PF (3rd row) methods. (a) Tracking of eyes on the dataset of *face.avi*; (b) Tracking of hand with conclusion on the dataset of *hand.avi*.

Fig. 5. Experiment with the dataset of *soccer.avi*, the tracking results by the proposed, MS, and PF are illustrated in 1st, 2nd, and 3rd row respectively

5   Conclusions

This study presents a fused approach for the efficient and robust object tracking. To represent the target more robust, both color and LBP features are adopted. To improve the tracking efficiency, the mean shift method is introduced to boost the performance of traditional particle filter algorithm. MS preserves the diversity of particles and reduce the required number of particles, the particle filter restrains the defects local optimum. Experiments with several datasets with illumination change, occlusion and appearance change demonstrate the improvements by the proposed algorithm in both robustness and efficiency.

Acknowledgments. This work was supported in part by the National Natural Science Foundation of China (NSFC, grant no. 61002040), NSFC-GuangDong (grant no. 10171782619-2000007), and the Introduced Innovative R&D Team of Guangdong Province-Robot and Intelligent Information Technology R&D Team.

References

1. Yilmaz, A., Javed, O., Shah, M.: Object tracking: A survey. ACM Journal of Computing Surveys 38, 13–57 (2006)
2. Comaniciu, D., Ramesh, V., Meer, P.: Kernel-based object tracking. IEEE Transactions on Pattern Analysis and Machine Intelligence 25, 564–577 (2003)
3. Isard, M., Blake, A.: Condensation—Conditional Density Propagation for Visual Tracking. International Journal on Computer Vision 25, 5–28 (1998)
4. Brasnett, P., Mihaylova, L., Bull, D., Canagarajah, N.: Particle Filtering with Multiple Cues for Object Tracking in Video Sequences. Image and Vision Computing 25, 1217–1227 (2007)
5. Hui, T., Yiqin, C., Tingzhi, S.: Face Tracking using Multiple Facial Features based on Particle Filter. In: 2nd International Asia Conference on Informatics in Control, Automation and Robotics, vol. 3, pp. 72–75. Elsevier, Wuhan (2010)
6. Tang, S.L., Kadim, Z., Liang, K.M., Lim, M.K.: Hybrid Blob and Particle Filter Tracking Approach for Robust Object Tracking. In: International Conference on Computational Science, vol. 1, pp. 2549–2557. Elsevier, Wuhan (2010)
7. Kwon, J., Lee, K.M., Park, F.C.: Visual tracking via geometric particle filtering on the affine group with optimal importance functions. In: International Conference on Computer Vision and Pattern Recognition, pp. 991–998. IEEE Press, Miami (2009)
8. Kwon, J., Lee, K.M.: Visual tracking decomposition. In: International Conference on Computer Vision and Pattern Recognition, pp. 1269–1276. IEEE Press, San Francisco (2010)
9. Comaniciu, D., Ramesh, V., Meer, P.: Real-time tracking of non-rigid objects using mean-shift. In: International Conference on Computer Vision and Pattern Recognition, vol. 2, pp. 142–149. IEEE Press, Hilton Head Island (2000)
10. Fang, J., Yang, J., Liu, H.: Efficient and robust fragments-based multiple kernels tracking. International Journal of Electronics and Communications 65, 915–923 (2011)
11. Leichter, I., Lindenbaum, M., Rivlin, E.: A probabilistic framework for combining tracking algorithms. In: International Conference on Computer Vision and Pattern Recognition, vol. 2, pp. 445–451. IEEE Press, Washington (2004)
12. Deguchi, K., Kawanaka, O., Okatani, T.: Object tracking by the mean-shift of regional color distribution combined with the particle-filter algorithms. In: International Conference on Pattern Recognition, vol. 3, pp. 506–509. IEEE Press, Cambridge (2004)

Locality Preserving Kernel Hybrid Discriminate Analysis for Dimensional Reduction

Shijin Ren[1,*], Xiaoping Liu[2], Maoyun Yang[1,2], and Guiyun Xu[2]

[1] School of Computer Science & Technology,
Jiangsu Normal University, Xuzhou, Jiangsu 221116, China
{sjren_phd,ymaoyun}@163.com
[2] School of Mechanical and Electrical Engineering,
CUMT, Xuzhou, Jiangsu 221116, China
lxpgzk@sina.com, xuguiy@163.com

Abstract. Hybrid discriminant analysis (HDA) combining principal component analysis (PCA) with linear discriminant analysis (LDA) can achieve better performance for samples following complex distribution. However, HDA can not work well for complex and nonlinear distributed data. As a result, a locality preserving HAD (LPKHDA) algorithm is proposed by combining the kernel method with manifold learning, overcoming the shortcomings of manifold learning and kernel methods. According to kernel-induced selection criterion, the optimal kernel parameter of LPKHDA can be achieved efficiently through gradient method and a boosted LPKHDA algorithm based on Adaboost idea is implemented. Extensive experiments are conducted to evaluate the proposed algorithm.

Keywords: Locality preserving, kernel hybrid discriminant analysis, manifold learning, model selection, kernel-induced space, dimensional reduction.

1   Introduction

Over the past decades, many dimensional reduction methods, such as principal component analysis (PCA), linear discriminant analysis (LDA), are applied in many fields [1-4]. However, PCA might outperform LDA for small sample size (SSS) problem [3,5], while LDA outperforms PCA in supervised learning. It is necessary to integrate PCA and LDA into a unified framework. The proposed methods include PCA+KFDA[6],PCA+LDA[7], hybrid discriminant analysis(HDA) etc [8]. HDA can extract global and discriminant   features from data set, outperforming PCA, LDA and PCA+LDA[8]. However, HDA model parameters are difficult to be estimated in practice and may fail to discover more complex and nonlinear relationship that exists in the data. Both PCA and LDA are not applicable for non-uniformly distributed or imbalanced data since they have a huge tendency to cluster dominant data set rather than the small samples.

---

* Corresponding author.

F.L. Wang et al. (Eds.): CMSP 2012, CCIS 346, pp. 16–23, 2012.

Manifold learning is a promising technique for nonlinear dimension reduction. It can discover intrinsic geometrical structure embedded in low-dimension space, which can reflect the inherent structure of the high-dimensional original data and preserve the useful information as much as possible [9]. The geometrically motivated manifold learning has been paid much attention and proved to be a powerful nonlinear dimensionality reduction tool. The other approach is kernel-based methods (like KPCA) can not explicitly uncover the manifold structure of data and don't take the local structure into account [10]. Furthermore, in many applications, the mapped data in feature space may not be linearly separable and the optimal kernel parameter could not easily be determined. However, more comprehensive kernel function inevitably results to reduce the performance of the model [11].

Considering the above discussion, a locality preserving HAD (LPKHDA) algorithm in kernel-induced space is presented. Firstly, the input data is mapped into high dimensional feature space, HDA is built in this space. Secondly, we incorporate manifold learning into KHDA to discover local manifold structure. Finally, the optimal kernel parameter of LPKHDA is achieved efficiently through gradient optimization method in term of model selection criterion in the kernel-induced space. In simulation, we implement a boosted LPKHDA algorithm.

The rest of this paper is organized as follows. In section 2, KHDA algorithm is deduced. LPKHDA is derived by incorporating locality preserving into KHDA in Section 3. Section 4 gives kernel-induced space-based model selection.The experimental results are given in Section5. In Section 6, the conclusions and the future work are discussed.

2   KHDA

HDA integrating PCA and LDA in a unified framework is formulated as [9]

$$J(\mathbf{w}) = \arg\max_{\mathbf{w}} \left| \mathbf{w}^T \left[(1-\lambda)\mathbf{S}_B + \lambda\mathbf{S}_\Sigma \right] \mathbf{w} \right| / \left| \mathbf{w}^T \left[(1-\lambda)\mathbf{S}_w + \eta\mathbf{I} \right] \mathbf{w} \right| \qquad (1)$$

where $\mathbf{S}_w, \mathbf{S}_B$ are within-class and between-class scatter matrices respectively , λ is weighted parameter, η is regularization that deal with the singularity issue of $\mathbf{S}_w$, $\lambda, \eta \in [0,1]$, $\mathbf{S}_\Sigma$ is total scatter matrix, $\mathbf{I}$ is $N \times N$ identity matrix. With different values of (λ, η), Eq.(1) provides a rich set of alternatives to PCA and LDA. As a result, HDA can keep a balance between clustering and separating, effectively overcoming issues resulting from non-uniform distribution and imbalanced data sets.

Aiming at the data with complex and nonlinear characteristics, we extend HDA to KHDA through kernel trick. Assume a matrix $\mathbf{X} = [\mathbf{x}_1, \mathbf{x}_2, \cdots, \mathbf{x}_N] \in \mathbb{R}^{d \times N}$ composes of C class data sets, where $\mathbf{x}_i \in \mathbb{R}^d$ is a sample. Let $\mathbf{x}_i^{(l)}$ and ω_l be class label of l_{th} class data, $i = 1, 2, \cdots, N$, $\mathbf{m}_l$ and N_l denote means and the number of samples which share the same class label $\omega_l, l = 1, 2, \cdots, C$, $\sum_{l=1}^{C} N_l = N$.

Given a nonlinear map $\phi(\cdot): R^d \rightarrow R^{n_F}$, the input data is mapped into high dimensional space and the condition $k(\mathbf{x}_i, \mathbf{x}_j) = \phi(\mathbf{x}_i)^T \phi(\mathbf{x}_j)$ holds, The matrices are defined as $\boldsymbol{\Phi}_b = \left(1/\sqrt{N}\right)\left[\sqrt{n_1}\left(\mathbf{m}_\phi^{(1)T} - \mathbf{m}_\phi^T\right); \cdots; \sqrt{n_C}\left(\mathbf{m}_\phi^{(C)T} - \mathbf{m}_\phi^T\right)\right]$,

$\boldsymbol{\Phi}_w = \left[\boldsymbol{\Phi}^{(1)}; \boldsymbol{\Phi}^{(2)}; \cdots; \boldsymbol{\Phi}^{(C)}\right]$, $\boldsymbol{\Phi}_t = \left(1/\sqrt{N}\right)\left[\phi(\mathbf{x}_1)^T - \boldsymbol{\mu}_\phi^T; \cdots; \phi(\mathbf{x}_N)^T - \boldsymbol{\mu}_\phi^T\right]$,

$\boldsymbol{\Phi}^{(l)} = \left(1/\sqrt{N}\right)\left[\phi(\mathbf{x}_1^{(l)})^T - \boldsymbol{\mu}_\phi^{(l)T}; \cdots; \phi(\mathbf{x}_{n_l}^{(l)})^T - \boldsymbol{\mu}_\phi^{(l)T}\right]$,where $\boldsymbol{\mu}_\phi^{(l)} = (1/n_l)\sum_{i=1}^{n_l} \phi(\mathbf{x}_i^{(l)})$,

$\boldsymbol{\mu}_\phi = (1/N)\sum_{i=1}^N \phi(\mathbf{x}_i)$. Let $\mathbf{S}_t^\phi$, $\mathbf{S}_b^\phi$ and $\mathbf{S}_w^\phi$ be total, between-class and within-class scatter matrices for the mapped data points, these matrices are given as $\mathbf{S}_t^\phi = \boldsymbol{\Phi}_t^T \boldsymbol{\Phi}_t$, $\mathbf{S}_b^\phi = \boldsymbol{\Phi}_b^T \boldsymbol{\Phi}_b$, $\mathbf{S}_w^\phi = \boldsymbol{\Phi}_w^T \boldsymbol{\Phi}_w$ and $rank\left(\mathbf{S}_t^\phi\right) = rank\left(\mathbf{S}_b^\phi\right) + rank\left(\mathbf{S}_w^\phi\right)$, $\mathbf{S}_t^\phi = \mathbf{S}_b^\phi + \mathbf{S}_w^\phi$ .The optimization problem of KHDA can be written as

$$J\left(\mathbf{w}_\phi\right) = \arg\max_{\mathbf{w}_\phi} \mathbf{w}_\phi^T\left[(1-\lambda)\boldsymbol{\Phi}_b^T\boldsymbol{\Phi}_b + \lambda\boldsymbol{\Phi}_t^T\boldsymbol{\Phi}_t\right]\mathbf{w}_\phi \Big/ \left(\mathbf{w}_\phi^T\left((1-\lambda)\boldsymbol{\Phi}_w^T\boldsymbol{\Phi}_w + \eta\mathbf{I}\right)\mathbf{w}_\phi\right) \quad (2)$$

Assume $\mathbf{w}_\phi$ lies in span of the data points, i.e. $\mathbf{w}_\phi = \boldsymbol{\Phi}_t^T\boldsymbol{\beta}$, the optimization problem shown in Eq. (2) gives rise to

$$J(\boldsymbol{\beta}) = \arg\max_{\boldsymbol{\beta}} \boldsymbol{\beta}^T\left[(1-\lambda)\boldsymbol{\Omega}_b^T\boldsymbol{\Omega}_b + \lambda\boldsymbol{\Omega}_t^T\boldsymbol{\Omega}_t\right]\boldsymbol{\beta} \Big/ \left(\boldsymbol{\beta}^T\left((1-\lambda)\boldsymbol{\Omega}_w^T\boldsymbol{\Omega}_w + \eta\boldsymbol{\Omega}_t\right)\boldsymbol{\beta}\right) \quad (3)$$

Where, $\boldsymbol{\Omega}_t = \mathbf{P}\left[k(\mathbf{x}_i, \mathbf{x}_j)\right]_{i,j=1}^N \mathbf{P}^T$, $\mathbf{P} = \mathbf{I}_N - (1/N)\mathbf{1}_N\mathbf{1}_N^T$, $\mathbf{I}_N$ is $N \times N$ identity matrix, $\mathbf{1}_N^T$ is $1 \times N$ vector of ones, the definitions of $\boldsymbol{\Omega}_b, \boldsymbol{\Omega}_w$ are similar to $\boldsymbol{\Omega}_t$. The solution of KHDA is the eigenvector of the following generalized eigen-problem associated with the largest eigenvalue:

$$\left[(1-\lambda)\boldsymbol{\Omega}_b^T\boldsymbol{\Omega}_b + \lambda\boldsymbol{\Omega}_t^T\boldsymbol{\Omega}_t\right]\boldsymbol{\beta} = \rho\left((1-\lambda)\boldsymbol{\Omega}_w^T\boldsymbol{\Omega}_w + \eta\boldsymbol{\Omega}_t\right)\boldsymbol{\beta} \quad (4)$$

Where, $\eta > 0$ which depends on the number of samples is small. Just as KCCA, KPCA and KLDA[13,14], KHDA can discover manifold embedded in high-dimensional feature space to some extent and is difficult to take the local structure of data into account. To uncover global and local information of data points, LPKHDA is developed by combining manifold learning and KHDA.

3   LPKHDA

In this section, KHDA is rewritten in the framework of least square support vector machine (LSSVM), and then locality preserving KHDA is deduced.

In the framework of LSSVM, The equivalent formulation of KHDA is given as

$$J(\boldsymbol{\beta}, \mathbf{e}) = \arg\max_{\mathbf{w},\mathbf{e}} \frac{\gamma}{2}\boldsymbol{\beta}^T\left[(1-\lambda)\boldsymbol{\Omega}_b^T\boldsymbol{\Omega}_b + \lambda\boldsymbol{\Omega}_t^T\boldsymbol{\Omega}_t\right]\boldsymbol{\beta} - \frac{1}{2}\boldsymbol{\beta}^T\mathbf{K}\boldsymbol{\beta} - \frac{v_2}{2}(1-\lambda)\mathbf{e}^T\mathbf{e} \quad (5)$$

$s.t. \ \mathbf{e} = \boldsymbol{\Omega}_w\boldsymbol{\beta}$

where, γ, v_2 are positive regularization coefficients. The solution to the optimization problem in Eq.(5) is given by proposition 1.

Proposition 1. Given a positive kernel function $k : R^d \times R^d \to R$ satisfying $k(\mathbf{x}, \mathbf{z}) = \phi(\mathbf{x})^T \phi(\mathbf{z})$, $\gamma, v_1, v_2 \in R^+$ and $v = 1/\lambda$ are regularization coefficients, the optimization problem in Eq.(5) turns out to a generalized eigen-problem

$$\left[(1-\lambda) \mathbf{\Omega}_b^T \mathbf{\Omega}_b + \lambda \mathbf{\Omega}_t^T \mathbf{\Omega}_t \right] \boldsymbol{\beta} = v \left(\mathbf{K} + v_2 (1-\lambda) \mathbf{\Omega}_w^T \mathbf{\Omega}_w \right) \boldsymbol{\beta} \tag{6}$$

Proof: Using Lagrange multipliers, this optimization problem in Eq.(5) can be formulated as

$$L(\boldsymbol{\beta}, \mathbf{e}, \boldsymbol{\tau}) = \frac{\gamma}{2} \boldsymbol{\beta}^T \left[(1-\lambda) \mathbf{\Omega}_b^T \mathbf{\Omega}_b + \lambda \mathbf{\Omega}_t^T \mathbf{\Omega}_t \right] \boldsymbol{\beta} - \frac{1}{2} \boldsymbol{\beta}^T \mathbf{K} \boldsymbol{\beta} - \frac{v_2}{2} (1-\lambda) \mathbf{e}^T \mathbf{e} - \boldsymbol{\tau}^T (\mathbf{e} - \mathbf{\Omega}_w \boldsymbol{\beta})$$

where $\boldsymbol{\tau}$ is Lagrange multiplier vector. According to KKT condition, the derivative of $L(\boldsymbol{\beta}, \mathbf{e}, \boldsymbol{\tau})$ with respect to $\boldsymbol{\beta}, \mathbf{e}, \boldsymbol{\tau}$ is computed and set zeros. Thus, we have

$$\delta L / \delta \boldsymbol{\beta} = \gamma \left[(1-\lambda) \mathbf{\Omega}_b^T \mathbf{\Omega}_b + \lambda \mathbf{\Omega}_t^T \mathbf{\Omega}_t \right] \boldsymbol{\beta} - \mathbf{K} \boldsymbol{\beta} + \left(\boldsymbol{\tau}^T \mathbf{\Omega}_w \right)^T = 0 \tag{7}$$

$$\delta L / \delta \mathbf{e} = \boldsymbol{\tau} - v_2 (1-\lambda) \mathbf{e} = 0, \quad \delta L / \delta \boldsymbol{\tau} = \mathbf{e} - \mathbf{\Omega}_w \boldsymbol{\beta} = 0 \tag{8}$$

Define $v = 1/\lambda$, according to Eq.(7)-(8), the optimization problem in Eq.(5) reduces to a generalized eigen-problem expressed as

$$\left[(1-\lambda) \mathbf{\Omega}_b^T \mathbf{\Omega}_b + \lambda \mathbf{\Omega}_t^T \mathbf{\Omega}_t \right] \boldsymbol{\beta} = v \left(\mathbf{K} + v_2 (1-\lambda) \mathbf{\Omega}_w^T \mathbf{\Omega}_w \right) \boldsymbol{\beta} \qquad \blacksquare$$

Define $v' = v/v_2$, $v_1 = 1/v_2$, the Eq.(6) is then written as

$$\left[(1-\lambda) \mathbf{\Omega}_b^T \mathbf{\Omega}_b + \lambda \mathbf{\Omega}_t^T \mathbf{\Omega}_t \right] \boldsymbol{\beta} = v' \left(v_1 \mathbf{K} + (1-\lambda) \mathbf{\Omega}_w^T \mathbf{\Omega}_w \right) \boldsymbol{\beta} \tag{9}$$

Let $\boldsymbol{\beta}_1, \cdots, \boldsymbol{\beta}_M$ be eigenvectors corresponding to the largest eigenvalue of the above eigenproblem, the nonlinear features can be yielded via

$$\mathbf{z}_i = \left[z_i^{(1)}, \cdots, z_i^{(M)} \right] = [\boldsymbol{\beta}_1, \cdots, \boldsymbol{\beta}_M]^T \mathbf{K}_{\mathbf{x}_i}, \quad \mathbf{K}_{\mathbf{x}_i} = [k(\mathbf{x}_1, \mathbf{x}_i), \cdots, k(\mathbf{x}_N, \mathbf{x}_i)]^T, \quad M \le d.$$

Denote $\mathbf{Z} = \left\{ z_i^{(d)} \right\}_{i=1}^N$, after λ is given, the optimal $v^*, \boldsymbol{\beta}^*$ can be obtained by solving the following optimization problem

$$CS_1(\boldsymbol{\beta}, \eta) = \max_{d \in \{1, 2, \cdots, N\}} \left((1-\lambda) \mathbf{S}_b^{\left(z^{(d)} \right)} + \lambda \mathbf{S}_t^{\left(z^{(d)} \right)} \right) \Big/ \left((1-\lambda) \mathbf{S}_w^{\left(z^d \right)} + \eta \boldsymbol{\beta}^T \mathbf{K} \boldsymbol{\beta} \right) \tag{10}$$

where $\mathbf{S}_w^{\left(z^{(d)} \right)}$ is within-class scatter matrix associated with data set $\mathbf{Z}$.

Now, we deduced LPKHDA algorithm by incorporating locality preserving into KHDA. For the dataset $\left\{ \phi(\mathbf{x}_i) \right\}_{i=1}^N$, we refer to [14] and have

$$\mathbf{w}_\phi^T \mathbf{S}_\Xi^\phi \mathbf{w}_\phi = \sum_{i=1}^n \left\| \mathbf{w}_\phi^T \left(\phi(\mathbf{x}_i) - \mathbf{m}^\phi \right) \right\|^2 \quad , \qquad \mathbf{w}_\phi^T \mathbf{S}_B^\phi \mathbf{w}_\phi = \sum_{l=1}^C N_l \left\| \mathbf{w}_\phi^T \left(\mathbf{m}_l^\phi - \mathbf{m}^\phi \right) \right\|_2^2 \quad ,$$

$$\mathbf{w}_\phi^T \mathbf{S}_w^\phi \mathbf{w}_\phi = \sum_{l=1}^C \sum_{i=1}^{N_l} \left\| \mathbf{w}_\phi^T \left(\phi(\mathbf{x}_i) - \mathbf{m}_l^\phi \right) \right\|^2 , \quad \text{where} \quad \mathbf{m}^\phi = \mu^\phi , \ \mathbf{m}_l^\phi = \mu_l^\phi . \text{ Note that } \mathbf{S}_\Xi^\phi = \mathbf{S}_b^\phi + \mathbf{S}_w^\phi ,$$

Inspired from manifold learning theory, we incorporate the locality preserving into KHDA. Now, the globally nonlinear problem can be divided into multiple locally sub-linear problems via the locality similarity matrices, and vice versa, these linear problems can be combined to approximate original problem. So the LPKHDA can be expressed as

$$\max_{\mathbf{w}_\phi} \frac{1}{2N} \mathbf{w}_\phi^T \sum_{i=1}^N \sum_{j=1}^N \left(\phi(\mathbf{x}_i) - \phi(\mathbf{x}_j) \right) \left(S_{ij}^x \right)^2 \left(\phi(\mathbf{x}_i) - \phi(\mathbf{x}_j) \right)^T \mathbf{w}_\phi -$$
$$\lambda \mathbf{w}_\phi^T \sum_{l=1}^C \frac{1}{2N_l} \sum_{i=1}^{N_l} \sum_{j=1}^{N_l} \left(\phi(\mathbf{x}_i^{(l)}) - \phi(\mathbf{x}_j^{(l)}) \right) \left(S_{ij}^{(l)} \right)^2 \left(\phi(\mathbf{x}_i^{(l)}) - \phi(\mathbf{x}_j^{(l)}) \right)^T \mathbf{w}_\phi - \frac{1}{2} \left\| \mathbf{w}_\phi \right\|^2 \tag{11}$$

$$s.t. \ (1-\lambda) \mathbf{w}_\phi^T \sum_{l=1}^C \frac{1}{2N_l} \sum_{i=1}^{N_l} \sum_{j=1}^{N_l} \left(\phi(\mathbf{x}_i^{(l)}) - \phi(\mathbf{x}_j^{(l)}) \right) \left(S_{ij}^{(l)} \right)^2 \left(\phi(\mathbf{x}_i^{(l)}) - \phi(\mathbf{x}_j^{(l)}) \right)^T \mathbf{w}_\phi = 1 \tag{12}$$

Where $\mathbf{S}_x = \left[S_{ij}^x \right]_{i,j=1}^N , \mathbf{S}_{(l)} = \left[S_{ij}^{(l)} \right]_{i,j=1}^{N_l}$ are similarity matrices shown as Ref[15]. Similar to Ref[15], the Eq. (11) can be rewritten as

$$\max_{\mathbf{w}_\phi} \ \frac{1}{2N} \mathbf{w}_\phi^T \mathbf{X}^\phi \mathbf{S}_{xx} \mathbf{X}^{\phi T} \mathbf{w}_\phi - \lambda \mathbf{w}_\phi^T \sum_{l=1}^C \frac{1}{2N_l} \mathbf{X}_l^\phi \mathbf{S}_{\mathbf{x}^{(l)}\mathbf{x}^{(l)}} \mathbf{X}_l^{\phi T} \mathbf{w}_\phi - \frac{1}{2} \left\| \mathbf{w}_\phi \right\|^2 \tag{13}$$

$$s.t. \ (1-\lambda) \mathbf{w}_T^\phi \sum_{l=1}^C \frac{1}{2N_l} \mathbf{X}_l^\phi \mathbf{S}_{\mathbf{x}^{(l)}\mathbf{x}^{(l)}} \mathbf{X}_l^{\phi T} \mathbf{w}_\phi = 1$$

where $\mathbf{S}_{xx} = \mathbf{D}_{xx} - \mathbf{S}_x \circ \mathbf{S}_x$, $\left(\mathbf{S}_x \circ \mathbf{S}_x \right)_{i,j} = \left(\mathbf{S}_x \right)_{i,j}^2$, $\mathbf{S}_{\mathbf{x}^{(l)}\mathbf{x}^{(l)}} = \mathbf{D}_{\mathbf{x}^{(l)}\mathbf{x}^{(l)}} - \mathbf{S}_{\mathbf{x}^{(l)}} \circ \mathbf{S}_{\mathbf{x}^{(l)}}$,

$\mathbf{X}^\phi = \left[\phi(\mathbf{x}_1), \cdots, \phi(\mathbf{x}_N) \right]$, $\mathbf{X}_l^\phi = \left[\phi(\mathbf{x}_1^{(l)}), \cdots, \phi(\mathbf{x}_{N_l}^{(l)}) \right]$, $\mathbf{D}_{xx} = diag\left\{ d_{xx}^1, \cdots, d_{xx}^N \right\}$,

$d_{xx}^m = \sum_{n=1}^N \left(\mathbf{S}_x \right)_{mn}^2$, , $\mathbf{D}_{\mathbf{x}^{(l)}\mathbf{x}^{(l)}} = diag\left\{ d_{\mathbf{x}^{(l)}\mathbf{x}^{(l)}}^1, \cdots, d_{\mathbf{x}^{(l)}\mathbf{x}^{(l)}}^{N_l} \right\}$, $d_{\mathbf{x}^{(l)}\mathbf{x}^{(l)}}^i = \sum_{j=1}^{N_l} \left(\mathbf{S}_{\mathbf{x}^{(l)}} \right)_{ij}^2$,

$i,j = 1,2,\cdots,N_l$, $m,n = 1,2,\cdots,N$ .Obviously, $\mathbf{S}_{xx}$ is similar to Laplacian matrix of LPP. Noting that $\mathbf{w}_\phi = \boldsymbol{\beta}^T \boldsymbol{\Phi}_t$, the solution to LPKHDA can be yielded by solving the following eigenproblem

$$\left[\frac{1}{N} \lambda \mathbf{K}_x \mathbf{S}_{xx} \mathbf{K}_x - (1-\lambda) \sum_{l=1}^C \frac{1}{2N_l} \mathbf{K}_{\mathbf{x}^{(l)}} \mathbf{S}_{\mathbf{x}^{(l)}\mathbf{x}^{(l)}} \mathbf{K}_{\mathbf{x}^{(l)}} \right] \boldsymbol{\beta} = v \left((1-\lambda) \sum_{l=1}^C \frac{1}{N_l} \mathbf{K}_{\mathbf{x}_l} \mathbf{S}_{\mathbf{x}^{(l)}\mathbf{x}^{(l)}} \mathbf{K}_{\mathbf{x}_l} + \eta \mathbf{K} \right) \boldsymbol{\beta} \tag{14}$$

where $\mathbf{K}_x = \left[k(\mathbf{x}_i, \mathbf{x}_j) \right]_{i,j=1}^N \in R^{N \times N}$, $\mathbf{K}_{\mathbf{x}^{(l)}} = \left[k(\mathbf{x}_i^{(l)}, \mathbf{x}_j^{(l)}) \right]_{i,j=1}^{N_l} \in R^{N_l \times N_l}$. $\boldsymbol{\beta}^{(p)}$ denotes eigenvector corresponding to the p_{th} largest eigenvalue, $p = 1,2,\cdots,M$, the features are generated by projecting $\phi(\mathbf{x})$ in $\mathbf{w}^{(p)}$.

4   A Kernel-Induced Space Selection Approach to Model Selection

As we know, class separation information should be preserved as much as possible in the optimal kernel feature space F^*. Due to F^* changing with kernel function parameter and $tr(\mathbf{AB}) = tr(\mathbf{BA})$, $tr(\mathbf{A}+\mathbf{B}) = tr(\mathbf{A})+tr(\mathbf{B})$ ($tr(\cdot)$ is trace of matrix), LPKHDA model selection criterion established   is given as following

$$CS(\theta) = \left(tr\left(\mathbf{S}_\Xi^{\phi L}\right) - (1-\lambda)tr\left(\mathbf{S}_w^{\phi L}\right)\right) \Big/ \left((1-\lambda)tr\left(\mathbf{S}_w^{\phi}\right) + \eta N\right) \tag{15}$$

where, $\mathbf{S}_w^{\phi L} = \sum_{l=1}^{C}(1/2N_l)\mathbf{X}_l^{\phi}\mathbf{S}_{\mathbf{x}^{(l)}\mathbf{x}^{(l)}}\mathbf{X}_l^{\phi T}$ and $\mathbf{S}_\Xi^{\phi L} = (1/2N)\mathbf{X}^{\phi}\mathbf{S}_{\mathbf{xx}}\mathbf{X}^{\phi T}$ are total and within-class scatter matrices with locality preserving, they   are formulated as

$$tr\left(\mathbf{S}_w^{\phi L}\right) = \sum_{l=1}^{N_l}(1/N_l)\left(tr\left(\mathbf{D}_{\mathbf{x}^{(l)}\mathbf{x}^{(l)}}\mathbf{K}^{(l)}\right) - \mathbf{1}_{N_l}^T\mathbf{K_s}^{(l)}\mathbf{1}_{N_l}\right) \quad , \quad tr\left(\mathbf{S}_\Xi^{\phi L}\right) = $$

$(1/N)\left(tr\left(\mathbf{D}_{\mathbf{xx}}\mathbf{K}\right) - \mathbf{1}_N^T\mathbf{K_s}\mathbf{1}_N\right)$ .where $\mathbf{K_s}^{(l)} = \left[k\left(\mathbf{x}_i^{(l)},\mathbf{x}_j^{(l)}\right)\left(S_{ij}^{(l)}\right)^2\right]_{i,j=1,2,\cdots,N_l}$,

$\mathbf{K_s} = \left[k\left(\mathbf{x}_i,\mathbf{x}_j\right)\left(S_{ij}^x\right)^2\right]_{i,j=1,2,\cdots,N}$, $\mathbf{K}^{(l)} = \left[k\left(\mathbf{x}_i^{(l)},\mathbf{x}_j^{(l)}\right)\right]_{i,j=1,2,\cdots,N_l}$. In practical application, RBF function is often employed as kernel function. In order to ensure the numerical stability of $tr\left(\mathbf{S}_w^{\phi L}\right)$. The kernel function is modified as Ref[15] . The criterion in (15) turns out to $CS_{\mu'}(\theta)$. The optimal θ^* is obtained through gradient descent. Derivate $CS_{\mu'}(\theta)$ with respect to θ , the gradient is

$$\frac{\partial CS_{\mu'}(\theta)}{\partial \theta} = \left(\left(\frac{\partial tr\left(\mathbf{S}_\Xi^{\phi L}\right)}{\partial \theta} - \beta\frac{\partial tr\left(\mathbf{S}_w^{\phi L}\right)}{\partial \theta}\right)\left(\beta tr\left(\mathbf{S}_w^{\phi}\right) + \eta N\right) - \beta\frac{\partial tr\left(\mathbf{S}_w^{\phi L}\right)}{\partial \theta}\left(tr\left(\mathbf{S}_\Xi^{\phi L}\right) - \beta tr\left(\mathbf{S}_w^{\phi L}\right)\right)\right)\Big/\left(\beta tr\left(\mathbf{S}_w^{\phi}\right) + \eta N\right)^2$$

$$\partial tr\left(\mathbf{S}_\Xi^{\phi L}\right)\Big/\partial \theta = 1/N\left(tr\left(\mathbf{D}_{\mathbf{xx}}\,\partial \mathbf{K}/\partial \theta\right) - \mathbf{1}_N^T\,\partial \mathbf{K_s}/\partial \theta\mathbf{1}_N\right)$$

$$\partial tr\left(\mathbf{S}_w^{\phi L}\right)\Big/\partial \theta = \sum_{l=1}^{N_l}1/N_l\left(tr\left(\mathbf{D}_{\mathbf{x}^{(l)}\mathbf{x}^{(l)}}\,\partial tr\mathbf{K}^{(l)}/\partial \theta\right) - \mathbf{1}_{N_l}^T\,\partial tr\mathbf{K_s}^{(l)}/\partial \theta\mathbf{1}_{N_l}\right)$$

where $\partial tr(\mathbf{K})/\partial \theta = \left[\|\mathbf{x}_i - \mathbf{x}_j\|^2 \exp\left(-\|\mathbf{x}_i - \mathbf{x}_j\|^2/2\theta^2\right)/\theta^3\right]_{i,j=1}^N$, $\partial \mathbf{K_s}/\partial \sigma =$

$\left[\left(S_{ij}^x\right)^2\partial k\left(\mathbf{x}_i,\mathbf{x}_j\right)/\partial \theta\right]_{i,j=1}^N$. $\partial tr\left(\mathbf{K}^{(l)}\right)/\partial \theta$ and $\partial tr\left(\mathbf{K_s}^{(l)}\right)/\partial \theta$ can be deduced in a similar way.

In this paper, we must search for optimal $\left(\lambda^*,\eta^*\right)$ in parameter space. Inspired from the idea in Ref [6], we propose an alternative LPKHDA method called boosted LPKHDA by introducing Adaboost idea into LPKHDA. The implementation procedure of Boosted LPKHDA is similar to Ref [3].

5   Simulation

In the following, we use UCI data set and face data set to evaluate our method. To demonstrate the superiority of Boosted LPKHDA over competing methods, we comprehensively compare its classification performance with that of state-of-the-art manifold learning methods.

(1) UCI data sets

We evaluate the algorithm on 4 UCI and face recognition data sets. 400,200,170 and 400 samples are randomly drawn from Banana, Breast Cancer, Heart and Ringnorm data sets respectively to form training subsets, the remain samples form test subsets. In the application, the number of the wake classifiers for Boosted HDA and Boosted LPKHDA is eight and eight (λ,η) are sampled from [0,1]. The results are demonstrated in table 1. it can be deduced from table 1 that KFDA doesn't always outperform local LFDA, which illustrated that kernel-trick or manifold learning methods can not always effectively tackle complex and nonlinear relationship existing in the samples. However, the proposed algorithm excels other nonlinear dimensional reduction methods.

Table 1. Classification error mean (%) and standard variance on UCI data set

	Heart	Breast-cancer	Banana	Ringnorm
KPCA	22.6±0.33	33.1±0.47	10.8±0.06	19.7±0.8
LPP	23.8±3.3	33.5±4.6	13.6±0.7	20.6±1.1
PCA	24.3±3.5	34.5±5.2	11.8±0.8	21.6±1.4
KFDA	21.3±0.34	28.9±0.48	10.8±0.47	16.8±1.1
LFDA	21.9±0.8	34.4±4.3	13.9±0.9	21.3±1.6
Boosted HDA	17.9±2.71	28.3±1.53	11.6±0.6	18.5±0.7
FDA	22.6±3.1	32.9±2.5	12.7±0.8	20.2±1.9
Boosted PKHDA	14.2±0.62	23.8±1.36	8.9±0.23	15.7±1.2

(2) Face recognition

We perform face recognition on ORL, PIE and Yale datasets. We select five subjects labeled as C05, C07, C09, C27, C29 from PIE, each contains 168 images. Three and six images of each individual are randomly drawn from ORL and Yale to form training and test subsets that are not intersected with each other. All images are rotated, gray scaled, aligned, cropped, resized and normalized to a resolution of 32x32 with zero mean and one variance. Every method independently performs ten times on each data base. the average recognition rate prediction is taken as the evaluation of each method. The experimental results are shown in table 2. From table 2, we can see that the proposed algorithm can also work on the data that manifold learning methods can not perform well.

Table 2. Face recognition (%) and the number of reduced dimension

	PIE	ORL	Yale165
KPCA	61.36 (137)	85.71 (45)	73.22 (36)
LPP	67.22 (67)	78.5 (35)	78.13(41)
KFDA	79.22 (134)	85.23(39)	81.76 (33)
LFDA	80.68 (128)	84.16(34)	82.37(37)
LNMF	82.82 (175)	80.11(40)	83.14(45)
Boosted HDA	81.25(119)	85.38(41)	82.5(36)
Boosted LPKHDA	85.74(122)	87.63(36)	86.67(35)

6   Conclusion

LPKHDA can discover the local manifold embedded in high-dimension space and descript global information of data, relaxing the constraints on kernel function for kernel-based methods and the manifold learning, and has the following merits: (a) Preserving local and discriminative features can be obtained; (b) greatly reducing the complexity of mapped data geometrical structure;(c) obtaining the optimal kernel parameter and avoiding computational issue. The results of simulations show satisfactory performance of LPKHDA.

References

1. Zhao, H., Yuen, P.C., Kwok, J.T.: A Novel Incremental principal component analysis and its application for face recognition. IEEE Trans. System, Man, and Cybernetics-Part B:Cybernetics 36(4), 873–886 (2006)
2. Duda, R., Hart, P., Stork, D.: Pattern Classification, 2nd edn. Wiley, New York (2001)
3. Lu, Y., Tian, Q.: Discriminant subspace analysis: An adaptive approach for image classification. IEEE Trans. Multimedia 11(7), 1289–1300 (2009)
4. Sui, J., Adali, T., Pearlson, G.: A CCA+ICA based model for multi-task brain imaging data fusion and its application to schizophrenia. NeuroImage 51, 123–134 (2010)
5. Tao, Q., Wu, G., Wang, J.: The theoretical analysis of FDA and applications. Pattern Recognition 39(6), 1199–1204 (2006)
6. Chen, C., Yang, J., Yang, J.: A face recognition method by fusing PCA and LDA. Control & Decision 19(10), 1147–1151 (2004)
7. Skrobot, V.L., Castro, E.V.R., Pereira, R.C.C.: Use of principal component analysis and linear discriminant analysis in gas chromatographic data in the investigation of gasoline adulteration. Energy & Fuels 21(6), 3394–3400 (2007)
8. Yu, J., Tian, Q., Rui, T.: Integrating discriminant and descriptive information for dimension reduction and classification. IEEE Trans. Circuits and Systems for Video Technology 17(3), 372–377 (2007)
9. Roweis, S.T., Saul, L.K.: Nonlinear dimensionality reduction by locally linear embedding. Science 290, 2323–2326 (2000)
10. Shao, J., Rong, G., Jiming, L.: Learning a data-dependent kernel function for KPCA-based nonlinear process monitoring. Chemical Engineering Research and Design 87, 1471–1480 (2009)
11. Sun, T., Chen, S.: Locality preserving CCA with applications to data visualization and pose estimation. Image and Vision Computing 25, 531–543 (2007)
12. Liu, X., Xu, G.: PSO-Based Uncorrelated hybrid discriminant analysis algorithm. Applied Mechanics and Materials 109, 671–675 (2012)
13. Zhang, J., Huang, H., Wang, J.: Manifold learning for visualizing and analyzing high-dimensional data. IEEE Trans. Intelligent Systems 10, 1541–1672 (2010)
14. Horikawa, Y.: Use of Autocorrelation Kernels in Kernel Canonical Correlation Analysis for Texture Classification. In: Pal, N.R., Kasabov, N., Mudi, R.K., Pal, S., Parui, S.K. (eds.) ICONIP 2004. LNCS, vol. 3316, pp. 1235–1240. Springer, Heidelberg (2004)
15. Wang, L., Chan, K.L., Xue, P., et al.: A kernel-induced space selection approach to model selection in KLDA. IEEE Trans. Neural Networks 19(12), 2116–2122 (2008)

Investigation of Directional Traffic Sign Feature Extracting Based on PCNN in Different Color Space[*]

Mengjun Wang[**], Lu Yang, Xia Wang, and Jianfei Liu

School of Information Engineering,
Hebei University of Technology, Tianjin, 300401, China
{Mengjun Wang,wangmengjun}@hebut.edu.cn

Abstract. For the first time in this paper, directional traffic signs feature extracting based on Pulse Coupled Neural Network (PCNN) in different color space are investigated. Entropy series is extracted from the image of traffic sign in both RGB model and HSV model. Each entropy series of R, G, B, H, S, V color space is used as feature vector for recognition, match analysis is carried out by minimum variance. Experiments are carried out based on the directional signs class in national standard GB5768-1999 database. Experiment results show that feature vector based on Entropy series in B color space get the higher recognition rates than the other color space, with 50 iteration and 5×5 convolution kernel matrix of PCNN.

Keywords: Traffic sign recognition, Pulse Coupled Neural Network, entropy sequence, color space.

1   Introduction

Traffic sign recognition (TSR) is an important part of the Intelligent Transportation Systems (ITS), the recognition result is not only to remind drivers of traffic safety information, but also be used as the autopilot overall coordination of the joint input. For traffic sign recognition system, feature extraction is the identification process. The most obvious features are color and shape information. For example, color information is used at HSV model and RGB model [1-3]. But color information is only used in the detection step. Shape information is used to detect the round, triangle and hexagon for traffic signs [3-5].

PCNN is derived from the Echorn's neuron model. Echorn's neuron model is developed by simulating the activities of the visual nerve cell based on the observation of the visual cortex nerve cell of cats. Researches on PCNN and its applications have developed greatly in recent years, it can used to image segmentation, noise reduction, image smoothness, and feature extraction. Pulse coupled neural network (PCNN) has been used to deal with the traffic signs [6, 7]. While extracting the features, gray images is adopted. Color information is more important in TSR system because of the

[*] Project supported by College Technology and Research Youth Foundation of Hebei Province (No. 2010121).
[**] Corresponding author.

F.L. Wang et al. (Eds.): CMSP 2012, CCIS 346, pp. 24–31, 2012.

particularity color of traffic signs. The main colors adopted in traffic sign system are blue, yellow, red, and black. Examples of traffic sings from Chinese national standard GB5768-1999 database are shown in Fig.1.

Fig. 1. Examples of traffic signs in Chinese national standard GB5768-1999 database

Taking into account the specificity of the color of road signs, for the first time in this paper, traffic sign feature extracting based on Pulse Coupled Neural Network (PCNN) in different color space are investigated. Each entropy series of traffic images in R, G, B, H, S, V color space is extracted as feature vector for recognition, to find out the optimal color space for feature extraction.

The paper is organized as follows. Section 2 addresses the theory of PCNN. Section 3 addresses the traffic images and entropy series of images. Section 4 reports the experimental results. Finally, Section 5 summarizes the paper.

2   Description of PCNN Model

In image processing, PCNN model is organized as a one lever 2-D network, which has the same size with the input image. Each neuron is corresponding with a pixel in the image. The basic PCNN neuron is shown in Fig.2. There are three components in the neuron: input part, linking park, pulse generator. The PCNN neuron accepts the feeding input and the linking input, and then generates the internal activity. Feeding input is the basic input from the neuron's, which consists of the neighboring pixels of corresponding pixels in the input image. Linking input is the input of lateral connections with neighboring neurons. After compared to a dynamic threshold, Feeding input and Linking input are then combined to create the internal state.

For the convenience of simulation, the PCNN is described as iteration equations as follows [7]:

$$F_{ij}[n] = e^{-\alpha_F} F_{ij}[n-1] + V_F \sum_{kl} M_{ijkl} Y_{ij}[n-1] + S_{ij} \qquad (1)$$

$$L_{ij}[n] = e^{-\alpha_L} L_{ij}[n-1] + V_L \sum_{kl} W_{ijkl} Y_{ij}[n-1] \qquad (2)$$

$$U_{ij}[n] = F_{ij}[n](1 + \beta L_{ij}[n]) \qquad (3)$$

$$T_{ij}[n] = T_{ij}[n-1]e^{-\alpha_T} + V_T Y_{ij}[n] \qquad (4)$$

$$Y_{ij}[n] = \begin{cases} 1 & U_{ij}[n] > T_{ij}[n] \\ 0 & U_{ij}[n] \le T_{ij}[n] \end{cases} \qquad (5)$$

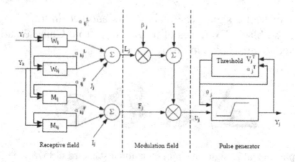

Fig. 2. Basic PCNN neuron

In these equations, S_{ij} is the input stimulus, it is the normalized gray level of image pixel in (i, j) position in image processing. $F_{ij}[n]$ is the feedback input of the neuron in (i, j), $L_{ij}[n]$ is the linking item, $U_{ij}[n]$is the internal activity of neuron, $T_{ij}[n]$ is the dynamic threshold. $Y_{ij}[n]$ is the pulse output of neuron with the binary value 0 or 1. M and W are the constant synaptic inter-connecting weight matrices for the feeding and the linking input, which dependant on the distance between neurons. Generally, M and W refer to the Gaussian weight functions with the distance, normally $W=M$. β is the linking coefficients; indicate the linking strength of PCNN. α_F, α_L, α_T are the attenuation time constants of $F_{ij}[n]$, $L_{ij}[n]$, $T_{ij}[n]$, respectively. V_F, V_L, $V_T$denote the inherent voltage potential of $F_{ij}[n]$, $L_{ij}[n]$, $T_{ij}[n]$, respectively.

For the feeding channel, $\alpha_F$determines the decay rate of feeding channel. Larger α_F causes faster decay. V_F can enlarge or reduce the influence from surrounding neurons. Matrix W refers to the mode of inter-connection among neurons in the feeding receptive field. Generally, the size of W denotes the size of the feeding receptive field. The value of matrix element w_{ijkl} determines the synaptic weight strength. In most cases, this channel is simplified via $\alpha_F =0$ and $V_F=0$.Different from the feeding channel, the link channel usually keep itself as it is. The link channel also has three parameters (α_L, V_L, and M) that have the same function to the parameters (α_F, V_F, and W), respectively. Usually, the inter-connection employs the Gaussian weight functions with the distance. The linking coefficient β is an important parameter, because it can vary the weighting of the linking channel in the internal activity. Hence, its value is usually depended on different demands. For example, if much influence from the linking channel is expected, β should be given larger value. All neurons often have the same value of β.

3   Traffic Signs Feature Extraction

When the equations are running iteratively, the PCNN will output a sequence of binary images. The output of PCNN varies in a period which is related with the properties of the input image and the parameters of PCNN. The aim of our research is finding a suitable parameter set and iteration times to produce an ideal segment binary image.

A 2-D image ($m \times n$) can be thought as a PCNN neuromime with $m \times n$ neurons, and the gray level of pixels is the input of neuron as S_{ij}. One pixel's pulsating output can activate other corresponding pixels having the approximate gray level in the neighborhood and let them generate pulsating output binary image $Y[n]$. $Y[n]$ contains important information of the image, including regional information, edge, and texture features. It can be used to create a 1-D signal vector including some interesting features with respect to invariance and uniqueness. The transforms for the binary images to signal vector include the following methods.

$$\text{Time series } V_1 [n] : V_1[n] = \sum Y_{ij}[n] \qquad (6)$$

Let $H(P)$ behalfs of the entropy of output binary image, it can be defined as the following equation.

$$H(P) = -P_1 \log_2(P_1) - P_0 \log_2(P_0) \qquad (7)$$

Where P_1 is the probability of 1 in a binary image, P_0 is the probability of 0 in a binary image during the cyclic iteration operation.

$$\text{Entropy series } V_3[n]: \; V_3[n] = -\sum P \times \log_2 P \qquad (8)$$

Fig. 3. Directional signs class in national standard GB5768-1999 database

The entropy series and the time signature have the similar characteristic, the entropy series is also invariant under simple transformations, such as rotation, scaling and translation.

Entropy series of PCNN is used to extract the one-dimensional characteristics of images, which usually can be used as the image feature vector of the road traffic signs. Then, each entropy series of R, G, B, H, S, V color space is used as feature vector for recognition, match analysis is carried out by minimum variance. Experiments are carried out based on the directional signs class in national standard GB5768-1999 database, all the signs are shown in Fig.3.

4   Experiments and Result Discussion

Road traffic sign images in the standard library are color images. While used for PCNN feature extraction, grayscale images are adopted in order to reduce computation, no color information is available. But color information is more important in TSR

system because of the particularity color of traffic signs. To utilize the color information with less computation, we summarized the characters of traffic signs' colors. In
national standard GB5768-1999 traffic sign database, different traffic sign classes have
different primary colors. The primary color of directional signs class is blue, the primary color of warning signs class is yellow, and the primary color of warning signs class
is yellow, while the primary color of prohibition signs class is red. So PCNN entropy
sequence is extracted in different color space. Entropy sequence is the extracted one-
dimensional feature series using PCNN. Experiments are carried out in directional
signs class. Entropy series is extracted from the image of traffic sign in both RGB
model and HSV model. Each entropy series of R, G, B, H, S, V color space is used as
feature vector for recognition, match analysis is carried out by minimum variance.

In the experiment, the parameters of PCNN are shown in Table. I. $L_{ij}[n]$, $U_{ij}[n]$,
$Y_{ij}[n]$ matrices are initially set to zero. M and W are set as equation 9. The number of
iterations is 50, $N=50$. The dimension of the vector of lip region based on PCNN is 50.

$$W = M = \begin{bmatrix} 0 & 0.2 & 0.25 & 0.2 & 0 \\ 0.2 & 0.5 & 1 & 0.5 & 0.2 \\ 0.25 & 1 & 0 & 1 & 0.25 \\ 0.2 & 0.5 & 1 & 0.5 & 0.2 \\ 0 & 0.2 & 0.25 & 0.2 & 0 \end{bmatrix} \tag{9}$$

Table 1. Parameters of PCNN

paramerters	α_F	α_L	α_E	V_F	V_L	V_E	β
Value	0.1	1.0	1.0	0.5	0.2	27	0.1

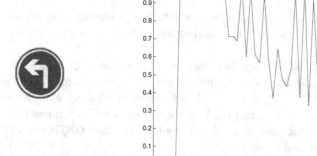

Fig. 4. Turn Left Traffic sign and its Entropy sequence in Blue color space

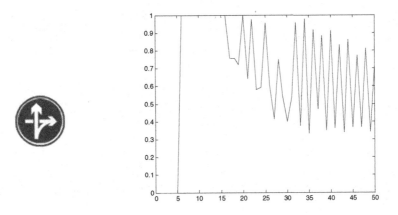

Fig. 5. Straightforward Across and Turn Right traffic sign and its Entropy sequence in Blue color space

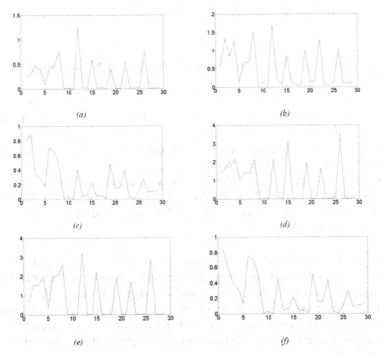

Fig. 6. Variance value of entropy series between Turn Left and 29 directional signs in the *R, G, B, H, S, V* color spaces

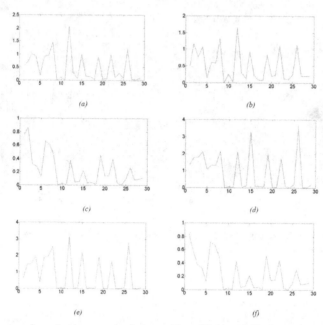

Fig. 7. Variance value of entropy series between Turn Right and 29 directional signs in the *R, G, B, H, S, V* color spaces

From Fig.4 to Fig.5 show Turn Left and Straightforward Across and Turn Right traffic signs and their entropy series on blue color space as examples. Then classified processing goes along in directional signs class based on minimum variance of entropy series in both RGB model and HSV model.

Fig.6 *(a)* to *(f)*, is the variance value of entropy series between Turn Left and 29 directional signs in the *R, G, B, H, S, V* color spaces respectively, and Fig.7 *(a)* to *(f)*, is the variance value of entropy series between Turn Right and 29 directional signs in the *R, G, B, H, S, V* color spaces respectively.

In these figures, the X-axis represents the 29 directional signs; the Y-axis represents the variance value of entropy sequence between test image and 29 standard directional signs. Where the minimum variance value appeared at X-axis is the result of test image. The correct location of Turn Left sign and Turn Right is 9 and 11 respectively. From the experiment result, we can see the minimum variance value appeared at 9 and 11 location only in *B* color space. In other color space, *R, G, H, S, V*, the classified results may be confused because of the multiple minimum variance values appeared at different locations.

5   Conclusion

For the first time in this paper, directional traffic signs feature extracting based on Pulse Coupled Neural Network (PCNN) in different color space are investigated. Entropy series is extracted from the image of traffic sign in both RGB model and

HSV model. Each entropy series of *R, G, B, H, S, V* color space is used as feature vector for recognition, match analysis is carried out by minimum variance. Experiments are carried out based on the directional signs class in national standard GB5768-1999 database. Experiment results show that feature vector based on Entropy series in *B* color space get the higher recognition rates than the other color space, with 50 iteration and 5 × 5 convolution kernel matrix of PCNN. So color information is more important in TSR system. Appropriate feature extracting means should be adopted according with the particularity color characters of traffic signs. For different traffic sign classes, feature extracting should be carried out in different color space.

References

1. Merve, C.K., Muthittin, G., Sima, E.U.: Traffic sign recognition using Scale invariant feature transform and color classification. In: 23rd International Symposium on Computer and Information Sciences, pp. 1–6. IEEE Press, New York (2008)
2. Joshi, M., Gingh, M.J., Dalela, S.: Automatic Colored Traffic Sign Detection using Optoelectronic Correlation Architectures. In: IEEE International Conference on Vehicular Electronics and Safety, pp. 75–78. IEEE Press, New York (2008)
3. King, H.L.: Intra color-shape classification for traffic sign recognition. In: International Computer Symposium, pp. 642–647 (2010)
4. Chen, H.B., Wang, Q., Xu, X.R., et al.: Line detection in traffic sign image based on improved Hough transforms. Opt. Precision Eng. 17(5), 1111–1118 (2009)
5. Andrey, V., Jo, K.H.: Automatic Detection and Recognition of Traffic Signs using Geometric Structure Analysis. In: International Joint Conference on SICE-ICASE, pp. 1451–1456 (2006)
6. Rughooputh, S.D.D.V., Buootun, H., Rughooputh, H.C.S.: Pulse coupled neural networks for sign recognition for navigation. In: IEEE International Conference on Industrial Technology, vol. 1, pp. 89–94. IEEE Press, New York (2003)
7. Wang, Z.H.B., Ma, Y.D., Cheng, F.Y., et al.: Review of pulse-coupled neural networks. Image and Vision Computing 28(10), 5–13 (2010)

A Novel Framework about Multi-focus Image Fusion

Xiaoqing Luo[1], Xiaojun Wu[1], and Zhancheng Zhang[2]

[1] School of Internet of Things Jiangnan University, Wuxi, Jiangsu
214122, People's Republic of China
{xiaoqing_luo_jnu,xiaojun_wu_jnu}@163.com
[2] Suzhou Institute of Nano-tech and Nano-bionics, Suzhou, Jiangsu
215123, People's Republic of China
cimszhang@163.com

Abstract. Multi-focus image fusion aims to combine a set of images that are captured from the same scene but with different focuses for producing another sharper image. To tackle the above challenge, a novel framework about multi-focus image fusion is proposed, which belongs to the fusion method based on transform domain. The regions of input image are divided to three categories: detail, plain and transition. Selecting the appropriate decision index and combining with the global and local information to achieve image fusion. This framework is flexible and generic and brings in fusion images with higher spatial resolution.

Keywords: Multi-focus, image fusion, framework, transform.

1 Introduction

Multisensor image fusion has become an area of intense research in the past few years. The fused image should be more useful for human visual or machine perception[1]. Since optical imaging cameras cannot capture objects at various distances all in focus, several images with different sharp parts are fused to get one image with all the objects focused. In this paper, we will focus on multi-focus image fusion. A simple method is to perform a simple normalized aggregation of the images. The main drawback is that all information content within the images are treated the same. A normalized weighted aggregation approach to image fusion can be used[2]. Li et al. introduced a method based on the selection of image blocks from source images[3]. The basic idea of these kind of methods is how to design focus measures to choose the clearer image blocks from source images to construct the fused image[4][5].

Recently, multi-resolution analysis has become a widely adopted technique perform image fusion[6][7]. The wavelet-based statistical feature can be used to sharpness measure[8]. In addition, according to region content the wavelet coefficients are defined different fused strategy, which is more effecient. One limitation of pixel or decomposition coefficients based methods is that they are sensitive to noise or misregistration. Therefore, some researchers proposed to fuse images using region-based methods in a wavelet decomposition framework[9][10]. The key challenge of multi-focus image fusion is proper to judge the type of local content and design fused

F.L. Wang et al. (Eds.): CMSP 2012, CCIS 346, pp. 32–37, 2012.
© Springer-Verlag Berlin Heidelberg 2012

strategy. To tackle the above challenge, A novel framework is proposed, which is based on multi-resolution transform. The input image is partitioned into regions, which are divided to three categories: detail, plain and transition. The type of region is distinguished by sharpness criterion and similarity measure. The detail and plain region adopt global fusion means and the transition region use local fusion means for high frequency. The fusion framework adequately considers the information feature of image, and exploits the advantage of region-based and pixel-based fusion method to design fusion strategy. Experimental results show that the approach is capable of image fusion with higher image quality.

2   Novel Multi-focus Image Fusion Framework

Fig.1 is the framework of multi-focus image fusion. Where A and B are the source images, LA and LB are the low frequency information of source image, HA and HB are the high frequency information of source image, F is the fusion image. LF and HF is the low and high frequency information of fusion image.

First, the source images are decomposed into low and high frequency information. At the same time, we can partition A and B into corresponding regions. The easiest way is to partition windows. Second, some common fusion means are used to fuse low frequency parts such as weighted average et al. For high frequency parts, the fusion

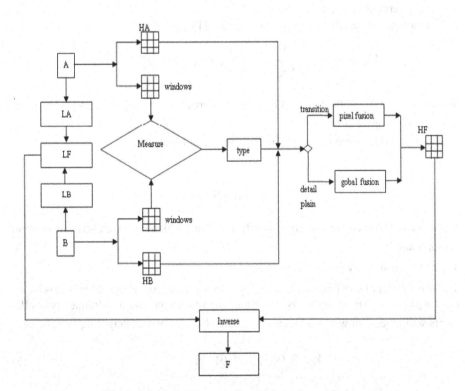

Fig. 1. Schematic diagram of multi-focus image fusion

strategy is designed by the type of regions. The regions are divided into three types: detail, plain and transition. When the image is out-focus, the detail region become blur from clear and the plain region basically unchanged. The transition region include the boundary between focus and out-focus, which is made up of clear pixels and blur pixels. The sharpness and similarity function are used to determine the type of region. If the corresponding region has the large difference of sharpness, we think it as detail region. Otherwise, it is the other types. We use similarity function to further distinguish plain and transition region based on sharpness function. The corresponding region of plain type has high degree of similarity, transition type is exactly the opposite. According to region type, we select different fusion means. Owing to the particularity of transition region, we achieve the fusion based on pixel. However, the other types are fused by global information of region. This framework based on windows and take advantage of the superiority of local and global fusion to design the fusion strategy according the content of image, which more reasonable and robust. At last, the fusion result is obtained by inverse transformation with fused low and high frequency information.

3   Concrete Realization of Fusion Framework

The concrete realization of fusion framework is described as follows:

1. The region is simplified for window.
2. The variance is selected as sharpness function[11].

$$Variance = \frac{1}{M \times N} \sum_x \sum_y \left(f(x, y) - \mu \right)^2 \qquad (1)$$

Where M and N are the row and column of source images and $f(x, y)$ is the pixel gray, μ is the gray mean.

3. The vector difference [12] is defined as similarity function.

$$S_{mv} = 1 - \frac{|a - b|}{|a| + |b|} \qquad (2)$$

Where m and v represent the corresponding region, which are stretched out column vector a and b.

4. The fusion strategy can be defined as:

The wavelet detail coefficients are used together with a decision algorithm that is based on sharpness and similarity measures. Thus, the fused high and low frequency coefficients set in the i-th windows region $y_{i,F}$ are obtained by the weighting factors, i.e.

$$y_{i,F} = \omega_{i,A} y_{i,A} + \omega_{i,B} y_{i,B} \qquad (3)$$

where $\omega_{i,A}$ and $\omega_{i,B}$ are the weighting factors, which are determined by $\omega_{i,B} = 1 - \omega_{i,A}$. When the low frequency coefficients are fused, $\omega_{i,A} = 0.5$. Otherwise, $\omega_{i,A}$ is defined as

$$\omega_{i,A} = \begin{cases} 1 & if\ abs(\Delta u) > T_1\ \&\&\Delta u > 0 \quad type:det\,ail \\ 0 & if\ abs(\Delta u) > T_1\ \&\&\Delta u < 0 \quad type:det\,ail \\ \dfrac{E_{i,A}}{E_{i,A} + E_{i,B}} & if\ abs(\Delta u) < T_1\ \&\&S_{i,AB} > T_2\ type:plain \end{cases} \quad (4)$$

$if\ abs(\Delta u) < T_1\ \&\&S_{i,AB} \leq T_2\ type:transition$

$$y_{i,F(x,y)} = \omega_{i,A} y_{i,A(x,y)} + \omega_{i,B} y_{i,B(x,y)} \quad (5)$$

$$\omega_{i,A(x,y)} = \begin{cases} 1 & grad_{i,A(x,y)} > grad_{i,B(x,y)} \\ 0 & grad_{i,A(x,y)} < grad_{i,B(x,y)} \end{cases} \quad (6)$$

$$\Delta u = sharpness(i,A) - sharpness(i,B); \quad E_i = \sum_x \sum_y y_{i,(x,y)}^2$$

where the coefficient T_1 and T_2 are the threshold of the difference of sharpness and similarity measure. E_i is the region energy. And $grad_{i,(x,y)}$ is the gradient and $\omega_{i,(x,y)}$ is the weighting factor of pixel (x, y) in the region of input images.

4   Experimental Results

In this section, the Clock images are employed to do the image fusion experiment. the source images are from http://www.imagefusion.org/. The image size is 232×232. The parameters of the proposed methods are experimentally set as $T_1 = 0.05$ and $T_2 = 0.6$. The size of windows is 5×5. The above parameter settings is experimentally selected. Fig.2 shows the clock images using different image fusion approaches. Fig.2(a) is the left focus image and Fig.2(b) is the right focus image. Fig.2(c) is the multi-focus fusion imge using the DWT method[6]. Fig.2(d) is the normalized weighted aggregation approach (J.Tian's method[2]). Fig.2(e) is the multifocus image fusion using morphological wavelets (Ishita De's method[7]).Fig.2(f) shows the fusion result based on the selection of image blocks from source images (Wei huang's method[4]). Fig.2(g) shows the fusion result using the proposed method.

Table 1 shows the values of the seven object evaluation parameters to test the effectiveness by comparing the parameter values of the fusion images in Fig.2. The object evaluation including[11]:mean(U), variance(V), entropy(E), mutual information

(MI), spatial frequency(SF), gradient(G) and running time(t). With the biggest V, SF and G, the fusion image of Fig.2(g) is the clearest. The values of U, E and MI of Fig.2(g) are larger, which means the fusion image get abundant information. The only shortcoming is the running time have a little long, which can solve by enhancing hardware. As expected, most evaluation criteria show that the quality of Fig.2 (g) is the best. The novel framework about multi-focus image fusion is superior to weighted aggregation approach and selection of image blocks from source images et al.

(a) source image A (b) source image B   (c) the DWT method (d) J.Tian's method

(e) Ishita De's method   (f) Wei huang's method   (g) the propose method

Fig. 2. the source images and fusion images

Table 1. Values of the object evaluations for fusion images in Fig.2

Images /statistics	U	V	E	MI	SF	G	t
Fig.2(c)	102.8308	46.1398	5.0797	7.1224	11.7789	7.4669	0.5350
Fig.2(d)	102.9316	46.9342	5.0985	7.6020	14.9038	9.1135	15.2210
Fig.2(e)	102.4358	47.1059	5.1049	7.7083	15.9267	9.9196	0.6080
Fig.2(f)	102.6793	46.9547	5.1012	8.5963	15.9532	9.8424	1.9330
Fig.2(g)	102.8290	47.2443	5.1034	7.8681	16.3470	9.9610	5.2570

5   Conclusion

A novel framework about multi-focus image fusion is proposed. The selecting principles of different subband coefficients obtained by the wavelet decomposition are discussed in detail. The averaging scheme is presented for the lowpass subband coefficients. Based on the region type, a global scheme combined with the local scheme is put forward for the bandpass directional subband coefficients fusion. The judge of region type is a key step, which can use sharpness and similarity function. It is important to note that the proposed fusion algorithm outperforms some typical methods. Experimental results validate the effectiveness of the proposal.

Acknowledgments. This work was supported by the National Natural Science Foundation of P.R. China (Grant No.:60973094,61103128) and 111 Project of Chinese Ministry of Education (Grant No. B12018), Key Grant Project of Chinese Ministry of Education (Grant No.: 311024), Scientific Research Foundation for new Scholars (Grant No.: 1255210232110940).

References

1. Goshtasby, A.A., Nikolov, S.: Image fusion: adbances in the state of the art. Information Fusion 8(2), 114–118 (2008)
2. Tian, J., Chen, L., Ma, L., et al.: Multi-focus image fusion using a bilateral gradient-based sharpness criterion. Optics Communications 284, 80–87 (2011)
3. Li, S., Kwok, J.T., Wang, Y.: Combination of images with diverse focuses using the spatial frequency. Information Fusion 2, 169–176 (2001)
4. Huang, W., Jing, Z.: Evaluation of focus measures in multi-focus image fusion. Pattern Recognition Letters 28, 493–500 (2007, 2008)
5. Huang, W., Jing, Z.: Multi-focus image fusion using pulse coupled neural network. Pattern Recognition Letters 28, 1123–1132 (2007)
6. Li, H., Manjunath, B.S., Mitra, S.K.: Multisensor image fusion using the wavelet transform. Graphical Models and Image Processing 57, 235–245 (1995)
7. De, I., Chanda, B., Chattopadhyay, B.: Enhancing effective depth-of field by image fusion using mathematical morphology. Image and Vision Computing 24(12), 1278–1287 (2006)
8. Tian, J., Chen, L.: Adaptive multi-focus image fusion using a wavelet-based statistical sharpness measure 92, 2137–2146 (2012)
9. Nikolov, S.G., Lewis, J.J., O'Callaghan, R.J., et al.: Hybrid fused displays: between pixel- and regionbased image fusion. In: Proceedings of 7th International Conference on Information Fusion, Stockholm, Sweden, pp. 1072–1079 (June 2004)
10. Piella, G.: A general framework for multiresolution image fusion: from pixels to regions. Information Fusion 4(4), 259–280 (2003)
11. Luo, X., Wu, X.: New metric of image fusion based on region similarity. Optical Engineering 49(4), 047006-1–047006-13 (2010)
12. Thung, K.-H., Paramesran, R., et al.: Content-based image quality metric using similarity measure of moment vectors. Pattern Recognition 45, 2193–2204 (2012)

Calibration System for the Cross-Correlation Algorithm Based on OpenCV[*]

Min Chen and Hongrong Wang

Fujian University of Technology,
Department of Computer and Information Science
Fuzhou, PRC China
chenmin@fjut.edu.cn

Abstract. The application of cross-correlation algorithm should be preceded by the calibration system validating the precision and accuracy of the algorithm. Selected adjacent two images from the video stream of the moving target, and calculate the displacement of the moving target, and then the vector information can be obtained according to the time interval set in the video capture rate. Cross-correlation algorithm in order to reduce computation, the image on the equivalent land is divided into several regions, the sub-regions of the same location is calculated. The selection of the size of the sub-regions will affect the accuracy of measurement results, so the image calibration system using a variety of images to find the association between the size of the sub-regions and the intensity of the images. This will reduce the generation of error, and founded a basement for the subsequent processing. Because the selection of the sub-regions size will affect the accuracy of measurement results, the image calibration system testing images with variety intensities to find the association between the size of the sub-regions and the image intensities. This will reduce the generation of error, and lay a good foundation for the subsequent processing. The development of the image calibration system is developed under Windows, using C/C++ programming languages, and the openCV open source image library.

Keywords: calibration system, cross-correlation algorithm, sub-region, openCV

1   Introduction

Cross-correlation technique has been successfully applied in many fields[1]; its development was based on information theory and stochastic process theory. In the cross-correlation algorithm, the image of the moving target is a random distribution of the digital field, using the correlation search technology to extract the displacement

---

[*] This research was supported by the general project of the Natural Science Foundation of Fujian Province (No. 2008F3003), General project of the Fujian Province Department of Education Technology (No. JB08193), research project of Fujian University of Technology (No. GY-Z0803).

F.L. Wang et al. (Eds.): CMSP 2012, CCIS 346, pp. 38–45, 2012.

information[2].Cross-correlation technique is to measure the same target displacement in the movement in the adjacent two images, combined with the frame rate, displacement divided by the reciprocal of the frame rate (i.e. the time interval) to get the velocity[3]. In order to validate the correctness and reliability of the algorithm, it is necessary to calibrate and clarify the accuracy of the algorithm.

Calibration of the algorithm by computing the image of the different particle density was calculated and analyzed to select the most suitable size of the sub-region[4]. Cross-calibration of the correlation algorithm is to enable the measurement of the algorithm can be applied to the speed of the image of the particle motion in a variety of situations, and as much as possible to minimize the error introduced by the algorithm itself. Meanwhile, the cross-correlation algorithm in the calculation, by using the fast Fourier transform in order to improve computing speed[3], to reduce the computational complexity and improve the program timeliness.

OpenCV is Intel ® Open Source Computer Vision Library. It consists of a series of C functions and a small amount of C++ classes, and many common image processing and computer vision algorithms[5]. Algorithm is the standard functions on the basis of openCV provided.

2   Calculation Method

2.1   Principle of the Cross-Correlation Algorithm

The algorithm is calculation of the cross-correlation function of two adjacent images using FFT (Fast Fourier Transform)[6]. The first step is to convert the information of the two sub-regions from the spatial to the frequency domain, and then do the convolution of two Fourier spectrums, and then Fourier's inverse transformation to restore it to the spatial domain. The proceeds of a cross-correlation function, the location of its maximum value is the particle displacement coordinates of the demand area.

2.2   Calculation Steps

Division of the Sub-region

The selection of the sub-region size is very important in the cross-correlation calculation. The larger region is set, it will has more information in it, more computation time will needed to calculate, also more noise will be produced to, reducing the correlation of the two sub-region. Instead, the smaller sub-region will contain little information, the less effective bubble pairs will reduced, or even unable to meet the necessary conditions for correlation analysis, which will affect the reliability and correctness of the analysis results. Therefore, the choice of a suitable size of sub-region will reduce the impact of the noise to be reduced to the lowest level, reduce the amount of calculation of the correlation analysis, and while at the same time improve the accuracy and reliability of the results of the analysis. According to the Nyquist sampling theorem, the sampling frequency is greater than the twice of highest signal frequency, the signal will be reconstructed without distortion[7]. Therefore, the size of the sub-region should be chosen at least three times larger than the bubble maximum displacement in the sub-region.

The division of the sub-region often is unable to accommodate the sub-region at the image edge, as shown in the dashed box in figure 1. In order ensure the sub-region of the same size, it is necessary to shift left of the region. The same method is used for the Y-direction.

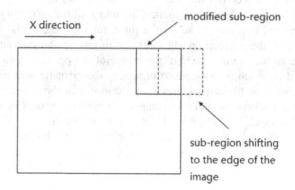

Fig. 1. The diagram of the division

Application of the Algorithm

The actual implementation of the cross-correlation algorithm is equivalent to two images divided into multiple sub-districts, cross-correlation calculations on the two sub-zones in the two images on the same location. The detailed calculation steps of the algorithm as shown below in figure 2.

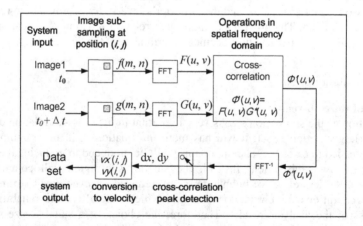

Fig. 2. Numeric processing flow-chart of cross-correlation algorithm

3   Performance Tests

To verify the algorithm, the image shift technique is used on a variety of densities images, so that the particle motion in the image displacements is the same and the displacements are known. The two images before and after the shifting are calculated by the cross-correlation algorithm.

Low-Density Image Test

A pair of single moving particle images is selected, as shown in figure 3.

Fig. 3. A pair of images with single moving particle

Amount of the translation of these two pictures is unknown, the particle motion in these two apparently difficult to see with the naked eye, but you can roughly estimate that this is a small displacement values, and their cross-correlation calculation result (unit: pixels) is:

Table 1. low density x and y displacement

Sub-region No.	X displacement	Y displacement
-	2	1

Because of the single moving particle, the images are not divided into sub-regions, the whole images have been calculated, the single-particle displacement is (2, 1).

Another low-density images before and after the shifting are shown in figure 4.

Fig. 4. Low-density images before and after the shifting

The actual shifting of this group of pictures are (10, -3), matching experimental results (10, -3).

Medium-Density Image Test

A pair of single moving particle images is selected, as shown in figure 5.

Fig. 5. Medium-density particle motion images

This group of medium-density particle motion image size is 256*256, take the sub-area size is 8*8, and the offset is 2, part of the calculation result is:

Table 2. Medium density x and y displacement

Sub-region No.	X displacement	Y displacement
...		
9517	0	0
9518	0	0
9519	0	0
9520	0	0
9521	0	0
9522	0	0
9523	0	0
9524	0	0
...		

The image is divided into 15 500 sub-areas, but part of the results shows above that the sub-region size selected is too small, many sub-regions do not contain enough information to calculation, the result does not have representative.

Take the sub-area size is 20*20, and the offset is 10, part of the calculation result is:

Table 3. Medium density x and y displacement with lager sub-region

Sub-region No.	X displacement	Y displacement
...		
27	1	1
28	1	1
29	1	1
30	1	1
31	2	1
32	2	1
33	2	1
34	2	1
...		

From the calculation results can be seen that the size of the sub-region has eliminated most of the data redundancy.

High-Density Image Test

High density images before and after shifting as shown in figure 6, (7, -9) is the given displacement. Displacement is very small, the changes are hard to be seen.

Fig. 6. High-density image pairs before and after shift

The sub-regions of a variety of sizes calculated by the velocity vectors are shown in figure 7 and figure 8. The number n-m each marked at the upper half of the figure, in which n means the size of the sub-regions in the calculation, m is the offset.

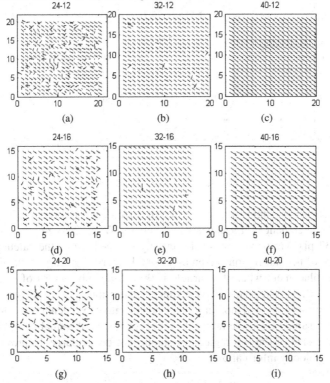

Fig. 7. (a-i) subplot: 24,32,40 offset:12~20

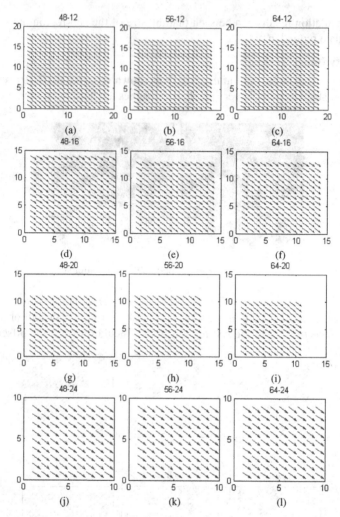

Fig. 8. (a-l) subplot: 48, 56, 64 offset: 12~24

It can be seen from figure 7 and 8, when the size of the sub-regions is taken as 24 pixels, the displacement vector appears more errors. When the size of the sub-regions is taken as 32 pixel error vector is substantially reduced, while the calculated results when the size of the sub-regions taken as 40 pixel no error appears, indicating that the maximum displacement when the particle is 9pixel the sub-regions of size> 32pixel. That is, when the sub-region size is 4 times greater than the displacement, several sizes of the sub-region will not introduce errors into the calculation. On the other hand, with the same offset, the larger the sub-region size, the smaller numbers of the vectors, so the size of the sub-regions of should not be too large, to prevent lose the details of the velocity information.

4   Conclusions

Cross-correlation algorithm first divides the image into a number of the sub-regions with the same size, and then each pair sub-regions are calculated to obtain the velocity vector, yielding statistical average velocity vectors. The choice of the sub-regions size is particularly critical, made too small, and easy to produce more redundant data and error; made too much, will lose details. Therefore, several tests are conducted to select the sub-regions size. From which, it shows that the images with different densities, the size of the selected sub-area related with the movement of the particle displacement. When the size of sub-region is four times larger than the displacement, the speed information can be basically restored; the size of the sub-regions will not introduce error. The above discussion laid a solid foundation for the applications of the cross-correlation algorithm.

Acknowledgment. This work was supported by the general project of the Natural Science Foundation of Fujian Province, and the general project of the Fujian Province Department of Education Technology, and the research project of Fujian University of Technology.

References

1. Zhang, Z.H., Yang, H.Y.: Use Cross-correlation To Discern Content of An Image. Microcomputer Information 31 (2009)
2. Wong, W.G., Liao, G.X., Wang, X.S.: DPIV image diagnosis method research. Fire Safety Science 8(4), 1–7 (1999)
3. Chen, M., He, J.H., Ji, Y.J., Chen, L.Y.: Researches on the Measurement of Bubble Velocity Based on Cross-Correlation. Photonica Sinica 34(8), 1254–1256 (2005)
4. Sun, H.Q., Kang, H.G.: DPIV flow field measurement technology of data processing. Journal of Dalian University of Technology 40(3), 364–367 (2000)
5. Yu, S.Q.: "openCV Overview",
   http://www.opencv.org.cn/index.php/OpenCVoverview
6. Kang, H.G., Wang, P.R., Sun, H.Q.: Cross-correlation technique applied research in ocean engineering. Ocean Technology 22(4), 58–61 (2003)
7. Willert, C.E., Gharib, M.: Digital particle image velocimetry. Experiments in Fluids 10(4), 181–193 (1991)

Audio-Visual Emotion Recognition
Based on Facial Expression and Affective Speech

Shiqing Zhang[1,2,*], Lemin Li[1], and Zhijin Zhao[3]

[1] School of Communication and Information Engineering,
University of Electronic Science and Technology of China,
Chengdu 611731, China
[2] School of Physics and Electronic Engineering, Taizhou University,
Taizhou 318000, China
[3] School of Communications Engineering, Hangzhou Dianzi University,
Hangzhou 310018, China
tzczsq @163.com

Abstract. In this paper, the performance of audio-visual emotion recognition integrating facial expression and affective speech is investigated. The local binary patterns (LBP) features are extracted for facial image representations for the single facial expression recognition. Three typical acoustic features including prosody features, voice quality features as well as the Mel-Frequency Cepstral Coefficients (MFCC) features are extracted for the single speech emotion recognition. Then, we fuse the two modalities, i.e. facial expression and affective speech, and performed audio-visual emotion recognition at the feature-level. The support vector machines (SVM) is used for all the emotion classification. Experimental results on the publicly available eNTERFACE'05 emotional audio-visual database demonstrate that the presented method of audio-visual expression recognition obtains an accuracy of 66.51%, giving better performance than the mono-modality.

Keywords: Emotion recognition, Local binary patterns, Acoustic features, Support vector machines.

1 Introduction

Research on understanding and modeling human emotions, i.e., affective computing [1], is currently a very active topic within the engineering community. Facial expression and speech are two main vehicles of human emotion expressions, since people mostly rely on facial expression and speech to understand someone's affective states [2]. In recent years, recognizing human emotions from facial expression and speech, i.e., audio-visual emotion recognition, has increasing attracted extensive attention within artificial intelligence field due to its important applications to human-computer interaction [3].

---

* Corresponding author.

F.L. Wang et al. (Eds.): CMSP 2012, CCIS 346, pp. 46–52, 2012.

Previous work on emotion recognition focused on recognizing human emotions by using a single modality, such as the single affective speech signals or the single facial expression. Motivated by very little work done on audio-visual emotion recognition, in this work we investigate the performance of audio-visual emotion recognition integrating facial expression and affective speech. At first, we extracted the relevant features from affective facial images and speech signals. And the popular support vector machines (SVM) [4] classifier is trained separately with face and acoustic features for mono-modal emotion recognition. Then, we fuse affective face and speech modalities for classification into combined emotion categories at the feature-level. To evaluate the performance of audio-visual emotion recognition, the publicly available eNTERFACE'05 emotional audio-visual database [5] is used for audio-visual emotion recognition experiments.

2   Feature Extraction

In this section, the details of feature extraction from facial images and affective speech are given in brief.

2.1   Facial Feature Extraction

Since the local binary patterns (LBP) [6, 7] has a predominant characteristic, that is, LBP tolerates against illumination changes and operates with its computational simplicity, we adopted LBP for facial image representations for facial expression recognition.

The process of LBP features extraction generally is consisted of three steps: firstly, a facial image is divided into several non-overlapping blocks. Secondly, LBP histograms are computed for each block. Finally, the block LBP histograms are concatenated into a single vector. As a result, the facial image is represented by the LBP code.

The cropped facial images of 110×150 pixels contain facial main components such as mouth, eyes, brows and noses. The LBP operator is applied to the whole region of the cropped facial images. For better uniform-LBP feature extraction, two parameters, i.e., the LBP operator and the number of regions divided, need to be optimized. Similar to the setting in [8], we selected the 59-bin operator, and divided the 110×150 pixels face images into 18×21 pixels regions, giving a good trade-off between recognition performance and feature vector length. Thus face images were divided into 42 (6×7) regions, and represented by the LBP histograms with the length of 2478 (59×42).

2.2   Acoustic Feature Extraction

Although there is no general agreement regarding the best features for speech emotion recognition, the most widely used acoustic features are prosody features, voice quality features as well as the spectral features. In our work, the extracted prosody features contain pitch, intensity and duration. And the representative voice quality features include the first three formants (F1, F2, F3), spectral energy distribution, harmonics-to-noise-ratio (HNR), pitch irregularity (jitter) and amplitude irregularity (shimmer). As the representative spectral features, the popular Mel-Frequency Cepstral Coefficients (MFCC) is extracted. Some typical statistical parameters such as mean, standard derivations (std), median, quartiles, and so on, are computed for each extracted feature. These extracted acoustic features from emotional utterances, 204 in total, are shown in Table 1.

Table 1. Acoustic feature extraction

Feature types	Feature groups	Statistics
Prosody features	Pitch	maximum, minimum, range, mean, std, first quartile, median, third quartile, inter-quartile range, the mean-absolute-slope
	Intensity	maximum, minimum, range, mean, std, first quartile, median, third quartile, inter-quartile range
	Duration	total-frames, voiced-frames, unvoiced-frames, ratio of voiced vs. unvoiced frames, ratio of voiced-frames vs. total-frames, ratio of unvoiced-frames vs. total-frames
Voice quality features	Formants	mean of F1, std of F1, median of F1, bandwidth of median of F1, mean of F2, std of F2, median of F2, bandwidth of median of F2, mean of F3, std of F3, median of F3, bandwidth of median of F3
	Spectral energy distribution	band energy from 0 Hz to 500 Hz, band energy from 500 Hz to 1000 Hz, band energy from 2500 Hz to 4000 Hz, band energy from 4000 Hz to 5000 Hz.
	HNR	maximum, minimum, range, mean, std
	Jitter, Shimmer	Jitter, Shimmer
Spectral features	MFCC	mean, std of the first 13 MFCC, and their first-deltas and second-deltas

3   Support Vector Machines for Emotion Classification

Support vector machines (SVM) [4] is based on the statistical learning theory of structural risk management which aims to limit the empirical risk on the training data and on the capacity of the decision function. The basic concept of SVM is to transform the input vectors to a higher dimensional space by a nonlinear transform, and then an optimal hyperplane which separates the data can be found.

Given training data set $(x_1, y_1), ..., (x_l, y_l), y_i \in \{-1, 1\}$, to find the optimal hyperplane, a nonlinear transform, $Z = \Phi(x)$, is used to make training data become linearly dividable. A weight w and offset b satisfying the following criteria will be found:

$$\begin{cases} w^T z_i + b \geq 1, & y_i = 1 \\ w^T z_i + b \leq -1, & y_i = -1 \end{cases} \tag{1}$$

We can summarize the above procedure to the following:

$$\min_{w,b} \Phi(w) = \frac{1}{2}(w^T w) \tag{2}$$

Subject to $y_i(w^T z_i + b) \geq 1, \quad i = 1, 2, ..., n$

If the sample data is not linearly dividable, the following function should be minimized.

$$\Phi(w) = \frac{1}{2} w^T w + C \sum_{i=1}^{l} \xi_i \tag{3}$$

whereas ξ can be understood as the error of the classification and C is the penalty parameter for this term.

By using Lagrange method, the decision function of $w_0 = \sum_{i=1}^{l} \lambda_i y_i z_i$ will be

$$f = \text{sgn}\left[\sum_{i=0}^{l} \lambda_i y_i (z^T z_i) + b\right] \tag{4}$$

From the functional theory, a non-negative symmetrical function $K(u,v)$ uniquely defines a Hilbert space H, where K is the rebuild kernel in the space H:

$$K(u,v) = \sum_i \alpha \varphi_i(u) \varphi_i(v) \tag{5}$$

This stands for an internal product of a characteristic space:

$$z_i^T z = \Phi(x_i)^T \Phi(x) = K(x_i, x) \tag{6}$$

Then the decision function can be written as:

$$f = \text{sgn}\left[\sum_{i=1}^{l} \lambda_i y_i K(x_i, x) + b\right] \tag{7}$$

The development of a SVM emotion classification model depends on the selection of kernel function. There are several kernels that can be used in SVM models. These include linear, polynomial, radial basis function (RBF) and sigmoid function.

$$K(x_i, x_j) = \begin{cases} x_i^T x_j & Linear \\ (\gamma x_i^T x_j + coefficient)^{degree} & Polynomial \\ \exp(-\gamma | x_i - x_j |^2) & RBF \\ \tanh(\gamma x_i^T x_j + coefficient) & Sigmoid \end{cases} \tag{8}$$

4   Audio-Visual Emotion Database

The publicly available eNTERFACE'05 audio-visual emotion database [5] is used for experiments. It contains six basic emotions, i.e., anger, disgust, fear, joy, sadness, and surprise. 43 non-native (eight female) English speaking subjects from 14 nations posed the six basic emotions with five sentences. Each subject was told to listen to six successive short stories, each of them intended to elicit a particular emotion. They then had to react to each of the situations by uttering previously read phrases that fit the short story. Five phrases are available per emotion, as "I have nothing to give you! Please don't hurt me!" in the case of fear. Two experts judged whether the reaction expressed the intended emotion in an unambiguous way. Only if this was the case was a sample (= sentence) added to the database. Therefore, each sentence in the database has one assigned emotion label, which indicates the emotion expressed by the speaker in this sentence.

5   Experiment Study

5.1   Experiment Setup

All extracted features, including the LBP features and the acoustic features, were normalized by a mapping to [0, 1] before anything else. In all classification experiments, the SVM classifier is used. We used the LIBSVM package [9] to implement SVM algorithm with radial basis function (RBF) kernel, kernel parameter optimization, one-against-one strategy for multi-class classification problem. A 10-fold cross validation scheme is employed in 6-class emotion classification experiments, and the average results are reported. Our experiment configuration is Intel CPU 2.10 GHz, 1G RAM memory, MATLAB 7.0.1 (R14).

5.2   Experimental Results and Analysis

We firstly employed the extracted LBP features with the length of 2478 to perform the single facial expression recognition. Then, the extracted 204 acoustic features are directly used to perform the single speech emotion recognition. Finally, we integrated the extracted LBP features and the acoustic features and performed audio-visual emotion recognition experiments at the feature-level fusion. The experimental results are given in Table 2. As shown in Table 2, the performance of audio-visual emotion recognition comes up to an accuracy of 66.51%, outperforming the single facial expression recognition and the single speech emotion recognition. This indicates that fusion of facial expression and affective speech at the feature-level achieves better performance than the used mono-modality (i.e., facial expression or affective speech).

Table 2. Comparison of Emotion Recognition Results

Methods	Facial expression	Affective speech	Audio-visual
Accuracy	62.79%	44.73%	66.51%

To further explore the recognition results of different kinds of emotions when performing audio-visual emotion recognition, the confusion matrix of audio-visual emotion recognition results is given in Table 3. The confusion matrix of the results in

Table 3 indicates that three emotions, i.e., anger, joy and sadness, can be recognized . well. In detail, the recognition accuracy is 81.86% for anger, 73.02% for joy, and 74.88% for sadness. The other four emotions are classified badly with an accuracy of less than 61%.

Table 3. Confusion Matrix of Audio-Visual Emotion Recognition Results at the Feature Level

	Anger	Disgust	Fear	Joy	Sadness	Surprise	Accuracy
Anger	176	13	9	4	2	11	81.86%
Disgust	28	112	24	25	10	16	52.09%
Fear	23	21	122	6	27	16	56.74%
Joy	7	25	5	157	4	17	73.02%
Sadness	4	11	26	2	161	11	74.88%
Surprise	12	17	26	16	14	130	60.46%
Overall accuracy							66.51%

6   Conclusions

This paper has presented a method of audio-visual emotion recognition based on facial expression and affective speech. We separately performed facial expression recognition and speech emotion recognition, and then fused facial expression and speech modalities for classification into combined emotion categories at the feature-level. The experimental results on eNTERFACE'05 audio-visual emotion database show that the performance of audio-visual emotion recognition integrating facial expression and affective speech is better than the performance obtained by the single facial expression or by the single affective speech.

References

1. Picard, R.: Affective computing. MIT Press, Cambridge (1997)
2. Cowie, R., Douglas-Cowie, E., Tsapatsoulis, N., Votsis, G., Kollias, S., Fellenz, W., Taylor, J.G.: Emotion Recognition in Human-Computer Interaction. IEEE Signal Processing Magazine 18(01), 32–80 (2001)
3. Jaimes, A., Sebe, N.: Multimodal human-computer interaction: A survey. Computer Vision and Image Understanding 108(1-2), 116–134 (2007)
4. Cortes, C., Vapnik, V.: Support-vector networks. Machine Learning 20(3), 273–297 (1995)
5. Martin, O., Kotsia, I., Macq, B., Pitas, I.: The eNTERFACE'05 Audio-Visual Emotion Database. In: 22nd International Conference on Data Engineering Workshops Atlanta, Atlanta, GA, USA (2006)
6. Ojala, T., Pietikäinen, M., Mäenpää, T.: Multiresolution gray scale and rotation invariant texture analysis with local binary patterns. IEEE Transactions on Pattern Analysis and Machine Intelligence 24(7), 971–987 (2002)

7. Huang, D., Shan, C., Ardabilian, M., Wang, Y., Chen, L.: Local Binary Patterns and Its Application to Facial Image Analysis: A Survey. IEEE Transactions on Systems, Man, and Cybernetics, Part C: Applications and Reviews 41(99), 1–17 (2011)
8. Shan, C., Gong, S., McOwan, P.: Facial expression recognition based on Local Binary Patterns: A comprehensive study. Image and Vision Computing 27(6), 803–816 (2009)
9. Chang, C., Lin, C.: LIBSVM: a library for support vector machines (2001), Software available at http://www.csie.ntu.edu.tw/cjlin/libsvm

Propagation-Aware Online Packet Classification for Live Video Streaming over DiffServ Networks

Hao Liu, Jing Li, and Shang-He Yang

Engineering Research Center of Digitized Textile & Fashion Technology,
Ministry of Education, Donghua University, Shanghai, China
{liuhao,lijing,yangsh}@dhu.edu.cn

Abstract. Although a two-class DiffServ network provides certain transmission quality guarantees for live video streaming, the received video quality may still be seriously degraded if it lacks an effective online classification mechanism for video packets. By analyzing the available coding information in encoded frames and error-propagation effect in future frames, a propagation-aware online packet classification scheme is proposed to timely classify different packets in the current frame. Simulation results show that the proposed scheme can significantly increase the determination accuracy of traffic classes, and thus effectively improve loss resilience of live video streaming over the two-class DiffServ network.

Keywords: Live video streaming, Two-class DiffServ, Packet classification, Loss resilience, Error propagation.

1 Introduction

Due to the good scalability and manageability, the Differentiated-Services (DiffServ) network is a very promising architecture for next generation Internet, where a two-class DiffServ network is the most common DiffServ architecture [1]. In a two-class DiffServ network, video packets are classified into two traffic classes: high-reliability traffic class and best-effort traffic class. The packets as the high-reliability traffic class are transmitted with nearly no packet loss. Correspondingly, the packets as the best-effort traffic class will experience the traditional best-effort forwarding, and some packets may be lost due to time-varying transmission errors, buffer overflow or delay bound violation [2]. In the prevalent coding standards (e.g. H.264) for live video streaming, the sophisticated prediction mechanism creates strong dependency between video packets. Consequently, packet loss may result in serious error propagation and substantially deteriorate the received video quality. Due to limited transmission resources and complex coding mechanism, how to improve loss resilience is still a big technical challenge for live video streaming over DiffServ networks. For loss-resilience packet classification, one critical aspect is to evaluate the possible transmission distortion of different packets. The transmission distortion of a video packet may be computed by an analysis-by-synthesis approach [3], where each packet is analyzed by simulating its unique loss and decoding with a given error-concealment method. Based on the analysis-by-synthesis approach, the offline

F.L. Wang et al. (Eds.): CMSP 2012, CCIS 346, pp. 53–60, 2012.
© Springer-Verlag Berlin Heidelberg 2012

simulations in [4] have demonstrated that there is a strong linear correlation between the error-propagation distortion and the motion reference ratio. However, it is impractical for live video streaming to directly use the analysis-by-synthesis approach, where the video packets of the current frame are encoded and classified on-the-fly, and the transmission distortion after the current frame cannot be timely obtained. Therefore, it would be useful that the transmission distortion of future frames could be online estimated according to the current coding results.

For live video streaming over DiffServ networks, some online packet classification techniques have been proposed. Based on the group-of-pictures (GOP) structure, the frame type is directly used to classify video packets [5]: I-frame packets and B-frame packets respectively have high and low loss-resilience importance, and the packets with the same frame type have the degressive importance in a GOP. However, the predetermined metric may result in mistaken classification of packet importance for different video sequences. Further, Przylucki [6] proposed an online packet classification scheme to provide unequal loss protection for important packets, and the scheme focuses on the effect of erroneous packets within a frame while the issue of time-varying error propagation between frames has not been considered. By analyzing the available coding information in encoded frames and error-propagation effect in future frames, we will propose a propagation-aware online packet classification scheme to timely classify different packets in the current frame.

2   Packet Classification of Live Video Streaming

For live video streaming over a two-class DiffServ network, the sender must assign a traffic class to each packet in the current frame. According to the loss-resilience importance of different packets, all packets in a frame need to be timely partitioned into two traffic classes: high-reliability traffic class and best-effort traffic class. "p_h" and "p_b" respectively denote the packet loss probability of high-reliability traffic class and that of best-effort traffic class. Fig. 1 illustrates an example of online packet classification in a frame, where one row of macroblocks is encoded into a packet and each packet with a resynchronization point can be decoded independently. In Fig. 1, two packets are classified as the high-reliability traffic class, and the remaining packets are classified as the best-effort traffic class.

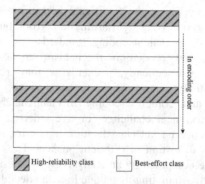

Fig. 1. An example of online packet classification in a frame

The packets in the current frame are stored in a buffer for the online packet classification. The GOP length "N_g" denotes be the fixed frame amount of each GOP. Typically, Frame n ($n{\geq}1$) is equally fragmented into "M" ($M{\geq}1$) slices. Let "K" and "N_P" respectively be the total macroblock amount of each packet and the total pixel amount of each packet. For each frame, "η" denotes the amount of packets as the high-reliability traffic class. In encoding order, "$P_{n,m}$" denotes the packet belonging to Slice m ($1{\leq}m{\leq}M$) of Frame n, and "$S_{n,m}$" denotes the size of Packet $P_{n,m}$. "$f(n,m,j)$" denotes the jth original pixel belonging to the Packet $P_{n,m}$. When a video packet is lost due to network congestion, all frames in the same GOP are impaired due to error propagation, and this phenomenon causes significant degradation of received video quality. Fig. 2 illustrates the error-propagation effect induced by a lost packet, where only one packet of Frame 2 (marked as a black rectangle) is lost, and the subsequent shadow areas with different grayscales denote the possible error-propagation region.

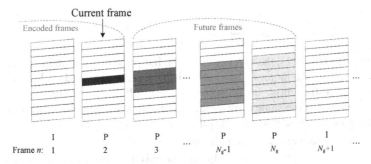

Fig. 2. The error-propagation effect when a video packet is lost

For live video streaming, its end-to-end distortion consists of two additive parts: 1) source-coding distortion induced by lossy compression; 2) transmission distortion induced by packet losses. Often the source-coding distortion and transmission distortion are uncorrelated with each other. For a video packet, larger transmission distortion indicates higher loss-resilience importance. The transmission resources of a frame mainly depend on the amount of important packets. Our objective is to seek an optimal classification policy that reduces the transmission distortion under the resource constraints.

3   Propagation-Aware Online Packet Classification

After encoding the current Frame n, all packets belonging to Frame n can form a packet queue: $Q = \left\{ P_{n,1}, P_{n,2}, \cdots P_{n,m}, \cdots P_{n,M} \right\}$. For the packet classification of the queue Q, three online packet classification schemes will be investigated.

(1) In-order packet classification

In a video frame, the latter packet in encoding order may depend on the coding information of the former packet. The traffic class of each packet can be predetermined according to its encoding order. In encoding order, the former η

packets of each frame are directly classified as the high-reliability traffic class, i.e. from top to bottom. Regardless of transmission distortion, the remaining packets are classified as the best-effort traffic class.

(2) Content-aware online packet classification

In correspondence to the Pixel $f(n,m,j)$, "$\hat{f}(n,m,j)$" and "$\tilde{f}(n,m,j)$" respectively denote its reconstructed value at the sender and that at the receiver. If the Pixel $f(n,m,j)$ is lost, the pixel-copy error concealment is performed, i.e. "$\tilde{f}(n,m,j) = \hat{f}(n-1,m,j)$". By using the coding side information, the instantaneous transmission distortion "$D_i(n,m)$" of the Packet $P_{n,m}$ can be simply calculated by the mean square error (MSE) between the Packet $P_{n,m}$ and its reference Packet $P_{n-1,m}$:

$$D_i(n,m) = \frac{1}{N_P} \cdot \sum_{j=1}^{N_P} [\hat{f}(n,m,j) - \tilde{f}(n,m,j)]^2$$

$$= \frac{1}{N_P} \cdot \sum_{j=1}^{N_P} [\hat{f}(n,m,j) - \hat{f}(n-1,m,j)]^2 \tag{1}$$

Based on the Equation (1), the content-aware online packet classification assumes that the Packet $P_{n,m}$ with the larger $D_i(n,m)$ value is more important, and is classified as the high-reliability traffic class. In the content-aware online packet classification, each packet in a frame has the same error-propagation effect, which may result in mistaken classification of packet importance for different video sequences.

(3) Propagation-aware online packet classification

When a video packet is lost, the induced transmission distortion can propagate to subsequent frames in a GOP. Based on the above content-aware online packet classification, we further propose the propagation-aware online packet classification scheme. Although the prevalent coding standards introduce multiple macroblock modes for luminance component, all macroblocks can be classified into two basic types: Inter-macroblock with inter-frame motion reference and Intra-macroblock without inter-frame motion reference. Due to the temporal correlation, the coding results of encoded frames are often used to timely estimate the related information of future frames. Frame $n1$ and Frame $n2$ are two consecutive encoded P-frames that are closest to Frame n. "$K_{inter}(n1,m)$" and "$K_{inter}(n2,m)$" respectively denote the amount of Inter-macroblocks in Packet $P_{n1,m}$ and that in Packet $P_{n2,m}$. The error-propagation effect of Packet $P_{n,m}$ is regarded as a degressive process of $D_i(n,m)$ in its GOP. When the reconstructed pixel is regarded as a low-pass filter output of the original pixel by removing certain energy, the coefficient "α_m^n" denotes the residual energy ratio for the error-propagation effect [4]. Since Ref. [4] does not provide any explicit estimation method, α_m^n is estimated by using the coding side information from two previous P-frames:

$$\alpha_m^n = \frac{\sum_{j=1}^{N_P} [\hat{f}(n1,m,j) - \hat{f}(n2,m,j)]^2}{\sum_{j=1}^{N_P} [f(n1,m,j) - f(n2,m,j)]^2} \tag{2}$$

To estimate the error-propagation effect in future frames, the error-propagation count "EPC(n,m)" of the Packet $P_{n,m}$ is used to approximate the motion reference ratio in the current GOP:

$$\text{EPC}(n,m) = \beta_1 \cdot \sum_{\theta=n+1}^{n_{last}} \left[\alpha_m^n \cdot \frac{K_{inter}(n1,m)}{K} \right]^{(\theta-n)} + \beta_2 \cdot \sum_{\theta=n+1}^{n_{last}} \left[\alpha_m^n \cdot \frac{K_{inter}(n2,m)}{K} \right]^{(\theta-n)} . \quad (3)$$

where "n_{last}" denotes the last frame in the current GOP that contains the Packet $P_{n,m}$; "β_1" and "β_2" ($\beta_1 + \beta_2 = 1$) are two weighting parameters whose values can be empirically set to "$\beta_1 = 0.8$" and "$\beta_2 = 0.2$". The error-propagation effect among future frames is approximated as a frame-by-frame decaying process. After encoding the Frame n, "$GTD(n,m)$" denotes the normalized GOP-level transmission distortion induced by the lost Packet $P_{n,m}$, where only Packet $P_{n,m}$ is lost and other packets in the same GOP are error-free.

$$GTD(n,m) = \frac{D_i(n,m) \cdot \left[\text{EPC}(n,m) + 1 \right]}{S_{n,m}} . \quad (4)$$

Based on the Equation (4), the propagation-aware online packet classification assumes that the Packet $P_{n,m}$ with the larger $GTD(n,m)$ value is more important, and is classified as the high-reliability traffic class. According to one of the aforementioned three online packet classification schemes, the sender can timely determine the traffic class for each packet in the current frame.

4   Simulation Results

By using H.264 reference software JM17.0 [7], three typical CIF (4:2:0) sequences, namely *Akiyo*, *Foreman* and *Football*, are encoded at their typical bitrates. The GOP structure is an I-frame followed by a serial of P-frames. The default error concealment in JM17.0 decoder is performed. After each frame is encoded, the most important packets are classified as the high-reliability traffic class, while other packets in the same frame are classified as the best-effort traffic class. Without loss of generality, the high-reliability packet loss probability p_h is equal to 0%, and the best-effort packet loss probability p_b varies from 0% to 20%. For each frame, the amount of high-reliability packets "η" includes four typical values from low ($\eta=1$) to high ($\eta=4$) so as to highlight the characteristics of the proposed scheme. For its simplicity and mathematical tractability, the two-state Markov channel model has been widely used to generate different packet loss patterns for the Internet. Before each simulation run, the channel model is reinitialized by a time-based seed. We run 10 simulations with each η value, and calculate the peak signal-to-noise ratio (PSNR) of each received frame. For a given p_b value and a test sequence, "PSNR(p_b)" denotes the average PSNR over 40 different simulations with four typical η values. The main simulation parameters are listed in Table 1.

Table 1. Main simulation parameter settings

Parameters	Values
Target bitrate	128 kbps(*Akiyo*), 256 kbps (*Foreman*), 384 kbps (*Football*)
Target frame rate	15 fps
Codec	H.264 JM17.0, Main profile, Level 2
GOP structure	IPPP···IPPP···
GOP length (N_g)	15 frames
Intra refresh	Off
Rate control	Enable
Slice mode	Fixed macroblock number in a slice
η	1, 2, 3, 4
Streaming protocols	RTP/UDP/IP
Channel model	Two-state Markov
p_h	0%
p_b	0%, 1%, 3%, 5%, 10%, 15%, 20%

Here we examine and compare the loss-resilience performance of three online packet classification schemes: (a) the traditional in-order packet classification (IPC). In encoding order, the former η packets of each frame are classified as the high-reliability traffic class; (b) the content-aware online packet classification (COPC). The COPC scheme is similar to the classification mechanism in [6]; (c) The proposed propagation-aware online packet classification (POPC).

Fig. 3 depicts the PSNR(p_b) curve as a function of the best-effort packet loss probability p_b. We can see that the POPC scheme consistently outperforms two reference schemes for different p_b values. Since the IPC scheme only takes into account the spatial-temporal position of a packet in a GOP, some important packets cannot avoid the losses which result in significant PSNR(p_b) drop. For very low p_b=1%, the loss-resilience performance is very close due to the isolated error effect. For p_b=3%, the PSNR(p_b) differences of the POPC and COPC schemes are relatively insignificant. For p_b=5-15%, the PSNR(p_b) differences of the POPC and COPC schemes are relatively significant. We can also see that PSNR(p_b) drops down sharply in the range of p_b=15-20%. The reason is that burst packet losses in this p_b range often result in the whole-frame losses, and the error concealment in the JM decoder cannot recovery whole-frame loss well.

For three online packet classification schemes, Fig. 4 further demonstrates an empirical cumulative distribution function (CDF) of the frame-by-frame PSNR in all simulations. Since the issue of time-varying error propagation between frames is still ignored, the distortion estimation of the COPC scheme cannot adapt the actual conditions well, especially for serious packet losses and high-dynamic video content. Since the GOP-level transmission distortion is effectively estimated, the POPC scheme is more accurate than other two online classification schemes, and thus achieves better loss-resilience performance.

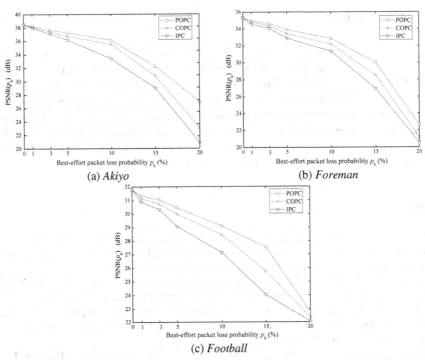

Fig. 3. The PSNR(p_b) curve as a function of the best-effort packet loss probability p_b

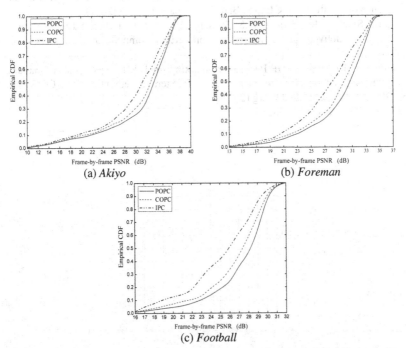

Fig. 4. The empirical CDF comparison of the frame-by-frame PSNR in all simulations

5   Conclusion

Different video packets in a frame usually exhibit different loss-resilience importance and different error propagation characteristics. For live video streaming over a two-class DiffServ network, we have proposed a propagation-aware online packet classification scheme to estimate and compare the GOP-level transmission distortion of video packet in a frame. Under the resource constraints, the proposed scheme can adaptively be aware of non-stationary error-propagation effect, and thus significantly improve the determination accuracy of traffic classes and the loss resilience for live video streaming over the two-class DiffServ network.

References

1. Zhang, F., Macnicol, J., Pickering, M.R., Frater, M.R., Arnold, J.F.: Efficient Streaming Packet Video over Differentiated Services Networks. IEEE Trans. Multimedia 8(5), 1005–1010 (2006)
2. Chen, L.S., Liu, G.Z.: A Delivery System for Streaming Video over DiffServ Networks. IEEE Trans. Circuits and Systems for Video Technology 20(9), 1255–1259 (2010)
3. Masala, E., De Martin, J.C.: Analysis-by-Synthesis Distortion Computation for Rate-distortion Optimized Multimedia Streaming. In: IEEE International Conference on Multimedia & Expo., Baltimore, USA, pp. 345–348 (2003)
4. Zhang, Y.F., Qin, S.Y., He, Z.H.: Transmission Distortion-optimized Unequal Loss Protection for Video Transmission over Packet Erasure Channels. In: IEEE International Conference on Multimedia & Expo., Barcelona, Spain, pp. 1–6 (2011)
5. Ke, C.H., Shieh, C.K., Hwang, W.S., Ziviani, A.: A Two Markers System for Improved MPEG Video Delivery in a DiffServ Network. IEEE Communications Letters 9(4), 381–383 (2005)
6. Przylucki, S.: Efficiency of IP Packets Pre-marking for H264 Video Quality Guarantees in Streaming Applications. In: Kwiecień, A., Gaj, P., Stera, P. (eds.) CN 2012. CCIS, vol. 291, pp. 120–129. Springer, Heidelberg (2012)
7. H.264/MPEG-4 AVC Reference Software,
   http://iphome.hhi.de/suehring/tml/download/jm17.0.zip

Color Image Segmentation Using Gaussian Mixture Model and EM Algorithm

Zhaoxia Fu[1,2] and Liming Wang[1]

[1] Science and Technology on Electronic Test &
Measurement Laboratory and Key Laboratory of Instrumentation Science &
Dynamic Measurement(Ministry of Education),
Information and communication engineering institute,
North University of China, Taiyuan, 030051, China
[2] Party school of shanxi provincial committee of the C.P.C, Taiyuan, 030006, China
fzx2005@163.com, wlm@nuc.edu.cn

Abstract. The segmentation of color image is an important research field of image processing and pattern recognition. A color image could be considered as the result from Gaussian mixture model (GMM) to which several Gaussian random variables contribute. In this paper, an efficient method of image segmentation is proposed. The method uses Gaussian mixture models to model the original image, and transforms segmentation problem into the maximum likelihood parameter estimation by expectation-maximization (EM) algorithm. And using the method to classify their pixels of the image, the problem of color image segmentation can be resolved to some extent. The experiment results confirm this method validity.

Keywords: Gaussian mixture model, EM algorithm, image segmentation, random variable.

1 Introduction

Image segmentation is the most important issue on automatic image analysis and pattern recognition. According to some features of the image or similar criteria of feature set, it is carried on the grouping cluster to the pixels, and the image is divided into a series of meaningful and different regions. The quality of image segmentation and regional boundaries precision immediately influence the following region description and image analysis and understanding, and they are important technical aspects in the image analysis, processing, understanding.

Traditional techniques of image segmentation can be divided into edge-based segmentation and region-based segmentation. The former is called for edge extraction from the target segmentation objects. The latter often determines the object boundary through spatial partial characteristic of the image, such as gray, texture, and other statistical properties of pixels. EM algorithm is a region segmentation method based on statistical pattern recognition, which has speediness and wide adaptability. The paper proposes a method of image segmentation based on Gaussian mixture model

F.L. Wang et al. (Eds.): CMSP 2012, CCIS 346, pp. 61–66, 2012.

and EM algorithm on this basis, using the maximum likelihood estimation and EM algorithm to achieve the purpose of color image segmentation.

2   Gaussian Mixture Model and EM Algorithm

2.1   Gaussian Mixture Model (GMM)

Gaussian mixture model [1] is a statistical model that can well describe spatial distribution and characteristics of the data in the parameter space. Gaussian mixture model is defined as the m-linear combination of Gaussian density function, i.e.,

$$p(x) = \sum_{i=1}^{M} \pi_i N_i(x \mid \mu_i, C_i) \tag{1}$$

where $N_i(x \mid \mu_i, C_i)$ denotes a bivariate or trivariate normal distribution with mean vector μ_i and a covariance matrix C_i. π_i is a mixture proportion for each group, and it is regarded as the ith prior probability of Gaussian distribution that data sample produces. These prior probabilities should satisfy

$$\sum_{i=1}^{M} \pi_i = 1 \quad \text{and} \quad 0 \le \pi_i \le 1 \tag{2}$$

For a given mixture model, using the model for data classification or clustering must also determine unknown parameters that the various Gaussian components of the model contain, and these unknown parameters are π_i, μ_i and C_i. There are many ways to estimate these parameters, and the most commonly way is EM algorithm based on the maximum likelihood estimation [2-6]. Maximum likelihood estimation enables the likelihood function maximization to obtain the parameter estimated value. In practice, the likelihood function is used the logarithmic form to express frequently.

Implied variables can not be directly observed, and any model with implied variables can be classified as incomplete data problems. In practice, a number of questions belong to incomplete data problems. For the clustering problem, we can assume that there is a discrete value of the implied variable Z and its value is $\{z_1, z_2, ..., z_k\}$. The value of the implied variable is unknown corresponding to all n objects. The purpose of clustering is to estimate Z corresponding to each observation value $x(i)$, $(1 \le i \le n)$.

If $X = \{x_1, x_2, ..., x_n\}$ is a data set composed of n observed vectors, then $Z = \{z_1, z_2, ..., z_n\}$ denotes n values of the implied variable Z corresponding to the observed data elements respectively, i.e., z_i is associated with data element x_i and z_i denotes an invisible cluster label of data element x_i.

The density function $p(x \mid \theta_i)$ of region segmentation using Gaussian function is modeled as

$$p(x \mid \theta_i) = N(x \mid \mu, C) = \frac{1}{(2\pi)^{\frac{D}{2}} |C|^{1/2}} \exp\left\{-\frac{1}{2}(x-\mu)^T C^{-1}(x-\mu)\right\} \tag{3}$$

For the whole image X (contains s pixels), the formation probability is

$$p(X \mid \pi, \mu, C) = \prod_{j=1}^{s} \left\{ \sum_{i=1}^{M} \pi_i N(x_j \mid \mu_i, C_i) \right\} \tag{4}$$

So solution of the above question is the one of the maximum likelihood estimation of the parameter $\theta = (\pi_1, \pi_2, ..., \pi_M, \mu_1, \mu_2, ..., \mu_M, C_1, C_2, ..., C_M)$.

2.2 EM Algorithm

EM algorithm is an alternative algorithm for the maximum likelihood estimation in the practical application, and it is an iterative optimization algorithm solving the likelihood function, which can guarantee that each iteration of the likelihood function is non decreasing. The iterative process can be divided into two steps: the first step is called the E step, which is based on the parameters of the initial value or the previous iterative value to calculate the expectation of the likelihood function; the second step is called the M step, which transforms the likelihood function maximization so as to obtain the new parameter value. The specific process of EM algorithm is repeated until convergence of the two steps.

For a Gaussian mixture model with M Gaussian components, if we know from which each data x_k is Gaussian component, then determine the parameters $(\pi_1, \pi_2, ..., \pi_M, \theta_1, \theta_2, ..., \theta_M)$ of a Gaussian mixture model and clustering algorithm easily, $\theta_i = (\mu_i, C_i)$; Conversely, if we know these parameters $(\pi_1, \pi_2, ..., \pi_M, \theta_1, \theta_2, ..., \theta_M)$, then will determine each data x_k is most likely which Gaussian component generates. However, both of which are unknown, they can be seen as implied variables, so we can use EM algorithm for incomplete data to estimate the parameters.

When the number of Gaussian components of Gaussian mixture model is M, and the number of data is N, the E step is expected to

$$Q(\theta \mid \theta^{(t)}) = \sum_{l=1}^{M} \sum_{i=1}^{N} \gamma(Z_{il}) \log \pi_l + \sum_{l=1}^{M} \sum_{i=1}^{N} \gamma(Z_{il}) \log N(x_i \mid \theta_l) \tag{5}$$

where $N(x_i \mid \theta_l)$ is the probability distribution of x_i for the lth Gaussian component; $\gamma(Z_{il})$ is the posterior probability of the lth Gaussian component, and it can be obtained by

$$\gamma(Z_{il}) = \frac{\pi_l N(x_i \mid \theta_l)}{\sum_{j=1}^{M} \pi_j N(x_i \mid \theta_j)} \tag{6}$$

After obtaining $Q(\theta \mid \theta^{(t)})$, we may use the following formulas to re-estimate every parameter of Gaussian mixture model in the M step.

$$\pi_l^{(t+1)} = \frac{1}{N} \sum_{i=1}^{N} \gamma(Z_{il}) \tag{7}$$

$$\mu_l^{(t+1)} = \frac{1}{N\pi_l^{(t+1)}} \sum_{i=1}^{N} x_i \gamma(Z_{il}) \tag{8}$$

$$C_l^{(t+1)} = \frac{1}{N\pi_l^{(t+1)}} \sum_{i=1}^{N} (x_i - \mu_l^{(t+1)})^2 \gamma(Z_{il}) \tag{9}$$

The E step and the M step form the iterative relations, they are repeated until all values have been convergence.

3   Segmentation Using Gaussian Mixture Model and EM Algorithm

Suppose $x_i = (x_i^R, x_i^G, x_i^B)$ is a pixel of color image, where x_i^R, x_i^G, x_i^B is the RGB components of the pixel respectively, $(i = 1, 2, ..., N)$. Image segmentation process is as follows:

a) Choose M, which is the number of region you want to segment, and then initialize θ, $\theta = (\pi_1, \pi_2, ..., \pi_M, \mu_1, \mu_2, ..., \mu_M, C_1, C_2, ..., C_M)$. To a color image, we determine subjectively that it is mixed by m single Gaussian. The initial value of each parameter is:

$$\pi_1^0 = \pi_2^0 = ... = \pi_M^0 = \frac{1}{M} \tag{10}$$

where μ_l^0 and C_l^0 are given by the above formula (8), (9), $(l = 1, 2, ..., M)$.

b) Use the above formula (7), (8) and (9) in the iterative EM algorithm to calculate the final θ, $\theta = (\pi_1, \pi_2, ..., \pi_M, \mu_1, \mu_2, ..., \mu_M, C_1, C_2, ..., C_M)$. In this procedure code of the paper, the iterative terminal condition is that absolute value of the difference is less than 10^{-6} between this result and the previous result.

c)   According   to   the   final   obtained   parameter $\theta = (\pi_1, \pi_2, ..., \pi_M, \mu_1, \mu_2, ..., \mu_M, C_1, C_2, ..., C_M)$, we mark each pixel x_i in the color image. The mark formula is as follows:

$$I_i = \max \left\{ E[\ln p(X, Z | \pi, \mu, C)] = \sum_{i=1}^{N} \sum_{l=1}^{M} \gamma(Z_{il}) \{\ln \pi_l + \ln N(x_i | \mu_l, C_l)\}, l = 1, 2, ..., M \right\} \tag{11}$$

4   Experimental Results

In the following experiments, the original color images are flower, tiger, bear in Figure 1. The number M of segmentation is respectively 2,5,10. The segmentation results show in Figure 2, 3, 4.

From the above results, we can see that Gaussian mixture model responses the distribution of color image information to a certain extent. When the value of M increases, the segmentation effect will make better in the experiments.

Fig. 1. Original images: (a) flower, (b) tiger, (c) bear

(a)   (b)   (c)

Fig. 2. Segmentation results $(M = 2)$

Fig. 3. Segmentation results $(M = 5)$

Fig. 4. Segmentation results $(M = 10)$

5   Conclusions

Gaussian mixture model is a half-parametric density estimation method, which fuses the merit of parameter estimation and non-parametric estimation, and does not limit to the specific form of the probability density function. Moreover the complexity of the model is only related with solution problems, and has nothing to do with the size of sample set. In this algorithm, we use Gaussian mixture model to describe a color image, and use EM algorithm to estimate the various parameters of Gaussian model to achieve image segmentation. This method's merit lies in using the randomness of the image, might give a stable result. But here uses only the image's color information, the segmentation effect is not very ideal. This indicates that if we make full use of the image's edge, texture and other features, will obtain better segmentation results.

Acknowledgment. This work was supported in part by the National Natural Science Foundation of China (NSFC) under Grant No. 61071193.

References

1. Permuter, H., Francos, J., Jermyn, I.H.: Gaussian mixture models of texture and colour for image database retrieval. In: Proc. of the IEEE International Conference on Acoustics, Speech and Signal Processing (2003)
2. Maclean, J., Jepson, A.: Recovery of ego-motion and segmentation of independent object motion using the EM algorithm. In: Proceedings BMVC, pp. 175–184 (1994)
3. Yuille, A.L., Stolorz, P., Utans, J.: Statistical physics, mixtures of distributions, and the EM algorithm. Neural Computation 6, 334–340 (1994)
4. Moss, S., Hancock, E.R.: Registering incomplete radar images using the EM algorithm. Image and Vision Computing 15, 637–648 (1997)
5. Cho, W.H., Kim, S.H., Park, S.Y., Park, J.H.: Mean field annealing EM for image segmentation. In: International Conference on Image Processing, vol. 3, pp. 568–571 (2000)
6. Park, J.-H., Cho, W., Park, S.: Deterministic Annealing EM and Its Application in Natural Image Segmentation. In: Zhang, J., He, J.-H., Fu, Y. (eds.) CIS 2004. LNCS, vol. 3314, pp. 639–644. Springer, Heidelberg (2004)

Cognitive Semantic Model for Visual Object Recognition in Image

Sieow Yeek Tan and Dickson Lukose

Artificial Intelligence Center, MIMOS Berhad,
Technology Park Malaysia, Bukit Jalil, Kuala Lumpur, Malaysia
{tan.sy,dickson.lukose}@mimos.my

Abstract. The paper presents a hierarchical semantic model to perform object recognition in 2D images using cognitive neuroscience vision process. The proposed model contains two vital parts: Object-Features (OF) Conceptualization and Concept Recognition (CR). The model facilitates combination of multiple visual descriptors in the OF conceptualization and the CR process. The model comprises four major operation layers: Image Components Extraction (IE Layer), Visual Content Extraction (CE Layer), Visual Content Matching (CM Layer) and Object Recognition (OR Layer), arranged hierarchically from bottom (IE Layer) to top (OR Layer). The OR layer incorporates Multi-Level Thresholds technique, which defines various threshold values to control and finalize CR process. The experiments performed involved two types of visual descriptors: Color and Edge Directivity Descriptor (CEDD) and Fuzzy Color and Texture Histogram (FCTH). They were carried out using 9 set of images dataset. Different threshold values were tested to validate the feasibility and accuracy of the proposed model. Intensive empirical assessment has been performed and the results are promising.

Keywords: Object Recognition, Image Understanding, Multiple Feature Descriptors, Hierarchical Semantic Model.

1   Introduction

Recognizing the content of image in term of objects has been a challenging problem in computer vision since the past decades. Some of the popular methods in addressing this problem are based on hierarchical approaches, which is inspired by the hierarchical nature of visual cortex [1-2]. The performance of hierarchical approaches has been always outperforming the single-template object recognition systems [3-4]. Nevertheless, in detecting certain type of objects, for instance faces, cars, pedestrians; single-template systems are still able to exhibit excellent performance [5-7].

We believe biological inspired hierarchical architecture with supervised learning will be a powerful method in solving visual object recognition problem. It can surpass some of the general purpose machine learning methods. Studies [1-2] have shown a concrete positive results in adopting such approach. In this paper, we propose a novel model, which is referring to human vision object recognition stages, according to

F.L. Wang et al. (Eds.): CMSP 2012, CCIS 346, pp. 67–78, 2012.
© Springer-Verlag Berlin Heidelberg 2012

cognitive neuroscience of visual object recognition mechanisms. Our model consists of four layers of operational stages, corresponding to four high-level processing stages proposed in human vision [8-9]. Stage 1 involves the image information extraction from multiple parts of an image into image components. It is like a human is having visual attention on multiple regions of an observed image. Stage 2 is the low-level processing of these components in preparing visual representations used for further analysis. Stage 3 involves the matching process of these visual representation towards the structural descriptions stored in memory. Stage 4 involves the operation of assigning semantic attributes from memory to the visual representation. The semantic attributes are conceptualized together with various image features in an Object-Features knowledge-base (OF KB), analogue to the structural capturing of visual representation in human memory. Low-level features are extracted from images and registered with a respective concept in OF KB. Such OF conceptualization is considered as supervised learning process, which is similar to the teaching and learning scenario for human being.

Recognition of visual objects essentially involves the computation of low-level visual information from different parts of an image at initial state. Some of the commonly used visual information has been encoded into a standard set of visual descriptors (VD), such as Colour Layout Descriptor, Colour Structure Descriptor, Dominant Colour Descriptor and Edge Histogram Descriptor [10-11], which have been proposed in MPEG-7 [10]. Recent examples of visual descriptors, such as Scale Invariant Feature Transform (SIFT) [12], Speeded-Up Robust Feature (SURF) [13] and Orientated FAST and Rotated BRIEF (ORB) [14], were developed to achieve a better features representation of an object. Researchers [15-18] have shown ways in recognizing single or multiple objects, by using single or combinations of the above mentioned feature descriptors.

We propose the use of two VD as the low-level features, namely Color and Edge Directivity Descriptor (CEDD) [19] and Fuzzy Color and Texture Histogram (FCTH) [20]. Both of the descriptors have been proven very effective against recognizing building concept from natural type of images [21]. Besides, their effectiveness has been recognized via the usage in various image annotation and retrieving systems [22, 23]. Feature descriptors CEDD and FCTH are made to be compact descriptors, which can not only effectively encoded the visual content such as colour, texture and edge, but also maintain its computation efficiency. An image is able to encode into these descriptors regardless its width, height and resolution. Similar to human recognition process, we are not paying very much attention to the size of an image while recognizing the objects in the image. In term of resolution, low resolution will contribute to poor descriptors encoding and lead to poor object recognition rate, where it has a similar analogy to normal human vision.

The paper is organized as follows: Section 2 describes the Semantic Hierarchical Object Recognition Model. The process of objects and visual features knowledge construction are elaborated in details. The explanation of the hierarchical object recognition model and illustration of the recognition process using the proposed model is given. Section 3 reveals the details of computation of the hierarchical model and the methodology analysis for each layer. The experiment image dataset and setup details are specified in Section 4. The results are finally discussed in Section 5, followed by a conclusion and future works in the last section.

2   Semantic Hierarchical Object Recognition Model

2.1   Objects and Visual Features Knowledge Construction

In the knowledge construction stage, a pre-defined concept representing an object will be fused with visual features and store in OF KB. We propose a simple model to mimic the example-based visual learning mechanism of human being. It contains three major steps, which are (i) Low-level Visual Feature Extraction (LVFE), (ii) Concept & Low-Level Visual Features Fusion (CLVF) and (iii) Concept & Low-level Visual Features Registration (CLFR), as shown in Figure 1. In LVFE process, the low-level features of a given image are extracted and encoded into different type of VD. The type of low-level features in used depends on the VD set engaged in the recognition model. We denote the set of VD as F, where $F = \{f_k \mid k=1,...,N_f\}$. f_k is the kth type of extracted feature vector and N_f is representing the number of the descriptor type. Different VD engines are required to generate different types of feature vectors. Hence, k descriptor engines are required to generate the descriptors set of F.

In the CLVF process, a concept that corresponds to the given image is paired with a respective set of VD, according to $\delta_j^{(c)} = (c, F_j)$; where c is a teaching concept. Consequently, several similar images representing a same concept can be used to produce different $\delta_j^{(c)}$, where $j \in [1,N_t^{(c)}]$ and $N_t^{(c)}$ is the total number of training images. Thus, we denote:

$$\delta^{(c)} = \left\{ \delta_j^{(c)} \middle| j \in [1, N_t^{(c)}] \right\}; c \in C \tag{1}$$

where C is the set of total concepts available in the OF KB. Finally, the CLFR process stores all the $\delta^{(c)}$ values into the OF knowledge-base. Thus, this model is not limiting the number of VD in use, training images for a specific concept and concepts trained.

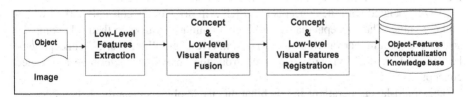

Fig. 1. Object-Features Conceptualization Process Flow

2.2   Hierarchical Object Recognition Model Overview

We proposed four layers of operations in our Hierarchical Object Recognition Model, from low-level image properties processing to high-level object identification, which adopting the multi-layer cognitive computation architecture. The layers include: (i)

Image Components Extraction (IE) layer, (ii) Visual Contents Extraction (CE) layer, (iii) Visual Content Matching (CM) layer and (iv) Objects Recognition (OR) layer. They are hierarchically organized as the illustration shown in Figure 2, capturing an image as input and the identified objects as output.

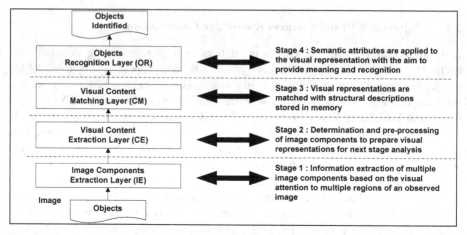

Fig. 2. Hierarchical Objects Recognition Model (Left Column) mapping to the High-level human vision object recognition stages according to cognitive neuroscience of visual object recognition process (Right Column)

In the IE layer, multiple regions from different parts of an input image are required to be identified. The regions are different in size and located randomly around the image. We introduced a Random Location Subwindows (RLS) mechanism for this operation. The mathematic model is explained in details next section. The next layer that linked directly to IE layer is CE layer. The operation in CE layer is to extract the low-level visual information from these multiple targeted regions. The information is encoded into different type of VD, respective to what have been used in OF conceptualization. In the CM layer, the encoded visual information will then be compared to the pre-registered information in OF KB. The comparison of the extracted VD and all the VD associated with the concepts in OFKB will drive every concept marked with a ranking value. The concepts that record higher similarity values in their VD comparison will score a higher ranking value. Thus, in OR layer, all the marked concepts will be analysed. A decision will be derived from the analysis to determine a detected concept.

This multi-layer operations in-combination enable objects in an image being identified, simulates the object recognition states in human vision, as shown in Figure 2. Various image components being extracted from multiple parts of an image without the needs of prior object segmentation process. Together with the low-level image processing that is performed on these specific parts. They are analogue to the process of a human is getting visual attention on certain parts of the image. In addition, the VD comparison in OF KB process as the similar analogy to the neuron firing mechanism for information searching in human memory. If the comparison of the features belonged to a specific object has achieved certain level of similarity, a decision will be made in the brain that the object has been recognized. Figure 3 further illustrates the details of the proposed model analogue to the human visual recognition mechanism.

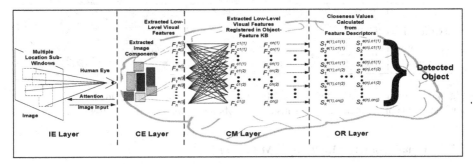

Fig. 3. Hierarchical Objects Recognition Model analogy to the human visual recognition

3   Hierarchical Model Computation and Analysis

3.1   Image Components Extraction (IE Layer)

The RLS mechanism plays the most important role in this layer. RLS generates random size regions, to be located randomly on an input image. We denote the region and image as e and I respectively. Although the width, d_w; height, d_h and the location (x, y), of the regions is randomly generated, the values are required to follow certain range. Equation $e = (x, y, d_w, d_h)$ represents parameters of the generated region, where $x \in [1, I_w\text{-}V_{max}]$; $y \in [1, I_h\text{-}V_{max}]$; $d_w, d_h \in [V_{min}, V_{max}]$. V_{min} and V_{max} are pre-defined values. I_w and I_h are the width and height of the input image respectively. The sub-window regions are allowed to overlap each other. Thus, the evaluation of a detected object located around the same regions is validated with respect to its extracted features. Image components, e_i will be extracted from the image, according to the RLS mechanism and form a set of elementary images, represented as $\Psi_{IE}(I)$, where $\Psi_{IE}(I) = \{e_i \mid i = 1,.., N_e\}$. N_e is the number of RLS pre-defined. Figure 4 shows the RLS placed on the image and the components extracted from the respective image.

3.2   Visual Contents Extraction (CE Layer)

Given a set of elementary images $\Psi_{IE}(I)$, which is the components extracted from image I, the low-level features of these components will be extracted in this layer. The low-level features information will be encoded into a set of VD, which will produce different types of feature vector. In this case, we denotes $f_k^{e(i)}$ as the kth type of feature vector extracted from elementary image of e_i. Let Ψ_{CE} be the outcome of the operation from this layer, with the input of elementary images set, we have:

$$\Psi_{CE}(\Psi_{IE}(I)) = \left\{ f_k^{e(i)} \middle| k = 1,.., N_f; i = 1,.., N_e \right\} \qquad (2)$$

Image Type	Sample Images

Fig. 4. Random Location Subwindows (RLS) placements displayed on the input images (Upper row) and some of the image components extracted based on the RLS (Lower row)

3.3   Visual Content Matching (CM Layer)

This layer is to perform the calculation of feature vector closeness. The closeness between the feature vectors generated from each elementary image with the feature vectors obtained from each concept registered in OF KB will be calculated. We propose Cosine Similarity to measure the closeness between these two feature vectors. Assumed the type k^{th} of feature vector extracted from component e_i is denoted as $f_k^{e(i)}$, which is one of the elements obtained from Ψ_{CE}. Also, assumed type k^{th} and j^{th} feature vector belonged to a concept c; obtained from OF KB, is denoted as $f_k^{c(j)}$. The Cosine Similarity of these two vectors is defined as $S_k^{e(i),c(j)}$ where

$$S_k^{e(i),c(j)} = \frac{(f_k^{e(i)} \cdot f_k^{c(j)})}{\|f_k^{e(i)}\| \times \|f_k^{c(j)}\|} \tag{3}$$

Consequently, for each of the image components will draw a similarity value of S, with respect to each of the training items that belonged to a specific registered concept. Let Ψ_{CM} be the outcome of the matching operation from this layer, we have:

$$\Psi_{CM}(I) = \left\{ S_k^{e(i),c(j)} \middle| k \in [1, N_f]; i \in [1, n(\Psi_{IE}(I))]; j \in [1, n(\delta^{(c)})] \right\} \tag{4}$$

where $c \in C$ known as the total concepts available in OF KB as shown in eq. (1).

3.4   Objects Recognition (OR Layer)

The operations from previous layers have enabled a similarity value being drawn to each registered concepts in OF KB. Further analysis based on these values is required to draw a decision for object identification. We proposed a method called Multi-Level Thresholds (MLT) to analyse the similarity values and derive a conclusion. The MLT model defined as below:

$$\omega_3^{(c)}(I) = \frac{1}{N_e}\sum_{i=1}^{N_e} \alpha_3(\omega_3(c,i)) \text{ where } c \in \boldsymbol{C}, N_e = n(\Psi_{\text{IE}}(I)) \text{ and}$$

$$\alpha_3(\omega_3(c,i)) = 1 \; \forall \; \omega_3(c,i) \geq t_3 \; ; \; \alpha_3(\omega_3(c,i)) = 0 \; \forall \; \omega_3(c,i) < t_3 \text{ where}$$

$$\omega_3(c,i) = \frac{1}{n(\delta^{(c)})}\sum_{j=1}^{n(\delta^{(c)})} \alpha_2(\omega_2(c,i,j)) \text{ where}$$

$$\alpha_2(\omega_2(c,i,j)) = 1 \; \forall \; \omega_2(c,i,j) \geq t_2 \; ; \; \alpha_2(\omega_2(c,i,j)) = 0 \; \forall \; \omega_2(c,i,j) < t_2 \text{ and}$$

$$\omega_2(c,i,j) = \frac{1}{N_f}\sum_{k=1}^{N_f} \alpha_1(\omega_1(c,i,j,k)) \text{ where}$$

$$\alpha_1(\omega_1(c,i,j,k)) = 1 \; \forall \; \omega_1(c,i,j,k) \geq t_1 \text{ and}$$

$$\alpha_1(\omega_1(c,i,j,k)) = 0 \; \forall \; \omega_1(c,i,j,k) < t_1 \text{ where } \omega_1(c,i,j,k) = S_k^{e(i),c(j)} \text{ and}$$

$S_k^{e(i),c(j)}$, refer to eq. (3) are the elements obtained from the outcome of the operation Ψ_{CM}; referring to eq. (4).

From the MLT model, it is easy to observe that we have introduced three level of threshold values, which are t_1, t_2 and t_3. They are required to be defined prior to the recognition process. All calculations are normalized, adapted to a fixed range of threshold values between 0 and 1. t_1 is the threshold value controlling the closeness measurement between the VD from the component images with the VD from teaching concept. It is also known as Single Feature Level (SFL) threshold. t_2 is observed as Feature Set Level threshold. For each item that is registered under a training concept, a vote will be considered only if the total of the single feature closeness values in its associated feature set has exceeded the t_2 threshold. Essentially, for all the items registered under a specific concept, some are marked as voted and some are not. If the total number of marked items exceeded the threshold t_3, then the concept is considered exist in the particular image components.

The final level of threshold in MLT model is defined as t, namely Attention Threshold (AT). By increasing this threshold value, it indicates higher attention power is needed for the model to recognize an object and vice versa. Thus, define if $\omega_3^{(c)}(I) \geq t$, then we conclude that the specific concept c has being identified in the image I.

4   Experiment Environment Setup

4.1   Experiment and Training Image Dataset

We examined our model with 9 concepts, which are Building, Human, Vehicle, Tiger, Sea, Cloud, Tree, Lion and Grass. Our experiment dataset for each concept comprises of 600 colour, natural images, generally downloaded from the Internet. 200 of them were made as training images. Image that was prepared as a specific concept will only contain the concept as the major content of it. For example, the image that is showing concept of 'Building' will only contain building as the major content while image that is showing concept of 'Sky' will only have sky as the major content. Figure 5 shows some of the sample images available from the dataset. It is important to note that the size of the images can be varying in pixel, averagely ranging between 100 and 3000, or even more. The resolution of the images is not a vital parameter of concern.

Fig. 5. Sample of experiment images containing concept 'Building' (3 images from the left) and concept 'Sky' (3 images from the right) as primary content

On the other hand, for each of the target concept, we have prepared a set of negative example of images, where the images contain totally non-related content with respect to the target concept. For example, if the target concept is 'Building', then the negative example of images will not contain any content of 'Building'. It may be composed from the set of images from target concept 'Sea' or 'Sky'. Figure 6 shows the sample images to further understand the negative example of images. We collected 400 negative images for each target concept included in our experiment dataset.

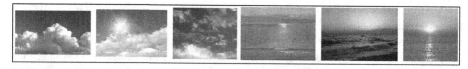

Fig. 6. Sample of negative images for concept 'Building', which totally not contain any content of building

4.2   Experiment Environment Setup

We have performed an empirical study on the performance of our proposed model, particularly in recognizing individual object represented as the primary content of an image, through multiple set of experiments. Throughout the experiments, we set the RLS number, N_e as 15. The width and height of the RLS will be varying randomly from one and others, ranging from 50 to 150 pixels, which have parameterized as V_{min} and V_{max} respectively. We have suggested CEDD and FCTH as the VD to be used in our experiments. We are interested to study the cases of VD to be used individually and hybrid in our model. Thus, we parameterized 3 sets of F, where F_1 only contains the VD type of CEDD, F_2 only contains FCTH and F_3 contains both. We identified 200 training images for each of the concepts, which have parameterized as $n(\delta^{(c)})$ where $c \in$ {Building, Human, Vehicle, Tiger, Sea, Cloud, Tree, Lion, Grass}.

Considering the threshold values discussed in the MLT model, we pre-set t_1 values ranging from 0.5 to 0.75, taking an incremental step of 0.05, for the purpose of empirical study. t_2 and t_3 are constantly set to 1.0 and 0.5 respectively. Finally, we set the Attention Threshold value, t, to 0 and 0.5.

5   Discussion of Experiment Results

We have adopted the Receiver Operator Characteristic (ROC) curve in evaluating the performance of our model. In ROC space, one plots the False Positive Rate (FPR) on the *x*-axis and the True Positive Rate (TPR) on the *y*-axis. The FPR measures the fraction of negative examples that are detected as positive. The TPR measures the fraction of positive examples that are correctly labelled. Thus, FPR(*c*) is defined as *FP / (FP + TN)* and TPR(*c*) is defined as *TP / (TP + FN)*. *TP*, *FP*, *TN* and *FN* are known as True Positive, False Positive, True Negative and False Negative where TP is examples correctly recognized as positive, FP is negative examples incorrectly recognized as positive. *TN* corresponds to negative examples correctly identified and *FN* refers to positive examples incorrectly recognized as negative. They are referred as the four categories of a confusion matrix [24].

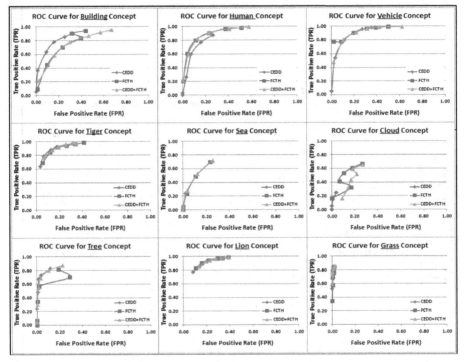

Fig. 7. Receiver Operator Characteristic (ROC) curve analysis for all experimented concepts with Attention Threshold setting, *t* = 0

In this paper, we intend to evaluate the performance of the proposed model with respect to the Attention Threshold effect towards the changes of the SFL threshold, when using different type of feature descriptors. Every concept image dataset as well as the negative image dataset will be supplied to be recognized by the model, with different parameters settings. Each case of experiment will produce its unique confusion matrix and represented in ROC curve shown in Figure 7. The area under the curve in ROC space reveals the performance of the algorithm.

The model achieves almost 1.0 TPR value when recognizing certain concepts, for example 'Building', 'Human', 'Vehicle' and 'Tiger' by using just CEDD descriptors. This shows the colour and edge information was being captured and contributing as one of the factors in recognizing the image content. Also, the result marked relatively high accuracy with the use of FCTH feature descriptor alone. This demonstrates that the model is able to capture texture feature as another vital factor in performing content recognizing task. On the other hand, the model seems not to perform well in detecting the concept 'Sea' and 'Cloud'. The image content of both concepts contains very rare contrast features in term of texture and edge. Thus, feature descriptors CEDD as well as FCTH contribute poorly in the model for recognizing such concepts. Consequently, the performance of using both descriptors in hybrid has also been affected due to this reason.

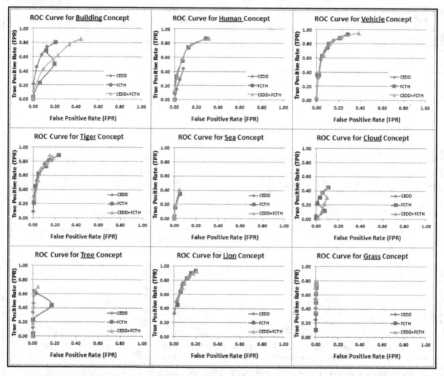

Fig. 8. Receiver Operator Characteristic (ROC) curve analysis for all experimented concepts with Attention Threshold setting, $t = 0.5$

The hybridization of two descriptors has obviously outperformed the use of single descriptor in every experiment case. The performance of the model has obtained a better consistency. This has proved that the model is having a better performance with the increasing uses of visual descriptor type. However, with the increment of Single Feature Level threshold, the accuracy dropped gradually. This is because a higher closeness between the trained features and the extracted feature are required to derive a matching decision. The ROC curves shown in Figure 7 reveal a good recognition performance of the proposed model as overall. The au-ROC for each of the experimented concepts has scored a high value.

Experiments have carried out by setting the model with a low attention power and a higher attention power, where the Attention Threshold setting, t is set to 0 and 0.5 respectively. Lower attention power setting enable the model to recognize a concept when just a few image components reveal the existence of the concept, where higher attention power setting requires more positive regions from the image to conclude a detected concept. Therefore, the performance of the model shown in ROC curves from Figure 8 has slightly dropped if compared to result shown in Figure 7.

6   Conclusion and Future Work

In this paper, a novel computational model in detecting concept from 2D images is presented. The model is with reference to cognitive neuroscience vision object recognition process. It contains of four major operation layers, including a Multiple Level Thresholding technique in recognizing the objects. The model exhibits the capability in facilitating various VD in combination to contribute their roles. Experiment results have shown the fusion of multiple VD for concepts detection is feasible.

A more comprehensive evaluation of the proposed model, especially based on other thresholding parameters has been undertaken. Immediate work includes using more types of VD, especially those proposed by MPEG-7 standard, to perform object detection. The effectiveness and robustness in using multiple low-level features will be experimented and evaluated. The works of optimizing the usage of various threshold values in achieving higher accuracy and better performance of the model are highly focused. We envision detecting more objects that is available in natural images, such as sand, rock, tree, road, mountain, flower and etc.

References

1. Walther, D., Koch, C.: Attention in Hierarchical Models of Object Recognition. Computation Neuroscience 165, 57–78 (2007)
2. Serre, T., Wolf, L., Bileschi, S., Riesenhuber, M., Poggio, T.: Robust Object Recognition with Cortex-Like Mechanisms. IEEE Transactions on Pattern Analysis and Machine Intelligence 29(3), 411–426 (2007)
3. Serre, T., Wolf, L., Poggio, T.: Object Recognition with Feature Inspired by Visual Cortex. In: Proceedings of CVPR 2005, vol. 2, pp. 994–1000 (2005)
4. LeCun, Y., Huang, F.J., Bottou, L.: Learning Method for Generic Object Recognition with Invarance to Pose and Lighting. In: Proceedings of CVPR 2004. IEEE Press (2004)
5. Schneiderman, H., Kanade, T.: A Statistical Method for 3D Object Detection Applied to Faces and Cars. In: CVPR, pp. 746–751 (2000)
6. Mohan, A., Papageorgiou, C., Poggio, T.: Example-based Object Detection in Images by Components. PAMI 23, 349–361 (2001)
7. Viola, P., Jones, M.: Robust Real-Time Face Detection. In: ICCV, vol. 20(11), pp. 1254–1259 (2001)
8. Humphreys, G.W., Price, C.J., Riddoch, M.J.: From Objects to Names: A Cognitive Neuroscience Approach. Psychological Research 62, 118–130 (1999)

9. Frintrop, S., Rome, E., Christensen, H.I.: Computational Visual Attention Systems and Their Cognitive Foundation: A survey. ACM Trans. Applied Perception 7(1) (2010)
10. Martinez, J.M.: Mpeg-7 Overview,
    `http://www.chiariglione.org/mpeg/standards/mpeg-7/mpeg-7.htm`
11. Manjunath, B.S., Ohm, J.-R., Vasudevan, V.V., Yamada, A.: Color and Texture Descriptors. IEEE Transactions on Circuits and Systems for Video Technology 11(6), 703–715 (2001)
12. Lowe, D.G.: Object Recognition from Local Scale-Invariant Features. In: International Conference on Computer Vision, Corfu, Greece, pp. 1150–1157 (1999)
13. Bay, H., Tuytelaars, T., Van Gool, L.: SURF: Speeded Up Robust Features. In: Leonardis, A., Bischof, H., Pinz, A. (eds.) ECCV 2006. LNCS, vol. 3951, pp. 404–417. Springer, Heidelberg (2006)
14. Rublee, E., Rabaud, V., Konolige, K., Bradski, G.: ORB: An Efficient Alternative to SIFT or SURF. In: International Conference on Computer Vision, Barcelona (2011)
15. Zhang, Q., Izquierdo, E.: A Multi-feature Optimization Approach to Object-Based Image Classification. In: Sundaram, H., Naphade, M., Smith, J.R., Rui, Y. (eds.) CIVR 2006. LNCS, vol. 4071, pp. 310–319. Springer, Heidelberg (2006)
16. Zhang, Q., Izquierdo, E.: Combining low-level features for semantic extraction in image retrieval. EURASIP Journal on Advances in Signal Processing 2007(4), 1–12 (2007)
17. Lowe, D.G.: Distinctive Image Features from Scale-Invariant Keypoints. International Journal on Computer Vision 60(2), 91–110 (2004)
18. Pavel, F.A., Zhiyong, W., Feng, D.D.: Reliable Object Recognition Using SFIT Features. In: Multimedia Signal Processing, MMSP 2009 (2009)
19. Chatzichristois, S.A., Boutalis, Y.S.: CEDD: Color and Edge Directivity Descriptor: A Compact Descriptor for Image Indexing and Retrieval. In: Proceedings of the 6th International Conference on Computer Vision Systems, Santorini, Greece (2008)
20. Chatzichristois, S.A., Boutalis, Y.S.: FCTH: Fuzzy Color and Texture Histogram - A Low Level Feature for Accurate Image Retrieval. In: Proceedings of the Ninth International Workshop on Image Analysis for Multimedia Interactive Services, pp. 191–196 (2008)
21. Tan, S.Y., Bong, C.W., Lukose, D.: Building Detection with Loosely-Coupled Hybrid Feature Descriptors. In: Anthony, P., Ishizuka, M., Lukose, D. (eds.) PRICAI 2012. LNCS, vol. 7458, pp. 552–563. Springer, Heidelberg (2012)
22. Lux, M., Chatzichristois, S.A.: LIRE: Lucene Image Retrieval – An Extensible Java CBIR Library. In: ACM International Conference on Multimedia 2008 (ACM MM), Open Source Application Competition, Vancouver, British Columbia, pp. 1085–1087 (2008)
23. Zagoris, K., Chatzichristois, S.A., Papamarkos, N., Boutalis, Y.S.: IMG(ANAKTISI): A Web Content Based Image Retrieval System. In: 2nd International Conference on Similarity Search and Applications (SISAP), pp. 154–155. IEEE Computer Society, Prague (2009)
24. Jess, D., Mark, G.: The relationship between precision-recall and roc curves. Technical report #1551, University of Madison (2006)

Image Retrieval Based on Color-Spatial Distributing Feature

Qian Zhao[1,2], Jialin Cao[1,2], and Yueli Hu[2]

[1] Dept. of Electronic Science and Technology, Shanghai University of Electric Power,
Shanghai, 200090, China
[2] School of Mechatronics Engineering and Automation, Shanghai University,
Shanghai 200072, China

Abstract. In allusion to the problems that the traditional image retrieval method is prone to lose the spatial information of colors, an image retrieval method based on color-spatial distributing feature is proposed. According to visual attention computational mode, the weighted histogram which reflects the pixel position importance are constructed after all pixels are weighed by the pixel color contrast in multi-scale neighborhoods. In the meantime, the spatial relationship feature of same or similar colors is considered by colors distributing cohesion. The experiments show that the method mentioned above has high accuracy and its retrieval results match human visual percept well.

Keywords: Image Retrieval, Color Histogram, spatial cohesion, image similatity.

1   Introduction

With the development of multimedia network technology and rapid growth of image application, large numbers of people are using the internet for searching and browsing through different multimedia databases. Content-based image retrieval (CBIR) has become increasingly important in recent decades, which early usually uses color, texture, shape, spatial relationship etc. low-level features to describe image content, and take them as the retrieval index. Color is the most intuitive and distinct visual feature, For every object all has their own color features and the same kind of object often has similar color information, color features have been applied widely in image retrieval. Since color histogram is usually easy to extract , fairly convenient to design similarity measures and fairly insensitive to variations originated by camera rotation or zooming (Del Bimbo, 1999;Smeulders, et al., 2000), color histogram is the most traditional and the most widely used way to represent color patterns in an image. But the conventional color histogram retrieval method is prone to lose the spatial information of colors and have the higher feature dimensions[1], which results in poor retrieval accuracy. Stricker M et al. [2] propose a method based on color block histogram and color block moment, which firstly divides the image into some block and then calculates color histogram of each block. LI[3] think that human eyes are

F.L. Wang et al. (Eds.): CMSP 2012, CCIS 346, pp. 79–86, 2012.
© Springer-Verlag Berlin Heidelberg 2012

naturally drawn towards the center of an image. So weighted values are measured for each sub-block according to the Euclidean distance between a certain sub-block and the central sub-block. This method can not consider image local relativity and debase retrieval performance. Wangxiangyan[4] introduce a color block histogram image retrieval method based on visual weight of sub-block calculated by the color complexity measure of pixels to improve the method of Li. These methods use rectangle blocking color histogram which is sensitive to variations originated by camera rotation and increase. SUN Jun-ding [5] apply normalized annular color histogram and color distribution entropy to describe spatial information of colors. Xing Qiang [6] propose an image retrieval method based on the weighted chromaticity histogram, the gray value of pixel has been weighted based on the proportion of the chromaticity represented by the pixel in the raw image. But the retrieval results should be improved.

According to human visual attention mechanism, pixels with higher color difference with respect to their multi-scale neighborhoods can quickly arouse the attention of the observers, the weighted histogram based color contrast is constructed which reflects the importance of each pixel in the raw image. Based on the case that the same or similar color pixels spread in the image, such as scattered, concentrated, color distributing cohesion is used to represent the spatial distribution of color simultaneously. Therefore, the whole image's content can be expressed from general statistic to spatial distributing by the two kinds of features. The experiment results show that the method can gain very good retrieval results which match human visual percept well.

2   Weighted Color Histogram Based on Color Contrast

2.1   Traditional Color Histogram

For a given image $I(N_1 \times N_2)$, $N_1 \times N_2$ is the size of image, $I(x, y)$ is color value of the pixel point (x, y) , the normalization color histogram of quantized image of I is calculated as follows:

$$H = (h[1], h[2], \cdots, h[i], \cdots, h[n]) \tag{1}$$

$$\sum_{k=1}^{n} h[i] = 1, \, 0 \leq h[i] \leq 1,$$

Where i represents a color in the color histogram after quantization, $h[i]$ is the frequency of pixels in color i , n is the number of bins in the color histogram.

$$h[i] = \frac{\sum_{x=1}^{N_1} \sum_{y=1}^{N_2} f(x, y, i)}{N_1 * N_2} \tag{2}$$

$$f(x, y, i) = \begin{cases} 1, & Q(T * I[x, y]) = i \\ 0, & otherwise \end{cases} \tag{3}$$

Where Q denotes quantized process of HSV color space and T is conversion from RGB to HSV. Given a query image I_1 and a database image I_2, Measure distance d between the normalization color histograms of the two quantized image is calculated as formula (4).

$$d_h(I_1, I_2) = \sum_{i=1}^{n} \frac{|h(I_{1i}) - h(I_{2i})|}{1 + h(I_{1i}) + h(I_{2i})} \tag{4}$$

$h(I_{1i})$ and $h(I_{2i})$ stand for the frequency of color value i in I_1 and I_2 respectively. Traditional distance of color histogram is only according to a single statistical index of pixel frequency of the same color value and does not consider importance difference of pixel position and the spatial relationship (scattered or concentrated)of colors in the image. So it's ability to distinguish images is very limited and two image with different content may have the same or similar color histogram.

2.2   Color Contrast Calculation

For an image, not all part of it is important, some parts of the image are more prominent than other parts because they can quickly arouse the attention of the observers, which reflect the high-level semantic concept of salience object in the image. so in this paper all pixels are weighed by the color attention measure, and the weighted histogram which can imply pixel position importance are cumulate.

Itti et al. (1998) have built a computational model of saliency-based spatial attention derived from a biologically plausible architecture. For a color input image, the model computes a saliency map from maps for color, luminance, and orientation contrasts at different scales. But this saliency map is 1/256 size of the original image and the object in the original image is usually separated into some disjointed parts in the saliency map. These results are disadvantage for subsequent image processing. Vision attention value is simulated as local contrast of an image region with respect to its neighborhood at various scales [11]. So the color contrast $S(x, y)$ for a pixel at position (x, y) in the image is determined as follows:

$$S(x, y) = \frac{1}{3}[D_{\frac{w}{2}}(x, y) + D_{\frac{w}{4}}(x, y) + D_{\frac{w}{8}}(x, y)] \tag{5}$$

$$D_t(x, y) = d(c(x, y), m_t(x, y))$$

$D_t(x, y)$ is a Euclidend distance between the pixel at position (x, y) and the aver age vectors of $t \times t$ neighbor region around (x, y), Since perceptual difference in CIELab color space is approximately Euclidian, so CIELab color space is used in attention calculation, $c(x, y)$ denotes color vectors at position (x, y): $[L, a, b]^T$; $m_t(x, y)$ denotes the average vectors of $t \times t$ neighbor region around $(x, y) : [L, a, b]^T, t = \{\frac{w}{2}, \frac{w}{4}, \frac{w}{8}\}, w = \min(m, n)$, and m, n is width and height of the image. When the image is polluted by noise, $c(x, y)$ in the Equation(5) will be replaced by a small neighbor region of position (x, y), such as 5x5、7x7. Thus equation(5) can be changed as follows:

$$D_t(x, y) = d(\bar{c}(x, y), m_t(x, y)) = \sqrt{(\bar{L} - L_m)^2 + (\bar{a} - a_m)^2 + (\bar{b} - b_m)^2} \qquad (6)$$

2.3   Weighted Color Histogram

After color contrast $S(x, y)$ of each pixel in the image is calculated according to Equation (5), $S(x, y)$ should be normalized into $[0,1]$ and then be denoted by $\tilde{S}(x, y)$. $\tilde{S}(x, y)$ can reflect importance of every pixel, the bigger $\tilde{S}(x, y)$ is, the more important the corresponding pixel is, so all the pixels are weighed by $\tilde{S}(x, y)$ and then cumulate to construct weighted color histogram. Equation(2) for the frequency of pixels in traditional color histogram will be modified as follows:

$$h'[i] = \frac{\sum\limits_{i=1}^{N_1} \sum\limits_{j=1}^{N_2} \tilde{S}(x, y) f(x, y, i)}{\sum\limits_{k=i}^{n} \sum\limits_{i=1}^{N_1} \sum\limits_{j=1}^{N_2} \tilde{S}(x, y) f(x, y, i)} \qquad (7)$$

Obviously, the weighted color histogram can present the significance of colors in an image well. The more contrast these pixels are with respect to its neighborhood at various scales, the greater the visual attention is, corresponding to these pixels the bigger the weighted value is. In a word , the weighted color histogram can reflect the importance of pixels position. These are similar to human   visual attention mechanism.

3   Spatial Relations in Images

Weighted color histogram includes position information of each pixel and make important pixels with higher weighted value. But the spatial relations of the pixels with similar color play also an important role to improve the retrieval performance. Dispersed pixels and concentrated pixels like color block may have the same statistic, in fact they reflect different image information for observer. In this paper, the spatial relationship of color is considered by the same or similar color distributing cohesion [12].

For a given image I , $I(x,y)$ denotes color value of the pixel of position (x,y), $A_i = \{(x,y)|(x,y) \in I, I(x,y) = i, 1 \le i \le n\}$ is the set of all pixels with color i, n is the number of color category, n_i expresses the number of pixels in the A_i. Let $c_i = (x_i, y_i)$ be the spatial central position of all the pixels in the A_i , where x_i and y_i are defined as

$$x_i = \frac{1}{n_i} \sum_{(x,y) \in A_i} x \; ; \; y_i = \frac{1}{n_i} \sum_{(x,y) \in A_i} y \tag{8}$$

ρ_i expresses distributing cohesion of the same or similar color and is defined as

$$\rho(i) = (\frac{1}{n_i} \sum_{k=1}^{n_i} \sqrt{(x_k - x_i)^2 + (y_k - y_i)^2})^{-1} \tag{9}$$

Where, (x_k, y_k) is the coordinates of pixel in set A_i. If $\rho(i)$ is very big, that means the color distribution is relatively scattered. On the contrary, it means the color distribution is relatively concentrated.

4   Similarity Measures for Ranking Images

Given a image I , the feature vector of I is $(h'(I_1)$, $\rho(I_1)$; $\cdots$, $h'(I_i), \rho(I_i), \cdots, h'(I_n), \rho(I_n),)$, in which $h'(I_i)$ is the weighted frequency of color value i, $\rho(I_i)$ expresses the cohesion of all pixels with color value i, n is the number of color category. Assume that a query image I_1 and a database image I_2, the distance d between the two image is changed as d'.

$$d'_h(I_1, I_2) = \sum_{i=1}^{n} \frac{|h'(I_{1i}) - h'(I_{2i})|}{1 + h'(I_{1i}) + h'(I_{2i})} \times \frac{|\rho(I_{1i}) - \rho(I_{2i})|}{1 + \rho(I_{1i}) + \rho(I_{2i})} \tag{10}$$

Similarity Measures of two images include two parts, the first term of equation (10) takes into account weighted color histogram, which is based on the consideration importance of pixel position, namely that pixels with larger color contrast are more likely to attract human attention than ones with smaller color contrast. The second term of equation (10) takes into account the similarity of the pixels with similar color distributing cohesion. The smaller $d'_h(I_1, I_2)$ is , the more similar the images I_1 and I_2 are. The image retrieval methods deliver the database images with the small-est $d'_h(I_1, I_2)$ to the user.

5   Experimental Results and Analysis

In this section, we conduct image retrieval experiments on the proposed techniques and system. Corel Photo Gallery is used as the image database, which contains 1000 JPEG images with size of 384x256 or 256x384 pixels. These images are composed of 10 semantic categories, such as Africa, buildings, horses, elephants, dinosaurs, flowers, buses, beach, mountains, and food. Each category includes 100 images. 6 images are selected randomly as query images from each of 5 image semantic categories and hence, a total of 30 query images are taken in our experiments. For each query, we select the top k results from the query results to compute precision, i.e. p_k. p_k is defined as the proportion of the relevant images retrieved in the top k retrieved images according to the similar distance. The average precision ($\overline{p}_k$) of 6 retrieval results are regarded as retrieved precision of each semantic category. Three methods, namely traditional color histogram retrieval (TCHR),weighted color based color contrast histogram retrieval (WCHR) and combining weighted color histogram and cohesion (WCHCR), are compared with $\overline{p}_k$ when $k = 10,20,30$ .The comparison can be shown in the Table 1. We can see that the method proposed (WCHCR) in this paper has the higher average precision than that of TCHR and WCHR.

Table 1. Comparison of average precision

Testing image	$\overline{P}_{10}$			$\overline{P}_{20}$			$\overline{P}_{30}$		
	TCHR	WCHR	WCHCR	TCHR	WCHR	WCHCR	TCHR	WCHR	WCHCR
Buses	68	70	74	60	62	65	50	56	58
Beach	59	61	65	54	55	56	48	50	55
Flowers	81	84.7	87.0	71.5	80.2	83.3	58.6	70.3	80.4
Horses	88.3	93.3	95.0	78.5	83.2	85.3	70.9	72.1	78.3
Food	73	76.1	81.3	67.5	73.8	75.2	60.2	62.9	67.1

A retrieval result of three retrieval methods is shown in Fig.1. The query image is the upper-left corner image of each block of images, 30 images which are the most similar to the query image have been output. The results are ranked in ascending order of similarity to the query image from left to right and then from top to bottom. The traditional color histogram can only reflect the statistical characteristics but its ability to distinguish images is very limited, Thus, the false retrieval rate is very high, it can be seen in Fig.1(a). Weighted color histogram retrieval (WCHR) considers significance of each pixel and the retrieval results are improved, such as Fig.1(b). While , the output result in Fig.1(c) takes significance of each pixel and spacial color distributing information of the same color into consideration, by this way, the retrieval results will be much better in accordance with the visual perspective.

Fig.1(a). Retrieval results of the TCHR

Fig.1(b). Retrieval results of the WCHR

Fig.1(c). Retrieval results of the proposed algorithm (WCHCR)

Fig. 1. Retrieval Results Comparison of the different algorithms

6   Conclusions

An image retrieval algorithm based on color contrast and cohesion is presented in this paper. Unlikely traditional image retrieval method only using pixel statistical characteristics, the method not only utilizes significance of each pixel, but also spacial color distributing information of the same color. Experimental results show that the proposed method has better image retrieval effectiveness than the classic histogram and the weighted color histogram method.

References

1. Lew, M.S., Sebe, N., Djeraba, C., Jain, R.: Content-based multimedia information retrieval: state of the art and challenges. ACM Transactions on Multimedia Computing, Communications, and Applications 2(1), 1–19 (2006)
2. Stricker, M., Dimai, A.: Color Indexing with Weak Spatial Constraints. In: Proc. of the IS&T/SPIE Conf. on Storage and Retrieval for Image and Video Databases IV (1996)
3. Li, X.L.: Image retrieval based on perceptive weighted color blocks. Pattern Recognition Letters 24(12), 1935–1941 (2003)
4. Wang, X.-Y., Yang, H.-Y., Zheng, H.-L., et al.: A Color Block-histogram Image Retrieval Based on Visual Weight. Acta Automatica Sinica 10, 1489–1492 (2010)
5. Sun, J.-D., Wu, X.-S.: Image Retrieval Based on Color Distribution Features. Journal of Optoelectronics Laser 17(8), 1009–1013 (2006)
6. Xing, Q., Yuan, B.-Z., Tang, X.-F.: A fast image retrieval method based on weighted chromaticity histogram. Journal of Computer Research and Development 42(11), 1903–1910 (2005)
7. Yoo, H.-W., Park, H.-S., Jang, D.-S.: Expert system for color image retrieval. Expert Syst. Appl. 28(2), 347–357 (2005)
8. Nezamabadi-pour, H., Kabir, E.: Image retrieval using histogramsof uni-color and bi-color and directional changes in intensity gradient. Pattern Recognit. Lett. 25(14), 1547–1557 (2004)
9. Smith, J.R., Chang, S.F.: Tools and techniques for color image retrieval. In: Sethi, I.K., Jain, R. C. (eds.) Storage Retrieval for Image and Video Databases IV, IS&T/SPIE Proceedings, vol. 2670, pp. 426–437 (1996)
10. Wang, H.-L., Zhao, H.-F., Luo, B.: Image retrieval based on local color and spatial features. Computer Technology and Development 16(1), 76–79 (2006)
11. Achanta, R., Hemami, S., Estrada, E., et al.: Salient regiondetection and segmentation. In: Proceedings of the 6th International Conference on Computer Vision Systems, Santorini, pp. 66–75 (2008)
12. Ding, G., Dai, Q., Xu, W.: A Method for Image Retrieval Technique Based on Local Distribution Features of Interest Points. Journal of Optoelectronics Laser 16(9), 1101–1106 (2005)

Wavelet Domain Distributed Information Entropy and Genetic Clustering Algorithm for Image Retrieval

Kamil Moydin[1] and Askar Hamdulla[2]

[1] Institute of Information Science and Engineering Xinjiang University, Urumqi 830046
[2] College of Software, Xinjiang University, Urumqi 830008
askar@xju.edu.cn

Abstract. After segmenting the image into several sub-images, each sub-image is taken through three level wavelet transform, and then the texture images are obtained. Meanwhile, the distributions of each sub-image's information entropy are calculated. Such a way, both the global wavelet texture information and the spatial distribution of information entropy are effectively used as the main retrieval characteristics. On this basis, the genetic clustering algorithm used for the image clustering, and the likelihood between the query example image and corresponding image's cluster center is calculated. Experimental results show that the method presented in this paper has good retrieval performance.

Keywords: Image retrieval, wavelet transform, wavelet histogram, wavelet information entropy distribution, genetic clustering.

1 Introduction

In recent years, because of the urgent needs, CBIR (Content-based Image Retrieval) technology has been get widespread concern and rapid development. Because of good spatial frequency characteristics and transform mechanism consistent with human vision system, the wavelet transform occupied an important position in the new generation of still image compression standard (JPEG2000) and moving image compression standard (MPEG24). So, study image indexing technology based on wavelet domain has great significance. This paper proposes an effective image retrieval new method based on wavelet information distribution entropy, and its main idea is: on the basis of image segmentation, calculate the wavelet information entropy of each sub image by applying wavelet and information entropy theory, and take it as image features to do image retrieval. This method is characterized by: (1) Feature extraction from the segmented sub image greatly reduces the computational complexity. At the same time, the representation of image features has good tightness. (2) It could effectively reduce the feature dimensions of images, and then the speed of retrieval is greatly improved.

F.L. Wang et al. (Eds.): CMSP 2012, CCIS 346, pp. 87–94, 2012.

2   Discrete Wavelet Transformation

Wavelet is a powerful mathematical tool that can deal with multi scale visualized information, wavelet representation of image gives the image change information in different scales.

Suppose $U(x, y)$ is a separable two dimensional scale function that is

$$U(x, y) = U(x)U(y) \qquad (1)$$

In which, $U(x)$, $U(y)$ is one dimensional scale function, if $7 (x)$, $7 (y)$ are corresponding wavelet , Then we can determine following three two-dimensional base wavelet :

$$7^1(x, y) = U(x)7(y)$$
$$7^2(x, y) = 7(x)U(y)$$
$$7^3(x, y) = 7(x)7(y) \qquad (2)$$

According to the two dimensional wavelet, image's two-dimensional discrete wavelet transform [2] is given:

$$\begin{cases} f^0_{2j+1}(m, n) = \{[\ f^0_{2j}(\ x, y)*U(\ -x, -y) \ ] \}(\ 2m, 2n \ ) \\ f^1_{2j+1}(m, n) = \{[\ f^0_{2j}(\ x, y)*7^1(\ -x, -y) \ ] \}(\ 2m, 2n \ ) \\ f^2_{2j+1}(m, n) = \{[\ f^0_{2j}(\ x, y)*7^2(\ -x, -y) \ ] \}(\ 2m, 2n \ ) \\ f^3_{2j+1}(m, n) = \{[\ f^0_{2j}(\ x, y)*7^3(\ -x, -y) \ ] \}(\ 2m, 2n \ ) \end{cases} \qquad (3)$$

Where, $f^0_{20}(\ x, y)$ is original image, after discrete wavelet transform, the image is decomposed into 1/4 size's sub images, the high-frequency part detail image and low-frequency part approximate image on horizontal, vertical, diagonal direction, each image obtained according to second decimation filter. Approximated image $f^0_{2j+1}(x, y)$ decomposed into 2^{j+1} smaller scale image in the same way, so that the original image decomposed into multi-resolution multiple sub images with different space and different frequency. Framework of the discrete wavelet decomposition of the image shown in Figure 1 .

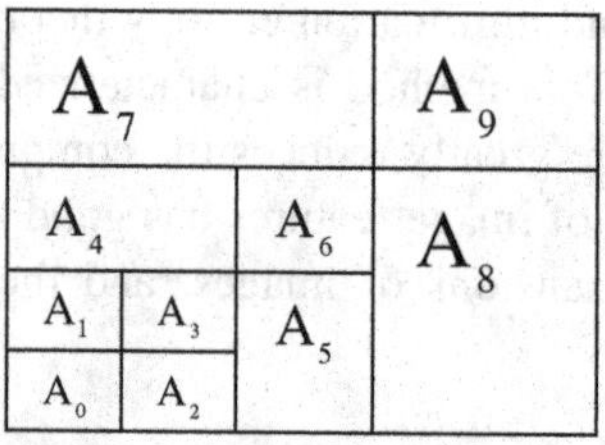

Fig. 1. Image discrete wavelet decomposition framework

3   Calculation of the Sub-image Wavelet Histogram

The steps of calculating the sub-image wavelet histogram is as follows:

Step1: First, divide the image into $n \cdot n$ size of sub-images, thus calculating the global features of the image is converted into calculating the local features.

Step2: According to the equation (3), do three level wavelet decomposition for each sub-image, the first level of a sub-band composed of { A_7, A_8, A_9 }, the second level of sub-band composed of { A_4, A_5, A_6 }, the third level of sub-band composed of { A_0, A_1, A_2, A_3 }. The coefficients of the ten wavelet sub-band are used in the generation process of image features.

Step3: takes the absolute value of those coefficients calculated from all ten wavelet sub-band which produced by 3 layer wavelet decomposition. And it compared with a predefined threshold S_i, the wavelet coefficient which greater than the threshold is 1, the wavelet coefficient which less than the threshold is 0. The mean of each sub-band take as the threshold and it make the threshold is adaptive. Experiments show that the mean of each sub-band as the threshold has better retrieval accuracy than using the fixed threshold.

4   The Calculation of Wavelet Information Entropy

Set vector $v = [\ x_1, x_2 ... x_n\ ]$, assume that the probability of $x_i \in v$ is $p_i = P(\ x_i\ )$, then the information entropy of v can expressed by the following formula:

$$E_v = -\sum_{i=1}^{n} p_i log p_i \qquad (4)$$

The information entropy was originally proposed by Shannon [3], it means that it is just the probability distribution function for a random variable. The information entropy has the following characteristics: symmetry, non-negative, deterministic, scalable, additively, extremality and so on. In reference paper [4], information entropy is used for image retrieval for the first time. Due to the fact that the used information entropy is one-dimensional, so the retrieval accuracy is low. Reference [5] applying distributed information entropy to obtain more satisfactory results. After normalizing the calculated wavelet texture histogram h, $h = [h_1, h_2, ..., h_{2N}]$, normalized texture histogram can be taken as a probability density function of different texture pixels in the whole image space. According to the information entropy theory, texture information entropy of a sub-image can be expressed as:

$$E = -\sum_{i=1}^{2N} h_j log_2(h_j) \qquad (5)$$

Texture information entropy of all sub-images can be expressed as:

$$E_i = - \sum_{i=1}^{2N} h_{i,j} log_2(h_{i,j}), i = 1, 2, ..., M; \ j = 1, 2, ..., 2^N \qquad (6)$$

Where, M is the number of sub-image block, N is the number of sub-band of the sub-images, take N = 10 in this paper.

5   Genetic Clustering Algorithm

Clustering image library [6] is to divide images in the library into some category according to their feature similarity. Suppose the feature vector set of all images in image library is $Z = \{Z_1, Z_2, ... Z_n\}$, Z_i is the feature vector of ith image in the library. At this moment, the clustering process is equivalent to divide the feature vector in the feature library into k classes according to the distances from each other (this paper uses Euclidean distance). The commonly used method is to choose an image as a rallying point for each class to represent this class, and calculate the distance between the rallying point and other images in this class, take the average as a measure of clustering result's standard. Rallying point set R is a subset of Z.

This paper uses a clustering algorithm proposed in literature [7] as a basic method of data clustering. Assume that data set D has different t types of data, each data has m features, in which has m_C classified feature and m_N numeric feature, $m = m_C + m_N$. Might as well put classification features before numerical features, Use D_i $(1 \leq i \leq m)$ to express the number i^{th} feature set.

Definition 1: given a cluster C, $a \in D_i$, the frequency of a in C defined as the number of times a appear in the projection of C on D_i, and expressed by $FreqcD_i(a)$,

$$FreqcD_i(a) = |\{ object \ | object \in C, object . D_i = a\}| \qquad (7)$$

Definition 2: Given a cluster C, the cluster summary information of C defined as: $CSI = \{kind, n, Summary\}$, in which kind is the category of cluster, $n = |C|$ is the size of C, Summary composed of two part: frequency information with different value in classification features and the centroid of numerical features, that is :

$$Summary = \{(Stat_i, Cen) | Stat_i = \{(a, FreqcD_i(a) | a \in D_i\} \qquad (8)$$

In which, $1 \leq i \leq m_C$, $Cen = (c_{m_C+1}, c_{m_C+2}, ..., c_{m_C+m_N})$

Comparison of the distinguished levels of a feature on a classified cluster need to consider two factors: one is the value differences of two clusters on those features sets, the second is the sizes of two clusters, for this put forward definition 3.

Definition 3: The distinction degree on feature D_i of cluster C_1 and C_2 defined as:

$$d_i(\, kind_{C1}, kind_{C2} \,) = \frac{\left| C_1 \right| \cdot \left| C_2 \right|}{\left| C_1 \right| + \left| C_2 \right|} dif(\, C_i^{(1)}, C_i^{(2)} \,) \qquad (9)$$

where , $kind_{C1}$ and $kind_{C2}$ is the category of C_1 and C_2 , $dif(\, C_i^{(1)}, C_i^{(2)} \,)$ expressed the difference on D_i of two clusters.

For numeric feature D_i

$$dif(\, C_i^{(1)}, C_i^{(2)} \,) = \left| C_i^{(1)} - C_i^{(2)} \right| \qquad (10)$$

For classified feature D_i

$$dif(\, C_i^{(1)}, C_i^{(2)} \,) = 1 - \frac{1}{\left| C_1 \right| \bullet \left| C_2 \right|} \sum_{P_i \in (C_1 | D_i) \cap (C_2 | D_2)} Freq_{C_1} D_i(\, p_i \,) \bullet Freq_{C_2} D_i(\, p_i \,) \qquad (11)$$

Definition 4:　The distinction degree of feature D_i defined as

$$f_i = \frac{Max_i - Min_i}{Mean_i} \qquad (12)$$

In which, Max_i , Min_i , $Mean_i$ is the max, min and average value of $d_i(\, kind_{C1}, kind_{C2} \,)$ obtained in definition 3 while C_1 , C_2 traverse the cluster one time.

Because of the relationship between features, the importance of remaining features may change after removing some of the features. So, it may need for multi-step options, until the results are stable. This paper proposes a feature selection algorithm based on clustering. The clustering does not use the flag, but the use flags to logo on the clustering results, using voting mechanism to determine the category of each cluster, and using category differences between the clusters to determine the importance of features and then select the feature subset. The algorithm is described as follows:

Step1: Random selecting the clustering threshold, and use clustering algorithm to cluster the data set D. Use voting mechanism to determine each cluster categories, obtain clustering results with category information $C = \{ \, C_1, C_2, ..., C_k \, \}$;

Step2: according to definition 3, calculate the discriminative degrees between any cluster and the other cluster on the feature (indicating two categories information);

Step3: calculate average value of discriminative degrees between each feature obtained from step (2) and different categories;

Step4: calculate average value $Mean_i$ of discriminative degrees between each feature D_i and different categories. And further calculate the maximum Max_i and minimum Min_i of average discriminative degrees between each feature and different categories;

Step5: calculate discriminative degrees between each feature D_i and different categories $f_i = \dfrac{Max_i - Min_i}{Mean_i}$;

Step6: according to descending order f_i, obtain f_i^* (i=1, ..., m) on the feature $D_1 \sim D_m$;

Step7: Find the point or inflection point i_0 of the dramatic changes in the line chart of f_i^* (i=1, ..., m). $f_i^* \sim f_{i_0}^*$ is the selected feature subset;

6   Image Retrieval Algorithm

The content-based image retrieval algorithm presented in this paper is described as follows:

Step1: taking the discrete wavelet transform, extract wavelet texture histogram feature vector of the sub-image retrieved in the Image Library, and compose feature library expressed by equation (3).

Step2: after cluster feature database with using the genetic clustering algorithm described above, obtain each image class and its cluster center.

Step3: put in the query sample images and extract the feature vectors

Step4: calculating the distance between the points of target image and cohesion image in each category, to determine the target image belongs to which category (minimize the distance between the image points for this category cohesion).

Step5: according to the similarity of size, returns the retrieved images.

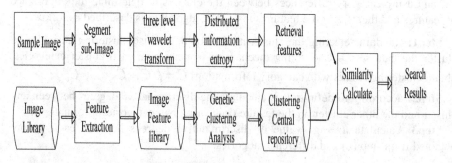

Fig. 2. Procedures of algorithm

7   Experimental Results

The experimental system implemented by the Matlab7 based GUIDE environment, we selected 6000 colored picture of 10 class from the internationally accepted standard video library Corel 10, including landscapes, flowers, figures, cars, animals, etc. use recall, precision, retrieval speed to evaluate the retrieval system's performance. Figure 3 shows 14 images after retrieving the flower image by using the retrieval method proposed in this paper, the first one is the image retrieval sample.

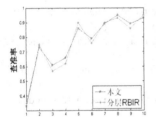

Fig. 3. results of flower retrieval

We implemented a prototype image retrieval system in platform of Matlab7.0. Under the same hardware and software environment, we compare the performance of the algorithms proposed in this paper and [8] algorithm. Comparative experimental results are as shown in Fig.4, Fig.5, and Fig.6.

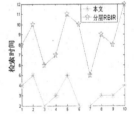

Fig. 4. Comparison of precision   **Fig. 5.** Comparison of recall   **Fig.6.** Comparison of time

In order to test the retrieval effectiveness of the algorithm, firstly selecting 10 categories of images in the image database to composed a set of queries, and then tests the retrieval performance of different algorithms. We use of "precision" and "recall" as the evaluation criteria of the algorithm retrieval effectiveness. Fig.4 and Fig.5 shows that the contrast curve line of precision and recall related to the FWIDET in this paper and layered RBIR on image database. It can be seen from Fig.4 and Fig.5 that retrieval effectiveness of the algorithm presented in the paper and effectiveness of layered RBIR is similar. Fig.6 shows that the retrieval speed is improved a lot, which is due to clustering, and the search take place only in the corresponding class which sample query image belong to. It reduces the number of images comparisons, and improves the retrieval speed and retrieval accuracy, and decreases the semantic gap between low-level features and high-level semantics.

8   Conclusions

This paper presents an algorithm for image retrieval based on wavelet domain distributed information entropy. It is different from the traditional methods of image retrieval which use of wavelet texture. The algorithms presented in this paper use not only the global information of wavelet texture, but also the information entropy of domain distributed information. Experimental results compare with similar method show that the method presented in this paper has higher performance of image retrieval.

Acknowledgments. This work is supported by Program for New Century Excellent Talents in University (NCET-10-0969), Natural Science Foundation of China (No. 61065001).

References

1. Smeulders, A.W.M., Worring, M., Santini, S., et al.: Content based image retrieval at the end of the early years. IEEE Transactions on Pattern Analysis and Machine Intelligence 22(12), 1349–1380 (2000)
2. Castleman, K.R.: Digital image processing, pp. 261–304. Electrical Industrial Publishing Company, Beijing (1998)
3. Shannon, C.E.: A Mathematical theory of communication. Bell Systems Technical Journal 27, 379–423 (1948)
4. Zachary, J.M.: An Information theoretic approach to content based image retrieval, pp. 45–62. Louisiana State University and Agricultural and Mechanical College (2000)
5. Sun, J.D., Zhang, X.M., Cui, J.T., et al.: Image retrieval based on color distribution entropy. Pattern Recognition Letters 27(10), 1122–1126 (2006)
6. Wang, X.P., Cao, L.M.: Genetic Algorithm: Theory, Application and Realized. Xi'an Jiaotong University Press, Xi'an (2002)
7. Jiang, S.Y., Song, X.Y., et al.: A clustering based method for unsupervised intrusion detections. Pattern Recognition Letters 27(7), 802–810 (2006)
8. Sun, Y.Q., Ozawa, S.J.: A hierarchical approach for region based image retrieval. In: IEEE International Conference on Systems, Man and Cybernetics, vol. 1, pp. 1117–1124 (2004)
9. Aulia, E.: Hierarchica indexing for region based image retrieval. Louisiana State University (May 2005)

A New Automated Image Registration Method
Based on Corners[*]

Jin-jian Lv, Gang Deng, and Bo Xu

Air Force Early-warning Academy, Wuhan, 430019, China
{lvjj1979,dgang1978,sheep258}@yahoo.com.cn

Abstract. Image registration plays an import role in image processing and computer vision. A new automated image registration method based on corners is proposed in this paper. Corners are extracted by an improved technique based on Harris and then compose virtual triangles. According to the principle that the corresponding virtual triangles are similar in the reference and sensed images under the similarity transformation, the most similar two virtual triangles can be found. Their corresponding vertexes are used as control points and the parameters of similarity transformation are obtained. The proposed method is guaranteed to register images if only three corresponding corners are extracted from the reference and sensed images. Another advantage of the proposed method is that there is theoretically no limited to scale, translation and rotation of two images. The experiment results prove that the proposed method is accurate and robust.

Keywords: feature extraction, corners, virtual triangle, similarity transformation, automated image registration.

1 Introduction

Image registration is a fundamental task in image processing used to match a pair of images taken at different times, different sensors, or from different viewpoints [1]. It is a classical problem of several applications areas such as defense surveillance, remote sensing, medical imaging, computer vision and so on. In these applications, users generally use manual registration which is not feasible in cases where a large number of images need to be registered. Thus, there is a critical need for automated techniques that require little or no operator supervision.

The current automated registration techniques can be classified into two broad categories: area-based and feature-based techniques [2]. In the area-based algorithms, a small window of points in the sensed image is compared statistically with windows of the same size in the reference image. The centers of the matched windows then are used as control points to solve for the transformation parameters between the two images. Although it is implemented simply, a majority of it have the limitation of registering only images with small misalignment. It becomes unreliable when the images have multiple modalities and the gray-level characteristics vary.

---

[*] This work is supported by the Postdoctoral Science Foundation of China (20110431889).

F.L. Wang et al. (Eds.): CMSP 2012, CCIS 346, pp. 95–102, 2012.
© Springer-Verlag Berlin Heidelberg 2012

In contrast, the feature-based methods are more robust and more suitable in these cases. There are two critical procedures generally involved in the feature-based techniques: feature extraction and feature correspondence. Spatial features usually include points, edges, boundaries, road intersections, and special structures. The most desired features are points, because their coordinates can be directly used to determinate the parameters of a transformation function that registers the images. Corners are one of point features in common use. There are many mature methods to extract corners, so the difficulty of the methods based on corners is corners matching. A variety of techniques are used to match corners, such as relaxation [3-4], Hausdroff distance and its related methods [5-7], relatively distance and histogram clustering [8-11] and so on. But they have many limitations to corners extracted from the reference and sensed images. The number of corners should be equal and simple transformation exist between them etc. This limits the application of the methods based on corners. In most existing corner-based techniques, corners correspondence is still the most challenging problem.

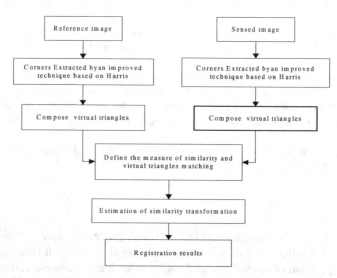

Fig. 1. Overview of the proposed method

To solve the problems of the aforementioned methods, a new automated image registration method based on corners is proposed in this paper. The critical elements for the proposed registration method are explored. These elements include corners extraction, corners matching and transformation parameter estimation. The overview of the method is shown as fig.1. Corners are extracted by an improved technique based on Harris and then compose virtual triangles. Corresponding corners are matched by virtual triangles rather than corners themselves. The similarity transformation is used to transform the sensed image into reference image in this paper. The proposed method is guaranteed to register images if only three corresponding corners are extracted from the reference and sensed images. Another advantage of the method is that there is theoretically no limited to scale, translation and rotation of two images.

2   Corners Extraction

The method[12] proposed by Harris et al is verified as a good method. Given a 2D image, we will get the gradient $\Delta I(x,y)$ of the 2D image $I(x,y)$ where:

$$\Delta I(x,y) = \begin{pmatrix} \partial I(x,y)/\partial x \\ \partial I(x,y)/\partial y \end{pmatrix} = \begin{pmatrix} I_x \\ I_y \end{pmatrix} \tag{1}$$

Where I_x, I_y denote the x, y directional derivatives respectively. Harris detector is based on the following cornerness measure:

$$W(x,y) = \det(C_I) - k\, trace^2(C_I) \tag{2}$$

Where $k = 0.04$, $\det(\bullet)$ denotes the determinant, the matrix C_I represents the averaged dyadic product of the gray-value gradient:

$$C_I = \begin{bmatrix} \overline{I_x^2} & \overline{I_x I_y} \\ \overline{I_y I_x} & \overline{I_y^2} \end{bmatrix} \tag{3}$$

Where $trace(\bullet)$ represents the trace of matrix:

$$trace(C_I) = \overline{I_x^2} + \overline{I_y^2} \tag{4}$$

Where $\overline{\bullet}$ represents the local average.

The intensity of reference and sensed images taken under different conditions is different commonly and it will be difficult to extract corresponding corners. Furthermore, if we compute cornerness measure of each pixel in the two images, the computing complexity will be large. Therefore, an improved technique based on Harris is presented as following:

a. Firstly, the contrasts of the reference and sensed images are enhanced by histogram equalization respectively. The histogram of the equalized reference image is used to specify the histogram of the equalized sensed image and the new sensed image is obtained. The new sensed image and the equalized reference image will be more similar [13] and the corresponding corners in two images will be extracted easily.

b. Compute cornerness measure only in pixels whose gradient amplitude is larger than an experiential threshold rather than all pixels of the image. Usually, 20% of the total pixels are sufficient because these pixels represent structure information of the image [14]. The computing complexity reduces and the most corners can be extracted.

However, the number of corners extracted by the upper method is still large. In order to reduce the computing complexity ulteriorly and make corners dispersing the whole image extensive, extracted corners are processed in the following:

a. Given corners extracted from the two images are $L_R = \{(X_i,Y_i), i=1,2,\cdots,M\}$ and $L_S = \{(x_j,y_j), j=1,2,\cdots,N\}$, where M, N are the number of corners respectively, according to the value of cornerness measure $W(x,y)$, sort the corners and get sorted corners, represented by $L_R^{'} = \{(X_i^{'},Y_i^{'}), i=1,2,\cdots,M\}$ and $L_S^{'} = \{(x_j^{'},y_j^{'}), j=1,2,\cdots,N\}$.

b. Starting from the first of $L_R^{'}, L_S^{'}$, select one corner at a time, guaranteeing the Euclidean distance between the second selected corner and the first selected corner less than a preset thresh. Repeat the process until the desired number is achieved or no more corners remain in $L_R^{'}, L_S^{'}$. The final extracted corners are $P = \{(X_i,Y_i), i=1,2,\cdots,m\}$ and $Q = \{(x_j,y_j), j=1,2,\cdots,n\}$, in this paper, $m,n \le 30$.

The flowchart of the improved technique based on Harris is shown as fig.2.

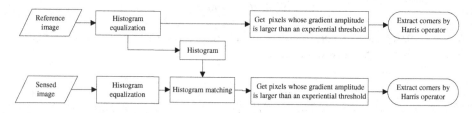

Fig. 2. Flowchart of the improved technique based on Harris

3   Virtual Triangles Matching

3.1   Some Definitions

Definition 1: Select randomly three points from $P = \{(X_i,Y_i), i=1,2,\cdots,m\}$ or $Q = \{(x_j,y_j), j=1,2,\cdots,n\}$, then connect them orderly to compose triangle. We call the triangle as virtual triangle because it is not exist in the images actually.

Definition 2: We call the random two virtual triangles in reference and sensed images as a virtual triangles pair.

Definition 3: If three corresponding vertexes of a virtual triangles pair are corresponding corners, we call them as a matching virtual triangles pair.

3.2   Virtual Triangles Matching

If the relation of two images is similarity transformation, a matching virtual triangles pair in them are similar. Virtual triangles matching are based on the principle.

Given random three points in $P = \{(X_i,Y_i), i=1,2,\cdots,m\}$ are p_1, p_2, p_3, random three points in $Q = \{(x_j,y_j), j=1,2,\cdots,n\}$ are q_1, q_2, q_3. $\Delta p_1 p_2 p_3$ and $\Delta q_1 q_2 q_3$ compose a virtual triangles pair shown as fig.3.

Fig. 3. A virtual triangles pair

l_{12}, l_{13}, l_{23} and $l'_{12}, l'_{13}, l'_{23}$ are the lengthes of three sides of $\Delta p_1 p_2 p_3$ and $\Delta q_1 q_2 q_3$ respectively, where l_{ij} and l'_{ij} (i =1, 2, 3; j =1, 2, 3) represent the distances between p_i and p_j , q_i and q_j :

$$l_{ij} = \sqrt{(X_i - X_j)^2 + (Y_i - Y_j)^2} \qquad l'_{ij} = \sqrt{(x_i - x_j)^2 + (y_i - y_j)^2} \qquad (5)$$

L and L' are the perimeters, S and S' are the areas of $\Delta p_1 p_2 p_3$ and $\Delta q_1 q_2 q_3$ respectively:

$$L = l_{12} + l_{13} + l_{23} \qquad L' = l'_{12} + l'_{13} + l'_{23} \qquad (6)$$

$$S = \sqrt{\frac{L}{2}(\frac{L}{2} - l_{12})(\frac{L}{2} - l_{13})(\frac{L}{2} - l_{23})} \qquad S' = \sqrt{\frac{L'}{2}(\frac{L'}{2} - l'_{12})(\frac{L'}{2} - l'_{13})(\frac{L'}{2} - l'_{23})} \qquad (7)$$

Under the similarity transformation, if $\Delta p_1 p_2 p_3$ and $\Delta q_1 q_2 q_3$ are a matching virtual triangles pair, they should be similar:

$$\frac{l_{12}}{l'_{12}} = \frac{l_{13}}{l'_{13}} = \frac{l_{23}}{l'_{23}} = \sqrt{\frac{S}{S'}} \qquad (8)$$

Because of noise and other reasons, the location of extracted corners perhaps have a little excursion from their real location. So $\Delta p_1 p_2 p_3$ and $\Delta q_1 q_2 q_3$ can not be absolute similar:

$$\frac{l_{12}}{l'_{12}} \approx \frac{l_{13}}{l'_{13}} \approx \frac{l_{23}}{l'_{23}} \approx \sqrt{\frac{S}{S'}} \qquad (9)$$

In order to find the most similar matching virtual triangles pair, we define the measure of similarity as following:

$$\min((1 - \frac{l_{12}}{l'_{12}} / \sqrt{S/S'})^2 + (1 - \frac{l_{13}}{l'_{13}} / \sqrt{S/S'})^2 + (1 - \frac{l_{23}}{l'_{23}} / \sqrt{S/S'})^2) \qquad (10)$$

According to the measure of similarity, we can gain the most similar matching virtual triangles pair to achieve virtual triangles matching. Their corresponding vertexes are used as control points.

4   Estimation of Similarity Transformation

Similarity transformation is used in this paper. Suppose (X_1,Y_1), (x_1,y_1), (X_2,Y_2), (x_2,y_2) and (X_3,Y_3), (x_3,y_3) are coordinates of three corresponding vertexes of the most similar matching virtual triangles pair gained in section 3. The lengthes of three corresponding sides of them are denoted as $l_{12}, l'_{12}, l_{13}, l'_{13}, l_{23}, l'_{23}$. $\theta_1, \theta'_1, \theta_2, \theta'_2, \theta_3, \theta'_3$ are the angles between three corresponding sides and horizontal orientation respectively.

The scale s can be estimated as following:

$$s = \left(\frac{l_{12}}{l'_{12}} + \frac{l_{13}}{l'_{13}} + \frac{l_{23}}{l'_{23}} \right) / 3 \tag{11}$$

Computing the rotation angle θ by formulation (12):

$$\theta = (\theta_1 - \theta'_1 + \theta_2 - \theta'_2 + \theta_3 - \theta'_3)/3 \tag{12}$$

Via (X_1,Y_1), (x_1,y_1), (X_2,Y_2), (x_2,y_2), (X_3,Y_3), (x_3,y_3) and formulation (10), we can get three horizontal and vertical translation: $\Delta x_1, \Delta y_1, \Delta x_2, \Delta y_2, \Delta x_3, \Delta y_3$. And $\Delta x, \Delta y$ can be computed:

$$\begin{cases} \Delta x = (\Delta x_1 + \Delta x_2 + \Delta x_3)/3 \\ \Delta y = (\Delta y_1 + \Delta y_2 + \Delta y_3)/3 \end{cases} \tag{13}$$

5   Experimental Results

The reference image and the sensed image are shown as fig.4. Corners extracted by an improved technique based on Harris are denoted as red "+" dots in fig.5. The registration result of the proposed method is shown as fig.6.

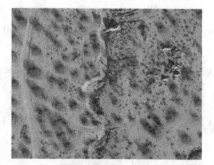 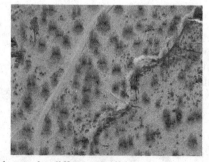

Fig. 4. Reference and sensed image taken under different conditions

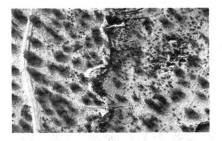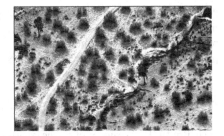

Fig. 5. Corners extracted by an improved technique based on Harris

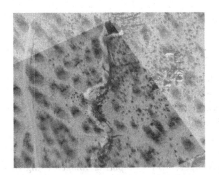

Fig. 6. Registration result of proposed method   **Fig. 7.** Registration result of manual method

Table 1. Comparison between the manual method and the proposed method

Parameters / Methods	Model parameters				Errors		
	s	$\theta(\circ)$	Δx	Δy	$xError$	$yError$	$RMSE$
Manual method	1.004	29.06	-189.052	276.506	1.223	0.971	2.071
Proposed method	1.005	29.62	−187.496	274.282	1.301	0.890	1.938

The manual registration result is compared to that of the proposed automated algorithm. The result of this comparison is shown in Table 1.

6   Conclusions

A new automated image registration method based on corners is proposed in this paper. Corners are extracted by an improved technique based on Harris firstly and then compose virtual triangles. Corresponding corners are gained by matching virtual triangles rather than corners themselves. Parameters of similarity transformation are estimated by the coordinates of corresponding corners. The performance of the proposed algorithm has been demonstrated by registering two images taken under different conditions. Registration accuracy of proposed method is comparative with manual method. The method is also robust since it overcomes the limitations of corners correspondence of existing methods mentioned in section I. Further goal for us is to improve registration accuracy of the proposed method in the future.

References

[1] Brown, L.: A survey of image registration techniques. ACM Computer Surveys 24(4), 325–376 (1992)

[2] Zitova, B., Flusser, J.: Image registration methods: a survey. Image Vision Computing 21, 977–1000 (2003)

[3] Ranade, S., Rosenfeld, A.: Point pattern matching by relaxation. Pattern Recognition 12, 269–275 (1980)

[4] Ton, J., Jain, A.K.: Registering Landsat images by point matching. IEEE Trans. on GRS 27, 642–651 (1989)

[5] Stockman, G.C., Kopstein, S., Benett, S.: Matching images to models for registration and object detection via clustering. IEEE Trans. on PAMI 4, 229–241 (1982)

[6] Goshtasby, A., Stockman, G.C.: Point pattern matching using convex hull edges. IEEE Trans. on Systems, Man, and Cybernetics 15, 631–637 (1985)

[7] Goshtasby, A., Stockman, G.C., Page, C.V.: A region based approach to digital image registration with subpixel accuracy. IEEE Trans. on GRS 24, 390–399 (1986)

[8] Huttenlocher, D.P., Klanderman, G.A., Rucklidge, W.J.: Comparing images using the Hausdorff distance. IEEE Trans. on PAMI 15, 850–863 (1993)

[9] Huttenlocher, D.P., Rucklidge, W.J.: A multi-resolution technique for comparing images using the Hausdorff distance. In: Proceedings of the IEEE Conference on Computer Vision and Pattern Recognition, New York, pp. 705–706 (June 1993)

[10] Olson, C.F., Hutenlocher, D.P.: Automatic target recognition by matching oriented edge pixels. IEEE Transactions on Image Processing 6, 103–113 (1997)

[11] Zhou, P., Tan, Y., Xu, S.-S.: A New Method of Image Registration Based On Corner Detection. Transaction of USTC 32(4), 455–461 (2002)

[12] Harris, C., Stephens, M.: A combined corner and edge detector. In: Proceedings of the 4th Alvey Vision Conference, pp. 147–151 (1988)

[13] Tuo, H., Zhang, L., Liu, Y.: Multi-sensor aerial image registration using direct histogram specification. In: Proceedings of the 2004 IEEE International Conference on Networking, Sensing & Control, Taipei, Taiwan, pp. 807–812 (2004)

[14] Keller, Y., Averbuch, A.: Implicit similarity: a new approach to multi-sensor image registration. In: Proceedings of the 2003 IEEE Computer Society Conference on Computer Vision and Pattern Recognition (2003)

Symmetric Normal Inverse Gaussian and Structural Similarity Based Image Denoising

Yuanjiang Li[1,2] and Yuehua Li[1]

[1] School of Electronic Engineering and Optoelectronic Technology,
Nanjing University of Science and Technology, Nanjing, China
hmb4507@njust.edu.cn
[2] Institute of Electronic and Information, Jiangsu University of Science and Technology,
Zhenjiang, 212003, China
Lyj@bitai.com

Abstract. An image denoising method based on symmetric normal inverse Gaussian (SNIG) model within the framework of non-local means (NLM) is proposed in this paper. We use Structural Similarity (SSIM) to compute the value of SSIM between the reference patch and its similar versions, and remove the dissimilar pixels. Besides, the SNIG model is adopted to adjust the coefficients of these patches with low SSIM in DT-CWT domain. Experiments show that the proposed method has the capacity to denoise effectively, improves the peak signal-to-noise ratio of the image, and keeps better visual result in edges information reservation as well.

Keywords: Non local-mean (NLM), image denoising, Symmetric normal inverse Gaussian, Structural Similarity.

1   Introduction

In the area of image processing, wavelet-based methods have strong impact on various applications such as denoising, restoration, super-resolution and so on. The key point of this method is to adjust the coefficient of images in wavelet domain based on some explicit or fuzzy prior information. The method based on the wavelet provides good approximations in estimation problems in [1]. In [2], a Gaussian probability density function (Gaussian PDF) is proposed for updating the image coefficients. Further, because the discrete wavelet transform (DWT) is not shift-invariant and lack good directionality, it results in pseudo-Gibbs phenomena in [3]. Besides, the dual-tree complex wavelet transform (DT-CWT) has been proposed for overcoming the problem, which is employed to decompose the image to seven sub bands in order to reduce the speckle noise in [4]. However, wavelet-based methods depend on the accuracy of prior information.

Compared with wavelet methods, non-local methods for image processing are research hot points due to its simple and model-free advantage in the recent years. Buades et al [5] presented a non-local means (NLM) denoising method based on the self-similarity of images in the spatial domain. Its main core is to use the weighted

F.L. Wang et al. (Eds.): CMSP 2012, CCIS 346, pp. 103–111, 2012.

average of all pixels for estimating the noisy pixel. Especially, the weight reveals the similarity between the patch centered at the noisy pixel and others, meanwhile improved denoising performance of NLM owes to the similarity comparison based on patches. But the tradition NLM method is fit for the small size image with high signal noise ratio due to its computational complexity. Denoising and restoration are different research direction in image processing, but they are faced with a challenging problem, which is to preserve the detail (such as edge, texture) and reduce the noise from their observed but degraded images.

In this paper, an improved version of NLM is proposed to reduce the effect of noise and acquire the reliable information of images. In the algorithm, we firstly use Structural Similarity (SSIM) [6] to compute the value of SSIM between the reference patch and its similar versions. Then the improved NLM is used to estimate the patch with high value of SSIM, meanwhile the SNIG model is adopted to adjust the coefficients of these patches with low SSIM in DT-CWT domain. Thus, the proposed algorithm demonstrates its effective capacity to denoise and keeps better visual result in edges information reservation experimentally.

2   Related Work

Given this model, f is the degraded version of the original noiseless image z. n is the random noise. So, the relationship at pixel i is $f_i = z_i + n_i$. The NLM method obtains the new value at pixel i, f using a weighted average of all pixels in the image:

$$\hat{f_i} = \frac{1}{C(i)} \sum_j w(i, j) f_j,$$ (1)

where $C(i) = \sum_j w(i,j)$, especially, the weight $w(i,j)$ measures the contextual similarity between pixel i and j based on the distance. In the option of NLM, $w(i,j)$ adopts the structure similarity between the corresponding patches centered at i and j instead of the point similarity. Because single pixel is not enough to show the structure information, NLM has the advantage of describing the details such as texture. Suppose N_i and N_j are the patches or blocks centered at pixel i and j with fixed size of $K \times K$, respectively. Let $f(N_i)$ denote all the pixels which are limited to the given patch, such that $f(N_i) = \{f_i, i \in N_i\}$. Buades et al [5] proposed the definition of weights as follow:

$$w(i, j) = \exp(\frac{-\| f(N_i) - f(N_j) \|_2^2}{(h\sigma_n)^2}).$$ (2)

where $\|\bullet\|_2$ is a Gaussian weighted Euclidean distance function, σ_n is the noise variance, h is the decay parameter.

Compared with other excellent methods, NLM still has unignored issues. According to the nature of non-local algorithm, the patches are computed across the whole image for obtaining the weight of these corresponding pixels. The drawback is reduced to three aspects. Firstly, the computational complexity influences the efficiency strongly. The operation of weighed averaging across entire images is fully responsible for this defect. Secondly, the result of NLM is a spatial mean theoretically. The more corresponding pixels are used to average, the better should the effect of denoising be, but this assumption is usually impossible or impracticable. Not all pixels on the image are fit for estimating the reference pixel due to the discrepancy of structure of different regions, so the result of NLM depends on the matched pixels and appropriate weight primarily. However, traditional NLM covers a hypothetical condition that noise images include enough similar patterns, or all pixels of degraded images are suitable for estimating the specific pixel. Natural images are packed with a large amount of information such as edges, texture and so on. To conclude, the improvement of the NLM method includes chiefly three points. One is fast algorithm; another is adaptive classification of pixels based on the information of image patches and the other is the way of obtaining weights. As shown in Eq. (2), the weight $w(i, j)$ not only reflects the Gaussian weighted Euclidean distance of N_i and N_j, but also describes the structural similarity of i and j. The greater the weight is, the more similar the pixels are. Although the dissimilar pixels have small weights, the impact of them towards denoising is not neglected. Simultaneously, N_i and N_j are inevitably corrupted by noise, which results in the poor weight of similar pixels. Consequently, we propose a modified NLM method combined with SNIG model, which is known as "SNIG-NLM".

3   Proposed Method

The "SNIG-NLM" method is divided into two steps. Firstly, we use SSIM to remove these dissimilar patches from all neighborhoods of the reference patch, which is the same as the ridding of unmatched pixels. Secondly, if all neighborhoods have low value of SSIM, the SNIG model is adopted to adjust the coefficients in DT-CWT domain of patches, and then repeat the first step.

In the framework of NLM method, the search range of similar patches across the whole image. Although we restrict the range in a rectangular window, dissimilar pixels still exist around the estimated one and exert their influence on the denoised result. The reason is that the patch (or pixels) belonged to texture region takes part in denoising the reference pixel of flat region. In order to remove the unfit pixels, we use the evaluation criterion based on Structural Similarity (SSIM) [6] to remove the dissimilar pixels.

In the first step, given the reference block Z_{x_R} and the candidate match block Z_{x_x}, the SSIM index is defined as

$$SSIM(Z_{x_R}, Z_x) = \frac{(2\mu_{Z_{x_R}}\mu_{Z_x} + C_1)(\sigma_{Z_{x_R}Z_x} + C_2)}{(\mu_{Z_{x_R}}^2 + \mu_{Z_x}^2 + C_1)(\sigma_{Z_{x_R}}^2 + \sigma_{Z_x}^2 + C_2)},$$

(3)

where $\mu_{Z_{x_R}}$, μ_{Z_x} is the mean intensity of Z_{x_R} and Z_x respectively, $\sigma_{Z_{x_R}}$, σ_{Z_x} is the standard deviation, $\sigma_{Z_{x_R}Z_x}$ is the correlation coefficient corresponds to the cosine of the angle between the vectors Z_{x_R} - $\mu_{Z_{x_R}}$ and Z_x - μ_{Z_x}, C_1 and C_2 are small constants which eliminates unstable results when either $(\mu_{Z_{x_R}}^2 + \mu_{Z_x}^2)$ or $(\sigma_{Z_{x_R}}^2 + \sigma_{Z_x}^2)$ is very close to zero.

The SSIM index that values between -1 and 1 achieves its maximum value of 1 only if the two compared blocks are exactly the same. In order to restrict it between 0 and 1, SSIM index is taken by absolute value.

The bigger is the value of SSIM, the structure between the reference patch and its corresponding ones is more similar. If the SSIM of the neighboring patches is greater than 0.4, they are allowed to participate in the weighted operation, which is shown as

$$SSIM(Z_{x_R}, Z_x) > 0.4$$

(4)

For reducing the effect of noise, we propose an operation about weight refinement based on SSIM, which is written as

$$w(i,j) = \exp(\frac{-\| f(Z_{x_R}) - f(Z_x) \|_2^2 + SSIM(Z_{x_R}, Z_x)}{(h\delta_n)^2})$$

(5)

If the SSIM's value of all neighbourhoods is lower than 0.4, we use the SNIG model to adjust their coefficients in DT-CWT domain. In order to obtain the patch with less noise, a Bayesian MAP estimator is developed by adopting the SNIG PDF for modeling the details of image and using the GGD PDF for modeling the noise. The SNIG PDF is given by [7]

$$P_f(f) = A\frac{K_1(\alpha\sqrt{\delta^2 + f^2})}{\sqrt{\delta^2 + f^2}}$$

(6)

where $A = \dfrac{\alpha\delta\exp(\alpha\delta)}{\pi}$, and K_1 is the modified Bessel function of the second kind. α controls the shape of SING model. δ is a scale parameter. In [8], the GGD PDF is expressed as

$$GG_{\sigma_x,\beta}(x) = C(\sigma_x, \beta)\exp\{-[\alpha(\sigma_x, \beta)|x|]^\beta\}$$

(7)

where $\quad \alpha(\sigma_X, \beta) = \sigma_X^{-1} \left[\dfrac{\Gamma(3/\beta)}{\Gamma(1/\beta)} \right]^{1/2} \quad \bullet$ and $\quad C(\sigma_X, \beta) = \dfrac{\beta\alpha(\sigma_X, \beta)}{2\Gamma(1/\beta)}$,

$C(\sigma_X, \beta)$ is normalization factor. $\Gamma(t) = \displaystyle\int_0^\infty e^{-u} u^{t-1} du$ is the function of $\Gamma \bullet$Here,

σ_X is the variance of signal, which controls the diffusion of GGD model, and β is a shape parameter. We suppose that the distribution of the noise in each sub band of DT-CWT is GGD model.

In [9-10], the Bayesian MAP estimator is shown as

$$\hat{f} = \arg\max P(g - f)P_f(f) \tag{8}$$

where g is the transformed version of degraded patch in DT-CWT domain. Besides, an approximate solution of (8) is acquired, which is

$$\hat{f} = sign(g)\max(|g| - C \bullet \delta_\tau^2 |M|, 0) \tag{9}$$

where C is the regularization parameter, which is important to preserve the edge and reduce the noise. δ_τ represents the correlation of sub bands, and

$$M = \frac{\beta g}{\sigma_X \beta + \alpha\delta^2} + \frac{\alpha g}{\sqrt{\delta^2 + g^2}} \frac{\sigma_X \beta}{K_1(\alpha\sqrt{\delta^2 + g^2})} \tag{10}$$

We need to estimate the parameter $\delta_\tau, \alpha, \beta, \sigma_X, \delta$, and C. For easy computation, we assume $\alpha = \beta$ and $\sigma_X = \delta$. The estimation of σ_X is proposed by Donoho [11], which is obtained as

$$\sigma_X = median(|y(k.l)|)/0.6475 \tag{11}$$

where $y(k.l)$ is the coefficient of every sub band of the DT-CWT. Especially, $\sigma_{X_1} \in HH_1$, $\sigma_{X_2} \in HH_2$. To obtain the SNIG parameter α or the GGD parameter β, we use the proposed approach by Wang [12]. The parameter β is estimated as

$$\beta \approx R^{-1}\left(\frac{\sigma_{X_1}}{\sigma_{X_2}}\right) \tag{12}$$

where $R(x) = \dfrac{\Gamma^2(2/x)}{\Gamma(1/x)\Gamma(3/x)}$.

We adopt the discrepancy iterative method in [13] based on Morozov equation for solving the regularization parameter C. It is expressed as

$$\phi(C) =\| g - f \|^2 - \| \kappa \|^2 \tag{13}$$

where κ is the noise of imaging system. According to the work of [14], κ is set to $4\| \sigma_{x_2} \|^2$. In order to calculate (11) for getting the approximate solution of C, the Newton iteration method is used. The approximate equation of (13) is shown as

$$\phi(C)+\phi'(C)(C_{k+1} -C_k) = 0 \tag{14}$$

$$C_{k+1} = C_k - \frac{\phi(C)}{\phi'(C)} \tag{15}$$

k denotes the number of iterations. $\phi'(C)$ is the derivative of $\phi(C)$. The condition of stopping iterations is $\phi(C) \le 10^{-6}$ or the maximum number of iterations is 200.

The proposed method can be summarized as follow:

1. Compute the SSIM of the reference patches and their neighboring versions.
2. If the value of SSIM belonged to some corresponding patches are more than 0.4, then apply the improved NLM method to process these patches.
3. If no corresponding patches satisfy the rule about SSIM, then apply the DT-CWT on the log-transformed patches.
4. Estimate the parameter of SNIG and GGD model, then obtain the MAP estimate from (6).
5. Perform an exponential transformation of the result from Step 4.
6. Compute (12) and update the regularization parameter C. If the terminating condition is met, the restoration is accomplished, Otherwise iterating the process from Step1 to Step 6.

4   Experiment Results

To investigate the effectiveness of the proposed image denoising methods, we compare the denoised results of traditional NLM [5], BM3D [15] and BLS-GSM [16] with SNIG-NLM.

Suppose the noiseless image is available, and its noisy version is produced by adding zero-mean white Gaussian noise with δ_n =20. The test image is grayscale Lena with the size 512×512. Figure 1 shows the original image and various denoised versions.

Among these methods, BM3D is the most effective algorithm for denoising, which relies on the structure of blocks. Its denoising result is prior to other existing methods in terms of both visual quality and PSNR. Comparing with the results of BLS-GSM and NLM, the great majority of texture and geometric structure are still clear with fewer nicks in Figure 2 (e) and (f). So the result of NLM-SNIG shown in Figure 2 (f) is close to BM3D in preserving details and keeping smooth within the homogeneous area.

Fig. 1. The denoising experiment on the standard image:(a)the original image;(b)the noisy image(σ_n =20);(c) image denoised by BLS-GSM;(d)image denoised by NLM;(e) image denoised by BM3D; and (f) image denoised by SNIG-NLM

Based on a detailed analysis of the denoised results, BLS-GSM generates some discontinuous information during the course of denoising, and destroys the flatness of homogeneous area shown in Figure 2 (c). Especially, the effect is revealed around the edge of hat obviously. Moreover, NLM method usually leads to two drawbacks such as excessive smoothness of edges, decreasing the contrast of images. Both of them give rise to the lost of important details. For example, the breach appears on the mouth of 'Lena', which makes the contour of mouth broken. So the denoised result of NLM is the worst within these methods on the visual effect, which is also presented on the table of PSNR displayed subsequently.

Table 1. PSNR values (dB) obtained by different methods applied on different test images and different noise level

	BLG-GSM(dB)	BM3D(dB)	NLM (dB)	SNIG-NLM (dB)
Boats				
σ_n =10	33.58	33.91	32.88	33.70
σ_n =25	29.37	29.62	28.61	29.55
σ_n =50	26.36	26.78	25.21	26.70
σ_n =100	23.74	23.97	22.16	23.85
Lena				
σ_n =10	35.59	35.92	34.33	35.88
σ_n =25	31.73	32.07	30.47	31.97
σ_n =50	28.64	29.06	27.30	28.95
σ_n =100	25.68	25.95	23.75	25.80

SNIG-NLM method has the good capability of removing noises and preserving details, which is close to BM3D. From the visual effect, the proposed method is more desirable than these methods such as BLS-GSM and traditional NLM, which is owed to the combination of NLM and adaptive shrinkage based on SNIG model. The PSNR values for implementations using different images and different noise levels are listed in Table 1.

From the table above, it is easy to evolve several conclusions. Firstly, our results confirm that the traditional NLM method is less effective than other approaches due to the effect of dissimilar patches (or pixels). Therefore the PSNR of NLM is the lowest at the same noise level. Secondly, the proposed method outperforms BLS-GSM and NLM in terms of PSNR, and comes close to BM3D. In addition, it consistently provides good results for images with kinds of noise levels, and provides relatively stable PSNR that gains over BLG-GSM by about 0.23 dB and NLM by about 1.1 dB on average. We attribute the advantageous performance of NLM-SNIG to the adaptive shrinkage based on SNIG model and the proper selection of similar patches.

5   Conclusions

In this paper, the goal of the proposed method is applied to improve the resolution of images using the SNIG and GGD model in the framework of NLM. We use Structural Similarity (SSIM) to compute the value of SSIM between the reference patch and its similar versions, and remove the dissimilar pixels. Besides, the SNIG model is adopted to adjust the coefficients of these patches with low SSIM in DT-CWT domain. In the process of adjusting the coefficients, we use a MAP estimator to restrict the bad effect for obtaining the real detail based on SNIG PDF model and make use of Newton iteration method to update the regularization parameter C. Experiments show that the proposed method has the capacity to denoise effectively, improves the peak signal-to-noise ratio of the image, and keeps better visual result in edges information reservation as well.

Acknowledgments. The authors would like to thank the anonymous reviewer and editors for their helpful comments and suggestions. This work is supported by National Natural Science Foundation of China under Grants 60901008 and 61001010, National Ministry Foundation of China under Grants 9140A05070910BQ02 and 51305050102, University Science Research Project of Jiangsu Province under Grants 11KJB510020, University Postgraduate Research and Innovation Project of Jiangsu Province under Grants CXLX12_0199.

References

1. Mallat, S.: A Wavelet Tour of Signal Proc. Academic, San Diego (1998)
2. Gupta, Chauhan, R.C., Saxena, S.C.: Locally adaptive wavelet domain Bayesian processor for denoising medical ultrasound images using speckle modelling based on Rayleigh distribution. IEE Proceedings on Vision, Signal and Image Processing 152, 129–135 (2005)

3. Selesnick, I.W., Baraniuk, R.G., Kingsbury, N.: The dual tree complex wavelet transform-A coherent framework for multiscale signal and image processing. IEEE Signal Processing Magazine 22, 123–151 (2005)
4. Bhuiyan, M.I.H., Omair Ahmad, M., Swamy, M.N.S.: Wavelet-based Despecking Of Medical Ultrasound Images With The Symmetic Nomrmal Inverse Gaussian Prior. In: ICASSP, pp. 721–724 (2007)
5. Buades, A., Coll, B., Morel, J.M.: The staircasing effect in neighborhood filters and its solution. IEEE Transaction on Image Processing 15, 1499–1505 (2006)
6. Wang, Z., Simoncelli, E.P.: Stimulus synthesis for efficient evaluation and refinement of perceptual image quality metrics. In: Human Vision and Electronic Imaging IX, Proc. SPIE, vol. 5292 (2004)
7. Hanssen, A., Oigard, T.A.: The normal inverse Gaussian distribution for heavy-tailed processes. In: Proc. IEEE EUEASIP Workshop on Nonlinear Signal and Image Processing (2001)
8. Mallat, S.: A theory for multiresolution signal decomposition: the Wavelet representation. IEEE Trans. Patten Analysis and Machine Intelligence 11, 674–693 (1989)
9. Bhuiyan, M.I.H., Omair Ahmad, M., Swamy, M.N.S.: Spatially adaptive wavelet-based method using the Cauchy prior for denoising the SAR images. IEEE Trans. on Circuits, Systems and Video Technology (2007)
10. Hyvarinen, A.: Sparse code shrinkage: Denoising of non-Gaussian data by maximum likelihood estimation. Neural Computation 11, 1739–1768 (2007)
11. Donoho, D.L., Johnstone, I.M.: Denoising by thresholding. IEEE Trans. on Information Theory 41, 613–627 (1995)
12. Wang, T.-Y., Li, Z.-M.: A Fast Parameter Estimation of Generalized Gaussian Distribution. Chinese Journal Of Engineering Geophysics 3, 172–176 (2006)
13. Tang, X.-J., Liu, J., Tian, J.-W.: Restoration of discrepancy iterative images using mechanism for evaluating noise. J. Huazhong Univ. of Sci & Tech (Nature Science Edition) 35, 60–61 (2007)
14. Zeng, S.-Y., Ding, L.-X., Kang, L.-S.: A method to approach optimal restoration in image restoration problems without noise energy information. Acta Mathematica Scientia 23, 512–520 (2003)
15. Dabov, K., Foi, A., Katkovnik, V., Egiazarian, K., et al.: Image denoising with block-matching and 3D filtering. In: Pro. SPIE Electronic Imaging: Algorithms and Systems V, vol. 6064A-30 (2006)
16. Portilla, J., Strela, V., Wainwright, M., Simoncelli, E.P.: Image Denoising using Scale Mixtures of Gaussians in the Wavelet Domain. IEEE Transactions on Image Processing 11, 1338–1351 (2003)

An Improved Edge Detection Method
Based on Composite Morphology[*]

Yi Zhang[**], Xin Jiang, Zhen-Dong Wang, and Jiang Yue

Jiangsu Key Laboratory of Spectral Imaging & Intelligent Sense,
Nanjing University of Science and Technology, Nanjing 210094, China
zhy441@sina.com

Abstract. In order to make the morphological edge detection method have strong anti-noise and accurate edge extraction ability, an improved edge detection method based on composite morphology is proposed. Firstly, two different sets of structural elements are constructed. Then an improved morphology gradient operator is used in edge detection. Finally, the final edge is obtained according to the weights which are determined by the extended spatial frequency. The simulation results show that the method can extract more complete and coherent image edge, and it also has a strong noise-restrain ability.

Keywords: edge detection, Top-hat transform, composite morphology.

1 Introduction

The image edge is the part of the image where grayscale or structure has undergone significant change , it is extremely important for the description of image structure and image feature information , so edge extraction is a hot issue in image processing and analysis techniques. Traditional edge extraction method using the maxima of First-order differential gradient of the edge region or the second derivative zero-crossing value to locate the edge, such as Robert operator, Prewitt operator, Sobel operator and Canny operator [1-2], but these algorithms are sensitive to noise, the image edge is prone to the problem of missed or double-pixel edge. The more obscure, less smooth and fractured edge will have a greater impact on the image analysis and processing. In recent years, some new methods such as wavelet transform [3], neural network method was proposed, but these algorithms have a poor positioning ability and large amount of calculation.

Mathematical morphology is a nonlinear image processing means. The basic idea is to use the mutual operation between structural elements and edge areas to extract the image edge. Morphological edge extraction method not only has strong anti-noise

---

[*] Foundation item: Project (61071147) supported by the National Natural Science Foundation of China.

[**] Corresponding author. Vice Researcher.

F.L. Wang et al. (Eds.): CMSP 2012, CCIS 346, pp. 112–119, 2012.
© Springer-Verlag Berlin Heidelberg 2012

ability, but also the maximum extent possible to retain the characteristics of the original image [4-5].

In this paper, with studying composite morphological edge detection method, we propose an improved composite morphological edge extraction method. Using Composite morphological features to improve the morphological gradient operator, and synthesize the final edge with the adaptive weights, the simulation results show that the method has a strong ability to suppress noise, the extracted edge is more smooth, consistent and complete.

If you have more than one surname, please make sure that the Volume Editor knows how you are to be listed in the author index.

2   Improved Multi-structure and Multi-faceted Morphology Edge Detection Method

2.1   Basis for the Work

Method of morphological edge extraction is achieved by using morphological gradient, it can get the image edge on the basis of retaining the image texture features information very well. Common morphological gradient operator is defined as:

$$g = (f \oplus b) - (f \ominus b) \tag{1}$$

As to extract better edge in the image contains more noise, we have introduced the anti-noise morphological gradient operator, such as anti-noise dilation and erosion morphological gradient operator, which is defined as:

$$g_4 = (f \circ b) \oplus b - (f \bullet b) \ominus b \tag{2}$$

The choice of structural elements in morphology will directly affect the image processing results. In the actual image, the edge information is very rich. It is difficult to get the edge full detected in morphological operations using a single fixed structure element, so composite morphological methods can be used to extract the image edges, common-used composite morphology include multiple-scale morphology, multi-structure morphology and multi-faceted morphology [6].

Different composite morphological methods have specific algorithms, but the basic idea is basically the same. That is applying different size, shape or orientation of the structural elements to morphological operations synthetically, finally we synthesis the final edge by average weights.

The following pictures are the edge extraction results of the three composite morphological method, the selected image is one of the NASA AVIRIS image.

Equations should be punctuated in the same way as ordinary text but with a small space before the end punctuation mark.

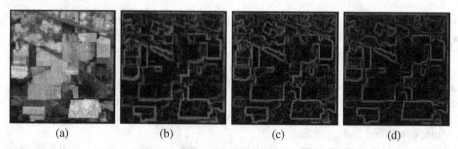

(a)	(b)	(c)	(d)

Fig. 1. Composite morphological edge extraction results: (a) The input image (b) Multi-scale morphology extraction (c) Multi-structure morphology extraction (d)Multi-faceted morphology extraction.

2.2   Image Preprocessing

The image noise is inevitable in the image processing, traditional method to remove noise is the whole image smoothing filter, this method can remove image noise, but it will weaken the details in the image.

Filtering on the basis of preserving more image detail, this paper presents a Top-Hat transform-based filtering method. The basic approach is to use the Top-Hat transform to detect the image gray peak and valley regions [7], and then for these areas to locate the noise in the image, finally filter the area of the detected to realize filtering of noise region.

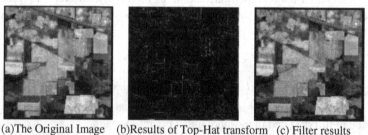

(a)The Original Image   (b)Results of Top-Hat transform   (c) Filter results

Fig. 2. Image preprocessing

2.3   Algorithm and Implementation Steps

Different size, shape and orientation of structural elements can form different composite morphological methods. These methods have their respective advantages, such as multi-scale morphology using different sizes of structural elements , the extracted edge is more complete and comprehensive; multi-structure morphology using different shapes of structural elements, it can extract more complex edge, its noise immunity is also strong [8-10]; multi-faceted morphology using a linear structural elements in different directions, it can retain the edge direction information very well, and can extract more delicate and smooth edges [11].

Therefore, we can use two or three of the above methods according to the specific image to construct a more comprehensive composite morphology. The method of edge extraction in this paper based on multi-faceted morphology and the multi-structure morphology, the algorithm is as follows:

(1)Select M different shape of the structural elements to construct multi-structure elements set$\{B_M\}$ and select N different directions of linear structural elements to construct multi-faceted structural elements set $\{B_N\}$;

(2) To the structural elements in the two structural elements set, we use the anti-noise dilation and erosion morphological gradient operator to extract edge.

(3) We synthesize new edge by the weights of obtained edge image:

$$G = \sum_{n=1}^{K} w_n g_n \tag{3}$$

G is the synthetic image edge, K is the number of extracted edge (K = M + N), g_n is the extracted edge from the respective structural element, w_n is the weights for each edge.

Figure 3 shows the results of extracted edge by the multi-faceted and multi-structure morphology.

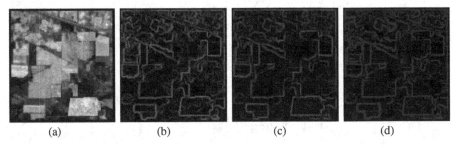

(a)   (b)   (c)   (d)

Fig. 3. Composite morphological edge extraction (a) Input image (b)Results of multi-structure morphology (c)Results of the multi-faceted morphology (d) Results of the multi-faceted and multi-structure morphology

For the above-mentioned composite morphological operations, we are using the anti-noise dilation and erosion morphological gradient operator to extract edge as show in formula (2). The operator is actually obtained by combining the morphological filtering and morphological gradient edge extraction, so it has strong anti-noise ability and good edge extraction results.

Actually ,the gradient operator used in the two operations is a single structural elements .As we known, the advantages of multi-structure morphology is able to extract the complex image edge and have strong noise suppression capability , the advantages of multi-faceted morphology is good at retaining the edge direction information and accessing to get the more delicate and smooth edges.

Therefore, we can improve multi-faceted and multi-structure morphology algorithm. That is the multi-structure morphology play a major role in noise suppression, the multi-faceted morphology play a major role in edge detection. Improved anti-noise dilation and erosion gradient operator can be defined as [12-13]:

$$g = (f \circ b_1) \oplus b_2 - (f \bullet b_1) \ominus b_2 \qquad (b_1 \neq b_2) b \qquad (4)$$

Among them, the gradient operator use different shapes of the structural elements in the opening and closing stage and different directions of linear structural elements in the dilation and erosion stage.

In addition, the above-mentioned final edge is synthesized with the average weights, this method allows the contributions from each edge to the final edge are average, but actually edge extracted from different structural elements are not the same. For this we can introduce an image evaluation parameters to construct the weights of each edge, we usually use the information entropy, spatial frequency and the average gradient as edge detection evaluation parameters, we choose the extended spatial frequency to determine the value of the weights.

Spatial frequency is an important indicator reflecting the sharpness of the image, it can describe image edge information and details very well, extended spatial frequency take gray-scale changes in the two pairs of angular direction of the ordinary spatial frequency into account, which is defined as follows:

$$HF = \left[\frac{1}{M \times (N-1)} \sum_{m=1}^{M} \sum_{n=2}^{N} (f(m,n) - f(m,n-1))^2 \right]^{\frac{1}{2}} \qquad (5)$$

$$VF = \left[\frac{1}{(M-1) \times N} \sum_{m=2}^{M} \sum_{n=1}^{N} (f(m,n) - f(m-1,n))^2 \right]^{\frac{1}{2}} \qquad (6)$$

$$DF_1 = \left[\frac{1}{(M-1) \times (N-1)} \sum_{m=2}^{M} \sum_{n=2}^{N} (f(m,n) - f(m-1,n-1))^2 \right]^{\frac{1}{2}} \qquad (7)$$

$$DF_2 = \left[\frac{1}{(M-1) \times (N-1)} \sum_{m=2}^{M} \sum_{n=2}^{N} (f(m-1,n) - f(m,n-1))^2 \right]^{\frac{1}{2}} \qquad (8)$$

$$SF = \left[HF^2 + VF^2 + DF_1^2 + DF_2^2 \right]^{\frac{1}{2}} \qquad (9)$$

Which DF_1 and DF_2 are respectively the space frequencies of the two pairs of angle direction . SF is the extended spatial frequency.

The improved composite morphological edge detection algorithm is as follows:

(1)Select M different shape of the structural elements to construct multi-structure elements set$\{B_M\}$ and select N different directions of linear structural elements to construct multi-faceted structural elements set $\{B_N\}$;

(2) Using the morphological gradient operator extract edge as show in formula(2), in each operator b_1 is selected from structural elements set$\{B_M\}$, b_2 is selected from structural elements set $\{B_N\}$.

(3) Calculate extended spatial frequency SF of the obtained image edge, and then calculate the weights of each edge of the image:

$$w_i = \frac{SF_i}{\sum_{n=1}^{K} SF_n} \tag{10}$$

(4) Weighted obtained image edge,finally synthesize the new edge, namely:

$$G = \sum_{n=1}^{K} w_n g_n \tag{11}$$

Among them, G is the new edge image, K is the number of extracted edge (K=M×N), g_n is the extracted edge with different structural element, w_n is the weights for each edge of the weighted synthesis.

3   The Simulation Results

The comparison results of improved multi-structure and multi-faceted morphological edge detection and the conventional edge detection are shown in Figure 4, the selected multi-structure elements are square, diamond, and disc-shaped structural elements scale of 2 , the selected multi-faceted structural elements set are linear structural elements of 0 °, 45 °, 90 °, 135 ° direction.

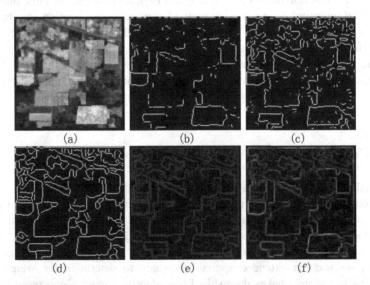

Fig. 4. Comparison of the edge extraction results (a) Input image (b)Prewitt operator results (c) Log operator results(d) Canny operator results(e)Conventional morphological extracted results (f)Results of improved morphological method

For noise image, processing image with various edge detection method, simulation results are shown in Figure 5.

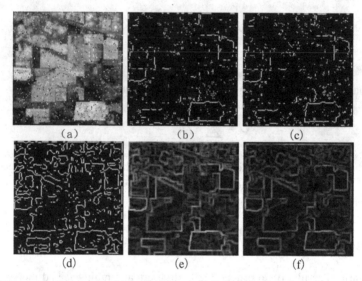

(a)   (b)   (c)

(d)   (e)   (f)

Fig. 5. Edge extraction results for noise image (a) Image with Gaussian noise (b) Prewitt operator results (c) Log operator results (d) Canny operator results (e) Conventional morphological extracted results (f) Results of improved morphological method

From the simulation results in Figure 4 and Figure 5, we can see edge information obtained by improved edge detection method is more comprehensive and the edge is smoother and more consistent. For the noise image, the advantages of edge extracted by improved multi-structure and multi-faceted morphological methods are more obvious, it is not only has strong ability in noise suppression, the extracted edge compared to that extracted by conventional morphological is more sharp .It also provides a very good condition for the subsequent image analysis or target recognition.

4   Conclusion

Improved composite morphological edge extraction method proposed in this paper compared to the conventional morphological edge extraction method has a stronger noise immunity, and the extracted edge is also more accurate. The image before processing need to go through a transformation based on the top-hat filter, and then extract the edge with multi-structure and multi-faceted morphological methods. In addition, we use the extended spatial frequency to determine the weight of the synthetic edge, which makes the method has adaptive capacity, and more objective. Compared to traditional morphological edge detection algorithm, it can maximize the advantages of edge detection accuracy and noise suppression ability with the structural elements of different shapes and different directions in the edge extraction.

The simulation results show that the edge information obtained by improved edge detection method is more comprehensive and the edge is smoother and more consistent. For the noise image, the edge extracted by improved method is sharp and also has a strong ability in noise suppression.

References

1. Zhang, B., He, S.-X.: Improved edge-detection method based on the Canny Algorithm. Infrared Technology 28(3), 165–169 (2006)
2. Demigny, D., Kamle, T.: A discrete expression of Canny 's criteria for step edge detector performances evaluation. IEEE Transactions on Pattern Analysis and Machine Intelligence 19(6), 1199–1211 (1997)
3. Schmeelk, J.: Wavelet transforms on two- dimensional images. Mathematical and Computer Modeling 36(7/8), 939–948 (2002)
4. Yang, H., Zhang, J.-W.: Research on application of mathematical morphology in edge detection of image. Journal of Liaoning University 32(1), 50–53 (2005)
5. Jing, X.-J., Ma, Y.-X., Qu, E.: Morphological filter based on genetic learning. Communication and Information Technology 1(12/14), 749–752 (2005)
6. Cui, Y.: Image processing and analysis - mathematical morphology method and its application. Science Press, Beijing (2000)
7. Jackway, P.T.: Improved morphological Top-Hat. IEEE Electronics Letters 14(6), 1194–1195 (2000)
8. Luo, X.-G., Liu, T., Peng, C.-L., Wen, L.: Correction edge-detection algorithm based on multi-structure morphology of the medical image. Journal of Biomedical Engineering 1(26), 177–180 (2009)
9. Zhao, Y.Q., Gui, W.H., Chen, Z.C.: Edge detection based on multi-structure elements morphology. In: Proceeding of the 6th World Congress on Intelligent Control and Automation, WCICA 2006, vol. 2, pp. 9752–9798 (2006)
10. Song, J., Delpe, J.: The analysis of morphological filters with multiple structuring elements. Computer Vision Graphics and Image Processing 50, 308–328 (1990)
11. Liang, Y., Li, T.-M.: The application of image edge detection with multi-direction morphological structuring elements. Journal of Yunnan University 21(5), 392–394 (1999)
12. Agam, G.: Regulated morphological operations. Pattern Recognition 32, 23 (1999)
13. Huang, J.-L., Zhou, H.: An Image edge detection method of multi-structural elements and multi-scale based on morphology. Microelectronics and Computer 8(26), 76–79 (2009)

Image Compression Based on Hierarchical Clustering Vector Quantization*

Shi Wang, Long Ye, Wei Zhong, and Qin Zhang

Key Lab of Media Audio & Video of Ministry of Education,
Communication University of China, Beijing 100024, China
hfwangshi168@126.com, {yelong,wzhong,zhangqin}@cuc.edu.cn

Abstract. Vector quantization (VQ) is an efficient tool for lossy compression due to its simple decoding algorithm and high compression rate. The key technique of VQ is the codebook design. In this paper, based on fuzzy c-means clustering algorithm, we firstly generate the initial classified codebooks according to the image features of different blocks. And then the proper codebooks are selected by adjusting the PSNR thresholds which are based on the quality of the reconstructed image. Since the proposed hierarchical clustering VQ framework is more adaptable to the specific regions of an image, we can reconstruct the different regions of the image hierarchically. Experimental results show that the proposed coding framework can achieve satisfactory quality measured by PSNR while reducing the codebook size significantly.

Keywords: vector quantization, hierarchical clustering, image compression, fuzzy c-means.

1 Introduction

Vector quantization (VQ) is an important technology for image compression to generate a significant codebook which can represent the large amounts of image data [1]. The process of the codebook generation can be regarded as a data clustering process. Training vectors are classified into the specific codebook which contains much smaller size of codewords based on the minimization of average distortion between the training vectors and codebook vectors. The size of the codebook is much less than that of original image data, and thus the purpose of higher image compression rate is definitely achieved.

VQ consists of three parts, codebook design, encoding and decoding. The most important technique of a VQ algorithm is the codebook generation. In 1980 based on a training sequence, an iterative design algorithm was proposed by Linde, Buzo and Gray (LBG) [2] to generate a locally optimal codebook. Although this LBG algorithm has a solid theoretical foundation and its implementation is simple, it is very sensitive to the initial codebook and thus easy to fall into local optimum. In recent years, there

---

* This work is supported by the National Natural Science Foundation of China under grant Nos. 60832004 and 61101166.

F.L. Wang et al. (Eds.): CMSP 2012, CCIS 346, pp. 120–128, 2012.

are several non-iterative codebook generation algorithms have been proposed [3]-[8]. The pairwise nearest neighbor (PNN) algorithm [3, 4] generates hierarchical clustering using a sequence of merging operations until the desired number of clusters is reached. The progressive constructive clustering (PCC) algorithm [5] searches the training sequence only once and generates the codewords progressively based on the given threshold. Other algorithms, such as Kekre's efficient fast algorithm (KEFA) [6, 7] and simple codebook generation (SCG) [8], can reduce the computational complexity and improve the speed of the codebook generation because there is no need to compute the Euclidean distance. However, both of these iterative and non-iterative traditional algorithms cannot make the generated codebook adaptive to different structures or regions of an image. To this purpose, the hierarchical VQ (HVQ) [9] was proposed to increase the compression ratio based on the different regions of an image. Other HVQ algorithms, such as the hierarchical multirate VQ (HMVQ) [10] and the edge modified VQ (EMVQ) [11], can also improve the compression result according to the different features or structures of the image. All of the above HVQ techniques aim to reduce the compression rate while the reconstructed images still get decent perceptual qualities.

In this paper, we propose a new HVQ framework in which the codebook design is performed by clustering algorithms, which are frequently used in pattern recognition. Based on the fuzzy set theory, we introduce the fuzzy c-means (FCM) [12, 13] algorithm to generate the codebooks for the specific blocks of a certain image and then these hierarchical codebooks are used to reconstruct the different regions of the image. Our hierarchical clustering framework consists of three steps: the original image is firstly split into blocks to form various dimensional vectors; secondly, these different dimensional vectors are clustered by the FCM algorithm to generate HVQ initial codebooks; finally, the original image is divided to regions with different size which are quantized hierarchically by the codebooks. Experiments on the basic testing images demonstrate that the proposed hierarchical clustering VQ framework is more adaptable to the specific regions of an image than the traditional methods with a significantly reduced codebook size.

The outline of this paper is organized as follows. Section 2 introduces FCM clustering algorithm to generate the codebook. A new HVQ framework is proposed in Section 3. Experiments on the basic testing images are given in Section 4. Finally, some conclusions are drawn in Section 5.

2   Fuzzy c-Means Algorithm

In this section, we first introduce the FCM algorithm laying the foundation for the proposed HVQ framework. The fuzzy clustering model [14] was firstly proposed by Ruspini in 1969. In this model, the FCM clustering algorithm can classify the raw data $X^k = \{x_1, x_2, ..., x_N\}$ into the finite set $V = \{v_1, v_2, ..., v_c\}$. It is based on the minimization of an objective function called c-means function and can be defined as:

$$\min J_m(X;U,V) = \sum_{i=1}^{c} \sum_{j=1}^{N} u_{ij}^m d_{ij}^2, \tag{1}$$

where

$$u_{ij} \in [0, 1], \ 1 \le j \le N, \ 1 \le i \le c, \tag{2}$$

$$\sum_{i=1}^{c} u_{ij} = 1, \ 1 \le j \le N, \tag{3}$$

$$0 < \sum_{j=1}^{N} u_{ij} < N, \ 1 \le i \le c, \tag{4}$$

where m $(m > 1)$ is the fuzzy weight component, c donates the number of the clusters, N donates a set of raw data X. The matrix $U = [u_{ij}]$ with size $c \times N$ represents fuzzy partitions and u_{ij} is the membership value of x_j belonging to v_i. d_{ij}^2 is the squared inner-product distance norm which can be defined as

$$d_{ij}^2 = \left\| x_j - v_i \right\|^2 = (x_j - v_i)^T (x_j - v_i). \tag{5}$$

Refs. [12, 13] give an iterative algorithm to get the solution of the FCM's objective function. This algorithm firstly initializes the matrix $U = [u_{ij}]$ and computes the center of each cluster,

$$v_i^{(k+1)} = \sum_{j=1}^{n} (u_{ij}^{(k)})^m x_j / \sum_{j=1}^{n} (u_{ij}^{(k)})^m, \ 1 < i < c. \tag{6}$$

Then update $U^{(k)} = u_{ij}^{(k)}$ to $U^{(k+1)} = u_{ij}^{(k+1)}$ by

$$u_{ij}^{(k)} = 1 / \sum_{r=1}^{c} \left(\frac{d_{ij}^{(k)}}{d_{rj}^{(k)}} \right)^{\frac{2}{m-1}}. \tag{7}$$

If $\left\| U^{(k+1)} - U^{(k)} \right\| < \varepsilon$, then stop. Otherwise $k = k+1$ and goto (6).

The FCM algorithm is a local optimum search clustering algorithm based on the finding cluster centers by iteratively adjusting their positions and evaluation of an objective function which is similar to k-means. The quality of clustering depends on the initialization of cluster centers, which will determine the converging speed and accuracy. Comparing to the traditional k-means, the FCM algorithm allows more flexibility by introducing the possibility of memberships to clusters.

3   Hierarchical Vector Quantization

It is well known that an image consists of many blocks with varying size. Some small blocks are used in high-detail regions and the other large blocks in low-detail regions. So we can definitely divide an image into blocks and sub-blocks according to the features of the image. Therefore, image blocks containing low-detail information can be encoded at a lower bit-rate, such as the smooth background region of the image. Other image blocks which include the structural region and edge of the image may consist of the high-detail information which can be encoded at a higher bit-rate. And thus we can make our codec more adaptive to the different regions of the original image.

In the proposed HVQ framework, we first divide the original image into blocks and sub-blocks. All of these blocks with varying size can be described as training vectors. After training these different-length vectors by the FCM algorithm, we generate the codebooks which contain different numbers of codewords or atoms. And then based on the quality of the reconstructed image, we choose our codebook by setting up threshold which is measured by PSNR. The lower dimensional the codeword is, the higher PSNR threshold should be adopted. If the PSNR value of the reconstructed image is lower than the minimum of the PSNR threshold, we end our program and the hierarchical codebooks have been chosen.

In summary, the proposed hierarchical clustering VQ framework can be described as follows:

Step 1: Divide the original image into N non-overlapping various dimensional blocks such as blocks with different size 2×2, 4×4... .

Step 2: by using the FCM algorithm, the codebooks with different size, such as 16, 32, 64..., are generated and the original image is then reconstructed by the generated codebooks.

If the PSNR value of the reconstructed image $\geq \sigma_{\dim}$, where $\sigma_{\dim}$ is the threshold measured by PSNR for different dimensions of the codeword size,

The codebook is chosen and the searching is ended in this dimension.

Then go to Step 1 for higher dimensional blocks.

Else if the PSNR value of the image reconstructed by highest-sized codebook $\leq \sigma_{TH_m}$,

The searching program is ended.

Step 3: the original image is divided into sub-blocks and blocks. The different regions are reconstructed by different codebooks.

If the PSNR value of the block $\geq \sigma_m$,

High dimensional codebook is chosen.

Else if the PSNR of the sub-block which belongs to the current block $\geq \sigma_m$,

Low dimensional codebook is chosen.

Else

There is no proper codebook and the image reconstruction is ended.

Step 4: adjust the thresholds in this framework $(\sigma_{\dim}, \sigma_m)$ according to the reconstructed image result measured by PSNR. The chosen of the thresholds $(\sigma_{\dim}, \sigma_m)$ will be discussed in Section 4.

Next we will consider the calculation of the bit rate in the proposed HVQ scheme. We know that in the non-hierarchical VQ algorithm, by using a codebook with quite few codewords compared to the number of image vectors, the resulting bit rate can be calculated as follows,

$$R = \log_2(N_c)/S, \tag{8}$$

where N_c is the codebook size and S is the number of codeword pixels. As for the HVQ scheme, the total bit rate is

$$R = \left[\sum_{i=1}^{n} \log_2 (N_{ci}) \times N_{bi} \right] \Big/ M ,\tag{9}$$

where N_{bi} is the number of blocks which are decoded by the codebooks C_i, n is the total number of the layers and M is the total pixels in the original image.

Here for clear illustration, we give an example shown in Fig. 1 to demonstrate the calculation of the total bit rate in different layers.

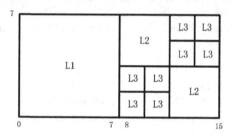

Fig. 1. Blocks and sub-blocks of the image

Let us suppose all of the layers in Fig. 1 are reconstructed by $N_{ci} = 2^5$ codewords. As shown in Fig. 1, there are three different layers to form this image. So the total bit rate can be calculated as

$$R = (1 \times 5 + 2 \times 5 + 8 \times 5) / (16 \times 8)$$
$$= 0.430 \text{ bpp.}$$

Therefore the code length of every layer is $\log_2 (2^5) = 5 \; bit$. For the same length of the codewords in every layer, the choice of the codebooks in different layers becomes ambiguous. In order to solve this problem, 2 more bit information ($\log_2 4 = 2 \; bit$) is added in the code length to indicate the exact codebook. And thus (9) can be rewritten as

$$R = \left[\sum_{i=1}^{n} \log_2 (N_{ci} + t) \times N_{bi} \right] \Big/ M ,\tag{10}$$

where t ($0 \leq t \leq ceil \lceil \log_2 s \rceil$) is the extra bit information, s is the number of the equal value in N_{ci}. By using (10), the bit rate of the proposed HVQ can be calculated as

$$R = [1 \times (5+2) + 2 \times (5+1) + 8 \times (5+0)] / (16 \times 8)$$
$$= 0.461 \text{ bpp.}$$

With the proposed HVQ framework, we can reconstruct the image hierarchically by the different codebooks which are generated by different layers of the image.

4   Experiments

In this section, we illustrate the performance of our hierarchical clustering VQ framework. Firstly we give an example of the codebook generation, and then we use our framework on some basic testing images and compare our framework result with that of traditional algorithms.

For the codebook generation by executing the FCM algorithm, we can generate different codebooks varying from codeword dimensions and numbers. The different codebook size can be chosen as $M = 16$, 32, 64, 128, etc and the different dimensions of codewords can be $D = 2 \times 2$, 4×4, etc . Fig. 2 demonstrates an example of a codebook whose size is $M = 32$ and dimension is $D = 4 \times 4$.

Fig. 2. A codebook with size $M = 32$ and dimension 4×4

Then we take 256×256 grayscale Lena image as an example to illustrate our hierarchical clustering VQ framework. By using the codebooks generated by the FCM algorithm, the experimental PSNR results of the reconstructed image are given in Table 1, with three codeword sizes (2×2, 4×4, 8×8) and varying vector dimensions (from 16 to 256).

Table 1. The experimental PSNR results of the reconstructed image with three codeword sizes (2×2, 4×4, 8×8) and varying vector dimensions (from 16 to 256)

codebook size	codeword dimension		
	2×2	4×4	8×8
16	28.74	24.78	20.91
32	**30.37**	**25.41**	21.27
64	31.93	26.05	21.96
128	33.47	26.43	22.42
256	35.00	26.80	**22.72**

In the design procedures shown in Section 3, here we choose $\sigma_{\dim 2\times 2} = 30$ for dimension 2×2, $\sigma_{\dim 4\times 4} = 25$ for dimension 4×4 and $\sigma_m = 25$, due to the reason that the typical values for PSNR in lossy image compression are above 30 dB and acceptable values for wireless transmission quality loss are about 20 dB to 25 dB. The experimental results shown in Table 1 are illustrated in Fig. 3, together with the choice of the thresholds $\sigma_{\dim}$ and σ_m.

With the reasonable threshold $\sigma_{\dim}$ and σ_m, we can select the proper codebooks for the original image. In the case of image Lena, we choose the hierarchical codebooks with size $M = 32$ and dimensions being respectively 4×4 and 2×2. Then by executing Step 3 in Section 3, we can get the structure (edge and adjacent) regions denoted by black and blue sub-blocks and other smooth background regions by green blocks, as shown in Fig. 4. Since the structure regions contain high-detail information of the image which are very important features for perceptual quality, we select codebook with dimension 2×2 to code this type of region. For low-detail smooth background regions, another codebook with dimension 4×4 is chosen. By choosing the codebooks with different dimensions for different regions, we can obtain the reconstructed image by our hierarchical clustering VQ framework in Fig. 5. The specifications of the reconstructed image are $\text{PSNR} = 29.40$, $\text{SSIM} = 0.81$ and $\text{bpp} = 0.68$.

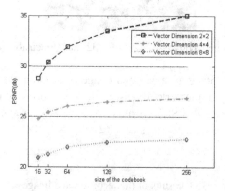

Fig. 3. The experimental results shown in Table 1 together with the choice of the thresholds $\sigma_{\dim}$ and σ_m. The upper black line is the threshold $\sigma_{\dim}$ and the lower is σ_m

Fig. 4. Hierarchical VQ blocks (black and blue are structure region of the image and green are normal smooth region)

Further some more basic grey-level images are tested in our hierarchical clustering VQ framework, namely Airplane, Baboon, Cameraman, Fruits, Boats and Bridge. Here we also choose two hierarchical codebooks which are generated with dimensions 2×2 and 4×4 respectively. The experimental results are shown in Table 2. Comparisons between our framework and some traditional algorithms, such as LBG, KEFA, OPNN, SCG, are also given in Table 3.

Fig. 5. The reconstructed image by our hierarchical clustering VQ framework

Table 2. The experimental results on some testing images by the proposed framework

Image	Proposed method			
	PSNR	SSIM	Bpp	Codebook size
Lena	29.40	0.81	0.68	32+32
Airplane	30.84	0.89	0.86	64+128
Baboon	26.90	0.83	1.08	32+64
Cameraman	30.86	0.88	0.66	32+64
Fruits	29.41	0.75	0.69	32+16
Boats	29.82	0.86	0.79	32+64
Bridge	26.71	0.84	1.15	32+64

Table 3. Our method compare with others in codebook size and PSNR

Image		Proposed	LBG	KEFA	OPNN	SCG
Lena	PSNR	**29.40**	27.47	29.32	28.73	29.24
	Codebook size	**32+32**	256	256	128	128
Cameraman	PSNR	**30.86**	26.37	26.84	27.23	29
	Codebook size	**32+64**	256	256	256	256
Boats	PSNR	**29.82**	27.47	26.92	**30.55**	29.56
	Codebook size	**32+64**	256	256	256	256
Bridge	PSNR	**26.71**	23.57	25.41	**26.82**	**26.90**
	Codebook size	**32+64**	256	256	256	256

From Tables 2 and 3, we can see that compared with traditional algorithms, our hierarchical clustering VQ framework can achieve higher PSNR performance with much smaller codebook size. This is attributed to the codebook generation with smaller vector dimension for structure regions. For this reason, the reconstruction quality measured by PSNR and SSIM can be improved significantly with much smaller codebook size at the cost of slight increase in compression rate.

5   Conclusion

In this paper, a new hierarchical clustering VQ framework is proposed. It can generate the codebooks with different sizes and dimensions according to the different information regions, making it more adaptable to the specific regions of an image. By applying our framework to some basic testing images, the experimental results demonstrate the superiority of the proposed framework to other traditional algorithms. In the future work, the traditional FCM algorithm should be optimized to avoid falling into the local optimum. Besides, we can add more layers and higher dimensional codewords to reduce the compression bit rate in our framework.

References

1. Gray, R.M.: Vector quantization. IEEE ASSP Magazine, pp. 4–29, (1984)
2. Linde, Y., Buzo, A., Gray, R.M.: An algorithm for vector quantizer design. IEEE Transactions on Communications COM-28, 84–95 (1980)
3. Equitz, W.H.: A new vector quantization clustering algorithm. IEEE Transactions on Acoustics, Speech and Signal Processing 37(10), 1568–1575 (1989)
4. Somasundaram, K., Vimala, S.: Fast codebook generation for quantization using ordered pairwise nearest neighbor with multiple merging. In: IEEE International Conference on Emerging Trends in Electrical and Computer Technology, pp. 581–588 (2011)
5. Akrout, N.M., Prost, R., Goutte, R.: Image compression by vector quantization: a review focused on codebook generation. Image and Vision Computing 12(10), 627–637 (1994)
6. Kekre, H.B., Sarode, K.T.: Centroid based fast search algorithm for vector quantization. International Journal of Imaging 1(A08), 73–83 (2008)
7. Kekre, H.B., Sarode, K.T.: Fast codebook search algorithm for vector quantization using sorting technique. In: ACM International Conference on Advances in Computing, Communication and Control, pp. 23–24, (2009)
8. Vimala, S.: Techniques for generating initial codebook for vector quantization. In: International Conference on Electronics Computer Technology, vol. (4), pp. 201–208 (2011)
9. Samet, H.: The quadtree and related hierarchical data structure. Computer Surveys 16, 187–260 (1984)
10. Yu, P., Venetsanopoulos, A.: Hierarchical multirate vector quantization for image coding. Signal Processing: Image Communication 4(6), 497–505 (1992)
11. Yu, P., Venetsanopoulos, A.: Hierarchical finite state vector quantization for image coding. Signal Processing VI: Theories and Applications, 1223–1226 (1992)
12. Klir, G.J., Yuan, B.: Fuzzy sets and fuzzy logic theory and applications, pp. 358–362. Prentice-Hall Inc., Upper Saddle River (1995)
13. Pal, N.R., Bezdek, J.C.: On cluster validity for the fuzzy c-means model. IEEE Transactions on Fuzzy System 3, 370–372 (1995)
14. Baraldi, A., Blonda, P.: A survey of fuzzy clustering algorithms for pattern recognition-part I and II. IEEE Transactions on Systems, Man, and Cybernetics-Part B: Cybernetics 29(6) (1999)

The Characteristics of Region Gradient for Image Inpainting

Xueyi Ye, Wentao He, Huahua Chen, and Wangbing Li

The Lab of Pattern Recognition and Information Security,
College of Communication Engineering, Hangzhou Dianzi University,
Hangzhou, 310018, China
{xueyiye,iseealv}@hdu.edu.cn, hewentao2003@126.com,
lwb5082298@163.com

Abstract. The TV model is one of the most classic models in the field of image inpainting. Having analyzed the computing essences and numerical implementation process of the TV model, we find that it is easy to resulting in the edge region fuzzy or fracture of inpainted images using the model. Accordingly, an improved TV model based on characteristics of region gradient is proposed in this paper. Here, the region gradient characteristics are mainly decided by the region direction variable of a pixel and used in the original TV calculating model. Therefore, the gradient value reflects the image feature more accurately and the iterative repair makes full use of the neighborhood's information of a pixel, by which the edge of the missed region is protected and repaired better. Simulation results demonstrate the validity of the proposed model by yielding excellent visual effect and showing some significant performances improvement over the primitive TV model in terms of subjective or objective image quality measures.

Keywords: Characteristics of region gradient, total variation, digital image inpainting.

1 Introduction

Image inpainting is the art of filling the missing data in an image or painting with available information from their surroundings so that the restored image or painting seems as natural as its original version [1, 2]. Recently, the technology has been widespread concern of the domestic and foreign experts, some experts have applied inpainting techniques in de-interlacing [3], image compression [4] and automatic image recovery [5].

The existing digital image restoration models are separated into two types: the geometric inpainting and the texture synthesis based on image restoration. At present, the TV model [6] is one of the most classic algorithms in the field of image inpainting. However, the drawback of the TV model is poor in large-scale region inpainting, both the calculation of gradient and the numerical implementation only used the (x, y) direction information of image, and ignored the role of several points in other two directions, which leads the restoration effect is not nature[7].

F.L. Wang et al. (Eds.): CMSP 2012, CCIS 346, pp. 129–136, 2012.

Focusing on the computing essence and the numerical implementation of the TV model, we find the actual situation that the TV model using the information only in two directions during the gradient value calculation and the numerical implementation, so an image inpainting algorithm based on characteristics of region gradient is presented in this paper. In the new model, the gradient value of a pixel in an image is decided by the partial derivative along the four directions. It not only reflects the image feature more accurate and makes the diffusion intensity in edge more moderate, but also makes full use of the neighborhood's information in the process of iterative repair. Experimental results prove that the inpainting performance of the proposed method is better than the original algorithm.

2   The TV Model for Inpainting

Chan et al presented the TV inpainting model in 2002. The following is to illustrate the TV model by a schematic diagram of typical geometric image in need of inpainting.

Let u be an image to be repaired, let Ω be an inpainting domain with piecewise smooth boundary $\partial\Omega$ and E denotes any fixed closed domain in the complement Ω^c, so that $\partial\Omega$ lies in the interior of $E \cup \Omega$, seeing Figure (1).

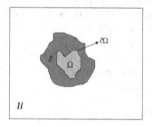

Fig. 1. Schematic diagram of image in need of inpainting

The image inpainting model based on the TV model is as follows:

$$-\nabla \cdot (\frac{\nabla u}{|\nabla u|}) + \lambda_e (u - u^0) = 0 \qquad (1)$$

Here the extended Lagrange multiplier λ_e is given by

$$\lambda_e = \begin{cases} \lambda, (x,y) \in E \\ 0, (x,y) \in \Omega \end{cases} \qquad (2)$$

Now, we discretized the TV model. For a given target pixel O, let $P = \{E,N,W,S\}$ denote its four adjacent pixels, and $p = \{e,n,w,s\}$ denote the corresponding four midway points (not directly available from the digital image), see figure (2).

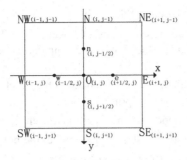

Fig. 2. Target pixel and its adjacent pixels

Given $v = \dfrac{\nabla u}{|\nabla u|} = \hat{D} \cdot \nabla u = \left(\dfrac{1}{|\nabla u|} u_x, \dfrac{1}{|\nabla u|} u_y \right) = (v^1, v^2)$, hence the target pixel O is discretized by central differencing:

$$\frac{\partial u}{\partial t} = \nabla \cdot v_O = \left[\frac{\partial v^1}{\partial x} \right]_O + \left[\frac{\partial v^2}{\partial y} \right]_O \approx \frac{v_e^1 - v_w^1}{h} + \frac{v_s^2 - v_n^2}{h} \qquad (3)$$

Where h denotes the grid size, which is always taken to be 1 in image processing. Next, take the midpoint e, for example:

$$v_e^1 = (\frac{1}{|\nabla u|} u_x)_e = (\frac{1}{|\nabla u_e|}) \left[\frac{\partial u}{\partial x} \right]_e = (\frac{1}{|\nabla u_e|}) \cdot \frac{u_E - u_O}{h} \qquad (4)$$

$$|\nabla u_e| = |(u_e^1, u_e^2)| = |(\left[\frac{\partial u}{\partial x} \right]_e, \left[\frac{\partial u}{\partial y} \right]_e)| = \frac{1}{h} \sqrt{(u_E - u_O)^2 + [(u_{NE} + u_E - u_{SE} - u_S)/4]^2} \qquad (5)$$

Similar discussion applies to the other w, s, n to obtain v_w^1, v_s^2, v_n^2. Therefore, at a pixel O, (1) and (3) is discretized to

$$\sum_{p \in \Lambda} \frac{1}{|\nabla u_p|} (u_O - u_p) + \lambda_e(O)(u_O - u_O^0) = 0 \qquad (6)$$

3   The Characteristics of Region Gradient for TV Model

Considering the computing essence of (1), the diffusion intensity and diffusion direction are determined by $v = \dfrac{\nabla u}{|\nabla u|} = \hat{D} \cdot \nabla u = \left(\dfrac{1}{|\nabla u|} u_x, \dfrac{1}{|\nabla u|} u_y \right) = (v^1, v^2)$. When inpainting, the size of diffusion coefficient decides the magnitude of smoothing effect (that is the size of diffusion intensity) in different image feature. The image inpainting should have a large diffusion in the smooth region; on the contrary, the image inpainting should have a large diffusion. However, in the original TV algorithm, computing the gradient value of the diffusion only considered the change of image in (x, y) direction and used the partial derivative in (x, y) direction, without taking into account the change in other directions. Considering (9) from the numerical implementation of TV model, the TV model inpainting algorithm is actually a weighted algorithm. In figure (3), the inpainting of the point (i, j) used smoothing iterations only in two directions, the value obtained by weighting the four point of its neighborhood, while the other points $(i+1, j+1)$, $(i-1, j+1)$, $(i+1, j-1)$, $(i-1, j-1)$ of its neighborhood did not participate in the inpainting process of point (i, j) . Nevertheless, in the most part of the edge, the point is always in the edge. That makes the inpainting possibly have a big diffusion at the edge structure and a small diffusion at the smooth region so that the inpainting result is ambiguous.

In the process of original TV algorithm, the expression form of gradient is as (7):

$$\nabla u = (u_x, u_y) = (\frac{(u(i+1, j) - u(i, j)}{h}), (\frac{u(i, j+1) - u(i, j)}{h})) \tag{7}$$

After rotating the Cartesian coordinate system $\pi/4$ along the counter clockwise, the expression form of gradient is unchanged, but the neighborhood point has changed to other four point, the distance between point (i, j) and its neighborhood point is $\sqrt{2}h$, see figure(3). Now, we re-express the gradient as (11):

$$\nabla u = (u_m, u_n) = (\frac{(u(i+1, j-1) - u(i, j)}{\sqrt{2}h}), (\frac{u(i+1, j+1) - u(i, j)}{\sqrt{2}h})) \tag{8}$$

The expression (8) contains the information in two diagonally opposite direction. Consequently, we combine (7) and (8), increase the partial derivativein other two directions to assist calculating the gradient value, see figure (3). Defined u_m is the partial derivative along the top-right direction, u_n is the partial derivative along the bottom-right direction. we express the region gradient form $\nabla^{\wedge} u = (u_x, u_m, u_n, u_y)$. The partial derivative along the four directions is expressed as (9).

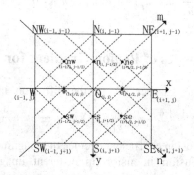

Fig. 3. Schematic diagram of the four directions

$$\begin{cases} u_x = \dfrac{u(i+1,j)-u(i,j)}{h} \\[2mm] u_m = \dfrac{u(i+1,j-1)-u(i,j)}{\sqrt{2}h} \\[2mm] u_n = \dfrac{u(i+1,j+1)-u(i,j)}{\sqrt{2}h} \\[2mm] u_y = \dfrac{u(i,j+1)-u(i,j)}{h} \end{cases} \qquad (9)$$

Therefore, $\dfrac{\partial u}{\partial t} = \nabla^\wedge \cdot (\dfrac{\nabla^\wedge u}{|\nabla^\wedge u|}) = \nabla^\wedge \cdot (Ku_x, Ku_m, Ku_n, Ku_y)$, where $K = \dfrac{1}{|\nabla^\wedge u|}$,

$\nabla^\wedge \cdot () = (\dfrac{\partial}{\partial x}, \dfrac{\partial}{\partial m}, \dfrac{\partial}{\partial n}, \dfrac{\partial}{\partial y})^T$. T is transpose of the vector.

Given $v = \dfrac{\nabla^\wedge u}{|\nabla^\wedge u|} = K \cdot \nabla^\wedge u = (Ku_x, Ku_m, Ku_n, Ku_y) = (v^1, v^2, v^3, v^4)$, thus the target pixel O is

discretized by central differencing as follows:

$$\dfrac{\partial u}{\partial t} = \nabla \cdot v_O = \left[\dfrac{\partial v^1}{\partial x}\right]_O + \left[\dfrac{\partial v^2}{\partial m}\right]_O + \left[\dfrac{\partial v^3}{\partial n}\right]_O + \left[\dfrac{\partial v^4}{\partial y}\right]_O \approx \dfrac{v_e^1 - v_w^1}{h} + \dfrac{v_{ne}^2 - v_{sw}^2}{\sqrt{2}h} + \dfrac{v_{se}^3 - v_{nw}^3}{\sqrt{2}h} + \dfrac{v_s^4 - v_n^4}{h} \qquad (10)$$

As the distance of adjacent pixels is small, we consider the distance between NE and O is equal to the distance between E and O , both are h . Let $h=1$. Now we only consider the inpainting part.

Next, take the midpoint e and ne , for example:

$$\begin{cases} v_e^1 = [Ku_x]_e = K_e \cdot \left[\dfrac{\partial u}{\partial x}\right]_e = K_e(u_E - u_O) \\[2mm] v_{ne}^2 = [Ku_m]_{ne} = K_{ne} \cdot \left[\dfrac{\partial u}{\partial m}\right]_{ne} = K_{ne}(u_{NE} - u_O) \end{cases} \qquad (11)$$

According to the central differencing, we can get (12) and (13):

$$\begin{cases} [u_x]_e = u_E - u_O \\[2mm] [u_m]_e = \dfrac{u_E + u_{NE} - u_O - u_S}{2} \\[2mm] [u_n]_e = \dfrac{u_E + u_{SE} - u_O - u_N}{2} \\[2mm] [u_y]_e = \dfrac{u_E + u_{SE} - u_N - u_{NE}}{4} \end{cases} \qquad (12)$$

$$\begin{cases} [u_x]_{ne} = \dfrac{u_{NE} + u_E - u_O - u_N}{2} \\[2mm] [u_m]_{ne} = u_{NE} - u_O \\[2mm] [u_n]_{ne} = u_E - u_N \\[2mm] [u_y]_{ne} = \dfrac{u_E + u_O - u_N - u_{NE}}{2} \end{cases} \qquad (13)$$

Similar discussion applies to the w, sw, se, nw, s, n to obtain $v_w^1, v_{sw}^2, v_{se}^3, v_{nw}^3, v_s^4, v_n^4$.

Substituting $v_w^1, v_{sw}^2, v_{se}^3, v_{nw}^3, v_s^4, v_n^4$ into (13), we get:

$$u_O = \frac{K_e u_E + K_w u_W + K_{ne} u_{NE} + K_{sw} u_{SW} + K_{se} u_{SE} + K_{nw} u_{NW} + K_s u_S + K_n u_N}{K_e + K_w + K_{ne} + K_{sw} + K_{se} + K_{nw} + K_s + K_n} \tag{14}$$

Adding the denoising part to (19), we obtain the new algorithm as show (20):

$$\sum_{p \in \Lambda} \frac{1}{|\nabla^\wedge u_p|}(u_O - u_p) + \lambda_e(O)(u_O - u_O^0) = 0 \tag{15}$$

Where $P \in \{NW, N, NE, E, SE, S, SW, W\}$, $p \in \{nw, n, ne, e, se, s, sw, w\}$.

Obviously, from (8) and (14), we can see that the proposed method adds more useful neighborhood information when calculating the gradient value, which can reflect the characteristics of image more accurately, and also adds four neighborhood information when calculating the weighted sum of (9). Therefore, the characteristic of region gradient for TV model is superior to the original TV model.

4   Experiments and Analysis

In this section, we illustrate the proposed algorithm with numerical simulations. We compare the inpainting effect between the original TV model and the new algorithm based on the inpainting result has tended to stabilize. At last, we compare the mean square error (MSE) of two algorithms. Color images are considered as a set of three images, and the above described technique is applied independently to each one, the obtained components are then combined to give the final results. This paper tests the new algorithm effect for vertical edges and tilt edges through the special images inpainting, figure 5-6 show some real images inpainting results of the two algorithms.

4.1   The Special Images Inpainting

Our first experiment (Figure 4) is the inpainting of two broken edges by a white bar. When inpainting to stabilize, from figure 4(b), (c), the new algorithm can protect and inpainting the edge.

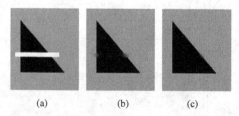

(a)   (b)   (c)

Fig. 4. Test vertical edges and tilt edges: (a) damaged image (b) result with original TV algorithm (c) result with new algorithm

4.2   The Real Image Inpainting

Figure 5 is the inpainting result of lady, the sub-image is enlargement image of local region. From figure 5 (c), the result is close to what one would expect, although the final image had a little   indentation. From the sub-image of figure 5 (b), at the palm, some edges are not inpainting completely and a bit fuzzy, but in sub-image of figure 5 (c), the connection of edge is more natural.

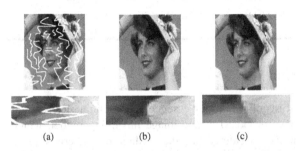

(a)   (b)   (c)

Fig. 5. Lady Image inpainting result: (a) damaged image and local enlargement image (b) result with original TV algorithm and local enlargement image (c) result with new algorithm and local enlargement image

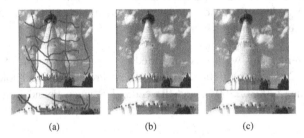

(a)   (b)   (c)

Fig. 6. Natural color image inpainting result: (a) damaged image and local enlargement image (b) result with original TV algorithm and local enlargement image (c) result with new algorithm and local enlargement image

In figure 6, we display the result for temple color image, where we applied our method to three channels simultaneously. Relatively speaking, the final result is good for this numerical scheme of our algorithm.

By both subjective observation and mean square error evaluations with respect to the originals, we conclude that the proposed method gives satisfactory output for structural inpainting. Table 1summarizes the inpainting results through the MSE obtained on two different algorithms.

MSE is defined as (16):

$$MSE = \frac{1}{m \times n} \sum_{i=1}^{m} \sum_{j=1}^{n} \left[u(i,j) - \hat{u}(i,j) \right]^2 \tag{16}$$

Where $u(i, j)$ denotes the repaired image, $\hat{u}(i, j)$ denotes the original image, m,n is the size of image.

Table 1. Performance comparisons between proposed algorithms through the MSE

Experimental image	Image size	Break size	mean square error (MSE)	
			TV algorithm	New algorithm
Figure 5	256*256	4162	8.3580	7.789
Figure 6	230*172	3605	10.6040	7.9721

5   Conclusion

Based on the analysis of computing essence and the numerical implementation of the TV model, we have proposed a new image inpainting model, which re-pressed the gradient function and considered that the gradient characteristic of a pixel should be determined by the region direction variable of a pixel and used in the original TV calculating model, which makes full use of neighborhood information in inpainting of pixel and progressively propagates neighborhood information into damaged region, hence, it can restore edge successfully. Experimental results showed in our examples demonstrate the high performance of the proposed model which has demonstrated great efficiency in inpainting the damaged images.

Acknowledgements. This work was supported by the Natural Science Foundation of China (No.60802047, No. 61001216), the Key Project of Technology Plan of Zhejiang Province (2008C21092), and the Natural Science Foundation of Zhejiang Province (R1090138).

References

1. Bertalmio, M., Sapiro, G., Caselles, V., et al.: Image inpainting. ACM Press/Addison-Wesley Publishing Co. (2000)
2. Zhang, H.-Y., Peng, Q.-C.: A Survey on Digital Image Inpainting. Journal of Image and Graphics 12(1), 1–10 (2007)
3. Ballester, C., Bertalm, I.O.M., Caselles, V., et al.: An inpainting-based deinterlacing method. IEEE Transactions on Image Processing 16(10), 2476–2491 (2007)
4. Liu, D., Sun, X., Wu, F., et al.: Image compression with edge-based inpainting. IEEE Transactions on Circuits and Systems for Video Technology 17(10), 1273–1287 (2007)
5. Rane, S.D., Sapiro, G., Bertalmio, M.: Structure and texture filling-in of missing image blocks in wireless transmission and compression applications. IEEE Transactions on Image Processing 12(3), 296–303 (2003)
6. Chan, T.F., Shen, J.: Mathematical models for local nontexture inpaintings. SIAM Journal on Applied Mathematics, 1019–1043 (2001)
7. Li, J.-J., Zhang, C.-M., Fan, H., et al.: Image Inpainting Algorithm Based on Fractal Theory. Chinese Journal of Electronic. (10), 2430–2435 (2010)

Automatic Image Annotation
Based on Region Feature

Ke Chen[1,2], Jinxiang Li[2], and Liang Ye[2]

[1] JiangSu Province Support Software Engineering R&D Center for Modern Information
Technology Application in Enterprise, Suzhou, 215100, China
szchenke@126.com
[2] Suzhou Vocational University, Suzhou, 215104, China
{ljx,ye1}@jssvc.edu.cn

Abstract. An automatic image annotation approach is proposed to bridge the semantic gap issues in image retrieval. It begins with building connection between semantic concept and image region by image segmentation, and then extracting visual features from image region in order to find the correlativity between semantic concept and image region in the annotated image while annotation, calculating the similarities between different image regions to annotate the unannotated target images, using the given correlativity as a priori knowledge. Experiments conducted on a 2000 image dataset demonstrate the effectiveness and efficiency of the proposed approach for image annotation.

Keywords: Semantic Concept, Image Region, Visual Features, Priori Knowledge, image retrieval.

1 Introduction

The study on management technology of multimedia data has always been an important direction in the whole database study. Comparing with classic database, the multimedia data are different with characteristics like large quantity, unstandard format and so on. How to bring the multimedia data into the handlerable range of database management system is the most important problem need to be solved for adapting the database management for new using demands. The image data used as main part of multimedia data, has mostly been stored and managed as general data type. What actually been stored is just a document name, the system can reach expected effects such as showing and reading images by calling this document while using. However, storing and showing image data effectively are way far from enough, besides, it should be flexible enough for handling various kinds of contents included, such as retrieval the interested image content from a large mass image database, getting images which fit for some criterion of semantic constraints and visual feature. i.e. a image data should be generally stored and managed as a dataset instead of an independent data document. Image contents need to be organized systematically and managed by database management technology, by this way users can take advantages in using, managing and manipulating image data.

F.L. Wang et al. (Eds.): CMSP 2012, CCIS 346, pp. 137–145, 2012.
© Springer-Verlag Berlin Heidelberg 2012

Effective image description method makes base for image data management. During the recent few years people have been doing abundance of image description related researches. These researches are different from the traditional method which merely takes one aspect as describing target, they pay more and more attention to the combination of semantic and content, they help to obtain high-level semantic indirectly from the low-level visual features and annotate the image automatically.

Automatic annotation is a challengeable but important task for the content-based image retrieval work. Using the annotated image collection, it will figure out the relationship model between the semantic concept space and the visual feature space automatically, and then use this model to annotate the unspecified target images, more specifically to say, it's trying to build a bridge between high-level semantic and low-level visual features, therefore, to some extend, this method will help to handle the mostly semantic gap problems based on the using of different image retrieval methods. If this automatic annotation method is feasible, then the current image retrieval problems will be translated into text information retrieval problems, which has been maturely mastered by people, and it will be widely used in fields like biomedical sciences, business, military, education, digital library and internet retrieval, and so on.

The outline of the paper is as follows. We discuss related work in section 2. Section 3 describes the automatic image annotation algorithm in detail. Extensive experimental results are shown in Section 4. Finally, conclusions are given in Section 5.

2   Related Work

With the development of the Internet, bringing new challenges to annotation image technology. There have been a lot of algorithms presented for automatic image annotation, which seeks to find keywords that best describe the visual content of an image. The research on automatic image annotation has proceeded along two categories, probabilistic modeling method and classification method. The basic idea of the former is to determine the joint probabilities between annotations and image visual content. The representative works are Cross-Media Relevance Model (CMRM) [1], Continuous Relevance Model (CRM) [2], and Multiple Bernoulli Relevance Model (MBRM) [3]. The method of the second category attempts to infer the correlations between semantic words with images by learning classifiers, which include content-based annotation methods with Support Vector Machine [4], estimating the visual feature distributions associated with each keyword [5], and asymmetrical support vector machine-based MIL algorithm [6].

In the last few years, segmentation has been used as a preprocessing tool for image annotation. Images can be segmented in regions, cluster similar regions and then use these regions as the region semantics. For instance, general purpose segmentation algorithms like Blobworld [7] and Normalized-cuts[8] to extract regions. These algorithms do not always produce good segmentations, but are useful for building and testing models. Duygulu et al. [9] segmented images into blobs, extracted features from them, and trained the correspondence between features and keywords with the EM algorithm. Mori et al. [10] segmented images into grids, clustered them, and obtained the word distributions for a cluster from the keywords in it. Finally, they annotated an input image by calculating suitable keywords from the distributions of the clusters similar to the grids of the input image.

3   Proposed Algorithm for Annotated Images

The primary goal of the section is to select series keywords to describe un-annotated image based on region features relevancy. First, using the image segmentation algorithm produces the regions of each image, and then establishing the relevancy between regions with keywords as a priori knowledge. Finally, through calculation the similarity of un-annotated image regions with each training image's to annotate the un-annotated image.

3.1   Image Segmentation Using K-Means Clustering Algorithm

Images can be segmented into regions by the K-means algorithm which is an unsupervised learning algorithm that classifies a given data set into multiple classes through a certain number of clusters based on their inherent distance from each other. The algorithm assumes that the data features form a vector space and tries to find natural clustering in them. The points are clustered around centroids $k_i \forall i = 1 \cdots k$ which are obtained by minimizing the objective.

$$V = \sum_{i=1}^{k} (\sum_{x_c \in K_i} \| x_c - k_i \|^2) \tag{1}$$

Where there are k clusters K_i, i=1,2,...,k and k_i is the centroid of all the points $x_c \in K_i$

As a part of this project, an iterative version of the algorithm was implemented. The algorithm takes a 2 dimensional image as input. Various steps in the algorithm are as follows:

a) Compute the histogram of the intensities.
b) Place K points into the space represented by the objects that are being clustered. These points represent initial group centroids.
c) Repeat the steps d-e until the cluster labels of the image does not change anymore.
d) Cluster the points based on distance of their intensities from the centroid intensities.

$$c^{(i)} = \arg \min_j \| x^{(i)} - k_j \|^2 \tag{2}$$

e) Recalculate the new centroid for each of the clusters.

$$k_i = \frac{\sum_{i=1}^{m} 1\{c^{(i)} = j\}x^{(i)}}{\sum_{i=1}^{m} 1\{c^{(i)} = j\}} \tag{3}$$

Where m is the number of clusters to be found, i iterates over the all the intensities, j iterates over all the centroids.

Now for every image can be segmented into several regions.

3.2   Region Similarity Measure

A region can be described in many aspects, such as the color, texture, shape and size of the region. Among them the color histogram computed with the RGB color space is an effective descriptor to represent the object color feature statistics. We uniformly quantize each color channel into16 levels and then the histogram of each region is calculated in the feature space of $16 \times 16 \times 16 = 4096$ bins.

Bhattacharyya coefficient is a divergence-type measure which has a straightforward geometric explanation, so we choose to use the Bhattacharyya coefficient $\tau(R, Q)$ to measure the similarity between two regions R and Q. If two regions have similar contents, their histograms will be very similar, and hence their Bhattacharyya coefficient will be very high.

$$\tau(R,Q) = \sum_{u=1}^{4096} \sqrt{Hist_R^u \cdot Hist_Q^u} \tag{4}$$

Where HistR and HistQ are the normalized histograms of R and Q, and the superscript u represents the uth element of them.

The region histograms are local histograms and they reflect the local features of images, hence such cases that two perceptually very different regions may have very similar histograms are rare, and the higher the Bhattacharyya coefficient between R and Q is, the higher the similarity between them is.

The score of $\tau(R, Q)$ can be normalized into a range of 0 and 1 as follow:

$$\text{sim}(R, Q) = 1\text{-norm}(\tau(R, Q)) \tag{5}$$

3.3   The Correlation between Regions with Keywords Measure

Given images of a training collection T, we should first segment them into region sets $R=\{R_1, R_2, \cdots, R_m\}$ using the image segmentation algorithm proposed in section 3.1, next manually assign keywords to every region of R in order to establish the correlation between regions and keywords. Let W be the annotation vocabulary, $W = \{ w_1, w_2, \cdots, w_n \}$, where $w_1, w_2, \cdots, w_n$ is co-occurrence keyword corresponding to every region in the set of regions $R=\{R_1, R_2, \cdots, R_m\}$.

We employ joint probability $P(w_i, R_j)$ to present the correlation between keyword w_i and region R_j, and use the probability of keyword w_i for the annotation of the region R_j. The joint probability $P(w_i, R_j)$ is estimated similar to CRCM probabilistic model as follows:

$$
\begin{aligned}
P(w_i, R_j) &= \sum_{J \in T} P(J) P(w_i, R_j \mid J) \\
&= \sum_{J \in T} P(J) P(w_i \mid J) P(R_j \mid J)
\end{aligned}
\tag{6}
$$

$$
P(w_i \mid J) = \alpha \frac{\#(w_i, J)}{\mid J \mid} + (1 - \alpha) \frac{\#(w_i, T)}{\mid T \mid}
\tag{7}
$$

$$
P(R_j \mid J) = \beta \frac{\#(R_j, J)}{\mid J \mid} + (1 - \beta) \frac{\#(R_j, T)}{\mid T \mid}
\tag{8}
$$

Where, J *is an instance of T* and represents the test image, $\#(w_i, J)$ means the actual number of time that the word w_i occurs in the semantic concept of image J, $\#(w_i, T)$ is the total number of times occurs in all semantic concepts in the training collection T. Equally, $\#(R_j, J)$ reflects the actual number of times that the region R_j occurs in the image J, and $\#(R_j, T)$ sums the number of occurrences of region R_j in the training collection T. $\mid J \mid$ is the total count of all words and regions occurring in the image J, and $\mid T \mid$ is the total size of the training collection T.

3.4   Image Annotation and Retrieval

The correlation of keywords with regions established based on a training collection of image that is used as a priori knowledge and is combined with the lower feature of the regions to annotate the un-annotated image. Suppose given a collection S of un-annotated image, first using the image segmentation algorithm to extract the region sets $R'=\{R'_1, R'_2, \cdots, R'_k\}$ for an un-annotated image I from S, and then predicting the probabilities $P(w_i \mid R'_t)(i = 1, 2, \cdots, n)$ for every region of R' as follows:

$$
P(w_i \mid R'_t) = \sum_{j=1}^{m} (sim(R'_t, R_j) \cdot P(w_i, R_j))
\tag{9}
$$

Where $sim(R'_t, R_j)$ and $P(w_i, R_j)$ can be estimated from equations (1) – (3), the $sim(R'_t, R_j)$ stands for the similarity between un-annotated region R'_t and annotated region R_j, likewise the $P(w_i, R_j)$ is the correlation between words and region.

Through calculation the similarity of un-annotated image regions with each training image's and the correlation of keywords with regions to select the final words that have the highest probability under $P(w_i \mid R't)$ and use the words as candidate annotation for region R'_t.

4   Experimental Results

4.1   Experiments Design

We conduct our experiments with Ground Truth Database which is originated from the Object and Concept Recognition for Content-Based Image Retrieval research team of the University of Washington. We choose 2000 images annotated with keywords from Ground Truth Database as our Image dataset. The dataset is divided into two parts: 1500 image for training and the rest 500 images for test. Each image is segmented into 1-10 regions and is annotated with 1-5 words.

As used by previous researchers, the quality of automatic image annotation is measured through the process of retrieving the test images with a semantic keyword. For each keyword, precision can be defined as the number of retrieved relevant images N_a divided by the total number of retrieved images N_b, and recall is the number of retrieved relevant images N_a divided by the total number of relevant images in database N_c.

$$\Pr ecision = \frac{N_a}{N_b} \qquad \operatorname{Re} call = \frac{N_a}{N_c} \tag{10}$$

F1 measure is computing as follows:

$$F1 = \frac{2 \times \text{Precision} \times \text{Recall}}{\text{Precision} + \text{Recall}} \tag{11}$$

We compute the average precision and recall over all the words occurring in the test images to evaluate the performance. There are totally 60 words in the test set.

4.2   Results and Discussions

This section shows some illustrative examples of the annotations generated by our approach. The average precision, recall and F1 for CMRM and our approach on 60 mostly used keywords are reported in Table 1, and some test images with the annotations generated by the CMRM and our approach are shown in Table 2. It is observed that the proposed approach can yield better precision than CMRM.

Table 1. Comparing our method with the CMRM

Models	CMRM	Our Method
Recall	32.14%	35.29%
Precision	37.55%	39.45%
F1	34.64%	37.26%

Table 2. Automatic annotations compared with the CMRM

Image	Original Annotation	CMRM Annotation	Our Method Annotation
	sky rocks water beach	sky mountain stone water	sky clouds rock trees water
	tree fields sky	tree sky water fields	sky tree fields
	buildings leafless trees sky	trees snow sky	trees ground sky
	trees ground trail people	people field hill	trees people grass ground

Fig.1 shows the results of the proposed algorithms with the number of test images. The horizontal axis gives the different values of testing images, the bars denotes the corresponding, precision, recall and F1 value. Fig.2 shows results of the proposed algorithms with the number of the annotations m evaluated, the horizontal axis gives the different values of annotations m, the bars denotes the corresponding precision, recall and F1 value.

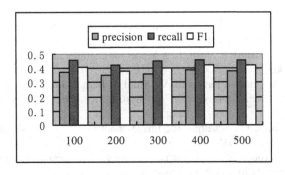

Fig. 1. Performance of different number of test image

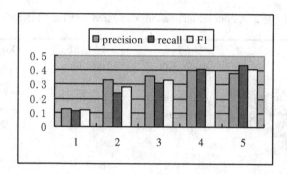

Fig. 2. Performance with different values of annotation m

5   Conclusions and Future Work

We propose an automatic image annotation method based on region feature related. General processes are: segmenting the image, extracting visual features of each region, building the connection between image region and semantic concept, then figuring out the joint probability in between, make clear the semantic by using keywords relating method and considering the similarity of region features, finally fulfill the automatic image region semantic annotation. Experiments show that the proposed algorithm will help to get much better recall and precision.

Acknowledgment. This work was supported by the Innovation Team Grant of SuZhou Vocational University NO.3100124 and the Open Foundation of SuZhou Vocational University No. 2011SZDYJ07.

References

1. Jeon, J., Lavrenko, V., Manmatha, R.: Automatic Image Annotation and Retrieval Using Cross-media Relevance Models. In: Proc. ACM SIGIR, pp. 119–126 (2003)
2. Lavrenko, V., Manmatha, R., Jeon, J.: A Model for Learning the Semantics of Pictures. In: Proc. NIPS (2003)
3. Feng, S.L., Manmatha, R., Lavrenko, V.: Multiple Bernoulli relevance models for image and video annotation. Trans. Circuits and Systems for Video Technology 13(1), 26–38 (2003)
4. Cusano, C., Ciocca, G., Schettini, R.: Image annotation using SVM. In: Proc. Internet Imaging, pp. 330–338 (2004)
5. Carneiro, G., Vasconcelos, N.: A database centric view of semantic image annotation and retrieval. In: Proc. ACM SIGIR, pp. 559–566 (2005)
6. Yang, C.B., Dong, M., Hua, J.: Region-based Image Annotation using Asymmetrical Support Vector Machine-based Multiple-Instance Learning. In: Proc. CVPR, pp. 2057–2063 (2006)

7. Carson, C., Thomas, M., Belongie, S., Hellerstein, J.M., Malik, J.: Blobworld: A system for region-based image indexing and retrieval. In: Third Int. Conf. on Visual Information Systems, Amsterdam (1999)
8. Shi, J., Malik, J.: Normalized cuts and image segmentation. IEEE Transactions on Pattern Analysis and Machine Intelligence 22(8), 888–905 (2000)
9. Duygulu, P., Barnard, K., de Freitas, J.F.G., Forsyth, D.: Object Recognition as Machine Translation: Learning a Lexicon for a Fixed Image Vocabulary. In: Heyden, A., Sparr, G., Nielsen, M., Johansen, P. (eds.) ECCV 2002, Part IV. LNCS, vol. 2353, pp. 97–112. Springer, Heidelberg (2002)
10. Mori, Y., Takahashi, H., Oka, R.: Image-to-word transformation based on dividing and vector quantizing images with words. In: Proceedings of the International Workshop on Multimedia Intelligent Storage and Retrieval Management (1999)

A New Stereo Matching Method
Based on the Adaptive Support-Weight Window

Liansheng Sui, Bo Gao, and Bo Zhang

School of Computer Science and Engineering,
Xi'an University of Technology,
Xi'an, 710048, China
liudua2010@gmail.com,
gaobo_xaut@126.com,
175531358@qq.com

Abstract. We propose a new stereo matching approach based on the adaptive support-weight of local window. First, we use the truncated absolute differences cost function to compute the disparity space image. Second, we redefine the support-weight of a local window which is evaluated according to two factors such as color difference and space distance between a pixel and its center pixel in the local window. Finally, we aggregate the matching cost based on the support weight and use the winner-take-all method to compute the disparity map. In order to improve method's speed, we design an efficient support-weight calculation way. The results of the experiment show that our approach can compute the accurate disparity than other methods.

Keywords: stereo matching, support-weight, disparity map.

1 Introduction

The stereo matching problem has been an important research topic in the field of computer vision for many years. In a binocular stereo system, we usually use two cameras located in different viewpoints to shoot a same scene and capture a pair different images. For a point of an object surface in 3D space, two imaging points are formed in every image and matched. Given an imaging point in one image, how to search its matched point in the other is difficult. Currently, the image pairs used in almost all algorithms are rectified with epipolar lines, and matched points are in the same scanning line. For rectified image pairs, we can search a matching point in a one dimension scanning line instead of in a two dimension image plane. A disparity is the difference of horizontal coordinate between two matched points. If an imaging point coordinate and its disparity in one image are known, the matched point coordinate in the other can be computed. Thus, how to compute the disparity map for all imaging points in the image pair is the key in binocular stereo system.

Scharstein and Szeliski have studied and analyzed a large number of binocular stereo matching algorithms, and proposed an approach used to evaluate these

F.L. Wang et al. (Eds.): CMSP 2012, CCIS 346, pp. 146–153, 2012.
© Springer-Verlag Berlin Heidelberg 2012

algorithms [1]. They have divided these algorithms into two categories: local and global approach. Affected by various factors such as illumination, noise, shading, lacking of texture, repetitive pattern and so on, stereo matching is usually ambiguous. In order to remove ambiguity and obtain correct disparity, local approaches compute the support weight in a local window to increase the signal-to-noise ratio. But if the spanning depth of the local window is discontinuous, these approaches will lead the foreground fattening. Using global approaches, the modeling of the stereo matching is set to an energy function minimum problem and the disparity map is obtained by optimization algorithm. Because of the shortcoming of the modeling, the energy of the real disparity map is not the minimum of the energy function, so the energy of the disparity map solved by the global approach is lower than the energy of the real disparity map. Meanwhile, it is a NP-hard problem to search the minimum of the function itself, and the time complexity is high [2].

Although the precision of local approaches is not as good as global, the speed is faster. Thus these approaches are widely used in the real time systems which not require high precision [3]. In general, the stereo matching usually includes four steps: matching cost computation, cost aggregation, disparity computation and disparity refinement. Local approaches only include first three steps and the research is focused on the cost aggregation [4]. Researchers have proposed many methods from the two dimension aggregation to three dimension aggregation such as shift-table window [1,5], adaptive window [6,7,8,9,10,11] and adaptive support-weight window [12,13,14,15,16,17,18,19,20]. Shift-table window method makes use of many different windows to improve the precision of the matching. These windows are obtained by placing the unknown matching pixel on different positions of a fixed window. This method evaluates the cost of different windows and chooses the window of the smallest cost as the support-window of the unknown matching pixel. Different from shift-table window, adaptive window improve the matching's precision by the way of changing the size of window. The method based on the adaptive support-weight window computes different weight for every pixel in the support-window of the unknown matching pixel, and according to the weight ratio aggregate the matching cost of every pixel to final cost.

In this paper, we propose a new stereo matching method based on adaptive support-weight window. First, we use the truncated absolute differences cost function to compute the disparity space image (DSI). Second, we redefine the support-weight of the local window which is different from the idea of the papers [13, 15 and 17]. In a local window, the weight of every pixel is evaluated according to two factors such as color difference and space distance between it with center pixel, and affection produced by these factors are not independent. Finally, we aggregate the matching cost based on the new defined weight and use the winner-take-all method to compute the final disparity map. At the same time, we use an efficient support-weight calculation way in order to improve method's efficiency. The results of the experiment show that the accurate disparity map is evaluated with this method.

This paper is organized as follows. Section 2 introduces the principle of the method. Section 3 shows the results of the method's experiment. Section 4 gives conclusion and discussion.

2   Principle of the Method

2.1   Computation of DSI

The DSI is based on the two-dimension coordinate system of the image and formed by introducing a disparity axis which is perpendicular to the two-dimension coordinate plane. For an image pair, each element DSI (x, y, d) represents the matching cost of the pixel (x, y) in a referenced image under the disparity d. In this paper, we use the truncated absolute differences (TAD) to compute the matching costs for all pixels of an image. For a color image, we decompose it into three channel image R, G and B, and compute the DSI of various channels respectively. Then, we add the DSI from various channels to obtain the entire. The computation of DSI matching cost can be as follows:

$$DSI\ (x, y, d) = \min\{ \sum_{c \in \{R, G, B\}} | L_c (x, y) - R_c (x + d, y) |, T \} \tag{1}$$

In above Equation, the $L_c(x, y)$ is the intensity value of the pixel (x, y) in the c channel component of the referenced image, and $R_c (x+d, y)$ is the intensity value of the pixel $(x+d, y)$ in the corresponding channel of the target image. The symbol T denotes the truncated threshold value. Compared with other matching cost, TAD effectively reduces the negative effects of inaccurate matching and enhances the reliability.

2.2   Definition on the Support-Weight of Local Window

The purpose of the cost aggregation is to aggregate the pixel's cost that has the same disparity to improve the noise-signal ratio and obtain the correct disparity. However, the disparity is what we want to solve and unknown for an image pair. We have to introduce some hypothesizes in order to evaluate correct disparity. In a nature scene, an object surface is consisted of small different color blocks, and a block with the same color usually has the same disparity. Meanwhile, an object surface is usually continuous. Therefore the disparity can be considered invariable in a certain range in the surface of the object, and two factors such as color difference and space distance from any one pixel to the center of the local window are important for computing cost aggregation.

In order to evaluate the color difference, we use the CIELab color space. The CIELab color model can imitate human eye's non-linear perception which has the characteristic of perception consistency. The perception consistency means that the same color variation can produce the same diversification of visual importance. We use the CIELab color space to compute the color difference between the pixel (x', y') and (x, y) which is expressed as follows:

$$\Delta c(x', y', x, y) = \sqrt{(l(x', y') - l(x, y))^2 + (a(x', y') - a(x, y))^2 + (b(x', y') - b(x, y))^2} \tag{2}$$

In Equation (2), $l(x, y)$, $a(x, y)$ and $b(x, y)$ are the three CIELab color space components of the pixel (x, y). The space distance between (x', y') and (x, y) is computed as follows:

$$\Delta s(x', y', x, y) = \sqrt{(x'-x)^2 + (y'-y)^2} \qquad (3)$$

In the papers [13, 15 and 17], the support-weight of a local window is computed by considering color difference and space distance are independent. But for two planes which have same color and are located in different depth, the corresponding imaging planes have different colors. So we think that color difference and space distance are not independent for computing the support-weight in the local window, and redefine its computation as follows:

$$W(x', y', x, y) = \exp(-\frac{\Delta c(x', y', x, y) * \Delta s(x', y', x, y)}{r}) \qquad (4)$$

In Equation (4), the parameter r results from the experiment for an image pair.

2.3   Cost Aggregation

Based on the support-weight defined by Equation (4), we use the symmetrical strategy to aggregate the matching cost. The formula to aggregate the matching cost is expressed as follows:

$$C(x, y, d) = \frac{\sum_{(x',y') \in N(x,y)} W(x', y', x, y) * W(x'+d, y', x+d, y) * DSI(x', y', d)}{\sum_{(x',y') \in N(x,y)} W(x', y', x, y) * W(x'+d, y', x+d, y)} \qquad (5)$$

In above equation, $N(x, y)$ is the support window of the pixel (x, y) in the reference image, $W(x', y', x, y)$ is the weight of the neighbor pixel (x', y') in the support window , $W(x'+d, y'+d, x, y)$ is the weight of the corresponding pixel $(x'+d, y)$ in the target image, and DSI (x', y', d) is the matching cost of the pixel (x', y') in the reference image under the disparity d.

Given a range of disparity, we can compute many matching costs for a pixel in the reference image with equation (5). Next, we use the winner-take-all (WTA) to choose the optimized disparity for this pixel that has the lowest matching cost. The WTA strategy can be expressed as follows:

$$disp\ (x, y) = \arg \min_{d \in D}\ C(x, y, d) \qquad (6)$$

In equation (6), the symbol D denotes the range of disparity.

2.4   Calculation of the Support-Weight

From the above description, given many possible disparities, we know that the support-weight the weight in many local window must be computed. Hence the method needs to consume a lot of time. In order to improve method's efficiency, we use the following the support-weight calculation way.

Suppose that the pixels p and q of the reference image are in the same scanning line and p is in the left side of q ($q = p+1$). Given the number of possible disparity is n, when we evaluate the disparity of p, n support windows in the target image which centered with pixel $p+d_1$, $p+d_2$,..., $p+d_n$ are produced for all possible disparity d_1, d_2,..., d_n. Similarly, when we evaluate the disparity of q, n support windows which centered with pixel $q+d_1$, $q+d_2$, ..., $q+d_n$ are produced. Because there is $d_n = {_{dn-1}}+1$ and $q = p+1$, so there is $q+d_1=p+d_2$, $q+d_2=p+d_3$, ..., $q+d_{n-1}=p+d_n$. Thus, when we deal with p the weights of the support window which centered with pixels $p+d_2$, $p+d_3$, ..., $p+d_n$ respectively are computed, and when we deal with q only the weight of the support window centered with the pixel $q+d_n$ is need to compute.

3   Experiment

In this section, we carry out the experiment on the four images of the Middblebury database such as Tsukuba, Venus, Teddy and Cones [18]. We use the method proposed in the paper [4] to evaluate the final disparity map, and compare our approach with other excellent local method introduced in the paper [19]. The paper [4] evaluates the disparity map according to NOCC and DISC. The NOCC represents the error rate of the whole image except the shading region, and the DISC represents the error rate of the discontinuous region.

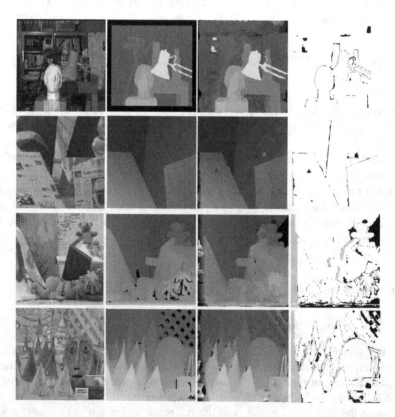

Fig. 1. From left to right they are the reference image, the ground truth, our result and the Bad pixels (error>1) on Tsukuba, Venus, Teddy and Cone

Fig. 1 shows the results of above four images used with our approach. In experiments, we set the size of support window to 31, and set r to 80, T to 30. Meanwhile, we use the median filter to smooth the disparity maps. For the leftmost pixels in a scanning line in the reference image, the corresponding disparity can be evaluated because they do not have matched pixel in the target. In our approach, we simply regard the disparity of the valid leftmost pixel as their disparity. Although we do not have implemented occlusion processing, disparity refinement and so on, our method still obtain accurate depth boundary.

Fig. 2 shows the affection of the size of support window on our approach performance. From the Fig.2, we know that the NOCC and DISC arrive the lowest point when the size of window is about 31 pixels for Tsukuba (a) and Venus (b).

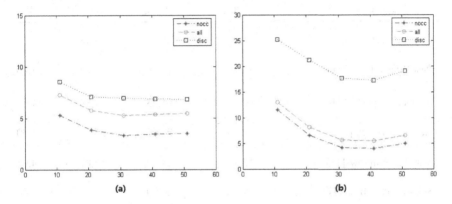

Fig. 2. The affection of the sizeof support window on Tsukuba and Venus

Table 1. Comparison between our approach and others on Tsukuba and Venus

Images	Tsukuba		Venus	
Parameters	NOCC	DISC	NOCC	DISC
Our approach	2.56	7.45	1.27	11.30
Fast Bilateral 39_3 [17]	2.95	8.69	1.15	6.64
Segment Support[14]	2.15	7.22	1.38	6.25
Adaptive Weight[13]	4.66	8.25	4.61	13.20
Variable Windows[10]	4.28	14.26	5.99	9.17
Segmentation based [11]	4.53	13.10	6.91	17.25
Shiftable Windows[1]	7.58	21.61	7.79	13.93

Table 1 shows the comparison between our method and others on Tsukuba and Venus. Table 2 shows the comparison on Teddy and Cone. From Table 1 and 2, we know that the performance of our approach is almost as good as the paper [14, 17], and better than other papers. On the whole, the results of all methods on Tsukuba and Venus are better than Teddy and Cones. This is because that the latter has not only a lager disparity range but also is more complexity scene.

Table 2. Comparison between our approach and others on Teddy and Cones

Images	Teddy		Cones	
Parameters	NOCC	DISC	NOCC	DISC
Our approach	11.00	20.9	7.78	13.60
Fast Bilateral 39_3 [17]	10.70	20.80	5.23	11.40
Segment Support[14]	10.54	21.23	5.83	11.83
Adaptive Weight[13]	12.70	22.40	5.50	11.90
Variable Windows[10]	13.48	24.69	7.87	14.94
Segmentation based [11]	10.94	24.09	7.67	16.16
Shiftable Windows[1]	17.19	29.78	10.27	22.12

4   Conclusion

This paper proposes a new stereo matching method based on adaptive support-weight window. When computing the support weight of every pixel in a local window, we use color difference and space distance between this pixel and the center of the window, and these two factors are not independent. The experiment shows that our approach can obtain the accurate disparity map, especially for the image pair with small disparity range. Furthermore, the control parameters needed by our approach are less. However, our approach is insufficient to images with high texture and repetitive pattern. In the future, we will use color segmentation technique and the edge detection information to improve performance.

Acknowledgment. This research was supported by Foundation of Shaanxi Education Department of Shaanxi Province under grant 11JK1032.

References

1. Scharstein, D., Szeliski, R., Zabih, R.: A Taxonomy and Evaluation of Dense Two-Frame Stereo Correspondence Algorithms. International Journal of Computer Vision 47(1), 7–42 (2002)
2. Tappen, M.F., Freeman, W.T.: Comparison of graph cuts with belief propagation for stereo, using identical MRF parameters. In: ICCV, vol. 2, pp. 900–907 (2003)
3. Brown, M.Z., Burschka, D., Hager, G.D.: Advances in Computational Stereo. IEEE Transactions on Pattern Analysis and Machine Intelligence 25(8), 993–1008 (2003)
4. Tombari, F., Mattoccia, S., Di Stefano, L., Addimanda, E.: Classification and Evaluation of Cost Aggregation Methods for Stereo Correspondence. In: IEEE Conference on Computer Vision and Pattern Recognition, pp. 1–8 (2008)
5. Bobick, A.F., Intille, S.S.: Large occlusion stereo. International Journal of Computer Vision 33(3), 181–200 (1999)
6. Kanade, T., Okutomi, M.: A Stereo Matching Algorithm with an Adaptive Window: Theory and Experiment. IEEE Transactions on Pattern Analysis and Machine Intelligence 16(9), 920–932 (1994)
7. Boykov, Y., Veksler, O., Zabih, R.: A Variable Window Approach to Early Vision. IEEE Trans. PAMI 20(12), 128–1294 (1998)
8. Veksler, O.: Stereo Correspondence with Compact Windows via Minimum Ratio Cycle. IEEE Transactions on Pattern Analysis and Machine Intelligence 24(12) (2002)
9. Adhyapak, S., Kehtarnavaz, N., Nadin, M.: Stereo Matching via selective multiple windows. Journal of Electronic Imaging 16(1) (2007)
10. Veksler, O.: Fast variable window for stereo correspondence using integral images. In: Proc. Conf. on Computer Vision and Pattern Recognition, pp. 556–561 (2003)
11. Gerrits, M., Bekaert, P.: Local Stereo Matching with Segmentation-based Outlier Rejection. In: Proc. Canadian Conf. on Computer and Robot Vision, pp. 66–73 (2006)
12. Xu, Y., Wang, D., Feng, T., Shum, H.Y.: Stereo computation using radial adaptive windows. In: IEEE International Conference on Pattern Recognition, vol. 3 (2002)
13. Yoon, K.J., Kweon, I.S.: Adaptive Support-Weight Approach for Correspondence Search. IEEE Transactions on Pattern Analysis and Machine Intelligence 28(4), 650–656 (2006)
14. Tombari, F., Mattoccia, S., Di Stefano, L.: Segmentation-Based Adaptive Support for Accurate Stereo Correspondence. In: Mery, D., Rueda, L. (eds.) PSIVT 2007. LNCS, vol. 4872, pp. 427–438. Springer, Heidelberg (2007)
15. Gu, Z., Su, X.Y., Liu, Y.K., Zhang, Q.: Local Stereo Matching with Adaptive Support-weight, Rank Transform and Disparity Calibration. Pattern Recognition Letters 29(9) (2008)
16. Hosni, A., Bleyer, M., Gelautz, M., Rhemann, C.: Local Stereo Matching Using Geodesic Support Weights. In: IEEE International Conference on Image Processing, pp. 2093–2096 (2009)
17. Mattoccia, S., Giardino, S., Gambini, A.: Accurate and Efficient Cost Aggregation Strategy for Stereo Correspondence Based on Approximated Joint Bilateral Filtering. In: Zha, H., Taniguchi, R.-i., Maybank, S. (eds.) ACCV 2009, Part II. LNCS, vol. 5995, pp. 371–380. Springer, Heidelberg (2010)
18. The Middlebury Computer Vision Pages, http://vision.middlebury.edu
19. Computer vision laboratory, http://www.vision.deis.unibo.it/spe/SPEresultsTAD.aspx
20. Mattoccia, S.: A locally global approach to stereo correspondence. In: IEEE Workshop on 3D Digital Imaging and Modeling (2009)

Trademark Image Retrieval
Based on Improved Distance Measure of Moments

Yan Shao and Zhong Jin

School of Computer Science and Engineering
Nanjing University of Science and Technology,
Nanjing, China
{shaoyan,jinzhong}@patternrecognition.cn

Abstract. Zernike moments and Pseudo-Zernike moments are widely used as shape descriptors in trademark image retrieval. One moment is a complex number that contains magnitude and phase. In a classical way, Euclidean distance is used for computing distance between two moments, only taking the magnitude information into consideration. When retrieving binary trademark image, this paper conducts a comparison between the classical and the improved distance measure of Zernike moments and Pseudo-Zernike moments. With the demonstration of two experiments, it proposes to apply the improved distance measure of Pseudo-Zernike moments to binary trademark image retrieval in that the improved one takes both magnitude and phase information into account and achieves more accuracy than the classical one.

Keywords: Moments, Distance measure, Retrieval, Phase.

1 Introduction

As a sign of a corporation, trademark plays an important part in industry and commerce. Not only does it identify the producer of commodity and service, but also represents the reputation of the corporation for its quality and reliability [1]. With the rapid increasing number of registered trademarks, it is urgently necessary to establish an accurate and efficient trademark image retrieval system, which is used to avoid similar trademarks registered repeatedly and spitefully.

Since first introduced by Teague [2] and Teh [3], Zernike moments and Pseudo-Zernike moments have been extensively studied and widely used in pattern recognition and image analysis as global feature descriptions due to the advantages of rotation invariance and robustness to deformations [3-8]. Recently, efforts have been devoted to improve the computation time and accuracy of the moments [9-13].

One moment is a complex number that contains magnitude and phase. But the classical way and all the modified way mentioned above to measure the distance of two moments only take into account the moment magnitude. Though losing the phase information allows the invariance to rotation, it also limits the ability of retrieving the rotation angle between two similar images and the accuracy of image retrieval.

F.L. Wang et al. (Eds.): CMSP 2012, CCIS 346, pp. 154–162, 2012.
© Springer-Verlag Berlin Heidelberg 2012

To compensate for this shortage, Jerome Revaud proposes a new distance measure of Zernike moments which takes both magnitude and phase into consideration [14]. With reference to Revaud's improvement idea, this paper will improve the distance measure of Pseudo-Zernike moments through the calculation of both magnitude and phase and propose a new method for binary trademark image retrieval.

2 Improved Distance Measure of Zernike Moments

2.1 Zernike Moments

In recent years, Zernike moment has been used widely in pattern recognition and image analysis as a shape descriptor. Zernike moments of a given image are calculated as correlation values of the image with a set of orthogonal Zernike basis functions mapped over a unit circle.

A basis function for Zernike moments is defined with the order of Zernike moments n and a repetition m constrained by n with the following condition: $D = \{(n, m) \mid n \geq 0, n > |m|, n - |m| \; is \; even\}$. In Eq. (1), (x, y) is the pixel value of the image and $(\; r, \theta\;)$ is the polar coordinate position.

$$V_{nm}(x, y) = V_{nm}(r, \theta) = R_{nm}(r) \exp(im\theta) \tag{1}$$

and

$$R_{nm}(r) = \sum_{s=0}^{(n-|m|)/2} (-1)^s \frac{(n-s)!}{s! \times \left(\frac{n+|m|}{2} - s\right) \times \left(\frac{n-|m|}{2} - s\right)!} r^{n-2s} \tag{2}$$

Then a Zernike moment can be expressed as:

$$Z_{nm} = \frac{n+1}{\pi} \int_0^{2\pi} \int_0^1 f(r, \theta) R_{nm}(r) \exp(-im\theta) r dr d\theta \tag{3}$$

2.2 Distance Measure of Zernike Moments[14]

Apparently, Z_{nm} is a complex number. In a classical way, Euclidean distance is used for computing distance between two Zernike moments, only taking the magnitude information into consideration without the phase information. Let I and J be two different images and Z_{nm}^I and Z_{nm}^J represent Zernike moments of image I and J, the classical distance measure can be simply expressed as:

$$d_{ZMs}^2 = \sum \sum \left(\left|Z_{nm}^I\right| - \left|Z_{nm}^J\right|\right)^2, \qquad (n, m) \in D \tag{4}$$

Though losing the phase information can allows the invariance to rotation, it also makes a negative impact on estimating the degree of similarity between two images. In order to ameliorate this situation, an improved distance measure of Zernike moments is proposed by Jerome Revaud. The improved method takes both magnitude and phase into account.

We express J image rotated by φ as $(J * R_\varphi)$ and define the distance between I and $(J * R_\varphi)$ as Eq. (5), where Z_{nm}^I and Z_{nm}^J represent Zernike moments of image I and J.

$$d^2(\varphi) = \sum\sum \frac{\pi}{n+1}\left[\left|Z_{nm}^I\right|^2 + \left|Z_{nm}^J\right|^2 - 2\left|Z_{nm}^I Z_{nm}^J\right| \cdot \cos\left(m\varphi + [Z_{nm}^J] - [Z_{nm-}^I]\right)\right],$$

$$x^2 + y^2 \leq 1 \quad and \quad (n, m) \in D \tag{5}$$

Then, we can get the minimize distance between I and J by finding an optimal angle φ to minimize the expression mentioned above. We can simplify the process of computing $d^2(\varphi)$ by removing the constant part. The left part can be equivalently expressed as a sum of n cosines by aggregating the cosine terms that own the same frequency. After the pretreatment, the problem can be turned to finding out the minimum of a 2π-periodic function. As usual, we would use gradient descent to get the extremum. In order to extract the global minimum of Eq. (5) efficiently, we would use Nyquist-Shannon sampling theorem to restrict the search.

After all, the minimum of the expression is just the minimal distance between two images and the corresponding φ is just the optimal angle to make two images most similar. Then the improved distance measure of Zernike Moments can be simply expressed as:

$$d_{ZMs}^2 = \min\left(d^2(\varphi)\right), \qquad (n, m) \in D \tag{6}$$

3   Improved Distance Measure of Pseudo-Zernike Moments

3.1   Pseudo-Zernike Moments

Be similar to Zernike moments, the kernel of Pseudo-Zernike moments is a set of orthogonal Pseudo-Zernike polynomials which have properties analogous to those of Zernike polynomials. These polynomials have the form of Eq. (1) and are defined over the polar coordinate space inside a unit circle, too. Yet, the distinction is that Zernike radial polynomials are replaced by Pseudo-Zernike radial polynomials as follows:

$$R_{nm}^{'}(r) = \sum_{s=0}^{n-|m|} (-1)^s \frac{(2n+1-s)!}{s! \times (n-|m|-s)! \times (n+|m|+1-s)!} r^{n-s},$$

$$n > |m| \geq 0 \tag{7}$$

The Zernike moment Z_{nm} in Eq. (3) becomes Pseudo-Zernike moment P_{nm} if the radial polynomial in Eq. (7) is used to compute the polynomial with the condition, n-|m|= even, eliminated. So P_{nm} can be expressed as:

$$P_{nm} = \frac{n+1}{\pi} \int_0^{2\pi} \int_0^1 f(r, \theta) R_{nm}'(r) \exp(-im\theta) r dr d\theta \qquad (8)$$

3.2   Distance Measure of Pseudo-Zernike Moments

In the classical way to measure the similarity of two Pseudo-Zernike moments, just like Eq. (9), Euclidean distance also only takes the moment magnitude information into account. P_{nm}^I and P_{nm}^J represent Pseudo-Zernike moments of two different images I and J.

$$d_{PZMs}^2 = \sum\sum \left(\left| P_{nm}^I \right| - \left| P_{nm}^J \right| \right)^2, \qquad (n, m) \in D \qquad (9)$$

Since the Pseudo-Zernike polynomials are also a complete set of functions orthogonal on the unit disk, Revaud's improvement idea of calculating both magnitude and phase is also applicable to improve the distance measure of Pseudo-Zernike moments. We can describe the minimum distance between image I and J using the following expression:

$$d_{PZMs}^2 = \min\left(d^2(\varphi) \right), \qquad (n, m) \in D \qquad (10)$$

where $d^2(\varphi)$ is computed as:

$$d^2(\varphi) = \sum\sum \frac{\pi}{n+1} \left[\left| P_{nm}^I \right|^2 + \left| P_{nm}^J \right|^2 - 2 \left| P_{nm}^I P_{nm}^J \right| \cdot \cos\left(m\varphi + [P_{nm}^J] - [P_{nm}^I] \right) \right], \qquad (11)$$
$$x^2 + y^2 \leq 1 \qquad and \qquad (n, m) \in D$$

4   Experiments

In this section, we will use a trademark database including 1500 binary trademark images of BMP format with 111 × 111 resolution, of which 100 images are generated via 10 kinds of deformation of 10 images in the database. The 100 deformed images and their original images are shown in Fig. 1[15].

We will do two experiments to compare the trademark retrieval performance between the classical and the improved distance measure of Zernike moments and Pseudo-Zernike moments.

● One of the experiments is to proof-test the ability of finding original images through using the 100 deformed images as query images.
● The other experiment is to use 10 original images to retrieve their deformed images in the database.

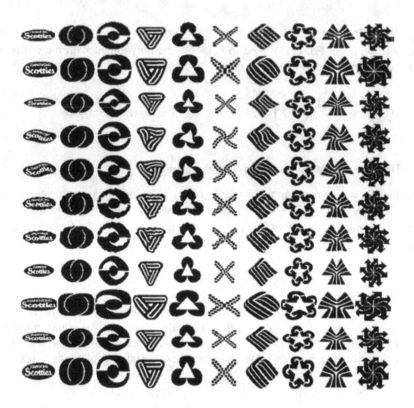

Fig. 1. 10 trademark images (in Line 1) and the corresponding 10 deformed images for each

4.1   Experiment I

With the increase of matrix order and feature dimension, the descriptive power of the image will enhance, which, yet, also results in information redundancy and dimension curse. Therefore, in this experiment, 100 deformed images are set as query images. Then, in different dimensions, improved and classical distance measure are carried on respectively to examine the ability of each measure to retrieve original images of these 100 deformed images during the other 1400 images in the database. The retrieval performance is measured using Accumulative frequency (AF) [15] as follows and higher value of AF means better retrieval performance.

$$AF(n) = \frac{original\ images\ within\ n\ positions}{N} \times 100\% \qquad (12)$$

where N=100 is the number of query images.

The retrieval results of the two measures of Zernike moments (ZMs) and Pseudo-Zernike moments (PZMs) are listed in Table 1. The results indicate that, using Zernike moments as a shape descriptor, the retrieval in 36 dimensions of the feature matrix is better enhanced than that in 30 dimensions, whereas 42 dimensions involves much more calculation yet without significant enhancement. Using Pseudo-Zernike moments, the amount of computation in 36 dimensions is less than that in 45 dimensions and 55 dimensions, but the retrieval precision is similar to that in 45 dimensions and 55 dimensions. Thus, both for Zernike moments and for Pseudo-Zernike moments, the retrieval in 36 dimensions achieves the best overall performance. What's more, in these three feature dimensions in this experiment, the retrievals of the improved distance measure are better than those of the classical one, especially, the capability to retrieve the original image as the most similar one. The last, of the four methods, we can clearly figure out the improved distance measure of Pseudo-Zernike moments performs best.

Table 1. The retrieval results of the classical and the improved distance measure of Zernike moments and Pseudo-Zernike moments with different n

method AF(n)		n=1	n=2	n=3	n=5	n=8	n=10
Classical Distance Measure of ZMs in Eq. (4)	30 dimensions	63%	69%	73%	79%	83%	87%
	36 dimensions	66%	75%	79%	82%	87%	89%
	42 dimensions	67%	76%	80%	85%	89%	90%
Improved Distance Measure of ZMs in Eq. (6)	30 dimensions	68%	77%	81%	85%	88%	90%
	36 dimensions	72%	77%	83%	86%	90%	90%
	42 dimensions	76%	84%	87%	91%	92%	92%
Classical Distance Measure of PZMs in Eq. (9)	36 dimensions	72%	80%	82%	86%	91%	92%
	45 dimensions	74%	82%	83%	87%	92%	93%
	55 dimensions	73%	83%	86%	90%	92%	93%
Improved Distance Measure of PZMs in Eq. (10)	36 dimensions	77%	85%	89%	92%	93%	93%
	45 dimensions	80%	84%	87%	92%	94%	94%
	55 dimensions	82%	86%	88%	92%	93%	94%

4.2   Experiment II

In this experiment, we use the 10 original images shown in the first line of Fig. 1 as query images. For each query image, the 10 deformed images listed below it in Fig. 1

are regarded as its highly similar images. Furthermore, for each query image, our aim is to retrieve as many deformed images as possible from the other 1499 images.

Just as is illustrated in Experiment I, the overall performance of both Zernike moments and Pseudo-Zernike moments in 36 dimensions is the best; therefore, in Experiment II, the comparison is conducted in 36 dimensions. First, we compute Zernike moments and Pseudo-Zernike moments of each image. Then, classical and improved way to measure similarity of these moments are respectively carried on between every query image and the other 1499 images in the database. At last, the mean Recall Ratio of each method is calculated for the final comparison of retrieval capabilities. From the retrieval results, the most similar K images to the query image are selected. In this experiment, we assign 16 to K. Parts of the results are illustrated in Fig. 2.

Fig. 2 shows that being used in binary trademark image retrieval, just like classical way to measure the similarity of moments, the improved one also has rotation invariance and can well retrieve images after rotation. However, for other geometrical deformation, the retrieval capability of the improved distance measure is much better than the classical one. Moreover, the arrangement sequence of the retrieved similar images basically satisfies human vision.

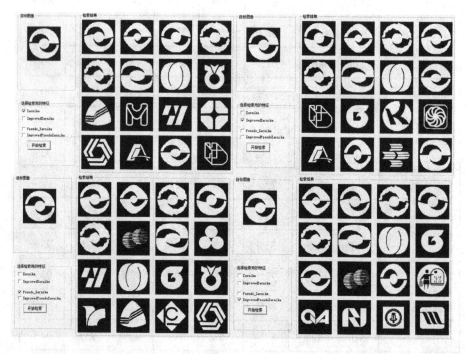

Fig. 2. The figure shows the retrieval results of the classical way and the improved way to measure similarity of Zernike moments and Pseudo-Zernike moments. The 16 best retrievals for the query image are displayed, which are ordered by distance measure.

Table 2. MR of each method

method	Classical Distance measure of ZMs	Improved Distance measure of ZMs	Classical Distance measure of PZMs	Improved Similarity Measure of PZMs
MR	77%	79%	79%	82%

In the application of trademark image retrieval, we usually use the Recall Ratio of the retrieval to present the capability of every retrieval method. Higher value of R means better performance. Since single image retrieval result is insufficient to prove the performance of the retrieval method, hence, we will respectively calculate the Recall Ratio for each query image and then average the results. The performance measure used in the experiment is expressed as:

$$MR = \frac{sum\ of\ similar\ images\ retrieved}{M \times K} \times 100\% \tag{13}$$

where M=10 is the number of query images and K=10 is the number of similar images for each query image. The calculation results are listed in Table 2.

This experiment also proves that the performance of the improved distance measure of moments is better than the classical one. And of all, the improved measure of Pseudo-Zernike moments has the highest retrieval precision.

5   Conclusion

In this paper, based on the comparison of the classical and the improved distance measure of Zernike moments and Pseudo-Zernike moments, a new method for binary trademark retrieval is proposed, that is, the improved measure of Pseudo-Zernike moments. Just as is illustrated in the two experiments, the new method can achieve more accuracy than the other three methods. Yet, the new trademark retrieval can be further polished up. For instance, in the future, it can be combined with Multi-Feature extraction to achieve a better result.

References

1. Xia, S.: Introduction to Trademark Law. China University of Political Science and Lao Press, Beijing (1989)
2. Teague, M.: Image Analysis via the General Theory of Moments. J. Optical Soc. Am. 70(8), 920–930 (1980)
3. Teh, C.H., Chin, R.T.: On image analysis by the method of moments. IEEE Transaction on Pattern Analysis and Machine Intelligence 10(4), 496–513 (1988)

4. Kim, Y.S., Kim, W.Y.: Content-based trademark retrieval system using visually salient feature. In: IEEE Computer Society Conference on Computer Vision and Pattern Recognition, pp. 307–312 (1997)
5. Eakins, J.P., Boardman, J.M., Graham, M.E.: Similarity retrieval of trademark images. IEEE Transactions on Multimedia 5(2), 53–63 (1998)
6. Chong, C.-W., Raveendran, P., Mukundan, R.: Translation Invariants of Zernike Moments. Pattern Recognition 36, 1765–1773 (2003)
7. Belkasim, S., Hassan, E., Obeidi, T.: Radial Zernike Moment Invariants. In: International Conference on Computer and Information Technology, pp. 790–795 (2004)
8. Huang, S., Wu, X.: Multi-feature Trademark Image Retrieval Based on Integrated Distance Function. Manufacturing Information Engineering of China 38(7), 74–78 (2009)
9. Bin, Y., Xiong, P.: Improvement and Invariance Analysis of Zernike Moments. In: International Conference on Communications, Circle and Systems and West Sino Expositions, vol. 2, pp. 963–967 (2002)
10. Kotoulas, L., Andreadis, I.: Real-Time Computation of Zernike Moments. IEEE Transactions on Circuits and Systems for Video Technology 15(6), 801–809 (2005)
11. Shao, J., Ma, D.: A New Method for Comparing Zernike Circular polynomials with Zernike Annular polynomials in Annular Pupils. In: 2010 International Conference on Computer, Mechatronics, Control and Electronic Engineering (CMCE), pp. 229–232 (2010)
12. Chong, C.W.: An efficient algorithm for fast computation of Pseudo-Zernike moments. International Journal of Pattern Recognition and Artificial Intelligence 17(6), 1011–1023 (2003)
13. Xia, T., Zhou, W., Li, S.: A new algorithm for fast computation of Pseudo-Zernike moments. Chinese Journal of Electronics 33(7), 1295–1298 (2005)
14. Jerome, R., Guillaume, L., Atilla, B.: Improving Zernike Moments Comparison for Optimal Similarity and Rotation Angle Retrieval. IEEE Transactions on Pattern Analysis and Machine Intelligence 31(4), 627–636 (2009)
15. Irwin, K., Zhong, J.: Integrated probability function and its application to content-based image retrieval by relevance feedback. Pattern Recognition 36, 2177–2186 (2003)

Fast Vanishing Points Detection
for Omnidirectional Images

Wenting Duan and Nigel M. Allinson

School of Computer Science,
University of Lincoln, U.K.
{wduan,nallinson}@lincoln.ac.uk

Abstract. This paper presents a novel method for extracting the dominant vanishing directions from omnidirectional images using the detected conics and
lines. The method assumes the camera system has vertically aligned optical axis
and is partially calibrated, i.e. only mirror parameter and FOV are known.
Based on the geometric properties of catadioptric line projection, the algorithm
fully recovers the other camera calibration parameters, cluster the detected conics and use the conic intersections to derive the vanishing points (VPs). The approach shows applying certain geometric constraints can enable fast conic
grouping and VPs detection. The efficiency of our method has been validated
by experiments on real images (publicly available).

Keywords: Vanishing points, conic detection and grouping, catadioptric
camera, calibration.

1   Introduction

The extraction and utilisation of information about camera parameters and scene
geometry using vanishing points (VPs) is an important topic of research in computer
vision and photogrammetry. Catadioptric cameras, those which have a field of view
greater than 180 degrees, are becoming increasingly important and widely used in
areas such as robot navigation [1][2] and 3D reconstruction [3][4], and model acquisition for virtual reality [5]. Therefore, the development of techniques for VPs detection
in catadioptric images is a research priority. Catadioptric systems are classified into
two groups; 'central' if the system possesses a unique effective viewpoint, otherwise
'non-central'. A unique effective viewpoint allows image mapping from the catadioptric image plane to a perspective plane giving the orientation of any part of the scene.
Hence, in most cases, the central catadioptric system is preferable. Compared with
perspective projection, the projection geometry of central catadioptric system is much
more complicated. Lines which are not coplanar with the mirror axis of a catadioptric
camera are projected to conics in the image plane. The other lines that are coplanar
with the mirror axis are projected as radial lines (principal point centred). This case
happens when the optical axis is vertically aligned, i.e. the camera system is placed
with its optical axis orthogonal to ground. This is very easy to achieve with a tripod or

F.L. Wang et al. (Eds.): CMSP 2012, CCIS 346, pp. 163–170, 2012.
© Springer-Verlag Berlin Heidelberg 2012

flat surface. In most applications especially in robotics, a catadioptric system is commonly observed that it has a vertical orientation.

A three step process of catadioptric image projection model was developed by Barreto [8] where the non-linearity of the image formation is isolated in a single function ℏ. Under Barreto's unifying projection model, a set of parallel lines intersect in two antipodal points in the sphere and these two points corresponds to the vanishing direction of this set of parallel lines. Hence the task of extracting the vanishing direction is actually to detect the intersection points of a group of 'parallel' conics from the omni-directional image. As pointed out by Barreto, under the central catadioptric projection, a line in the 3D world is generally mapped into a small arc. Our challenge lies in accurate conic fitting and grouping since this directly affect the accuracy of estimated conic intersection.

Compared to the existing techniques for conic fitting and VPs detection[6][9][10], our approach only require partially calibrated catadioptric system and assume vertical aligned optical axis. We show how geometric features presented in a vertical oriented catadioptric image can be used to reduce the search space when applying RANSAC algorithm for VPs detection. The rest of the paper is distributed as follows. In Section 2, the unifying model for catadioptric image formation and the projection of two parallel 3D lines is briefly explained. The geometric properties involved in the proposed approach are also introduced. In Section 3, the new method for extracting conics and their associated VPs is presented. Section 4 shows the verification of the proposed method. The method is tested on real images which are publicly available. Finally we conclude in Section 5.

2   Central Catadioptric Projection

2.1   Unifying Model

The unifying model of central catadioptric projection developed by Barreto [8] is shown in Figure 1(a). A 3D world point X is projected on the unit sphere at X_C. The unit sphere is centred at the focal point of the mirror and denoted as O. The unifying model represents this transformation by a 3×4 matrix $P = R[I \mid -C]$. After the transformation $X_C = PX$, the point X_C is then mapped to the point $\bar{x}$ in the canonical plane Π_∞. This transformation is modelled using function $\hbar$, in which the non-linearity of the mapping is embedded. The point O_C with coordinates $(0, 0, -\xi)^T$ is the other projection centre which re-projects the point X_C on the unit sphere to $\bar{x}$ in the sensor plane Π_∞. The function $\hbar$ is written as

$$\hbar(x) = \begin{bmatrix} x \\ y \\ z + \xi\sqrt{x^2 + y^2 + z^2} \end{bmatrix} \tag{1}$$

Finally, a collineation H_C is applied to transform $\bar{x}$ to obtain the point $\hat{x}$ in the catadioptric image plane, i.e. $\hat{x} = H_C\bar{x}$. H_C is written as

$$H_C = K_C R_C M_C \text{ where } M_C = \begin{bmatrix} \psi - \xi & 0 & 0 \\ 0 & \xi - \psi & 0 \\ 0 & 0 & 1 \end{bmatrix} K_C = \begin{bmatrix} r \cdot f_e & s & u_0 \\ 0 & f_e & v_0 \\ 0 & 0 & 1 \end{bmatrix} \quad (2)$$

M_C changes according to the mirror type and shape, K_C is the camera calibration matrix and R_C is the rotation matrix of the mirror relative to the camera. The majority of the catadioptric sensors commercially available have their mirror accurately aligned with the camera. Therefore, the rotation matrix $R_C = I$. Generally, the calibration of a central catadioptric system is to obtain mirror parameter ξ and the intrinsic parameter matrix K_C.

2.2 Projection of Lines in Catadioptric Cameras

As shown in Figure 1(b), a line l in space intersect the unit sphere through the origin O creating a plane $\Pi = (n_x, n_y, n_z, 0)^T$. The unit sphere based representation of line is then defined as $n = (n_x, n_y, n_z)$. The image conic which is the catadioptric projection of line l in the canonical image plane is expressed as

$$\bar{\Omega} = \begin{bmatrix} n_x^2(1 - \xi^2) - n_z^2\xi^2 & n_x n_y(1 - \xi^2) & n_x n_z \\ n_x n_y(1 - \xi^2) & n_y^2(1 - \xi^2) - n_z^2\xi^2 & n_y n_z \\ n_x n_z & n_y n_z & n_z^2 \end{bmatrix} \quad (3)$$

In the catadioptric image plane, we have our conic image as

$$\hat{\Omega} = H_C^{-T} \bar{\Omega} H_C^{-1} \quad (4)$$

2.3 Computation of Catadioptric Line Images (CLIs)

For the computation of CLIs, we adopt the analytical process proposed by Bermudez-Cameo et al [10]. If a point lies on a conic, their relationship can be expressed as $x^T \Omega x = 0$. When the catadioptric camera parameters are known, only two points are required to fit a CLI. Suppose some points $\hat{x}$ is known to be lie on a CLI in the image plane, these points are firstly transformed back to the canonical plane Π_∞ using the inverse of the collineation matrix H_c via $\bar{x} = H_c^{-1}\hat{x}$. For each point $\bar{x} = (\bar{x}, \bar{y}, \bar{z})$, compute

$$\gamma = -\frac{\bar{z}}{1-\xi^2} + \frac{\xi}{1-\xi^2}\sqrt{\bar{z}^2 + (\bar{x}^2 + \bar{y}^2)(1 - \xi^2)} \quad (5)$$

If two points $\bar{x}_1 = (\bar{x}_1, \bar{y}_1, \bar{z}_1)$ and $\bar{x}_2 = (\bar{x}_2, \bar{y}_2, \bar{z}_2)$ are given in the canonical plane, to estimate the normal n, we just need to solve the following linear system

$$\begin{pmatrix} \bar{x}_1 & \bar{y}_1 & \gamma_1 \\ \bar{x}_2 & \bar{y}_2 & \gamma_2 \end{pmatrix} \begin{pmatrix} n_x \\ n_y \\ n_z \end{pmatrix} = \begin{pmatrix} 0 \\ 0 \end{pmatrix} \quad (6)$$

Once n is estimated, the image conic is computed using equation (3) and (4).

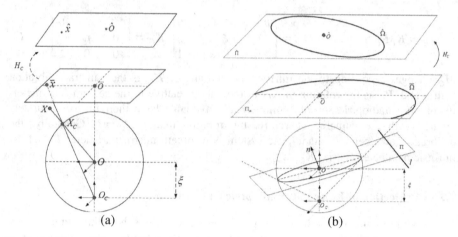

Fig. 1. (a) The unifying model for image formation of central catadioptric cameras; (b) Line image formation of central catadioptric systems

2.4   Vanishing Points and Geometric Properties

A set of parallel lines is projected as a set of conics intersecting at two common points $\widehat{F}$ and $\widehat{B}$ in the image plane. The orientation of the line $\widehat{\mu}$ passing through $\widehat{F}$ and $\widehat{B}$ is the vanishing direction of this set of conics. Hence, $\widehat{F}$ and $\widehat{B}$ are simply defined as the vanishing points of parallel lines in catadioptric image plane. When the central catadioptric camera has a vertical aligned optical axis, there are three important geometric properties which can be used to facilitate camera calibration and VPs detection.

1. For the set of lines that are parallel to the mirror axis of the camera, the lines are projected as radial lines intersecting at the principal point $\widehat{O}$.
2. In the case of parallel line group orthogonal to the mirror axis, the principal point $\overline{O}$ lies in the middle of the line segment connecting intersecting points $\overline{F}$ and $\overline{B}$ in the canonical plane Π_∞, i.e. $|\overline{FO}| = |\overline{OB}|$. If matrix H_C is affine, $|\widehat{FO}| = |\widehat{OB}|$.
3. The horizon conic $\widehat{\Omega}_h$ is the projection of lines which are orthogonal to the mirror axis and lies on the same plane as the focal point O of the unifying model (i.e. the focal point of the mirror). For any parallel line group orthogonal to the mirror axis, their intersecting points $\widehat{F}$ and $\widehat{B}$ always lie on the horizon conic $\widehat{\Omega}_h$.

2.5   Calibration of Central Catadioptric System

Assuming the central catadioptric system is placed orthogonal to a horizontal surface in a man-made environment, a high number of parallel lines from man-made structures (e.g. walls, doors, and windows) which are either orthogonal to or coplanar with the mirror axis are projected onto the catadioptric image plane. With known mirror parameter ξ and elevation angle α above horizon, we can recover the rest of catadioptric system parameters $\{f_e, r, s, u_0, v_0\}$ through the boundary ellipse $\widehat{\Omega}_b$.

If $s \neq 0$ and $r \neq 1$, the mirror boundary $\widehat{\Omega}_b$ are projected to an ellipse

$$Ax^2 + 2Bxy + Cy^2 + 2Dx + 2Ey + F = 0 \tag{7}$$

The principal point $\left(u_0 = \frac{BE-CD}{AC-B^2}, v_0 = \frac{BD-AE}{AC-B^2}\right)$ is the centre of the boundary ellipse. The aspect ratio $r = \sqrt{-B^2/A^2 + C/A}$. For parameter skew s, we first compute the eigenvectors v_1, v_2 of matrix $A_s = \begin{bmatrix} A & B \\ B & C \end{bmatrix}$. If the angle between eigenvectors v_1, v_2 are denoted as τ, $s = \cos \tau$. Once parameters u_0, v_0, r and s are known, then the image plane can be transformed to a plane with $s = 0$ and $r = 1$. In this way, the boundary ellipse is transformed to a circle with centre u_0, v_0 and a known radius $\hat{R}_b$. Once $\hat{R}_b$ is known, the focal length f_e is calculated using the formula

$$f_e = \hat{R}_b(\xi - \sin(\alpha))/\cos(\alpha)\sqrt{1 - \xi^2} \tag{8}$$

3   VPs Detection Approach

Based on the geometric properties stated in Section 2.4 and calibration parameters derived in Section 2.5, an approach for VPs Detection in central catadioptric image is developed. In this section, we demonstrate how the geometric constraints are applied in the method to reduce the search space for both CLIs and VPs detection.

3.1   Detection of CLIs from Real Images

First of all, we apply Canny edge detection to an example of catadioptric image (Figure 3(a)). The detected edge points are shown in Figure 3(b). The orientation of each edge point is obtained after using the Canny edge detector, then the edge orientation span is divided into a set of k ranges. The edges are labelled with their associated value of k corresponding to the orientation range that they belong to. The edge points from every five consecutive labels are grouped together for connected component analysis. Edge lists formed after connected component analysis with supporting points fewer than N pixels are removed. The results at this stage are shown in Figure 3(c). From Figure 3(c), it is also not difficult to find out that there are mainly three types of edge lists: first, projection of lines planar to the mirror axis, i.e. straight line segments pointing towards the centre of the image; second, projection of parallel lines orthogonal to the mirror axis; third, arc segments of mirror boundary. Following the calibration process described in Section 2.5, we can fit the ellipse and carry out the circle transformation of the image boundary to obtain image centre (Figure 3(d)). Then the straight lines segments pointing towards the centre are grouped. A line l_i connecting the endpoints (e_{1i}, e_{2i}) of each edge list is drawn and its direction β_i is computed. Another line l_i^c is drawn to connect one of the endpoint e_{1i} and the estimated image centre (u_0, v_0) and again the line's direction β_i^c is obtained. The line segments pointing towards the image centre can be found by using $|\theta_i^c - \theta_i| < \tau$, e.g. within $\tau = 10°$ of orientation difference in our experiment. The filtered results are shown in Figure 3(e) and (f).

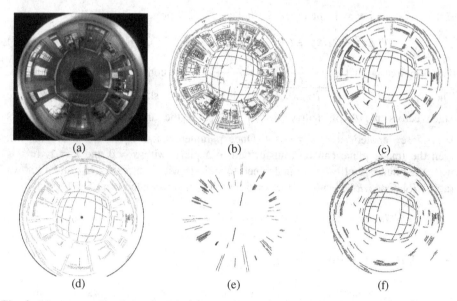

Fig. 2. (a) an example of catadioptric image; (b) the detected edge points of the image; (c) detected lines and arc segments; (d) detected mirror boundary arc segments; (e) grouped radial lines; and (f) arc segments with radial lines and mirror boundary filtered out.

For each edge points $\hat{x}_i$ of the conic segments, their relative distances d_i and orientations θ_i to the image centre are computed.

$$d_i = \sqrt{(\hat{x}_i - u_0) + (\hat{y}_i - v_0)} \quad \text{and} \quad \theta_i = \text{atan}((\hat{y}_i - v_0)/(\hat{x}_i - u_0)) \tag{9}$$

Since the longer segments provide more information for conic fitting, it is first used as the reference arc. The search range of conic segments belonging to the same conic is limited to ones with θ_i within 60 degrees to the reference arc (both clockwise and anticlockwise). Then we use d_i of each conic segment to search for conic segments with distance of close value, hence the search space for potential conic segments lying on the same conic is further reduced. Lastly, the estimated n_r and n_s for both reference arc and searched arcs are compared. They belong to the same conic if the difference between n_r and n_s are small (less than 0.02 in our experiment). Then the reference arc and its associated arcs are combined and the rest conic segments continue with the process.

3.2   Detection of VPs and Conic Grouping

Once the CLIs are detected, we can carry out the detection of VPs and conic grouping simultaneously. Using geometric property 2 stated in Section 2.4, the VPs $\hat{F}_i$ and $\hat{B}_i$ of a CLI C_i can be found by enforcing the constraints the conics have common points $\hat{F}_i$ and $\hat{B}_i$ and $|\hat{F}\hat{O}| = |\hat{O}\hat{B}|$. The geometric property 3 then can be used to assess the accuracy and validity of the estimated $\hat{F}_i$ and $\hat{B}_i$. Since the horizon conic

$\widehat{\Omega}_h$ is a circle if H_C is affine (i.e. $s = 0$ and $r = 1$), it can be calculated from the calibration parameters. The centre of the horizon circle $\widehat{\Omega}_h$ is the image centre (u_0, v_0), its radius R_h is obtained using $R_h = f_e\sqrt{1 - \xi^2}/\xi$. Hence, the validity of the estimated VPs can be checked by measuring if they lie on or close to the horizon circle. In this way, the conics which are not orthogonal to the mirror axis are eliminated. The conics are grouped simply by checking their VPs distance to the other validated VPs.

4   Experiment

The proposed method is tested on real images. The omnidirectional image database from the University of Amsterdam [12] is used. These omnidirectional images were taken by a central catadioptric system consisting of a perspective camera and a hyperbolic mirror. The image size is 1024×768 pixels. The elevation angle (i.e. FOV above horizon) of the catadioptric system is 0.4887 radians. The mirror parameter ξ is given by the manufacturer as 0.9886. The rest of the camera and geometric parameters calibrated for the catadioptric system is shown in Table 1.

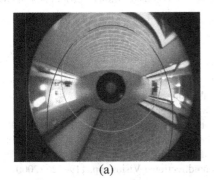 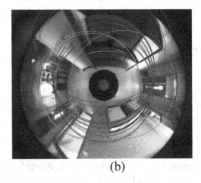

(a)   (b)

Fig. 3. (a) The results of conic fitting: green conic is detected using constrained method and the blue conic section is detected using unconstrained method; (b)The detected CLIs and VPs: different sets of conics are shown in different colour.

Table 1. Camera and geometric parameters obtained from real images

	f_e	R_b	u_0	v_0
Average value	1764.8	451.93	530.79	389.16
Standard deviation	± 4.07	± 1.04	± 1.69	± 1.44

For conic fitting, the results from unconstrained method to constrained method (i.e. introduced in Section 2.3) are highly different as shown in Figure 3(a). The unconstrained approach can be unreliable and inaccurate when edge points are not well distributed along their corresponding conic. Figure 3(b) shows an example of grouped CLIs and their corresponding vanishing points. The accuracy of the vanishing points are measured against the horizon circle. From our experiment, the average error of detected vanishing points location are 0.71 pixels with standard deviation 1.78. This is to say, given reliable camera calibration, our approach can achieve high accuracy and the same time reduce search space for both conic and VPs detection.

5   Conclusion

This paper first showed geometric properties such as boundary circle can be used to recover camera parameters if only mirror parameters are known. The mirror axis are assumed to be vertically aligned. Once the catadioptric camera is calibrated, geometric features such as relation between horizon circle and vanishing points are used to facilitate the localisation of VPs and conic grouping. Compared with the method shown in Bazin et al [6] and Bermudez-Cameo et al [10], where RANSAC algorithm is used to exhaustively search CLIs and VPs, our method shows the advantage of largely reduce the search space by applying geometric constraints. To show the effectiveness of proposed approach we tested it with real images that are publicly available on line. The experiment shows the average deviation of results from theoretical VPs' value (estimated using calibration parameter and horizon circle) is less than 1 pixel. Our future work include using detected VPs and derived geometric properties in 3D reconstruction and scene structure recovery.

References

1. Winters, N., Gaspar, J., Lacey, G., Santos-Victor, J.: Omnidirectional Vision for Navigation. In: Proc. IEEE Workshop Omnidirectional Vision, pp. 21–28 (2000)
2. Benosman, R., Deforas, E., Devars, J.: A New Catadioptric Sensor for Panoramic Vision of Mobile Robots. In: Proc. IEEE Workshop Omnidirectional vision, pp. 112–118 (2000)
3. Taylor, C.: Video Plus. In: Proc. IEEE Workshop Omnidirectional Vision, pp. 3–10 (2000)
4. Sturm, P.: A Method for 3D Reconstruction of Piecewise Planar Objects from Single Panoramic Images. In: Proc. IEEE Workshop Omnidirectional Vision, pp. 119–126 (2000)
5. Peleg, S., Ben-Ezra, M., Pritch, Y.: Omnistereo: Panoramic Stereo Imaging. IEEE Trans. on Pattern Analysis and Machine Intelligence 23(3), 279–290 (2001)
6. Bazin, J., Kweon, I., Demonceaux, C., Vasseur, P.: UAV Attitude Estimation by Vanishing Points in Catadioptric Images. In: IEEE ICRA, pp. 2743–2749 (2008)
7. Geyer, C., Daniilidis, K.: A Unifying Theory for Central Panoramic Systems and Practical Implications. In: Vernon, D. (ed.) ECCV 2000. LNCS, vol. 1843, pp. 445–461. Springer, Heidelberg (2000)
8. Barreto, J.: General Central Projection Systems, Modeling, Calibration and Visual Servoing. PhD thesis, University of Coimbra (2003)
9. Barreto, J., Araujo, H.: Direct Least Square Fitting of Paracatadioptric Line images. In: Computer Vision and Pattern Recognition Workshop, pp. 78–87 (2003)
10. Bermudez-Cameo, J., Puig, L., Guerrero, J.J.: Hypercatadioptric Line Images for 3D Orientation and Image Rectification. In: Robotics and Autonomous Systems (2012)
11. Kŏsecká, J., Zhang, W.: Video Compass. In: Heyden, A., Sparr, G., Nielsen, M., Johansen, P. (eds.) ECCV 2002, Part IV. LNCS, vol. 2353, pp. 476–490. Springer, Heidelberg (2002)
12. Zivkovic, Z., Booij, O., Krose, B.: From Images to Rooms. Robotics and Autonomous Systems 55(5), 411–418 (2007)

Detection of Laser Concentric Circles Based on Gradient Hough Transform

Yuehuan Lou

Department of Computer Science and Technology
Shanghai University of Electric Power,
China
louyuehuan@yahoo.com.cn

Abstract. It is presently difficult to realize automation, numerical expression and real-time processing in the measurements for center of laser concentric circles. To solve this problem, a new real-time processing method based on Gradient Hough Transform algorithm is presented, in which invalid accumulation in common Hough Transform by using gradient direction information of image edge can be greatly resolved, and the coordinates of the center of circle can be quickly detected. It is proved, for the most part, that the method can satisfy with practical application on highly precise measuring of collimation.

Keywords: Laser Concentric Circles, Gradient Hough Transform, Circle detection

1 Introduction

In recent years there has appeared a kind of laser collimating instruments that are also named laser verticality instruments based on laser. It forms collimating lines whose center is circle interference fringes by using its excellent collimation and coherence. The prime means at present is using chess grids to gain circle center[1]. This method is simple and easy to be done, but the precision is not high because of man-made means, and can't be achieved automatic measurement.

Aiming at the problem, it brings out the method that CMOS image sensor is regarded as receiver, to capture the laser beam image in which diffraction fringes form concentric circles. And now, the critic problem is to find an algorithm that center of concentric circles can be calculated out. As we all know, Hough Transform (HT) is an effective method for circle detection. However, it has been prevented from being used for practical computer vision tasks because of long computation time and large memory requirements. Lei Xu[2] develops a novel algorithm called the Randomized Hough Transform (RHT) to complete the task of extracting global features such as line segments from a binary image. The algorithm overcomes most problems associated with the standard HT scheme, including speed and memory consumption. There are many researchers develop different algorithms for RHT[3-5].

F.L. Wang et al. (Eds.): CMSP 2012, CCIS 346, pp. 171–176, 2012.

2   Principle of Circle Detection Based on Hough Transform

In image space, three points which are not in the same line are chosen randomly, and they are mapped to a point in parameter space. This is a multi-to-one mapping, and it voids huge calculation brought by one-to-multi mapping in tradition Hough transform. A circle has geometric property that two perpendicular bisectors of non-parallel chords on the circle intersect in the center of circle. In order to simplify the process, only three points are selected to confirm a circle. The principle of Hough transform is shown in Fig.1.

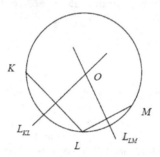

Fig. 1. Principle of Hough transform in circle detection

As shown in figure 1, in the circle O, three different points K, M, L are selected. According to the geometric property of circle, the perpendicular bisector L_{KL} of LM and the perpendicular bisector L_{LM} of LM intersect in the center of circle O. It is supposed that the coordinates of the three point K, M, L are (x_K, y_K), (x_M, y_M), (x_L, y_L) respectively. The equations of L_{KL} and L_{LM} are:

$$y = k_{KL}x + d_{KL} \tag{1}$$

$$y = k_{KM}x + d_{KM} \tag{2}$$

The parameters k_{KL}, d_{KL}, k_{LM} and d_{LM} in Eq.(1) and Eq.(2) are calculated as follow:

$$k_{KL} = \frac{x_K - x_L}{y_K - y_L} \tag{3}$$

$$d_{KL} = \frac{y_K + y_L - k_{KL}(x_K + x_L)}{2} \tag{4}$$

$$k_{LM} = \frac{x_L - x_M}{y_L - y_M} \tag{5}$$

$$d_{LM} = \frac{y_L + y_M - k_{KM}(x_L + x_M)}{2} \tag{6}$$

In simultaneous equation system (1) and (2), the coordinate of the circle center (x_C, y_C) and radius of the circle r_C can be resolved by the following equations:

$$x_C = \frac{d_{KL} - d_{LM}}{k_{KL} - k_{LM}} \tag{7}$$

$$y_C = k_{KL}x_C + d_{KL} \tag{8}$$

$$r_C = \sqrt{(x_K - x_C)^2 + (y_K - y_C)^2} \tag{9}$$

It concludes that three points which are not in the same line map to a point (x_C, y_C, r_C) in the parameter space. In this paper, it is supposed that three points make up a point-group in image space and a vector $P = (x, y, r)$ represents the point in parameter space. So a point-group in a circle in image space maps to a vector P_i in parameter space. In image space, n point-groups are selected and mapped to n vectors $P_1 P_2 \dots P_n$ in parameter space. If the point-groups are selected from the same circle, they will be mapped to the same vector in parameter. In all the vectors, the one which has the max count number is the parameter of the circle.

3   Gradient Hough Transform Algorithm

Randomized Hough Transform is multi-to-one mapping and the parameters are saved and accumulated in the memory units. Lots of invalid parameters are produced when doing randomized sampling, and these invalid parameters occupy lots of memory units and make invalid accumulation[6]. For example, there have N circles whose size is q, and have n points which are not on the circles, the probability that 3 points are selected at the same circle by random sampling is expressed as follow:

$$p = \frac{NC_q^3}{C_{(Nq+n)}^3} = \frac{Nq(q-1)(q-2)}{(Nq+n)(Nq+n-1)(Nq+n-2)} \tag{10}$$

If $n = 0$, Eq.(10) can be simplified,

$$P = \frac{NC_q^3}{C_{Nq}^3} = \frac{Nq(q-1)(q-2)}{Nq(Nq+n-1)(Nq-2)} \approx \frac{1}{N^2} \tag{11}$$

It is obvious that the probability P is in inverse proportion to the mounts of circles N, when N increases, invalid accumulations are more and more. So it is impractical for our concentric circles detections.

For this, it brings out Gradient Hough Transform. As we all know, the line along the gradient direction[7, 8] in the circle edge of image passes the center of circle. Because of concentric circles, there has only one center, if we select the two random points in the circle edge, the two lines along the gradient directions cross at the center. We suppose two points, C_a and C_b, and their gradient directions are expressed by $dy/dx |C_a$ and $dy/dx |C_b$, their coordinates are (X_{Ca}, Y_{Ca}) and (X_{Cb}, Y_{Cb}), so we can figure out the center which is expressed (X_o, Y_o) by using Eq.(12) and Eq.(13).

$$\frac{dy}{dx}\Big| C_a = \frac{Y_o - Y_{Ca}}{X_o - X_{Ca}} \tag{12}$$

$$\frac{dy}{dx}\Big| C_b = \frac{Y_o - Y_{Cb}}{X_o - X_{Cb}} \tag{13}$$

The detailed algorithm steps are described as follows:

Step 1: We can clearly see that, the center is located at the light spot nearby. An estimated value can be found by searching the center of light spot with 5×5 template, we define it with (X_p, Y_p), this template can decrease the influence of image noise.

Step 2: At the same time of thresholding, we need account the values of their gradient directions.

Step 3: In order to improve transform speed, the binary image need be filtered again. We define a circle that the center is (X_p, Y_p), the radius is 100 pixels, if the effective pixels which are not in the place of circle will be thrown off.

Step 4: Select two effective pixels at random, the probable center can be figure out by using previous algorithm, that is (X_o, Y_o). When the coordinates satisfies the condition that:

$$\left[(X_o - X_p)^2 + (Y_o - Y_p)^2\right]^{\frac{1}{2}} < 20 \tag{14}$$

Then apply for a memory, plus 1 in corresponding units, and record the coordinates, find the accumulated maximum value when the operation is finished, the corresponding coordinates are the center of concentric circles.

4   Experimental Results and Analysis

The experiment is testing the verticality of elevator track, which is evaluated by measuring spot center coordinates of different locations. The image accepted by CCD which is far from collimating instrument more than 5 meters is diffraction circles. Fig.2 shows the results of edge extraction and center position by computing the concentric circles images at the distance of 10, 20 and 40 meters. It can be seen that there are many pixels of ring edge at the distance of 10 and 20 meters, which can be detected easily and accurately. The number of pixels of circle edge decreases with the increasing distance because the edge of circle is relatively vague, which can be eliminated by median filter algorithm, at the same time, diffraction rings will also be a corresponding reduction in the number. Running time of detecting center coordinates is mostly less than 100ms, which meets the requirements of quasi-real-time measurement. Shown from Fig.2, it can be found that the pixels of circles are discontinuous, but there almost have no influence on detection by running Gradient Hough Transform extraction algorithm. Based on statistical thinking, the algorithm can finds out the maximum extent possible center by same class assembling. At the same time, the effective pixels extracted at random need not be located at the same circle, so long as the results are given to precise positioning. Experimental data show that the quasi-real-time requirements can be acquired, measuring accuracy is also high, which is lower than 3 pixels of experimental measurement error.

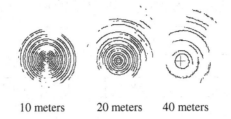

10 meters   20 meters   40 meters

Fig. 2. The results of edge detection and center calculation of different position

In order to test the validity of algorithm, this means can be adopted that averages results of repeated measuring same image replacing result of single measuring. Table 1 shows the center coordinates of ten consecutive measurements for above three images.

Table 1. The center coordinates of different position

Measuring	Coordinates(X_i, Y_i)		
times	10 meters	20 meters	40 meters
1	(161,114)	(144,137)	(159,130)
2	(161,116)	(145,139)	(157,134)
3	(162,115)	(144,139)	(159,133)
4	(161,116)	(144,138)	(158,132)
5	(162,115)	(146,140)	(160,133)
6	(161,116)	(145,137)	(158,129)
7	(161,114)	(145,140)	(160,135)
8	(162,114)	(144,139)	(157,130)
9	(160,115)	(145,139)	(159,113)
10	(162,115)	(144,138)	(157,133)
Average	(161.3,115.0)	(144.5,138.6)	(158.4,132.2)

Seen from that, the results prove that the algorithm is effective and accurate. The average value of 10 times of measurements is also given in Table 1. The following is standard deviation σ of X and Y calculated by Eq.(15).

$$\sigma = \sqrt{\frac{\sum_i^n v_i^2}{n-1}} \tag{15}$$

Where n is measuring times, V_i is standardized residual, Table 2. shows the results of standard deviation gained by calculating above 3 sets of data. It also illuminates that the Gradient Hough Transform algorithm is effective to apply to collimating measurement.

Table 2. The standard deviation of 10 times of results

Measuring distance	10 meters	20 meters	40 meters
σ_x	0.7	0.7	1.2
σ_y	0.8	1.1	1.9

In summary, the method of laser collimation based on Gradient Hough Transform can realize automation, digitization, and measurement of quasi-real-time, and eliminate the rough error which is brought out by human. The system can be applied to highly precise track measurements and fundamental collimating measurements. There have wide prospects.

References

1. Peng, Y.X., Xie, H.Y.: Detection Techniques for Center of Laser Beams. In: Proceeding of Measuring Instruments Conference of China, pp. 73–76 (2003)
2. Xu, L., Oja, E., Kultanen, P.: Randomized HoughTransform(RHT): Basic Mechanisms, Algorithms, and Computational Complexities. J. Computer Vision Graphics Image Process: Image Understanding 57(2), 131–154 (1993)
3. Ma, W.-J., Li, Q.-Q.: An Improved Method of Circle Detection Based on Randomized Hough Transform. Information Technology & Informatization, 128–130 (2006)
4. Yue, J., Xiang, X.-Z.: An improved algorithm of Hough circle detection. J. Applied Science and Technology, 74–76 (2006)
5. Xia, L., Cai, C., Zhou, C.P., Ding, M.Y.: New fast algorithm of Hough transform detection of circle. J. Application Research of Computers 24(10), 196–200 (2007)
6. Shu, Z.L., Qi, F.H.: A novel algorithm for fast circle detection using randomized Hough transform. J. Computer Engineering 29(6), 87–88 (2003)
7. Wang, J., Wang, X.T., Xu, X.G.: Fast circle detection using randomized Hough transform based on gradient. J. Application Research of Computers. 23(8), 1646–167 (2006)
8. Zhao, G.X., Huang, S.: An improved randomized Hough method of circle detection. J. Computer Technology and Development 18(4), 77–79 (2008)

A Fuzzy Background Modeling Approach for Motion Detection in Dynamic Backgrounds

Zhenjie Zhao[1], Thierry Bouwmans[2], Xuebo Zhang[1,*], and Yongchun Fang[1]

[1] Institute of Robotics and Automatic Information System,
Nankai University, China
[2] Laboratory of Mathematics, Images and Applications,
University of La Rochelle, France
thierry.bouwmans@univ-lr.fr,
{zhaozj,zhangxb,yfang}@robot.nankai.edu.cn

Abstract. Based on Type-2 Fuzzy Gaussian Mixture Model (T2-FGMM) and Markov Random Field (MRF), we propose a novel background modeling method for motion detection in dynamic scenes. The key idea of the proposed approach is the successful introduction of the spatial-temporal constraints into the T2-FGMM by a Bayesian framework. The evaluation results in pixel level demonstrate that the proposed method performs better than the sound Gaussian Mixture Model (GMM) and T2-FGMM in such typical dynamic backgrounds as waving trees and water rippling.

Keywords: T2-FGMM, MRF, motion detection, dynamic backgrounds.

1 Introduction

Motion detection is commonly utilized as a pre-processing step in such many computer vision tasks as object detection, recognition, tracking, etc. The aim of motion detection is to separate the foreground (FG) in which we are interested from the background (BG), where background subtraction is the most commonly utilized method, surveys in [1, 2, 3]. Among many background subtraction methods, the statistical method, especially Gaussian Mixture Model (GMM), which is originally proposed by Stauffer and Grimson [4], is the most famous and effective one. On the basis of GMM, the authors of [5] introduced some spatial-temporal constraints to enhance the performance of background subtraction. Although GMM works well in multimodal background, it cannot yield satisfactory solution for dynamic backgrounds. Based on this reason, an online auto-regressive model was proposed by Monnet *et al.* to deal with dynamic backgrounds [6]. Besides, inspired by biological vision, Mahadevan and Vasconcelos proposed a new method in [7] for highly dynamic scenes. More recently, El Baf *et al.* [8, 9] found that the T2-FGMM [10] presents good performance for dynamic scene modeling. Unfortunately, spatial-temporal constraints are not considered in these works.

---

* Corresponding author.

F.L. Wang et al. (Eds.): CMSP 2012, CCIS 346, pp. 177–185, 2012.

In this paper, we successfully introduce the spatial-temporal constraints into the T2-FGMM by the MRF framework to achieve superior modeling performance for dynamic backgrounds. Different to [5], this work can deal with dynamic scenes well since the fuzzy method is used. Firstly, the output of T2-FGMM is regarded as the initial labeling field of the MRF. Then, the local energy of the labeling field is elegantly combined with that of the observation by a Bayesian framework. The Iterated Conditional Modes (ICM) algorithm, due to its calculation efficiency, is employed to obtain the maximum a posterior probability (MAP). The contribution of this paper is that we successfully combine the spatial-temporal prior and the observation of the T2-FGMM to achieve satisfactory performance for dynamic backgrounds. The experiment results show that the designed method behaves better than GMM and T2-FGMM in such typical dynamic backgrounds as waving trees and water rippling.

The rest of the paper is organized as follows: state of the art and some recent works are reviewed briefly in Section 2. Section 3 is the basic principle of T2-FGMM. Section 4 gives the details of the designed background modeling approach. Experiment results are shown in Section 5, and the conclusion is provided in Section 6.

2   Related Works

The common approach for background subtraction is to give an appropriate background model, which aims to deal with the challenges such as illumination variant, dynamic backgrounds, camouflage, shadows, etc. Wren *et al.* [11] model the background as a single Gaussian in the system called "Pfinder", which aims to detect people indoors. But this method cannot handle the outdoor scenes well, since the distribution of gray-level value outdoors is multimodal. Stauffer and Grimson [4] model the background as a Gaussian Mixture Model, which can deal with the multimodal background well. But the update of GMM's parameters cannot accommodate with the rapidly changing scenes, such as sudden illumination changes, dynamic backgrounds, etc. Non-parametric methods are proposed in [12, 13], which are more flexible for the rapid variation of the background at the price of heavy computation. Compared with the model-based methods above, the data-based methods have lower computation complexity, and can handle part of the background challenges with the well-designed processes of initialization and update like Vibe [14]. The self-organizing approach for background subtraction proposed by Maddalena *et al.* [15] may be one of best methods for the moment, which learns background motion in a self-organizing manner through the technique of the neural network. Other recent works using fuzzy approaches can be found in [16].

3   Type-2 Fuzzy Gaussian Mixture Model

T2-FGMM [10] consisting of K components of multivariate Gaussian with an uncertain mean vector is described as: $p(x) = \sum_{k=1}^{K} \omega_k \eta(x; \mu_k, \Sigma_k)$, where ω_k denotes the weight of the k-th Gaussian satisfying $\sum_{k=1}^{K}\omega_k = 1$ and $\omega_k > 0 (k=1,\cdots,K)$, and

the Gaussian distribution η is: $\eta(x;\mu_k,\Sigma_k) = \dfrac{1}{\sqrt{(2\pi)^d \Sigma_k}}\prod_{m=1}^{d}\exp[-\dfrac{1}{2}(\dfrac{x_m - \mu_{k,m}}{\sigma_k})^2]$,

where $\mu_{k,1} \in [\underline{\mu_{k,1}},\overline{\mu_{k,1}}],\cdots,\mu_{k,d} \in [\underline{\mu_{k,d}},\overline{\mu_{k,d}}]$, x presents the d-dimensional observation vector, μ_k is the uncertain mean vector, and the diagonal covariance matrix is denoted as: $\Sigma_k = diag\{\underbrace{\sigma_k,\cdots,\sigma_k}_{d}\}$ for simplicity. Each exponential component is the

Gaussian primary membership function (MF), whose uncertainty is described by the secondary MF defined as an uniform distribution. The distance of the upper and the lower primary MF denotes the uncertainty of the observation x. As the uncertain mean can handle dynamic backgrounds better than the uncertain variance [8, 9], we will only use the uncertain mean in this paper.

4   Improved T2-FGMM by MRF

T2-FGMM does not consider the spatial-temporal constraints and its performance needs be improved for dynamic scenes. Meanwhile, MRF gives a framework to add the prior to the observation in computer vision [17]. Based on this observation, we fuse them together to form a fuzzy background modeling approach for motion detection in dynamic scenes. This section provides the details of the proposed method.

4.1   Model Maintenance

The model maintenance is made like the original GMM [4] with the learning rate α. For each frame, a new observation x in a pixel position is used to match and update the background model. The match process will be introduced in 4.2. For the case an observation x matches one of the K Gaussians, the parameters are updated as:

$$\omega_{k,t+1} = (1-\alpha)\omega_{k,t} + \alpha,$$

$$\mu_{k,m,t+1} = (1-\rho)\mu_{k,m,t} + \rho x_{m,t+1},$$

$$\sigma_{k,m,t+1}^2 = (1-\rho)\sigma_{k,m,t}^2 + \rho(x_{m,t+1} - \mu_{k,m,t+1})^2,$$

and $\rho = \alpha\eta(x;\mu_k,\Sigma_k)$. If no match is found with any of the K Gaussians, then the least probable Gaussian is replaced with a new one, and the parameters are: $\omega_{k,t+1}$ = low prior weight, $\mu_{k,t+1} = x_{t+1}$, Σ_k = large initial varaince.

4.2   Foreground Detection

Firstly, the Gaussians are ordered decreasingly by the ratio ω_k/σ_k. Then we define c_f as the maximum portion of x that belongs to FG, similar as [18]. And the first B

Gaussians whose total weight exceeds $1-c_f$ will be viewed as a background distribution: $B = \arg\min_b (\sum_{k=1}^b \omega_k > (1-c_f))$. A match test is made by the distance between two bounds of the primary MF's log-likelihood interval for each pixel: $H(\mathrm{x}_{m,t}) = |\ln(\underline{h}(\mathrm{x}_{m,t})) - \ln(\overline{h}(\mathrm{x}_{m,t}))|$, where $\underline{h}(\mathrm{x}_{m,t})$ is the lower MF and $\overline{h}(\mathrm{x}_{m,t})$ is the upper MF. For the case of the uncertain mean, we have:

$$H(x_{m,t}) = \begin{cases} \dfrac{2\xi |x_{m,t} - \mu_{k,m}|}{\sigma}, \text{if } x_{m,t} \leq \underline{\mu_{k,m}} \text{ or } x_t \geq \overline{\mu_{k,m}} \\ \dfrac{|x_{m,t} - \mu_{k,m}|}{2\sigma_k^2} + \dfrac{\xi |x_{m,t} - \mu_{k,m}|}{\sigma_k} + \dfrac{\xi^2}{2}, \text{otherwise} \end{cases}, \tag{1}$$

where ξ is an arbitrary constant, which controls the interval between $\underline{\mu_{k,m}}$ and $\overline{\mu_{k,m}}$: $\underline{\mu_{k,m}} = \mu_{k,m} - \xi\sigma_k$, $\overline{\mu_{k,m}} = \mu_{k,m} + \xi\sigma_k$, $\xi \in [0,3]$, and $x_{m,t}$ is the observation at time t, channel m. The classification will be made by: $\sqrt{\sum_{m=1}^d H(x_{m,t})} < \varsigma\sigma_k$, where ς is a constant threshold determined experimentally. If the previous condition is satisfied, then x_t match the Gaussian. If no match is found for all K Gaussians, then x_t is labeled as FG. In the case that a match is found, if it happens in the top B Gaussians, then x_t is labeled as BG, otherwise x_t will still be labeled as FG. After all the match test for every pixel, we get the initial labeling field as l_0.

4.3   Labeling Field Optimization

The initial labeling field is usually not optimal, and it can be possibly improved with the spatial-temporal constraints. Based on this idea, we utilize MRF model to further optimize the labeling field.

Spatial and Temporal Prior Determination

The set of sites and labels are: $S = \{1, 2, \cdots, p \times q\}, L = \{0,1\}$, where p, q denote the number of the image's row and column, respectively. In the set L, 0 denotes the background, and 1 denotes the foreground.

For the spatial neighborhood system, let the neighbors of pixel i consists of 8 nearest pixels, with the specific definition as: $N_i = \{j \mid 0 < dist(pixel_i, pixel_j) < 2\}$, where $dist(pixel_i, pixel_j)$ is the pixel distance between i and j. And the spatial energy function of i is defined as:

$$U_s(i) = \sum_{j \in N_i} V_s(i, j), \text{ where } V_s(i, j) = \begin{cases} -\beta, \text{ if } l_j = l_i \\ \beta, \text{ if } l_j = l_i \end{cases}. \tag{2}$$

Similar as the spatial neighborhood system, the temporal neighborhood system at time $t+1$ is set as follows: $\Omega_i = \{ j_t \mid 0 < dist(pixel_{i_t}, pixel_{j_t}) < 2 \}$, and the temporal energy function is chosen as:

$$U_e(i) = \sum_{j \in \Omega_i} V_e(i, j), \text{ where } V_e(i, j) = \begin{cases} -\beta', \text{ if } l'_j = l^{t+1}_i \\ \beta', \text{ if } l'_j \neq l^{t+1}_i \end{cases}. \tag{3}$$

Therefore, the total prior energy can be calculated as:

$$U(l) = U_e(l) + U_s(l) = \sum_i U_e(i) + \sum_i U_s(i). \tag{4}$$

According to the Hammersley-Clifford theorem, the prior distribution $P(l)$ is a Gibbs distribution [17]: $P(l) = \dfrac{1}{Z} \times \exp(-\dfrac{U(l)}{T})$, where Z is a positive constant for normalization, and T denotes the temperature constant.

Likelihood Function Calculation

Though the background obeys the distribution of GMM, we adopt the most probable Gaussian for simplicity: $p(x_t \mid 0) = \dfrac{1}{\sqrt{(2\pi)^d \Sigma_k}} \prod_{m=1}^{d} \exp[-\dfrac{1}{2}(\dfrac{x_{m,t} - \mu_{k,m,t}}{\sigma_{k,t}})^2]$. It is reasonable to adopt a single Gaussian because x is most likely to be unimodal at any time t, and GMM can handle multimodal background at a long time. The foreground distribution is also adopted as a Gaussian. It has the same variance with the background but a different mean, which guarantees the foreground is totally different from the background: $p(x_t \mid 1) = \dfrac{1}{\sqrt{(2\pi)^d \Sigma_k}} \prod_{m=1}^{d} \exp[-\dfrac{1}{2}(\dfrac{x_{m,t} - \mu'_{k,m,t}}{\sigma_{k,t}})^2]$. The relationship of $\mu_{k,m,t}$ and $\mu'_{k,m,t}$ is: $\mid \mu_{k,m,t} - \mu'_{k,m,t} \mid = 2.5\sigma_{k,t}$.

Posterior Probability Maxmization

Given the observation filed $X = \{x_1, x_2, \cdots, x_{p \times q}\}$ and the spatial-temporal prior, our work now is to maximize the posterior probability and obtain a better labeling field:

$$l^* = \arg\max p(X \mid l)P(l), \tag{5}$$

Where $P(l)$ is the Gibbs distribution, and $p(X \mid l)$ is the likelihood function we have just explained.

We adopt the ICM method to optimize l^*. Although ICM cannot guarantee the solution of global maximum, it is highly efficient and yields satisfactory results. The process for each frame is described as follows:

1. Use the T2-FGMM's output as the initial labeling field, and 0 for background, 1 for foreground;

2. Add the spatial and temporal prior to each pixel, and calculate the local energy of each pixel by combining the prior and the likelihood;
3. Compute the global energy, and if the increment is small than a threshold (set 10), stop to get the final labeling field, otherwise, go to 2 to continue.

5   Experiment Results

Two typical dynamic backgrounds, waving trees and water rippling from the new dataset [19], are used to evaluate the effectiveness of the proposed method in comparison with GMM and T2-FGMM. The parameters of the algorithms are shown in Table. 1 (the parameters for GMM and T2-FGMM are from the works [4], [8, 9]).

Table 1. Parameters of GMM, T2-FGMM and our method

	K	α	c_f	ξ	ς	β	β'
GMM	3	0.001	0.25	--	--	--	--
T2-FGMM	3	0.001	0.25	2	2.5	--	--
Our method	3	0.001	0.25	2	2.5	0.9	2.8

To evaluate the methods in pixel level, false positive (FP), false negative (FN), true positive (TP), true negative (TN) are used. P denotes the background, and N denotes the foreground. T presents the judgment of correct classification, and F presents the judgment of wrong classification. Statistical metrics give an overall performance in a much fairer way in dynamic backgrounds. False positive rate (FPR), Percentage of Bad Classification (PBC), F-measure are given as follows:

$$\text{FPR} = \frac{\text{FP}}{\text{FP+TN}}, \text{PBC} = 100 \times \frac{\text{FN+FP}}{\text{FN+FP+TN+TP}}$$
$$\text{recall} = \frac{\text{TP}}{\text{TP+FN}}, \text{precision} = \frac{\text{TP}}{\text{TP+FP}}, F = 2 \times \frac{\text{recall} \times \text{precision}}{\text{recall} + \text{precision}}. \tag{6}$$

5.1   Waving Trees

We use the "overpass" sequence to test the waving trees situation. Fig. 1 shows the input images, ground truth and the output of GMM, T2-FGMM and the proposed approach. The evaluation of these three approaches in pixel level is shown Table. 2 and Fig. 3. The results show that our method can restrain the dynamic background better than GMM and T2-FGMM. At the same time, the overall performance is better than GMM and T2-FGMM as well.

Table 2. The statistical results of GMM, T2-FGMM and the proposed method

	FPR	PBC	F-measure
GMM	0.751	11.387%	0.937
T2-FGMM	0.039	2.251%	0.988
Our method	0.034	1.510%	**0.992**

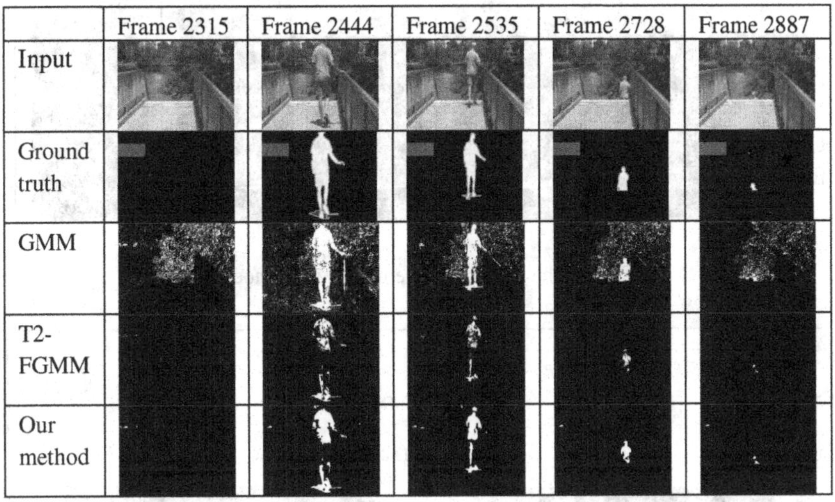

Fig. 1. The representative result of "overpass", the 1st row is the input frames, the 2nd row is the ground truth, the 3rd row is the GMM's output, the 4th row is the T2-FGMM's output, the 5th row is our method's output

5.2   Water Rippling

We use the "canoe" sequence to test the water rippling situation. Fig. 2, Fig. 3 and Table. 3 are the experimental results. Similar to the waving trees situation, our method can perform better than GMM and T2FGMM in both local and overall evaluations.

Table 3. The statistical results of GMM, T2-FGMM and the proposed method

	FPR	PBC	F-measure
GMM	0.905	33.219%	0.792
T2-FGMM	0.044	2.968%	0.985
Our method	0.032	2.397%	**0.988**

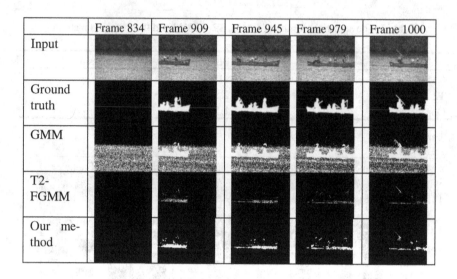

Fig. 2. The representative results of "canoe"

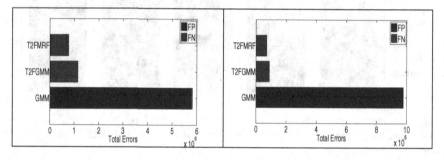

Fig. 3. The 1st column is the total errors of the sequence "overpass", 2nd column is the total errors of the sequence "canoe"

6   Conclusion

We have developed a new method for motion detection in dynamic backgrounds based on T2-FGMM and MRF. The proposed method achieves superior performance than GMM and T2-FGMM, and it is different to other approaches based on Bayesian method since the fuzzy model is used, which aims to handle the problem of dynamic backgrounds. Furthermore, the proposed method can be extended to detect shadow easily. The future work is to develop a more effective likelihood function of the background and the foreground to make the method more robust.

Acknowledgments. This work is supported in part by Specialized Research Fund for the Doctoral Program of Higher Education of China under Grant (20090031110035), National Natural Science Foundation of China (61203333), and the Fundamental Research Funds for the Central Universities.

References

1. Radke, R.J., Andra, S., Al-Kofahi, O., Roysam, B.: Image change detection algorithms: a systematic survey. IEEE Transactions on Image Processing 14(3), 294–307 (2005)
2. Piccardi, M.: Background subtraction techniques: a review. In: IEEE International Conference on Systems, Man and Cybernetics, vol. 4, pp. 3099–3104 (2004)
3. Brutzer, S., Hoferlin, B., Heideman, G.: Evaluation of background subtraction techniques for video surveillance. In: CVPR 2011, pp. 1937–1944 (2011)
4. Stauffer, C., Grimson, W.: Adaptive background mixture models for real-time tracking. In: IEEE CVPR 1999 (1999)
5. Zhou, Y., Xu, W., Tao, H., Gong, Y.: Background segmentation using spatial-temporal multi-resolution MRF. In: IEEE Workshops on Application of Computer Vision, vol. 1, pp. 8–13 (2005)
6. Monnet, A., Mittal, A., Paragios, N., Ramesh, V.: Background modeling and subtraction of dynamic scenes. In: CVPR 2003, vol. 2, pp. 1305–1312 (2003)
7. Mahadevan, V., Vansconcelos, N.: Background subtraction in highly dynamic scenes. In: CVPR 2008, pp. 1–6 (2008)
8. El Baf, F., Bouwmans, T., Vachon, B.: Type-2 Fuzzy Mixture of Gaussians Model: Application to Background Modeling. In: Bebis, G., Boyle, R., Parvin, B., Koracin, D., Remagnino, P., Porikli, F., Peters, J., Klosowski, J., Arns, L., Chun, Y.K., Rhyne, T.-M., Monroe, L. (eds.) ISVC 2008, Part I. LNCS, vol. 5358, pp. 772–781. Springer, Heidelberg (2008)
9. El Baf, F.,Bouwmans, T., Vachon, B.: Fuzzy Statistical Modeling of Dynamic Backgrounds for Moving Object Detection in Infrared Videos. In: IEEE CVPR Workshops, pp. 60–65 (2009)
10. Zeng, J., Xie, L., Liu, Z.: Type-2 fuzzy Gaussian mixture models. Pattern Recognition 41(12), 3636–3643 (2008)
11. Wren, C., Azarbayejani, A., Darrell, T., Pentland, A.: Pfinder: Real-time tracking of the human body. PAMI 19(7), 780–785 (1997)
12. Kim, K., Chalidabhongse, T.H., Harwood, D., Davis, L.S.: Real-time foreground-background segmentation using codebook Model. Real-Time Image 11, 172–185 (2005)
13. Elgammal, A., Harwood, D., Davis, L.: Non-parametric Model for Background Subtraction. In: Vernon, D. (ed.) ECCV 2000. LNCS, vol. 1843, pp. 751–767. Springer, Heidelberg (2000)
14. Barnich, O., Van Droogenbroeck, M.: ViBe: A Universal Background Subtraction Algorithm for Video Sequences. Image Processing 20(6), 1709–1724 (2011)
15. Maddalena, L., Petrosino, A.: The SOBS Algorithm: What Are the Limits? In: IEEE Workshop on Change Detection, CVPR 2012 (2012)
16. Bouwmans, T.: Background Subtraction for Visual Surveillance: A Fuzzy Approach. In: Bouwmans, T. (ed.) Handbook on Soft Computing for Video Surveillance, ch. 5. Taylor and Francis Group (2012)
17. Li, S.: Markov Random Field Models in Computer Vision. In: Eklundh, J.-O. (ed.) ECCV 1994. LNCS, vol. 801, pp. 361–370. Springer, Heidelberg (1994)
18. Zivkovic, Z.: Improved Adaptive Gaussian Mixture Model for Background Subtraction. In: International Conference on Pattern Recognition, vol. 2, pp. 28–31 (2004)
19. IEEE CVPR 2012 Workshops on Change Detection (2012),
   http://www.changedetection.net

A Multi-view Fuzzy Matching Strategy
with Multi-planar Homography

Jie Shao[1] and Nan Dong[2]

[1] Shanghai University of Electric Power,
Department of Computer and Information Engineering, Shanghai 200090
[2] Chinese Academy of Sciences,
Shanghai Advanced Research Institute, Shanghai 201203

Abstract. Occlusions and incorrect detection make it very difficult to combine information from all views correctly in multi-view surveillance. As a result, we proposed a fuzzy matching strategy using a multi-planar homography constraint. Different from conventional methods which determine relationships of blobs based on their locations on the ground plane corresponding to the feet of the people, our method employs a statistical strategy. First, we divide each target into several parts, and project them onto different planes in the space. Then overlapped parts in different planes will be recorded. The optimal pairs appear based on a voting strategy. Experimental results are shown in scenes from different view points and light conditions. The algorithm is able to accurately match target blobs in all views. It is ideally suitable for conditions with not enough features.

Keywords: multi-view, fuzzy strategy, multi-planar homography.

1 Introduction

Multi-view collaborative sensing is one of the most challenging tasks in intelligent video sensing. It is implemented based on single view target detection and multi-view target matching. Multi-view target matching is one of the research directions of digital image registration, and also the pre-processing stage of digital image mosaic and 3D reconstruction. In the area of multiple targets sensing, a detected blob is no longer guaranteed to be a single person, but may belong to several people. Even worse, a person might be completely occluded by other people. As a result, with the help of target matching, we could mix data from different view points together, to enrich our information, and get more accurate results. As the example of a multiple pedestrian tracking system mentioned in [1], a multiple blob tracker is employed and the position of head is used to locate each pedestrian. Its performance decreases when targets are close to each other and occluded. However, if targets are tracked in cameras of different positions contemporarily, detection and tracking accuracy will be efficiently increased [2].

Different from static image registration methods, the results of multi-view target motion matching do not only rely on static feature matching, but their spatio-temporal

F.L. Wang et al. (Eds.): CMSP 2012, CCIS 346, pp. 186–193, 2012.

motion features in most of the cases. For example, in [3], they applied planar homography to project blobs of each view images onto the ground plane, and then particle filtering works in the 3D space. This kind of conventional methods is based on the assumption that feet of all the pedestrians are on the ground all the time. It is not real in some situations, like the moments of jumping, running and so on. Besides, as the area of feet is very small in most of the images, a foreground blob may not have accurate feet area after target detection, or a blob could be bigger or smaller than its real size. Arsic D.[4] proposed an idea of multi-Layer homography for a more precise 3D reconstruction of the scenery. Khan and Shah [5,6] proposed their multi-view image association method from a novel point. One of the views is set as the reference view, and then the foreground likelihood maps from all the other views are warped on to the reference view to produce a 'synergy map', which is used to obtain pixels that represent ground plane locations of people in the scene. It effectively decreases computational costs in 3D tracking but does not increase matching accuracy. In addition to these achievements, Javed et al. [2] obtain relationships between objects based on FOV of different cameras.

In most existing cases, methods based on planar homography are not reliable, so they are often followed by modification approaches based on color distribution or key points matching. Cai et al. [7] selected N points belonging to the medial axis of the upper body as the feature for tracking, and then tracked based on geometric parameters like position and velocity. Delamarre et al. [8] used only contours of the silhouettes of the person to form its 3D geometric model. With the help of the extension of Annealed Particle Filtering, Deutscher et al. [9] tracked complex human movements without the use of extra constraints such as labeled markers, pose assumptions, restricted movement or color coding. Besides, in [10], kernel color histogram based mean shift method is used in multiple camera tracking. But color histogram is unstable in the condition of light variation, and it is also not suitable for blobs with small size.

Based on the above considerations, if we make full use of spatio-temporal information composed of all views, not only modification process like feature matching could be largely simplified or even be omitted, but the performance of the whole matching method could also be improved. Borrowed the idea of multi-planar homography from [4], and associated it with multi-part color histogram confidence mentioned in [11], we proposed a multi-part fuzzy matching method based on multi-planar homography in this paper. It is cooperated with a voting strategy to obtain the final result. The method is composed of three steps: 1. foreground blob modeling; 2. multi-part fuzzy projection; 3. voting strategy.

2   Foreground Blob Modeling

After our pixel-based background subtraction, blob analysis is performed on the background-subtracted images based on morphological operators to connect clustered pixels and remove isolated noise like ``salt \& pepper'' noise and diminutive clusters of pixels. The details of the process are presented in [12].

3   Multi-part Fuzzy Projection

Assuming that the homogeneous coordinates of point p in world coordinate system are $(X_W, Y_W, Z_W, 1)$, its corresponding image coordinates are (u, v) when the camera coordinates are (X_C, Y_C, Z_C). According to equ. (1), if (u, v) are known, we could project p onto the space plane with fixed Z_W [13].

$$Z_C \begin{bmatrix} u \\ v \\ 1 \end{bmatrix} = K \begin{bmatrix} R & t \end{bmatrix} \begin{bmatrix} X_W \\ Y_W \\ Z_W \\ 1 \end{bmatrix} \tag{1}$$

R is a orthogonal identity matrix with the size of 3×3. It is a rotation parameter. t is a translation parameter. Both R and t is decided by the world coordinates of the camera. Matrix K is a intrinsic parameter of the camera.

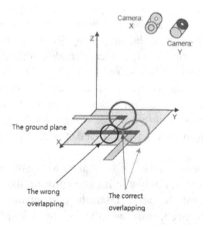

Fig. 1. Sketch map of multi-view ground plane warping

In order to decrease the computational costs, a rectangle is used to represent each foreground blob. In that case, warping a foreground blob onto a space plane has become the process of computing corresponding values of (X_W, Y_W) with the coordinate input of rectangle corners. On the ground plane, $Z_W = 0$. After warping, a rectangle will become an irregular quadrilateral on the plane. Based on the conventional assumption that feet area are always on the ground, the irregular quadrilateral areas belonging to the same target are sure to overlap, and the overlapping area on the ground plane is related to warped feet area, shown in Fig.1. Camera X and camera Y are two different views, and there are four irregular quadrilaterals on the ground plane. The two yellow ones are warped foreground blobs from the image captured by camera X, and the other two green ones are warped foreground blobs from the image captured by camera Y. As the sketch map shown in Fig.1, there are three overlapping areas. Two of them painted in red are warped feet areas, but the other one is not, which means the overlapped two blobs are not belonging to the same target.

There may be two reasons for the problem: 1. inaccurate feet areas, which means there may be differences between the target area and its detected foreground blob. And feet areas may not be on the ground at that moment. 2. There is more than one target in the scene, and the warped foreground blobs are extended to large quadrilaterals, so that different areas of the quadrilaterals are possible to overlap, like the wrong overlapping in Fig.1.

A multi-part fuzzy projection method is proposed to decrease the above errors. The method is shown in Fig.2.

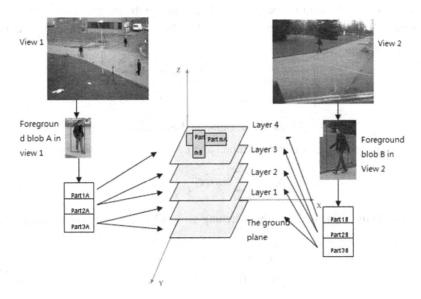

Fig. 2. multi-part fuzzy projection

There are images of two views at the same frame in Fig.2. Foreground blobs of the same person are picked up from two images respectively, and they are called blob A and blob B. When a person stand on the ground, its feet are on the ground plane with $Z_W = 0$. And when Z_W changes, the planes in the 3D space will always have a cross section with the body of the person until Z_W is bigger than the height of the person Z_{height}. From the bottom to the top, the cross section of the body belongs to its feet, legs, the upper body and the head respectively. The key idea of multi-part fuzzy projection is that when the value of Z_W is bigger than 0 and smaller than Z_{height}, and if we project foreground blobs onto planes of different Z_W, all the projection areas of the same target will overlap, and the overlapping area is corresponding to the body of the height Z_W. As a result, a foreground blob is equally divided into three parts, called part 1 to part 3 from top to bottom. The space from 0 to Z_{height} is also equally divided into 5 sub-spaces. As a result, there are 6 boundary planes, called the ground plane, layer 1 to layer 4, and the top layer from bottom to top. Except the top layer whose Z_W is Z_{height}, there are 5 planes left. As the pointing directions of the arrows shown in Fig.2, part 1 of the blob is projected onto layer 4, part 2 is projected onto layer 3 and layer 2, and part 3 is projected onto layer 1 and the ground plane.

4   Voting Strategy

In the previous section, all the parts of the foreground blobs are projected onto different planes. Assuming i and j are two warped blobs on the plane n, $Score_{i,j}^n$ is the state of overlapping between i and j.

$$\begin{cases} Score_{i,j}^n = 1 & i \cap j \neq 0 \\ Score_{i,j}^n = 0 & i \cap j = 0 \end{cases} \tag{2}$$

The $Score_{i,j}^n$ of all the planes are accumulated according to equ. (3), where $S_{i,j}$ shows the relationship between projection i and j.

$$S_{i,j} = \sum_{n=0}^{5} score_{i,j}^n \tag{3}$$

According to the value of $S_{i,j}$, the matching probability $p_{i,j}$ between i and j is set below:

$$\begin{cases} p_{i,j} = 1 & S_{i,j} \geq Thr \\ p_{i,j} = 0 & S_{i,j} < Thr \end{cases} \tag{4}$$

Thr is the threshold of the matching probability.

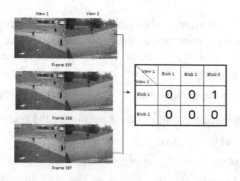

Fig. 3. Voting result

Taking Fig.3 as an example, there are images of frame 395, 396 and 397 from two different views. Images in the left column are from view 1 and the images in the right column are from view 2. There are 3 people in the left images in this three consecutive frames, and 2 targets (1 person and 1 car) in the right images.

The values of $p_{i,j}$ are shown in the right table. Targets in the images are labeled with different red numbers in the center. From left to right the blobs are labeled 3, 1, and 2 in view 1. In view 2, the person is labeled 1 and the car is labeled 2. As the final statistical table shown in the right of the images, there is only one "1", which means only blob 3 in view 1 is matched with blob 1 in view 2.

Fig. 4. Matching result

The proposed method could effectively modify the detection errors caused by occlusions. In Fig. 4, there are 3 people in the middle of the right image occluded by each other. There are also three blobs in the left image. The final matching result based on the proposed method is shown in table 1. Blob 1, 2, and 3 in the left image are all corresponding to blob 3 in the right image.

Table 1. Voting Result

Image A \ Image B	Blob 1	Blob 3	Blob 4
Blob 1	0	1	0
Blob 2	0	1	0
Blob 3	0	1	0

5   Experimental Result and Analysis

The proposed method is implemented on standard PC hardware (2 Quad CPU at 2.66GHz) with C language in the environment of Visual Studio 2005. It is one step of multi-view pedestrian surveillance system. The detection results are from GMMs based background subtraction method, and the tracking step after target matching is implemented by parallel particle filtering. The whole system runs with the speed of 5 fps without program optimization. All the experimental videos are from dataset of PETS 2009. The positions of 8 fixed cameras are shown in the left image of Fig. 5, and the scene is at a crossroad of the campus. From the map of the exhibition we could find that cameras 2, 5, 6, 7, 8 are near the area of interest, while the other 3 cameras are far away.

Fig. 5. Experimental environment and results

We take images from camera 1 and camera 7 as examples. Matching results based on the proposed method is shown in the right two images of Fig.5. The top two images and the bottom two images are from two different frames, and the left images are from camera 1 and the right images are from camera 7. Targets in the rectangles of the same color are the recognized as the same person. There are light variation and great changes of target size in two different views, but our method has shown to be effective.

However, there are still some errors can't be resolved by our method. Like two pedestrians walking shoulder by shoulder in the right side of Fig. 4 (a), as they are captured only by one camera, the merging blob can't be split due to lack of information. In other situations, if only part of the target is detected, or one target is split into several foreground blobs, correct matching could not be obtained as well. As a result, in the above situations, feature matching is needed in post processing.

6   Conclusion

A multi-planar homography based multi-view fuzzy matching method is proposed in this paper. Foreground blobs in different views belonging to the same target are classified and grouped. The matching result is applicable for the following process like target tracking and behavior analysis in multi-view target surveillance. Different from conventional methods which determine locations on the ground plane according to the feet of the people, we present a novel multi-planar homography constraint, and apply a multi-part fuzzy warping strategy, so that different parts of foreground blobs are warped onto different planes in a fuzzy logic. Experimental results show that our method is more robust and effective in real applications when there are inaccurate detection results.

References

1. Zhong, F., Qin, X., Chen, J., Hua, W., Peng, Q.: Confidence-Based Color Modeling for Online Video Segmentation. In: Zha, H., Taniguchi, R.-i., Maybank, S. (eds.) ACCV 2009, Part II. LNCS, vol. 5995, pp. 697–706. Springer, Heidelberg (2010)
2. Javed, O., Rasheed, Z., Alatas, O., et al.: Knight: a real-time surveillance system for multiple overlapping and on-overlapping cameras. In: Proceedings of the IEEE International Conference on Multimedia and Expo, vol. 1, pp. 6–9 (2003)
3. Du, W., Piater, J.: Multi-camera People Tracking by Collaborative Particle Filters and Principal Axis-Based Integration. In: Yagi, Y., Kang, S.B., Kweon, I.S., Zha, H. (eds.) ACCV 2007, Part I. LNCS, vol. 4843, pp. 365–374. Springer, Heidelberg (2007)
4. Arsic, D., Hristov, E., Lehment, N., Hornler, B., Schuller, B., Rigoll, G.: Applying Multi-Layer Homography for Multi-camera Person Tracking. In: Second ACM/IEEE International Conference on Distributed Smart Cameras, pp. 1–9 (2008)
5. Khan, S.M., Shah, M.: Tracking Multiple Occluding People by Localizing on Multiple Scene Planes. PAMI 31(3), 505–519 (2009)
6. Khan, S.M., Shah, M.: A Multiview Approach to Tracking People in Crowded Scenes Using a Planar Homography Constraint. In: Leonardis, A., Bischof, H., Pinz, A. (eds.) ECCV 2006. LNCS, vol. 3954, pp. 133–146. Springer, Heidelberg (2006)
7. Cai, Q., Aggarwal, J.: Tracking human motion using multiple cameras. In: Proceedings of the International Conference on Pattern Recognition, Vienna, Austria, pp. 68–72 (1996)
8. Delamarre, Q., Faugeras, O.: 3D articulated models and multi-view tracking with physical forces. Computer Vision and Image Understanding 81, 328–357 (2001)
9. Deutscher, J., Davision, A., Reid, I.: Automatic partitioning of high dimensional search spaces associated with articulated body motin capture. In: Proceedings of the IEEE Conference on Computer Vison and Pattern Recognition, Kauai, Hawaii, vol. 2, pp. 669–676 (2001)
10. Taj, M., Cavallaro, A.: Multi-camera track-before-detect. In: Proc. of ACM/IEEE Int. Conf. on Distributed Smart Cameras (ICDSC 2009), Como, IT, pp. 1–6 (2009)
11. Shao, J., Dong, N., Liu, F., Li, Z.: A close-loop tracking approach for multi-view pedestrian tracking. Journal of Computational Information Systems 7(2), 539–547
12. Shao, J., Dong, N., Liu, F., Li, Z.: A close-loop tracking approach for multi-view pedestrian tracking. Journal of Computational Information Systems 7(2), 539–547
13. Zhang, Z.: A Flexible New Technique for Cmera Calibration. IEEE Transactions on Pattern Analysis and Machine Intelligence 22(1), 1330–1334 (2002)

Research on Displacement Parameters Measurement Based on Binocular Vision and Image Processing Technology

En-xiang Du[1], Wei Wang[1], Fu-quan Zhao[1], and Jingjing Ren[2]

[1] Department of Arm's Engineering, Academy of Armored Force Engineering,
Beijing 100072, China
[2] LangFang Advanced Technical School, Langfang Hebei, China, 065000

Abstract. According to the demand of related performance test of the weapon system, the displacement parameters measurement based on binocular vision and image processing technology and the corresponding solution design has been put forward, the displacement parameter test of muzzle under the complex environment has been solved.

Keywords: binocular vision   image processing   displacement parameter.

1   Forward

Displacement parameters measurement of the muzzle is always a big problem in artillery test. The reason is that strong vibration impact, cigarette, flame and shock wave exists in the muzzle in lunch process. So conventional techniques are always difficult to work. In order to carry on measurement, sometimes, some additional devices used to be installed in the muzzle, thus the structure of the barrel may be changed and the true motion state of the muzzle may be influenced. According to the demand of related performance test of the weapon system, the displacement parameters measurement based on binocular vision and image processing technology and the corresponding solution design has been put forward in this text.

2   The Solution Design on Displacement Parameters Measurement Based on Binocular Vision and Image Processing Technology

2.1   The Principle of Displacement Parameters Measurement Based on Binocular Vision and Image Processing Technology

The displacement parameter measurement system based on binocular vision and image processing technology is composed of light source of muzzle, two high-speed cameras and signal processor, as Fig. 1 shows. The light source is fixed to the barrel, so it moves with the barrel, which is the checkpoint of muzzle motion.

F.L. Wang et al. (Eds.): CMSP 2012, CCIS 346, pp. 194–199, 2012.

The high-speed camera1 is installed on the left of the muzzle, from which the motion trail of light source up and down and back and forth direction can be get. And the high-speed camera2 is installed under the muzzle with getting the light source left and right and before and after direction. The image data of high speed camera1 and camera2 will be processed in the signal processor to get the 3D motion trail of light source from different direction.

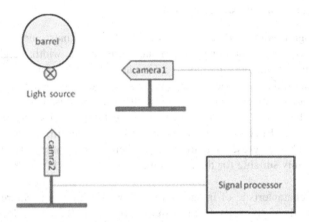

Fig. 1. The principle of displacement parameters measurement based on binocular vision and image processing technology

2.2   Image Processing Technology on Displacement Parameters Measurement

The digital image detection based on computer vision is the brand-new technology in the measuring field in recent years. It is a comprehensive measuring system based on optics, which involve optoelectronics, computer technology, laser technology, image processing technology, etc. The measurement method based on image sensor is non-contact, high-speed and the dynamic range is large and it has a enriched amount of information, etc. And it is convenient to connect with computer, so that it is very easy to process the image data. Thus the image sensor is used widely in non-contacting measuring field.

2.3   The Algorithm on Displacement Parameters Measurement

The light source detection, light source outline detection, motion trail of light source measuring, binocular vision image information fusion and non-contacting measuring is involved in the measure algorithm.

(a) The detection of light source

The image histogram is a kind of very important and practical tool in image processing, in which the grey level of image is summarized. It is the function of statistics features of grey level and the value of grey level in mathematics, in which the frequency or probability of each grey level in the one image histogram is counted. The grey level value distribution of the image is offered in the histogram. In the coordinates of the grey level histogram, the abscissa means the grey level of each image pixel and the vertical coordinate means the frequency or probability of image pixel in different grey level. Thus the image histogram can be adopted in the light source detection.

(b) The detection of light source outline

The shape-recognition method can be summed up for two kinds: one is a kind of discernment based on object border which include girth, angle, width, height, diameter, etc. Its description method includes chain-yard, B-spline function, FDs, auto-regression model (AR) and Hough-vary etc. Among them FDs is one of widely used features. The other method that is a kind of discernment based on object coverage areas which include area, roundness and moment features, etc. Its description method includes Run-length Encoding, Quad-tree and Moment Descriptor etc. The moment features is one of widely used features among them. Above-mentioned two kinds of methods are mainly suitable for the discernment of the closed boundary or the region of a plane.

The overall characteristic of image can be showed in moment features, which offers different kinds of geometry features information. And 0-3 orders features of moment can describe the overall characteristic of image, and the high-order moment includes more meticulous detail but is relatively sensitive to the noise. The moment features has very important application in the image analyzing and discernment. Any image can be regarded as a two-dimensional probability density function f (x, y), the general definition of its moment Φpq is as follows:

$$\Phi_{pq} = \iint_{\xi} \psi_{pq}(x, y) f(x, y) dx dy, \qquad p, q = 0, 1, 2, 3 \cdots \qquad (1)$$

ζ is the domain of $f(x, y)$, $\psi_{pq}(x, y)$ is moment weight function, it is continuously.

In polar coordinates (r, θ)

$$\Phi_{pq} = \iint_{\xi} r^{p+q+1} \psi_{pq}(\theta) f(r, \theta) dr d\theta, \qquad p, q = 0, 1, 2, 3 \cdots \qquad (2)$$

The improved algorithms based on the border of region to calculate moment invariants can be applied in the border of the close areas which is not overlapped. But in practical application, overlap and cross in the structure is unavoidable and the method of chain-yard to show the structure is often difficult. In addition, in order to unite structure moment and regional moment, a new moment feature that is suitable to region, closed and unclosed areas has been proposed, which is defined relative moment and used in shape-recognition. And the discrete calculating methods of relative moment have been proposed.

The formation of image of light source in muzzle is a dot and the outline features of light source can be obtained by adopting the moment features and dots measurement algorithms to realize. The image measurement can be used to measure roundness errors in the dot measurement algorithms. Thus the homogeneity that the energy of laser faculae distributed can be appraised. The border of laser faculae can be drawn out by image pretreatment, and then the biggest inscribed circle and minimum circumscribed circle of the laser outline can be found by adopting the method of vector and by which the issue of regional peak value in optimized algorithm can be overcome. And a kind of roundness calculating formula can be designed to appraise the quality of laser beam.

The optimized algorithm and hereditary algorithm is effective algorithms by which roundness can be calculated accurately and fast. In the former algorithm the centre of least-square circle is usually defined as the initial value. According to different method, the direction and step which the centre of a circle moves can be confirmed and the centre of a circle which meets the minimum regional condition can be found. This is an optimization question of multiple-peak value and may converge to locally optimal solution. The latter algorithm is time-consuming. The geometry method is applied to the roundness evaluation in recent years. Firstly convex hull of a set of point S is constructed, and then the farthest and nearest Voronoi circles can be constructed, finally the centre of the circle can be found. This method is more ocular and accurate than others and can also solve the question of muti-centres at the same time.

(c) Realization of the displacement parameter measurement algorithms.

Based on the exactly gathering each frame of image, after the grey level mutation, grey level histogram statistics and image two-valued processing, then the luminous points become white and the background become black. In the edge detection, the edge of object in each image is different from the whole character, which is often appeared in discontinuous form, thus the edge of the object become the most remarkable part in the image and this local character can be distinguished that   the method is called edge detection. The edge character can be drawn by the mutation of the grey level, the color and the structured texture, and then the edge of the object can be regarded as the boundaries of different areas.

Edge Trim: The method of image two-valued processing and skeletonization is usually divided into zoom and pivot transform. The original image can be reconstructed by the Anti-pivot transform to Axial skeleton, which is an important expression method of the image two-valued processing.

Judging the form of luminous points: By calculating the moment features of the pretreatment image, whether the luminous point is normal or not cab be judged.

Calculating of roundness: The computing method of biggest inscribed circle is finished by iteration. Finding any point as the centre of the circle. Calculating the distance from the point to the edge. Choosing the point whose distance is minimum as the direction vector. Moving in the opposite direction to the next centre of the circle by a certain step. When three points in edge whose distance to a point is minimum and equal are found, this point is the centre of the inscribed circle.

Assessing the quality of the luminous point: Adopting the roundness calculation formula weighs the quality of the laser luminous point, thus whether the luminous point is normal or not can be judged.

Position the light source according the temporal relations. Merging the light source position in each time-sequence image frame of two signals to form the three-dimensional motion trace light source, and then three-dimensional errors can be calculated up and down, sideways and front-to-back.

Fig. 2 below shows the flow chart of displacement parameters measurement based on image processing technology.

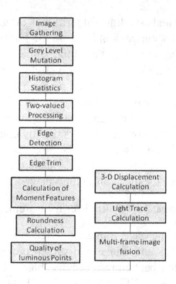

Fig. 2. The flow chart of displacement parameters measurement based on image processing technology

3   Conclusion

According to the demand of related performance test of the weapon system, the displacement parameters measurement based on binocular vision and image processing technology and the corresponding solution design has been put forward and by which the test results are more ocular and accurate. Thus the problem of the displacement parameter test of muzzle under the complex environment has been solved.

References

1. Cooper, P.A.: Modeling and Simulation of Space Station Freedom Berthing Dynamics and Control. NASA-TM-109151 (1994)
2. Ashrafiuon, H.: Modeling of a Deformable Manikin Neck for Multi-body Dynamic Simulation. AD-A313744 (1995)

3. Cox, P.A.: Muzzle Motion of the M68 105mm Gun. AD-A062296 (1978)
4. Hanaged, S.: Problem of the Dynamics of a Cantilever Beam Attached to a Moving Base. J. Guidance. Control and Dynamics 12(3) (1989)
5. Kwak, B.M.: Dynamic Analysis and Optimal Design Formulation of a Weapon-vehicle System. AD-780 918 (1974)
6. Zhang, Y.: International Scientfic Instruments Directiry (1987)
7. Peng, X., Peng, Y., Qiao, L.: The Study on Boundary Scan Test in Mixed Circuit System (2004)

Vehicle Tracking in Video Based on Pixel Level Motion Vector

Yang Xiong[1], Xiaobo Lu[1], Zhou Zhu[2], and Weili Zeng[2]

[1] School of Automation, Southeast University, Nanjing, 210096, China
xbdgyf@live.cn, xblu2008@yahoo.cn
[2] School of Transportation, Southeast University, Nanjing, 210096, China
zhu_zhou@qq.com, zengwlj@yahoo.com.cn

Abstract. In this paper, the problem of missing vehicles halfway in previous approach of vehicle tracking based on motion vector is studied, and a vehicle tracking algorithm based on pixel level motion vector is proposed. In the proposed algorithm, blocks of vehicles are shifted by pixel level motion vector which is acquired directly by block matching method, and overlapping between blocks contained in a single vehicle is allowed. By the experiments, the proposed algorithm was proved to be very successful. It can track vehicles farther than block level motion vector based approach.

Keywords: vehicle tracking, vehicle detection, block matching, motion vector.

1 Introduction

In recent years, traffic monitoring has become a popular research area for the development of efficient intelligent transportation systems. It is very important to achieve reliable vehicle detection and tracking for the sake of estimating traffic parameters and analysis individual behavior of vehicles. Among various approaches, video based systems provide more flexible solutions for traffic monitoring [1].

There are many related works of vehicle tracking in video stream images. Optical flow based tracking [2] has much computational costs that computation is done in every pixels of the frame. It is not very robust against noise and illumination and hard if objects with large homogeneous area in motion. Mean-shift based tracking [3] has been used for simple implementation and quick detection, but it is difficult to overcome the problem of scale variation. 3D model based tracking [4] requires a lot of 3D models of vehicles, so it is not adapted to general traffic images. Zhou Zhu employs motion vector [5] method to shift vehicles among images, and resolve occlusion problem by MRF model [6]. Among these methods, motion vector method dispense with a priori knowledge of vehicle shape and 3D model, moreover, it is robust against scale variation. However, experiments using previous motion vector based approach showed that some vehicles lost in tracking while they were in the image in fact. To solve this problem, a tracking algorithm based on pixel level motion vector is proposed in this paper.

F.L. Wang et al. (Eds.): CMSP 2012, CCIS 346, pp. 200–206, 2012.
© Springer-Verlag Berlin Heidelberg 2012

The remainder of this paper is organized as follows. An overview of the vehicle tracking algorithm based on block level motion vector is stated in Section 2. The proposed vehicle tracking algorithm based on pixel level motion vector is described in Section 3. The experiment results are shown in Section 4. The Conclusion is contained in Section 5.

2   Block Level Motion Vector

An image of 640×480 pixels is divided into 80×60 blocks, where each block consists of 8x8 pixels. The blocks at which the difference between intensities and those at the background image is smaller than a threshold value is regarded as background blocks, and the other blocks is regarded as foreground blocks. A vehicle is described by a group of foreground blocks with the same vehicle ID. Blocks in each frame image are given background ID at the beginning. Vehicles are shifted from the current image to the next image based on motion vector estimated by block matching.

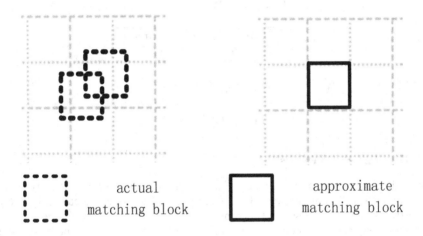

Fig. 1. Different actual matching blocks enjoy the same approximate matching block

Due to dividing an image into non-overlapping blocks, it is necessary to normalize motion vector form pixel level to block level, in other words, both the horizontal and vertical components of a motion vector must be rounded to integral multiples of side length of block. For convenience, the block which is shifted from last frame image based on pixel level motion vector is called the actual matching block, and the block which is shifted from last frame image based on block level motion vector is called the approximate matching block. When different actual matching blocks enjoy the same approximate matching block as shown in Fig.1, only one of them can be reserved. Therefore, some vehicle blocks are lost in shifting processing. Blocks reduction can cause vehicle location inaccuracy, and even missing vehicle halfway.

3   Pixel Level Motion Vector

To solve the problems of losing vehicle blocks in block level motion vector based tracking, this paper provides an vehicle tracking algorithm based on pixel level motion vector to ensure that the vehicles can be tracked farther. In this algorithm, an image of 640 × 480 pixels is divided into 633 × 473 blocks, where each block consists of 8x8 pixels, namely, each pixel at the left and top region consisted by pixels corresponds to a block. The flow chart is shown in Fig. 2.

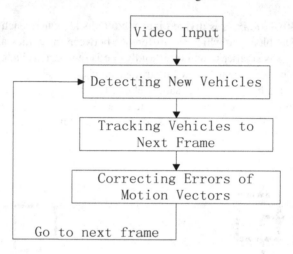

Fig. 2. Flow Chart

3.1   Detecting New Vehicles

Set up a detecting area on the entrance of the scene as shown in Fig.3. It is assumed that all vehicles will come through the detecting line. Therefore, we can assign new vehicle IDs only to the foreground regions in the detecting area. The foreground regions can be obtained by calculating the difference between the kth frame image and the background image of the input video. A connective region where each pixel has a larger difference than a threshold value is regarded as a foreground region.

Fig. 3. New blocks of a vehicle in the detecting area

If a foreground region are partially overlap a vehicle previously detected, assign the corresponding old vehicle ID to the blocks in the foreground region. Otherwise, give them a new vehicle ID.

3.2   Tracking Vehicles to Next Frame

The motion vector of a block is the result of the coordinate of the matching block in the next frame image subtracting the coordinate of the current block. The matching extent between two blocks is examined by the *MAD* (mean absolute difference) between them in this paper. The *MAD* is calculated as Formulas (1).

$$MAD[B_{k-1}(x_1, y_1), B_k(x_2, y_2)] = \frac{1}{64} \sum_{(x,y) \in B_{k-1}(x_1,y_1)} |I_{k-1}(x, y) - I_k(x + dx, y + dy)| \qquad (1)$$

where $B_{k-1}(x_1,y_1)$ represents the block whose coordinate is (x_1,y_1) in the kth frame image, $B_k(x_2,y_2)$ represents the block whose coordinate is (x_2,y_2) in the kth frame image, $MAD[B_{k-1}(x_1,y_1), B_k(x_2,y_2)]$ represents the *MAD* between $B_{k-1}(x_1,y_1)$ and $B_{k-1}(x_1,y_1)$, $I_{k-1}(x,y)$ represents the intensity of the pixel at (x,y), (dx,dy) represents (x_2-x_1,y_2-y_1).

According to the principle of the least *MAD*, the motion vector of a block is gotten as Formulas (2).

$$(V_x, V_y)_{1,1,k-1} = \arg \min_{(dx,dy)} MAD[B_{k-1}(x_1, y_1), B_k(x_1 + dx, y_1 + dy)] \qquad (2)$$

where $(V_x, V_y)_{1,1,k-1}$ indicates the motion vector of $B_{k-1}(x_1,y_1)$.

Shift all vehicle blocks to the next image based on the pixel level motion vector estimated by block matching, and assign them the corresponding vehicle ID. Unless different blocks in the kth frame image enjoy the same matching block in the $k+1^{th}$ frame image, all the blocks belong to vehicles can be inherited in next frame image.

3.3   Correcting Errors of Motion Vectors

Although pixel level motion vector is more accurate than block level motion vector, the block matching method can't assure all motion vectors are right. Sometimes, some errors occur in bounding blocks of vehicles, where very poor texture exists. Since those errors should lead to segmentation errors, it is necessary to correct errors of motion vectors after shifting vehicles to the next frame.

At first, check whether each block with a vehicle ID is a background block or not, give the background blocks the background ID. Thus, a lot of wrong matching blocks can be filtered out as shown in Fig. 4. However, if a block of one vehicle in the kth frame image is wrongly matched with a block of another vehicle in the k+1th frame image as shown in Fig. 5(a). The background block verification method for correct errors of motion vectors described above will lose efficacy. In fact, the segmentation errors can be easily corrected just by giving the overlapping foreground blocks among different vehicles the background ID as shown in as shown in Fig. 5(b). Thanks to the high blocks inheriting rate achieved in the process of shifting vehicles, the wrongly matched blocks are abandoned vehicle IDs safely, and using the remained vehicle blocks still can keep vehicles tracked.

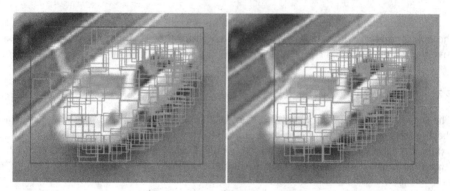

Fig. 4. The comparison between vehicle without filtering out background blocks (as shown in the left) and with filtering out background blocks (as shown in the right)

Fig. 5. The comparison between vehicles without filtering out overlapping blocks (as shown in the left) and with filtering out overlapping blocks (as shown in the right)

4 Experiment Results

Algorithm in this paper is written in C++ language, and runs in VS2010 compiler environment. Test PC uses Intel Pentium Dual 1.6GHz CPU and 2G memory. The experiment has realized the algorithm described in the paper and compared with previous algorithm. Fig.6 and Fig.7 show the tracking results in the 136th and 152th frame images in the same traffic video using pixel level motion vector method and block level motion vector method.

In the 136th frame image, it is event that the blocks belong to the 1st vehicle tracked based on block level motion vector was less than those based on pixel level motion vector. The contrast is more shape between the two methods in the 152th frame image, the 1st vehicle tracked based on block level motion vector was lost, while the 1st vehicle tracked based on pixel level motion vector still existed.

Fig. 6. The experiment results comparison between tracking by pixel level motion vector method (as shown in the left) and block level motion vector method at the 136th frame (as shown in the left)

Fig. 7. The experiment results comparison between tracking by pixel level motion vector method (as shown in the left) and block level motion vector method at the 152th frame (as shown in the left)

5   Conclusion

By the experiments, the proposed algorithm that tracking vehicles based on pixel level motion vector was proved to be robust against scale variation in vehicle segmentation as well as the previous approach that tracking vehicles based on block level motion vector. Moreover, the proposed algorithm can solve the problem exist in block level motion vector, which is losing right matching blocks belong to vehicles, and then vehicles can be tracked farther and more accurate. However, we should point out that the larger number of blocks increased the amount of calculation when shifting vehicles to the next image, which needs to be resolved in further study.

Acknowledgments. This work was supported by the National Natural Science Foundation of China under grant 60972001, the Program Sponsored for Scientific Innovation Research of College Graduate in Jiangsu Province under grant CXZZ_0163, and the Scientific Research Foundation of Graduate School of Southeast University under grant YBJJ1140.

References

1. Ki, Y.K., Lee, D.Y.: A traffic accident recording and reporting model at intersections. IEEE Transactions on Intelligent Transportation Systems 8, 188–194 (2007)
2. Nejadasl, F.K., Gorte, B.G.H., Hoogendoorn, S.P.: Optical flow based vehicle tracking strengthened by statistical decisions. Journal of Photogrammetry and Remote Sensing 61, 159–169 (2006)
3. Ha, D.B., Zhu, G.X., Zhao, G.Z.: Vehicle Tracking Method Based on Corner Feature and Mean-shift. Computer Engineering 36, 197–200 (2010)
4. Zhang, Z., Huang, K., Tan, T.: 3D Model Based Vehicle Tracking Using Gradient Based Fitness Evaluation under Particle Filter Framework. In: 2010 20th International Conference on Pattern Recognition (ICPR), pp. 1771–1774 (2010)
5. Zhu, Z., Lu, X., Wei, Y.: Real-time vehicle tracking system based on motion vector. Journal of Transportation Engineering and Information 5, 110–115 (2007)
6. Kamijo, S., Matsushita, Y., Ikeuchi, K.: Occlusion Robust Tracking utilizing Spatio-Temporal Markov Random Field Model. In: IEEE ICPR, pp. 142–147 (2000)

Alpha Matting Using Immune Feature Extraction Network

Hong Ge[1,2], Xueming Yan[1], Kazunori Okada[2], and Yan Li[1]

[1] School of Computer Science, South China Normal University, Guangzhou, 510631,
Guangdong, China
[2] Department of Computer Science, San Francisco State University, San Francisco,
94132, CA, USA
gehong2012@gmail.com, Xueming126@126.com, kazokada@sfsu.edu,
yanli@scnu.edu.cn

Abstract. Image matting is inherently an ill-posed problem of determining the mixing parameter, "alpha", for each pixel in an "unknown" area of an image. Although there were many approaches designed to solve this problem successfully, their performance decreases rapidly both in accuracy and speed when matting the images with complex texture or color due to poor choices of the sample pairs of foreground and background. In this paper, an AIS (Artificial Immune System) algorithm—IFEN (Immune Feature Extraction Network) is used to improve the quality of sample pairs by extracting "feature" foreground/background pairs from the original randomly sampled pairs. The experimental results show that the performance of matting is promoted significantly by our method.

Keywords: image matting, IFEN, Robust matting, Guided filter.

1 Introduction

Matting refers to the problem of soft and accurate foreground extraction from an image as proposed first by Poter & Duff in 1984 [1], and plays an important role in image and video editing. Formally, an input image is modeled as a convex combination of a foreground image F_z and a background image B_z as

$$I_z = \alpha_z F_z + (1 - \alpha_z)B_z \tag{1}$$

where z = (x, y) refers to the image coordinates, and   are the pixels' foreground opacities [2]. For natural images, F_z and B_z are not constrained to particular values. Thus, all variables on the right-hand side of Eq.(1) become unknown, making the problem of computing an alpha matte ill-posed.

To address the ill-posed nature of the matting problem, most existing approaches require additional constraints in the form of user input, known as trimaps. A trimap divides an image into three regions, identifying pixels as known foreground with

F.L. Wang et al. (Eds.): CMSP 2012, CCIS 346, pp. 207–214, 2012.
© Springer-Verlag Berlin Heidelberg 2012

$\alpha_z = 1$ or as known background with $\alpha_z = 0$. The remaining unconstrained pixels are marked as unknown. The goal of a digital matting algorithm is then to compute the values of α_z, F_z and B_z for all pixels labeled as unknown in a trimap.

Matting techniques proposed previously can be categorized into sampling-based methods [4,5], affinities-based methods [6], or a combination of the two [7,8]. The combined methods became recently popular, where local affinities are employed in their optimization steps for solving or refining the matte. Although various successful examples [3] have been shown for these approaches, their performance rapidly degrades, when foreground and background patterns become complex, due to two key factors.

First, sampling pairs of foreground and background pixels is an important factor for accuracy of matting because in many images the foreground and background regions contain significant textures and/or discontinuities, thus direct color sampling may become erroneous. Second, once the pairs of foreground and background are sampled, determining α_z for each unknown pixel requires the solution of a large linear system, whose size is directly proportional to the number of the unknown variables, making the matting a time-consuming procedure. One of the solutions to improve the efficiency of matting is to develop a method to choose the best pairs of foreground and background samples for unknown pixels, which can promote the matting accuracy and improve the time-complexity at the same time.

To this goal, Wang et al. [7] proposed a robust matting method by optimizing color samples. They proposed an evaluation function to sample best color pairs of foreground and background for a specific unknown pixel, so the matte only needs to be (re)computed for a small portion of the image at a time. But, long or complex foreground's boundaries are still monotonous and time-consuming to trace. In [8], Gastal et al. carefully sampled the pairs of foreground and background in a small neighborhood, pronouncing that their approach could generate high-quality mattes up to 100 times faster than the previous techniques. However, the accuracy of their method was shown to decrease largely when the assumption that the true foreground and background colors of the unknown pixels can be explicitly estimated by analyzing nearby known pixels did not hold. This indicates that it is not enough just to decrease the size of the sampled color pairs in order to improve the performance of matting both in accuracy and the speed.

In this paper, we propose a modified matting method named IFENRM based on the Robust Matting algorithm proposed in [7]. The IFENRM exploits an artificial immune system [9], known as immune feature extraction network (IFEN) proposed in [10], to address the accuracy-efficiency tradeoff in the image matting.

One of the key factors which make the Robust Matting robust and efficient method is to use an optimized color sample. However, the optimized color samples are selected from a large original sample set, which are collected spreading foreground and background samples along the boundaries of known foreground and background regions. This original sample set is surely a large one, so the optimization will be time-consuming and the optimized samples probably become the simple averages of the full sample space [7].

IFEN is designed to effectively extract a feature subset from an original raw dataset by using the computational principles inspired by the immune system [10]. Our proposed method applies IFEN to extract an optimal foreground/background pair set from the original sample set, then use the Robust Matting method on this "best" and small set of foreground/background pairs directly to gain the resulting alpha matting. The size of the searching space for the Robust Matting method is decreased greatly and the quality of the candidate foreground/background pairs are improved a lot, so that both the accuracy and the speed of matting can be promoted.

Next, in Section2, we introduce the basic framework of our proposed matting solution with IFEN; in section3, the experimental results are presented. Finally, conclusions are put forward in Section4.

2   Image Matting Based on IFEN

The procedure of the proposed matting method based on IFEN is shown in Fig. 1. The first step of matting is to provide a trimap, which segments the input image into three regions: definitely foreground Fg, definitely background Bg and unknown Cz. The second step is to collect the original sample set from boundary of foreground and background. Then, the "best" set of foreground and background pairs are extracted from the original sample set by IFEN. Next, for each pixel I_z in the unknown area, implement matting using the Robust Matting on the optimal foreground/background pair set, resulting in the alpha matte of the input image as a set of estimated α_z^*. Finally, in order to prevent discontinuities in the resulting matte, an additional step, matte smoothing, is used to ensure the local smoothness of the final alpha values, while maintaining its distinct features.

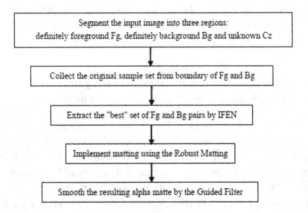

Fig. 1. Flowcharts of IFEN-based matting

Fig. 1 shows the overall procedure of the proposed IFENRM matting. The following explains several key steps in our matting method in detail.

1) Sampling foreground and background pixels: In this step, we first collect the foreground and background samples along the boundary outlines of known regions to construct an original foreground and background set, as shown in Fig. 2. The red line indicates the outline of foreground region while the green line is the outline of background region.

The reason for sampling the foreground/background pairs is two-fold: one is the assumption that the true foreground and background colors should be similar to some pixels in the neighborhood of the unknown pixel. Second is that using more samples near outlines was not shown to improve the matting performance, allowing us to use only pixels on the outlines as the original sample pairs.

Fig. 2. An example of matting with a trimap. Left: the original image, Middle: the trimap, Right: outline of foreground (red) and background (green) of the trimap.

2) Optimizing the original sample set by IFEN: IFEN is used to produce the best pairs of foreground and background pixels from the original foreground/background pair set. The original foreground/background pair set is a set consisting of each possible pair of the original foreground and background set. Here, we apply IFEN to extract the best subset of foreground/background pairs from the original foreground /background pair set.　IFEN is a biologically-inspired algorithm. The flowchart of the IFEN is shown in Fig.3. We interpret the basic immune system-inspired functions of IFEN for the context of the matting application as follows:

Antigen: a pixel I_z in the unknown region.

Antigen set: a set of pixel samples in the unknown region;

Antibody: a pair of foreground and background, such as (F^i, B^j) ;

Original antibody network: a set of pairs of foreground/background samples in the known area initialized by the original foreground/background pairs; at the end of IFEN, the resulting antibody network yields the best pairs of foreground/background.

Affinity computing: the affinity of a sampled foreground/background pairs should be proportional to the accuracy of evaluating a given unknown pixel by the sampled pairs. In [7], they chose a foreground/background pair that maximizes an energy confidence measure for evaluating unknown pixels. We adopt this confidence formula in [7] as the affinity between an antigen and an antibody:

$$aff_{gb}((F^i, B^j), I) = \exp\left\{ -\frac{R_d(F^i, B^j)^2 \cdot \omega(F^i) \cdot \omega(B^j)}{\sigma^2} \right\} \qquad (2)$$

Where, F^i is the ith foreground sample and B^j is the jth background sample. $R_d(F^i, B^j)$ is the distance between the foreground/background pair:

$$R_d(F^i, B^j) = \frac{\left\| I - (\hat{\alpha}F^i + (1 - \hat{\alpha})B^j) \right\|}{\left\| F^i - B^j \right\|}$$

Where, $\hat{\alpha}$ is the estimated alpha value defined by:

$$\hat{\alpha} = \frac{(I - B^j)(F^i - B^j)}{\left\| F^i - B^j \right\|^2}$$

And, $\omega(F^i)$ and $\omega(B^j)$ are two weights defined as:

$$\omega(F^i) = \exp\left\{ -\left\| F^i - I \right\|^2 / D_F^2 \right\}$$

And

$$\omega(B^j) = \exp\left\{ -\left\| B^j - I \right\|^2 / D_B^2 \right\}$$

On the other hand, the affinity between two antibodies is defined as:

$$aff_{bb} = \left\| (F^i, B^j) - (F^u, B^v) \right\| + \sqrt{(i - u)^2 + (j - v)^2} \tag{3}$$

Hypermutation: antibody's hypermutation operation in IFEN is to bring change to the antibody network, so we design the hypermutation used in matting as:

$$(i_k, j_k) = (i, j) + \mathrm{int}(\omega\beta R^k) \tag{4}$$

Where $\beta = 0.5$, (i, j) and (i_k, j_k) refer to the current indexes of foreground/background pair and the indexes in the k-th hypermutation, respectively. R^k is a random number with normal distribution. ω is the maximum indexes of foreground and background. More details of this procedure refer to [10].

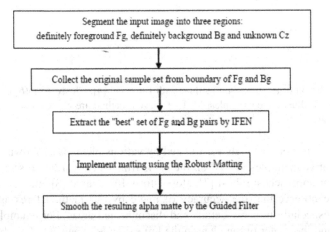

Fig. 3. The flowchart of IFEN

3) Implement matting using the Robust Matting: using the Robust Matting method in [7] to each pixel in the unknown area to compute the resulting alpha matte α^*. The procedure of the Robust Matting references to [7].

4) Smoothing the resulting alpha matte: this step is to smooth the matte estimated by the above procedure. We adopt the Guided Filter proposed in [11] to realize the final matte α. We use α^* to represent the resulting alpha matte.

3   Results

We have implemented the proposed technique using Matlab2010, and assessed its quality in two types experiments described in this section.

First, the accuracy of the alpha matting is evaluated against varying levels of tri-map quality as shown in Fig. 4. A series of trimaps with declining accuracy is created by iteratively dilating the unknown regions. Because the foreground/background pairs are sampled from the pixels of trimap outlines, the better the trimap, the better the quality of the sampled pairs and of the resulting matte. We compare our IFENRM method with Bayesian [4], closed-form [6] and robust [7] approaches in terms of the mean square error (MSE) between the estimated mattes and the corresponding ground-truths created by a variety of matting methods with extensive manual user assistance. With the quality level of trimap declining, the MSE increases for all approaches, however the quality decrease by our method is smaller than others, indicating the robustness of our proposed method against the quality of trimaps.

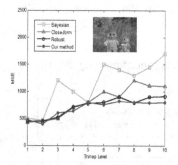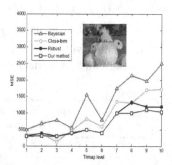

Fig. 4. Comparison of the proposed method with Bayesian [4]. Closed-form[6] and Robust [7] methods for two illustrative examples. MSEs for each method are plotted against the accuracy levels of trimaps.

Second, we present the mattes estimated by various methods as shown in Fig. 5 for three illustrative examples. Based on the same trimaps shown in the second row, we compare four approaches: robust [7], closed-form [6], shared [8] and our IFEN-based method. We observe that the accuracy of matte by our method fares against other techniques especially in some details and disconnected areas. For example, the edge of the leaf and the center of the plant in the left example image could not be identified correctly by the closed-form method. While the robust and the shared methods could classify these interior parts relatively well, some details of the foreground edges were not delineated satisfactorily. The proposed method yielded a favorable result both in the details of the edge and the disconnected parts in the interiors. The similar outcome was observed for the other two images, such as the tail and the top of head of the animal and the hair tip of the girl. Because of the feature data extraction of IFEN, the resulting foreground/ background pairs are limited to the smaller and best pairs and can include the features involving pixels both in the known and the unknown regions. Therefore, the alpha values estimated for some pixels in those unknown area can be more accurate than those with randomly sampled feature pairs.

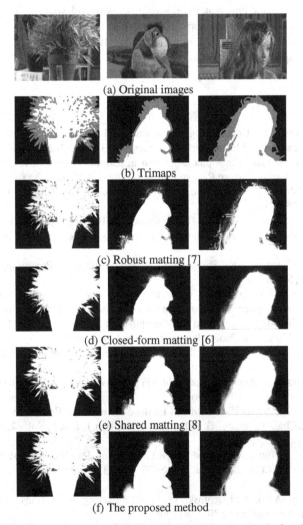

(a) Original images

(b) Trimaps

(c) Robust matting [7]

(d) Closed-form matting [6]

(e) Shared matting [8]

(f) The proposed method

Fig. 5. Qualitative comparison of estimated mattes by various methods for three illustrative natural image examples

4 Conclusion and Future Work

In this paper, we propose a new matting method based on IFEN which focuses on optimizing the foreground/background pairs to estimate the alpha values. Our experimental results show that our method significantly improves the accuracy of matting. Our method can easily learn more general color model in both linear and nonlinear cases, which then are used in computing alpha values of unknown pixels more effectively. Moreover, the promising results of the proposed method also inspire further exploration of the works in the field of intelligent information processing techniques, such as neural network and genetic algorithms, as useful sources for improving the performance of existing matting approaches such as [12,13].

Our future work includes adopting different IFEN operations and testing the overall matting approaches with more data.

References

1. Porter, T., Duff, T.: Compositing digital images. In: The 11th Annual Conference on Computer Graphics and Interactive Techniques, vol. 3, pp. 253–259 (1984)
2. Ruzon, M.A., Tomasi, C.: Alpha estimation in natural images. In: IEEE Conference on Computer Vision and Pattern Recognition, vol. 1, pp. 18–25 (June 2000)
3. Wang, J., Cohen, M.F.: Image and Video Matting: A Survey. Computer Graphics and Vision 3, 97–175 (2007)
4. Chuang, Y., Curless, B., Salesin, D., Szeliski, R.: A Bayesian approach to digital matting. In: Proc. of IEEE Computer Vision and Pattern Recognition, vol. 2, pp. 264–271 (December 2001)
5. Sun, J., Jia, J., Tang, C.-K., Shum, H.-Y.: Poisson matting. In: Proceedings of ACM Siggraph, pp. 315–321 (April 2004)
6. Levin, A., Lischinski, D., Weiss, Y.: A closed form solution to natural image matting. In: IEEE Conf. on Computer Vision and Pattern Recognition, pp. 228–242 (June 2008)
7. Wang, J., Cohen, M.F.: Optimized color sampling for robust matting. In: IEEE Conference on Computer Vision and Pattern Recognition, pp. 1–8 (June 2007)
8. Gastal, E.S.L., Oliveira, M.M.: Shared sampling for real-time alpha matting. Computer Graphics Forum 29, 575–584 (2010)
9. Hart, E., Timmis, J.: Application areas of AIS: the past, the present and the future. Applied Soft Computing 8, 191–201 (2008)
10. Ge, H., Yan, X.: A Modified Artificial Immune Network for Feature Extracting. In: Tan, Y., Shi, Y., Chai, Y., Wang, G. (eds.) ICSI 2011, Part I. LNCS, vol. 6728, pp. 408–415. Springer, Heidelberg (2011)
11. He, K., Sun, J., Tang, X.: Guided Image Filtering. In: Daniilidis, K., Maragos, P., Paragios, N. (eds.) ECCV 2010, Part I. LNCS, vol. 6311, pp. 1–14. Springer, Heidelberg (2010)
12. Levin, A., Rav-Acha, A., Lischinski, D.: Spectral matting. IEEE Trans. on Pattern Analysis and Machine Intelligence 30, 1–8 (2008)
13. Zheng, Y., Kambhamettu, C., Yu, J., Bauer, T., Steiner, K.: Fuzzy matte: A computationally efficient scheme for interactive matting. In: IEEE Conference on Computer Vision and Pattern Recognition, pp. 1–8 (June 2008)

Gaussian Particle Filter Based Algorithm for Tracking of a Dim Moving Point Target in IR Image Sequences

Dilmurat Tursun and Askar Hamdulla

Institute of Information Science and Engineering, Xinjiang University, Urumqi, 830046, China
askar@xju.edu.cn

Abstract. In order to solve the problems of deviations with large error occurred at the sharp corners of motion trajectories and poor stability of tracking algorithm presented in previous paper, and further make improvements to the tracking precision, in this paper the rather appropriate state model is established first of all, and then the effective observations are collected by using spatial-temporal detection and fusion in which the brightness information of the target included in the decision criteria for the first time. Under the different circumstances of Gaussian noise and non-Gaussian noise, the experimental results show that take the Gaussian particle filter as the tracking algorithm which has no use of re-sampling could have effectively improved the precision of algorithm for tracking dim moving point target in IR image sequences, and has a good real-time performances and good stability.

Keywords: target detection and tracking, IR image sequences, dim moving point target, Gaussian particle filter.

1   Introduction

Dim moving target tracking refers to the process of analyzing the motion states of the target formed by Infrared thermal imaging. Steady, high precision algorithm for tracking of IR target has a very important application prospect in military research field such as guidance, reconnaissance etc. The essence of the target tracking procedure is determination process of the target's positions in IR image sequences. In the case of low SNR Infrared image sequences, the infrared dim point target contains less information, no texture, no shape, no size features are available, resulting in dim target detection and tracking was not accurate enough indeed. In the paper [1, 2, 3], accomplish the target tracking task based on probabilistic data association particle filter, but found that the tracking trajectory in the corner will appear deviation, tracking errors are large, algorithm's stability is not good enough.

On the analysis of the existing literatures, in order to solve the problem of target tracking error, first of all, this paper established a more appropriate state model for target movement. Then, after going through the process of space-time domain decision fusion according to the characteristics of target, and combined with the target's intensity information get the final effective measurements, then apply the Gaussian particle filter algorithm for real-time target tracking.

F.L. Wang et al. (Eds.): CMSP 2012, CCIS 346, pp. 215–223, 2012.

2   The Observation Model of Image Sequences

The model of IR image sequences is defined in paper [3, 4], that is

$$F(x, y, k) = F_T(x, y, k) + F_B(x, y, k) + N(x, y, k) \; , \quad k = 1, 2, 3... \quad (1)$$

Where, (x, y) coordinates of the image pixels, k is the frame number, F_T is modeling for target pixel's space-time information, F_B is modeling for background pixel's space-time information, $N(x, y, k)$ is the background clutter which follow Gaussian distribution that $N(0, \sigma_B^2)$.

3   The Algorithm for Detection of Effective Measurements

When the state transition model is more close to the actual target motion, target tracking algorithm will have strong robustness. And when the observation model preserves the perfect target features, the target tracking algorithm will have high accuracy.

3.1   The State Model of Target Movement

We can get the information from thermal imaged target in infrared image sequences such as position (x, y), velocity (v_x, v_y), As well as the target gray level value I, then dim moving target's state transition equation can be expressed as a formula (2) shown below:

$$X(k+1) = FX(k) + Gv(k) , \quad k = 1, 2, 3... \quad (2)$$

In which, $X(k) \in R^n$, $X(k) = (x, y, v_x, v_y, \Delta_x, \Delta_y)$ is the state of the system at time k, Δ_x , Δ_y are the velocity innovation at time k, v_x , v_y are the velocity. In a short period of time, because of the movement of infrared long distance target is closely related to the velocity and velocity innovation at last moment k-1, so the target velocity innovation of next frame can be defined as formula (3), shown below;

$$\Delta = v_k - 2v_{k-1} + v_{k-2} \; , \quad k = 3, 4, 5... \quad (3)$$

In which, v_k is velocity of target at current frame, if $k < 2$ 时，$\Delta = 0$, $v(k) \in R^n$ is normalized procedural noise, G is a coefficient matrix, stands for the radius of the particle beam, F is a transfer matrix that its definition is shown in formula (4):

$$F = \begin{bmatrix} 1 & 0 & T & 0 & T & 0 \\ 0 & 1 & 0 & T & 0 & T \\ 0 & 0 & 1 & 0 & 0 & 0 \\ 0 & 0 & 0 & 1 & 0 & 0 \\ 0 & 0 & 0 & 0 & 1 & 0 \\ 0 & 0 & 0 & 0 & 0 & 1 \end{bmatrix} \quad (4)$$

In which, T is the image acquisition time interval.

3.2   The Measurement Model of Target

The measurement model [4] at time k can be defined as formula (5) shown below:

$$z(k+1) = h_k(X(k), e(k)) , \quad k = 1, 2, 3 \ldots \tag{5}$$

In which, $z(k) \in R^{n_z}$ is observation vector at time k, each observation measurement are formed from its location and intensity, that is $z(k) = (x, y, I)$, and $e(k) \in R^n$ is the observation noise.

There are have less information inside the tracking window that the detection algorithm dependent on, and resulting in the true measurements are missed or mixed with false measurements, so that the localization of the target is often inaccurate and incomplete. The current detection algorithm does not fully consider the IR target's intensity and its distribution characteristic that the detected measurements included false or missed measurements. In order to improve the tracking accuracy of dim moving target, this paper used spatial and time domain information of target and background pixels, and put forward a new detecting algorithm.

Because of atmosphere's heat diffusion phenomenon, the point targets in images obtained by the infrared sensors appeared in the shape of circular or elliptic, and its grayscale values are follow two-dimensional Gaussian distribution which defined as formula (6) shown below :

$$s(\mu, v) = s_{max} \exp\left\{-\frac{1}{2}\left[\frac{(\mu - \mu_0)^2}{a_\mu^2} + \frac{(v - v_0)^2}{a_v^2}\right]\right\} \tag{6}$$

In which, a_μ^2 and a_v^2 are the target's intensity distribution area, (μ_0, v_0) is Gaussian distribution center, $|\mu - \mu_0| < a_\mu$ and $|v - v_0| < a_v$ are the diffusion levels of target intensity, while $a \to 0$, the point spread function tends to δ function. Based on the target gray level value and its distribution characteristics, the proposed algorithm is as follows:

Step1: the image sequences are putted into the system, and a window is opened at the predicted position, and the frame differences are taken in time domain, adaptive threshold detection in spatial domain are taken in that tracking window respectively. We can see from the paper [3], the residual noise of the differenced image will obey Gaussian distribution with a mean of 0, The time-domain differential frame operator is given in formula (7),

$$|I_k(x, y) - I_{k-1}(x, y)| > 3\sigma_1 \tag{7}$$

Where, σ_1 is the variance of the residual noise in the tracking window; Within the tracking window, according to the local advantages of target intensity, make an adaptive decision based on the mean and variance of target's gray level value, it's decision criteria is given in formula (8) shown below:

$$I_k(x, y) - Mean(I_k \_ w) > Th * \sigma_2 \qquad (8)$$

Where, $Mean(I_k \_ w)$ is the mean value of pixel's intensity in tracking window, σ_2 is the variance. Th is an adjustable parameter that its parameter's selection is related to the fluctuation degree of background pixel's gray level value.

Step2: take the binarization operation on the raw measurements detected by thresholding the pixels in time differenced image and adaptive decision in the tracking window, and store the location and gray level values corresponding to those measurements;

Step3: Clustering the measurements of time domain differenced frame of image, find its cluster center Z_c; and also clustering the measurements of adaptive detection, find its cluster center Z_a;

Step4: Compare the coordinates of Z_c and Z_a:

（1）If $|Z\_c - Z\_a| \leq 1$, compute average coordinate position Z_cent of Z_c and Z_a, regard it as position of fusion center. According to variance α in formula (6), set the measure $\lambda\alpha$, usually λ take values in [1.5, 2.5]. Within the tracking window, divide the raw measurements detected by parallel way of decision in differenced frame of image and adaptive thresholding into two parts, the Figure1 given for this purpose. Within the elliptical area, will carry out logical "or" operation to measurements those came from differenced image detection and adaptive decision, and carry out logical "and" operation to measurements those of outside elliptical area.

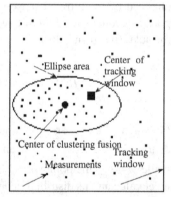

（2）If $|Z\_c - Z\_a| > 1$, in tracking window, carry out logical "or" operation to measurements those came from differenced image detection and adaptive decision.

Fig. 1. Measurements in tracking window

Step5: By decision fusion of Step4, according to the advantages of local intensity of target in tracking window and the statistics of gray value, set the threshold, get the measurements at time k, that is $z(k) = (x, y, I)$. The effective measurement detection algorithm is shown in Figure 2:

4   The Tracking Algorithm Based on Gaussian Particle Filtering

For nonlinear filtering problem, particle filter can be adapted well to Gaussian, or non Gaussian noise environments. The N sampling points $\{x_j, \ j=0,1,2,...,k\}$

independently extracted from filter probability distribution $p(x_k \mid z_{1:k})$, and can approximate the posterior probability density by using weighted summation method. For the target tracking task, it means to get the state of moving target as well. We can get the posterior probability distribution $p(x_k \mid z_{1:k})$ through the recursion shown below on the condition of given priori probability density.

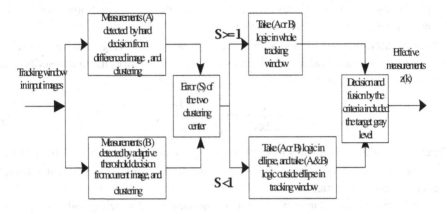

Fig. 2. The scheme of effective measurements detection

State prediction:

$$p(x_k \mid z_{1:k-1}) = \int p(x_k \mid x_{k-1}) p(x_k \mid z_{1:k-1}) dx_{k-1} \tag{9}$$

Filtering update:

$$p(x_k \mid z_{1:k}) = \frac{p(z_k \mid x_k) p(x_k \mid z_{1:k-1})}{p(z_k \mid z_{1:k-1})} \tag{10}$$

Where $p(x_{k-1} \mid z_{1:k-1})$ is the posterior probability distribution at time k-1, $p(x_k \mid x_{k-1})$ is a first order Markov process, can be obtained by system equation(2); $p(z_k \mid x_k)$ is likelihood function, can be obtained by observation equation (5). From formula (10), we can see that the state posterior probability distribution can be obtained through the correction to priori probability by using observations z_k.

According to the assumption that the target's true measurements obey Gaussian distribution [5], this paper uses the algorithm of Gaussian particle filter for target tracking in which take the Gaussian density as approximation of the posterior probability density by using importance sampling method, then updating the state's mean and covariance matrix. Compare to particle filtering, there is no need to resample, and does not exist particle degradation problems [2, 6, 7], so that reduces the complexity and computation load of particle filter. The Gaussian particle filter tracking algorithm is described as below:

Step1: Initialize the particle samples: Get target information at time k=1 by detection procedure, create initial sample set $\left\{X_i, \frac{1}{n}\right\}_{n=1}^{N}$, in which N is particle number, $n=1,2...N$, particle sample obey Gaussian distribution, and are sampled in random way;

Step2: By use of the effective measurement detection algorithm presented in this paper, get measurements $z(k)$ at time k;

Step3: according to the measurements $z(k)$, assign the weights to the particles based on the Gaussian posterior probability density, its density function described as the formula (11) shown below:

$$W_k^n(X_k | Z_{1-k}) = \frac{1}{\sqrt{2\pi}C}\exp\left\{\frac{(S_m-O)^2}{2C^2}\right\}, \quad m=1,2,3,...N \tag{11}$$

Where, S_m is the coordinates of particle m , S_m-O is the innovation of particle m; O , C are the clustering center of measurements and covariance matrix of relative clustering center of particles;

Step4: Estimate the target position by using normalized weight, and estimate the speed and speed innovations of target in next frame by using prior two frames and current frame tracking information;

Step5: If tracking is not over, then go back to step1.

5   Experimental Results and Analysis

5.1   Experimental Environment and Results

This paper uses the infrared image sequence for validation, Experiments completed by Matlab7.0 on the PC with Intel(R) Pentium(R) processor 1.80GHz 512MB storage. The SNR of image sequences defined as formula (12) shown below:

$$SNR = 10\log\frac{\mu-Mean}{\sigma} \tag{12}$$

In which u is the average grayscale value of target, σ is a standard deviation of target area, $Mean$ is mean of target area. Tracking performance is validated by using absolute error which defined as formula (13) shown below:

$$Error = TrackPo - X\_true \tag{13}$$

Where, $TrackPo$ is estimated target position, X_true is true target position. The target take uniform movement in 1-40 frames, accelerated movement in 41-70 frames, decelerated movement in 71-120 frames, accelerated movement in 121-180 frames. Then, we collected a total of 180 infrared image sequences, and set the target size of 3x3 pixels, rectangular tracking window size of 9x9 pixels. Target image occupied a circular area, set $\lambda\alpha=2$, the particle number is 200.

Experimental data setup: In the case of the strong background fluctuation, we add white noise on the IR image sequences. its deviation is 0.0001, SNR is 7db, and are tracked by the algorithm of paper [1] and of this paper separately; then add random speckle (non Gaussian noise) to IR image sequences, the mean is 0, deviation is 0.0005, SNR is 7db, use the algorithm presented in this paper, and the adaptive threshold is taken to Th=2, initial state of target is [39 83 0.8 0.3 0 0]. The comparisons of trajectory of tracking algorithm between paper [1] and this paper are shown in Figure 3 and Figure 4 respectively.

The comparisons of absolute tacking error under different noise types and different tracking algorithms presented in this paper and paper [1] is shown in Figure 5. After 50 times of Monte-Carlo experiments, the average detection and tracking time are given in Table 1.

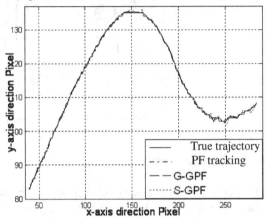

Fig. 3. Whole trajectory of tracking algorithms

5.2   Analysis of the Results

We can see from the Figure 3 and Figure 4, the algorithm presented in this paper can effectively tracking the dim moving target in IR image sequences. Figure 5 shows that the absolute tracking error is much smaller, the error fluctuation is smaller, the stability is better, the noise type's influence to target tracking accuracy is smaller than paper [1], and no error drift phenomenon occurred. But all have better real-time efficiency.

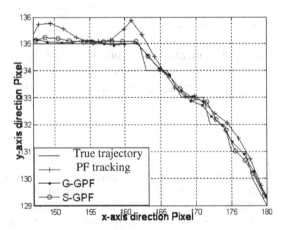

Fig. 4. Local trajectory of tracking algorithms

Table 1. Comparison of single frame detection time and tracking time

	Single frame Detection time (s)	Tracking time of 180 frames (s)
PF	0.003386	13.459407
G-GPF	0.006666	13.480746
S-GPF	0.006658	13.480316

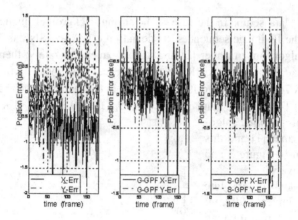

Fig. 5. Comparison of absolute tracking error

6   Conclusions

This paper take the velocity innovation into the state model, implement the decision fusion in time and spatial domain according to the local intensity of target, and get the final effective observation measurements, then used Gaussian particle filter tracking the target. Experimental results show that its time complexity and computational load are similar to standard particle filter tracking, but the tracking accuracy is improved and stability is increased indeed.

Acknowledgments. This work was supported by Natural Science Foundation of China (61263038), Key Technologies R&D Program of China (2009BAH41B03), and Program for New Century Excellent Talents in University (NCET-10-0969).

References

1. Dilmurat, T., Xiang, G.Y., Askar, H.: A Particle Filter Based Algorithm for State Estimation of Dim Moving Point Target in IR Image Sequence. In: Proc. 2nd Int. Symposium on Intelligent Information Technology Application, pp. 127–131 (2008)
2. Xiang, G.Y., Askar, H.: Particle Filter and Data Association Method Based Algorithm for Tracking Multiple Point Targets in IR Image Sequences. Journal of Optoelectronics Laser 20(2), 244–247 (2009)
3. Askar, H., Wang, B.Z.: PDAF Based on CFAR Performance Comparative Research in Tracking Dim Point Moving Target Technology. Computer Engineering and Applications 3(45), 168–171 (2009)
4. Wu, B., Ji, H.B.: Research on IR Dim Small Target Detection, Doctoral Thesis of UEST of Xian of China (2008)
5. Askar, H.: IRST System Improvements for Detection and Tracking of Dim Moving Point Targets in Heavy Clutter. Doctoral Thesis of UEST of China (2003)

6. Zhang, C.C., Yang, D.G.: Tracking Method of IR Small Target Based on Particle Filter. Modern Defence Technology 36(2), 124–128 (2008)
7. Samond, D.J., Birch, H.A.: Particle Filter for Track-before-detect. In: IEEE Proceedings of the American Control Conference, pp. 3755–3760 (2001)
8. Cheng, S.Y., Zhang, J.Y.: Research on Air-to-sea Bearing-Doppler only TMA by Gaussian Particle Filtering. Journal of Projectiles Rockets Missiles and Guidance 3, 286–289 (2006)

Moving Shadow Detection in Video Surveillance Based on Multi-feature Analysis

Wei-Gang Chen

School of Computer and Information Engineering,
Zhejiang Gongshang University, Hangzhou, China

Abstract. Moving object detection and segmentation in video surveillance systems has to deal with moving cast shadows to avoid unwanted misclassification which may interfere with the true shape and size of moving objects. This paper proposes an approach for detecting and removing moving shadows making integrated use of intensity, chromacity and texture features. Moving foreground detection is carried out by locally evaluating normalized square sum of frame difference. A significance test on the distribution of the local sum is performed to classify each pixel into foreground and background. Then, intensity and chromacity features are used to exclude foreground pixels from further evaluation. In the final step, texture features in a local region are encoded as histograms of oriented gradient (HOG). Shadow detection is performed by measuring dissimilarity between tow HOGs. Results on various test sequences and real surveillance sequences, which contains shadows range from dark and small to light and large, show the effectiveness of the proposed approach.

Keywords: motion segment, shadow detection, video surveillance.

1 Introduction

Detecting moving objects in video sequences is a key operation for many applications, including traffic monitoring, people tracking, and object recognition. When the video data is captured by a fixed camera, adaptive Gaussian mixtures have been proved to be effective for modeling complex, non-static backgrounds [1]. The foreground objects can then be segmented by subtracting the current image from the reference background model. Despite this success, approaches based on background subtraction fail to distinguish between the actual moving object and its shadow silhouette. This is due to the fact that shadows and objects share some important visual features.

It is often necessary to separate moving objects from their shadows. Fig. 1 shows an application scenario, i.e., vision-based vehicle detection, which is an important technical fundamental for many applications related to intelligent transport systems, such as intelligent parking, automatic license plate recognition, or measurement of traffic parameters, like vehicle count, speed, and flow. In these systems, if cast shadows are misclassified as parts of moving vehicles, it can lead to the problem of prematurely trigger, i.e., trigger the camera to take picture before the vehicle entering an appropriate position (see Fig.1 (b) for details). As a result, subsequent analysis tasks (e.g., license plate recognition) will fail.

F.L. Wang et al. (Eds.): CMSP 2012, CCIS 346, pp. 224–231, 2012.

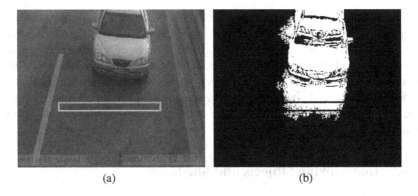

(a)   (b)

Fig. 1. An application scenario. (a) Original image; (b) Results of motion detection.

Many works have been done on differentiating shadows from moving objects. Several different features have been explored in these works, including intensity, chromacity, and edge information [2,3].

Intensity: In comparison with the reference background, the shadow pixels decrease their intensity, as they are blocked from the illumination source. Generally, the reduction rate changes smoothly between neighboring pixels [4]. A reliable background image is crucial for the methods that rely on intensity. An approximated background information is not helpful for shadow detection, even worse, may induce error classification.

Chromacity: Chromacity is an objective specification of the quality of a color regardless of its luminance. Most shadow detection methods use the assumption that shadow regions become darker, but retain their chromacity. For instance, in the HSV color space, the hue as well as the saturation components of shadow pixels change, but within a certain limit [5]. In the RGB color space, shadow pixels are more saturated toward blue. As a result, these pixels falling on neutral surfaces, such as asphalt roads, tend to be more blueish [6].

Geometry: Although methods that use geometry features generally segment moving regions from the static background using background subtraction, these methods do not rely heavily on the estimated background model, which is the case of methods using intensity feature. Instead, these methods usually impose limitation on application scenarios. For example, the object type was specified as pedestrians in [7] and as vehicles in [8]. Furthermore, these two methods require objects and shadows to have different orientations.

Textures: Shadow regions generally do not have strong edges. Compared with the reference background, edge magnitude values of shadow pixels are lower, while shadows do not significantly modify the edge gradient direction at any pixel [4]. Some methods exploit the fact that shadow regions retain most of their texture [2].

This paper propose a robust multi-feature approach for shadow detection and removing. The method uses both spectral (specifically, intensity and chromacity) and texture features, and evaluates these features by one scan. First, a simple intensity constraint, which ensures that a moving pixel can not be a shadow if it has higher intensity in current frame than in the background image, is imposed. Then, the chromacity features

(specifically, for outdoor environment, shadow pixels falling on neutral surfaces tend to be more blueish) are also exploited. Finally, the texture features are characterized by the distribution of local edge directions. If the textures of a small region centered at a candidate pixel are correlated to the background reference, the pixel is classified as shadow. We continue the paper as follows. In Section 2, we describe the method for detecting foreground pixels first, and then present the method for removing shadows. Experimental results are presented in Section 3, and our conclusions are drawn in Section 4.

2   Detecting Moving Objects and Shadows

2.1   Moving Foreground Detection

The first step of the proposed algorithm is change detection, which calculates the change mask by thresholding the difference image $D = \{d_k(\mathbf{p})\}$, with $d_k(\mathbf{p}) = I_k(\mathbf{p}) - I_{k-1}(\mathbf{p})$, where $I_k(\mathbf{p})$ and $I_{k-1}(\mathbf{p})$ are the image values at pixel $\mathbf{p}$ of two consecutive input frames. Under the hypothesis that no change occurred at position $\mathbf{p}$, i.e., the null hypothesis H_0, the corresponding difference follows a Gaussian distribution with mean zero and variance σ^2 which is equal to twice the variance of the camera noise. To make the detection more reliable, the decision to be taken should not be based on $d_k(\mathbf{p})$ only. Instead , we evaluate a normalized square sum of the frame differences [9]:

$$\Delta_k(\mathbf{p}) = \sum_{\mathbf{p}' \in W(\mathbf{p})} \frac{d_k^2(\mathbf{p}')}{\sigma^2} \tag{1}$$

where $W(\mathbf{p})$ is a window of observation centered at position $\mathbf{p}$.

A significance test [9] on the distribution of Δ is performed to assess whether the null hypothesis can be accepted or not. Under the null hypothesis, the normalized square sum $\Delta_k(\mathbf{p})$ is known to obey a χ^2 distribution with N_w degrees of freedom, where N_w denotes the number of pixels within the window $W(\mathbf{p})$ which is of size 3×3 in our experiments. Coupling the threshold t_s to the rate of false alarms associated with the test is reasonable and feasible. Given an acceptable false alarm rate α, t_s can be determined using

$$\alpha = \Pr(\Delta_k(\mathbf{p}) > t_s \,|\, H_0) \tag{2}$$

In the following steps, the background images will serve as the references for the subsequent assessment. So, a reliable background information is needed. In this work, following the approach of [10], we use a stationary map, the value in which indicates that the corresponding pixel keeps stationary for how many consecutive frames, to record the history of frame difference mask. Specifically, for pixels labeled as 'changed' in the difference mask, the corresponding value in the stationary map is cleared to zero. For these labeled as 'unchanged', the corresponding value is increased by one [10]. If the value in the stationary map exceeds a predefined threshold, the background is updated in a causal low-pass filtering manner as depicted as follows:

$$B_k(\mathbf{p}) = \eta B_{k-1}(\mathbf{p}) + (1 - \eta) I_k(\mathbf{p}) \tag{3}$$

where B_k (.) is the current background image, $\eta \in (0, 1)$ is a weight.

The variance σ^2 that characterizes the noise level presents in the video sequence is crucial for calculating the local sum Δ in Eq. (1). The algorithm described in [11] is adopted in this paper. For reducing the computation cost, the estimation is integrated in the process of calculating the local sum. That is both the Δ computation and the convolution for noise estimation (see [11] for details) are completed in one scan.

2.2 Shadow Elimination Based on Intensity and Chromacity

After the variation detection, the pixels in the input image are classified into two categories: foreground and background. The former consists of moving objects, the moving cast shadows, and the false positive pixels. The goal of the following step is to eliminate the shadows and false positives by using simple intensity and chromacity features. In our system, we propose the use of YCbCr color space. The reason is that this format is typically used in video surveillance systems for video coding. Using the same, instead another, format for object segmentation will avoid the extra computation required in color conversion.

In real-world outdoor scenes, the shadows are formed when the light source is blocked. So, the shadow pixels decrease their intensity in comparison with the reference background. Further observation suggests that blue component of a shadow pixel may be enhanced by the reflection of the sky in blue spectrum [10]. Therefore, we use the following simple assumptions to eliminate shadow pixels in this stage: (1) A foreground pixel cannot be a shadow if it has higher Y component value in current frame than in background; (2) A foreground pixel cannot be a shadow if it has higher Cr or lower Cb value in current frame than in background.

In order to suppress the influence of noise, decision like we are faced with is usually based on evaluating a set of pixels inside a small region instead of a single pixel. We thus compute the local mean of Y, Cr and Cb components inside a 3×3 sliding window of current frame and the background. These mean values are then evaluated using above mentioned two heuristic rules. For every pixel in the set of moving pixels in the frame difference mask, if either of the rules is satisfied, it can be excluded from further evaluating.

2.3 Shadow Elimination Based on HOG

We have observed that local textures can be described rather well by the local intensity gradients. In the shadow detection scenarios, an important fact that shadows pixels decrease their intensity in comparison with the reference background, however do not significantly modify the gradient directions, can be exploited. In this paper, we make use of histograms of oriented gradient (HOG), which is first introduced by N. Dalal and B. Triggs [12] to solve pedestrian detection issues and has shown superior performance to most other existing feature sets, as feature descriptor.

An overview of the HOG descriptors can be described as follows: First, the image gradients are computed by convolving the original image with a horizontal gradient kernel $[-1, 0, 1]$ and a vertical gradient kernel $[-1, 0, 1]^T$, respectively. At each pixel, the orientation of the gradient, which covers a range of $0° - 180°$, is quantized to a given number of directions. For pixels remain to be evaluated, the local texture feature is encoded as an HOG obtained from a fixed size (8×8 in our work) cell centered at the candidate position. For each cell, an 1-D histogram of gradient directions is accumulated using gradient magnitude of each pixel as weight. The histogram is then normalized so that its sum equals unity, and the descriptor vector can be treated as a probability distribution.

Let $H_{x,y}^{(c)}$ be the HOG of the cell corresponding to pixel (x, y) in current frame, and $H_{x,y}^{(b)}$ be the HOG in background. The dissimilarity between the two histograms is measured using the formula below, which is a measure derived from the so-called histogram intersection [13]:

$$\hat{d}_{x,y} = 1 - \sum_i \min\left(H_{x,y}^{(c)}(i) - H_{x,y}^{(b)}(i) \right) \qquad (4)$$

If $\hat{d}_{x,y}$ is great than a threshold, the candidate pixel can be excluded from being a shadow, otherwise, it is removed from the foreground mask.

2.4 Post-Processing

After the steps mentioned above, object masks are generated. However, due to the camera noise and irregular object motion, there generally exist some noise regions in the mask. Therefore, a post-processing step to remove these small isolated regions is necessary. In this paper, we propose to use morphological filters for this purpose. The open operation, which is defined as an erosion followed by a dilation using the same structure element for both operations, is employed [14].

3   Experimental Results

We perform simulations on three test sequences: *Highway I, Highway III, Campus* [15] and a number of real surveillance sequences, which contains shadows range from dark and small to light and large.

Fig. 2 shows some detection results for the *Highway I* sequence and two real surveillance sequence (*Road I and Road II*) in our approach. The second row is the results of change detection. The fifth row shows the results after shadow elimination using multi-feature. We can find that the moving cast shadows attached to the vehicles are exactly removed from the foreground. As a result, the problem of prematurely trigger in vision-based vehicle detection systems can be well solved.

We manually marked the shadow regions in these sequences as the ground-truth data. To compare the performance of the proposed algorithm with existing methods, the simulation results of these methods are quantitatively evaluated in terms of *shadow detection rate η* and *shadow discrimination rate ξ*, which were presented in the benchmark paper [5] as the performance metrics, and defined as follows:

$$\eta = \frac{TP_S}{TP_S + FN_S} \qquad (5)$$

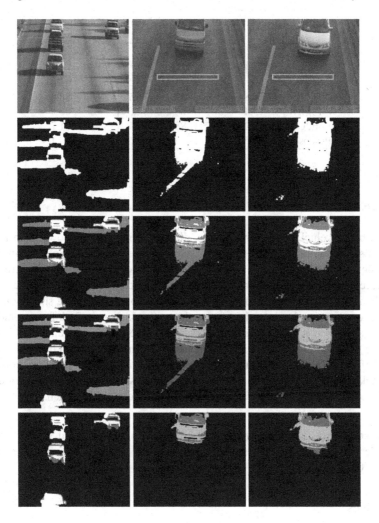

Fig. 2. Detection results on three test sequences, *Highway I* and two real sequences (from left to right). From the top to bottom are: original images; results of change detection; results after shadow elimination based on intensity and chromacity features (pixels excluded from further evaluation are depicted with high intensity); results after shadow elimination based on texture features (object pixels are depicted as red).

$$\xi = \frac{TP_F}{TP_F + FN_F} \tag{6}$$

where TP and FN stand for the number of true positive and false negative pixels, and the subscript S stands for shadow and F for foreground. The average values of η and ξ are included in Table I for comparison.

Table 1. Quantitative comparison of the proposed method

Method	Highway I		Campus		Road I	
	η (%)	ξ (%)	η (%)	ξ (%)	η (%)	ξ (%)
SP[5]	59.6	84.7	72.4	74.1	87.1	86.3
DNM1[5]	69.8	76.9	82.9	86.7	89.2	88.1
GMSM[16]	75.4	74.7	66.2	72.3	85.7	86.4
RatioEdge[16]	67.2	90.2	88.0	97.7	88.4	91.2
Proposed	68.6	87.5	84.3	85.6	90.3	89.1

4   Conclusion

In vision-based vehicle detection systems, differentiating cast shadows from moving objects is significant and remains largely unsolved. We proposed a robust method for shadow detection and removing which makes integrated use of intensity, chromacity and texture features. After motion detection, foreground pixels are evaluated using following heuristic rules by one scan: (1) A foreground pixel cannot be shadow if it has higher Y component value in current frame than in background; (2) A foreground pixel cannot be shadow if it has higher Cr or lower Cb value in current frame than in background. (3) The texture features are characterized by the distribution of local edge directions. If the textures of a small region centered at a candidate pixel are correlated to the background reference, the pixel is classified as shadow. Results on various real surveillance sequences show the effectiveness of the proposed approach.

Acknowledgments. This work was supported by the Zhejiang Natural Science Foundation under Grant Y1110809, and Zhejiang Public Welfare Project under Grant 2011C24008.

References

1. Stauffer, C., Grimson, E.: Learning Patterns of Activity Using Real-Time Tracking. IEEE Trans. Pattern Anal. Mach. Intell. 22(8), 747–757 (2000)
2. Sanin, A., Sanderson, C., Lovell, B.C.: Shadow Detection: A Survey and Comparative Evaluation of Recent Methods. Pattern Recognition 45(4), 1684–1695 (2012)
3. Chen, W.-G., Xu, B.: Detecting Moving Shadows in Video Sequences Using Region Level Evaluation for Vision-based Vehicle Detection System. In: Inter. Conf. on Frontier of Computer Science and Technology, pp. 142–146 (2010)
4. Wang, Y., Loe, K.-F., Wu, J.-K.: A Dynamic Conditional Random Field Model for Foreground and Shadow Segmentation. IEEE Trans. Pattern Anal. Mach. Intell. 28(2), 279–289 (2006)
5. Prati, A., Mikic, I., Trivedi, M.M., Cucchiara, R.: Detecting Moving Shadows: Algorithms and Evaluation. IEEE Trans. Pattern Anal. Mach. Intell. 25(7), 918–923 (2003)
6. Cucchiara, R., Grana, C., Piccardi, M., Prati, A.: Detecting Moving Objects, Ghosts, and Shadows in Video Streams. IEEE Trans. Pattern Anal. Mach. Intell. 25(10), 1337–1342 (2003)

7. Hsieh, J.-W., Hu, W.-F., Chang, C.-J., Chen, Y.-S.: Shadow Elimination for Effective Moving Object Detection by Gaussian Shadow Modeling. Image and Vision Computing 21(6), 505–516 (2003)
8. Fang, L.Z., Qiong, W.Y., Sheng, Y.Z.: A Method to Segment Moving Vehicle Cast Shadow Based on Wavelet Transform. Pattern Recognition Letters 29(16), 2182–2188 (2008)
9. Aach, T., Kaup, A.: Bayesian Algorithm for Adaptive Change Detection in Image Sequences using Markov Random Fields. Signal Process.: Image Commun. 7(2), 147–160 (1995)
10. Chien, S.-Y., Ma, S.-Y., Chen, L.-G.: Efficient Moving Object Segmentation Algorithm Using Background Registration Technique. IEEE Trans. Circuits Syst. Video Technol. 12(7), 577–586 (2002)
11. Immerkaer, J.: Fast Noise Variance-Estimation. Computer Vision and Image Understanding 64(9), 300–302 (1996)
12. Dalal, N., Triggs, B.: Histograms of Oriented Gradients for Human Detection. In: IEEE Conference on Computer Vision and Pattern Recognition, pp. 886–893 (2005)
13. Brunelli, R., Mich, O., Modena, C.M.: A Survey on the Automatic Indexing of Video Data. Journal of Visual Communication and Image Representation 10(2), 78–112 (1999)
14. Soille, P.: Morphological Image Analysis: Principles and Applications, 2nd edn. Springer (2007)
15. http://cvrr.ucsd.edu/aton/shadow/
16. Zhang, W., Fang, X.Z., Yang, X.K., Wu, Q.M.J.: Moving Cast Shadows Detection Using Ratio Edge. IEEE Trans. Multimedia 9(6), 1202–1214 (2007)

Liquid Surface Location of Milk Bottle
Based on Digital Image Processing

Fujian Feng, Lin Wang, Qian Zhang, Xin Lin, and Mian Tan

Guizhou Key Laboratory of Pattern Recognition and Intelligent System,
Guizhou Minzu University, 550025 Huaxi, Guiyang, China
fujian_feng@163.com

Abstract. Liquid surface location plays an important role in the measurement scale automatic monitoring system. In this paper, we first propose a new method to segmentation milk bottles image by Shen algorithm and the projection statistics method. Secondly, liquid surface area was found out by scanning mark algorithm. Finally, the rough liquid surface was smooth by projection statistics method. The experimental results demonstrate the great robustness and efficiency of our method.

Keywords: Liquid surface location, Region mark, Shen algorithm, Projection.

1   Introduction

Manpower read on the liquid surface scale lines is widely used in industrial and agricultural production. Fig.1 shows the actual scene of the dairy farm workers to read the bottle scale. However, the subjective factors, artificial read the scale will lead to data errors, the reliability is not high, but time-consuming, it is difficult to meet the requirements of modern production in accuracy, efficiency, automation and security. In recent years, digital image processing and pattern recognition technology is widely used in image information extraction, information processing, pattern recognition, and the detection, measurement and control. This does not change the original equipment, only to add the appropriate image acquisition devices to complete the measurement of the production of automatic identification, low cost and high efficiency.

At presents, people have widely researched the method of measurement scale automatic recognition. Dual-threshold Hough transforms is applied to automatic index identification of index-instrument [1], [2], but it calculation is very complicated, and could not solve parameter problem. Nevatia [3] improved heuristic join algorithm.

However, the result of its edge detection is more sensitive and prone to fracture the short straight line. Multi-frame difference accumulation algorithms[4], solving automatic location of the digital region. But the milk will be spilled on the sidewall, and a large number of bubbles are generated in the liquid level position, so using the above methods to accurately locate the surface of milk becomes very difficult.

F.L. Wang et al. (Eds.): CMSP 2012, CCIS 346, pp. 232–239, 2012.

Fig. 1. The dairy farm workers to read the bottle scale   **Fig. 2.** Bottle image in the actual scene

In this paper, milk bottles image by preprocessing algorithms before liquid surface location. Then, the projection information which can reveal the overall scale regional in the milk bottles image is smooth by Shen algorithm. The exact location of the milk surface is detected by the minimum of the smooth histogram. This approach can solve the liquid level detection problem in a very straightforward and robust way under various conditions.

The remaining part of this paper is organized as follows. Section 2 introduces methods for image pre-processing. In section 3, the automatic segmentation of the scale regional is presented. The exact location of surface is described in section 4. Section 5 shows some experiment results. Finally, conclusions are drawn in Section 6 with the future work discussed as well.

2   Image Preprocessing

In Fig.2, we can see that difficult to extract feature information because of the complex background; leading to the recognition rate is reduced. Therefore, the image pre-processing has become the key steps of digital image processing technology. It includes the image edge detection [5], image binaryzation [6],[7],[8] and image segmentation [9] and so on.

2.1   Edge Detection

So far, there have been many maturity edge detection algorithms, Such as Sobel operator, mask touch algorithm, differential algorithm. We select Sobel operator (in Fig.3) to detect the image edge because the simple operators costs us a little computational time.

$$\begin{bmatrix} -1 & 0 & 1 \\ -2 & 0 & 2 \\ -1 & 0 & 1 \end{bmatrix} \qquad \begin{bmatrix} -1 & -2 & -1 \\ 0 & 0 & 0 \\ 1 & 2 & 1 \end{bmatrix}$$

(a)   (b)

Fig. 3. Soble operator: (a) horizontal operator, (b) vertical operator

From Fig.2, we can see that bottle image information (scale region, milk region and background region) consists of three parts. First, remove the interference from the scale and the scale line for position liquid level. Because the rich information of the horizontal edge of the scale and the scale line. In this step, we convolve the bottle image with horizontal Sobel operators. Edge detection results are shown in Fig.4.

Fig. 4. Detection results by horizontal Sobel operator   **Fig. 5.** Binary image

2.2   An Auto-Adaptive Threshold Binary Image

All milk bottle images are binarized by an auto-adaptive threshold. In Fig.4, we can see that Gray level higher part gathered at the scale regional component and the overall share of energy is relatively small. Threshold point in the background and the scale line is divided by three-quarters of the total energy. Given that H(i) is the gray histogram value in point i. The following equation is used to obtain optimal threshold value.

$$\sum_{i=0}^{T} H[i] \ge \frac{3}{4} \tag{1}$$

Fig.5 shows the binary image by above equation. The white part of the image is mainly distributed in the region of the scale. Therefore, the scale region can be segmented by this feature.

3   Automatic Segmentation of Scale Regional

From Fig.5, the higher part of the gray value distribution in the vertical direction of the scale regional. Therefore, we propose projection statistical algorithms for split the scale regional and non-scale regional. From fig.7 (a), we can see that the larger part of the statistical value corresponding scale regional. Non-scale area is split by removing the scale area.

In fact, these larger values corresponding to the larger local maxima. Shen algorithm [10] is introduced to find the maximum point in the statistical value. The Shen algorithm not only has the function of the low-pass filter, and can calculate the first derivative and second derivative. Given that I(x) is the original statistical signal and, Flow diagram are shown in Fig.6.

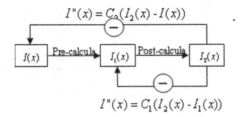

Fig. 6. Algorithm flowchart

Where, C1 and C2 are constant of not equal to 0.

We are easy to get a signal series of a first derivative and second derivative by Shen algorithm. Then, multiple maximum points are obtained by the first derivative equal to zero. The algorithm process is as follows.

1. I(x) is smooth by Shen algorithm in order to find out scale area. Smoothing process is as follows.

$$\begin{cases} I_1(x) = I(x) & x = 1 \\ I_1(x) = aI(x) + (1-a)I_1(x-1) & x = 2,3,...,W \end{cases} \tag{2}$$

$$\begin{cases} I_2(x) = I_1(x) & x = W \\ I_2(x) = aI_1(x) + (1-a)I_2(x-1) & x = 1,2,...,W-1 \end{cases} \tag{3}$$

Where, a is the smoothing parameter and 0<a<1.

2. Find I2'[x] is equal to 0 the maximum points from I2[x]. First and second extreme point corresponds to the scale region in Fig.7(c).
3. Scale area is located. The original image is split into the scale regional and non-scale regional, the left non-scale area is divided into five, where (2/5-4/5) as the sub-region to determine the milk surface.

Fig.7 gives an example that shows a milk bottles image and its automatic segmentation of scale area. It shows that the smoothing results of the projected image and the non-scale area are well described in a milk bottles image.

4   Liquid Surface Locations

4.1   Binarization of The N-Scale Area

Image binaryzation is the key of the accurate positioning of the surface. Image binaryzation methods in general are: the Oust threshold method [6], fuzzy clustering method [8] etc. but the production process in the bottle wall splash of milk and milk liquid bubbles. Therefore, using the above method of image binaryzation result is not satisfactory. From Fig.7(d), we can see that sub-image is composed by two parts of the milk region, sidewall and two main peaks on the histogram. Histogram results are shown in Fig.8.

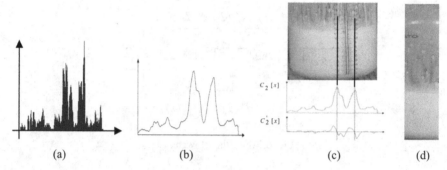

Fig. 7. A milk bottles image and its automatic segmentation of scale area: (a) Projection image; (b) Smooth the results; (c) Scale segmentation; (d) Non-scale area

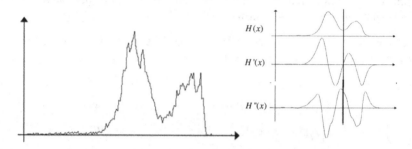

Fig. 8. The gray level histogram of the sub-region   **Fig. 9.** Smoothing the histogram, the first derivative and second derivative by Shen algorithm

In Fig.8, the rightmost peak corresponds to the region of the grayscale higher milk, while the left peak corresponding to the sidewall part. Milk area is split by finding the valley value between the right side of the peak and the left peak point as an adaptive segmentation threshold. In fact, the valley point position is seen as a minimum point. But, it is difficult using conventional mathematical methods to calculate the histogram of the first derivative and second derivative. However, in the above, we can easily calculate the derivative is 0 points and to determine the derivative of the positive and negative through the introduction of Shen algorithm. Then adaptive threshold is found by a valley point.

Fig.9 shows the sub-image histogram $H(x)$ by Shen filtering and its corresponding first derivative and second-order derivative ($H'(x)$, $H''(x)$).

In Fig.10(a), we can see that grayscale image is converted into binary image by threshold segmentation technique. However, the binary image due to background noise, and some small noise region, which affects the location of the accurate positioning surface. Therefore, these noise region needs to be cleared.

4.2   Region Marking Method for Noise Region

Fig.10(a) shows milk part is the largest in all white areas. Therefore, the largest area is found by the regional marking method. First, each region is marked through regional marking method, and calculates the area of these regions, and then the largest area is located by to remove the smaller the area, Fig.10(b) shows remove image noise by regional marking method.

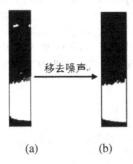

(a)   (b)

Fig. 10. Remove image noise: (a) Binary image after adaptive threshold; (b) Binary image of the removed noise

4.3   Liquid Surface Location

Fig.10(b) shows milk regional surface is not level, thus can not be used to liquid surface positioning. We propose a scanning method for solve this problem. Then, Split out a sub-region by scanning methods, including the background region and liquid region. Given that W is the region width and S is the liquid area. The following equation is used to obtain average height.

$$H = \frac{S}{W} \tag{4}$$

Fig.11 gives the process of our algorithm with sub-region by scanning methods.

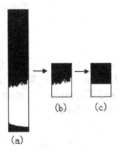

(b)   (c)

(a)

Fig. 11. Liquid surface locate: (a) Binary image of the removed noise; (b) Split out a sub-region by scanning methods; (c) liquid surface smooth results

5   Experimental Results

In this section, preliminary experiments for testing the feasibility and robustness of our method are conducted by applying the above-mentioned procedure. There are 300 images of this kind of images to be processed using our algorithm. The prospects of the bottle image is very complex, For example, light reflective, milk splashed on the sidewall, scale line and scale digital. The proposed algorithm can more accurately determine the location of the liquid surface for these images. Fig.12 shows the results using this set of images.

Fig. 12. Some experimental results

6   Conclusions and Future Work

Our preliminary experimental results show that proposed method is capable of finding exact surface location. In our algorithm, the milk bottles image is divided into the scale regional and non-scale regional, it reduces much noise interference. The gray histogram of non-scale regional is smooth by Shen algorithm; the algorithm can quickly find the zero point of the derivative. That makes it highly sensitive to transparent container surface detection. Another advantage of our method is that our approach is straightforward and simple.

Though the new method proposed in this paper is still in its stage of a prototype, it has already shown its potential for various implementations. This method can also be used for other transparent container surface detection. Our research will be carried on following this track.

Acknowledgements. This work was supported by the Guizhou Key Laboratory of Pattern Recognition and Intelligent System ([2009]4002) and National Natural Science Foundation of China (60965001) and Guizhou information processing and pattern recognition graduate education innovation base.

References

[1] Illingworth, J., Kittler, J.: A Survey of the Hough Transform. Compute Vision Graphics Image Process. 44(1), 87–116 (1988)
[2] Wei, Y., Yang, Y., Chen, W.: Application of Two Threshold Hough Transform in Automatic Index Identification of Index-instrument. China Instrumentation (10), 11–13 (2004)

[3] Nevatia, R., Babu, K.: Linear Feature Extraction and Description. Computer Graphics and Image Processing 13(3), 257–269 (1980)

[4] Yin, C., Liu, D., Song, J., Liu, T.: An Auto-Recognition Method for Digital Characters Based on Video Images. Microcomputer Information 24(10), 219–221 (2008)

[5] Heath, M., Sanocki, T., Bowyer, K., Sarkar, S.: Comparison of edge detectors: A methodology and initial study. Computer Vision and Image Understanding 69(1), 38–54 (1998)

[6] Sahoo, P.K., Soltani, Wong, A.K.C., Chen, Y.C.: A survey of Thresholding Techniques. Computer Vision, Graphics and Image Processing 41(2), 233–260 (1988)

[7] Chan, F.H.Y., Lam, F.K., Hui, Z.: Adaptive Threshold by Variational Method. IEEE Transactions on Image Processing 7(3), 468–473 (1998)

[8] Di Zenzo, S., Cinque, L., Levialdi, S.: Image Threshold using Fuzzy Entropies. IEEE Transactions on Systems, Man and Cybernetics, Part B: Cybernetics 28(1), 15–23 (1998)

[9] Li, H., Pan, Z., Wei, W.: Comparison for image segmentation based on different parameters estimate. Computer Engineering and Applications 44(10), 181–184 (2008)

[10] Shen, J., Castan, S.: An Optimal Linear Operator for Step Edge Detection. CVGIP: Graphical Models and Image Processing 54(2), 112–133 (1992)

Color Images Co-segmentation Based on Fuzzy Local-Entropy Classification

Hager Merdassi, Walid Barhoumi, and Ezzeddine Zagrouba

Research Team "Systèmes Intelligents en Imagerie et Vision Artificielle"
(SIIVA) – RIADI Laboratory, Institut Supérieur d'Informatique,
2 Rue Abou Rayhane Bayrouni, 2080 Ariana, Tunisia
hager.merdassi@hotmail.fr, walid.barhoumi@laposte.net,
ezzeddine.zagrouba@fsm.rnu.tn

Abstract. In this paper, we are interested in the unsupervised co-segmentation of color images. Solving this co-segmentation problem returns usually to optimize an energy function, which evaluates the similarity between the similar foreground objects in the input images. The objective is to evaluate the correspondence of foreground objects that penalizes the dissimilarity between them. To assess this correspondence existing techniques simply compare the histograms in the absence of any information of spatial coherence. The purpose of this paper is to integrate spatial information in order to avoid false detection. Indeed, in addition to the integration of the spatial information thanks to the use of the local entropy during the histogram computing, the main contribution of the proposed technique resides in the fuzzy local-entropy classification which allows to model the ambiguity of a pixel membership to a histogram bin. In particular, this permits to minimize over-segmentation and noise effects on the final co-segmentation results. Recorded results and the comparative study prove the accuracy of the proposed technique for color images co-segmentation.

Keywords: co-segmentation, histogram matching, local entropy, fuzzy classification.

1 Introduction

Object segmentation is a fundamental task in computer vision. Recently, existing techniques supply an additional image that can be sufficient to segment both images together in order to obtain higher accuracy than this achieved with either one alone. This task is called "co-segmentation" and refers to the simultaneous segmentation of similar foreground objects from two (or more) images [1]. The objective is to facilitate the detection of an object while profiting from the contrast of the similar objects as well as from the backgrounds appearances in the other views (Fig. 1). Most of existing automatic co-segmentation techniques formulated the problem as an energy minimization problem. Thus, solving the co-segmentation problem consists to minimize an energy function that evaluates the similarity between foreground objects (1). The first two terms are the Markov Random Field (MRF) energy terms for each image I_i ($i \in \{1,2\}$), E^d is a data term which is assumed to penalize solutions that are

F.L. Wang et al. (Eds.): CMSP 2012, CCIS 346, pp. 240–248, 2012.
© Springer-Verlag Berlin Heidelberg 2012

$$E_{\text{coseg}} = MRF_{I_1} + MRF_{I_2} + E(h_1, h_2), \text{ where, } \forall\, i \in \{1, 2\}, \ MRF_{I_i} = E_i^d + E_i^s. \quad (1)$$

inconsistent with the observed data and E^s is a smoothness term which enforces spatial coherence (1). The last term E is a global term that penalizes the difference between the foreground histograms h_1 and h_2 relatively to the pair of input images.

(a)   (b)

Fig. 1. Co-segmentation aims to facilitate the detection of the foreground object in (a) while exploiting the contrast in (b).

In [1, 2, 3] the problem was formulated as a MRF-based segmentation with a regularized difference of the two histograms. In [1], the L_1-norm is used in order to force foreground histograms of images to be similar while presenting a novel optimization scheme called trust region graph cuts. In [2], authors used the L_2-norm within a non-iterative half integrality-based algorithm. However, due to the presence of the histogram difference term, techniques based on L_1 and L_2-norms lead to complex optimization. Thus, rather than penalize the difference of the two foreground histograms, authors in [3] opted to reward the similarity and solved the problem optimally in polynomial time using a max-flow algorithm based on an appropriately constructed graph. More recently, authors in [4] proposed a histogram matching term that is able to perform scale-invariant co-segmentation. The scalable algorithm described in [5] is more general and can deal with more than two input images. Besides, it allows multiple objects to appear more than one time in an image. To do this, a common pattern discovery algorithm was incorporated with color, smoothness, confidence and locality cues to achieve accurate segmentation. In other works and differently to the energy minimization context, authors devoted the co-segmentation of an image group within a discriminative clustering framework [6]. For example, authors in [8] proposed a two level co-segmentation algorithm that iterates between segmenting images independently and using the produced segmentations to learn a SVM classifier separating foreground from background. In another work, to obtain multiclass co-segmentation, authors proposed an algorithm based on temperature maximization on anisotropic heat diffusion [7]. The common theme in unsupervised co-segmentation is enforcing consistency in appearance of segmented foreground and then aforementioned techniques extract the common foreground objects automatically without any user input. Many recent techniques look to apply a supervised co-segmentation which allows the user to indicate the foreground objects through simple scribbles [10]. For that matter, given a complete segmentation for some images, appearance models for the foreground/background classes can be then learned. Other works considered both supervised and unsupervised scenarios and the problem of co-segmentation was focused to detect multiple foreground objects while proposing less restrictive techniques based on a number of properties such as optimality guarantee and linear complexity [9]. In this paper, we are interested in the unsupervised co-segmentation of an image pair. We formulate co-segmentation as an energy minimization problem based on binary labeling (foreground *vs.* background). Thus, solving this problem returns to minimize an energy function, which evaluates the similarity between foreground objects by considering three terms: an intrinsic data term relating to the two processed images, a smoothness term which promotes a smooth segmentation of each image, and a correspondence term which penalizes the dissimilarity between foreground objects in the input images. To assess this correspondence, which strongly influences the final results, existing techniques simply compare the intensity histograms without considering the spatial coherence of neighboring pixels. For this, we propose to integrate the spatial information, by using the local-entropy during the histogram computing, in order to avoid false detections. Besides, we proposed a fuzzy classification technique in order to model the ambiguity of a pixel membership to a histogram bin, especially for pixels on bins' borders. This permits to optimize the final co-segmentation results, while minimizing noise effects. The rest of this paper is organized as follows. In Section 2, we describe the proposed technique based on fuzzy local-entropy classification. We show the experimental results in Section 3 and we produce conclusions and perspectives in Section 4.

2   Proposed Technique

As the co-segmentation goal is to segment common foreground objects from two images, we start by detecting the correspondence of these objects, which strongly influences the final results. Thus, given two images, I_1 and I_2, of the same size $M \times N$, the first step in the proposed technique consists to define the local-entropy for each color channel C_i of each image I_i ($C \in \{R,G,B\}$ and $i \in \{1,2\}$). This is done while considering the neighborhood of each pixel in order to characterize the texture of the input images, which provides information about the local variability of the intensity values. The objective behind the consideration of the local entropy $EC_i(j)$ of each pixel j in the color channel C_i, instead of its intensity, is to integrate the spatial information since neighboring pixels should have in general the same behavior (foreground *vs.* background), what allows particularly to avoid isolated pixels on the co-segmentation results (*c.f.* Section 3.). Given the number K of bins in the first image, each pixel is then associated to one of the K bins of the corresponding histogram, while producing the centers of bins to the second image in order to obtain the same classes for both images (Fig. 2). Then, for each color channel C_i, we define a binary matrix HEC_i (2) of size $K \times S$ where $S(=M.N)$ denotes the number of pixels in C_i.

$$\forall j \in C_i, \ \forall k \in \{1,...,K\}, \ HEC_i(j,k)=1 \ \Leftrightarrow \ EC_i(j) \in H_k, \tag{2}$$

where, H_k is the kth histogram bin. Next, we introduced a fuzzy classification technique in order to reclassify ambiguous pixels, which mainly appear on the borders of bins (Fig. 3). Indeed, the automatic pixels classification into a histogram provides K equally spaced containers, what leads to decrease the certainty of the correct belonging of a pixel into a bin, especially for those on the area χ "shared" by two bins (Fig. 3). Thus, our strategy consists to define a fuzzy membership degree $\mu_{B,Ci}(j)$, for each pixel j in each channel C_i, to the bin B to which pixel j belongs by default, as well as its fuzzy membership degrees $\mu_{B-l,Ci}(j)$ ($l \in [-1,1]$) to the neighboring bins $B-1$ and $B+1$ (3). This returns to define, relatively to each binary matrix HEC_i, a fuzzy membership matrix MC_i, where each pixel j has three fuzzy values (3) depending on its position in the corresponding bin. In fact, such that if $EC_i(j) \leq EC_i(c_B)$ then $l=-1$ else $l=1$, the membership degrees of pixel j to bins $B-1$, B and $B+1$ are defined as follows:

$$\mu_{B,C_i}(j) = 1 - \frac{|EC_i(j) - EC_i(c_B)|}{|EC_i(c_B) - EC_i(l_{B,B+l})|}, \quad \mu_{B+l,C_i}(j) = 1 - \mu_{B,i}(j) \text{ and } \mu_{B-l,C_i}(j) = 0, \quad (3)$$

where, c_B is the central pixel of bin B which belongs to color channel C, $l \in \{-1, 1\}$, $l_{B,B+1}$ (resp. $l_{B,B-1}$) is the local-entropy on the limit between bins B and $B+1$ ($B-1$ and B). For example, supposing that the red component of the input image is composed of four pixels ($S=4$); where $ER_l(j=1)=2.2$, $ER_l(j=2)=3.9$, $ER_l(j=3)=0.5$ and $ER_l(j=4)=4.45$; which will be classified into five bins ($K=5$) varying from 0 to 5, so that $ER_l(c_{B=k})=0.5*k$ for each k ($\in \{1,2,...,K\}$). Thus, the fuzzy local-entropy classification of these pixels allows to obtain the fuzzy matrix MR as illustrated by Fig. 4.

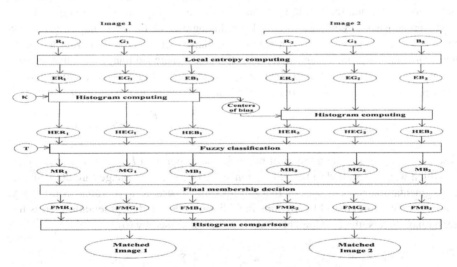

Fig. 2. Outline of the proposed histogram matching technique

Then, the fuzzy classification technique divides pixels into two groups. The first group contains the pixels with high membership degrees (≈ 1) to the default bin B.

However, given a threshold value "T" ($\in \,]0,1[$), the second group is composed of pixels with low non-null membership degrees ($\leq T$) and thus with high membership degrees to the bin $B-1$ or to the bin $B+1$. In this case, we define for each pixel j of the second group, the normalized distance $d(j, B+l)$ between this pixel and the bin $B-1$, or the bin $B+1$, and the default bin B in order to obtain the final classification by defining a final membership decision $FMC_i(j)$ (4) according to the nearest neighbors principle.

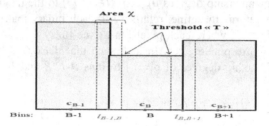

Fig. 3. Definition of the fuzzy membership degree $\mu_B(j)$ of a pixel j into a bin B

$$d(j, B+l) = \frac{|\,EC_i(j) - EC_i(c_{B+l})\,|}{n_l} \qquad (4)$$

where, $l \in \{-1, 0, 1\}$, n_l is the number of pixels in the bin $B+l$ and c_{B+l} is the center of the bin $B+l$. A low value of the normalized distance indicates that the pixel j and the set of pixels in $B+l$ are very similar, what indicates a low ambiguity between them. As a consequence, we modify the belonging of the pixel j to the bin $B+l$, depending on its position inside the bin B. Once the final membership matrixes are defined, the next step consists to compare the produced histograms of the two images, given the three color channels, while maximizing the similarity between them in order to obtain approximately the same foreground for each image ("matched image 1" and "matched image 2" in Fig. 2). In fact, two pixels in $I_1 \times I_2$ are similar only if they belong both to the same RGB bin H_k. This returns to resolve the following optimization problem:

$$\max \sum_{k=1}^{K} a_k b_k, \text{ such that } \sum_{k=1}^{K} a_k = Card(F_1) \text{ and } \sum_{k=1}^{K} b_k = Card(F_2), \qquad (5)$$

where, a_k (*resp.* b_k) is the number of pixels in the foreground F_1 (*resp.* F_2) of I_1 (*resp.* I_2) which were associated to the bin H_k. Once the two matched images are defined, the co-segmentation model also includes a global constraint to enforce consistency among the two foreground histograms in addition to the MRF segmentation terms for each image. Thus, the co-segmentation energy is expressed by (6):

$$\min \sum_{i=1}^{2} \left(\sum d_{i,j} x_{i,j} + \sum_{j \in V(q)} w_{jq} y_{i,jq} \right) - \lambda \sum_{k=1}^{K} \sum_{(j,q) \in (\cap I_1, H_k \times \cap I_2, H_k)} z_{jq}, \qquad (6)$$

$$\text{such that,} \begin{cases} \forall i \in \{1,2\}, \; x_{i,j} - x_{i,q} \leq y_{i,jq} \text{ and } x_{i,q} - x_{i,j} \leq y_{i,qj}; \\ \forall i \in I_1, \; z_{jq} \leq x_{i,j} \text{ and } \forall i \in I_2, \; z_{jq} \leq x_{i,q}. \end{cases}$$

where, $\{j,q\} \in \{1,..., S\}^2$, $d_{1,j}$ and $d_{2,j}$ are the deviation penalties charged for placing pixel j in the foreground of I_1 and I_2 respectively, $x_{i,j}$ is a binary variable indicating whether the pixel j is classified in the foreground in I_i, w_{jq} is the smoothness penalty which measures the cost of assigning different labels to two neighboring pixels j and q, λ is a coefficient expressing the relative weights of the two objectives, z_{jq} is a binary variable equals to 1 if $I_{i,j} \in F_1$ and $I_{i,q} \in F_2$, $V(q)$ is the neighborhood of pixel q and $\cap_{Ii,Hk}$ is the intersection between I_i and H_k. This model of co-segmentation attempts to simultaneously minimize smoothness and data terms in the MRF model for each image as well as to maximize the similarity between the foreground features in the two images (6). To resolve this minimization problem, we used an efficient max-flow-based algorithm applied on an appropriately constructed graph [3]. This non-iterative algorithm requires only one max-flow procedure, what allows to solve the problem optimally in a polynomial time. It produces more accurate segmentation results, while combining it with the proposed histogram matching technique,.

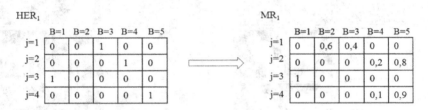

Fig. 4. An example of the fuzzy local-entropy classification

3   Experiments

In order to evaluate the quality of the proposed co-segmentation technique, this section is devoted to a comparison study with an efficient state-of-the-art technique [3]. This technique is the most similar technique, relatively the suggested one, since it is based on an energy minimization problem which was also solved using a max-flow procedure. We show in Fig. 5.a, the co-segmentation results obtained successively by [3] and by the proposed technique. It is clear that for the "stone" images pair, the over-segmentation effects (on the left border of the first image) was totally removed thanks to the fuzzy local-entropy classification. These effects are mainly due to the noise and especially to the existence of similar areas in the backgrounds of the images. For the "knut" images pair, we notice that our technique extracts successfully the object completely. In Fig. 5.b, we show a sample of the obtained co-segmentation results by the proposed technique, what confirms the aforementioned advantages. Moreover, given a co-segmentation ground truth [3], we evaluated objectively the results while measuring the miss-segmentation error for each image. Fig. 6.a illustrates the recorded error values for seven pairs of images while using the proposed technique and the one used in [3]. We remark that a clear difference occurs for the pairs "stone" (0.8% *vs.* 1.2%), "knut" (2.9% *vs.* 4.8%) and "amira" (12.6% *vs.* 13.1%)", and for the rest of pairs we recorded practically the same values. We used the same parameters for both techniques, such as the number of bins (Fig. 6.b.) and the value of λ (Fig. 7), which strongly affect the final results. Fig. 6.b presents the error value for the images pair "stone" while varying the number of histogram bins from 5 to 40. We remark that 10 bins per color channel works well since we obtain 0.8% as error value with the proposed technique, in contrast to [3] for which an error value of 1.2% was recorded. We can also note that starting from 15 bins, the error value increases remarkably for both techniques. Concerning the used value of λ, the extracted foregrounds were compared with these produced by [3] while varying the value of λ from 1 to 10^{-4} for the "stone" pair of images (Fig. 7). We can clearly deduce that, comparatively to [3], the proposed technique is much less sensitive to the value of λ.

(a)   (b)

Fig. 5. Subjective evaluation: (a) comparison of our results with those of [3]: the first row shows the images pair, second and third rows illustrate respectively the results of [3] and our results, (b) some results obtained by the proposed technique

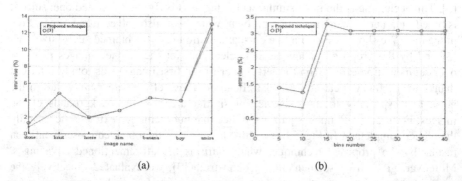

(a)   (b)

Fig. 6. Objective evaluation: (a) comparison of the error values of the proposed technique and those of [3], (b) influence of the bins number on the error value for the "stone" images pair

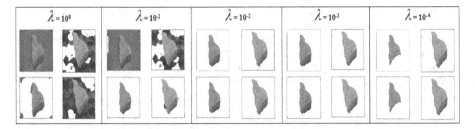

Fig. 7. Co-segmentation results while varying λ: the first row shows the co-segmentation results of [3] and our results are shown in the second row

4   Conclusion

We proposed a co-segmentation technique which allows the inclusion of the spatial information and the modeling of the ambiguity of a pixel membership to a histogram bin thanks to the use of the local-entropy throughout the histogram computing and to the fuzzy local-entropy classification. To resolve the energy minimization problem, we used a cost-efficient algorithm based on a max-flow procedure, which produces accurate segmentations and its combination with the proposed fuzzy local-entropy classification technique produces better results comparatively to existing techniques [1] [3]. As future works, we plan to extend the proposed technique to the general case of more than two images while constructing an efficient graph using the normalized cut which provides an unbiased measure of disassociation between subgroups of the graph and should produce more accurate segmentation, especially for textured images.

Acknowledgments. Authors would like to thank Dr. Vikas Singh, Biostatistics & Medical Informatics department at University of Wisconsin-Madison, for providing the implementation of [3] and for helpful discussions.

References

1. Rother, C., Minka, T., Blake, A., Kolmogorov, V.: Co-segmentation of image pairs by histogram matching: Incorporating a global constraint into MRFs. In: CVPR, New York (2006)
2. Mukherjee, L., Singh, V., Dyer, C.: Half-integrality based algorithms for cosegmentation of images. In: CVPR, Miami (2009)
3. Hochbaum, D.S., Singh, V.: An efficient algorithm for co-segmentation. In: International Conference on Computer Vision, Kyoto (2009)
4. Mukherjee, L., Singh, V., Peng, J.: Scale invariant cosegmentation for image groups. In: International Conference on Computer Vision and Pattern Recognition, Colorado (2011)
5. Chu, W.-S., Chen, C.-P., Chen, C.-S.: MOMI-Cosegmentation: Simultaneous Segmentation of Multiple Objects among Multiple Images. In: Kimmel, R., Klette, R., Sugimoto, A. (eds.) ACCV 2010, Part I. LNCS, vol. 6492, pp. 355–368. Springer, Heidelberg (2011)

6. Joulin, A., Bach, F., Ponce, J.: Discriminative clustering for image co-segmentation. In: CVPR, San Francisco (2010)
7. Kim, G., Xing, E.P., Fei-Fei, L., Kanade, T.: Distributed co-segmentation via submodular optimization on anisotropic diffusion. In: ICCV, Barcelona (2011)
8. Chai, Y., Lempitsky, V., Zisserman, A.: BiCoS: A bi-level co-Segmentation method for image classification. In: ICCV, Barcelona (2011)
9. Kim, G., Xing, P.: On multiple foreground co-segmentation. In: CVPR, Rhode Island (2012)
10. Batra, D., Kowdle, A., Parikh, D., Luo, J., Chen, T.: Interactively co-segmentating topically related images with intelligent scribble guidance. Computer Vision 93(3), 273–292 (2011)

An Effective TBD Algorithm for the Detection
of Infrared Dim-Small Moving Target in the Sky Scene

Lisha He, Lijun Xie, Tian Xie, Haibin Pan, and Yao Zheng

Center for Engineering & Scientific Computation, and School of Aeronautics and Astronautics,
Zhejiang University, Hangzhou, Zhejiang, 310027, PR China
helszju@163.com

Abstract. An effective algorithm for the detection of dim-small moving target in the infrared (IR) image sequence is described in this paper, which is based on the idea of Track-Before-Detect (TBD). To deal with the low signal to noise ratio (SNR) and high false alarm rate of the IR target detection in the sky scene, two of the Track-Before-Detect (TBD) methods are introduced: dynamic programming (DP) for the SNR enhancement by energy accumulation, and multistage hypothesis testing (MSHT) to lower the false alarm rate by threshold judgment. Furthermore, constraints as the stabilization of the energy and the continuity of the movement of IR dim-small target are applied to avoid the energy scatter. And based on MSHT, most of the false trajectories are eliminated to reduce the calculated amount and save the storage space. Simulation shows good results for the detection of IR dim-small moving target based on the algorithm we proposed.

Keywords: Track-Before-Detect, dynamic programming, multistage hypothesis testing, dim-small moving target.

1   Introduction

Detect-Before-Track (DBT) and Track-Before-Detect (TBD) are two categories of detection algorithm for IR dim-small moving target [1]. Research [1] [2] [3] shows that DBT algorithm adopts a "single-frame detection and multi-frame confirmation" strategy, and works well with the image sequence of high SNR by placing emphasis on the small target's spatial character rather than the temporal character during the detection procedure. Compared with TBD, the detection based on DBT is more fast, simpler and easier to implement in real-time, but may fail in the case of low SNR and target/background contrast. Figure 1 shows the flow chart of DBT algorithm.

Meanwhile, TBD algorithm adopts a "multi-frame detection" strategy [4-6] [10] to achieve the target, and both spatial and temporal information are needed when it works. The algorithm keeps tracking more than one candidate trajectories in the detecting process, and estimates a posterior probability for each one, which will be compared with a certain threshold at the end of the process. If one's posterior probability exceeds the threshold, it will be predicted as a target trajectory. It is suggested that TBD algorithm has a more complex structure and needs more computation and storage than DBT algorithm, but extremely effective in the low SNR environments. Figure 2 shows the flow chart of TBD algorithm.

F.L. Wang et al. (Eds.): CMSP 2012, CCIS 346, pp. 249–260, 2012.
© Springer-Verlag Berlin Heidelberg 2012

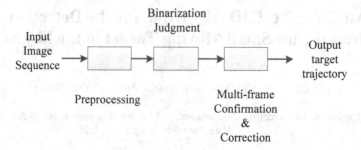

Fig. 1. Flow chart of DBT algorithm

This paper proposes an efficient algorithm for detecting IR dim-small moving target in the sky scene based on the idea of TBD. The detection work consists of preprocessing, energy accumulation and trajectory tracking & predication. The energy of dim-small moving target is cumulated along the optimal trajectory sought out by DP, which guarantees to eliminate the impact of low SNR. Pseudo trajectories and invalid candidate targets are rejected by MSHT threshold, which is of great benefit to decrease the calculation and storage load as well. Figure3 shows the process of our detection algorithm.

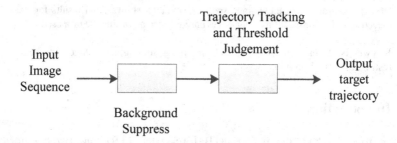

Fig. 2. Flow chart of TBD algorithm

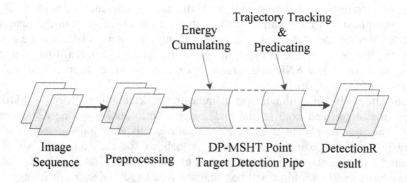

Fig. 3. IR dim-small moving target detection based on TBD algorithm

The following sections present the detection based on a TBD algorithm in detail. Section 2 develops a model of IR image sequence that contains dim-small moving target in the sky scene, and preprocesses the sequence by morphological filter. Section 3 describes the major detection algorithm, where the energy of IR dim-small moving target is accumulated without diffused by DP in section 3.1, MSHT threshold is set to reject invalid candidate trajectory by MSHT in section 3.2 and 3.3. Section 4 is the experimental results analyses. Section 5 gives the conclusion, and related references are listed in the last section.

2   Modeling and Preprocessing

2.1   Model of IR Image Sequence with Dim-Small Moving Target

The object will only occupy one or several pixels in the imaging plane when it is far away from the IR imaging system, although its actual diameter may be more than ten meters. In such situation, the amplitude of the noise signal presents to be similar with dim-small objects and the objects is totally mixed up with noise in IR images.

Ideally, assume that the noise in the IR image is conformed to Gaussian distribution, and IR image sequence meets the principle of superposition. If IR image sequence consists of N frames, each of them is of the size $M \times M$, $z(X_i)$ is the grayscale value for the pixel X_i in the i th frame of the IR image sequence, then the image Z is expressed as

$$Z = \{z(X_i)\} \quad \forall X_i \tag{1}$$

Thus the noise component $n(X_i)$ in position X_i meets the Gaussian distribution, that is $n(X_i) \to N(0, \sigma^2)$, σ^2 is the variance of the background. The grayscale $z(X_i)$ is defined as

$$z(X_i) = n(X_i) + T(X_i) \quad \forall X_i \tag{2}$$

Here $T(X_i)$ is the target component in position X_i.

If H_1 means there is a target at X_i, H_0 means there isn't a target at X_i, then

$$H_1 : z(X_i) = T(X_i) + n(X_i) \tag{3}$$

$$H_0 : z(X_i) = n(X_i) \tag{4}$$

Besides the Gaussian noise, background noises like clouds also exist in real IR images. Suppose the background noise in position X_i as $b(X_i)$ Thus the model of IR image is set as

$$H_1 : z(X_i) = b(X_i) + T(X_i) + n(X_i) \tag{5}$$

$$H_0 : z(X_i) = b(X_i) + n(X_i) \tag{6}$$

2.2   Top-Hat Filter

The background of IR image sequence is usually extensive and changes gently, accounting for the low-frequency part of the image spatial frequency spectrum, while the target is small and isolated like a bright point, accounting for the high-frequency part of the image spatial frequency spectrum. Thus high-pass filters are proper useful for preprocessing. As one of the high-pass filters, Top-hat is used to eliminate the element changes indistinctively and detect the element of high-frequency by morphological operation, as shown in equation (7).

$$Hat(f) = f - (f \circ b) \tag{7}$$

Here f stands for the grayscale image, b is the structure element, and $(f \circ b)$ means to do open operation on image f by the structure element b.

Figure 4 shows the original image and the preprocessing result in the form of grayscale image and histogram. The result indicates that Top-hat operator does well in burring and eliminating background noise like clouds.

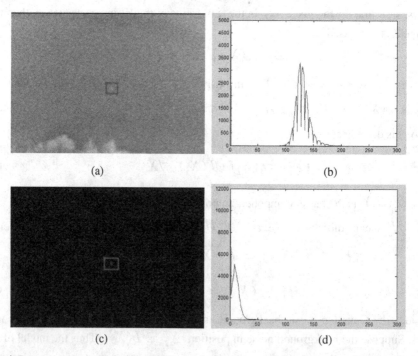

(a)   (b)

(c)   (d)

Fig. 4. Preprocessing by Top-hat: (a) The original IR image in the sky scene; (b) Histogram of the original grayscale image; (c) Preprocessing result by Top-hat filter; (d) Histogram of the preprocessing result

3   The Detection of IR Dim-Small Moving Target

3.1   Energy Accumulation Based on DP Algorithm

Based on the model developed above, the detection of IR dim-small moving target can be translated into a mathematical problem: to find an optimal energy accumulation path. This very optimal path is suggested to be the target trajectory we searched for in normal conditions. And the SNR of IR image sequence will be enhanced when the energy of dim-small target is accumulated by this path. Researches [1] [6] [7] have shown that DP is eminently suitable for the optimal path searching, which can be used to accumulate the energy of dim-small targets, and find out the linear motion trajectories.

DP algorithm complies with the rule that the maximum integrated energy should be the energy accumulated along the target trajectory. That is, if $E = \sum\limits_{i \in Traj} e_i$ is the energy integrated by the target trajectory, $E' = \sum\limits_{j \notin Traj} e_j$ is the energy by other invalid trajectory, then $E > E'$ is tenable. Here e_i is the energy of the ith frame.

Set $E_{max}(X_k, k)$ as the energy of pixel X_k accumulated along the optimal moving trajectory for k frames, initialized as 0 at the first frame, then

$$E_{max}(X_k, k) = \begin{cases} \max\limits_{x_{k-1} \in D_{k-1}} E_{max}(X_{k-1}, k-1) + z(X_k) & k=1,...N \\ 0 & k=0 \end{cases} \tag{8}$$

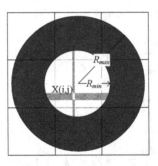

Fig. 5. Target status transition domain with $v \in [v_{min}, v_{max}]$, after temporal delay t, here $R_{min} = v_{min}t$, $R_{max} = v_{max}t$

Where D_{k-1} is a target status transition domain [9] that states the position and status of the target in the next frame after certain temporal delay. It performs as an annular region centered on current position (see Figure 5), affected by the velocity v and camera shake parameters.

Fig. 6. Energy scattering during the energy accumulation

DP algorithm enables dim-small moving target to be prominence with the energy integrated along the optimal trajectory, which guarantees the enhancement of SNR, but meanwhile inevitably introduces the problem of energy scattering. That is, the target is much lighter with the energy increased, but looks larger at the same time for the energy of neighborhood pixels also may be accumulated, shown in figure 6.

Dim-small targets can be considered as doing uniform rectilinear motion in a short period of time because IR image sequence is taken from long-distance. It is suggested that the energy and forward moving direction of dim IR target are relative stable and consecutive for frames but not of the Gauss noise, for which its distribution and movement are randomly. In this case, we find a way [7] to avoid the problem of energy scattering. That is, introduce an energy gradient threshold γ_E and a move transition threshold γ_d to bind the energy accumulation. The followed formulas show these constraints.

$$\exp(\frac{|\overline{Z_{E'}} - Z(X_k)|}{Z(X_k)}) \leq \gamma_E \quad k = 1,...N \tag{9}$$

Where $\overline{Z_{E'}} = \dfrac{E_{max}(X_{k-1}, k-1)}{k-1} \quad k = 1,...N$

$$\exp(-\frac{\overline{d}_{(k,k-1)}}{180}) \leq \gamma_d \quad k = 1,...N \tag{10}$$

Here $\overline{d}_{(k,k-1)}$ is the transition angle of pixel X_{k-1} moved from the (k-1)th frame to kth frame, defined as

$$\overline{d}_{(k,k-1)} = \begin{cases} |d(X_k,X_{k-1}) - d(X_{k-1},X_{k-2})| & |d(X_k,X_{k-1}) - d(X_{k-1},X_{k-2})| \leq 180° \\ 360 - |d(X_k,X_{k-1}) - d(X_{k-1},X_{k-2})| & 360 - |d(X_k,X_{k-1}) - d(X_{k-1},X_{k-2})| \geq 180° \end{cases} \tag{11}$$

3.2   The Principle of MSHT Algorithm

If IR dim-small target moves with the velocity $v \leq 1$, the excursion of target will be no more than one pixel per frame, and the size of target status transition domain is 3×3. Since the transition probability for each position is same in this domain, there are 9 candidate trajectories in the next frame starting from the current pixel, then 25 candidate trajectories in the next second frame. Realize that the number of candidate trajectories is increased exponentially, the more frames, the larger calculation amount. In allusion to this situation, Dr. S.D. Blostein from Queen's University first mentioned the MSHT algorithm [10] [11] in 1988. MSHT algorithm is another TBD algorithm, which can reduce the calculation amount and storage space by organizing candidate trajectories in the tree structure, hypothesis testing the tree for every frame, so as to abandon the invalid branch timely.

As shown in figure 7, a target is started from the node {1} in the first frame, and develops four candidate trajectories after three frames, as 1->1->1, 1->1->3, 1->1->4, 1->2->5, corresponding to four candidate targets. Here 1->1->1 means the coordinates of the target hasn't changed, 1->1->3, 1->1->4 means the target has moved one pixel at the third frame, 1->2->5 implies that the target has moved one pixel per frame. All these candidate trajectories are according with the status transition laws.

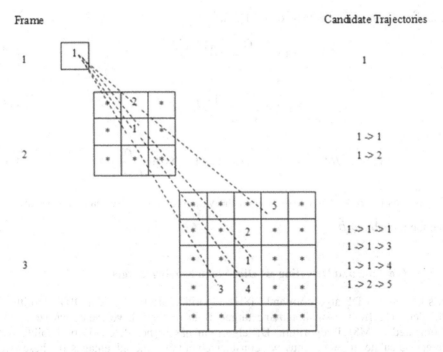

Fig. 7. The tree structure of candidate trajectories

MSHT algorithm has brought in two thresholds $[\hat{a}, \hat{b}]$ to binary hypothesis testing of the pixels. Assume H_1 as the hypothesis for the absence of the target, H_0 as the hypothesis for the presence of the target.

When $k \in (1, N-1)$,

$$\begin{cases} \sum_{i=1}^{k} Z(X_i) \geq \hat{a} & Traj \sim H_1 \\ \sum_{i=1}^{k} Z(X_i) \leq \hat{b} & Traj \sim H_0 \\ \hat{b} < \sum_{i=1}^{k} Z(X_i) < \hat{a} & \text{take another sample,} \end{cases} \tag{12}$$

When $k = N$,

$$\begin{cases} \sum_{i=1}^{k} Z(X_i) > \hat{V}_T & Traj \sim H_1 \\ \sum_{i=1}^{k} Z(X_i) \leq \hat{V}_T & Traj \sim H_0 \end{cases} \tag{13}$$

Let c_0, c_1 are two constants on $[0, 1]$, then

$$\hat{a} = \ln[\frac{1-(1-c_1)(1-\hat{\beta})}{(1-c_0)\hat{\alpha}}] \tag{14}$$

$$\hat{b} = \ln[\frac{(1-c_1)(1-\hat{\beta})}{1-(1-c_0)\hat{\alpha}}] \tag{15}$$

$$\hat{V}_T = \eta[\mu_1 \Phi^{-1}(c_0\hat{\alpha}) + \mu_0 \Phi^{-1}(c_1(1-\hat{\beta}))](\frac{\sigma}{\mu_1 - \mu_0}) \tag{16}$$

Thresholds $[\hat{a}, \hat{b}, \hat{V}_T]$ is involved with the value of SNR, false alarm rate $\hat{\alpha}$ and detection probability $\hat{\beta}$.

3.3   Tracking and Detecting IR Dim-Small Moving Target

It's known that DP algorithm and MSHT algorithm are two typical DBT algorithms for detecting IR dim-small moving target. Both of them have their own strengths. Compared to MSHT algorithm, DP algorithm has higher detection probability but larger calculate amount. Thus we consider combining the advantages of these two algorithms to detect IR dim-small moving target, aimed at obtaining high detection probability, and low computation and storage requirements.

Realize that the key point of DP algorithm and MSHT algorithm in detection is integrating the energy of dim-small target to enhance the SNR of IR image sequence, so the grayscale accumulation threshold acquired by MSHT also applies to DP algorithm.

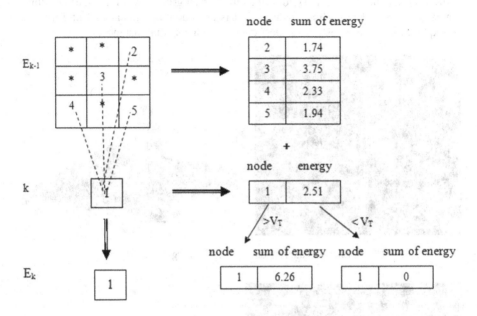

Fig. 8. The principle of DP-MSHT algorithm

A hypothesis testing threshold is brought into the DP energy accumulation process after combining with the MSHT algorithm in our work. For example, as shown in figure 8, define E_{k-1} as the accumulated energy matrix for the prior $(k-1)$ frames, for a certain pixel node {1} in the kth frame, there are 4 valid energy nodes, labeled as {2, 3, 4, and 5} according to the status transition law. Integrate the maximum energy node {3} among the four valid energy nodes with the current pixel node {1}. The energy of node {1} is accumulated while the integrated value exceeds a certain accumulated energy threshold V_T; otherwise the energy of node {1} turns to 0. Thus, the kth accumulated energy E_k in equation (8) is redefined as:

$$
E_k = \begin{cases} \max_{X_{k-1} \in D(k-1)}(E_{k-1}(X_{k-1})+Z(X_k)) & \begin{array}{l} E_{k-1}(X_{k-1})+Z(X_k)>V_T \\ X_{k-1} \in D(k-1) \end{array} \\ 0 & \begin{array}{l} E_{k-1}(X_{k-1})+Z(X_k)<V_T \\ X_{k-1} \in D(k-1) \end{array} \end{cases} \tag{17}
$$

4   Experimental Results

The IR image sequence we used for experiments is a real IR aircraft video taken by the FLIR camera system in the sky, with the size of 320×240. A dim-small target no more than 7 pixels is embedded in the clouds background, with the start coordination as (169,132). The motion of this target is considered as linear and uniform, for the sequence is taken by 30 frames per second in huge spatial distance.

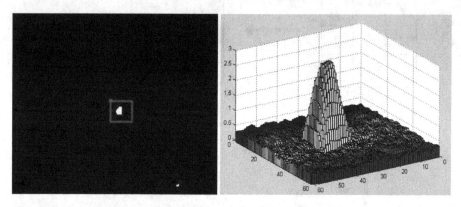

Fig. 9. Energy scattering during the DP energy accumulation

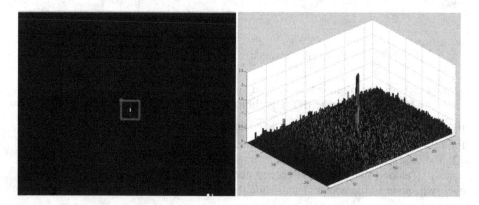

Fig. 10. Energy scattering is avoided by introducing the constraint conditions

Figure 9 is the grayscale and 3d mesh result of the energy accumulated by DP algorithm for 5 frames. It is confirmed that the energy of dim-small target is increased and diffused, for the bright spot in the image is larger and lighter contract with figure 6. Figure 10 presents that energy scattering is handled by taking the energy stability and the moving direction continuity of IR dim-small moving target in mind. We assume that the energy increases no more than 20%, and the transition angle not exceeds 90° in the experiment.

Figure 11 are experimental results based on DP algorithm and DP-MSHT algorithm. The first raw are original grayscale images of the 12th, 16th and 20th frames,

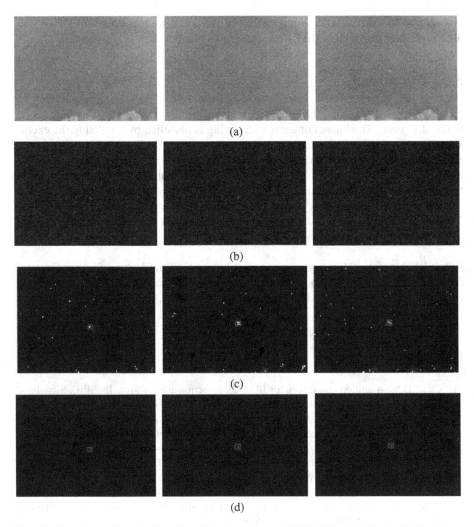

Fig. 11. Experimental results based on DP algorithm and DP-MSHT algorithm, with the target marked by red box. (a) Original grayscale images of the 12th, 16th and 20th frames; (b) Grayscale images of the three frames after preprocessed by Top-hat filter; (c) The detection results by DP algorithm; (d) The detection results by DP-MSHT algorithm.

each with the corresponding target coordinates as (169,134), (170,136), (170,135); the second raw are corresponding grayscale images after preprocessed by Top-hat filter; the third raw and the forth raw record the detection results by DP algorithm and DP-MSHT algorithm respectively. According to the results, both DP and DP-MSHT algorithms have detected dim-small moving target in these three frames, but much more noise and candidate targets are left in the result images based on DP algorithm, which may lower the detection probability of other frames. This phenomenon is improved obviously by the DP-MSHT algorithm shown in the fourth raw. There are less noise and almost no other candidate targets left in the result images based on DP-MSHT algorithm, thus proved this DBT algorithm has better detection performance.

5   Conclusions

This paper has discussed a TBD detection algorithm for IR dim-small moving target in the sky scene. The impact of energy scattering is dispelled by regulating the excursion of energy accumulation and the forward direction of IR dim-small moving target. False trajectories and candidate targets are rejected by the multi-stage threshold calculated by MSHT algorithm. Experimental results show that the algorithm presented in this paper has made some promotions on the detection performance, help to economize the resource, and promote the practical applicability of TBD algorithm in a way. The future work should still focus on keeping balance of the detection accuracy and calculation storage complexity of dim IR target detection.

Acknowledgments. This work is supported by the National Natural Science Foundation of China under grant No. 61008048. The authors wish to thank the contributions of the group of the Center for Engineering and Scientific Computation, Zhejiang University.

References

1. Chan, D.S.: A unified framework for IR target detection and tracking. In: SPIE, Signal and Data Processing of Small Targets, Orlando, pp. 66–76 (1992)
2. Jones, R., Svalbe, R.: Algorithms for the decomposition of gray scale morphology operations. IEEE Trans. on Pattern Analysis and Machine Intelligence 16, 581–588 (1994)
3. Boccignone, G., Chianese, A., Picariello, A.: Small target detection using wavelets. In: 14th International Conference on Pattern Recognition, pp. 1776–1778 (1998)
4. Zhang, C.C., Yang, D.G., Wang, H.Q.: Algorithm surveys for dim targets track–before–detect in infrared image. J. Laser & Infrared 37, 104–107 (2007)
5. Reed, I.E.: Application of 3-D Filtering to moving target detection. IEEE Transactions on Aerospace and Electronic Systems 19, 898–905 (1983)
6. Yair, B.: Dynamic programming solution for detecting dim moving targets. IEEE Transactions on Aerospace and Electronic Systems 21, 144–156 (1985)
7. He, L.S., Mao, L.J., Xie, L.J.: Dynamic programming algorithm for detecting dim infrared moving targets. In: MIPPR 2009, Proceedings of SPIE, vol. 7459 (2009)
8. Bai, X., Zhou, F., Jin, T.: Enhancement of dim small target through modified top-hat transformation under the condition of heavy clutter. J. Signal Processing, 1643–1654 (2010)
9. Ulisses, B.N., Manish, C., John, G.: Automatic target detection and tracking in forward-looking infrared image sequences using morphological connected operators. J. Electronic Imaging 13, 802–813 (2004)
10. Steven, D.B., Thomas, S.H.: Detection of small moving objects in image sequences using multistage hypothesis testing. In: International Conference on Acoustics, Speech, and Signal Processing, vol. 39, pp. 1611–1629 (1988)
11. Steven, D.B., Haydn, S.R.: A sequential detection approach to target tracking. IEEE Transactions on Aerospace and Electronic Systems 30, 197–211 (1994)

Moving Target Detection
Based on Improved Mixture Gauss Model[*]

Gang Liu[1,**], Yugan You[1], Siguo Zheng[2], and Fanguang Li[1]

[1] School of Electrical Power and Automation Engineering,
Shanghai University of Electrical Power, Shanghai 200090, China
[2] Shanghai Power Economic Research Institute,
Shanghai Municipal Electric Power Company, State Grid, Shanghai 200010, China
weimeiyefan@sina.com

Abstract. Based on mixture Gauss model to detect moving targets is easy to produce "ghosting", smear and background update problem caused by light mutation, so this paper proposes an improved mixture Gauss modeling method background update problem. This method combines the frame difference method to identify moving pixels and non-real motion pixels in the foreground image. By giving non-real pixels a larger learning rate to make them fast blending into the background, we solve the "ghost", smear and light mutations problems. The experimental results show that this algorithm can effectively detect moving targets.

Keywords: Moving object detection, Background subtraction, Gauss mixture model.

1   Introduction

Intelligent visual surveillance system is an important research field in computer vision, it has a wide range of applications in safety monitoring, communications, medical and other fields. In intelligent monitoring system, moving target detection is a fundamental and critical step. Moving target detection [1-2] is to real-time detect moving targets in a series of video sequences. At present the commonly used methods for target detection are background difference method, frame difference method and optical flow method. Among them, optical flow method's computation is more complex, its hardware requirement is very high, and it is not suitable for real-time

---

[*] Fund: This work was supported in part by National Natural Science Foundation of China (No.61203224/F030307), the Leading Academic Discipline Project of Shanghai Municipal Education Commission (No.J51303), and the Sic-Tech Innovation Foundation of Shanghai Municipal Education Commission (No.13YZ101.).

[**] Gang, Liu (1977.2-) is a master instructor and a via-professor in Shanghai University of Electrical Power, and mainly engages in the fields of the power quality analysis, the fault diagnosis and automatic control of substation equipment, the scene identification and planning of power plants, the multi-sensor image fusion and information fusion research.

F.L. Wang et al. (Eds.): CMSP 2012, CCIS 346, pp. 261–266, 2012.
© Springer-Verlag Berlin Heidelberg 2012

applications; frame difference method is relatively simple, real-time and has better adaptability to the dynamic environment, but can not completely extract all the relevant points of the target. Compare to the frame difference method, the background difference method can get more complete target, and its computation complexity is much lower than the optical flow computation, so the background difference method has been widely used.

2   Background Subtraction Method

Background subtraction [3-4] is simply using the current image subtracting the background image, select a suitable threshold for binarization of the differential image, you can accurately identify the location of moving targets. Its outstanding features are simple, fast and having good detection results, so it can be used in the occasion with high real-time requirement.

Suppose video image sequence at time t is I(x,y,t), the background image simulated by model is B(x,y,t), to do the subtraction of two images, we can get the difference image D(x,y,t). As the formula (1).

$$D(x, y, t) = | I(x, y, t) - B(x, y, t) | \qquad (1)$$

Then passed the threshold processing to get the two binary image BW(x,y,t).

$$BW(x, y, t) = \begin{cases} 1 & \text{if} (D(x,y,t) > T) \\ 0 & \text{otherwise} \end{cases} \qquad (2)$$

In formula (2), if the difference of the current frame and the background is greater than the threshold T, the binarized image is set to 1, indicating that the pixel in the movement area;otherwise the binary image is set to 0, indicating that the pixel is part of the background.

Although moving target detection based on the background difference method can get more complete extraction and moving object related informations than frame difference method, but with the passage of time, the scene may appear light change, wave reflection ,shaking trees and other external conditions changes , there may be some false movement, affect the effect of moving target detection.

3   Adaptive Mixture Gaussian Background Modeling

Mixture Gauss background model [5-6] is firstly proposed by Staufer and Grimson. This method uses Gaussian mixture modeling for each pixel, and uses pixel iterative for model parameters update, so as to effectively overcome the disturbance caused by the background image change, light gradient. After extracting and updating the background, the moving target can be very easy get by deducting the background.

In the video image sequence, according to the Gaussian function can modeling for each pixel (x_0, y_0) from 1 to t. Set to the time t, the finite set of pixel is $\{x_1, \ldots, x_t\} = \{I(x_0, y_0, s) \mid 1 \le s \le t\}$, where I is the video frame. If all the historical values of the pixel are approximated Through the K Gaussian functions, Then at time t, the probability of pixel value x_t belongs to the background is :

$$P(x_t) = \sum_{i=1}^{K} \omega_{i,t} * \eta(x_t, \mu_{i,t}, \Sigma_{i,t}) \tag{3}$$

Where x_t is the pixel values of the time t, usually constituted by the three channels' color values of red, green and blue. K is the number of mixture Gaussian model. The value of K generally depends on the available memory size and the computing power of system, under the normal circumstances, values are between 3 and 5. The greater the value of K, the stronger the ability to handle fluctuations, but the more time. $\omega_{i,t}$ is weights of the model i in the mixture Gaussian model at the time $t.\eta(\ )$ is i-th Gaussian distribution at the time t. Defined as follows:

$$\eta(x_t, \mu_{i,t}, \Sigma_{i,t}) = \frac{1}{(2\pi)^{\frac{n}{2}} |\Sigma_{i,t}|^{\frac{1}{2}}} e^{-\frac{1}{2}(x_t - \mu_{i,t})^T \Sigma_{i,t}^{-1}(x_t - \mu_{i,t})}, i = 1, 2 \ldots, K \tag{4}$$

Assuming the pixels of each color channel independently of each other and have same variance. So the covariance matrix is $\Sigma_{i,t} = \sigma^2_{i,t} I$. If $|x_t - \mu_{i,t-1}| \le \lambda \sigma_{i,t-1}$, means the x_t match the Gaussian model, update the model parameters:

$$\begin{cases} \omega_{i,t} = (1-\alpha)\omega_{i,t-1} + \alpha \\ \mu_t = (1-\rho)\mu_{t-1} + \rho X_t \\ \sigma_t^2 = (1-\rho)\sigma_{t-1}^2 + \rho(X_t - \mu_t)^T(X_t - \mu_t) \end{cases} \tag{5}$$

Where α is the weight update rate, ρ as a parameter update rate, $\rho = \alpha\eta(x_t, \mu_t, \sigma_t)$. The K Gaussian distributions arrangement in decreasing order of ω/σ, Meet the following type of pre-B models as the background:

$$B = \arg\min_b \left(\frac{\sum_{i=1}^{b} \omega_i}{\sum_{i=1}^{K} \omega_i} > T \right) \tag{6}$$

4   Improvement of Mixture Gaussian Model Algorithm

Mixture Gauss model effectively solves the pixel multi peak distribution problem, can be accurately modeling in the complex background image with the light gradient and branches shaking, but it still has the following disadvantages: 1. When the object in the background suddenly began to exercise, the revealed background area will be false detected as moving targets, to form the "ghost". 2. When the moving object became static, in a very long period of time it will still be judged as foreground, to form the "smear". 3. Light mutation. This paper uses an improved mixture Gauss model to solve these defects effectively.

4.1   The Elimination of "ghosting" and "smear"

The Gauss mixture model determine the foreground and background according to the Image pixel values. In the background, if the original stationary objects have a suddenly movement (such as a car drive away), the background which is covered by objects is revealed, these revealed part obviously can not match the long training background distribution so will be determined as the foreground to produce "ghosting". Similarly, when the moving object gradually be stationary into the background, in a long period of the time, it will still be judged as the foreground to produce "smear ". We can use the idea of the frame difference method to improve the algorithm to achieve the elimination of the above phenomenon.[7-8]

Figure 1(a) is the schematic diagram for the phenomenon of "ghosting". When object C1 moves from the frame k to C2 in frame k+1, the revealed background is A, the detected foreground is A+C2. Then object moves from C2 to C3 in frame k+2, the revealed background is A+B, the detected foreground is A+B+C3. It is easy to know that region A + C2 and the region A + B + C3 in Part A is the same, so make the foreground image of the frame k+2 and the hole image of the frame k+1 difference. Using appropriate threshold, if the difference does not exceed the threshold, the area A should be background. First correct error detection area in frame k+1 and establish a new Gauss model for the pixels on area A. Then take the current pixel value as the mean, take appropriate variance and weights to replace the lowest priority Gauss distribution of the original background distribution, updated them into the background distribution. So that we can eliminate the phenomenon of "ghost".

Figure 2(b) is the schematic diagram for the phenomenon of "smear". The object was still moving in frame k, the detected foreground is C1. The object has stopped since the frame k+1. Because of the update rule of the mixture Gaussian model, the background update rate of the area detected as foreground object is slow. So after this frame, object C will still be detected as the foreground in a long time. According to the above method, to make the foreground image C3 of the frame k+2 and the hole image of the frame k+1 difference, we will find the C3 area matches with the previous frame. It means the object has been static. First correct the foreground image of frame k +1 as the background and establish a new Gauss model for the pixels on area C2. Then take the current pixel value as the mean, take appropriate variance and weights to replace the lowest priority Gauss distribution of the original background distribution, updated them into the background distribution. So that we can eliminate the phenomenon of "smear".

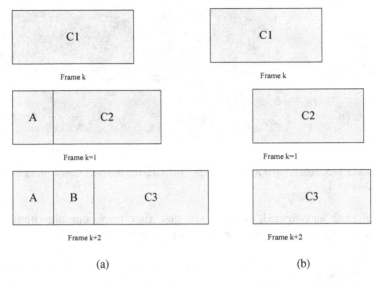

(a)   (b)

Fig. 1. (a) is the schematic diagram for the phenomenon of "ghosting", (b) is the schematic diagram for the phenomenon of "smear"

4.2   Light Mutation

The above method has a certain adaptability to light mutation. When the light suddenly changes, almost all the basic picture brightness are greatly change. If foreground pixels representing the whole image ratio of more than 50%, it was judged to be caused by light mutations. We need to initialize mixture Gauss model. After the initialization, the process is similer to the "ghosting" model. According to the above method, we can effectively detect the moving target.

5   Experimental Results

In order to test the effect of the proposed algorithm, we compared it with the classic mixture Gauss model.

(a)   (b)   (c)

Fig. 2. "ghosting"processing (a) Original image, (b) Classic mixture Gauss model, (c) The proposed algorithm

(a)   (b)   (c)

Fig. 3. "smear"processing (a) Original image, (b) Classic mixture Gauss model, (c) The proposed algorithm

From figure2 and figure3, we can see that after using our algorithm, it can effectively eliminate the phenomenon of "ghosting" and "smear".

6   Conclusion

This paper describes the basic mixture Gauss model modeling principle and parameter updating method. And on this basis, we use the frame difference method thought to improved mixture Gauss model. It effective solved the "ghosting" when static object re-sports and "smear" when moving object gradually be stationary into the background, in some degree weaken the effect to the mixture Gauss model caused by light mutation.

References

1. Liu, G., Li, J.: Moving target detection via airborne HRR phased array radar. Aerospace and Electronic Systems 37(3), 914–924 (2001)
2. Wang, P., Li, H., Himed, B.: Moving Target Detection Using Distributed MIMO Radar in Clutter With Nonhomogeneous Power. Signal Processing 55(10), 4809–4820 (2011)
3. Jung, C.R.: Efficient Background Subtraction and Shadow Removal for Monochromatic Video Sequences. IEEE Transactions on Multimedia 11(3), 571–577 (2009)
4. Suhr, J.K., Jung, H.G., Li, G., Kim, J.: Mixture of Gaussians-Based Background Subtraction for Bayer-Pattern Image Sequences. Circuits and Systems for Video Technology 21(3), 365–370 (2011)
5. Pyun, K.P., Lim, J., Won, C.S., Gray, R.M.: Image Segmentation Using Hidden Markov Gauss Mixture Models. Image Processing 16(7), 1902–1911 (2007)
6. Pyun, K., Lim, J., Gray, R.M.: A Robust Hidden Markov Gauss Mixture Vector Quantizer for a Noisy Source. Image Processing 18(7), 1385–1394 (2009)
7. Du, J., Hu, Y., Jiang, H.: Boosted Mixture Learning of Gaussian Mixture Hidden Markov Models Based on Maximum Likelihood for Speech Recognition. Audio, Speech, and Language Processing 19(7), 2091–2100 (2011)
8. Markley, S.C., Miller, D.J.: Joint Parsimonious Modeling and Model Order Selection for Multivariate Gaussian Mixtures. IEEE Journal of Selected Topics in Signal Processing 4(3), 548–559 (2010)

A Motion Descriptor Based on Statistics of Optical Flow Orientations for Action Classification in Video-Surveillance

Fabio Martínez[1,2], Antoine Manzanera[1], and Eduardo Romero[2]

[1] Unité d'Informatique et d'Ingénierie des Systèmes, ENSTA-ParisTech
antoine.manzanera@ensta-paristech.fr
[2] CIM&Lab, Universidad Nacional de Colombia, Bogota, Colombia
{fmartinezc,edromero}@unal.edu.co

Abstract. This work introduces a novel motion descriptor that enables human activity classification in video-surveillance applications. The method starts by computing a dense optical flow, providing instantaneous velocity information for every pixel. The obtained flow is then characterized by a per-frame-orientation histogram, weighted by the norm, with orientations quantized to 32 principal directions. Finally, a set of global characteristics is determined from the temporal series obtained from each histogram bin, forming a descriptor vector. The method was evaluated using a 192-dimensional descriptor with the classical Weizmann action dataset, obtaining an average accuracy of 95 %. For more complex surveillance scenarios, the method was assessed with the VISOR dataset, achieving a 96.7 % of accuracy in a classification task performed using a Support Vector Machine (SVM) classifier.

Keywords: video surveillance, motion analysis, dense optical flow, histogram of orientations.

1 Introduction

Classification of human actions is a very challenging task in different video applications such as surveillance, image understanding, video retrieval and human computer interaction [1, 2]. Such task aims to automatically categorize activities in a video and determine which kind of movement is going on. The problem is complex because of the multiple variation sources that may deteriorate the method performance, such as the particular recording settings or the inter-personal differences, particularly important in video surveillance, case in which illumination and occlusion are uncontrolled.

Many methods have been proposed, coarsely grouped into two categories: (1) the silhouette based methods, and (2) the global motion descriptors (GMDs). The silhouette based methods aim to interpret the temporal variation of the human shape during a specific activity. They extract the most relevant silhouette shape variations that may represent a specific activity [7, 8]. These approaches achieve high performance in data sets recorded with static camera and simple background, since they

F.L. Wang et al. (Eds.): CMSP 2012, CCIS 346, pp. 267–274, 2012.

need an accurate silhouette segmentation, but they are limited in scenarios with complex background, illumination changes, noise, and obviously, moving camera.

On the other hand, the GMDs are commonly used in surveillance applications to detect abnormal movements or to characterize human activities by computing relevant features that highlight and summarize motion. For example, *3d* spatio temporal Haar features have been proposed to build volumetric descriptors in pedestrian applications [6]. GMDs are also frequently based on the apparent motion field (optical flow), fully justified because it is relatively independent of the visual appearance. For instance, Ikizler *et al* [3] used histograms of orientations of (block-based) optical flow combined with contour orientations. This method can distinguish simple periodic actions but its temporal integration is too limited to address more complex activities. Guangyu et al [5] use dense optical flow and histogram descriptors but their representation based on human-centric spatial pattern variations limits their approach to specific applications. Chaudhry *et al* [4] proposed histograms of oriented optical Flow (HOOF) to describe human activities. Our descriptor for instantaneous velocity field is very close from the HOOF descriptor, with significant differences that will be highlighted later, and the temporal part of their descriptor is based on time series of HOOFs, which is very different from our approach.

The main contribution of this work is a motion descriptor which is both entirely based on dense optical flow information and usable for recognition of actions or events occurring in surveillance video sequences. The instantaneous movement information, represented by the optical flow field at every frame, is summarized by orientation histograms, weighted by the norm of the velocity. The temporal sequence of orientation histograms is characterized at every histogram bin as some temporal statistics computed during the sequence. The resultant motion descriptor achieves a compact human activity description, which is used as the input of a SVM binary classifier. Evaluation is performed with the Weizmann [8] dataset, from which 10 natural actions are picked, and also with the ViSOR video-surveillance dataset [9], from which 5 different activities are used. This paper is organized as follows: Section 2 introduces the proposed descriptor, section 3 demonstrates the effectiveness of the method and the last section concludes with a discussion and possible future works.

2   The Proposed Approach

The method is summarized on Figure 1. It starts by computing a dense optical flow using the local jet feature space approach [10]. The dense optical flow allows to segment the region with more coherent motion in a RoI. A motion orientation histogram is then calculated, using typically 32 directions. Every direction count is weighted by the norm of the flow vector, so an important motion direction can be due to many vectors or to vectors with large norms. Finally, the motion descriptor groups up the characteristics of each direction by simple statistics on the temporal series, whose purpose is to capture the motion nature.

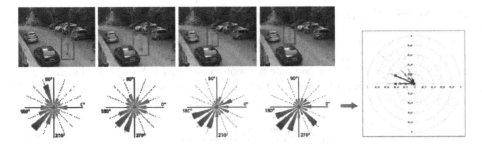

Fig. 1. General framework of the proposed method. First row: calculation of a dense optical flow. Second row: Orientation histograms representing the instantaneous velocities for every frame. Finally on the right, it is shown the descriptor made of temporal statistics of every histogram bin.

2.1 Optical Flow Estimation Using Local Jet Features

Several optical flow algorithms can be used within our method. They need to be dense and globally consistent, but not necessarily error-free, nor particularly accurate in terms of localization. In our implementation, we used the optical flow estimation based on the nearest neighbor search in the local jet feature space, proposed in [10]. It consists in projecting every pixel to a feature space composed of spatial derivatives of different orders and computed at several scales (the local jet): $f_{ij}^{\sigma} = f * \frac{\partial^{i+j} G_{\sigma}}{\partial x^i \partial y^j}$, where σ, the standard deviation of the $2d$ Gaussian function G_{σ} represents the scale, and $i + j$ the order of derivation. For each frame t and every pixel x, the apparent velocity vector $V_t(x)$ is estimated by searching the pixel associated to the nearest neighbor in the space of local jet vectors calculated at frame $t - 1$. The interest of this method is to provide a dense optical flow field without explicit spatial regularization, and an implicit multi-scale estimation by using a descriptor of moderate dimension for which the Euclidean distance is naturally related to visual similarity. In our experiments, we used 5 scales, with $\sigma_{n+1} = 2\,\sigma_n$, and derivatives up to order 1, resulting in a descriptor vector of dimension 15.

2.2 Motion RoI Segmentation

The dense optical flow can be used for a coarse spatial segmentation of potential human actions at each frame. First a binary morphological closing operation is performed on pixels whose velocity norm is above a certain threshold, to connect close motion regions. The resulting connected components may also be grouped according to a distance criterion, and the bounding boxes of the remaining connected components form the motion RoIs. We use this simple segmentation to eliminate noisy measurements outside the moving character (Single actions are considered in these experiments).

2.3   Velocity Orientations Histogram

The next step consists in coding the distribution of instantaneous motion orientations. For a non-zero flow vector V, let $\phi(V)$ denotes its quantized orientation. Based on the HOG descriptor [11], we compute the motion orientation histogram of each frame as the relative occurrence of flow vectors within a given orientation, weighted by the vector norm:

$$H_t(\omega) = \frac{\sum_{\{x; \phi(V_t(x))=\omega\}} \|V_t(x)\|}{\sum_{\{x; \|V_t(x)\|>0\}} \|V_t(x)\|}$$

where $\omega \in \{\omega_o \dots \omega_{N-1}\}$. ω_N the number of orientations was set to 32 in our experiments. This part of our descriptor, dealing with instantaneous velocity information, is almost identical to the HOOF descriptor of Chaudhry *et al* [4], except that the HOOF descriptor is invariant under vertical symmetry, i.e. it does not distinguish the left from the right directions. This property makes the HOOF descriptor independent to the main direction of transverse motions, but it also reduces its representation power, missing some crucial motion information, like antagonist motions of the limbs. For this reason, we chose to differentiate every direction of the plane, the invariance w.r.t. the global motion direction being addressed at the classification level.

2.4   Motion Descriptor

Finally, a description vector is computed to capture the relevant motion features. For n frames, it consists in a set of temporal statistics computed from the time series of histogram bins $H_t(\omega)$, as follows:

1. *Maximum:* $M(\omega) = \max_{\{0 \le t < n\}}\{H_t(\omega)\}$

2. *Mean:* $\mu(\omega) = \sum_{\{0 \le t < n\}} \frac{H_t(\omega)}{n}$

3. *Standard deviation:* $\sigma(\omega) = \sqrt{\sum_{\{0 \le t < n\}} \frac{H_t^2(\omega)}{n} - \mu(\omega)^2}$

We also split the sequence into 3 intervals of equal durations and compute the corresponding means as follows:

4. *Mean Begin:* $\mu_b(\omega) = \sum_{\{0 \le t < \frac{n}{3}\}} \frac{H_t(\omega)}{n/3}$

5. *Mean Middle:* $\mu_m(\omega) = \sum_{\{\frac{n}{3} \le t < \frac{2n}{3}\}} \frac{H_t(\omega)}{n/3}$

6. *Mean End:* $\mu_e(\omega) = \sum_{\{\frac{2n}{3} \le t < n\}} \frac{H_t(\omega)}{n/3}$

Some examples of human activities and their associated motion descriptor in the two datasets are shown in Figure 2. For each motion descriptor, the blue and gray lines respectively represent the maximum and mean values. The red square, yellow triangle and green disk represent the mean values for the beginning, middle and end portion of the sequence respectively. For readability purposes, the standard deviation is not displayed here. It turns out from our experiments that the aspect of the descriptor is visibly different for distinct human activities.

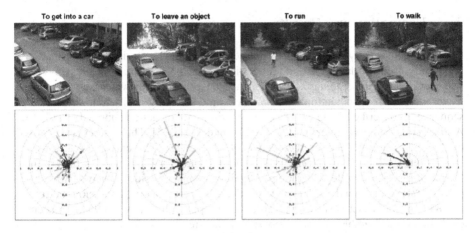

(a)ViSOR dataset

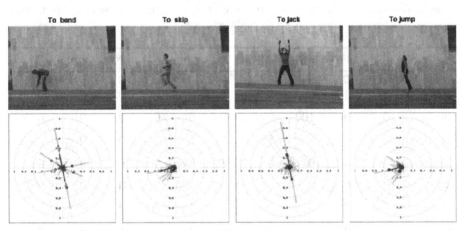

(b) Weizmann dataset

Fig. 2. Example of motion descriptors for human activities

2.5   SVM Classification

Classification was performed using a bank of binary SVM classifiers. The SVM classifier has been successfully used in many pattern recognition problems given its robustness, applicable results and efficient time machine. In our approach, we use the *one-against-one SVM multiclass classification* [12], where given k motion classes, $\frac{k(k-1)}{2}$ classifiers are built and the best class is selected by a voting strategy. The SVM model was trained with a set of motion descriptors, extracted from hand labeled human activity sequences (see next section). The Radial Basis Function (RBF) kernel was used [13].

3   Evaluation and Results

Our approach was evaluated in two datasets: The Weizmann dataset [14] that it is commonly used for human action recognition and the VISOR dataset [9], which is a real world surveillance dataset. Performance on each dataset was assessed using a leave-one-out cross validation scheme, each time selecting a different single action sequence, as described in the literature by previous human action approaches [15, 16]. A first evaluation was done over the Weizmann dataset [14]. This dataset is composed of 9 subjects and 10 actions recorded in 93 sequences. The classes of actions are "run", "walk", "skip", "jumping-jack" (jack), "jump-forward-on-two-legs" (jump), "jump-in-place-on-two-legs" (pjump), "gallop-sideway" (side), "wave-two-hands" (wav2), "wave-one-hand"(wav1) and "bend". The corresponding confusion matrix for the Weizmann dataset is shown in Table 1. Our approach achieves a 95 % of accuracy, which is comparable to results reported in the literature.

Table 1. Confusion matrix for the Weizmann dataset. Every row represents a ground truth category, while every column represents a predicted category.

Category	bend	jack	jump	pjump	run	side	skip	walk	wav1	wav2
bend	100	0	0	0	0	0	0	0	0	0
jack	0	100	0	0	0	0	0	0	0	0
jump	0	0	100	0	0	0	0	0	0	0
pjump	0	0	0	89	0	0	11	0	0	0
run	0	0	0	0	80	0	20	0	0	0
side	0	0	0	0	0	100	0	0	0	0
skip	0	0	0	0	0	20	80	0	0	0
walk	0	0	0	0	0	0	0	100	0	0
wav1	0	0	0	0	0	0	0	0	100	0
wav2	0	0	0	0	0	0	0	0	0	100

A second test was carried out with a dataset for human action recognition from a real world surveillance system (ViSOR: the Video Surveillance Online Repository) [9], which has been less used in the literature, but is more representative for video-surveillance applications. This dataset is composed of 150 videos, captured with a stationary camera, showing 5 different human activities: walking, running, getting into a car, leaving an object and people shaking hands, four of them shown in Figure 2. The high variability of this dataset is challenging: each activity is performed by several actors with different appearance, the background scene is usually different, and the motion direction, starting and halting points locations may be different for every video sequence. Evaluation was performed with 32 directions, corresponding to a descriptor dimension of 192, and obtaining an averaged accuracy of 96.7 %. Results obtained are shown in the confusion matrix (Table 2, top).

Table 2. Top: Confusion matrix. Row: ground truth / Column: predicted category. For example, row 4 means that out of all the "run" sequences, 96.43 % were classified correctly, and 3.57% were classified as "get into a car". Bottom: Statistical indices measured for each category.

Category	get car	leave object	walk	run	hand shake
get car	100	0	0	0	0
leave object	0	95	0	0	5
walk	0	0	92	8	0
run	3.57	0	0	96.43	0
hand shake	0	0	0	0	100

Action	Accuracy	Sensitivity	specificity	PPV	NPV
get car	98	100	94.9	96.6	100
Leave object	97	95	100	100	93
walk	95	91.7	100	100	88.9
run	94	96.4	90.4	92	95.6
hand shake	97	100	92.2	95.2	100
Average	96.2	96.6	95.5	96.8	95.5

The performance was also evaluated in terms of classical statistical indices (Table 2, bottom). Let *TP, TN, FP* and *FN* be the number of true positive, true negative, false positive and false negative, respectively, associated to each label. The *accuracy* is $Acc = \frac{TP+TN}{TP+TN+FP+FN}$, the *Sensitivity* is $Sen = \frac{TP}{TP+FN}$, the *specificity* is $Spec = \frac{TN}{TN+FP}$, the *Positive Predictive Value* is $PPV = \frac{TP}{TN+FP}$ and the *Negative Predictive Value* is $NPV = \frac{TN}{TN+FN}$. The obtained results demonstrate both good performance and a significant degree of confidence, using a very compact action descriptor of dimension 192. Our approach was also tested on the KTH dataset [14] but the results were significantly worse, with accuracy around 90 %. This is mainly due to a limitation of the local jet based dense optical flow, which needs enough scale levels to be effective and then provides poor results when the resolution is too low.

4   Conclusions and Perspectives

A novel motion descriptor for activity classification in surveillance datasets was proposed. A dense optical flow is computed and globally characterized by per-frame-orientation histograms. Then a global descriptor is obtained using temporal statistics of the histogram bins. Such descriptor of 192 characteristics to represent a video sequence was plugged into a bank of SVM binary classifiers, obtaining an average accuracy of 96.7 % in a real world surveillance dataset (ViSOR). For the classical human action dataset (Weizmann) our approach achieves a 95 % of accuracy.

A great advantage of the presented approach is that it can be used in sequences captured with a mobile camera. Future work includes evaluation on more complex scenarios. We also plan to adapt this method to perform on line action recognition system, by coupling it with an algorithm able to segment the video in space × time boxes containing coherent motion.

Acknowledgements. This work takes part of a EUREKA-ITEA2 project and was partially funded by the French Ministry of Economy (General Directorate for Competitiveness, Industry and Services).

References

1. Aggarwal, et al.: Human activity analysis: A review. ACM Computing Surveys 43, 1–43 (16), 3 (2011)
2. Poppe, R.: A survey on vision-based human action recognition. Image and Vision Computing 28, 976–990, 6 (2010)
3. Ikizler, N., et al.: Human Action Recognition with Line and Flow Histograms. In: 19th International Conference on Pattern Recognition (ICPR), Tampa, FL (2008)
4. Chaudhry, et al.: Histograms of oriented optical flow and Binet-Cauchy kernels on nonlinear dynamical systems for the recognition of human actions. In: IEEE Conference on Computer Vision and Pattern Recognition (CVPR), pp. 1932–1939 (2009)
5. Zhu, et al.: Action recognition in broadcast tennis video using optical flow and support vector machine, pp. 89–98 (2006)
6. Ke, Y., et al.: Efficient Visual Event Detection Using Volumetric Features. In: Int. Conf. on Computer Vision, pp. 166–173 (2005)
7. Weinland, D., Ronfard, R., Boyer, E.: Free viewpoint action recognition using motion history volumes. Computer Vision and Image Understanding, 249–257, 104 (2006)
8. Gorelick, L., Blank, M., Shechtman, E., Irani, M., Basri, R.: Actions as Space-Time Shapes. IEEE Trans. on Pattern Analysis and Machine Intelligence, 2247–2253, 12 (2007)
9. Ballan, L., Bertini, M., Del Bimbo, A., Seidenari, L., Serra, G.: Effective Codebooks for Human Action Categorization. In: Proc. of ICCV. International Workshop on VOEC (2009)
10. Manzanera, A.: Local Jet Feature Space Framework for Image Processing and Representation. In: Int. Conf. on Signal Image Technology & Internet-Based Systems (2011)
11. Dalal, N., et al.: Histograms of Oriented Gradients for Human Detection. In: Int. Conf. on Computer Vision & Pattern Recognition, pp. 886–893, 2 (2005)
12. Hsu, et al.: A comparison of methods for multiclass support vector machines. IEEE Transactions on Neural Networks 13, 415–425, 2 (2002)
13. Chang, C., et al.: LIBSVM: A library for support vector machines. ACM Trans. on Intelligent Systems and Technology 2, 21–27, 3 (2011)
14. Schuldt, et al.: Recognizing Human Actions: A Local SVM Approach. In: Proceedings of the 17th International Conference on Pattern Recognition, pp. 32–36, 3 (2004)
15. Wong, S.F., Cipolla, R.: Extracting spatiotemporal interest points using global information. In: Proc. IEEE Int. Conf. Computer Vision, pp. 1–8, 2 (2007)
16. Ballan, et al.: Human Action Recognition and Localization using Spatio-temporal Descriptors and Tracking (2009)

A Bayesian Online Object Tracking Method Using Affine Warping and Random KD-Tree Forest

Ming Xue and Shibao Zheng

Department of Electronic Engineering,
Shanghai Jiaotong University, 200240, Shanghai, China
{silas_xue,sbzh}@sjtu.edu.cn

Abstract. A Bayesian online object tracking method is proposed in this paper. Within the inference framework, estimation of the dynamical transition model and observation model is computed sequentially based on object appearance warping and KD-tree-based matching. Once the object to be tracked is located in the previous frame, the proposed method randomly samples structured local image patches in the current frame via Gaussian particle filtering within and around the previous target region to form the candidates. Then, a random KD-tree forest is established to organize the sampling data, and find the nearest neighbor (NN) to the object region in the previous frame. The information provided by the matching output is interpreted as the tracking result for the current frame. The trees update online until the tracking procedure is finished. Experiments demonstrate the efficiency and competitive performance of the proposed algorithm compared with some state-of-the-art works.

Keywords: object tracking, Bayesian framework, affine warping, random KD-tree forest.

1 Introduction

Object tracking has long been an important issue in image and video processing and been playing an important part in video surveillance. So far, a large number of algorithms have been proposed [13], but it still remains challenging due to the factors such as pose changes, illumination variation, background clutter, *et al.*.

In recent years, online object tracking has been popular in computer vision, image processing and machine learning [1-3, 7, 10, 11].Generally speaking, these algorithms can be categorized into discriminative and generative approaches. For the former part, discriminative methods formulate tracking as a classification problem which aims to distinguish the target from the background in each frame, and thus employs the information from both the target and the background [2, 3, 7]. In [2], Avidan makes a combination of weak classifiers into a strong one to form ensemble tracking. In [7], Grabner *et al.* propose an online boosting method to update discriminative features for tracking problem. Babenko *et al.* [3] propose multiple instance learning (MIL) framework which combine positive and negative samples into bags to learn a discriminative model for tracking. For the later part, generative methods formulate the

F.L. Wang et al. (Eds.): CMSP 2012, CCIS 346, pp. 275–282, 2012.
© Springer-Verlag Berlin Heidelberg 2012

tracking problem as searching for the regions which are most similar to the target region or model, based on either templates [1, 10] or subspace models [11]. For the stability of the observed image structure during tracking, Jepson *et al.* [10] propose an appearance model, which involves a mixture of stable image structure, learned over long time courses, along with two-frame motion information and an outlier process. An online EM-algorithm is used to adapt the appearance model parameters over time. Adams *et al.* [2] present a "Frag-Track" algorithm, in which the template object is represented by multiple image fragments or patches. Based on the integral histogram data structure, each patch votes on the possible positions and scales of the object in the current frame by comparing its histogram with the corresponding image patch histogram to find the object location in current frame. Instead of describing objects with a blob of pixels, David *et al.* [11] learn the eigenbases on-line during the object tracking process and estimate the motion parameter estimation with a particle filter. With respect to the template update, the algorithm concurrently develops an efficient subspace update algorithm that facilitates object tracking under varying pose and lighting conditions.

Inspired by the variant condensation algorithm by David *et al.*[11], which is originally proposed by Isard *et al.* [9], and the descriptor-based image matching algorithms with KD-trees [4, 12], in this paper, we propose a online Bayesian tracking method based on object appearance warping model and random KD-trees forest. The basic processing procedure is shown in Fig.1.

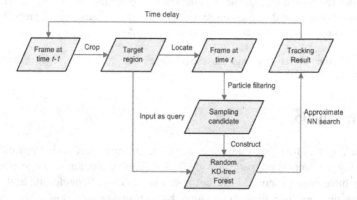

Fig. 1. Basic procedure of method

Once the object to be tracked is located and cropped as a patch in the previous frames, the proposed method randomly samples structured local image patches in the current frame via particle filtering within and around the previous target region to form the matching potential candidates, and change them into sequential pattern. Then, a k-d random forest is established to first organize the candidate data, and then find the nearest neighbor (NN) to the previous patch, which is inputted as a query point. The matching result responds to the tracking result in the current frame, and the forest model updates online in each frame to efficiently seize the possible changes of the object, until the tracking procedure is finished.

The rest of this paper is organized as follows: Section 2 describes the Bayesian tracking principle, which forms the basis of our approach. Section 3 describe the transition model dynamics, while in Section 4, the random KD-tree forest is described for observation matching. The evaluation and results of the proposed method are given in Section 5. A brief outlook on future improvement is given in Section 6.

2   Bayesian Particle Tracking Formulation

Generally speaking, the online object tracking problem could be interpreted as iterative and sequential estimation of the dynamical transition model and observation model. In propagational sense, it could also be cast as an inference task in a Markov model with hidden state variables. Within the Bayesian framework, the filtering process is a recursive estimation of time-evolving posteriori distribution of the target state given all the past observations, where namely the state at time t is modeled and computed based on the maximum a posterior (MAP) estimate of observations from the beginning to time t as follows,

$$p(\mathbf{X}_t \mid \mathbf{I}_{1:t}) = \alpha p(\mathbf{I}_t \mid \mathbf{X}_t)$$
$$\int p(\mathbf{X}_t \mid \mathbf{X}_{t-1}) p(\mathbf{X}_{t-1} \mid \mathbf{I}_{1:t-1}) d\mathbf{X}_{t-1} \tag{1}$$

where $\mathbf{X}_t$ is the state at time t, $\mathbf{I}_{1:t}$ refers to all the observations from the beginning to time t, and α is a normalization term. To sequentially estimate the hypothesized state output, it requires the definition of a dynamical state evolving model for estimation, and an observation likelihood model which measures the similar probability between the reference and current observation induced by the hypothesized state. Based on equation (1), the tracking process is managed by the observation model $p(\mathbf{I}_t \mid \mathbf{X}_t)$, which is the likelihood of $\mathbf{X}_t$ based on the observation of $\mathbf{I}_t$ at time t, and the 1st order Markovian transition model $p(\mathbf{X}_t \mid \mathbf{X}_{t-1})$, between two continuous states $\mathbf{X}_t$ and $\mathbf{X}_{t-1}$.

In this paper, we define that the state variable $\mathbf{X}_t$ describes the location and affine motion parameters of the target at time t, and directly use the pixels of target region as the observations rather than descriptors.

As demonstrated by numerous works in the object tracking literature [3, 7, 11], it is critical to construct an efficient dynamical transition model $p(\mathbf{X}_t \mid \mathbf{X}_{t-1})$ and an effective observation model $p(\mathbf{I}_t \mid \mathbf{X}_t)$. The next two sections describe the corresponding the details.

3   Dynamical Modeling by Affine Warping

Via affine image warping, a location of a target object in an image frame can be represented and transformed forwards and backwards between a typical image coordinate system and a coordinate system centering the target within a canonical box such as the unit square or any other distribution.

3.1   State and State Transition Dynamics Modeling

In this work, we follow the state modeling establishment proposed by David *et al* [11]. Thus, at time t, the information provided by the object consists of the six parameters, and more directly, the state at time t could be modeled as a 6-tuple set, which is

$$\mathbf{X}_t = (x_t, y_t, \theta_t, s_t, \alpha_t, \phi_t) \tag{2}$$

where x_t, y_t, θ_t, s_t, α_t and ϕ_t denote translation in horizontal and vertical direction separately, rotation angle, scale, aspect ratio, and skew direction at time t of the object.

Once the previous state is warped into a 'box' space and represented as a point, the surrounding points in such a space could possibly be state candidates, which potentially formulate the motion information in the current frame. The connection between the points corresponds to the state transition dynamics between previous states and current state. In a generic form, in this paper, we assume the dynamics between previous states and current state candidates could be modeled by Brownian particle motion, which means that the candidates points is a random movement of the previous state point. More specifically, for the 6-tuple set, we independently model each parameter in state $\mathbf{X}_t$ by a Gaussian distribution around its counterpart in state $\mathbf{X}_{t-1}$ with no bias, and thus

$$p(\mathbf{X}_t \mid \mathbf{X}_{t-1}) = \mathrm{N}(\mathbf{X}_t; \mathbf{X}_{t-1}, 0, \mathbf{\Psi}) \tag{3}$$

where $\mathbf{\Psi}$ is a diagonal covariance matrix whose elements are the corresponding variances of affine parameters. Please note that more complex model could be established to make the transition dynamics more practical to specific application.

3.2   Particle Sampling Based on Affine Transformation

Based on the assumption and modeling above, we could directly randomly sample the samples around the target region based on affine parameter, which is shown in Fig.2.

In the implementation, the affinity between 6-tuple parameter and canonical box could be computed by the following matrix representation [8]

$$\mathbf{p}' = \begin{bmatrix} \mathbf{A} & \mathbf{t} \\ \mathbf{0}^{\mathrm{T}} & 1 \end{bmatrix} \cdot \mathbf{p} \tag{4}$$

where $\mathbf{p} = (x, y, 1)^{\mathrm{T}}, \mathbf{p}' = (x', y', 1)^{\mathrm{T}}$ corresponds to the coordinate before and after the transform separately. Corresponding to (2), $\mathbf{A} = \begin{bmatrix} \theta_t & s_t \\ \alpha_t & \phi_t \end{bmatrix}$ is a 2×2 non-singular matrix, and refers to the composition of rotation and non-isotropic scaling, and $\mathbf{t} = (x_t, y_t)^{\mathrm{T}}$ is a translation vector.

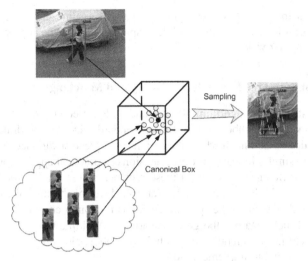

Fig. 2. Affine Particle Sampling

4   Random KD-Forest Observation Matching

After the paritcle candidate $\mathbf{X}_t$, and the corresponding image patch $\mathbf{I}_t$ are given, the following critical step is to model and estimate $p(\mathbf{I}_t \mid \mathbf{X}_t)$.

4.1   Modeling the Observation Estimation by Nearest-Neighbor-Based Appearance Similarity

We assume that an appearance model is constructed by estimating the similarity of a certain target candidate to the target observation in previous frame. Thus we could model the observation estimation based on a certain target candidate $\mathbf{X}_t$ is proportional to its likelihood to the target:

$$p(\mathbf{I}_t \mid \mathbf{X}_t) \propto \frac{1}{\hat{D}(\mathbf{X}_t, \mathbf{I}_{t-1}) + \varepsilon} \tag{5}$$

where $\hat{D}(\mathbf{X}_t, \mathbf{I}_{t-1})$ represents the similarity measurement between the observation of the state candidate $\mathbf{X}_t$ and the target observation $\mathbf{I}_{t-1}$, and ε is a small constant to prevent denominator of the right side in (5) from being zero. The similarity computation can be computed conducted by nearest neighbor image matching.

A nearest neighbor matching problem could be simply defined as follows: given a set of points $P=\{p_1, p_2, ..., p_n\}$ in a vector space $\mathbf{X}$, they would be preprocessed in such a way that given a new query point $q \in \mathbf{X}$, find the points in P that are nearest to q can be performed efficiently. In this paper, since the image patches are directly used rather than image features in matching, we will assume that $\mathbf{X}$ is a Euclidean vector space, yet it is noted that the Euclidean space could also be appropriate for most problems in computer vision.

4.2   Random KD-Tree Forest-Based Query and Matching

We use the Best Bin First algorithm [4] and random KD-tree Forest [12] to perform an approximate Nearest Neighbor search. In the standard KD-tree, the dimension which the data is divided is the one in which the data has the greatest variance. However, data variance is quite similar in many of the dimensions in practical application, and it does not make much difference in which of these dimensions the subdivision is made. We adopt the strategy of selecting at random (at each level of the tree) the dimension in which to subdivide the data. The split dimension is randomly chosen from the first D dimensions on which data has the greatest variance. Multiple trees are constructed in this way, different from each other in the choice of subdivision dimensions. We use the fixed value $D = 5$ in our implementation.

When indexing the trees, a single priority queue is maintained across all the randomized trees so that search can be ordered by increasing distance to each bin boundary [12]. The degree of approximation is determined by examining a certain number of leaf nodes, at which point the search is terminated and the best candidates returned. We directly use the FLANN library developed by the author for fast implementation.

5   Experimental Result

To evaluate performance of the proposed method, we collected a number of videos recorded in indoor and outdoor environments. The information and challenging factors of the test sequences are listed in Table 1.

Table 1. Information of test sequence

Name	Challenging Factors	Test Frame Range
Woman[1]	heavy occlusion	No. 1-100
Car[11]	illumination variation, distraction from other objects	No. 1-100
Face[3]	long-duration occlusion	No. 1-300

The proposed method is currently implemented with MATLAB, and it runs at about 2.5 frames per second on 600 particles on a standard 1.73 GHz computer with 1G RAM. We set the particle numbers to be 600, the number of trees is 4, and the object location in the first frame and x_t, $y_t, \theta_t, s_t, \alpha_t$ and ϕ_t in (2) are manually set in advance. For the same test sequence, the parameter of the proposed method is fixed.

Some tracking result frames are shown in Fig.3, which are used to illustrate the effectiveness. Moreover, a quantitative comparison with the classical methods in based on the total errors of center location in pixels is made, shown in Table II, in which the numbers corresponding to the least errors are in bold. The experimental results above demonstrate the effectiveness of the proposed online object tracking method.

Table 2. Total errors of center locations in pixels

Sequence	Mean Shift [6]	Variance Ratio [5]	Proposed
Woman	180	84	**16**
Car	3430	276	**92**
Face	3805	4041	**415**

Fig. 3. Several representative frames of 3 videos with bounding boxes located by proposed method(red), simple template matching method(white), mean shift method(blue),variance ration method(cyan) and ground truth(yellow)

6   Conclusions

In this paper, we propose an stepwise Bayesian object tracking framework. For sequential inference, we model the dynamical transition part based on particle filtering in an affine sampling space, and the observation part via candidate likelihood computation based on random KD-tree forest. The experiment demonstrates the effectiveness of the proposed tracker in indoor and outdoor environments.

Visual tracking is a challenging issue due to the complexity of the imaging environment. We plan to add template update scheme in the current framework so as for occlusion and illumination variation handling. Moreover, for specific applications, more efficient and robust observation model may need to be constructed to enhance robustness of the proposed algorithm.

Acknowledgment. We thank the reviewers for their comments and suggestions. This work was supported by grant No. 61171172 from NNSFC (National Natural Science Foundation of China) and No. 12DZ2272600 from STCSM (Science and Technology Commission of Shanghai Municipality, China).

References

1. Adam, A., Rivlin, E., Shimshoni, I.: Robust fragments-based tracking using the integral histogram. In: Proceedings of the 2006 IEEE Computer Society Conference on Computer Vision and Pattern Recognition, CVPR 2006, vol. 1, pp. 798–805. IEEE Computer Society, Washington, DC (2006)
2. Avidan, S.: Support vector tracking. In: Proceedings of the 2001 IEEE Computer Society Conference on Computer Vision and Pattern Recognition, CVPR 2001, vol. 1, pp. I-184–I-191 (2001)
3. Babenko, B., Yang, M.-H., Belongie, S.: Visual Tracking with Online Multiple Instance Learning. In: CVPR (2009)
4. Beis, J.S., Lowe, D.G.: Shape indexing using approximate nearest-neighbour search in high-dimensional spaces. In: Proceedings of the 1997 Conference on Computer Vision and Pattern Recognition (CVPR 1997), pp. 1000–1006. IEEE Computer Society, Washington, DC (1997)
5. Collins, R.T., Liu, Y.: On-line selection of discriminative tracking features. In: IEEE International Conference on Computer Vision, vol. 1, p. 346 (2003)
6. Comaniciu, D., Ramesh, V., Meer, P.: Kernel-based object tracking. IEEE Transactions on Pattern Analysis and Machine Intelligence 25, 564–577 (2003)
7. Grabner, H., Bischof, H.: On-line boosting and vision. In: 2006 IEEE Computer Society Conference on Computer Vision and Pattern Recognition, vol. 1, pp. 260–267 (2006)
8. Hartley, R.I., Zisserman, A.: Multiple View Geometry in Computer Vision, 2nd edn. Cambridge University Press (2004) ISBN: 0521540518
9. Isard, M., Blake, A.: Contour Tracking by Stochastic Propagation of Conditional Density. In: Buxton, B.F., Cipolla, R. (eds.) ECCV 1996. LNCS, vol. 1064, pp. 343–356. Springer, Heidelberg (1996)
10. Jepson, A.D., Fleet, D.J., El-Maraghi, T.F.: Robust online appearance models for visual tracking. In: CVPR (1), pp. 415–422 (2001)
11. Ross, D.A., Lim, J., Lin, R.-S., Yang, M.-H.: Incremental learning for robust visual tracking. Int. J. Comput. Vision 77(1-3), 125–141 (2008)
12. Silpa-Anan, C., Hartley, R.: Optimised kd-trees for fast image descriptor matching. In: IEEE Conference on Computer Vision and Pattern Recognition, CVPR 2008, pp. 1–8 (June 2008)
13. Yilmaz, A., Javed, O., Shah, M.: Object tracking: A survey. ACM Comput. Surv. 38 (December 2006)

A Methodology for Ground Targets Detection in Complex Scene Based on Airborne LiDAR

Jiafu Zhuang, Jie Ma[*], Yadong Zhu, and Jinwen Tian

State Key Laboratory of Multi-spectral Information Processing Technology,
Huazhong University of Science and Technology, Wuhan, China
majie.hust@sohu.com

Abstract. In this paper, an approach to detecting ground targets using LiDAR point data is proposed. First, outliers are weeded out and point cloud is divided into ground points and non-ground points. Second, the ground surface plane is fitted by ground points and then the relative elevations of all non-ground points are estimated. If the relative elevations of non-ground points exceed a predefined threshold, they will be removed. Subsequently, a 3D region growing algorithm based on the normal vector consistency is employed to generate potential ground targets. Geometric information is used for further filtration of these potential targets on the object level. Finally, the detection performance of the algorithm is analyzed. The experimental results show that the method proposed is effective.

Keywords: LiDAR, Detection, 3D Region growing.

1 Introduction

An airborne LiDAR system usually consists of a platform and a scanning laser sensor which are active sensors utilizing lasers to illuminate a scene and detectors to measure the return signals. It can take the initiative, real-time 3D information to a wide range of surface. The airborne LiDAR system will produce a large number of accurate 3D coordinates of discrete points after the laser scanning missions. How to detect ground targets from the large number of LiDAR points is mainly discussed in this article.

Although the point cloud gives a rich 3D information, many of the detection algorithms grid point cloud into a height image, or directly use range image or intensity image for segmenting and detecting the targets. HC Palm [1] extract edges, vertical structure features using image processing methods for target detection. M. Himmelsbach [3] divides point cloud into a number of grids. Each grid is assigned a value of the maximum absolute elevation difference of points locating in that grid. The edge of the target can then be extracted, around which indicates the existence of targets. Tomas Chevalier [5] estimates the ground surface by the watershed algorithm and then further estimate the relative height to ground of each non-ground points, following the L-shapes fitting method to achieve the targets. Christina [2][6] uses a local surface detection method to detect the targets.

---

* Corresponding author.

F.L. Wang et al. (Eds.): CMSP 2012, CCIS 346, pp. 283–290, 2012.

The proposed method in this paper is done on the 3D space. The detection method is mainly based on the following prior knowledge: elevation relative to ground surface of ground targets compared with that of buildings or trees is much lower; distribution of points of the same ground target is relatively compact while different ground targets are relatively far away from each other; ground targets has a sufficient flatness areas.

In this study, the sections are arranged as follows: (1) In section 2, we first remove the outliers from the data set. Then filter the points to separate the ground points from non-ground points. The ground points are later used to estimate the ground surface from which the relative height of non-ground points can be obtained to remove trees and high part of buildings. (2)In section 3, 3D region growing algorithm base on vector consistency is employed to detect and represent suspicious targets; (3)In section 4, experiment and conclusion.

2   Segment

2.1   Outlier Points Removal

The outlier is a point away from the landscape, such as systematic errors, noise, or birds. The outlier is usually classified as high outliers and low outliers. High outlier occurs when the laser beam hit the birds, low flying aircraft and noise points whose removal is relatively easy. The low outlier is generally caused due to multipath effects and other factors.

Assumed k nearest neighbours of LiDAR point $p_0(x_0, y_0, z_0)$ is, respectively for $p_1(x_1, y_1, z_1) \dots p_k(x_k, y_k, z_k)$. p_0 and $p_{1,2..k}$ together form the point set $\{I\}$ .Then the fitting plane of point set $\{I\}$ can be fitted by the least squares method. A point will be determined to be a outlier if the point to fitting plane distance is greater than a given threshold. The method can not only filter out the high outlier and low outlier, can effectively filter out for a few outliers close to each other.

2.2   Point Cloud Filtering

Point Cloud filtering is the process that removes the non-ground points from point cloud. The main purpose of the point cloud filtering in the subject of remote sensing is to filter out the non-ground points and generates DEM by the ground point, but in our proposed method, point cloud filtering is used to extract targets of interest by the non-ground points. ETEW (Elevation Threshold with Expanding the Window Filter) which is a point cloud filtering algorithm based on the slope change is adopted in this paper.

The abbreviated steps of ETEW are as follows: (1) data set is divided into an array of square cells. In each cells, only the elevation of the lowest point is retained. For the next iteration the cells are increased in size and the minimum elevation in each cell is determined. (2) each point in each cell minus the height of the minimum point in this cell. If the height difference is greater than the threshold, then those points are classified as non ground points. (3)The process is repeated with the cells and thresholds increasing in size until no points from the previous iteration are discarded.

(a)	(b)	(c)

Fig. 1. A case of point cloud filtering (a) original point cloud. (b) non-ground points. (c) ground points

Fig.1 (a) is a point cloud scene with building, trees, ground targets and ground. By applying ETEW filtering algorithm, the point cloud is divided into two parts: ground points and non-ground points. From Fig.1(c) objects such as building and trees and ground vehicles are removed correctly. It can also be seen that a large number of areas of the ground point cloud have no points.

2.3   Ground Estimation

The task in ground surface estimation is to identify data points that correspond to bare earth and then, based on this information interpolate the ground level at nearby positions. In this paper we use inpaint method proposed by Criminisi [7] to estimate the ground surface.

Fig. 2. Ground estimation from Fig. 1(c)

Fig.2 shows the result of the estimated ground surface. Even in the presence of a large area of the hole, the inpaint algorithm can also handle very well.

2.4   Objects Removal

Once the ground is estimated, for any point on the ground, given its X and Y coordinates, you can check out the corresponding elevation values.Usually only given the absolute elevation of a point there is no way to determine whether this point is a ground target point, the trees point or the buildings point. However, if given the relative elevation to the ground of a point, it will be easier to determine which class that point belongs to. It is know that the relative elevation to ground surface of ground targets is low, usually less than 4 meters, while that of trees and buildings is relatively high. According to this prior knowledge, a elevation threshold is set to get rid of a lot of trees points and building points. Unluckily, this method has a flaw, that is, the low part of trees and buildings will be also included.

Laser radar echo information can also be used to filter out some of the objects. Pulses with multiple echos and with large elevation difference between first echo and last echo are very likely to be reflected from the trees or the edge of the buildings.

Fig. 3. Result of objects removal

We can see from Fig 3 that almost civilian vehicles have been retained correctly. However, edge of the buildings and tree with low elevation are also mistaken as potential ground targets points which will inevitably bring adverse effect to the detection performance.

3   Detection of the Ground Targets

3.1   3D Region Growing Based on Vector Consistency

One of the basic problems of Region growing algorithm is to obtain the initial seed points. The initial seed points are extracted in the undivided original point cloud. First, the point cloud space is divided into a number of cells. Each cell is assigned as a value, that is, maximum absolute elevation difference which is the difference between the highest elevation and the lowest elevation in the cell. A cell will be marked as seed cell if the maximum absolute elevation difference of the cell is larger than a given thresold T_{thre}, consequently, the point with the highest elevation of the seed cell will be chosen as a initial seed point. T_{thre} has a large impact on detection performance. On this parameter, we will be in the experimental section for further analysis. Ground targets usually have a sufficient flatness plane. Points on the plane will produce high vector consistency. Region growing criteria is determined by this property.

Suppose that s is a seed point, $p_1, p_2 ... p_k$ are the nearest neighbors of s, respectively. $\vec{n}_s$ and $\vec{n}_1, \vec{n}_2 ... \vec{n}_k$ are the unit normal vector of s and $p_1, p_2 ... p_k$.

If p_i is not a seed point and satisfies condition (1), then A is added to the seed region.

$$\left| \vec{n}_s \bullet \vec{n}_i \right| > \cos(\theta_{thre}), \ i = 1, 2 \ldots k \tag{1}$$

Where, θ_{thre} is the angle threshold whose value reflects the consistency level of the normal vector between seed points and its neighboring points. If θ_{thre} has a higher value then it implies that seed points and its neighbors have a greater similarity in direction distribution.

The region growing process will be over when not any points meet the growth criteria.

3.2   Object-Level Filtering

The size of the ground targets is limited. For example the width of the civilian vehicle generally does not exceed 2 meters. The area, volume, length, width and height of ground targets are usually within a certain range. These features can be used to remove part of non-ground targets.

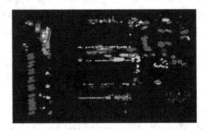

Fig. 4. Detected ground targets

Fig 4 shows the final result of detected ground targets. Almost all civilian vehicles have been successfully detected, however, some parts of building are mistaken as ground vehicles.

4   Experiments and Conclusion

4.1   Data Description

In this article, we choose several sets of point cloud data released by the Open Topography online test. Classification of each point as ground target or non-ground target point are artificial marked before the trial for each reference data. The point cloud data of the test includes the typical characteristics of the buildings, trees, ground targets, the steep slopes.

Table 1. The overview of the test data

scene id	points number	shot density:pts/m^2	Region characteristic
1	63440	4.03	civilian vehicles, trees, lake
2	14404	5.23	civilian vehicles, trees, buildings, slop
3	44000	11.5	military vehicles, trees, buildings

(a)   (b)   (c)

Fig. 5. Point cloud of scenes.(a)(b)(c) is the point cloud of scene1,2,3, respectly

4.2   Performance Analysis

This article discusses the effect of the maximum absolute elevation difference threshold T_{thre} and the angle threshold θ_{thre} on detection performance. T_{thre} will affect the selection of initial seed points. If T_{thre} is low, the opportunities of the ground target point being selected as the seed point will increase, but some low shrubs and buildings point will be added as well, which will lead to detection rate being higher whereas false alarm rate being uncertain. If T_{thre} is high, larger part of the ground target point will be not chosen as the seed point which may leads to the ground targets being dropped out and the declining of the detection rate. See Figure 6.

If angle threshold θ_{thre} is low, the detection rate and false alarm rate is correspondingly low. With the increase of the angle threshold, the detection rate will be increased. This is because, after the increase of the angle threshold, more ground target points and non-ground target points are joined in. As for the false alarm rate of change will depend on the distribution of the scene. See Figure 7.

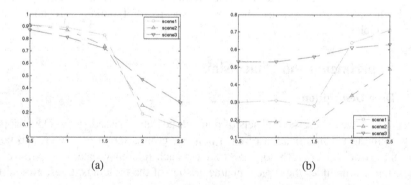

(a)   (b)

Fig. 6. T_{thre} on performance. $\theta_{thre} = 250$. Horizontal axis shows the value of T_{thre} (/m). (a)detection rate and the vertical axis the true target detections.(b)false alarm rate and the vertical axis the false target detections

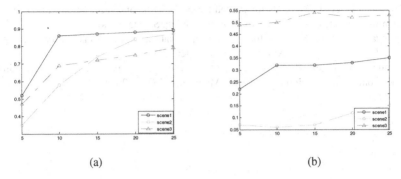

(a)   (b)

Fig. 7. θ_{thre} on performance. T_{thre} = 1.5m. Horizontal axis shows the value of θ_{thre} (/°). (a)detection rate and the vertical axis the true target detections.(b)false alarm rate and the vertical axis the false target detections

5   Conclusion

In this paper, for 3D laser radar target detection applications, a segment method combined with the 3D region growing algorithm based on vector consistency is proposed. Compared to the traditional 2D detection algorithm, the method in this paper can fully take advantage of 3D information of the point cloud to obtain better segmentation results and more accurately and efficiently to represent the targets with a high detection rate in the complex environment. In this paper, the bushes points, and the low building point filtering is not a good solution , how to deal with points of these types need further research.

Acknowledgements. The work in the paper is supported by National Science Foundation (61074156, 61104191) of China, Innovation Research Fund of Huazhong University of Science and Technology.

References

1. Palm, H.C., et al.: Detection of military objects in LADAR-images. Technical Report FFI/RAPPORT-2007/02472, Forsvarets forskningsinstitutt, Kjeller, Norway (2007)
2. Chevalier, T., Tolt, G., Andersson, P.: An approach to target detection in forested scenes. In: Proceedings of the SPIE - The International Society for Optical Engineering, vol. 6950, pp. 69500S-1–69500S-12 (April 3, 2008)
3. Himmelsbach, M., Luettel, T., Wuensche, H.-J.: Real-time object classification in 3D point clouds using point feature histograms. In: 2009 IEEE/RSJ International Conference on Intelligent Robots and Systems (IROS 2009), pp. 994–1000 (2009)
4. Li, J., Jiang, Y., Fan, R.: Recognition of Biological Signal Mixed Based on Wavelet Analysis. In: Jiang, Y., et al. (eds.) Proc. of UK-China Sports Engineering Workshop, pp. 1–8. World Academic Union, Liverpool (2007)

5. Chevalier, T., et al.: Methods for ground target detection and recognition in 3-D laser data. Scientific Report, FOI R–2150–SE, FOI, Linköping, Sweden (2006)
6. Grönwall, C., et al.: Methods for recognition of natural and man-made objects using laser radar data. In: Proc. SPIE, vol. 5412, pp. 310–320 (2004)
7. Criminisi, A., Perez, P., Toyama, K.: Object removal by exemplar-based inpainting. In: Proc. Conf. Comp. Vision Pattern Rec., Madison, WI (June 2003)

Wireless Video Measurement Based on Its Gabor Samples in High-Dimension Space

Jun Yang

School of Computer and Information Engineering, Shanghai University of Electric Power,
Shanghai 200090, China
mail_yangjun@hotmail.com

Abstract. Video measurement is an important issue in the wireless applications. Video's quality is poor when it is translated by channels. Since a frame of video can be considered as an image, its decomposed sub-images can be considered as point set in high-dimension space. Gabor filters can be used for image measurement for its biology characters. In this paper, firstly, an original image is transformed into frequency space with different scale and angle by performing analysis of Hue and Lightness in HSV space and combing these features in Gabor space. The synthesis image is generated with different scale and angle in different Gabor sub-space. With different sub-space, an algorithm is proposed to calculate its measurement based on Gabor features. The proposed method is constructive and proves the wireless video application system higher quality. Experimental results demonstrate advantages of the proposed method over FFT approaches.

Keywords: video measurement, Gabor filter, high-dimension space.

1 Introduction

Wireless communication technology gives new opportunities for video applications. Some mobile devices, such as digital television, digital cinema, wireless handset TV, have ability to play video. Sometimes, image quality plays a key role. Due to its biological similarity to human vision system, Gabor wavelets have been widely used in object recognition applications like fingerprint recognition [1], character recognition [2], etc.. Despite the success of Gabor-wavelet-based object recognition systems, both the feature extraction process and the huge dimension of Gabor features extracted demand large computation and memory costs, which makes them impractical for real applications[3]. In this paper, Gabor features are used to present original image. Gabor wavelets seem to be the optimal basis to extract local features for image quality presentation for several reasons:

1) Biological motivation: the shapes of Gabor wavelets are similar to the receptive fields of simple cells in the primary visual cortex.

2) Mathematical motivation: the Gabor filters are optimal for measuring local spatial frequencies.

F.L. Wang et al. (Eds.): CMSP 2012, CCIS 346, pp. 291–300, 2012.

User experience indicators can be considered as QoE (Quality of Experience, QoE). Sometimes, it can be quantified to reflect the network's quality about the gap between user's experience and hops. As we all know, for television programs, image eventually gives users the perception of influence eventually with audio-visual experience. From the channels between station and end user, source videos are often noised by different disturbed factors before signal reached terminator [6]. Therefore, image quality assessment is an important factor in the real practice and the measurement can be using in communication in order to improve a network's quality [7].

For an image quality assessment (IQA) problem, there are two different categories: subjective assessment by humans and objective assessment by algorithm automatically [8]. For human subjective assessment, an algorithm is defined by how well it correlates with human perception of quality. Among the algorithms, automatic "reduced-reference" (RRED Indices) image quality assessment (QA) algorithms from the point of view of image information change. Such changes are measured between the reference- and natural-image approximations of the distorted image. Algorithms that measure differences between the entropies of wavelet coefficients of reference and distorted images, as perceived by humans, are designed [9]. Feature similarity (FSIM) index for full reference IQA is proposed, which is a dimensionless measure of the significance of a local structure, is used as the primary feature in FSIM [10]. However, these models are algebra method and limited for video sequence or required more precise time. Some application is only make a measure between received image and original one. Meanwhile, real image is often chaotic sequence received or image quality is low. These methods are invalid for this kind of real application.

The paper is organized as follow. Section 2 gives basic definitions and description image calculation in high-dimension space based on Gabor filters; section 3 presents an algorithm of image measurement for coving features in high-dimension space. Results of different type images from video and measurement with real-noised image are provided in Section 4, with conclusions in Section 5.

2   Gabor Feature and Model

For wireless application, the signals are transmitted for source to user's destinations. Among this way, signals are often noised by out-side noise. The way is shown in figure 1.

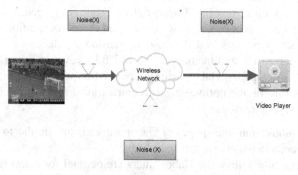

Fig. 1. Wireless video and noise

For real world, the received video quality is measured by reference objects. For vector in feature space, vector-valued image and its popularity is mainly due to its present in space. The definition of special exponent distribution is observed in the vector space. For Gabor space, the different channels give special distribution in high dimension space. We can define distance between vectors as

$$d_{i,j} = \sqrt{\sum_{i=1}^{M}\sum_{j=1}^{M} \| x_i - y_j \|^2} \tag{1}$$

where x_i is a value in vector X. Based on this measure, distribution between vectors in Gabor space is computed and filtered.

An input image is filtered with filters with various frequency and orientation at a channel. We can analysis these paralleling channels. For the customized regions have some common properties at different channels, we can separate special regions using there relationship of channels. The proposed paradigm is shown in Fig.2.

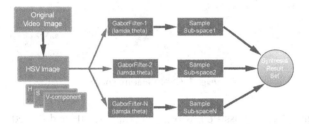

Fig. 2. Proposed Gabor Filters Process paradigm

The analysis can be performed in each filter channel using different scale and theta. It is possible to label customized regions in an out-put image.

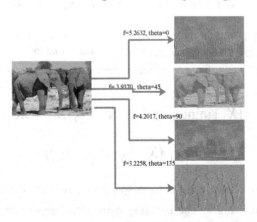

Fig. 3. The filtering results of Gabor

From Fig.3, we can find that the different level of features in Gabor space has its own properties. When performed by the algorithm, the (d) image is obtained which contains customized text features which is also has characteristic of readable letters for human beings.

For a digital image which size is $M \times N$, we denote is with f(x,y) as a point in high dimension space, where 0<x<M,0<y<N. It includes original image and noised image. In order to assert the image's quality, we define below scheme as Fig.4.

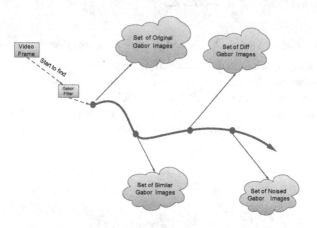

Fig. 4. Gabor feature space

In Fig.4, images are classified as original, similar, diff and noised images respectively. The main problem is to find sub-set of image in high dimension space. Its main idea is to find the points distribution of image in the high dimension space based on original image. Video quality is decrease when translating in network, such as cable network or wireless network. From the theory of geometrical learning [9], some similar objects in high dimension space are homeomorphism and can be measured as neighbors [10].

For the different points in hyper-space, covering entity can be made by adjust parameters [11]. For symbols $X_i \in B_i, X_i \neq Xo_i$, measure distance can be calculated by formula 2 and the shortest distance between current point to center point can be computed by formula 3.

$$X_j = \{X_k \mid \min(\rho(X_k, X_j)), X_k \in B_i\}, X_k \neq Xo_i \tag{2}$$

$$r_x = r - \min(\rho(X_i, Xo_i), \rho(X_j, Xo_i)) \tag{3}$$

When this operating is performed in hype-space for covering vectors of X_i, X_j, the result can be got like Fig.5. The covering parameters are shown in two-dimension space. The distance is described in formula 3.

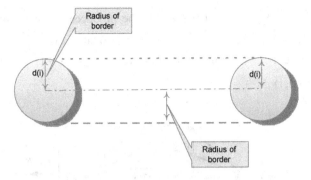

Fig. 5. Covering two neighbor points (2-Dim)

$$d^2(x,x_i,x_j)=\begin{cases}\|x-x_i\|^2, q(x,x_i,x_j)<0\\\|x-x_j\|^2, q(x,x_i,x_j)>\|x_i-x_j\|\\\|x-x_i\|^2-q(x,x_i,x_j)^2, \text{others}\end{cases} \tag{4}$$

Among this expression, where $q(x,x_i,x_j)$ is defined as below.

$$q(x,x_i,x_j)=\left\langle x-x_i,\frac{x_j-x_i}{\|x_j-x_i\|}\right\rangle \tag{5}$$

The definition of covering S can be shown in formula 6.

$$S(x,x_i,x_j,r)=\{x\mid d^2(x,x_i,x_j)<r^2\} \tag{6}$$

As for a sample pair, classifier $c:X \rightarrow Y$ is defined as the probability according to an unknown distribution D over $X\times Y$.

3   Algorithm

Suppose that in constructive neural network, the whole mapping objects are constructed step by step. Samples covering objects can be generated with different procedure number. The whole architecture is shown in Fig.6.

Let's consider the binary classification problem. The input space is X, an arbitrary subset of $\mathbb{R}^n$, and the output is $Y=\{0,1\}$ which is a binary classification problem. Therefore a pair of input and output can be symbolized as $z\equiv\{x,y\}$, $x\in X, y\in Y$. The output sequence of the Samples Mapping Objects can be written as $O = \{o_1, o_2, ..., o_p\}$ where $p(p \in Z_+)$ is the produced number which is determined in the process of network construction. The final output of constructive network is Y_i where i class denotation is $Y_i = \min\{i \mid Q(o_i) = 1\}$, Q is a function mapping $y_i \to \{0,1\}$.

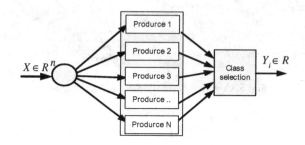

Fig. 6. Architecture of Mapping Objects

For   inside   neurons,   formula   is   described   as

$$\psi = f\left[\sum_{i=1}^{n} \left(\frac{w_j}{|w_j|} \right)^s \left| w_j(x_j - w_j') \right|^P - \theta \right]$$, where θ is threshold, S is sign

symbol, P is shape symbol, w' is center vector and w is direction vector. For RBF neuron, the parameters are given by $P = 2$, $w_j = 1$, $S = 1$. w_j' is center vector. For hyper-plane neuron, the parameters are given by $P = 1$, $w_j = 1$, $S = 1$. With different parameters, ψ gives different covering shapes in high dimension space in geometric viewpoint.

For constructive algorithm, let's consider hype-ball neurons in hidden layers where high priority level is characterized by small priority number. The general algorithm can be described as follows:

Input: Gabor Feature space data Set $X = \{X_1, X_2, ..., X_m\} \subset \mathbb{R}^n$, and the target is $Y \in R$. Priority number k=1 neuron sets $\{\psi\}$, $D' = \Phi$

Output: Samples Mapping Objects

Algorithm produce :

While $X \neq \phi$ do

For each X_i in X

$\to$ *get max sub set* $(X_{i,sub})$ *of* X_i *and its min Euclid distance* (d) *of* $X_{j, i \neq j}$

$\to$ *use hype-ball neuron* (ψ, d) *to cover* $X_{i,sub}$, *and set priority k to neuron* ψ

$\rightarrow add$ $X_{i,sub}$ *to temp set* $\overset{\circ}{D}$

End of for

$\rightarrow set$ $X - \overset{\circ}{D}$ *to* X, $\overset{\circ}{D} = \Phi$

k = k + 1

   End while

   For new coming data, the algorithm will update the produce number of neurons or add new neuron with a special value.

Input: new Gabor feature training

set $X' = \{X'_1, X'_2, ..., X'_m\} \subset \mathbb{R}^n$, $Y \in R$.

Output: Updated Produce Number of Mapping Objects
Algorithm Produce•
While $X' \neq \phi$ *do*

For each X'_i *in* X'

$\rightarrow$ *Get a consistent subset* $X'_{i,sub}$ *of* X_i *randomly* and then

do the following produce:
If covered($X'_{i,sub}$ *)*

do nothing
else

  if(misclassified($X'_{i,sub}$ *))*

  Adjust covering space range of hyper-ball neuron ψ *and adjust its priority number to lower one.*
else

  add new neuron with higher priority number k.
end if
end if

$\rightarrow add$ $X'_{i,sub}$ *to temp set* $\overset{\circ}{D}$

End of for

$\rightarrow set$ $X - \overset{\circ}{D}$ *to* X', $\overset{\circ}{D} = \Phi$
End while

   When new samples input into constructive neural network, the priority level of hidden neurons is strengthened or weaken. Using this method, the old information is not destroyed (forgot) after new data learning, but can be partly fetched at any latest priority. This produce is similar to man's learning procedure. As this updating and learning method is only to adjust the special priority level of neurons, therefore, it can process large data set with more effective heuristic algorithm.

   For sequence video frames, we will split it into some independent images and transform them into eigenvector in feature space using FFT. An image frame is spitted and transformed by FFT on each sub-block. The ultimate identify formula is written as

$$O_{AVLI} = \{O_{AVLI(1)}, O_{AVLI(2)}, ..., O_{AVLI(k)}\} \tag{7}$$

Where $O_{AVLI(i)}$ is the i piece time quantum. The last result is written as

$$\max\{count(i) \mid O_{AVLI(i)} = O_{AVLI(j)}, i \neq j\} \tag{8}$$

Where $count(i)$ is a function of taking sum number of same class in distinguished sequence and the value i gives the similar measure between the original image and compared one.

4   Experimental Results

In this paper, we proposed a new image quality assessment method for wireless videos. Through experiments, we verified that the proposed method represented actual subjective image quality very well. The test video sequence is collected from wireless source (TV), which is encoded by H.264 with image size of 320*240. 1) Using FFT. an image is split into 12*12 sub-blocks. Noised level is define from 0 to 5, the smaller is not noised.   2) Using Gabor filters, an images are transformed into different sub-space. In Fig.7, it gives the comparison between different type videos. The results indicate that the effect of proposed method for measure image based on point calculation in the high dimension space is coincidence with real condition, and the real life video sequence has some low accurate rate.

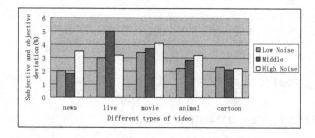

Fig. 7. Subjective and objective deviation with different noised images

From Table.1, it gives information that Gabor feature is superior to FFT method. On the other side, the sequence of image is not very required and its relation-ship can be covered in high-dimension space. From relative images, relation-ship of noised image and original image can be mapped into trends map which can gives information of image quality measure. Additionally, the biologic Gabor is more suitable for image quality measurement.

Table 1. Comparison Results between Gabor and FFT

Video Type	Video length	Noise Level	Sample Method	
			Gabor Filter	FFT
Train	60s	High	0.92	2.31
(300kbps)		Middle	1.03	1.80
		Low	0.67	1.90
Fire	60s	High	0.52	1.23
(300kbps)		Middle	1.02	2.12
		Low	0.44	1.51
River	60s	High	0.35	1.21
(300kbps)		Middle	1.23	2.84
		Low	0.61	1.34

5 Conclusions

We have proposed in this paper an image quality measurement based Gabor filter in high- dimension space. The contributions of this paper can be summarized as follows:

1. An idea of image presentation using Gabor video sequence measurement is proposed. Video image time is not aligned when performing testing produce. Method can be used for different type Video context with noise blind. The proposed method is robust.
2. The model is superior to FFT method. It used biologic image presentation and more suitable like human vision.

Experimental results indicate our method is effective in terms of accuracy, robustness, and stability for video quality assessment. The novelty of this solution is the direct embedding of finding reflecting parameters of image using points in high dimension space. It is a blind solution for video measurement. In addition, the proposed method allows simple and fast implementation for real-time mobile application. More studies in the aspect of geometry in high-dimension space should be invested in future.

Acknowledgement. This work is supported by National Natural Science Fund (61073189), Shanghai Technology Innovation Project (09160501700, 10110502200), and Leading Academic Discipline Project of Shanghai Municipal Education Commission (J51303). The authors are grateful for the anonymous reviewers who made constructive comments.

References

[1] Wang, W., Li, J.W., Huang, F.F., Feng, H.L.: Design and implementation of Log-Gabor filter in fingerprint image enhancement. Pattern Recognition Letters 29(3), 301–308 (2008)

[2] Zhang, B.C., Shan, S.G., Chen, X.L., Gao, W.: Histogram of Gabor phase patterns (HGPP): a novel object representation approach for face recognition. IEEE Transactions on Image Processing 16(1), 57–68 (2007)

[3] Bianconi, F., Fernandez, A.: Evaluation of the effects of Gabor filter parameters on texture classification. Pattern Recognition 40(12), 3325–3335 (2007)

[4] Myasnikov, V.V., Ivanov, A.A., Gashnikov, M.V., Myasnikov, E.V.: Computer program for automatic estimation of digital image quality 21(3), 415–418 (2011)

[5] ITU-T Recommendation BT.1788, Methodology for the subjective assessment of video quality in multimedia applications (2007)

[6] Soundararajan, R.: RRED Indices: Reduced Reference Entropic Differencing for Image Quality Assessment. IEEE Transactions on Image Processing 21(2), 517–526 (2012)

[7] Zhang, L., Mou, X., Zhang, D.: FSIM: A Feature Similarity Index for Image Quality Assessment. IEEE Transactions on Image Processing 20(8), 2378–2386 (2011)

[8] Ninassi, A., Meur, O.L., Callet, P.L., Barbba, D.: Does where you gaze on an image affect your perception of quality? Applying visual attention to image quality metric. In: Proc. IEEE Int. Conf. Image Process, ICIP 2007, vol. 2, pp. 169–172 (2007)

[9] Shoujue, W., Jiangliang, L.: Geometrical Learning, descriptive geometry, and biometric pattern recognition. Neuron Computing 67, 9–28 (2005)

[10] Wang, S.J.: Bionic (topological) pattern recognition–A new model of pattern recognition theory and its applications. Acta Electron. Sinica 30(10), 1–4 (2002)

[11] Zhu, S., Wang, Z., Liao, M.: Research on K-classification Covering for PONN. Computer Application 27(2), 330–332 (2007) (in Chinese)

The Image Analysis of the Level of a Fabric's Hairiness and Pilling Based on Matlab

Jianxia Su[1], Runping Han[1], Limin Shi[2], Hongyun Xiong[1], and Lu Qin[1]

[1] Information Engineering School of Beijing Institute of Fashion Technology,
Beijing, China
[2] Clothing Art and Engineering school of Beijing Institute of Fashion Technology,
Beijing, China
{Jianxia Su,Runping Han,Limin Shi,
Hongyun Xiong,ssybj}@sohu.com

Abstract. The abrasion resistance of shell fabric is one of the most important performance indexes of quality evaluation. The evaluation of level of fabric hairiness and pilling is usually confined to manual methods. This paper has studied the hairiness and pilling of shell fabric on the base of MATLAB. A series image analysis steps include image preprocessing, eigenvalue calculation and level judgment. Level critical value can be worked out by computer after the percentage of pilling part is calculated. Test shows that the process of this paper is practical and effective.

Keywords: fabrics, hairiness, pilling, level, image process.

1 Introduction

Nowadays, the increasingly high demand for the level of quality of life, aesthetics and comfort of the clothes become more and more important. A good clothes that has hair bulbs on the surface, not only affects the visual appearance, but also people looked uncomfortable and affect mood.

The durability of the fabric is the fabric to resist damage caused by various factors (mechanical, physical, chemical and microbiological) combined effects of performance under the conditions of use. Fabric in the course of damage, but in practice prove the wear and tear damage to one of the main characteristics of the fabric to resist wear and tear is hairiness and pilling, and the impact causes of fabric hairiness and pilling played a decisive role composition of the fibers of the fabric characteristics,structure and finishing.

The reserch on fabric hairiness and pilling is limited, it has a prospect of a large space. Using MATLAB image assessment level early pretreatment optimization (including cut-off including Figure, gray, wavelet filtering, noise removal, black and white, binarization, median filtering), re-use ratio in mathematics on from the area ratio of the ball part of the calculations and comparisons to obtain the cut-off value between each level, the final assessment of the level of the fabric pilling.

F.L. Wang et al. (Eds.): CMSP 2012, CCIS 346, pp. 301–308, 2012.

2   Pilling Fabric Image Preprocessing

The design of the fabric pilling rating by the image pre-pretreatment to pilling part of the area ratio calculated pilling fabric rating of three parts. Image preprocessing includes image capture, gray-scale, wavelet filtering, noise removed, black and white, binarization and median filter. The image capture in order to removal the impact of the sample picture due to the artificial hand-cutting and other external factors, reducing the difficulty of image processing, and improved pilling part of the area ratio of the percentage of accuracy. The gray scale is the first step in image processing. Wavelet filtering noise removal in order to exclude the image selected sweep fashionable can not be avoided in the dust impact to raise the ratio calculation accuracy. Black and white of the image into binary is to finish next processing. The binarization is to calculate the proportion of hairiness and pilling.

2.1   Image Read and Capture

Read in the image are the RGB model images, the RGB model and standardized simple normalized RGB model.

$$r = \frac{R}{R+G+B}, g = \frac{G}{R+G+B}, b = \frac{B}{R+G+B}. \tag{1}$$

r, g, b, said chromaticity coordinates, because only two chromaticity coordinates independent, ignored, expressed by the chromaticity space is two-dimensional. Preserved ingredients commonly known as a solid color, because the original brightness of the RGB color property in the standardization process to eliminate.

Fig. 1. The two images of the standards sample photos or test photos which are scanned by scanner are showed. The left is the original image, the right shows that a function is dedicated to the interception of the image rectangle

2.2   Image Graying

Color images often contain a large amount of color information, and will take up a lot of storage space. Technical operation of the system will reduce the speed, and thus by the image recognition processing color images converted to grayscale images. Selection criteria is the gray-scale transformation, the dynamic range of the pixel increases, the contrast of the image is strengthened, so that the images become clearer easy to identify. The image graying is the first step in image processing, and it is a very important step.

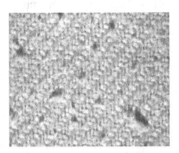

Fig. 2. Graying processing of image

2.3   Wavelet De-noising

Work to eliminate image noise is called the smoothing or filtering of the image. Smooth has two purposes: to improve the quality of the image and extract the object features. Image filtering methods are the wavelet filtering, average filtering, morphological filtering and median filtering. The wavelet filter is a simple and better method, it is the layers wavelet decomposition coefficient modulus is greater and smaller than a certain threshold value of the coefficient, respectively for processing, the wavelet coefficients reconstruction after processing a noise canceling after the image. The use of wavelet filtering can filter out some of the camera sometimes will affect the image produced by the effect of external factors, such as dust.

Wavelet analysis for image filter works as follows, a noisy image signal can be expressed as:

$$s(x, y) = f(x, y) + Ee(x, y) \quad (x, y = 0,...n-1) \tag{2}$$

Where s (x, y) is the noisy image signal; f (x, y) is the useful signal; e (x, y) is the noise signal; E is the noise intensity.

The noise signals are usually high-frequency signal, the useful signal is often a low frequency signal, De-noising to eliminate high-frequency signals while retaining the low-frequency signals. First, the wavelet decomposition of the image, it is because of the noise included in the higher frequency details; then use the threshold to handle the form of the decomposition of the wavelet coefficients for processing; Finally, the signal wavelet reconstruction can achieve the purpose of the image signal de-noising. Wavelet analysis for image de-noising process, broadly divided into the following paragraphs:

First is wavelet decomposition of the image signal. Select a suitable wavelet and the appropriate level of decomposition (denoted N), then treat the analysis of the image signal X N-layer decomposition.

Second is decomposition of high-frequency coefficients after threshold. Choose an appropriate threshold for each level of decomposition, and to quantify the layer of high-frequency coefficients of the soft threshold.

The last is reconstruction of image signal wavelet. Low frequency coefficients after threshold deal with layers of detail (high-frequency coefficient) of two-dimensional signal, wavelet reconstruction based on wavelet decomposition of the N layer approximation.

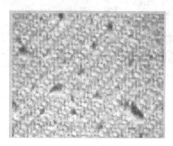

Fig. 3. The image after wavelet de-noising

2.4   Image Black and White

Corrosion is a process to eliminate the boundary points, the result is target decreased narrows and the hole increases, which can effectively eliminate isolated noise points. Expansion sucked in contact with the object of all backgrounds merged into objects in the process. The process of corrosion and expansion as the open operation, it has to eliminate small objects and thin at the separation of the role of objects and smooth larger objects boundaries.

Image minus operation is pre-operating as a complex image processing. It is using special function to do minus between images or constants. The functions will be two of the input image to do the corresponding pixel value minus, and then returns the result to the corresponding pixel of the output image. It treats the background to the current image of the morphological opening operation results, the background is then subtracted from the current image.

Fig. 4. The image after black and white preprocess

2.5   Image Binarization

Image binarization is the image of the whole image only black and white two colors represent pixel 0 and pixel 1.

Table 1. Pixels and images of the binary logic operations

P	Q	P and Q	P or Q	Not P
0	0	0	0	1
0	1	0	1	1
1	0	0	1	0
1	1	1	1	0

During the two values, the key point is to find the appropriate threshold, so its is important to separate the hair bulb part and no pilling fabric part. After binarization, the image can maintain a good prototype, will not throw away a useful shape, it does not produce additional vacancy. Threshold procedure is produced by user to specify a threshold or auto-generate by algorithm.The image in pixel gray value is less than the threshold, the pixel gray value is set to 0 or 255, or gray value is set for 255 or 0.

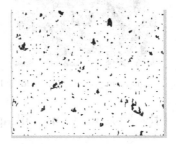

Fig. 5. The image after binarization

Fig. 6. If the image is not the white point of pilling characteristics part., then the image represented by black and white image should be reversed with the symbol "~" negated, otherwise the values obtained after the opposite.

2.6   Median Filtering

The median filtering is a nonlinear signal processing, the corresponding median filter is a nonlinear filter. Linear filtering smoothly reduces the noise, but it blurs the image edges and details. Nonlinear smoothing is to improve, that is, not all pixels with the average of the field instead of a linear smoothing, but to take a threshold, when the difference between the pixel gray value and the field average instead of at the threshold when the mean; whichever is the gray value when the difference between the pixel gray value and its field average is not greater than the threshold.

The median filter used in this paper is medfilter2 function. The value of each pixel from the input image pixel values to determine the corresponding pixel in the field, whose value is determined based on the median. The median sensitivity to outliers, the median filter can remove these outliers and does not decrease the image contrast. Usually median filter can filter out smaller hair noise, has a clearer distinction between the part of the hair bulb and none.

Fig. 7. The image preprocess after median filter

3   Area Calculate of the Hairiness and Pilling

In order to better identify the fabric pilling, the degree of fabric wearing must be ceded. The basis of classification is varied. In this paper, the ratio of the area of the hair bulb and o the total area of pilling is used to decide the levels. In other words, the proportion of the hair bulb area in the pilling fabric will determine the fabric hairiness and pilling level.

In this paper the known fabric sample standard photo will first be used on in the program, and each level of sample fabric pilling percentage values has been gotten, This would be used to decide the test sample's level. Among them, the best pilling is five, then four, three, two, the worst is one level. Then the ratio in the mathematical way is used to calculate the value of the boundaries between the various levels to determine the value of each level range.

3.1   Calculate the Hairiness and Pilling Part of the Area / Pixel

For the calculation of the hair bulb area, this paper is on the basis of the binarization. After binarization, the image pixel values only 0 and 1. The function 'bwarea' is dedicated to the calculation of the values of the two values of image pixels. Binarized interference such as part of pilling and non-pilling part may also interfere with each other, with a median filter, filtered through a small white spots, and the rest of the white point, which is recognized the hair bulb. Then 'bwarea' function calculates the value.

After image pre-processing, if the information you need is differ from the methods used, program should be adjusted with data consistent. Such as images, the black part is the hair bulb part of the required 'bwarea' function obtained is a part of pixels (white), should represent the first images of the hair bulb part as the representative of the pixels of the white one, and then subsequent processing.

```
picture = im2bw (~ midFilter);
 % inverted part of pilling into the white dots
total = bwarea (picture);
 % calculate the binary image pixels for an area
```

3.2   Calculate of the Entire Image Area / Pixel

Only the image pixels, the proportion of the hair bulb part of the whole image can be calculated. The 'size' function can be used to calculate the overall pixels. The key code is as follows:

```
[M, n] = size (picture);
% seek a long, wide pixel value
allarea = m * n;
% calculate the total area of pixels
```

3.3   Calculate the Proportion of Hairiness and Pilling

The pilling ratio of area is divided by the entire area of the hair bulb, then the final percentage can be calculated. The photos compared to the value of the test sample and standard samples, we the level of pilling can be calculated.

The key code   as follows:

```
q = total / allarea;% demand ratio
percent = q * 100;% to the ratio of percentage
```

This paper stresses the major design steps, produced a corresponding form interface for a program in MATLAB:

Fig. 8. The GUI by Matlab of the software

4   Conclusions

This paper discussed of the level of fabric hairiness and pilling after the image selected, interception, pre-treatment, to the end of a sliding scale, rating, and interface design. It realized the judging the level of hairiness and pilling program automatically instead of manual .

The software has been tested and the total efficiency is 90%, showing that auto pilling level teat faster and higher accuracy than artificial work. the accuracy and algorithm optimization remains to be improved.

Acknowledgments. This paper is sponsored by 2011ZK-07of Clothing Materials Research Development and of Evaluation of Beijing Key Laboratory and Kf2011-05 of Digital media and interactive media of Beijing Key Laboratory.

References

1. Jian, H., Chu, X.: Image processing application status and trends in the textile industry. China Textile University, 95–99 (1996)
2. The GBT 4802.1-2008 textile fabric pilling performance of the contents Part 1
3. Determination of the GBT propensity to surface fuzzing of textile fabric pilling performance Part 2
4. Zhou, Y.,Y., Pan, S., Gao, W.: Based on the standard sample according to the image analysis of fabric pilling ball ratings. Journal of Textile Research 30, 30–33 (2010)
5. Gao, S., Wang, L.: Matlab for pilling image wavelet de-noise processing of Textile Science and Technology. Computer Applications Edition 1, 37–39 (2005)
6. Shen, Y.: Textile pilling different ball test method comparison and evaluation. China Xianjian, 54–57 (2010)

An Improved Denoised 3D Edge Extraction Operator within Biomedical Images

Yu Ma [1,2], Yanning Zhang[1], Yougang Wang[2], Huilin Liang[2], and Shuang Xu[2]

[1] Institute of Computer Science, Northwestern Polytechnical University,
Xi'an, 710129, China
[2] Ning Xia University, Yin chuan, 750021, China
mayu.ningxia@gmail.com

Abstract. The previous 3D edge surface detector based on the Laplace and gradient operator can extract high accuracy edge surfaces with high efficiency in contrast with traditional isotropic surface extraction operator. However, the second derivatlive in the 3D detector shows natural sensitivity to noise, which generates the noise polluted 3D edge surfaces and noisy pieces. A novel denoising 3D edge detector is proposed; the noisy image is filtered by the 3D Gauss filter firstly, then edge surfaces are detected and extracted utilizing the traditional 3D edge surface detector. Furthermore, the extracted 3D noisy edge surface pieces are degraded by the tracking technique. Finally, the denoising 3D edge surfaces are converted to polygon pieces, then visualized the surface with combined image and graphic methods. Experimental results show that the proposed scheme suppresses noise and preserves edge surfaces than the traditional 3D edge surface detector.

Keywords: 3D edge surface detector, 3D Gaussian filter, denoising, tracking.

1   Introduction

Computed tomography (CT) and magnetic resonance imaging (MRI) produce the image sequence of two-dimensional (2D) cross-sectional slices which contain the three-dimensional (3D) information on the biomedical and industrial object [1]. However, the accompanying noise during image acquisition degrades the human interpretation or computer-aided analysis of the images. In a 3D reconstruction of biomedical images, it is a key step to extract the edge surfaces of the interesting organ or tissue from the 2D slices. However, the noises would lead to wrong or misleading edge surface structures in the images of the object. Therefore, denoising should be performed to improve the edge surface quality for more accurate diagnosis and applications. In this paper, we exploit a novel edge surface extraction detector based denoising in 3D volume data.

The Canny operator [2] is a classical traditional operator in 2D edge detection, which computes local maximum based gradient. The 3D edge detection operator is the extension of the 2D Canny Detector. In recent years many reports on the detection of the edge surface within 3D volume images have appeared in the literature [3], [4], [5], [6].

F.L. Wang et al. (Eds.): CMSP 2012, CCIS 346, pp. 309–316, 2012.
© Springer-Verlag Berlin Heidelberg 2012

Firstly, the edge surface is detected via the gradient and the zero crossing. Calculations of the gradient need to calculate the second derivative, which is the most frequent use of the Laplace operator. Here, we use the central difference to calculate the second derivative, and then compute the gradient and the gradient vector. After acquiring the zero crossing surfaces and the gradient surfaces, the whole edge surfaces are obtained by the methods. Experiments show that the result edge surfaces extracted by the traditional 3D edge detector can reach sub-voxel precision, can be widely used in three-dimensional biomedical image edge surface detection and extraction.

Although 3D edge detection operator shows high precision, location accuracy and detailed structure, as a differential operator, the Laplace operator has a natural sensitivity to noise. In our previous work, we have not considered the influence of the noise [3], [5], [6], lead to the distortion of the 3D edge surface, as shown in Figure 4 and Figure 8 (A).

There are several different denoising techniques, such as the spatial filters [7], the level set method [8], the nonlinear isotropic, the anisotropic diffusion [9], the wavelet transform [10] and the Wiener filter [11]. The essence of denoising executes smoothing, moreover preserves the sharp edge. The filtering method, an offline image processing approach, is often as effective as improving acquisition without affecting spatial resolution, and if properly designed, requires less time, and is usually less expensive. The Gaussian [12] filter is one of important preprocessing approaches for the images deteriorated by noises, which can reduce the influence of noise, avoid the inaccurate edge surface. The 3D Gaussian filter is an important preprocessing step in the edge extraction without loss of significant edge, as well as the high efficiency and simple realization. We take into account adding the 3D Gaussian filter to the 3D edge surface detector based on the Laplace and the zero crossing method, and overcome the defect proposed in our previous works. Furthermore, we employed coplanar tracking method to deduce the 3D noisy cracks after extracted the edge surfaces. It is the objective of this paper to investigate the improved denoising 3D edge surface detector based on the Laplace zero crossing method within 3D biomedical images. The structure of the paper is as follows, the first part discusses the related work of the traditional 3D edge detector, the 3D Gauss filter method is presented in the second part, and the third part investigates the improved 3D edge detector. Finally, the experimental result is given and analysed.

2   Related Work

The traditional 3D edge detector based on gradient and zero crossing can exactly locate the edge, however, it is a difficult point to determine the value of the gradient magnitude [3], [4]. The larger gradient value taken, the more detailed structure obtained, but brings the noisy edge surfaces, too many noises will pollute the significant 3D structure. Conversely, the less value generates the hole on the edge surfaces [3]. Ma Yu, the author of this article, and Lisheng Wang [5] attenuate the noises and fill the holes via the principle of coplanar, as well as the 3D region growing method, finally extract sub-voxel accuracy of the image edge. During the actual application of CT and MRI image, however, the users focus more on the organs and structures they are interested in. Ma Yu and Yanning Zhang further extend the tracking approach, select the interested region or structure in slice area, and extract the 3D edge surfaces interactively [6]. In all the previous methods, the denoising processing has not been considered. This paper is an extension of the aforementioned work. We first smooth the volume image by the 3D Gaussian operator before detecting the edge surface, as a result, the noise in the slice images are reduced greatly. Then the 3D coplanar tracking technique removes 3D noisy patches after edge surface detection.

3   The Edge Surface Detector

3.1   The Mathematical Model of the 3D Edge Detector

The Laplace operator is defined by:

$$\nabla^2 f = f_{xx} + f_{yy} + f_{zz},$$ (1)

where f_x is the first order derivative with respect to x and f_{xx} is the second order derivative with respect to x. The mathematical model of 3D edge detector includes the following definition:

$$\begin{cases} \nabla^2 f = 0, \\ \|\nabla f\| \geq T \end{cases}$$ (2)

where T is a predefined threshold of gradient magnitude. The Laplace isosurfaces are part of the special zero-crossing isosurfaces, together with the greater gradient magnitude isosurfaces constitute the 3D edge surfaces, and we call the traditional 3D edge surface detector. The detailed description of the 3D edge surface detector sees literature [3], [4], [5].

3.2   The 3D Gaussian Filter

Unfortunately, if the Gaussian filtering algorithm has not been exploited before the detection of the edge surface, the polluted surface appears in the extraction result, as illustrated in Figure 4 and Figure 8 (A).

The 3D Gaussian filter is an ideal smooth operator, not only reduces the noise, but also preserves the edge details as well. Another advantage of Gaussian smoothing operator is that the smoothing effect can be adjusted by choosing an appropriate value for the standard deviation. If a lower standard deviation is taken, only values inside a small number of neighbourhoods are smoothed; conversely, with a greater standard deviation, value over a large number of neighbourhoods are smoothed.

$$G(x, y, z) = \frac{1}{\sqrt{(2\pi)^3}\sigma^3} e^{-\frac{(x^2+y^2+z^2)}{2\sigma^2}}$$ (3)

where σ is the smoothing factor.

3.3   The Improved 3d Denoising Edge Detector

$$D(x, y, z) = I(x, y, z) * G(x, y, z) \qquad (4)$$

where $I(x, y, z)$ is noisy slice images, $G(x, y, z)$ is the Gauss filter function and $D(x, y, z)$ is the denoising image. From this and the improved denoising edge detector is:

$$\begin{cases} \nabla^2 D(x, y, z) = 0 \\ \|\nabla D(x, y, z)\| \geq T \end{cases} \qquad (5)$$

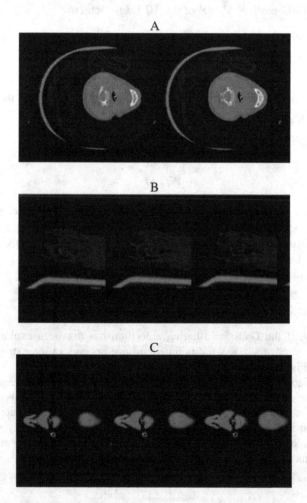

Fig. 1. The origin CT volume images with three views

4   Experimental Results

The denoising extraction algorithm investigated in this paper has been implemented using C++ under Microsoft Visual Studio; the OpenGL graphics system was also applied to well perform the extraction and rendering of 3D edge surfaces. Here we will present some experimental results using CT volume data, the volume size is 256×256×98 of a baby's head.

Figure 1 shows the original data with three views: Figure 1 (A) shows the coronal view, Figure 1 (B) corresponding the axial view and Figure 1 (C) corresponding to the sagittal view respectively.

As mentioned previously, however, as one of differential operators, the Laplace operator shows natural sensitivity to noise, they have never considered smoothing the volume image for denoising [3], [4], [5], [6], a key step in preprocessing within image analysis. High quality volume image without noise are certain immune to 3D edge surface detector, which can easily extract high accuracy edge surface, as depicted in Fig.2. But the noisy volume data lead to polluted edge surfaces. In order to further demonstrate, here we add Gaussian noise with mean 0 and variance 10 respectively, as shown in Fig.3, as a result, the noisy edge surface obtained in Fig.4.

Fig. 2. The extracted result of the 3D traditional edge detector from the unpolluted volumetric data

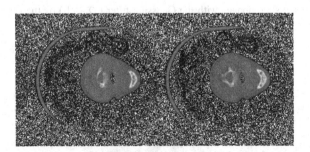

Fig. 3. Synthesis slice images added with Gaussian noise of mean=0, variance=10

Fig. 4. The noisy extracted edge surface extracted by the 3D traditional edge detector

If we implement the improved denoised method presented in this paper, the 3D Gauss filter is carried out before surface extraction, we can acquire the denoised volume images, and the sub-voxel edge surfaces can be extracted by the 3D edge surface detector. Furthermore, after the extraction, the further tracking denoising method in 3D field can purge 3D noisy patch [5], and we can obtain the final sub-voxel accuracy 3D edge surfaces, as described in Fig.6. Fig. 7 represents the other experimental result using the improved denoising edge surface detector for MRI human cervix with size of 128×128×98. Figure 7 (A) and Figure 7 (B) illustrate the comparison of extraction result between the traditional edge surface and the improved denoised edge detector; we can easily learn that the latter has a smoother and realistic surface obviously.

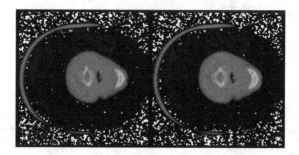

Fig. 5. The denoised slice images with the Gaussian filter ($\sigma = 1$) by the improved 3D edge surface detector

Fig. 6. The 3D edge surfaces extracted by the improved denoised 3D edge surfaces detector

A

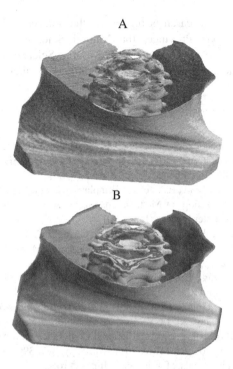

B

Fig. 7. The comparison between the tradition edge surfaces and the improved denoised detection algorithm

All the experiments were carried on a PC with a Pentium IV 2.6 GHz CPU and 1G byte dynamic RAM, using Visual C++ 6.0 and OpenGL. Although the new object is slightly changed by the improved 3D edge surface detector, it contains important features of the original object.

5   Conclusions

The sub-voxel 3D edge surfaces extracted from noisy volume data is exploited in this paper, via the method combination of the 3D Gauss filter and the traditional 3D edge surfaces detector based on Laplace and Gradient method. The previous work of the traditional 3D edge detector has not considered the affection of the noise [3], [4], [5], [6] due to the natural sensitivity of Laplace operator. As a result, the noisy edge surfaces appeared. The scheme proposed in this paper is an extension of previous work done by Ma Yu and Lisheng Wang [3], [4], [5], [6]; the former is the author of this paper. Firstly, the 3D Gauss filter denoises the noisy volume images, and then the sub-voxel edge surfaces are extracted. Furthermore, the extracted 3D noisy patches are removed by the tracking technique based on the coplanar principle within 3D cubes. Experimental results show the validity and effectiveness of the improved 3D denoised edge detection algorithm, which can overcome the shortcoming in the traditional 3D edge surface detector and easily be extended to other application and analysis within 3D biomedical and industrial images.

Acknowledgment. The research is funded by the Science and Technology Support Plan Project of Ningxia Province, the Natural Science Foundation of Ningxia (NZ0920), and in part by the National Natural Science Foundation of China (60961004), the National Natural Science Foundation of China (31060233).

References

1. Tang, Z.: 3D data visualization. Tsinghua University Press, Beijing (1999) (in Chinese)
2. Canny, J.: A computational approach to edge detection. IEEE Transaction on Pattern Analysis and Machine Intelligence 8(6), 679–698 (1986)
3. Wang, L., Wong, T.T., Heng, P.A., et al.: Template-matching approach to edge detection of volume data. In: Workshop on Medical Imaging & Argument Reality, Hong Kong, pp. 286–291. IEEE Computer Society (June 2001)
4. Heng, P.A., Wang, L., Wong, T.T., Leung, K.S., Cheng, J.C.: Edge surfaces extraction from 3D images. In: Sonka, M., Hanson, K. (eds.) Proc. Medical Imaging 2001, Image Processing, vol. 4322, pp. 407–416 (2001)
5. Ma, Y., Wang, L., Tang, Y.: A novel algorithm for tracking step-like edge surfaces within 3D images. Ji Suan Ji Fu Zhu She Ji Yu Tu Xing Xue Xue Bao/Journal of Computer-Aided Design and Computer Graphics 19(3), 329–333 (2007) (in Chinese)
6. Ma, Y., Zhang, Y., Wang, X., Li, Z., Rui, Y.: An automatic surface extraction for volume visualization. In: Proceedings-3rd International Conference on Measuring Technology and Mechatronics Automation, ICMTMA 2011, vol. 1, pp. 387–390 (2011)
7. Weeks, A.R.: Fundamentals of Electronic Image Processing. SPIE Optical Engineering Press and IEEE Press (1996)
8. Sethian, J.A.: Level Set Methods and Fast Matching Methods: Evolving Interfaces in Computational Geometry, Fluid Mechanics, Computer vision and Materials Science. Cambridge University Press (1999)
9. Clarenz, U., Diewald, U., Rumpf, M.: Nonlinear anisotropic diffusion in surface processing. In: Proceedings of IEEE Visualization 2000, pp. 397–405 (2000)
10. Sendur, L., Selesnick, I.W.: Bivariate shrinkage functions for wavelet-based denoising exploiting interscale dependency. IEEE Trans. Signal Process. 50(11), 2744–2756 (2002)
11. Marcos, M.F., Carlos, A.L., Juan, R.A., Westin, C.F.: Sequential Anisotropic Wiener Filtering Applied to 3D MRI Data. Magnetic Resonance Image 25, 278–292 (2007)
12. Schalkoff, R.J.: Digital Image Processing and Computer Vision. John Wiley and Sons (1989)

A Drogue Detection Method for Vision-Based Autonomous Aerial Refueling

Chunhua Song, Shibo Gao*, and Yongmei Cheng

College of Automation, Northwestern Polytechnical University, Xi'an 710072, China
gaohbob@gmail.com

Abstract. Drogue detection is important for vision-based autonomous aerial refueling. It is a difficult task due to disturbances caused by both the tanker wake vortex and atmospheric turbulence. In this paper, the problem of drogue detection is considered as moving object detection. A method based on multi-scale low rank and sparse decomposition is proposed for drogue detection. Firstly, the image sequences are decomposed by stationary wavelet transform respectively. Then the method based on low rank and sparse decomposition is employed on the low frequency sub-band image sequences of coarsest scale. After obtaining the object, the object is used as object confidence map to feedback the low sub-band image sequences of next fine scale for low rank and sparse decomposition. Thereinto, an alignment method is introduced into the low rank and sparse composition due to the vibration in the drogue video image. This method can overcome the influence of non-structure information, caused by atmospheric or aircrafts. The experimental results show that the proposed algorithm is effective in real autonomous aerial refueling data via multi-scale low rank and sparse decomposition for drogue detection under complex background.

Keywords: Image analysis, drogue detection, low rank, multi-scale.

1 Introduction

Autonomous aerial refueling (AAR) is one of the important challenges in modern aviation technology. There are two commonly used methods for aerial refueling [1, 2]: the probe-and-drogue refueling method, and the boom-and-receptacle method. The probe-and-drogue refueling system is the standard method for the USA Navy and the air forces of most other nations [3]. In this refueling method [2, 4], the tanker aircraft releases a long flexible hose that trails behind and below the tanker. At the end of the hose is a basket-shaped component called as drogue. The receiver aircraft has a probe that must be placed or docked into the drogue. This is the preferred method for small, agile aircraft because the hose and drogue are flexible and essentially passive during refueling. In addition, a human operator is not required on the tanker aircraft [3, 4]. The complete refueling procedure contains three phases [1, 2]: approach phase, refueling phase and separation phase. In the approach phase, as the tanker flies straight

---

* Corresponding author.

F.L. Wang et al. (Eds.): CMSP 2012, CCIS 346, pp. 317–324, 2012.

Fig. 1. The probe-and-drogue refueling system [2]

and level with no control over the drogue, the pilot of the receiving aircraft is responsible for linking the probe with the drogue. The probe-and-drogue refueling system is shown in figure 1.

Current technique applied in AAR systems is based on sensors such as laser, radar, global positioning systems (GPS) and inertial navigation systems (INS). The camera-based refueling technology has been recently proposed as an alternative to the above technologies [3, 5-7]. The landmark of drogue and computer vision algorithms is utilized for aerial refueling docking via the camera, which is installed on the probe. A camera-based refueling system has ideal characteristics for AAR [5]: cheap, low weight, and not requiring an active communication channel, etc. For vision-based AAR purposes, a key issue to determine relative orientation and position of the drogue and the probe accurately during the approach phase [8]. Then a robust relative navigation and control algorithm is integrated for adjusting the receiver aircraft. However, it is a difficult task to detect the drogue due to disturbances caused by both the tanker wake vortex and atmospheric turbulence [7]. In this paper, we discuss how to detect the drogue via the drogue video image, captured by the camera on the probe.

The drogue is aero dynamically stabilized. The movement of the drogue is irregular. But the tanker and the receiver aircrafts are stationary relatively in the early approach phase. The tanker releases the drogue step by step. And the drogue swing around because of the tanker wake vortex and atmospheric turbulence. In this view, the drogue is the only moving object in the approach phase during short period. So we can consider the problem of drogue detection as moving object detection. Traditional method of moving object detection is the background modeling [9] by mixture of gaussians [10] or stochastic approximation [11]. However, the sky background is changing at any time due to the fly of tanker and receiver aircraft. Moreover, the video of tanker and the drogue vibrate in the drogue video image, caused by the shake from the receiver aircraft. The drogue image sequences are shown in figure 2. The method of background modeling will be invalid in this case. In this paper, we present a new method based on multi-scale low rank and sparse decomposition (**Ms-Lrsd**) for drogue detection. Here the sparse object, which denotes the moving sparse object, can be considered as drogue via the low rank and sparse decomposition (**Lrsd**) on the image sequences. And the object in the low frequency sub-band image sequences of coarse scale is the object confidence map for the low sub-band image sequences of next fine scale for decomposition. The experimental results show that the proposed technique is effective in real AAR data via multi-scale low rank and sparse decomposition.

2   Drogue Detection via Ms-Lrsd

2.1   Object Detection Based on Lrsd

For the drogue image sequences $\{f_1, f_2, ..., f_T\}$ acquired by the camera on the probe, our purpose is to differentiate drogue from the image sequence, in which T denotes number of frames, and the size of each image f_t is $m \times n$. And the image at t-th frame can be decomposed into background b_t and object d_t, that is $f_t = b_t + d_t$. The object d_t is the expected drogue at t-th frame. If the image pixels at t-th frame are stacked as a column vector $F_i = vec(f_i)$, let $F = [F_1, F_2, ..., F_T] \in R^{mn \times T}$, then the decomposition of image sequences for moving object detection can be represented as $F = B + D$, where $B = [vec(b_1), ..., vec(b_T)] \in R^{mn \times T}$ and $D = [vec(d_1), ..., vec(d_T)] \in R^{mn \times T}$ are background term and object term, respectively. Here we discuss the intrinsic properties of background and object for decomposition [12]. Firstly, we assume that the videos are captured with no turbulence.

The background term B: The ideal background of each image in image sequences should be almost the same. So the linear correlations of background term are strong. That means the background term B should be a low rank matrix. The moving objects term D: The number of pixels occupied by the moving objects, which is drogue, is usually small compared to the total number of pixels in each image. It is a reasonable assumption for most realistic surveillance videos. Therefore, the foreground moving objects can be captured by restricting the number of nonzero entries, expressed as zero norm constraints. The combination with the above constraints on background term B and moving objects term D for decomposition of F is performed by solving the following low rank and sparse optimization, which can be described as [12, 13]

$$\min_{B,D} \left(rank(B) + \lambda \|D\|_0 \right), \ s.t. F = B + D \tag{1}$$

where λ is the weighting parameter, $rank(\cdot)$ denotes the rank of matrix, $\|\cdot\|_0$ denotes zero norm. The moving object D can be obtained by solving the above formula.

2.2   Multi-Scale Lrsd for Drogue Detection

We can see that the drogue has complete structure information from the figure 2. In order to overcome the influence of non-structure information, caused by atmospheric or aircrafts, we use a multi-scale method for moving objects detection, the objection are detected by fusion the multi-scale detection results via low rank and sparse decomposition. We use stationary wavelet transform (SWT) for images sequences decomposition. The SWT algorithm inserts $2j - 1$ zeroes between the filter coefficients at the resolution level j. The size of each wavelet sub-band equals to the size of the input image. Each image f_t can be decomposed into four parts at scale j:

one low-frequency sub-band f_t^j and three high-frequency sub-bands. Three high-frequency sub-bands images contain horizontal, vertical and diagonal detail information of image, such as edges or noise, respectively. While the low-frequency sub-band f_t^j reveals the structure information. The low-frequency sub-band image of coarse scale has better structure information than the low-frequency sub-band image of fine scale. Therefore, we employ the object in the low frequency sub-band image sequences of coarse scale as the object confidence map, similar to the object confidence map in [13], for the low sub-band image sequences of next fine scale for decomposition. We enforce the constraint object confidence map on the formula (1). The proposed method of multi-scale low rank and sparse decomposition for drogue detection can be expressed by

$$\min_{B^j, D^j} \left(rank\left(B^j\right) + \lambda^j \left\| \Gamma\left(D^{j+1}\right) \odot D^j \right\|_0 \right), \ s.t. \ F^j = B^j + D^j \tag{2}$$

where B^j and D^j is the background and object at scale j, $\odot$ denotes element-wise multiply. And $\left(\Gamma\left(D^{j+1}\right)\right)_{pq} = \begin{cases} 0, & D_{pq}^{j+1} \neq 0 \\ 1, & D_{pq}^{j+1} = 0 \end{cases}$ is the object confidence map at scale j. The object confidence map is used to encourage the sparse solutions D^j to be located on regions same with the object confidence map at scale $j+1$. Because of the vibration in the drogue video image, 2D parametric transformations is introduced into formula (2) to compensate for the background motion caused by shaking cameras on the probe, as shown in [12, 14], which can be used to model the translation, rotation and planar deformation of the background. That is

$$\min_{B^j, D^j, \tau^j} \left(rank\left(B^j\right) + \lambda^j \left\| \Gamma\left(D^{j+1}\right) \odot D^j \right\|_0 \right), \ s.t. \ F^j \circ \tau^j = B^j + D^j \tag{3}$$

where $F^j \circ \tau^j = \left[F_1^j \circ \tau_1^j, \ldots, F_T^j \circ \tau_T^j\right]$, and $F_t^j \circ \tau_t^j$ denotes the t-th frame after the transformation parameterized by vector $\tau_t^j \in R^p$ at scale j, where p is the number of parameters of the motion model ($p = 6$ for the affine motion and $p = 8$ for the projective motion). The problem described in formula (3) can be solved via binary matrix. Let $\left(I\left(D^{j+1}\right)\right)_{pq} = \begin{cases} 1, & D_{pq}^{j+1} \neq 0 \\ 0, & D_{pq}^{j+1} = 0 \end{cases}$, in which the 1 or 0 indicates the pixel belonging to object or not. Obviously, $\left\|D^j\right\|_0 = \left\|I^j\right\|_0$ and $\left\|\Gamma\left(D^{j+1}\right) \odot D^j\right\|_0 = \left\|\Gamma\left(I^{j+1}\right) \odot I^j\right\|_0$. As shown in [12], the objects should be contiguous pieces. Spatially or temporally neighboring image pixels should be encouraged to have similar labels. The Ising model is used to define the neighboring energy of I. The spatial smooth cost is given by $\sum_{(pq, \acute{p}\acute{q}) \in N} \left\| I_{pq} - I_{\acute{p}\acute{q}} \right\|$, which $(pq, \acute{p}\acute{q}) \in N$ is the set of neighboring pixels. It can be represented by $\left\| Avec(I) \right\|_1$, where A is an incidence matrix of neighboring pixels. And the $F^j \circ \tau^j = B^j + D^j$ can be expressed as $\min \left\| \left(F^j \circ \tau^j - B^j\right) \odot \left(I^j\right)^c \right\|_F^2$, where $\left(I^j\right)^c$ is the complementary set of I^j. Since matrix rank and the l_0-norm are not convex function, then replacing $rank\left(B^j\right)$ with sum of the singular values and $\|I\|_0$ with the l_1-norm $\|I\|_1$ can get exact solution by minimizing the convex surrogate. Our final optimization cost function can be rewritten as

$$\min_{B^j, I^j \in \{0,1\}, \tau^j} \frac{1}{2} \left\| \left(F^j \circ \tau^j - B^j \right) \odot \left(I^j \right)^c \right\|_F^2 + \gamma^j \left\| B^j \right\|_* + \lambda^j \left\| \Gamma \left(I^{j+1} \right) \odot I^j \right\|_1 + \theta^j \left\| Avec \left(I^j \right) \right\|_1 \tag{4}$$

where γ^j, λ^j and θ^j are non-negative parameters. We can see that the object confidence map, that is $\Gamma \left(D^{j+1} \right) = \left(I^{j+1} \right)^c$. For coarsest scale sub-band image sequences, the object confidence map is chosen as all ones matrix. The object detection results I^l of finest scale sub-band image sequences is the final detection result of drogue.

2.3   Solution for Optimization

Joint optimization over B^j, I^j and τ^j in formula (4) is difficult. An alternating algorithm is adopted to optimize the above cost function.

1. Update B^j, given I^j and τ^j: The idea of the singular value thresholding algorithm (SVT) [15] is used to update B^j, fixing sparse matrix I^j. Since $\min_{B^j} \frac{1}{2} \left\| \left(F^j \circ \tau^j - B^j \right) \odot \left(I^j \right)^c \right\|_F^2 + \gamma^j \left\| B^j \right\|_* = \min_{B^j} \frac{1}{2} \left\| \left(\left(F^j \circ \tau^j \right) \odot \left(I^j \right)^c - B^j \odot \left(I^j \right) \right) - B^j \right\|_F^2 + \gamma^j \left\| B^j \right\|_*$. Then singular value decomposition is done as $S \Sigma D^T = \left(F^j \circ \tau^j \right) \odot \left(I^j \right)^c - B^j \odot \left(I^j \right)$, and $\Sigma = diag \left(\sigma_1, ..., \sigma_r \right)$, $\sigma_1, ..., \sigma_r$ is the singular values ($\sigma_i \geq 0$). Then update B^j with SVT algorithm can be denoted as

$$\hat{B}_k = S \Psi_{\lambda_k} \left(\Sigma \right) D^T \tag{5}$$

where $\Psi_{\lambda_k} \left(\Sigma \right) = diag \left(\psi_{\lambda_k} \left(\sigma_1 \right), ..., \psi_{\lambda_k} \left(\sigma_r \right) \right)$, in which $\psi_{\lambda_k} \left(\sigma_i \right)$ is the soft thresholding operator, defined as $\psi_{\lambda_k} \left(\sigma_i \right) = \begin{cases} \sigma_i - \lambda_k, & \sigma_i > \gamma^j \\ 0, & \sigma_i \leq \gamma^j \end{cases}$.

2. Update I^j, given B^j and τ^j: Since

$$\min_{I^j \in \{0,1\}} \frac{1}{2} \left\| \left(F^j \circ \tau^j - B^j \right) \odot \left(I^j \right)^c \right\|_F^2 + \lambda^j \left\| \Gamma \left(I^{j+1} \right) \odot I^j \right\|_1 + \theta^j \left\| Avec \left(I^j \right) \right\|_1$$

$$= \min_{I^j \in \{0,1\}} \sum_{pq} \left[\frac{1}{2} \left(\left(F^j \circ \tau^j \right)_{pq} - B^j_{pq} \right)^2 \left(1 - I^j_{pq} \right) + \lambda^j \left(\Gamma \left(I^{j+1} \right) \right)_{pq} I^j_{pq} \right] + \theta^j \left\| Avec \left(I^j \right) \right\|_1 \tag{6}$$

$$= \min_{I^j \in \{0,1\}} \sum_{pq} \left[-\frac{1}{2} \left(\left(F^j \circ \tau^j \right)_{pq} - B^j_{pq} \right)^2 + \lambda^j \left(\Gamma \left(I^{j+1} \right) \right)_{pq} \right] I^j_{pq} + \theta^j \left\| Avec \left(I^j \right) \right\|_1$$

It is converted into a form of first-order Markov Random Field with binary labels. The graph cuts method can be used to optimize this problem [12].

3. Update τ^j, given B^j and I^j: $\min_{\tau^j} \left\| \left(F^j \circ \tau^j - B^j \right) \odot \left(I^j \right)^c \right\|_F^2$. The incremental refinement can be used to solve this parametric motion estimation problem [12, 14]. At each iteration, the τ^j is updated by

$$\hat{\tau}^j = \hat{\tau}^j + \arg\min_{\Delta\tau^j} \left\| \left(F^j \circ \hat{\tau}^j + J_{\hat{\tau}^j} \Delta\tau^j - B^j \right) \odot \left(I^j \right)^c \right\|_F^2 \tag{7}$$

where $\Delta\tau^j$ is a small increment and $J_{\hat{\tau}^j}$ is the Jacobian matrix $J_{\hat{\tau}^j} = \frac{\partial F^j}{\partial \tau^j}\Big|_{\hat{\tau}^j}$.

3   Experiments

We evaluate the performance of proposed algorithm on the real drogue image sequence. The bior1.3 wavelet is chosen for image sequences decomposition. Four scales decomposition is used for testing. The algorithm was tested on i5 3.1GHz Pentium CPU with 8 GB memory, through MATLAB implementation. The parameters are tuned according to [12], in which $\theta = 30\lambda$. There are 120 frames in the drogue image sequences. The size of the image is 432×576. The experimental results are shown in figure 2.

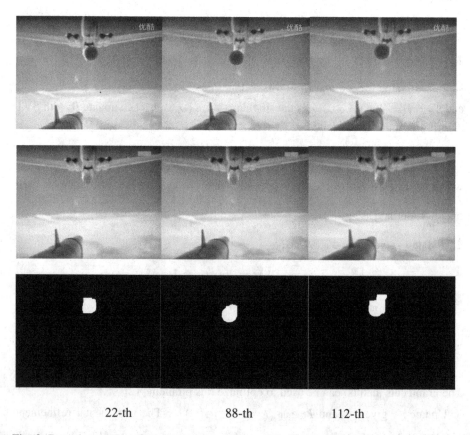

22-th   88-th   112-th

Fig. 2. Detection results of drogue image sequences. The first row shows the original visual image frames. The second row shows the estimated background image by our method. The third row shows the results of visual images by ours method.

We can see that the drogue is the moving object versus the tanker aircraft during short period. Our algorithm is to decompose the image sequences generating a background and the clear drogue region. The proposed method can align the image sequences for drogue detection in the presence of camera shake under complex background. The proposed method is able to distinguish drogue from backgrounds without any background modeling procedure.

4   Conclusion

This paper proposed a drogue detection method for vision-based AAR. The moving objects are detected as the sparse terms by decomposition. The approach is based on recent advances in efficient matrix rank minimization that come with theoretical guarantees. The experiments carried on real AAR video demonstrated that our proposed method is effective. This approach will be ideal for drogue detection under complex and uncontrolled scenes. The drawback of the vision-based techniques is the assumption that all the landmarks are always visible and functional. How to design reliable feature or landmarks in low visibility conditions, such as in a dark night or in a foggy environment, will be considered in our future work.

Acknowledgments. This work is supported by the Aviation Science Funds No.20105153022.

References

1. Mao, W., Eke, F.O.: A survey of the dynamics and control of aircraft during aerial refueling. Nonlinear Dynamics and Systems Theory 8(4), 375–388 (2008)
2. Chen, C.-I., Stettner, R.: Drogue tracking using 3D flash lidar for autonomous aerial refueling. In: Proc. SPIE, vol. 8037, p. 80370Q (2011)
3. Valasek, J., Gunnam, K., Kimmett, J., et al.: Vision-based sensor and navigation system for autonomous air refueling. Journal of Guidance, Control, and Dynamics 28(5), 832–844 (2005)
4. James, D., Theresa, S., John, V., et al.: Boom and receptacle autonomous air refueling using a visual pressure snake optical sensor. Journal of Guidance, Control, and Dynamics 30(6), 1753–1769 (2007)
5. Mahboubi, Z., Zico Kolter, J., Wang, T., et al.: Camera-based localization for autonomous UAV formation flight. In: Proceedings of the AIAA @ Infotech Conference (2011)
6. Giampiero, C., Marcello, R.N., Mario, L.F.: Simulation environment for machine vision based aerial refueling for UAVs. IEEE Trans. on Aerospace and Electronic Systems 45(1), 138–151 (2009)
7. Tandale, M.D., Bowers, R., Valasek, J.: Trajectory tracking controller for vision-based probe and drogue autonomous aerial refueling. Journal of Guidance, Control, and Dynamics 29(4), 846–857 (2006)
8. Soujanya, V., Giampiero, C., Marcello, R., et al.: Addressing corner detection issues for machine vision based UAV aerial refueling. Machine Vision and Applications 18(5), 261–273 (2007)

9. Oliver, N., Rosario, B., Pentland, A.: A bayesian computer vision system for modeling human interactions. IEEE Trans. on PAMI 22, 831–843 (2000)

10. Zivkovic, Z.: Improved adaptive gausian mixture model for background subtraction. In: ICPR, vol. 2, pp. 28–31 (2004)

11. Lopez-Rubio, E., Luque-Baena, R.M.: Stochastic approximation for background modelling. Computer Vision and Image Understanding 115(6), 735–749 (2011)

12. Zhou, X., Yang, C., Yu, W.: Moving object detection by detecting contiguous outliers in the low-rank representation. IEEE Trans. on PAMI 99 (to be published, 2012)

13. Oreifej, O., Li, X., Shah, M.: Simultaneous video stabilization and moving object detection in turbulence. IEEE Trans. on PAMI 99 (to be published, 2012)

14. Peng, Y., Ganesh, A., Wright, J., et al.: RASL: Robust alignment via sparse and low-rank decomposition for linearly correlated images. IEEE Trans. on PAMI 99 (to be published, 2012)

15. Cai, J., Candes, E., Shen, Z.: A singular value thresholding algorithm for matrix completion. SIAM J. on Optimization 20(4), 1956–1982 (2010)

Multi-phase Fusion of Visible-Infrared Information for Motion Detection

Yong Chen, Zhi-Ming Wang, and Hong Bao

Department of Computer Science and Technology, School of Computer and Communication,
University of Science and Technology, Beijing, 100083, China
yong.chen.jx.cn@gmail.com,
{wangzhiming,baohong}@ies.ustb.edu.cn

Abstract. A Multi-phase visible-infrared image fusion algorithm was proposed for bi-channel motion object detection. First of all, foreground detected separately by visible and infrared image was fused as foreground-fused image, and then an improved KIRSCH algorithm was used to calculate the complete contour from foreground-fused image, taking advantage of the complementary characteristics of the visible and infrared images by use of a fused image provided by channel-replacement-operation. At last, a complete moving target was obtained with the holes fill technology .Experimental results show that the proposed algorithm can effectively remove the shadow of the foreground in visible image, and access to the clear and complete moving target.

Keywords: image fusion, motion detection, motion contour, KIRSCH.

1   Introduction

Motion detection, as the basis of a whole monitoring system, is one of the key steps in the field of computer vision. It has a huge impact on subsequent target tracking, target recognition, behavior analysis, and intelligent search. However, due to the dynamic characteristics of the target, coupled with a variety of complex external conditions (such as the light changes, rain, lightning, etc.) and other disturbances (such as the impact of camera jitter, blocking, pore size, shadow, etc.), it has been the difficulty and hotspots of many related scholars.

For moving target detection, various methods from the literature were implemented and compared, including background subtraction, frames differential, optical flow, etc. Background subtraction [1] is the most simple motion detection algorithm, it can be more completely to get the prospects, but it is very sensitive to the selection of background model and the update strategy. Frames differential [2] as an improved method of background subtraction, is more sensitive to environmental noise, and it often turns out to be a moving object silhouette, which is not conducive to objective analysis and recognition. Optical flow [3] will be able to detect moving objects without any information of the test scenarios in advance. But the high-computation complexity made it is difficult to achieve a real-time processing.

F.L. Wang et al. (Eds.): CMSP 2012, CCIS 346, pp. 325–333, 2012.

By fusing visible and thermal infrared channel information, the integration of complementary information [4] is available to achieve moving targets detection quickly and accurately. Here, we propose a multi-phase visible-infrared image fusion strategy for motion detection. An improved KIRSCH algorithm is used to obtain the complete outline of the prospects in experimental materials. Also, the complementary characteristics of the visible and infrared images are obtained by use of the channel-replacement-operation. This method can not only effectively remove the shadow of the foreground in visible image, but also access to the clear and complete moving targets.

2   Method

2.1   Algorithm Framework

The algorithm processes framework as shown in Figure 1. First of all, after data registration [5, 6], the VI (visible image) and the IF (infrared image) are used to obtain the foregrounds respectively. Then these foregrounds are fused for new foregrounds, we call it the FFI (fused-foreground-image). At the same time, the original VI and IF are also integrated into a new image named FI (fused-image). Then, the FI, the FFI and the intensity channel of IF are input to an improved KIRSCH algorithm, and with the help of some image morphological operations, it turns out to be the complete targets.

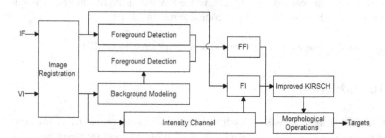

Fig. 1. Flowchart of the algorithm

2.2   Foreground Detection

With clear texture and color, frames differential is the best choice to get a more obvious contour for visible frame sequences. Since infrared images have complementary properties, and with a higher precision and recall rate [8]. GMM (Gaussian mixture model) [9] can extract the moving targets in a good performance. Each pixel value in infrared image to obey a certain distribution in the time axis, the distribution can be representing as a weighted superposition of K Gaussian distribution. For example, a pixel value at time t is expressed as X_t, which is a three-dimensional vector, then the distribution of X_t credited as $P(X_t)$:

$$P(X_t) = \sum_{i=0}^{k} w_{i,t} * \eta(X_t, \mu_{i,t}, \Sigma_{i,t}) \tag{1}$$

Here $w_{i,t}$ is the weight of the ith Gaussian distribution in our GMM at time t, and $\eta(X_t, \mu_{i,t}, \Sigma_{i,t})$ is the Gauss probability density function,

$$\eta(X_t, \mu_{i,t}, \Sigma_{i,t}) = \frac{1}{(2\pi)^{\frac{d}{2}}|\Sigma_{i,t}|^{\frac{1}{2}}} \exp^{\{-\frac{1}{2}(X_t-\mu_{i,t})^T\Sigma_{i,t}^{-1}(X_t-\mu_{i,t})\}} \tag{2}$$

$\mu_{i,t}$ and $\Sigma_{i,t}$ are the mean and covariance matrix of $\eta(X_t, \mu_{i,t}, \Sigma_{i,t})$, K is the number of Gaussian distribution, general value from 3 to 5. In order to reduce computation, we assume that R, G and B three-channel in the independent distribution with the same variance in this article. Then, the covariance matrix can be described as:

$$\Sigma_{i,t} = \sigma_k^2 I \tag{3}$$

The value of K is 5.

Now we start our process, when comes a new frame at time t, we initialize a Gauss distribution for an arbitrary pixel X_t with the following initialization parameters:

$$\begin{cases} w_{i,t} = 0.05, & \text{(a smaller value)} \\ \sigma_t^2 = 30 * 30, & \text{(a larger value)} \\ \mu_{i,t} = X_t, & \text{(the value of current pixel)} \end{cases} \tag{4}$$

This new Gauss distribution will be used to match with the existing N (0<=N<=K) Gaussian distributions in our GMM, in accordance with the following rules:

$$M_{i,t} = \begin{cases} 1, & \text{if } |X_t - \mu_{i,t}| < 2\sigma_{i,t}, \ i = 1,2,...,N, \ N \neq 0 \\ 0, & \text{else} \end{cases} \tag{5}$$

A background pixel was judged out when $M_{i,t}=1$ and what's more; we also update the parameters of the ith Gaussian distributions in our GMM, with renewal equations where   is the weight update rate and   as a parameter updating rate:

$$\begin{cases} w_{i,t} = (1 - \alpha)w_{i,t-1} + \alpha(M_{i,t}) \\ \mu_{i,t} = (1 - \rho)\mu_{i,t-1} + \rho X_t \\ \sigma_t^2 = (1 - \rho)\sigma_{t-1}^2 + \rho(X_t - \mu_t)^T(X_t - \mu_t) \\ \rho = \alpha * \eta(X_t, \mu_k, \sigma_k) \end{cases} \tag{6}$$

We choose the Gauss distribution matching with maximum weight to do the above operations when the current one matches multiple Gauss distributions.

If $M_{i,t}=0$ and N<K, a new Gauss distribution with initialization parameters is added also matching and update operations is necessary until N=K.

If N=K and the statistical number of frames used for training less than Learning-window [10] (the required minimum number of frames for Gaussian mixture model to establish, here we set Learning-window=100), we also initialize a new Gauss distribution to replace the one with minimum weights in the GMM. After the statistical number of frames exceeds over the Learning-window, that is, the Gaussian distribution represents the background with a larger $w_{i,t}$ and a minor $\Sigma_{i,t}$. Therefore, for a given pixel X_t, we first sort p_i from largest to smallest, here p_i is defined as:

$$p_i = w_i * |\Sigma_i|^{-\frac{1}{2}}, \quad i = 1, 2, ..., K \tag{7}$$

Now, we can assume that the Gaussian distribution represents the background with a larger probability will standing near the front. So, the background model will be established with the first B distributions if only meets the following conditions:

$$B = arg\ min_b(\textstyle\sum_{i=1}^k w_i > T) \tag{8}$$

T is considered to be a priori probability value, which is very essential for GMM. In this paper, we set $T=0.7$. Finally, a conditional probabilityP $P(X_t|bg)$ is set up to do the judgment.

$$P(X_t|bg) = \textstyle\sum_{i=0}^B w_{i,t} * \eta(X_t,\ \mu_{i,t},\ \Sigma_{i,t}) \tag{9}$$

If $P(X_t|bg) \geq T$, the current pixel will be sentenced to the background, else, the foreground.

2.3 Image Fusion for Foreground Detection

For original visible image and infrared image, we selected 6 simple image fusion methods from 13 summarized by Stephen R.Schnelle and Alex Lichen Chan [11, 12] for experimental comparison; frames differential and GMM are used for the results analysis. Results are shown in figure 2.

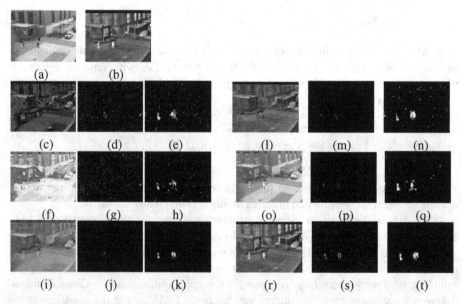

Fig. 2. Examples of original (a)visible and (b)infrared images, as well as fused images produced by (c)pix-and (f)pix-or (i)PCA-weighted average (l)Minimum (o)Maximum (r)channel-replacement; the second column shows the results by frames differential and the third column shows the results by GMM

The comparison among the 6 simple fusion strategies above shows that the results from channel-replacement strategy bring a surprising result not only with a clear texture but also an efficient shadow deduction. The channel-replacement strategy wins in comparison with other methods. For the channel-replacement strategy, here we replace the intensity channel of visible image with the same channel of infrared image. The first task is to obtain the intensity channel from RGB color images. the following transformation helps.

$$Y = 0.2989 * R + 0.5870 * G + 0.1140 * B \qquad (10)$$

2.4   Contour Extraction Based on Information Fusion

Multi-direction differential operator is one of the effective ways for image edge detection. Considering the contour extraction, we need a good precision and a high directivity. Kirsch operator is the best choice. The Kirsch operator is consists of eight 3x3 templates as figure 3 shows.

$$\begin{bmatrix} 5 & 5 & 5 \\ -3 & 0 & -3 \\ -3 & -3 & -3 \end{bmatrix} \begin{bmatrix} -3 & 5 & 5 \\ -3 & 0 & 5 \\ -3 & -3 & -3 \end{bmatrix} \begin{bmatrix} -3 & -3 & 5 \\ -3 & 0 & 5 \\ -3 & -3 & 5 \end{bmatrix} \begin{bmatrix} -3 & -3 & -3 \\ -3 & 0 & 5 \\ -3 & 5 & 5 \end{bmatrix}$$

$$\begin{bmatrix} -3 & -3 & -3 \\ -3 & 0 & -3 \\ 5 & 5 & 5 \end{bmatrix} \begin{bmatrix} -3 & -3 & -3 \\ 5 & 0 & -3 \\ 5 & 5 & -3 \end{bmatrix} \begin{bmatrix} 5 & -3 & -3 \\ 5 & 0 & -3 \\ 5 & -3 & -3 \end{bmatrix} \begin{bmatrix} 5 & 5 & -3 \\ 5 & 0 & -3 \\ -3 & -3 & -3 \end{bmatrix}$$

Fig. 3. Kirsch Operators

Each template represents a specific direction, we remark them as(from left to right, from top to bottom): K[0] (up)、K[1] (right-up)、K[2] (right)、K[3] (right-bottom)、K[4] (bottom)、K[5] (left-bottom)、K[6] (left)、K[7] (left-up). After operating with the 8 templates for any pixel, the maximum result is selected as the edge gradient value for the pixel. The flow diagram for contour extraction algorithm is shown in figure 4.

2.5   Threshold Selection

The algorithm repeatedly related to the selection of the threshold, for frame differential, a thread is needed for the binarization of the detected foreground image in VI. This binarization threshold is extracted from the histogram of the difference image, after histogram equalization of the difference image. We select the pixel value corresponding at the first trough as the binarization threshold, which can guarantee that most of the foreground pixels retained.

For contour extraction, a three threshold policy is put forward to ensure a complete object contour. The gradient size Thres_grad _val and gradient direction Thres_delta_dir of the contour pixel are used to promote a more complete and smooth outline. Besides, the threshold Thres_next_fg for limiting the detection range not only reduces the computational load but also the impact of background edge.

The selection of Thres_grad _val to adjust based on the foreground and background gray difference, a larger value is perfect for reducing the computation load and a smaller value to ensure a complete contour. The Thres_delta_dir selected according to the smoothness of contours, a smaller value is fit for smooth contours which can help to reduce the computation load, and a larger value will result a good behavior for some curved contours(no more than 5), Ideally, take the angle of the profile with a maximum degree of bending comparison rightly. A simple biselection is used for Thres_next_fg. The first step, a mean value T of intensity channel of IF is calculated as the initial value. For step 2, the pixels of intensity channel are divided into two sets G1 and G2 with threshold T:

$$G1 = \{Img\_fused.\,data[i][j] \mid Img\_fused.\,data[i][j] > T\} \tag{11}$$

$$G2 = \{Img\_fused.\,data[i][j] \mid Img\_fused.\,data[i][j] \leq T\} \tag{12}$$

Step 3, the mean value mean1 and mean2 are calculated for set G1 and G2 respectively, and new threshold T' is obtained through the following methods:

$$T' = (1/2)(mean1 + mean2) \tag{13}$$

Repeat the second step to the third step, until the difference between the adjacent two T' is less than a predefined value d (here we set d=0.01), then Thres_next_fg is preferable to the latest T'.

2.6   Morphological Hole Filling

Target, obtained after contour detection is only an empty profile, we need to fill it into a solid target. Line-scan-filling and Seed-filling are two typical filling algorithm. In our paper, Hole-filling based on contour [13] is adopted for Hole-filling. First of all, the circumscribed contour to the target area is found and marked, then a point in the area is selected as the seed to perform the region growing operation inside the contour until all the points are found. At last,he algorithm eliminates all the marks, and sets the target area foreground.

3   Experiments and Results

3.1   Experimental Results

To evaluate our proposed algorithm, we compare the experimental results with some other operation results by some commonly used moving target detection algorithms. Figure 6 shows the experimental results of the 156th video frame. Experimental data are from OTCBVS[7] .

3.2   Results Analysis

As shown in figure 6, (b) shows the results of frame difference method in visible image only, there have been some parts missing in (b), also (c) shows that the serious shadow of a great impact on the detection accuracy. Results of GMM in infrared

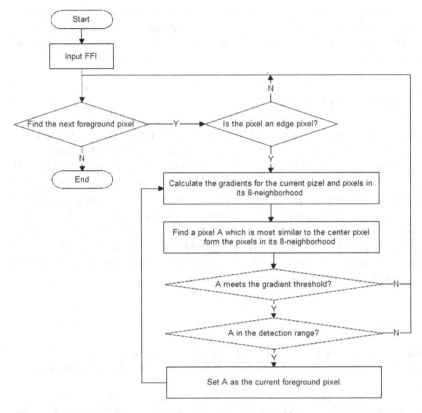

Fig. 4. Flow chart for contour extraction algorithm

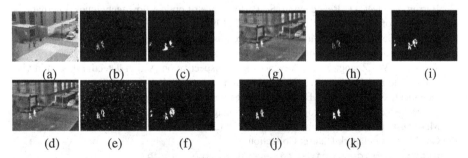

Fig. 5. Shows the (a)visible and (d)infrared images, and the (g)fused image, the second column shows the results by frame differential and the third column shows the results by GMM, (j)shows the temp result before hole filling and (k) shows the final result.

image only, as (e, f) shows, the halo effect and thermal noise are the stumbling blocks to achieve a complete and clear detection. The fusion-technology helps integrating the characteristics of both visual and infrared image, is favorable to moving target extraction. Image noise is significantly reduced in the fused image (shown in h, i), some incomplete parts will be improved by contour detection as a subsequent patches. More importantly, the image fusion can effectively remove the shadow in visible image. (j) shows the result of contour detection, and (k) show the final output of our algorithm, with a more complete outline and obvious boundary information, which is more appropriate in favor of track processing.

4   Summary and Conclusions

In this paper, we fused the visible and thermal infrared information to achieve the moving targets detection quickly and accurately. Here, we proposed a multi-phase information fusion algorithm for bi-channel motion detection. An improved KIRSCH algorithm was used to calculate the complete outline of the prospects in experimental materials. Also, the complementary characteristics of visible and infrared image are available for our detection by use of the channel-replacement-operation. This method can not only effectively remove the shadow of the visible image, but also access to the clear and complete moving target in poor lighting conditions. But when the heat of background is similar to foreground, the detected targets will turn out to be larger than the actual ones, which need to be improved in our future work.

References

1. Haritaoglu, I., Harwood, D., Davis, L.: W4: Real-time surveillance of people and their activities. IEEE Transactions on Pattern Analysis and Machine Intelligence 22(8), 809–830 (2000)
2. Lipton, A., Fujiyoshi, H., Patil, R.: Moving target classification and tracking from real-time video. In: IEEE Workshop on Applications of Computer Vision, Princeton, USA, pp. 8–14 (1998)
3. Barron, J., Fleet, D., Beauchemin, S.: Performance of optical flow techniques. International Journal of Computer Vision 12(1), 42–47 (1994)
4. Pohl, C., Genderen, J.L.: Multisensor Image Fusion in Remote Sensing Concepts, Methods and Applications. International Journal of Remote Sensing 9(5), 823–854 (1998)
5. Zhang, X.-W., Zhang, Y.-N.: Advances and perspective on motion detection fusion in visual and thermal framework. J. Infrared Millim. Waves 30(4) (August 2011)
6. Verstockt, S., Poppe, C., De Potter, P.: Silhouette Coverage Analysis for Multi-modal Video Surveillance. In: Progress In Electromagnetics Research Symposium Proceedings, Marrakesh, Morocco, March 20-23, vol. 1279 (2011)
7. OTCBVS Benchmark Dataset Collection, http://www.cse.ohio-state.edu/otcbvs-bench/
8. Ulusoy, H., Yuruk, H.: New method for fusion of complementary information from infrared and visual images for object detection. IET Image Processing 5(1), 36–48 (2011)
9. Zhang, L., Wu, B., Nevatia, R.: Pedstrian detection in infrared images based on local shape fetures. In: Fourth Joint IEEE Int. Workshop on Object Tracking and Classification in and Beyond the Visible Spectrum (OTCBVS 2007), in Conjunction with CVPR (2007)
10. Stauffer, C., Grimson, W.E.L.: Adaptive background mixture models for real-time tracking. In: Proceedings of the 1999 IEEE Computer Society Conference on Computer Vision and Pattern Recognition, Part vol. 2. IEEE Comput. Soc (1999)

11. Schnelle, S.R., Chan, A.L.: Enhanced Target Tracking Through Infrared-Visible Image Fusion. IEEE (2011)
12. Liu, Z., et al.: Object Assessment of Multiresolution Image Fusion Algorithms for Context Enhancement in Night Vision: A Comparative Study. IEEE Transactions on Pattern Analysis and Machine Intelligence 34(1) (January 2012)
13. Zhang, D.-C., Zhou, C.-G.: Hole-Filling Algorithm Based on Contour. Journal of Jilin University (Science Edition) 49(1) (January 2011)

A Porosity Simulation Method Using Cholesky Decomposition

Ting Zhang[1] and Yi Du[2]

[1] School of Computer and Information Engineering, Shanghai University of Electric Power, Shanghai 200090, China
[2] School of Computer and Information, Shanghai Second Polytechnic University, Shanghai 201209, China
tingzh@shiep.edu.cn, duyi@mail.ustc.edu.cn

Abstract. Porosity is an important parameter for the evaluation of transport properties in many scientific and engineering fields. However, it is quite difficult to predict the unknown porosity values only by some sparse conditional data in the process of simulation based on current popular interpolation methods. Therefore, some interpolation or extrapolation methods are used to estimate or predict the unknown porosity for better simulated results. Cholesky decomposition is introduced in the simulation and prediction of porosity distribution. The advantage is that this decomposition only needs to be performed once, multiple realizations are generated at the cost of a mere matrix multiplication. The major drawback is that, even if done only once, it is a very costly operation for large matrix and thus should be restricted to small fields and data sets. The simulation using Cholesky decomposition is the equivalent of the sequential Gaussian simulation algorithm with simple kriging and with an infinite data search neighborhood; all original conditioning data and previously simulated values are used in the kriging system at every node along the simulation path. The experimental results demonstrate that this method is practical.

Keywords: porosity, Cholesky decomposition, conditioning data, simulation, interpolation.

1   Introduction

Pores often exist in many materials, generated during material manufacturing processes. Porosity is an important property for the characterization of pores in fluids flow, which can reflect the structures of porous media and is quite significant in the fields such as catalysis, oil recovery, aging of building materials and so on. Because the prediction of transport properties in porous materials is of great importance in various fields, porosity must be available in order to predict the fluids flow properties quantificationally [1].

A proper interpolation method for porosity prediction or simulation is quite important and significant. When predicting the unknown porosity information, interpolation methods use some scattered points to estimate the unknown attributes of

F.L. Wang et al. (Eds.): CMSP 2012, CCIS 346, pp. 334–340, 2012.
© Springer-Verlag Berlin Heidelberg 2012

unsampled nodes to build an accurate and complete mathematical model according to some rules from math, physics and so on. Although a number of interpolation methods were introduced, the accurate simulation or prediction of porosity is still difficult to be realized.

Interpolation methods are mainly two types: "definite" methods and "indefinite" methods. The "definite" here means that the forms, parameters and results of interpolation functions are mostly definite. "Definite" methods include the inverse distance weighting method, the triangular mesh method, the basis function method, etc. The "indefinite" means that the forms of interpolation functions are indefinite and the selection of parameters in interpolation functions depends on the principles of statistics [1, 2]. The main "indefinite" interpolation methods are kriging and stochastic simulation in geostatistics. Kriging and stochastic simulation, both based on variogram which only describes the relations between two points in space and cannot reconstruct complex patterns such as curvilinear shapes, are called two-point geostatistics [3, 4].

Therefore, indefinite algorithms can normally be classified into two categories [5]. The first kind is that the interpolation algorithms which yield a unique interpolated result. These interpolation algorithms are usually low-pass filters which tend to smooth out local details of the spatial variability of the primary variable. They provide a local measure of uncertainty, e.g., a kriging variance.

Stochastic techniques which produce multiple possible realizations of the spatial distribution are the second one. Typically, these stochastic algorithms are full-pass filters which reproduce the full spectrum of the spatial variability. Fluctuations between the realizations of multiple stochastic results provide a visual and quantitative measure for the uncertainty about the underlying characteristics in the possible results.

Our paper mainly discusses the porosity simulation using Cholesky decomposition. It has the advantage of needing to be performed only once, multiple realizations are generated at the cost of a mere matrix multiplication. The major drawback of Cholesky decomposition is that, even if it is preformed only once, its operation is very costly for large matrix and thus should be restricted to small fields and data sets[6, 7].

The simulation using Cholesky decomposition is the equivalent of the sequential Gaussian simulation algorithm with simple kriging and with an infinite data search neighborhood; all original conditioning data and previously simulated values are used in the kriging system at every node along the simulation path. Experimental results show that the method is appropriate and practical.

2   Ideas and Methods

2.1   Cholesky Decomposition

If a square matrix A happens to be symmetric and positive definite, then it has a special, more efficient, triangular decomposition. Symmetric means that $a_{ij} = a_{ji}$ for i, $j = 1, \ldots, N$, while positive definite means that

$$v \cdot A \cdot v > 0, \quad \text{for all vectors v} \tag{1}$$

While symmetric, positive definite matrices are rather special, they occur quite frequently in some applications, so their special factorization, called Cholesky decomposition, is good to know about. When you can use it, Cholesky decomposition is about a factor of two faster than alternative methods for solving linear equations. Instead of seeking arbitrary lower and upper triangular factors L and U, Cholesky decomposition constructs a lower triangular matrix L whose transpose L^T can itself serve as the upper triangular part. In other words, we can have such equation [8]:

$$L \cdot L^T = A \tag{2}$$

This factorization is sometimes referred to as "taking the square root" of the matrix A. The components of L^T are of course related to those of L by

$$L_{ij}^T = L_{ji} \tag{3}$$

It is convenient, then, to have the factor L overwrite the subdiagonal (lower triangular but not including the diagonal) part of A, preserving the input upper triangular values of A. Only one extra vector of length N is needed to store the diagonal part of L. The operations count is $N^3/6$ executions of the inner loop (consisting of one multiply and one subtract), with also N square roots. As already mentioned, this is about a factor 2 better than LU decomposition of A (where its symmetry would be ignored).

A straightforward implementation of Cholesky decomposition is [8]:

```
SUBROUTINE choldc(a,n,np,p)
INTEGER n,np
REAL a(np,np),p(n)
      Note: Given a positive-definite symmetric matrix a(1:n,1:n), with physical
      dimension np, this routine constructs its Cholesky decomposition, A = L·L^T.
      On input, only the upper triangle of a needs to be given; it is not modified.
      The Cholesky factor L is returned in the lower triangle of a, except for its
      diagonal elements which are returned in p(1:n).
INTEGER i,j,k
REAL sum
      do  i=1,n
          do  j=i,n
              sum=a(i,j)
              do  k=i-1,1,-1 // subtract 1 each time
                  sum=sum-a(i,k)*a(j,k)
              enddo
              if(i equal j)then
                  if(sum less than or equal 0)
                  pause    'choldc failed'
                  p(i)=sqrt(sum)
              else
                  a(j,i)=sum/p(i)
              endif
          enddo
      enddo
return
END
```

You might at this point wonder about pivoting. The answer is that Cholesky decomposition is extremely stable numerically, without any pivoting at all. Failure of the above Cholesky decomposition, shown in the above choldc(a,n,np,p), simply indicates that the matrix A (or, with roundoff error, another very nearby matrix) is not positive definite. In fact, choldc is an efficient way to test whether a symmetric matrix is positive definite. (In this application, you will want to replace the pause with some less drastic signaling method.) Once your matrix is decomposed, the triangular factor can be used to solve a linear equation by back substitution. The straightforward implementation of this is as follows:

```
SUBROUTINE cholsl(a,n,np,p,b,x)
INTEGER n,np
REAL a(np,np),b(n),p(n),x(n)
    Note: Solves the set of n linear equations A·x = b, where a is a positive-
    definite symmetric matrix with physical dimension np. a and p are input as
    the output of the routine choldc. Only the lower triangle of a is accessed.
    b(1:n) is input as the right-hand side vector. The solution vector is returned in
    x(1:n). a, n, np, and p are not modified and can be left in place for successive
    calls with different right-hand sides b. b is not modified unless you identify b
    and x in the calling sequence, which is allowed.
INTEGER i,k
REAL sum
do i=1,n                        (Solve L · y = b, storing y in x)
    sum=b(i)
    do  k=i-1,1,-1 // subtract 1 each time
        sum=sum-a(i,k)*x(k)
    enddo
    x(i)=sum/p(i)
enddo
do i=n,1,-1 // subtract 1 each time        ( Solve L^T · x = y)
    sum=x(i)
    do k=i+1,n
        sum=sum-a(k,i)*x(k)
    enddo
    x(i)=sum/p(i)
enddo
return
END
```

A typical use of choldc and cholsl is in the inversion of covariance matrices describing the fit of data to a model. In many applications, one often needs L^{-1}. The lower triangle of this matrix can be efficiently found from the output of choldc:

```
do i=1,n
    a(i,i)=1/p(i)
    do  j=i+1,n
        sum=0.
    do k=i,j-1 // subtract 1 each time
        sum=sum-a(j,k)*a(k,i)
    enddo
    a(j,i)=sum/p(j)
    enddo
enddo
```

2.2   Simulation Method Using Cholesky Decomposition

Step 1: Transform the data into normal score space.
Step 2: Build the Covariance matrix.
Step 3: Solve the Cholesky decomposition.
Step 4: Multiply a vector of independent Gaussian random deviates with the result of Step 3.
Step 5: Back transform the Gaussian simulated field into the data space.
Step 6: Repeat from Step 4 for another realization.

3   Experimental Results and Analyses

Original data of porosity with the size of 80×80×40 voxels are shown in Fig. 1, which are respectively the exterior and cross-sections (X=40, Y=40, Z=20) of the original data. The experimental conditioning data composed of some sample points are shown in Fig. 2 in the region of 80×80×40 voxels. The background is set black to highlight the conditioning data of porosity. The sample data in Fig. 2 are actually extracted from original data, so we can evaluate our method by comparing the similarity between the simulated results and original data. The higher the similarity is, the better our method is.

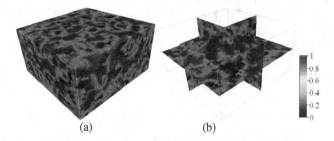

(a)   (b)

Fig. 1. Original data. (a) exterior; (b) cross-sections (X=40, Y=40, Z=20)

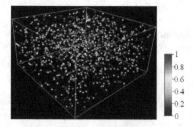

Fig. 2. Conditioning data

The region to be simulated has the size of 80×80×40 voxels. Our method was performed using the conditional data. The simulated result using Cholesky decomposition and the sample data is shown in Fig. 3. It is seen that the simulated result has similar structure with the original data.

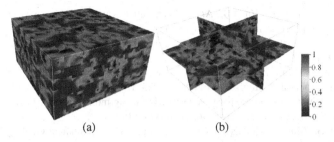

Fig. 3. Simulated result. (a) exterior; (b) cross-sections (X=40, Y=40, Z=20)

The average and variance of the simulated result and original data are respectively shown in Table 1, showing that the average and variance of the original data and simulated results are similar.

Table 1. The average and variance of original porosity data and simulated result

	original data	simulated result
porosity average	0.513	0.521
porosity variance	0.063	0.061

4   Conclusions

A porosity simulation method using Cholesky decomposition and conditioning data is proposed to realize the simulation of porosity. Cholesky decomposition has the advantage of needing to be performed only once, and then multiple realizations are generated at the cost of a mere matrix multiplication. The experimental results show that the simulated results are similar to the original porosity data, proving that our method is practical.

Acknowledgments. This work is supported by the Innovation Program of Shanghai Municipal Education Commission (09YZ454), and Shanghai Municipal Natural Science Foundation (No. 11ZR1413700, No. 12ZR1412000)

References

1. Zhang, T., Lu, D.T., Li, D.L.: Porous media reconstruction using a cross-section image and multiple-point geostatistics. In: Proceedings of ICACC 2009, Singapore, pp. 24–29 (January 2009)
2. Zhang, T., Lu, D.T., Li, D.L.: A statistical information reconstruction method of images based on multiple-point geostatistics integrating soft data with hard data. In: Proceedings of ISCSCT 2008, Shanghai, China, vol. 1, pp. 573–578 (December 2008)
3. Lu, D.T., Zhang, T., Yang, J.Q., Li, D.L., Kong, X.Y.: A reconstruction method of porous media integrating soft data with hard data. Chinese Science Bulletin 54(11), 1876–1885 (2009)

4. Remy, N., Boucher, A., Wu, J.B.: Applied Geostatistics with SGeMS: A Users' Guide, pp. 108–131. Cambridge University Press (2009)
5. Goovaerts, P.: Geostatistics for natural resources evaluation, pp. 54–80. Oxford University Press, New York (1997)
6. Yu, B.M., Li, J.H., Li, Z.H., Zou, M.Q.: Permeabilities of unsaturated fractal porous media. International Journal of Multiphase Flow 29, 1625–1642 (2003)
7. Okabe, H., Blunt, M.J.: Pore space reconstruction using multiple-point statistics. Journal of Petroleum Science and Engineering 46, 121–137 (2005)
8. Journel, A.G.: Markov Models for Cross-Covariances. Mathematical Geology 31(8), 955–964 (1999)

Reconstructing Porous Media Using MPS

Ting Zhang[1] and Yi Du[2]

[1] School of Computer and Information Engineering,
Shanghai University of Electric Power, Shanghai 200090, China
[2] School of Computer and Information,
Shanghai Second Polytechnic University, Shanghai 201209, China
tingzh@shiep.edu.cn, duyi@mail.ustc.edu.cn

Abstract. Multiple-point geostatistics (MPS) has been proved to be a powerful tool to capture curvilinear structures or complex features in training images. The three-dimensional reconstruction of porous media is of great significance to the research of mechanisms of fluid flow in porous media. However, it is quite difficult to reconstruct the unknown information only by some sparse known data in the process of reconstruction. Therefore, some interpolation methods are used to reconstruct the unknown region for better results. By reproducing high order statistics, MPS allows capturing structures from a training image, then anchoring them to specific model data. A training image is a numerical prior model which contains the structures and relationship existing in realistic models. The experimental results demonstrate that MPS is practical in porous media reconstruction.

Keywords: multiple-point geostatistics, search tree, porous media, reconstruction, interpolation.

1 Introduction

The pore structural characteristics have been the key to the studies on the mechanisms of fluids flow in porous media. The structural characterization and prediction of transport properties in porous materials is of great importance in various fields such as catalysis, oil recovery, aging of building materials, study of hazardous waste repositories, etc. These transport properties critically depend on the geometry and topology of the pore space, the physical relationship between rock grains and the fluids, and the conditions imposed by the flow process. Porous structural information must be available in order to predict the fluid flow properties quantificationally. The evolution of the modeling approaches for the representation of the porous structure is a result of advances in theoretical and experimental techniques as well as in computational resources [1, 2].

Because the complexity of the pore space morphology, the pore bodies and throats are usually represented by simplified shapes. Pore bodies have been represented by spheres or cubes, while pore throats have been represented by cylinders or other ducts with non-circular cross-sections. But because the real porous structures are quite

F.L. Wang et al. (Eds.): CMSP 2012, CCIS 346, pp. 341–348, 2012.

complex, the structures based on regular shapes cannot accurately describe the irregular geometry and topology of pore space, which has become an obstacle for the study of transport properties in porous media [3].

Information reconstruction for unknown regions is quite important and significant to the study of porous media. When reconstructing the unknown information, interpolation methods use some scattered points to estimate the unknown attributes of unsampled nodes to build an accurate and complete mathematical model according to some rules from math, physics and so on.

Although a number of interpolation methods were introduced, the accurate reconstruction of information is still difficult to be realized. Interpolation methods are mainly two types: "definite" methods and "indefinite" methods. The "definite" here means that the forms, parameters and results of interpolation functions are mostly definite. "Definite" methods include the inverse distance weighting method, the triangular mesh method, the basis function method, etc. The "indefinite" means that the forms of interpolation functions are indefinite and the selection of parameters in interpolation functions depends on the principles of statistics [1, 2]. The main "indefinite" interpolation methods are kriging and stochastic simulation in geostatistics. Kriging and stochastic simulation, both based on variogram which only describes the relations between two points in space and cannot reconstruct complex patterns such as curvilinear shapes, are called two-point geostatistics [3, 4].

Therefore, indefinite algorithms can normally be classified into two categories [5, 6]. The first kind is that the interpolation algorithms which yield a unique interpolated result. These interpolation algorithms are usually low-pass filters which tend to smooth out local details of the spatial variability of the simulated variable. They provide a local measure of uncertainty, e.g., a kriging variance.

Stochastic techniques which produce multiple possible realizations of the spatial distribution are the second type. Typically, these stochastic algorithms are full-pass filters which reproduce the full spectrum of the spatial variability. Fluctuations between the realizations of multiple stochastic results provide a visual and quantitative measure for the uncertainty about the underlying characteristics in the possible results.

Two-dimensional cross-sections of porous media are, in contrast to 3D images generated by direct imaging, often readily obtained and available at a high resolution, but they cannot include the three-dimensional information of porous media. Therefore, a method using MPS (multiple-point geostatistics) and three-dimensional volume data, which were obtained by synchrotron microtomography and were used as a 3D training image, is proposed to reconstruct porous media. "Training image" originally is a geological term which is used to describe the anisotropy in formation, the trend and distribution of geological bodies, etc. A training image of porous media includes different characteristics of pore spaces. After extracting these characteristics from a training image and then combining them into a "characteristics database", we can store the characteristics in a data structure called "search tree", which will be used again in the simulation process to "copy" those characteristics into reconstructed results according to the probability principle. Experimental results show that the method is appropriate and practical.

2   Ideas and Methods

2.1   Basic Concept of MPS

Kriging and stochastic simulation, both based on the variogram which only describes the relations between two points in space and cannot reconstruct complex patterns such as curvilinear shapes, are called two-point geostatistics. However, multiple-point geostatistics describes the relations of multiple points around a node to be simulated, so the disadvantages of two-point geostatistics are overcome. By reproducing high order statistics, MPS allows capturing structures from a training image, and then anchors them to specific model data. A training image is a numerical prior model which contains the structures and relationship existing in realistic models [2].

The training image is scanned using a data template τ_n that comprises n locations u_α and a central location u. The u_α is defined as: $u_\alpha = u + h_\alpha (\alpha=1,2,\ldots,n)$, where the h_α are the vectors describing the data template. For example, in Fig. 1(a), h_α are the 80 vectors of the square 9×9 template. In Fig. 1(b), h_α are the 26 vectors of the cubic 3×3×3 template with a blue center u.

Consider an attribute S that has K possible states $\{s_k; k=1,2,\ldots,K\}$. A data event d_n of size n, centered at location u, constituted by n vectors u_α in τ_n is defined as:

$$d_n = \{S(u_\alpha) = s_{k_\alpha} \; ; \alpha=1,2,\ldots,n\}. \tag{1}$$

where $S(u_\alpha)$ is the state at the location of u_α within the template. d_n actually means that n values $S(u_1)\ldots S(u_n)$ are jointly in the respective states $s_{k_1} \ldots s_{k_n}$. Fig. 2 illustrates the procedure of capturing a data event with a 5 × 5 template. And Fig. 3 illustrates two data events captured by the data templates displayed in Fig.1 (a) and (b) respectively. The different colors in the Fig. 3 mean different states of an attribute.

Scanning a training image using a data template is to get the probabilities of occurrences of the data events d_n, i.e., probabilities of the n vectors $u_1,\ldots,u_n$ within the τ_n jointly in the respective states $s_{k_1}, \ldots, s_{k_n}$ [6, 7]:

$$\text{Prob}\{d_n\} = \text{Prob}\{S(u_\alpha) = s_{k_\alpha} \; ; \alpha=1,2,\ldots,n\}. \tag{2}$$

In the process of scanning a training image using a given data template, it is a replicate when a data event in the training image has the same geometric configuration and the same data values as d_n associated with τ_n. Under the hypothesis of stationarity, i.e., the statistics are location-independent, the probability of occurrences of the data events d_n is the proportion of replicate number $c(d_n)$ found in the training image and the size of effective training image denoted by N_n [3, 8]:

$$\text{Prob}\{\; S(u_\alpha) = s_{k_\alpha} \; ; \alpha=1,2,\ldots,n\} \approx \frac{c(d_n)}{N_n}. \tag{3}$$

At any unsampled node u, we need to evaluate the cpdf (conditional probability distribution function) that the unknown attribute value $S(u)$ takes anyone of K possible states s_k given n nearest data denoted by $S(u_\alpha) = s_{k_\alpha}$ $(\alpha=1,2,\ldots,n)$. According to the Bayesian relation, the above cpdf is defined as:

$$\text{Prob}\{S(u)=s_k|d_n\}=\frac{\text{Prob}\{S(u)=s_k \quad and \quad S(u_\alpha)=s_{k_\alpha};\alpha=1,\cdots,n\}}{\text{Prob}\{S(u_\alpha)=s_{k_\alpha};\alpha=1,\cdots,n\}}. \tag{4}$$

where the denominator of (4) is the probability of conditional data event and can be inferred by (3); the numerator is the probability of occurrences of the conditional data event and u being the state s_k at the same time. The numerator can be obtained by the ratio denoted by $c_k(d_n)/N_n$, where $c_k(d_n)$ is the number of those replicates, among the $c(d_n)$ previous ones, associated to a central value $S(u)$ equal to s_k. The conditional probability can be defined as:

$$\text{Prob}\{S(u)=s_k \mid S(u_\alpha)=s_{k_\alpha};\alpha=1,\cdots,n\} \approx \frac{c_k(d_n)}{c(d_n)}. \tag{5}$$

Based on (5), the state of u can be drawn using Monte Carlo methodology. Because (5) adopts the idea of probability method, the drawn states of u are random, which can reflect prior probability models existing in the training image.

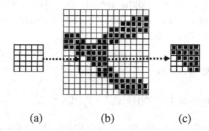

(a)   (b)

Fig. 1. Data templates.(a)a 2D data template;(b)a 3D data template

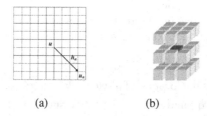

(a)   (b)   (c)

Fig. 2. Procedure of a data event captured by a 5 ×5 template. (a) a 5×5 data template;(b) a 15×15 training image;(c)a data event

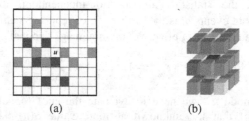

(a)   (b)

Fig. 3. Data events captured by the data templates displayed in Fig.1. (a) captured by a 2D data template;(b) captured by a 3D data template.

2.2   Accelerating Reconstruction by Search Tree

If a training image has to be scanned by data template anew at each unsampled node u to get its cpdf, then it will be extremely CPU-demanding. To avoid the repetitive scanning of the training image and reduce CPU time, the cpdf obtained from the training image is stored in a data structure called "search tree" [3]. The search tree stores the numbers of occurrences $c(d_n)$ and $c_k(d_n)$ found in the training image, from which the relation (5) can be calculated. The construction of the search tree is fast since it requires scanning the training image one single time prior to the image simulation. During the simulation, the required local cpdf at any unsampled node u is retrieved directly from the previous search tree, so the whole simulation process is greatly accelerated.

2.3   Porous Media Reconstruction Method Using MPS

Step 1. Scan the 3D training image of porous media using 3D data templates to build search trees;

Step 2. Assign the original hard data used as originally conditional data to the closest grid nodes;

Step 3. Define a random path visiting only once each unsampled node, i.e. the node to be simulated. At each unsampled location u, extract the conditional data events using the grid used in step 1. If no replicate of a data event can be found in the training image, the conditional probability of u is replaced by the marginal probability of each state s_k; otherwise, retrieve from the search tree the cpdf of occurrence of the conditional data event d_n. After that we can draw a simulated value for node u by using Monte Carlo methodology. The simulated value is then added to the conditional data which are used for conditioning the simulation at all subsequent nodes. Loop step 3 until all grid nodes are simulated. Then the stochastic structures of porous media are generated.

3   Experimental Results and Analyses

Two different smaller portions of volume data ($80 \times 80 \times 80$ voxels), obtained from volume data, were used as the training image and the true image respectively. Because the sample is homogeneous, we can approximately consider that the training image and the true image are similar in their structural characteristics. The porosities of these two images are 0.1745 and 0.1763 respectively, which are very close.

Fig. 4(a) is the exterior of the training image. The pore space is red and the grain is blue. Fig. 4(b) is the cross-sections in the X, Y and Z directions (X=40, Y=40, Z=40). Fig. 4(c) is the pore space of the training image when the grains are hidden. It is seen that the pore space in the training image has long-range connectivity and its shape is quite irregular.

The exterior, cross-sections (X=40, Y=40, Z=40) and pore space of the true image are shown respectively in Fig. 5 (a), (b) and (c). 0.5% sample points randomly collected from the true image were used as original conditional data, as shown in Fig. 5(d). The proportion of pore space points in the total points is 0.1742.

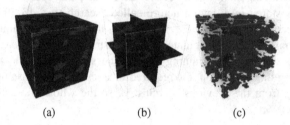

(a)   (b)   (c)

Fig. 4. The training image. (a) exterior; (b) cross-section(X=40, Y=40, Z=40); (c) pore space

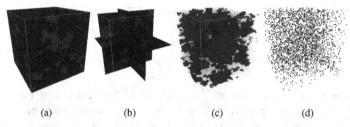

(a)   (b)   (c)   (d)

Fig. 5. The true image. (a) exterior; (b) cross-section(X=40, Y=40, Z=40); (c) pore space; (d) sample points

MPS reconstruction of porous media was made by using the training image and sample points. 3D data templates were used to simulate unsampled nodes. Fig. 6(a), (b) and (c) are respectively the exterior (80×80×80 voxels), cross-sections (X=40, Y=40, Z=40) and pore space of the image reconstructed by MPS. It is seen that the pore space in the horizontal and vertical cross-sections are irregular (shown in Fig. 6(b)), and that the pore space regenerates the long-range connectivity (shown in Fig. 6(c)) existing in the training image. The porosity of the reconstructed image is 0.1743 which is very close to that of the true image.

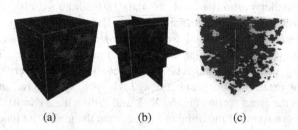

(a)   (b)   (c)

Fig. 6. The MPS-reconstructed image using grid data templates. (a) exterior; (b) cross-section (X=40, Y=40, Z=40); (c) pore space.

For comparison, two two-point geostatistical methods which are IK (indicator kriging) and one of the stochastic simulation methods, called SISIM (sequential indicator simulation), were used to reconstruct the sandstone images. All reconstructed images are 80×80×80 voxels. Fig. 7(a) and (b) are the exterior and pore spaces of porous media reconstructed by SISIM. Fig. 8(a) and (b) are the exterior and pore spaces of porous media reconstructed by IK. It is seen that the pore spaces reconstructed by SISIM and IK are quite different from that of the true image, proving that MPS is effective in reconstructing porous media.

(a)   (b)

Fig. 7. Images reconstructed by SISIM. (a) exterior; (b)pore space.

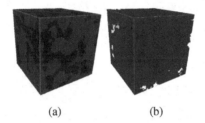

(a)   (b)

Fig. 8. Images reconstructed by IK. (a) exterior; (b)pore space.

4   Conclusions

A method using MPS and volume data of porous media to reconstruct porous media is proposed. 3D pore structures were acquired by synchrotron microtomography scanning, which provides the necessary training image for MPS reconstruction. The structural characteristics of the training image are extracted by using data templates, which will be copied to the reconstructed regions. The experimental results show that the reconstructed results are similar to the original data, proving that our method is practical.

Acknowledgments. This work is supported by the Innovation Program of Shanghai Municipal Education Commission (09YZ454), and Shanghai Municipal Natural Science Foundation (No. 11ZR1413700, No. 12ZR1412000).

References

1. Zhang, T., Lu, D.T., Li, D.L.: Porous media reconstruction using a cross-section image and multiple-point geostatistics. In: Proceedings of ICACC 2009, Singapore, pp. 24–29 (January 2009)
2. Zhang, T., Lu, D.T., Li, D.L.: A statistical information reconstruction method of images based on multiple-point geostatistics integrating soft data with hard data. In: Proceedings of ISCSCT 2008, Shanghai, China, vol. 1, pp. 573–578 (December 2008)
3. Strebelle, S.: Conditional simulation of complex geological structures using multiple-point statistics. Mathematical Geology 34(1), 1–21 (2002)
4. Okabe, H., Blunt, M.J.: Prediction of permeability for porous media reconstructed using multiple-point statistics. Physical Review E 70, 066135:1–066135:9 (2004)
5. Liu, Y.: Using the Snesim program for multiple-point statistical simulation. Computers & Geosciences 32(10), 1544–1563 (2006)
6. Lu, D.T., Zhang, T., Yang, J.Q., Li, D.L., Kong, X.Y.: A reconstruction method of porous media integrating soft data with hard data. Chinese Science Bulletin 54(11), 1876–1885 (2009)
7. Remy, N., Boucher, A., Wu, J.B.: Applied Geostatistics with SGeMS: A Users' Guide, pp. 108–131. Cambridge University Press (2009)
8. Goovaerts, P.: Geostatistics for natural resources evaluation, pp. 54–80. Oxford University Press, New York (1997)

Hierarchical Hole Filling for Novel View Synthesis[*]

Xin Du[1], Gang Ye[1], Yunfang Zhu[2], and Huiliang Shen[1]

[1] Department of Information Science and Electronic Engineering,
Zhejiang University,
Hangzhou, China
[2] College of Computer Science and Information Engineering,
Zhejiang Gongshang University,
Hangzhou, China
duxin@zju.edu.cn

Abstract. Novel view synthesis is a key technique in 3DTV. It usually uses depth maps as input. However, obtaining an accurate depth map from stereo images is hard even for the state-of-art stereo matching algorithms. When rendering based on the erroneous depth map, the resulting novel view will contain artifacts. In this paper, a new view synthesis method to eliminate image artifacts is proposed. Firstly, a bidirectional mapping method is introduced to get the initial virtual image. Secondly, a confidence map is built over the initial image, in which pixels with low value are regarded as artifacts and marked as "hole". Finally, these "holes" are filled up by the proposed Hierarchical Completion of Hole (HCH) method. Experimental results show that good results can still be acquired even with the input depth maps containing a large number of wrong pixels.

Keywords: View synthesis, 3DTV, Hole filling.

1 Introduction

Three-dimensional (3D) video technologies are becoming increasingly popular in our daily life. As it can provide a high-quality experience and immersive feeling, more and more people prefer to it. Novel view synthesis is one of the most important techniques in 3D video applications. It generates a new virtual view of the same scene through several images or streams captured by synchronized cameras. Moreover, free viewpoint video (FVV)[1] is another interesting application of novel view synthesis. FVV allows the user to freely look at arbitrary position of the scene as if it was captured by a real stereo camera.

---

[*] The authors would like to thank to Science Technology Department of Zhejiang Province under Grant 2010C31108, Zhejiang Provincial Natural Science Foundation of China under Grant LY12F01020, and National Science Foundation of China (NSFC) under Grant No. 61271339.

F.L. Wang et al. (Eds.): CMSP 2012, CCIS 346, pp. 349–357, 2012.

In general, novel view synthesis can be classified into three categories[2]: rendering with no geometry, rendering with implicit geometry, and rendering with explicit geometry. As the third type relies on only a few original images (e.g., simply one pair in our method), we discuss this situation only, which is called as depth image-based rendering (DIBR)[3]. Since the depth of every point is available in original images, the virtual view can be rendered by projecting the pixels of the original image to their proper 3D locations and re-projecting them onto the virtual view, also known as 3D warping[4].

However, obtaining accurate depth map is still a hard problem even for the state-of-art stereo matching algorithms. The rendering results based on erroneous depth map will contain obvious artifacts. Thus, the perceptual quality will be degraded significantly. Many works have been carried out on this aspect, such as smoothing the depth map[5, 6], depth-based in-painting[7], and so on.

In this paper, we propose a novel method for novel view synthesis, which consists of three major steps: bidirectional mapping, artifacts detection, and hierarchical completion of hole (HCH), as depicted in Fig.1. The rest of this paper is organized as follows. Section 2 describes the procedure of bidirectional mapping in detail. Then, detection of artifacts in initial novel view will be introduced in section 3. These artifacts will be corrected in section 4, and experiments will be conducted in section 4. Finally, the conclusion of this paper is drawn in section 6.

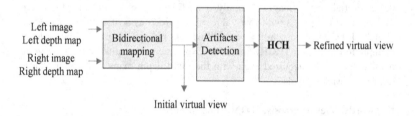

Fig. 1. Flowchart of the proposed method

2   Bidirectional Mapping

Assume the input stereoscopic images have been rectified, which means that for a pixel $P_l(x_l, y)$ in the left view, the correspondence point in the right view is $P_r(x_r, y)$, and the disparity is defined as: $d_l = x_l - x_r$. The synthesized view corresponds to a virtual viewpoint placed between left view and right view, which can be parameterized by s ($0 \leq s \leq 1$). So $s = 0$ means that the new viewpoint coincides with the left view, and $s = 1$ is with the right view. The mapping can be formulated by the following equation.

$$\begin{cases} x_l - x_v = s \cdot d_l \\ x_v - x_r = (1-s) \cdot d_r \end{cases} \qquad (1)$$

For a non-occluded pixel $P_v(x_v, y)$ in the synthesized image, its source may locates only in the left image I_l (occluded in right view), or only in the right image I_r (occluded in the left view), or in both images (can be seen both in the left view and the right image). So it should satisfy at least one part of eq.(1). Otherwise, it means that the point is not visible in both views, and will be marked as a hole directly.

Please note that the mapping described in eq.(1) is not a one-to-one mapping. Pixels that satisfying eq.(1) are regarded as candidates. We need to choose the correct (nearest) pixel from all the possible candidates. The criterion is to select the right pixel (either in left view or in right view) with the smallest depth value (or largest disparity value if disparity maps are used).

3   Artifacts Detection

Because of the hardness of depth estimation, the depth map may inevitably contain errors. When rendering based on erroneous depth maps, the resulting novel view will contain artifacts. An example is given in Fig.2, in which, (a) is the left image, (b) is the erroneous disparity map, and (c) is the initial novel view image. In the results, obvious artifacts (e.g., holes, wrong colors and edges) can easily be found.

In order to detect these artifacts, we build a confidence map for every pixel in the virtual view image according to the method proposed by Andrew J. Woods[8]. The idea of the method is that the novel view should have similar pixel intensities, gradients and Laplacians with the original image on the corresponding position. If none of similar region exists in either of the two original images, then this pixel will be given a low confident value. The corresponding confident map is shown in Fig.2(d). Pixels with low confident value below a given threshold are regarded as artifacts and marked as "Holes", which should be filled up to produce a good result.

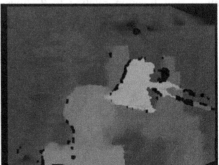

(a) Left image   (b) Disparity map

Fig. 2. Example of artifact detection

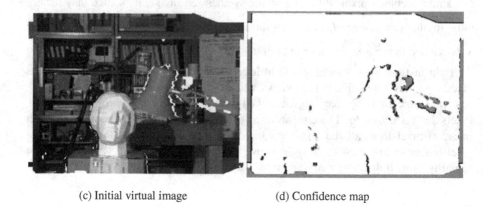

(c) Initial virtual image   (d) Confidence map

Fig. 2. (*continued*)

4   Hierarchical Completion of Holes

The artifacts in the initial virtual image have been detected and marked as "Holes". In this section, we will introduce a hierarchical completion of holes (HCH) method to fill up these "Holes".

Unlike traditional hole-filling methods (In-painting[7], interpolation, etc.) that use texture information directly from the surrounding area of the novel view image, our method uses the information from the original stereo images. It runs in a manner of re-matching, which searches the matching pixel from left image and right image, and then fills it. By this way, the refined virtual image will be more realistic with the original images.

We first introduce the notations used in the paper: for a pixel P, i denotes a neighboring location relative to P, thus P_i is the ith neighbor point of P. W_p^i represents a small, fixed-sized window around P_i, which should also contain P. The size of W_p^i is WN. In Fig.3, we give the eight cases of W_p^i when $WN = 3$.

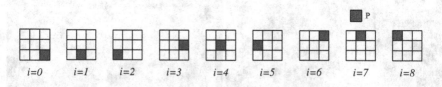

Fig. 3. The nine cases of W_p^i when $WN = 3$

The HCH method can be carried out by the following steps:

> **Setp1** Down-sampling the initial virtual image, original left and right image, and the confidence map respectively to build up the corresponding image pyramids $(R_0, R_1 ... R_{N-1})$. The image should be down-sampled until there are no large holes in the resulting R_{N-1} level initial virtual image.
>
> **Step2** Starting from R_{N-1}, apply our hole-filling algorithm to complete the initial virtual image in this pyramid level.
>
> **Step3** Propagate the refined result to the next level ($N = N-1$): fill up the holes in next level by replacing them by the corresponding pixel in this fixed level.
>
> **Step4** Repeat step2 and 3 until R_0 to acquire a hole-free refined virtual image.

In step2, for a hole pixel P's every searching window W_p^i in the initial virtual image of certain pyramid level, search its matching block V_p^i along the corresponding epipolar line (the same scan line if rectified) in the original images, the matching block should be the most similar patch to W_p^i, which should satisfy

$$V_p^i = \arg \min_{\tilde{V}_p^i \in \Phi} \left\{ d\left(\tilde{V}_p^i, W_p^i\right)\right\} . \tag{2}$$

Where Φ denotes the set of all searching windows, $d\left(\tilde{V}_p^i, W_p^i\right)$ is the distance measurement between two windows, which is usually defined as sum of squared difference (SSD) or sum of absolute difference (SAD). However, treating all points in the patch equally is not a good idea. Rather, points with large gradient should be paid more attention to than those with small gradient. In our implementation, stronger weights should be assigned to those points with larger gradient. Based on this, a new metric derived as

$$d\left(\tilde{V}_p^i, W_p^i\right) = \sum_{(\Delta x, \Delta y) \in WN} \left| P_k\left(\tilde{i}_x + \Delta x, i_y + \Delta y\right) - P_v\left(i_x + \Delta x, i_y + \Delta y\right)\right| \cdot \|\nabla P_v\| . \tag{3}$$

In Eq. (3), WN is the size of searching window, $\|\nabla P_v\|$ is the gradient magnitude. $P_v\left(i_x, i_y\right)$ is a pixel in W_p^i, while $P_k\left(\tilde{i}_x, i_y\right)$ is corresponding pixel in $\tilde{V}_p^i$. $k \in \{l, r\}$ means that $\tilde{V}_p^i$ can be from the left image or the right image. It is worth mentioning that during the similarity computation, the hole pixels must be excluded. Moreover, if the proportion of hole pixels $D_i > \eta$, this searching window is ignored. Since the down-sampling process will make the "hole" region smaller and smaller gradually. So there are must exist a certain pyramid level which satisfying the proportion requirement. The schematic diagram of matching process is shown in Fig.4.

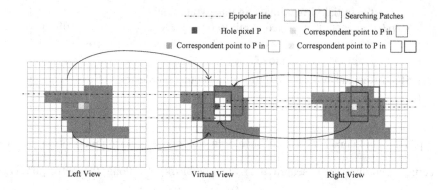

Fig. 4. Patch search(only part of patches are showed)

After get the matching patch V_p^i, the corresponding pixel of P is regarded as a candidate for completion, whose value C_i is used to fill up pixel P. The value of pixel P is the weighted average of matching pixels of all W_p^i, it will be

$$C = \frac{\sum w_i \cdot C_i}{\sum w_i} . \tag{4}$$

where w_i is the weight for the candidate of W_p^i, which can be defined as

$$w_i = (1 - D_i) \cdot s_i . \tag{5}$$

In Eq.(5), D_i is the percentage of hole pixels in W_p^i, s_i denotes the similarity metric between W_p^i and V_p^i, which can be obtained by

$$s_i = e^{\frac{d(V_p^i, W_p^i)}{2\sigma^2}} . \tag{6}$$

5 Experiment Results

We test the algorithm for different types of stereoscopic content, including the standard stereo image "Tsukuba" from Middlebury website, and stereoscopic video frames from the sequences "Door" and "Alt_moabit" from Mobile 3DTV[9]. The depth maps of these samples are generated by a simple method, in which obvious errors can be found (as shown in the following figures). The experimental parameters used are shown in Table 1. Without loss of generality, we set $s = 0.5$, thus the virtual view is placed exactly in the middle of the original views.

Table 1. Experimental parameters

s	WN	N	η	σ
0.5	5	4	0.7	10

In Fig.5, the result of "Tsukuba" is illustrated, the source image and depth image can be founded in Fig.2. From the result, we can find that the synthesized virtual image has been greatly improved.

Fig. 5. the refined virtual image of "Tsukuba"

Fig.6 gives a comparison of hole-filling between the proposed HCH method and In-painting method (implemented in openCV). Because the in-painting method fill up the "hole" pixels by only using the surrounding pixels, so the results are shown too smooth. Our method produces much better results.

The simple In-painting method may not be a good competitor. We further compare our results with the VSRS software[10], which can be thought of something like the state-of-the-art view synthesis approach used by most people. The results are shown in Fig.7. When erroneous depth maps are used, the outputs of VSRS method are greatly degraded. However, with the proposed HCH method, our results can still synthesize high-quality results.

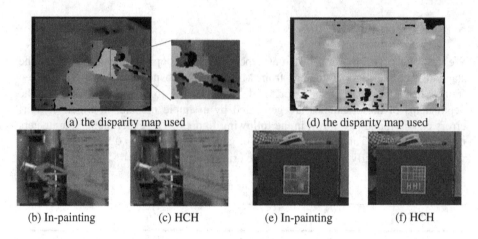

(a) the disparity map used   (d) the disparity map used

(b) In-painting   (c) HCH   (e) In-painting   (f) HCH

Fig. 6. Comparison of hole-filling with in-painting method

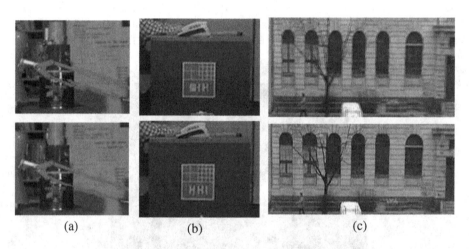

(a)   (b)   (c)

Fig. 7. Comparison of VSRS with the proposed method
First row: results of VSRS, second row: results by the proposed method

6   Conclusion

In this paper, a new method for novel view synthesis is proposed to deal with the situation that rendering high quality virtual image even with erroneous depth maps inputted. Three main steps are proposed: 1) generate the initial virtual image by bidirectional mapping; 2) detect the artifacts in initial virtual image and mark them as "holes"; 3) complete these "holes" with the proposed HCH algorithm. The effeteness of the proposed algorithm has been proven by experimental results.

References

1. Morvan, Y., Farin, D., De With, P.: System architecture for free-viewpoint video and 3D-TV. IEEE Transactions on Consumer Electronics 542, 925–932 (2008)
2. Harry, S., Sing, B.K.: Review of image-based rendering techniques. In: Proc. SPIE, vol. 4067, p. 2 (2000)
3. Christoph, F.: Depth-image-based rendering (DIBR), compression, and transmission for a new approach on 3D-TV. In: Proc. SPIE, vol. 5291, pp. 93–104 (2004)
4. McMillan Jr., L.: An Image-Based Approach To Three-Dimensional Computer Graphics [PhD Dissertation]. University of North Carolina (1997); Reader: Pizer, S.
5. Nquyen, Q.H., Do, M.N., Patel, S.J.: Depth image-based rendering from multiple cameras with 3D propagation algorithm. In: Proceedings of the 2nd International Conference on Immersive Telecommunications, Brussels, Belgium, pp. 1–6 (2009)
6. Wang, L.-H., Li, D.-X., Zhang, M.: Hierarchical Joint Bilateral Filtering for Depth Post-Processing. In: International Conference on Image and Graphics (ICIG), Washington, DC, pp. 129–134 (2011)
7. Oh, K.-J., Yea, S., Ho, Y.-S.: Hole-Filling Method Using Depth Based In-Painting For View Synthesis in Free Viewpoint Television (FTV) and 3D Video. In: Picture Coding Symposium, Chicago, USA (2009)
8. Andrew, J., Woods, N.S., Holliman, N.A.: Dodgson.: Adapting stereoscopic movies to the viewing conditions using depth-preserving and artifact-free novel view synthesis. In: Stereoscopic Displays and Applications, San Francisco, California (2011)
9. Europe's Seventh Framework Programme for research and technology development (FP7), http://sp.cs.tut.fi/mobile3dtv/
10. Tian, D., Lai, P.-L., Patrick, L.: View synthesis techniques for 3D video. In: Applications of Digital Image Processing XXXII, vol. 7443, pp. 74430T–74430T-11 (2009)

Illumination Invariant Face Recognition Based on Nonsubsampled Contourlet Transform and NeighShrink Denoise

Yuanyuan Ma, Suna Xia, Gangmin Zheng, and Xiaohu Ma

School of Computer Science and Technology, Soochow University,
Suzhou Jiangsu, China,
xhma@suda.edu.cn

Abstract. In order to eliminate the effect of illumination variations, in this paper, we propose a novel face recognition algorithm based on Nonsubsampled contourlet transform (NSCT) and NeighShrink denoise model. NSCT is a fully shift-invariant, multi-scale, and multi-direction transform, which can better preserve edges. Combined with NeighShrink denoise techniques that considers the correlation of neighboring contourlet transform coefficients, NSCT can represent illumination invariant more completely. Experimental results on the Yale B and CMU PIE face databases show that the proposed method achieves satisfactory recognition rates under varying illumination conditions.

Keywords: Face recognition, Illumination invariant, Nonsubsampled contourlet transform, NeighShrink denoise model.

1 Introduction

Face recognition is an important branch of biotechnology. It has been widely applied in the real world, in that its simplicity and non-contact. Face recognition under complex illumination situation will lead to a significant drop in recognition performance, due to shadows, uneven illumination.

Recently, numerous different approaches have been proposed to deal with this problem. Basically, these methods can be classified into three main categories: (1) compensation, (2) face modeling, and (3) invariant feature extraction. In the first category, face images are preprocessed using image processing techniques to normalize the images in order to obtain the stability of face image under illumination changes. These processes include histogram equalization (HE), block-based histogram equalization (BHE) [1]. Ping-Cheng Hsieh et al. [2] propose a shadow compensation approach based on facial symmetry and image average can solve the drawbacks of HE and BHE. The main idea of the methods in the second category is to represent the changes due to different illuminations in a subspace and estimate model parameters, such as spherical harmonic-based representations and 3D illumination subspace model [3]. In the third category, many algorithms have been presented to extract facial features which are invariant to illumination variations, such as self-quotient image [4]

F.L. Wang et al. (Eds.): CMSP 2012, CCIS 346, pp. 358–366, 2012.
© Springer-Verlag Berlin Heidelberg 2012

and "retinex" model. Compensation method which is simple and efficient, however, has difficulty with different lighting conditions and also, difficulty in achieving satisfactory results in practical applications. Face modeling can get excellent recognition rates. Otherwise, the algorithm is computationally intensive and is not very practical for usage in real time face recognition systems. Accordingly, it is very difficult to apply the approach in reality. Compared with the other two approaches, extracting illumination invariant features is a more effective approach for face recognition under various lighting conditions.

In order to obtain key facial features from face image under varying lighting, many approaches apply multiscale analysis method to extract key facial features in coarse-to-fine order. Xiaohua Xie et al. [5] suggest that illumination normalization should be performed mainly on large-scale features of the face image rather than on the original face image, proposing a method of normalizing both the Small- and Large-scale features of the face image. Lu-Hung Chen et al. [6] utilizes the scale invariant property of natural images to construct a Wiener filter approach to best separate the illumination-invariant features from an image. Goh et al. [7] proposes wavelet based illumination invariant preprocessing (WIIP) in face recognition. They decomposed a facial image into low and high frequency components using discrete wavelet transform (DWT) decomposition and set the illumination component as zero. Then both the processed illumination component was used to perform inverse DWT. Haifeng Hu [8] presented a discrete wavelet transform based illumination normalization approach, which can obtain the multi-scale smooth images while preserving the illumination discontinuities and can effectively reduce the halo artifacts in the normalized image. Cao et al. [9] presented a NeighShrink-based denoising model (IIE). This model uses neighboring wavelet coefficients to extract illumination invariant for face recognition. Multiscale facial structure representation (MFSR) [10] attempts to normalize varying illumination by modifying wavelet coefficients. Cheng et al. [11] proposed a method employing NormalShrink filter in NSCT domain to extract illumination invariant (NSNSCT).

In this paper, according to the NSCT multi-scale and multi-directional characteristics, taking into account the neighborhood of subband coefficients within, a novel illumination invariant extraction method was proposed to deal with the illumination problem based on Nonsubsampled contourlet transform and NeighShtink denoise. Experimental results on the Yale B, the CMU PIE face databases show that the proposed method is robust and effective for face recognition with varying illumination conditions.

2   Methodology

2.1   Retinex Illumination Model

According to Retinex theory, the image gray level can be assumed to be the product [12]

$$I(x, y) = R(x, y) \cdot L(x, y) \tag{1}$$

Where $R(x, y)$ is the reflectance and $L(x, y)$ is the luminance at each pixel (x, y). The reflectance component contains information about the object of the scene, and the illumination component contains only the light of illumination source. Generally speaking, it is an ill-posed problem to extract the reflectance and luminance components from a face image. A common assumption indicates that $L(x, y)$ changes slowly while $R(x, y)$ varies abruptly. This assumption is used to extract $R(x, y)$ by high-pass filter towards the logarithm of image in homomorphic filtering. Homomorphic filtering is performed by taking the log of each pixel, to enhance the contrast in dark regions and reduce contrast in bright regions. It improves the visibility of dark regions while maintaining the visual different of the light area. Taking logarithmic transform on Eq. (1), one can get

$$R'(x, y) \approx I'(x, y) - L'(x, y) \tag{2}$$

Where $R'(x, y) = \log(R(x, y))$, $I'(x, y) = \log(I(x, y))$ and $L'(x, y) = \log(L(x, y))$. The logarithm transform turns the multiplicative model into the additive model. As an additive model, classical image estimation techniques can be applied. Here, we are interested in R' because it includes the key facial feature for face recognition with varying illumination conditions. In this paper, the key facial feature R' is regarded as "noise" in the denoising model. Then we can get the illumination invariant feature through "reduction" operation.

2.2 Nonsubsampled Contourlet Transform

Wavelet transform is multi-resolution image decomposition tool which provide various channels representing the image feature by different frequency subbands at multi-scale. It is a famous technique in analyzing signals. Wavelets are good at isolating the discontinuities at edge points, but will not "see" the smoothness along the contours. Because wavelets are limited to using square-shaped brush strokes along the contour, using different sizes corresponding to the multiresolution structure of wavelets.

Nonsubsampled contourlet transform [13] which based on a nonsubsampled directional filter banks, is a flexible multiscale, multidirection and shift-invariant image decomposition. On the other hand, it explores effectively the smoothness of the contour by making brush strokes with different elongated shapes and in a variety of directions following the contour. In addition to this, it allows redundancy and it is possible to enrich the set of basic functions so that the representation is more efficient in capturing some signal behavior. Another important feature of NSCT is its stability that can threshold where the lack of shift-invariance causes pseudo-Gibbs phenomena around singularities.

2.3 NeighShrink Denoising Model

Illumination invariant can be estimated by Eq.2 after logarithmic transform. In order to extract robust illumination invariant R' under different illumination conditions, we lean upon an optimization problem, that is,

$$\arg \min R'^2 = \arg \min (I' - L')^2 \tag{3}$$

Eq.3 can be solved by image denoising techniques. Besides, NSCT-based denoising techniques can better preserve curve information in low frequency illumination fields than other multiscale analysis. There are several methods for image denoising, such as SureShrink, BayeShrink. However, these denoising methods tend to kill too many subbands coefficients that might contain useful image information in that not considering the correlation of subbands coefficients in a small neighborhood. Nevertheless, a large subbands coefficient will probably have large subbands coefficients at its neighbors. So NSCT based NeighShrink denoising model which consider the correlation of subbands can achieve satisfactory performance. First, decompose an image by NSCT, then apply NeighShrink denoising model to the subbands of NSCT by thresholding only the subband coefficients of the high sub-sands, while keeping the low resolution coefficients unaltered, which can enhance the edge-preserving ability in low frequency illumination fields. Finally, we reconstruct illumination component from the modified NSCT coefficients by inverse NSCT. $b_{j,k}$ is the high frequency coefficient at the k -th directional subband of the j -th scale. We require considering a neighborhood window B around it, such as 3×3, 5×5, 7×7, ect. Then we can get $S_{j,k}$ by Eq.4, which is the summation of squares of the high frequency coefficient in the neighborhood window B.

$$S_{j,k} = \sum_{b_{j,k} \in B} b_{j,k}^2 \tag{4}$$

The updated center pixel of the neighborhood window $b_{j,k}$ can be obtained by $S_{j,k}$. We can achieve all new coefficients according to the following formula.

$$\sigma_{j,k} = \max((1 - \frac{\lambda}{S_{j,k}}), 0) \tag{5}$$

$$b'_{j,k} = \sigma_{j,k} b_{j,k} \tag{6}$$

This parameter λ should be estimated strictly in a range of 0.1 to 0.5 to obtain the maximum recognition rate which can be obtained from the following experiment. It is necessary to note that the minimum of the shrinkage factor cannot be negative in order to avoid unsatisfactory results.

2.4   Algorithm

On the basis of the above descriptions, the proposed method for illumination invariant extraction can be described as follows:

Step1. Take the logarithm operation for the original face image $I(x, y)$ to get
$I'(x, y) = R'(x, y) + L'(x, y)$.

Step2. Perform NSCT transform of the logarithm facial image to obtain the low-pass subband and directional subbands.

Step3. Compute the shrinkage factor $b'_{j,k}$ at each directional subbands of each scale by using Eq. (4-6).

Step4. Reconstruct illumination $L'(x, y)$ from the modified NSCT coefficients by inverse NSCT.

Step5. Extract illumination invariant $R'(x, y)$ by Eq.2 and use the obtained $L'(x, y)$ for face recognition.

3   Experimental Results and Discussions

3.1   Datasets

To evaluate the performance of the proposed method for illumination invariant extraction, we have applied it to two well-known databases, the Yale face B database and the CMU PIE database. In the phase of recognition, PCA is employed to extract global feature, and the nearest neighbor classifier based on Euclidean distance is used for classification. The important statistics of these databases are summarized below:

- The Yale face database B totally contains images of 10 individuals in nine poses and 64 illuminations per pose. We only use the frontal face images under 64 illumination conditions for evaluation. All images are resized to 100×100 and roughly aligned between subjects. Generally, all the face images per subject can be divided into five subsets according to the angle of the light source directions, which are: Subset 1 (0-12°), Subset 2 (13-25°), Subset 3 (26-50°), Subset 4 (51-77°) and Subset 5 (above 78°). Fig. 1 shows the images under different illumination angles.

Fig. 1. The images under different illumination angles for the same person in the YaleB database

- The CMU PIE database contains 68 subjects with 1428 frontal face images under 21 different illumination conditions with background lighting off. All images from the database were simply aligned and resized to 100×100. Fig. 2 shows the different lighting images for a single subject.

Fig. 2. The images under different illumination angles for the same person in the CMU PIE database

3.2   Results

Experiments on The Yale Face Database B. In the proposed method, we use three-level NSCT decomposition, directions of decomposition in each scale are 2, 4 and 8, respectively, and the neighborhood window B is 5. $\lambda=0.1$ for training set and $\lambda=2$ for testing image. In our experiment, Subset 1 is used as training image samples, and the images from Subsets 2 to Subsets 5 are used as testing images, the results are given in Fig. 3 and the average results are given in Table. 1. Fig. 4 plots the recognition rate curves of the proposed method versus the parameter λ. It can be seen that the high recognition rate can be maintained for a range of λ from 0.1 to 0.5 for all subsets investigated.

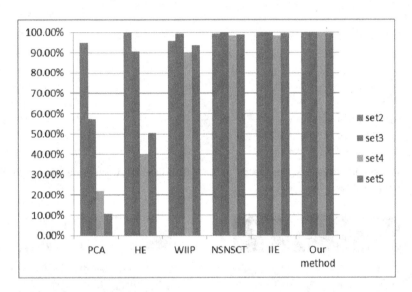

Fig. 3. Recognition rates when using images of subset 1 as training samples

Table 1. Average recognition rates when using images of subset 1 as training samples

Method	PCA	HE	WIIP	NSNSCT	IIE	Our method
Average recognition rate	46.29%	70.34%	94.67%	99.17%	99.51%	99.87%

It can be seen from Fig. 5 that the proposed method performs the best. Compared to PCA recognition rate is significantly improved. A 100% recognition rate is obtained with HE which from compensation method when the illumination angle is small. However, the recognition rates in bad illumination subset 4 and subset 5 are only 50%. So it is still difficult to deal with complicated illumination variations by HE. WIIP[8] , IIE[10] and NSNSCT[12] have a better performance in that they take into account the multi-scale feature. But the defects will appear when in some applications may need positive face images. We can see that from Fig. 5. From the above analysis, our method not only has a perfect performance but also can get a clearer positive light image of face.

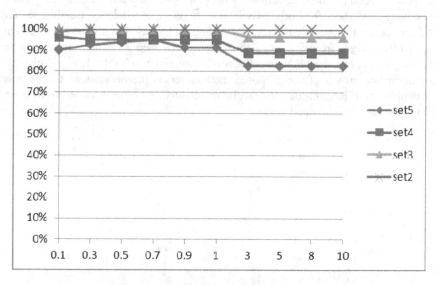

Fig. 4. Recognition rates versus parameter λ on Yale B database when using images of subset 1 as training samples

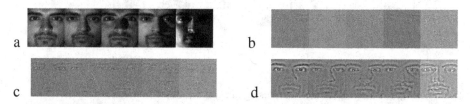

Fig. 5. Original images and illumination invariants for different method: (a) Original images, (b) WIIP, (c) IIE, (d) Our method

Experiments on the CMU PIE Face Database. In this experiment, we choose one image per subject for forming training set, and the other images for testing, where λ is 2. The recognition results are shown in Table 2. After changing the value of λ, we repeat the previous experiment and display the corresponding results in Fig. 6. Both the table and the figure further demonstrate the effectiveness of our method.

Table 2. Face recognition rates on CMU PIE database using one image as training samples

Method	PCA	HE	WIIP	NSNSCT	IIE	Our method
Face recognition	67.13%	99.85%	86.18%	96.18%	85.96%	99.93%

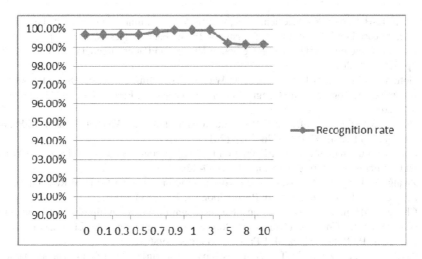

Fig. 6. Recognition rates versus parameter λ on CMU PIE database using one image as training samples

4   Conclusions

In this paper, a novel NSCT based illumination invariant extraction method with the consideration of correlation of neighboring coefficients is developed. The approach can better extract geometric structure without halo artifacts and pseudo-Gibbs phenomena around singularities, which attributes to the properties of nonsubsampled contourlet transform, that is, multiscale, multidirection analysis capability and shift-invariance. Meanwhile NeighShrink can avoid the omitting of useful subbands coefficients. Compared with other methods, it can turn out that the combination of NSCT and NeighShrink is a more effective approach for illumination invariant extraction. Experimental results on the Yale face database B and CMU PIE face database show that excellent recognition rates are achieved by the proposed method.

References

1. Xie, X., Lam, K.M.: Face Recognition under Varying Illumination based on a 2D Face Shape Model. Pattern Recognition 38(2), 221–230 (2005)
2. Hsieh, P.-C., Tung, P.-C.: Shadow Compensation based on Facial Symmetry and Image Average for Robust Face Recognition. Neurocomputing 73, 2708–2717 (2010)
3. Jacaobs, D.W.: Lambertian Reflectance and Linear Subspaces. IEEE Trans. on Pattern Analysis and Machine Intelligence 25(2), 218–233 (2003)
4. Sha, S., Raviv, T.R.: The Quotient Image: Class-based Re-rendering and Recognition with Varying Illuminations. IEEE Trans. on Pattern Analysis and Machine Intelligence 23, 129–139 (2001)
5. Xie, X., Zheng, W.-S., Lai, J., Yuan, P.C., Suen, C.Y.: Normalization of Face Illumination based on Large-and Small-scale Features. IEEE Trans. Image Processing 20(7), 1807–1821 (2011)

6. Chen, L.-H., Yang, Y.-H., Chen, C.-S., Cheng, M.-Y.: Illumination Invariant Feature Extraction based on Natural Images Statistics – Taking Face Images as an Example. In: IEEE Computer Society Conference on Computer Vision and Pattern Recognition, CVPR 2011, pp. 329–336 (2011)
7. Goh, Y.Z., Teoh, A.B.J., Goh, M.K.O.: Wavelet based Illumination Invariant Preprocessing in Face Recognition. In: Congress on Image and Signal Processing, vol. 335, pp. 421–425 (2008)
8. Hu, H.: Variable Lighting Face Recognition using Discrete Wavelet Transform. Pattern Recognition Letters 32(13), 1526–1534 (2011)
9. Cao, X.: Illumination Invariant Extraction for Face Recognition using Neighboring Wavelet Coefficients. Pattern Recognition 45, 1299–1305 (2012)
10. Zhang, T., Fang, B.: Multiscale Facial Structure Representation for Face Recognition under Varying Illumination. Pattern Recognition 42, 251–258 (2009)
11. Cheng, Y., Hou, Y., Zhao, C.: Robust Face Recognition based on Illumination Invariant in Nonsubsampled Contourlet Rransform Domain. Neurocomputing 73, 2217–2224 (2010)
12. Horn, B.K.P.: Robot vision. MIT Press, Cambirdge (1986)
13. da Cunha, A.L., Zhou, J.: The Nonsubsampled Contourlet Ttransform: Theory, Design, and Applications. IEEE Trans. on Image Processing 15(10), 3089–3101 (2006)

3D Mouse Realization in Autostereoscopic Display

Zhentang Jia and Yanfang Han

Shanghai University of Electric Power,
Shanghai, China
462458081@qq.com

Abstract. Based on the principle of autostereoscopic 3D display , a method was proposed to generate and show mouse symbol in 3D scene, which can be applied in any 3D applications. The X,Y coordinates were obtained by mouse moving, and Z obtained by mouse wheeling. Mouse symbols generated by virtual cameras from different view positions were multiplexed into the currently being displayed video contents in realtime, according to the optical principle of slanted lenticular. Experiment proved the effectiveness of the method.

Keywords: 3D mouse symbol, Autostereoscopic Display, Image multiplexing.

1 Introduction

The techniques of 3D display have been rapidly developed and widely used in recent years. In the existing kinds of 3D techniques, the naked eye 3D display which is also called autostereoscopic display is particularly appreciated, because one can perceive 3D vision without any accessories, such as glasses. Among the autostereoscopic displays, lenticular display and narrow-aperture display are the most commercially progressed ones[1].

On such display, most image objects seemed outside of the screen or behind of the screen surface. If the mouse symbol used to point a object still stays on the surface of screen, users will feel misplaced, uncomfortable, and even eye fatigue[2].

So, the paper presented a dynamic generation method of three dimension pointing symbol ,whose position can be adjusted freely in 3D space.

2 Principle of Lenticular 3D Display

Lenticular 3D display is similar to the narrow-aperture one in principle, both of them are composed of a LCD panel and a front positioned light splitting panel. The difference is that Lenticular display takes convex lens to split light , while narrow-aperture display uses parallax barriers[4]. Principle of the lenticular 3D display used in this paper is illustrated in figure 1.

Several sub-images are multiplexed into the lenticular display in special order[5], so that, for example, pixels of sub-image1 can only be seen by left eye, that of

F.L. Wang et al. (Eds.): CMSP 2012, CCIS 346, pp. 367–374, 2012.

sub-image2 by right eye. Those sub-images are pictures of an identical scene, captured from positions with slight separation. So, depth perception will be produced in human brain, as that be produced when see a real scene.

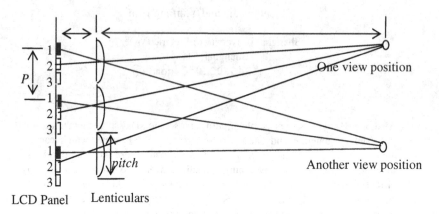

Fig. 1. Principle of lenticular 3D display

From figure-1, it can be seen that P, the distance of two adjacent pixels belonging to same sub-image , is slightly longer than actual lens pitch.

$$P = pitch + \frac{f}{F} pitch \tag{1}$$

Where, f is the focal length, F is the observe distance. The slanted lenticular display is generally used to reduce the Moiré patterns and to balance the resolution in vertical and horizontal directions.

3   Transformation of Mouse Coordinates

Coordinate systems are set as Figure 2, where (OXYZ) is the world coordinate, on which an initial camera is superposed. Image coordinate (xoy) is fixed at the plane Z=F, with original point on Z axis. So, mouse position M is extended to an arbitrary point in world coordinate M(X,Y,Z) , whose image point is $m_0(x_0,y_0)$ for the initial camera, and there is a projection relationship between M and m_0[3], as follow.

$$s\tilde{m}_0 = P\tilde{M} \tag{2}$$

Where, $\tilde{m}_0$ is the homogeneous coordinates of m0, $\tilde{M}$ is that of M, and P can be simplified as

$$P = \begin{bmatrix} F & 0 & 0 & 0 \\ 0 & F & 0 & 0 \\ 0 & 0 & 1 & 0 \end{bmatrix} \tag{3}$$

For perceptual intuition, we decompose the projection into analytic expression of components.

$$\begin{cases} x_0 = \dfrac{F}{Z} X \\[2mm] y_0 = \dfrac{F}{Z} Y \end{cases} \tag{4}$$

In order to get several sub-images of mouse symbol, a number of virtual cameras are set at different view positions. It can be realized by shifting camera along X axis. Here, taking 9 sub-image display device for example, we shift camera to 9 positions, with identical distance B between adjacent ones. Usually, B takes the value less than 65mm, which is the average distance between human's left and right eyes.

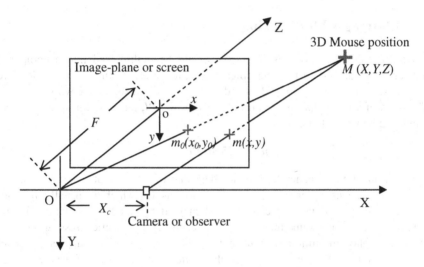

Fig. 2. Projection model of mouse position

It can be deduced from geometric relationship that , at a position where camera is shifted by X_c, image point m(x,y) has the relationship with mouse point M(X,Y,Z),

$$\begin{cases} x = \dfrac{F}{Z} X + (1 - \dfrac{F}{Z}) X_c \\[2mm] y = \dfrac{F}{Z} Y \end{cases} \tag{5}$$

where $X_c = n*B$, n = -4, -3, -2, -1, 0, +1, +2, +3, +4.

Then mouse positions in image plane (x,y) are transformed into pixel coordinates (u,v) in sub-images, according to the specified image resolution and pixel size. At the same time, the pixel coordinate usually takes the left-top corner as origin, while image coordinate origin is at center, so an origin translation should be considered.

$$\begin{cases} u = kx/w_{pix} + w_s/2 \\ v = ky/w_{pix} + h_s/2 \end{cases} \tag{6}$$

Where , w_{pix} is pixel width (usually equals to pixel height) in physical size, such as w_{pix}=0.266 mm for 23 inch LCD display; k is the scale factor from image plane to pixel plane; w_s, h_s are respectively the width and height of screen in pixel unit, for example w_s=1920, h_s= 1080.

In actual system, sub-images of pointing mark is not really generated, only the coordinate (u,v) is recorded instead. Mouse symbols will be drawn in realtime on the sub-images being displayed.

4   Sub-images Multiplexing

In 3D display device, several sub-images should be multiplexed into a composed image for show, according to a periodical order, as described in section 2. Here we denote the sub-image No. n with SI_n, and denote the multiplexed image with CI.

The pitch of a lenticular panel is usually given by *LPI*, meaning lines-per-inch. So the pitch can be worked out by

$$pitch = 25.4/LPI \tag{7}$$

The resolution of SI_n is generally smaller than that of CI, so that it is necessary to scale the sub-images up to the same resolution as CI which is usually the full resolution of display device. It can be implemented by pixel interpolation. In the following sections, we assume that both CI and each SI have identical resolution.

In LCD display, the minimum unit that can be operated individually is sub-pixel which is any of the three primary color components (R,G,B) of a pixel. For a pixel in CI , each sub-pixel may come from different sub-image. It is prerequisite to calculate the index of sub-image (or say sub-image number) for each sub-pixel R,G, and B, as the formula below.

$$\begin{cases} CI(u,v)_R = SI'_{nr}(u,v)_R \\ CI(u,v)_G = SI'_{ng}(u,v)_G \\ CI(u,v)_B = SI'_{nb}(u,v)_B \end{cases} \tag{8}$$

Where, SI' is scaled SI. The sub-pixel R of pixel CI(u,v) comes from the sub-pixel R of $SI'_{nr}(u,v)$ whose sub-image index is nr ,sub-pixel G from index ng, and sub-pixel B from index nb. It is obvious that the most important task is to calculate the sub-image index nr, ng, and nb.

From the geometric relations in Figure-3, we can get the formula to calculate sub-image index of each sub-pixel.

$$\begin{cases} n_r = \text{int}[(\textit{off}\text{-}w_{pix}/3)/w_{view}] \\ n_g = \text{int}[(\textit{off}\qquad)/w_{view}] \\ n_b = \text{int}[(\textit{off}+w_{pix}/3)/w_{view}] \end{cases} \qquad (9)$$

In which, int[] is a rounding operation to get integer; w_{pix} is the size of a pixel which equals to the dot pitch of screen, and w_{pix} /3 is the width of a sub-pixel; $w_{view}=P/N$, is the width shared by a sub-image within an effective pitch. P is the effective pitch of a lenticular line, N is the total number of sub-images. In the figure, as an example , $N=9$; $\textit{off}$ is the distance from the center of pixel to the edge of current lenticular pitch who covers the pixel. $\textit{off}$ can be worked out by the following formula .

$$\textit{off} = \{[u+0.5-\tan(a)\times(v+0.5)]\times w_{pix} + x0 + M\times P\}\bmod P \qquad (10)$$

Where, a is the slant angle of lenticular; x_0 is the start position of current lenticular unit on the top of screen . In fact, x_0 can be assigned with any value, such as zero, because sub-images are arranged in a recycling way, and the observer will move their head to find a suitable view position. M is a integer big enough, such as 5000, with the purpose to keep the value in curly braces greater than or equal to zero. The expression of $\textit{off}$ can also be written as

$$\textit{off} = (a\times u - b\times v + c)\bmod p \qquad (11)$$

But the slant angle is not obvious in this form, so it is not convenient for lenticular alignment.

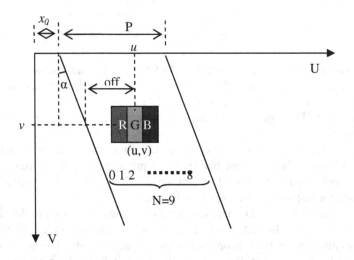

Fig. 3. Sub-Image index calculation

In addition, In order to speed up the processing in actual c++ programs, all variables are defined in integer type, taking micrometer as value unit. Thus , precision is kept high, and the function mod can also works properly.

5   Experiment Result

The proposed method was applied to an interactive stereo video display system. The display screen used in the experiment was YT-A215, which was a 21.5 inch Autostereoscopic 3D display produced by Shanghai Yingtong Communication Technology Co. Ltd. The dot pitch was 0.248mm, LPI of lenticular was 30, resolution was 1920x1080.   A video sequence of 9 sub-images was used in the test.

The world coordinate position of mouse mark was controlled by mouse device. Mouse moving was used to to control X and Y, mouse wheeling used to increase or decrease the value of Z. World coordinate was then projected onto image plane, and transformed onto pixel coordinates with necessary scaling.

In the projection model shown in Figure-2, we can take cameras as the observer's eyes, the image plane as LCD screen. Thus the distance between cameras and image plane corespondents to the observing distance, which was set at 0.8 m (F=0.8mm) in the experiment.

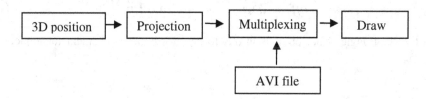

Fig. 4. Processing steps

A 3D video sequence was stored in a AVI file, with 9 sub-images arranged into nine-square grid in each frame. We fetched each frame, cut it into 9 sub-images, and drawn mouse mark onto each sub-images before multiplexed them together. Finally, the multiplexed 3D images was drawn on screen. Here we used cross mark "+" as mouse symbol .

Figure 5 shows the mouse symbols added on each sub-images, with mouse distance Z=1.1m. This is the case that mouse depth is greater than screen surface, or, in other words, mouse is behind screen surface. Figure-6 is the multiplexed 3D images used for display, in full size of 1920x1080.

Figure-7 shows the the 3D images with different mouse distance in detail. For (a), Z=1.1m, mouse is felt behind screen surface , (b). Z=0.8m=F. Mouse symbols of all sub-images are at same pixel coordinate, observer will feel that the mouse is just on the surface of screen.   (c). Z=0.6m, the mouse is felt in front of screen, or say outside of screen.

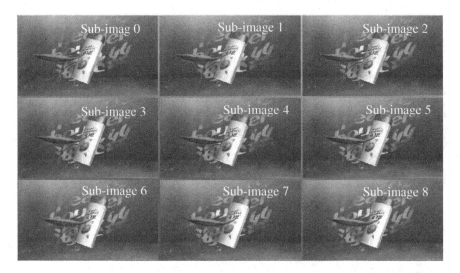

Fig. 5. Mouse symbols on each sub-images , with mouse distance Z=1.1m

Fig. 6. Multiplexed 3D image , with mouse distance Z=1.1m

The video images is also of 3D , and different depth can be perceived from different video objects. So, when the mouse is controlled to move along Z direction, it can be seen obviously that the mouse depth is changing, being felt moving through different layer of video objects.

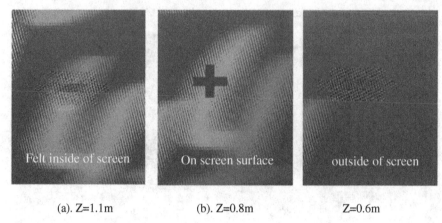

(a). Z=1.1m   (b). Z=0.8m   Z=0.6m

Fig. 7. Parts of 3D images in original resolution

6   Conclusion

The proposed method of 3D mouse realization was described in the paper, including mouse position controlling, coordinates projection, 3D image multiplexing, and display. Experiment showed that the method was effective. Users could get obvious depth perception of 3D mouse symbol in plat LCD screen..

But in current experiment, we didn't pick up the depth matched video object. This will be researched in future.

Acknowledgment. Thanks to the Project No.05DZ22305 supported by Science and Technology Commission of Shanghai Municipality.

References

1. Lim, H.S., Kim, S.-H., Lee, Y.-G., Park, H.W.: A Simultaneous View Interpolation and Multiplexing Method Using Stereo Image Pairs for Lenticular Display
2. Matusik, M., Pfister, H.: 3D TV: a scalable system for realtime acquisition, transmission, and autostereoscopic display of dynamic scenes. ACM Transactions on Graphics (TOG) 23(3), 814–824 (2004)
3. Xu, G., Zhang, Z.Y.: Epipolar geometry in stereo, motion and object recognition, a unified approach. Kluwer Academic Publishers (1996)
4. Park, D.H., Kim, K.G., Lee, C.H., et al.: Lenticular stereoscopic imaging and displaying techniques with no special glasses. In: Proc. of IEEE International Conference on Image Processing ICIP 1995, Washington, USA, October 23-26, vol. 3, pp. 137–140 (1995)
5. van Berkel, C., Clarke, J.A.: Characterization and Optimisation of 3D-LCD Module Design. In: Proc SPIE, vol. 3012, pp. 179–187 (1997)

Image Matching Based on 2DPCA-SIFT

Kun Lun Li, Qian Wu, Zhe Wang, Juan Zhang, and Qi Meng

College of Electronic and Information Engineering, Hebei University, Baoding, China
likunlun@hbu.edu.cn

Abstract. Image matching has become a hot topic of research in image processing, image retrieval and related fields. The SIFT (Scale Invariant Feature Transform) is a robust learning algorithm for extracting local features. However, at present several problems still exist in destroying the original data of internal spatial structure, and it will result in the curse of dimensionality. In this paper, we will present an algorithm based on 2DPCA-SIFT, which utilizes the original two-dimensional image to construct covariance matrix. From the experimental result we can see, the proposed algorithm integrally retains the image information of two-dimensional structure, and has higher matching accuracy.

Keywords: Image matching, Feature point matching, Feature extraction, SIFT (Scale Invariant Feature Transform), 2DPCA.

1   Introduction

Image matching is an important technology, which has been widely applied in remote sensing, pattern recognition, automatic navigation, medical diagnosis and computer vision, including object recognition and tracking. In practical applications, we try to make the features invariant to scale and zoom, rotate, blur, illumination and viewpoint transformation. For these differences, image feature points matching has a good adaptability, thus it becomes the mainstream in the current matching techniques. This method uses image gray variance to detect feature points, but it is sensitive for strong border [1]. Harris method detects the feature points through differential operation and auto-correlation matrix, but it is very sensitive for the scale variation [2].

Lowe D.G. (1999) proposed SIFT, which is a new point feature extraction method [3]. Lowe D.G. (2004) processed a further study to SIFT, which had well solved the image matching problem in the case of grayscale distortion, geometric distortion and partial occlusion between the two images, and successfully applied to target recognition, image restoration, image stitching and other fields [4].

On the basis of SIFT, [5] applies PCA (Principal Component Analysis) to normalize gradient patch in order to reduce the descriptor dimension. SURF (Speeded up Robust Features) [6] uses Hessian matrix to detect extreme points and describes a distribution of Haar-wavelet responses within interest points neighborhood to identify main direction and descriptors. [7] provides robustness to surface discontinuity and background change and [8] employs SIFT for extracting local image features and

F.L. Wang et al. (Eds.): CMSP 2012, CCIS 346, pp. 375–382, 2012.

constructing the probabilistic latent semantic analysis (PLSA) model, and introduces an unsupervised learning classification approach to wireless capsule endoscopy video segmentation. A novel method [9] is based on BFSIFT (bilateral filter SIFT) to find feature matches for synthetic aperture radar image registration. New AIR methods [10] is based on the combination of image segmentation and SIFT, it is complemented by a robust procedure of outlier removal and directly applied to remote sensing images.

In this paper, we propose an image matching algorithm based on the 2DPCA-SIFT, which uses 2DPCA (Two-dimensional PCA) [11] to describe SIFT feature vector, it retains the integrity of the image of the two-dimensional spatial structure information.

2   Instruction of SIFT

SIFT algorithm is one of the most representative methods to extract local invariant features. The algorithm mainly contains the following four steps: 1) Construct scale space. 2) Accurately locate the keypoint. 3) Assign orientation for each keypoint. 4) Generate keypoint descriptor.

2.1   Construct Scale Space

The scale space of an image is defined as a function, $L(x, y, \sigma)$, that is produced from the convolution of a variable-scale Gaussian, $G(x, y, \sigma)$, with an input image, $I(x, y)$:

$$L(x, y, \sigma) = G(x, y, \sigma) * I(x, y) \tag{1}$$

$$G(x, y, \sigma) = \frac{1}{2\pi\sigma^2} e^{-(x^2 + y^2)/2\sigma^2} \tag{2}$$

Where (x, y) is coordinate, σ is scale coordinate. $D(x, y, \sigma)$ can be computed from the difference of two nearby scales separated by a constant multiplicative factor k:

$$D(x, y, \sigma) = (G(x, y, k\sigma) - G(x, y, \sigma)) * I(x, y) = L(x, y, k\sigma) - L(x, y, \sigma) \tag{3}$$

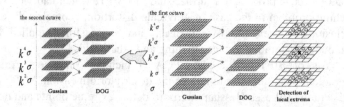

Fig. 1. Image pyramid and extrema detection

Fig. 1: For image pyramid, there are 4 octaves, and each octave has 5 scales. Initial image is repeatedly convolved with Gaussians to produce the set of scale space images. Maxima and minima of the difference-of-Gaussian images are detected by comparing a pixel (marked with $\times$) to its 26 neighbors in 3×3 regions at the current and adjacent scales.

2.2 Accurately Locate Keypoint

Brown's approach uses the Taylor expansion of the scale space function, $D(x, y, \sigma)$, to fit a 3D quadratic function of the candidate feature point to determine the interpolated location of the maximum:

$$D(X) = D(X_0) + \frac{\partial D^T}{\partial X} X + \frac{1}{2} X^T \frac{\partial^2 D}{\partial X} X \tag{4}$$

Where D and its derivatives are evaluated at the sample point, $X = (x, y, \sigma)^T$ is the offset from this point and $X_0 = (X_0, Y_0, \sigma_0)^T$ is the candidate extrema point. Taking the derivative of (4) formula with respect to X and getting the extreme location.

$$\frac{\partial D}{\partial X} = \frac{\partial D^T}{\partial X} + \frac{\partial^2 D}{\partial X^2} X = 0 \rightarrow \hat{X} = -\frac{\partial^2 D^{-1}}{\partial X^2} \frac{\partial D}{\partial X} \tag{5}$$

1) Reject low contrast points

The function value at the extremum, $D(\hat{X})$, which can be obtained by substituting equation (5) into (4). If $\left| D(\hat{X}) \right|$ is less than 0.03, it will be discarded, otherwise left.

$$D(\hat{X}) = D(X_0) + \frac{1}{2} \frac{\partial D^T}{\partial X} \hat{X} \tag{6}$$

2) Eliminate edge responses

The principal curvatures can be computed through a 2×2 Hessian matrix, H. The maximum eigenvalue is α, and the minimum eigenvalue is β, $\alpha = r\beta$, $T_r(H) = D_{XX} + D_{YY} = \alpha + \beta$, $Det(H) = D_{XX} D_{YY} - (D_{XY})^2 = \alpha\beta$, If $R < \frac{(r+1)^2}{r}$ (r takes 10), the keypoint will be left, otherwise discarded.

$$H = \begin{bmatrix} D_{XX} & D_{XY} \\ D_{YX} & D_{YY} \end{bmatrix} \tag{7}$$

$$R = \frac{T_r(H)^2}{Det(H)} = \frac{(\alpha + \beta)^2}{\alpha\beta} = \frac{(r+1)^2}{r} \tag{8}$$

2.3   Assign Orientation for Each Keypoint

In order to get rotation invariance for SIFT feature points, statistic each point's gradient magnitude and direction within a region around the keypoint. For each image sample, $L(x, y)$, in this kind of scale, the gradient magnitude, $m(x, y)$, and orientation, $\theta(x, y)$, is recomputed using pixel differences:

$$m(x, y) = \sqrt{(L(x+1, y) - L(x-1, y))^2 + (L(x, y+1) - L(x, y-1))^2} \tag{9}$$

$$\theta(x, y) = \tan^{-1}(\frac{L(x, y+1) - L(x, y-1)}{L(x+1, y) - L(x-1, y)}) \tag{10}$$

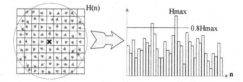

Fig. 2. Assign orientation for each keypoint

Fig. 2: Indicating the gradient magnitude and orientation of each sample point within keypoint neighborhood. These sample points are weighted by a Gaussian circular window with σ that is 1.5 times of the keypoint scale. The H max represents the main direction of the feature point, we consider the energy that is higher than $0.8 H$ max as the auxiliary direction.

2.4   Generate Keypoint Descriptor

The image is rotated to the main direction of this feature point. A 4×4 sub-region is chosen around each keypoint. There are 4×4 pixel points in each sub-region. Then the gradient orientation histogram of the 8 directions is calculated and sorted in each sub-region. SIFT features descriptor is a $4 \times 4 \times 8 = 128$ dimensional feature vector.

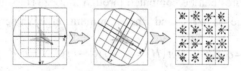

Fig. 3. The figure shows a 4×4 descriptor array computed from a 16×16 set of sample

3   Description of PCA-SIFT

The principal component analysis (PCA) is a linear transformation, which enables high-dimensional samples to project onto low-dimensional space. Yan Ke (2004) proposed PCA-SIFT which are the improved SIFT [5].

1) The image is rotated to keypoint's main direction. We choose a 41×41 patch around each keypoint, and calculate the horizontal and vertical gradient to form a $2 \times 39 \times 39 = 3042$ dimensional vector. These vectors form a matrix A, $n \times 3042$, n is the number of keypoints. The eigenvalues and eigenvectors of covariance matrix is calculated by $A = A - mean A$, $cov A = A^T A$. The first r eigenvectors are used to form a projection matrix w, $r \times 3042$. This projection is computed once and stored.

2) Build descriptor: Choosing the 41×41 patch around the keypoint to form a 3042 dimensional normalized gradient vector, x. We project x into our feature space using the stored eigenspace w, and generate a PCA-SIFT descriptor, $r \times 1$, where $r = 20$. At last we consider the similarity between feature vectors as matching pairs.

4   2DPCA-SIFT

PCA needs decomposing a non sparse matrix, $mn \times mn$, the high dimensional tensor model data were converted into vector model. To some extent, it would result in the curse of dimensionality. Compared with PCA, 2DPCA is a good solution, it is a quantum spatial learning method based on matrix pattern, and does not need to transform image ($m \times n$) into one-dimensional vector ($1 \times mn$) [11].

In this paper, we draw inspiration from 2DPCA and PCA-SIFT and propose feature points matching algorithm based on 2DPCA-SIFT. Main idea: Using SIFT to find keypoints and extract the location, scale, rotation invariant features, then using 2DPCA to reduce dimensionality to establish a more streamlined feature description.

Establish the 2DPCA-SIFT Descriptor:

1) Choose the 41×41 patch around the keypoint, a total of M image blocks, M is the number of keypoints.

2) Rotate image to main direction for each keypoint, calculate the horizontal and vertical gradient to form feature matrix, 39×78.

3) Use 2DPCA to reduce dimension.

The idea of 2DPCA is that the image A, ($m \times n$), is projected into X through linear transformation, $Y = A X$, so we will get an m-dimensional column vector, Y,.

2DPCA's core mission is to find the optimal projection vectors matrix X.

The specific processes are as follows:

a) Suppose the reference image having M feature points, $A_1, A_2, ..., A_M$, the A_i is denoted by an $m \times n$ matrix, the mean matrix of train samples:

$$\bar{A} = \frac{1}{M} \sum_{i=1}^{M} A_i \in R^{m \times n} \tag{11}$$

b) Get the projection matrix X by establishing the objective function. The total scatter of the project samples can be characterized by the trace of the covariance matrix of the projected feature vectors.

$$J(X)=tr(G)=tr\left\{\frac{1}{M}\sum_{i=1}^{M}[(A_i-\overline{A})X]^T[(A_i-\overline{A})X]\right\} \tag{12}$$

Where G_t is image covariance matrix, G denotes the covariance matrix of the projected feature vectors of the training samples, and $tr(G)$ denotes the trace of G:

$$G_t=\frac{1}{M}\sum_{i=1}^{M}(A_i-\overline{A})^T(A_i-\overline{A})\in R^{n\times n} \tag{13}$$

$$J(X)=tr(G)=tr\left\{\frac{1}{M}A^T\sum_{i=1}^{M}[A_i-\overline{A}]^T[A_i-\overline{A}]X\right\}=tr\left\{\frac{1}{M}X^TG_tX\right\} \tag{14}$$

The eigenvector of G_t that is corresponding to the largest eigenvalue λ_i is denoted by v_i. Where $v_i^T=(v_{i1},v_{i2},...,v_{in})$, $v_i^Tv_i=1$, $(i=1,2,...,n)$. It usually needs to select a series of projection axes, $X_1,X_2,...,X_r$ $(r=8)$ to compose projection matrix, which meet the standard orthogonal and maximize of $J(X)$.

$$\begin{cases}[X_1,X_2,...,X_r]=\arg\max J(X)\\ X_i^TX_j=0,i\neq j;i,j=1,2,...,r\end{cases} \tag{15}$$

$$w=(v_1,v_2,...,v_r) \tag{16}$$

c) Through linear transform we multiply image block, A_i, by the stored projection matrix, w, and use 2DPCA-SIFT to reduce to 8-dimensional. We use Euclidean distance as the similarity metric between these keypoints. That is:

$$\begin{cases}Y_{iA}=A_iw \ (i=1,2,...,M)=[Y_1^{(i)},Y_2^{(i)},...,Y_r^{(i)}]\\ Y_{jB}=B_jw \ (j=1,2,...,N)=[Y_1^{(j)},Y_2^{(j)},...,Y_r^{(j)}]\\ d(Y_{iA},Y_{jB})=\sum_{k=1}^{r}\left\|Y_k^{(i)}-Y_k^{(j)}\right\|_2\end{cases} \tag{17}$$

The nearest neighbor search is used to find the feature vector distance between the nearest neighbor and second nearest neighbor. When $D_{FirMin}/D_{SecMin}\leq Treshold$ (0.6), we regard the feature point as matching point.

5   Experiments and Analysis

In experiment, we compare 2DPCA-SIFT with PCA-SIFT and SIFT. We use the correct matching ratio as feature descriptor evaluation criteria. 2DPCA-SIFT is 8-dimension (see Fig. 7).

Fig. 4. The reference image and test image include six transformations

Fig. 5. Extract keypoints of the reference image and test image

Fig. 6. Matching result of 2DPCA-SIFT algorithm

In the paper, we use Mikolajczyk sequence images as data set, which contains 5 transformation sequences: (1) scaling and rotation, (2) blur, (3) illumination, (4) viewpoint, (5) JPEG compression. The experimental results show that, in response to the image of (1), (2), (4) and (5) variations, the correct rate of 2DPCA-SIFT is higher than PCA-SIFT and SIFT. For the image with (3) variation, the correct rate of 2DPCA-SIFT is lower than SIFT, but higher than PCA-SIFT.

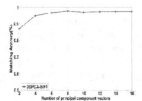
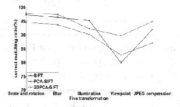

Fig. 7. The dimension of 2DPCA-SIFT

Fig. 8. Performance of three algorithms under 5 transformation sequences

6   Conclusions

This paper uses 2DPCA to describe SIFT keypoints around the local region image, these image matching experiments run in a series of variations. The proposed algorithm integrally retains image information, which avoids structuring scatter matrix in the high dimensional vector space, and reduces computation complexity and saves operating time. The experimental results show that: the algorithm has exceptional anti-scaling rotation ability and resistant to affine transformation and JPEG compression ability, which ensures higher matching rate, and reduces computation complexity. In addition in some cases, the dimension of feature matrix of the proposed algorithm still is sill very big, therefore the next research focus is to reduce the dimension.

Acknowledgments. Project is supported by the National Natural Science Foundation of China under Grant (No. 61073121), Natural Science Foundation of Hebei Province of China (No. F2009000215) and Medical Engineering Alternate Research Center Open Foundation of Hebei University (No. BM201102).

References

1. Moravec, H.: Towards automatic visual obstacle avoidance. In: Processing of the 5th International Joint Conference on Artificial Intelligence, p. 584 (1977)
2. Harris, C., Stephens, M.: A combined corner and edge detector. In: The Alvey Vision Conference, pp. 147–151 (1988)
3. Lowe, D.G.: Object recognition from local scale-invariant features. In: International Conference on Computer Vision, pp. 1150–1157 (1999)
4. Lowe, D.G.: Distinctive image features from scale-invariant keypoints. International Journal of Computer Vision 60(2), 91–110 (2004)
5. Ke, Y., Sukthankar, R.: PCA-SIFT: a more distinctive representation for local image descriptors. In: IEEE Computer Society Conference on Computer Vision and Pattern Recognition, pp. 511–517 (2004)
6. Bay, H., Tuytelaars, T., Van Gool, L.: SURF: Speeded Up Robust Features. In: Leonardis, A., Bischof, H., Pinz, A. (eds.) ECCV 2006. LNCS, vol. 3951, pp. 404–417. Springer, Heidelberg (2006)
7. Cui, C., Ngan, K.: Scale- and Affine-Invariant Fan Feature. IEEE Transactions on Image Processing 20(6), 1627–1640 (2011)
8. Yao, S., Guturu, P., Buckles, B.P.: Wireless Capsule Endoscopy Video Segmentation Using an Unsupervised Learning Approach Based on Probabilistic Latent Semantic Analysis With Scale Invariant Features. IEEE Transactions on Information Technology in Biomedicine 16(1), 98–105 (2011)
9. Wang, S., You, H., Fu, K.: BFSIFT: A Novel Method to Find Feature Matches for SAR Image Registration. Geoscience and Remote Sensing Letters 9(4), 1–5 (2011)
10. Goncalves, H., Corte-Real, L., Goncalves, J.A.: Automatic Image Registration Through Image Segmentation and SIFT. IEEE Transactions on Geoscience and Remote Sensing 49(7), 2589–2600 (2011)
11. Yang, J., Zhang, D., Frangi, A.F.: Two-Dimensional PCA: A New Approach to Appearance-Based Face Representation and Recognition. IEEE Transactions on Pattern Analysis and Machine Intelligence 26(1), 131–137 (2004)

Fabric Image Denoising Method Based on Wavelet-Domain HMT Model[*]

Qi Sun[1], Yaming Wang[1], and Chunxia Xu[2]

[1] College of Informatics & Electronics, Zhejiang Sci-Tech University, Hangzhou, China
sunqi@vip.sina.com, ywang@zstu.edu.cn
[2] Department of Computer, Zhejiang Industry Polytechnic College, Shaoxing, China
xcxbaby@126.com

Abstract. To deal with the problem of shape distortion and the poor adaptation in denoising of fabric textures, a denoising method based on hidden Markov tree (HMT) in wavelet domain for jacquard fabric images is proposed. The wavelet-domain HMT model is built and the parameters of HMT model are estimated by EM algorithm. Experimental results show that the method can effectively denoise fabric images and is a better method for fabric images than the classical image denoising methods. It also increases PNSR and perfectly preserves the shapes of fabric texture while denoising.

Keywords: Fabric Image, Wavelet-Domain HMT Model, Image Denoising.

1   Introduction

Fabric images usually have noise after fabric is scanned. This noise not only worsens the quality of the images and makes the images fuzzy, but also floods the shapes of fabric texture. It will lead to difficulties for the further fabric texture analysis and retrieval performance. So denoising is one of most important steps among a series of processing and computing on fabric images.

Image Denoising generally work based on the characteristics of real images, the statistical characteristics of noise and the regulation of spectral distribution [1]. At present, there are lots of methods for image denoising such as median filter [2], Wiener filter [3], edge preserving filter, partial derivative filter and wavelet image denoising [4]. However, these methods are easy to lose the details when denoising. Wavelet image denoising has become one of the main methods to denoise. This method can show structure and texture of an image respectively on different resolution scales because wavelet transform enjoys good localization in both time domain and frequency domain. But it produces shocking shadow on the edges of images due to its Gibbs-like artifacts and ignores the dependencies of wavelet coefficients between neighboring scales. If the dependencies of wavelet coefficients can be accurately

---

[*] Foundation item: The Program of National Science Foundation of China(No.61070063), Zhejiang Provincial Natural Science Foundation of China(Z1080702) and Zhejiang Province Department of Education (Y200909797).

F.L. Wang et al. (Eds.): CMSP 2012, CCIS 346, pp. 383–388, 2012.
© Springer-Verlag Berlin Heidelberg 2012

showed by a statistical model, the performance of denoising fabric images will be improved.

Hidden Markov models (HMMs) have been proposed and applied to image processing. In this paper we further survey the wavelet-domain hidden Markov tree model (HMT). Wavelet-domain HMT is a multidimensional Gaussian mixture model in which the hidden states have a Markov dependency structure. Thus the dependencies of wavelet coefficients can be captured through their hidden states. We also apply the wavelet-domain HMT model in fabric image denoising. The experiments show that the method is good for fabric image denoising.

2   Wavelet-Domain HMT Model

2.1   Theory

Wavelet coefficients between the neighboring scales of an image have the features of persistency and Non-Gaussian, so Crouse and his group proposed the wavelet-Domain Hidden Markov Tree model (HMT) [5] based on HMMs, which successfully captures the features of persistency and Non-Gaussian for a real image in the wavelet-domain. In order to match non-Gaussian of the wavelet coefficients, in HMT model probability density function(pdf) of wavelet coefficients is defined as a mixture Gaussian distribution model with hidden states and a probability tree is presented that the hidden states have a Markov dependency structure. The dependencies of wavelet coefficients are looked as the persistency of wavelet coefficients between the neighboring scales. So the wavelet coefficient is not only associated with the father scale's coefficient but also affects its offspring coefficients.

Because the topology of wavelet coefficients can be looked as a quad tree topology, the probability model for tree structure can present the dependencies of the wavelet coefficients along the scales shown in Fig. 1. Each black node in the figure 1 is a wavelet coefficient while each white node is it's corresponding hidden state. The links represent the dependencies between states. Each wavelet coefficients of scale J is associated with the four wavelet coefficients in scale J-1. In the wavelet-domain HMT model, each wavelet coefficient is defined as a Gaussian mixture model with m states and its corresponding hidden state is linked with four sub-variables in its next scale. Meanwhile, each parent-child state-to-state link has a state transition matrix that quantifies statistically the degree of dependencies of wavelet coefficients between the neighboring scales.

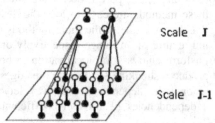

Scale J

Scale J-1

Fig. 1. 2-D HMT model, the black nodes are wavelet coefficients c_i, the white nodes are the corresponding hidden state s_i

Assumed that each wavelet coefficient c_i has a hidden state $s_i = \{S, L\}$ which cannot be observed, so c_i is corresponded with one of the two Gaussian mixture sources. State S is a Gaussian source with zero-mean and low variance σ_S^2 while L is with zero-mean and high variance σ_L^2. The pdf of wavelet coefficients is given by

$$f(c_i) = p_i^S g(c_i; 0, \sigma_S^2) + p_i^L g(c_i; 0, \sigma_L^2) \ , \tag{1}$$

where $g(x; 0, \sigma^2)$ is Gaussian distribution with mean 0 and variance σ^2, P_i^S and P_i^L is the probability that c_i is S and L respectively, $P_i^S + P_i^L = 1$. The state transition matrix is

$$A_i = \begin{bmatrix} \varepsilon_i^{SS} & \varepsilon_i^{SL} \\ \varepsilon_i^{LS} & \varepsilon_i^{LL} \end{bmatrix}, \tag{2}$$

where $\varepsilon_i^{SS} + \varepsilon^{SL} = 1$ and $\varepsilon_i^{LS} + \varepsilon_i^{LL} = 1$.

In case that the hidden State s_i of the wavelet coefficients is given, parent and child nodes of wavelet coefficients are independencies. The state s_i is only affected by its parent node and not associated with other random variables. The HMT model is expressed as

$$\theta = \{ \, p_0^L \, , \varepsilon_{i,\rho_i}^{mn}, \sigma_{i,m}^2 (m, n \in S, L) \}. \tag{3}$$

As in equation (3), the model is parameterized as follows: p_0^L is the probability mass function of the root node; $\varepsilon_{i,\rho(i)}^{mn} = P_{s_i|s_{\rho(i)}}(m \mid s_{\rho(i)} = n)$ is the transition probabilities that sub-state s_i is m if parent state $s_{\rho(i)}$ is n; $\sigma_{i,m}^2$ is the Gaussian mixture variance.

2.2 Applications to Image Denoising

In order to demonstrate the effectiveness of the HMT model for modeling an image's wavelet coefficients, first of all, the parameters of the model should be obtained. The parameters can be approached by the Expectation Maximization (EM) algorithm though training the current noise image or directly adopt the model parameters from the same type of images. If they are approached by EM algorithm, the image can be assumed noised by white Gaussian noise (The conclusion is also very effective for relative noise though this assumption is too harsh). The components of white Gaussian noise are independent and identically distributed with zero mean and known variance. The wavelet coefficient with noise can be defined as follows:

$$y_i = c_i + n_i \ , \tag{4}$$

where y_i is the wavelet coefficient of observation images, c_i is the wavelet coefficient of the original image, n_i is the noise wavelet coefficient (For Gaussian distribution, $n_i \sim N(0, \sigma_n^2)$).

If the hidden state s_i corresponded with c_i is known, the minimum-mean-square-error (MMSE) estimate of c_i can be obtained by the condition mean estimate of a Gaussian signal in Gaussian noise as

$$E(c_i \mid y_i, \ \theta) = \frac{\sigma_{i,m}^2}{\sigma_{i,m}^2 + \sigma_n^2} y_i \ . \tag{5}$$

Through the EM training to obtain the HMT model parameters, the posterior hidden state probability is $P(s_i \mid y_i, \theta)$ given the model θ and the observed wavelet coefficient y_i. So c_i can be obtained as:

$$c_i = E(c_i \mid y_i, \ \theta) = \sum p(s_i = m \mid y_i, \ \theta) \times \frac{\sigma_{i,m}^2 y_i}{\sigma_{i,m}^2 + \sigma_n^2} \ , \ m \in \{S, L\} \ . \tag{6}$$

The noise variance σ_n is obtained by a median estimate method raised by Donoho [6] as follows:

$$\sigma_n = \frac{median(abs(c_{i,j}))}{0.6745} \ , \tag{7}$$

where j is the scale of wavelet coefficients i is the wavelet coefficients number on this scale. Finally, the denoised image is achieved by the inverse DWT of this estimation of wavelet coefficients.

3   Simulation

In the experiment a $512*512$ Lena image is put with white Gaussian noise of mean 0 and variance 0.01. Then, respectively denoise it used by the methods including wavelet soft-threshold, median filter, Wiener filter and wavelet-domain HMT model. The result shows that Wavelet-domain HMT model on account of the dependencies of wavelet coefficients between scales has obvious advantages than other classical methods in Fig. 2. It keeps the shapes of the image and its PSNR is 1~2dB higher than other methods.

The experiment continues on a $512*512$ big jacquard fabric image. As the simulation results showed in Fig. 3, wavelet-domain HMT model on the fabric image also has a much better denoising effect than those classic methods. Its PSNR is the highest one. Yet wavelet-domain HMT needs parameter training and spends more time in the processing of denoising, which should be improved later.

Fig. 2. Comparation of denoising methods on a 512*512 Lena image

Fig. 3. Comparation of denoising methods on a 512*512 jacquard fabric image

4   Conclusion

This paper makes a research on the wavelet-domain HMT model and applies it on fabric images. The quad tree and probability of wavelet coefficients are discussed. Wavelet coefficients is defined as a mixture Gaussian distribution model with hidden states and a probability quad tree is presented that the hidden states have a Markov dependency structure. Thus, the HMT model built by the independencies of wavelet coefficients is used to denoise. The results show that wavelet-domain HMT model can effectively describe the characteristics of real image, improve PSNR of the fabric images and keep the fabric texture better.

Acknowledgments. Many people gave me support and help in the process of writing the paper. I'd like to give my many thanks to my friend, Miss Yanxi Zeng, who generously gave me her kindly help during writing.

References

1. Gonzalez, R.C., Woods, R.E.: Digital Image Processing. Prentice Hall, London (2001)
2. Ko, S.J., Lee, Y.H.: Center Weighted Median Filters And Their Applications To Image Enhancement. J. IEEE Trans., C. S 38, 984–993 (1991)
3. Rahamn, S.M., Hasan, M.K.: Wavelet-Domain Iterative Center Weighted Median Filter For Image Denoising. J. Signal P. 83, 1001–1012 (2003)
4. Fan, G.L.: Wavelet Domain Statistical Image Modeling and Processing. Ph.D.dissertation. University of Delaware, pp. 46–47 (2001)
5. Crouse, M.S., Nowak, R.D., Baraniuk, R.G.: Wavelet-Based Statistical Signal Processingusing Hidden Markov Models. J. IEEE Trans. S. P. 46, 886–902 (1998)
6. Donoho, D.L., Johnstone, I.M.: Ideal Spatial Adaptation Wavelet Shrinkage. J. Biometrika 81, 425–455 (1998)

Camera Calibration of the Stereo-Vision System with Large Field of View Based on Parallel Particle Swarm Optimization

Guangming Zhang, Yuming Chen, and Yuhao Yuan

School of Automation & Electrical Engineering,
Nanjing University of Technology, Nanjing, 211816

Abstract. Binocular vision calibration with Large Field of View (LFV) is a multi-parameter nonlinear complex problem. This paper utilizes particle swarm (PSO) algorithm to the multi-parameters optimization of binocular vision calibration. Considering radial distortion and tangential distortion of the camera model, this paper extends the standard particle Swarm Optimization (PSO) and proposes Parallel PSO Algorithms, this method improves the ability of searching the global optimal solution and the searching speed. Taking into account camera radial and tangential distortion, we achieve the global optimum of interior and exterior camera's parameters with this method in a large field of binocular vision system calibration. Experiments show that this method is simple, high precision, good stability. The interior and exterior camera's parameters are searched the global optimum solution, the result of the experiment indicated, the method is simple with high accuracy and good stability.

Keywords: Calibration of stereo-vision System, Parallel Particle Swarm Optimization, Large field of view.

1 Introduction

Binocular vision calibration is the most important aspect of stereo vision Inspection. The calibration parameters of the camera model are divided into internal and external parameters[1].According to the camera image model, binocular vision calibration is divided into the linear and non-linear calibration. The linear calibration idealizes the camera model, and solves the parameters with the linear equations, it is simple and fast, but its accuracy is poor. Considering the distortion parameters, non-linear calibration presents a nonlinear optimization method, such as the Levenberg_Marquardt (LM) optimization algorithm, Roger Tsai RAC two-step method [2]. However the optimized parameters are too many, the conventional algorithms compute complexity in the binocular stereo vision. The parameters must be set to a more appropriate initial value, so that it can get a better optimized solution [3]. With the increase of the parameters, the traditional algorithms often cannot find the optimal solution. The particle swarm optimization algorithm is a viable method of nonlinear optimization algorithm, it do not estimate the characteristics of the initial value, and achieves the good results

F.L. Wang et al. (Eds.): CMSP 2012, CCIS 346, pp. 389–395, 2012.

in many optimization problems, but it is easy to fall into local optimum [4,5]. Wang etc.[6] has proposed the parallel PSO algorithm of annealing algorithm, this algorithm is complex, the optimization time is relatively long, and online optimization is inappropriate. Gao etc. [7] has put forward the global particle swarm optimization algorithm, this algorithm can fast convergence and escape from local optimum, but the perturbations must be small. Combining the above ideas, this paper proposes the parallel PSO algorithm which's relatively simple and fast optimization so as to maintain the particle flying diversity, and it expands the scope of the solution space search. In the experiment, we compare the proposed algorithms with commercial software HALCON calibration algorithm; the experiment result has indicated this method has very high accuracy and easy operation. It not only takes advantage of PSO for the multiple parameters optimization capability, but also overcomes the shortcomings of PSO falling into local optimum, thus effectively has solved the nonlinear optimization problem of high-dimensional optimization of binocular vision calibration.

2   The Model of the Binocular Stereo Vision

Space point P image in the binocular vision system, assume the origin of the left camera image coordinate is the origin of the world coordinate system $O - x_w y_w z_w$, left camera pixel coordinate system is $O_l - u_l v_l$, right camera coordinate system is $O_r - x_{cr} y_{cr} z_{cr}$, its pixel coordinate system is $O_r - u_r v_r$, shown in Fig 1.

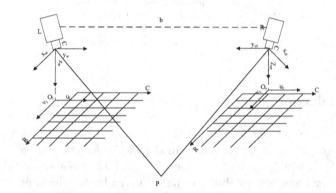

Fig. 1. Schematic diagram of a binocular stereo vision calibration

Homogeneous coordinates of the linear model of binocular vision system are:

$$s_l \begin{bmatrix} u_l \\ v_l \\ 1 \end{bmatrix} = \begin{bmatrix} a_{xl} & \gamma_r & u_{0l} & 0 \\ 0 & a_{yl} & v_{0l} & 0 \\ 0 & 0 & 1 & 0 \end{bmatrix} \begin{bmatrix} x_w \\ y_w \\ z_w \\ 1 \end{bmatrix} \quad (1)$$

$$s_r \begin{bmatrix} u_r \\ v_r \\ 1 \end{bmatrix} = \begin{bmatrix} a_{xr} & \gamma_r & u_{0r} \\ 0 & a_{yr} & v_{0r} \\ 0 & 0 & 1 \end{bmatrix} \begin{bmatrix} r_1 & r_2 & r_3 & t_x \\ r_5 & r_6 & r_7 & t_y \\ r_7 & r_8 & r_9 & t_z \end{bmatrix} \begin{bmatrix} x_w \\ y_w \\ z_w \\ 1 \end{bmatrix} \tag{2}$$

Where u_l, v_l, u_r, v_r are respectively left and right camera pixel rows (u axis), columns (v axis) pixel value; a_{xl}, a_{yl} a_{xr}, a_{yr} are respectively, u-axis and v-axis scale factor for left and right cameras, (that is $a_x = f / s_x$, $a_y = f / s_y$, where s_x, s_y are horizontal and vertical pixel spacing) ,non vertical factor of u-axis and v-axis in the left and right camera. Respectively left and right camera optical center u_{0l}, v_{0l}, u_{0r}, v_{0r}.

Given $m_l = [u_l, v_l]^T$, $m_r = [u_r, v_r]^T$, $X_w = [x_w, y_w, z_w, 1]^T$, the left and right camera's internal

parameters $A_l = \begin{bmatrix} a_{xl} & \gamma_r & u_{0l} & 0 \\ 0 & a_{yl} & v_{0l} & 0 \\ 0 & 0 & 1 & 0 \end{bmatrix}$, $A_r = \begin{bmatrix} a_{xr} & \gamma_r & u_{0r} \\ 0 & a_{yr} & v_{0r} \\ 0 & 0 & 1 \end{bmatrix}$, pose relationship with

the left and right camera and the world coordinate system is expressed as follows:

$$s_r m_l = A_l X_w$$
$$s_r m_r = A_r M_{lr} X_w \tag{3}$$

Formula (1) and (2) is a linear model of binocular stereo vision, the actual lens has varying degrees of distortion, lens distortion is mainly divided into radial distortion and tangential distortion [8,9], the non-linear expression as follows:

$$x' = x + \delta_x(x, y)$$
$$y' = y + \delta_y(x, y)$$
$$\delta_x(x, y) = x(1 + k_1 r^2 + k_2 r^4) + 2 p_1 xy + p_2 (r^2 + 2x^2)$$
$$\delta_y(x, y) = y(1 + k_1 r^2 + k_2 r^4) + 2 p_2 xy + p_1 (r^2 + 2y^2) \tag{4}$$

In the equation, (x', y') is the image plane coordinates which's described by a linear model, (x, y) is the actual image plane coordinate system with the lens distortion; in formula (4), $r = (x' - u_0)^2 + (y' - v_0)^2$, Where (u_0, v_0) are the exact coordinates for the light points. k_1, k_2, p_1, p_2 respectively are radial distortion and tangential distortion coefficients, the structures of the left and right camera are the same, so both the left camera and the right camera exist two types of distortion, they are $k_{l1}, k_{l2}, p_{l1}, p_{l2}$ and $k_{r1}, k_{r2}, p_{r1}, p_{r2}$.

3　Using Parallel PSO Algorithm to Optimize the Binocular Camera Parameters

The linear model resolution of the second section, which is the initial value of the parallel PSO algorithm optimizing. According to the principle of the parallel PSO, the solution steps are as follows:

Step1: the center coordinates of the identified point of the target are gotten with Gaussian filtering and sub-pixel edge detection , the features of image points of the left and right camera are matched with the epipolar constraint method, we acquire the target coordinate system $(x_p, y_p, 0)$ corresponding to the pixel coordinates points (u_l, v_l) and (u_r, v_r) of the left and right camera.

Step2: we do not consider the camera distortion, and calculate the initialized homography matrix H_l and H_r from the world coordinates to the image coordinates of the marked points. According to paper[10], we calculate internal parameters a_{xl}, a_{yl}, γ_l, u_{ol}, v_{ol}, s_l and a_{xr}, a_{yr}, γ_r, u_{0r}, v_{0r}, s_r as well as the external parameters M_{lr} of the left and right camera as the mean value. Considering the mean value distribution, M particles are randomly generated with the appropriate variance. According to mean value distribution, for $k_{l1}, k_{l2}, p_{l1}, p_{l2}$ and $k_{r1}, k_{r2}, p_{r1}, p_{r2}$, N particles are randomly generated with mean value distribution which is mean value 0, variance 0.5, the optimized parameters are make up of D = 26 dimensional space, and then we initialize the location of the particle swarm. The fitness functions as follow:

$$\text{Fitness} = \sum_{i}^{n}\sum_{j}^{m} \| m_{lij} - m(a_{xl}, a_{yl}, \gamma_l, u_{ol}, v_{ol}, s_l, k_{l1}, k_{l2}, p_{l1}, p_{l2}) \|^2 * \sum_{i}^{n}\sum_{j}^{m} \| m_{rij} - m(a_{xr}, a_{yr}, \gamma_r, u_{or}, v_{or}, s_r, k_{r1}, k_{r2}, p_{r1}, p_{r2}) \|^2.$$

Of which, m_{lij}, m_{rij} are respectively the actual pixel coordinates of the j th point of the i th calibration image of the binocular vision system. $m(a_{xl}, a_{yl}, \gamma_l, u_{ol}, v_{ol}, s_l, k_{l1}, k_{l2}, p_{l1}, p_{l2})$ and $m(a_{xr}, a_{yr}, \gamma_r, u_{or}, v_{or}, s_r, k_{r1}, k_{r2}, p_{r1}, p_{r2})$ are the coordinate values of the i th image's points being projected by formula (3).Randomly initialize the position and the speed of the particles in the particle swarm. Set the size of the group for K=M+N.

Step3: Calculate the fitness value of each particle Fitness (Objective function value).

Step4: Calculate the best location $p_{id} = (x_{i1}, x_{i2}, ..., x_{id})$ where the particle experiences. That is the location of the best fitness where the particle has experienced. From the following formula

$$p_{id}(t+1) = \begin{cases} p_{id}(t), & \text{fitness} > p_{id}(t) \\ x_i(t+1), & \text{fitness} < p_{id}(t) \end{cases} \qquad (5)$$

calculate the best location of the groups of all particles having experienced, that is the global optimum position.

Step 5: According to the formula (5) to optimize the speed and position of the particle.

Step 6: Judge the end conditions. Fitness value of the objective function is good enough or evolves to the pre-set number of iterations Maxiter; if not, returns to the Step 3 and continues.

4   Results

In order to test the effect of parallel particle swarm calibration algorithm. On a Windows XP platform, we use the Microsoft Visual C + + 6.0 to conduct the software programming, thus achieve extraction of the target point and the particle swarm calibration algorithm. The lens used in this experiment is the Computar F / 4 lens of the focal length of 8mm, CCD camera is a Basler PIA 2400-17gm industrial camera, with a resolution of 2448 (H) X 2050 (V), the unit pixel size of CCD image plane is 3.45um (H) X 3.45um (V). The planar circular target is a calibration board 500 * 500mm of HALCON, its accuracy is 0.01mm, and the measurement field of view area is 3500*2900mm, the farthest distance from the binocular visual system to calibration plate is 3000mm, this is a typical visual measurement of a long-range field of view, shown in Fig 2.

Fig. 2.   The field of view of binocular calibration

Using the parallel PSO algorithm, the binocular visual system shot a total of 17 pairs of images to obtain the data of the feature points, obtained the coordinates of the feature points on internal parameters of the binocular vision system and the external parameters of the binocular vision system as follows.

$$f_L = 7.95892\,\text{e-003},$$
$$k_1 = 3.71818\,\text{e+007}, k_2 = -5.05448\,\text{e+012},$$
$$p_1 = -8.41686\,\text{e-2}, p_2 = 2.59903\,\text{e-1}$$
$$f_R = 7.98422\,\text{e-003},$$
$$k_1 = -1.24486\,\text{e+007}, k_2 = -2.47384\,\text{e+011},$$
$$p_1 = -2.01358\,\text{e-2}, p_2 = -2.34705\,\text{e-2}$$
$$\alpha = 5.55693\,\text{e-1}\ ,\quad \beta = 1.71533\,\text{e-3}\ ,\quad \gamma = 5.05538\,\text{e-2}\ ,$$
$$T_x = 359.719, T_y = 344.427, T_z = 0.439258$$

Of which, k_1, k_2 are the lens lateral distortion coefficient, p_1, p_2 are the lens radial distortion coefficient. We compare the designed parallel PSO algorithm in the binocular calibration with HALCON [11]. This paper presents the standard errors of 90 points, which can be seen from Figure 3.

Table 1. The comparison of calibration to optimize the algorithm

	Execution time	Maximum error	Mean square error
HALCON	4.3s	0.17mm	0.0588398 m
Parallel PSO	7.6s	0.42mm	0.113173mm

From two aspects of the stability and accuracy of the algorithm, we can see from Table 1. The vision calibration algorithm is the preliminary work of vision measurement, and its calibration computation time has no affect on the process of measurement. Both the accuracy and repeat error rate of the calibration algorithm are critical for the vision measurement. From the above data, the parallel PSO binocular calibration algorithm is superior to binocular vision algorithm which is provided by HALCON.

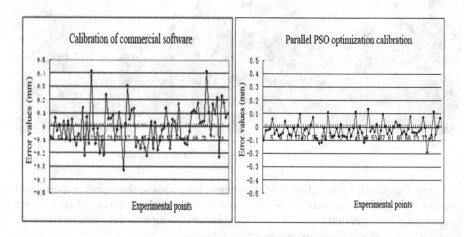

Fig. 3. The standard error of binocular calibration algorithm

5   Conclusion

This paper presents a stable, high-precision on-line vision calibration method. The camera model with the 30 internal and external parameters has considered all kinds of uncertain factors, such as the radial distortion, tangential distortion etc.; The process of calibration is divided into three steps of an ideal model parameter estimate, correction of distortion and global optimization, the proposed parallel PSO algorithm can effectively achieve the multi-parameter and nonlinear function optimization problems in the binocular vision, it is difficult to the traditional optimization methods. This calibration method is relatively simple, suitable for large field of the visual field measurement calibration and portable light pen vision measurement calibration.

References

1. Masaoka, S.: Three-dimensional human motion modeling by back-projection based on image-based camera calibration. IEEE Journal of Artificial Life and Robotics 4(1), 515–518 (2010)
2. Tsai, R.Y.: A versatile camera calibration technique for high-accuracy 3D machine vision metrology using off-the-shelf TV cameras and lenses. IEEE Journal of Robotics and Automaton 3(4), 323–344 (1987)
3. Huang, F., Huang, Y.: Online Calibration Technology of the Vision System in Intelligent Coordinate Measuring Machine. Semiconductor Optoelectronics 31(1), 67–70 (2010)
4. Du, W.L., Li, B.: Multi-strategy ensemble particle swarm optimization for dynamic optimization. Information Sciences 178(15), 3096–3109 (2008)
5. Zhang, F., et al.: Automatic Reconstruction of Distant Scenes from Wide Baseline Images. Journal of Computer-Aided Design & Computer Graphics 22(2), 256–263 (2010)
6. Wan, H., Cao, C.: Parallel particle swarm optimization based on simulated annealing. Control and Design 20(5), 499–503 (2005)
7. Gao, L., Li, R., Zou, D.: A Global Particle Swarm Optimization Algorithm. Journal of Northeastern University 32(11), 1538–1541 (2011)
8. Lou, X., Guo, M.: Methods of calibration improvement in the binocular vision system. Journal of Beijing Information Science & Technology University 25(1), 16–20 (2010)
9. Zhang, Y., Ou, Z.: A New Linear Approach for Camera Calibration. Journal of Image and Graphics 6(8), 727–731 (2001)
10. Steger, C., Uirich, M., Wiedemann, C.: Machine Vision Algorithms and Applications. Tsinghua University Press (2008)
11. Sun, J., Wu, Z., Liu, Q., Zhang, G.: Field calibration stereo vision senoor with large FOV. Optics and Precision Engineering 17(3), 633–640 (2009)

Biography

Guangming Zhang (1965-), male, professor, the Dean of the Automation and Electrical Engineering College in Nanjing University of Technology . Engaged in machine vision, intelligent control, and electromechanical integration study and so on.

A New Diversity Measure for Classifier Fusion

Ye Li[1], Li Xu[2], Ya Gang Wang[1], and Xiao Ming Xu[1]

[1] School of Optical-Electrical and Computer Engineering,
University of Shanghai for Science and Technology, Shanghai 200093 China
[2] Department of Electronics and Information Systems, Akita Prefectural University,
84-4 Ebinokuchi, Tsuchiya, Yuri-Honjo, Akita, 015-0055, Japan
{liye,ygwang}@usst.edu.cn, xuli@akita-pu.ac.jp,
xmxu@mail.usst.edu.cn

Abstract. The combination of multiple classifiers is one of the important topics in recent pattern recognition research. It is deemed that the diversity among the classifiers is a key issue in classifier combination. There are different diversity measures presented in the literature. In this paper, we first analyze several measures based on the oracle outputs of base classifiers while majority vote is taken as the combination method. Afterwards, we propose a new measure which overcomes the defects of the diversity measures analyzed. In order to illustrate the effectiveness of the proposed measure, a genetic algorithm based ensemble learning method is designed and compared on some UCI standard datasets to Bagging and Adaboost. The simulation shows that the proposed ensemble learning method gains better generalization performance over Bagging and Adaboost.

Keywords: pattern recognition, classifier fusion/combination, ensemble learning, diversity measure, genetic algorithm, majority vote.

1 Introduction

Classifier fusion means to train multiple classifiers and then combine their predictions in order to improve the classification performance in pattern recognition problems. It originates from the ground-breaking work of Hansen and Salamon [1] and afterwards has been well established as a research area. Ensemble learning usually comprises of two procedures, i.e. construction of base classifiers, and combination of the classifiers. By using the term "classifier fusion" one tends to focus mainly on how to combine the classifiers more effectively.

In classifier fusion, the classifiers need to be diverse in order to make some improvement [2-4]. That is, the classifiers should make errors on different objects. In classical ensemble learning algorithms such as Bagging [5] and Boosting [6], diversity is usually acquired by training the base classifiers on different sample subsets. In Bagging, the sample subsets are generated by resampling the training data with replacement. In Boosting, the sampling distribution is updated and the likelihood for objects misclassified by the previously generated base classifier is increased. While

F.L. Wang et al. (Eds.): CMSP 2012, CCIS 346, pp. 396–403, 2012.
© Springer-Verlag Berlin Heidelberg 2012

these algorithms seek diversity implicitly, many other algorithms use various statistics to qualify the diversity among base classifiers. Especially in selective ensemble learning methods, certain diversity measure is usually needed in order to select proper base classifiers to construct an ensemble with good generalization performance.

There are different diversity measures presented in the literature. Some of them are defined on the measurement level of base classifiers' outputs such as the percentage correct diversity measure [7] and the measure of fuzziness [8], while many other measures are based on the oracle outputs of base classifiers [1,3,9-16]. The measures usually can be categorized into either pairwise [9-12] or non-pairwise ones [1,3,7,8,13-16]. There are lots of studies on the relation between the ensemble performance and these measures [17-21]. Though some of the studies tends to conclude that the measures are naturally ineffective [17,18], there are proven connections between the diversity and the generalization performance of the ensemble.

In this paper, several popular diversity measures based on oracle outputs of base classifiers are investigated while taking majority vote as the combination method. We then introduce a new measure which overcomes the defect of them. In order to illustrate the effectiveness of the proposed measure, experiments are conducted by comparing a genetic algorithm based ensemble learning method, which uses the measure as the fitness function, to Bagging and Adaboost.

2 Analysis on Diversity Measures

2.1 Diversity Measures

1) Q-statistic [9]: Let $\mathbf{Z} = \{\mathbf{z}_1, \cdots, \mathbf{z}_N\}, z_j \in \mathfrak{R}^n$ be a labeled dataset and D_i be a classifier with the output of it being a binary vector $\mathbf{y}_i = [y_{1,i}, \cdots, y_{N,i}]^T$ ($i = 1, \cdots, L$) where $y_{j,i} = 1$, if D_i recognizes correctly object $\mathbf{z}_j$, and 0, otherwise. Then the Q-statistic for two classifiers D_i and D_k is defined as

$$Q_{i,k} = (N^{11}N^{00} - N^{01}N^{10}) / (N^{11}N^{00} + N^{01}N^{10}).$$ (1)

where N^{ab} is the number of objects for which $y_{j,i} = a$ and $y_{j,k} = b$. For a set of base classifiers, the averaged Q-statistic over all pairs of classifiers is

$$Q_{av} = \frac{2}{L(L-1)} \sum_{i=1}^{L-1} \sum_{k=i+1}^{L} Q_{i,k}.$$ (2)

2) Disagreement Measure [10]: This measure is the proportion of the objects on which one classifier is correct and the other is incorrect, i.e.,

$$Dis_{i,k} = (N^{10} + N^{01}) / N.$$ (3)

3) Double Fault [11]: This measure is the ratio between the number of objects misclassified by both classifiers and the total number of objects.

$$DF_{i,k} = N^{00} / N .$$ (4)

4) Correlation Coefficient [12]: The correlation between two base classifier outputs is defined as follows

$$\rho_{i,k} = (N^{11}N^{00} - N^{01}N^{10}) / \sqrt{(N^{11} + N^{10})(N^{01} + N^{00})(N^{11} + N^{01})(N^{10} + N^{00})} .$$ (5)

5) Entropy Measure: The measure is defined as

$$E = \frac{1}{N} \sum_{j=1}^{N} \frac{1}{(L - \lceil L/2 \rceil)} \min\{l(\mathbf{z}_j), L - l(\mathbf{z}_j)\},$$ (6)

where $l(\mathbf{z}_j)$ denotes the number of classifiers that correctly recognize $\mathbf{z}_j$.

6) Kohavi-Wolpert Variance: The measure is derived from the decomposition formula proposed in [14] as

$$KW = \frac{1}{NL^2} \sum_{j=1}^{N} l(\mathbf{z}_j)(L - l(\mathbf{z}_j)) .$$ (7)

7) Measure of Difficulty [1]: Let X be a random variable taking values in $\{0/L, 1/L, \cdots, 1\}$ and denoting the proportion of classifiers that correctly classify an object drawn randomly from the distribution of the problem. The measure of difficulty is defined as the variance of X. Diverse teams of base classifiers will have small variance.

$$\theta = \mathrm{var}(X)$$ (8)

8) Generalized Measure [15]: Let Y be a random variable denoting the proportion of classifiers out of L that fail on a randomly drawn object $\mathbf{x} \in \Re^n$. Denote by p_i the probability that $Y = i/L$ and by $p(i)$ the probability that i randomly chosen classifiers will fail on a randomly chosen $\mathbf{x}$. The generalized diversity measure is

$$GD = 1 - p(2) / p(1) ,$$ (9)

where $p(1) = \sum_{i=1}^{L} \frac{i}{L} p_i$ and $p(2) = \sum_{i=1}^{L} \frac{i}{L} \frac{i-1}{(L-1)} p_i$.

9) Coincident Fault Diversity [15]: This measure is a modification of the generalized diversity measure.

$$CFD = \begin{cases} 0 & p_0 = 1 \\ \frac{1}{1 - p_0} \sum_{i=1}^{L} \frac{L-i}{L-1} p_i & p_0 < 1 \end{cases} .$$ (10)

2.2   Case Study

Suppose that there are 3 base classifiers in the ensemble. We consider several representative cases as shown in Fig. 1.

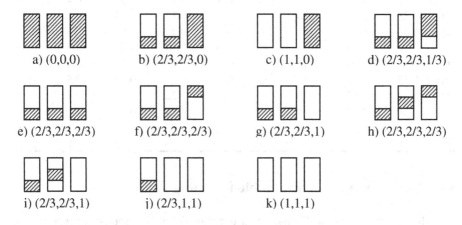

a) (0,0,0)   b) (2/3,2/3,0)   c) (1,1,0)   d) (2/3,2/3,1/3)

e) (2/3,2/3,2/3)   f) (2/3,2/3,2/3)   g) (2/3,2/3,1)   h) (2/3,2/3,2/3)

i) (2/3,2/3,1)   j) (2/3,1,1)   k) (1,1,1)

Fig. 1. Case study of the diversity measures, supposing that the ensemble comprises of 3 base classifiers. The shade stands for the part of objects misclassified and the number in the parentheses denotes the classification accuracy of each base classifier.

The values of the diversity measures can be calculated according to the formulas listed in the precedent section and the results are shown in Table 1. The up/down arrow in the table means that the bigger/smaller value the measure has, the more diverse the base classifiers are. From the table, we can get the following observations.

1. The values of E and KW are proportional to those of Dis_{av}, while the change of θ is very similar to that of ρ. In fact, it is pointed out by Kuncheva [17] that KW differs from Dis_{av} only by a coefficient. We imagine that other measures may have similar internal relation between them.
2. None of the measures can differentiate all the cases. For example, Q_{av} can not differentiate case d) and f), nor can it differentiate case g) and j). Though these cases are obviously different, Q_{av} takes the same value for them.
3. All the diversity measures except DF_{av} is irrelevant to the accuracies of the base classifiers.

Due to the defect of the discussed diversity measures as described in observation 2, one can not expect too much for obtaining an accurate description of the practical diversity among the base classifiers by them.

Table 1. The values of the discussed diversity measures for the cases described in Fig. 1

	$Q_{av}(\downarrow)$	$Dis_{av}(\uparrow)$	$DF_{av}(\downarrow)$	$P_{av}(\downarrow)$	$E(\uparrow)$	$KW(\uparrow)$	$\theta(\downarrow)$	$GD(\uparrow)$	$CFD(\uparrow)$
a)	1	0	1	-0.5	0	0	0	0	0
b)	0.11	0.44	0.33	0.17	0.67	0.15	0.10	0.4	0.67
c)	-0.33	0.67	0	-0.5	1	0.22	0	1	1
d)	-0.33	0.67	0.11	-0.33	1	0.22	0.03	0.75	0.83
e)	1	0	0.33	1	0	0	0.22	0	0
f)	-0.33	0.44	0.11	0	0.67	0.15	0.07	0.67	0.75
g)	0.56	0.22	0.11	0.17	0.33	0.07	0.10	0.5	0.5
h)	-1	0.67	0	-0.5	1	0.22	0	1	1
i)	-0.11	0.44	0	-0.33	0.67	0.15	0.03	1	1
j)	0.56	0.22	0	-0.33	0.33	0.07	0.03	1	1
k)	1	0	0	-0.5	0	0	0	1	0

3   New Measure for Ensemble Learning

Though it is argued that a diversity measure should not be another estimate for the classification accuracy [2,18], we think it is important and even necessary to take the classification accuracy into consideration. The diversity measure should be either positive or negative proportional to the generalization performance of the ensemble; otherwise, it is of no use for evaluating the performance of the base classifiers in the ensemble or the ensemble itself. Moreover, a diversity measure without considering the classification accuracy should still be used together with a certain measure concerning classification accuracy. Nevertheless, it is very difficult to make a tradeoff between the diversity and the accuracy. The 'good' diversity and 'bad' diversity proposed in [20] are also in line with this idea.

In this paper, we propose a new measure as follows where both the diversity and the accuracy are considered

$$DA = 1 - sqrt\left(\frac{2}{L(L-1)}\sum_{i=1}^{L-1}\sum_{k=i+1}^{L}\left(\frac{N_{i,k}^{00}}{N}\right)^2\right) - sqrt\left(\frac{1}{N}\sum_{j=1}^{N}\left(\frac{L-l(\mathbf{z}_j)}{L}\right)^2\right). \tag{11}$$

While the base classifiers should make errors on different objects, the double fault measure provides a way to evaluate this aspect. The second term in the proposed measure is similar to the double fault measure in that both of them are calculated based on the number of objects misclassified by both base classifiers. However, this term adopts the form of mean squared value in order to suppress large difference among the numbers of misclassified objects by each base classifier pair. That is, a large difference may deteriorate the performance of the ensemble.

On the other hand, for misclassified objects, the less the number of base classifiers misclassifying them, the more diverse the ensemble is. This idea introduces the third term in the proposed measure which also takes the form of mean squared value.

These two terms relate to each other to some extent. In some cases if the number of objects misclassified by each classifier pair is low, the third term would also take a low value; and vice versa. That is, both of them tend to be of low values when the base classifiers make errors on different objects and hence the intersections of the sets of objects misclassified individually by each classifier would have few objects. The difference between the terms is that the second one pairwisely evaluating the similarity between each pair of base classifiers while the third evaluates the similarity among all the base classifiers. Besides, the third term is helpful for choosing more accurate classifiers when the second term takes the same value for different ensembles.

The proposed measure will have a larger value if the base classifiers are more diverse and more accurate. The maximum of the new measure is 1 when each base classifier can recognize all the objects correctly.

Table 2 shows the calculation results of the proposed measure on the cases in Fig. 1. Here we ignore the results for from case a) to d) due to the fact that when constructing an ensemble, the accuracy of any base classifier should at least be better than 50% [1]. The measure values for from case e) to k) are monotonic increasing, which has an obvious relation to the accuracy of the ensemble. As expected, the proposed measure can obtain different values for case h), i), j) and k).

Table 2. The values of the proposed measure for the cases described in Fig. 1.

	a)	b)	c)	d)	e)	f)	g)	h)	i)	j)	k)
Div($\downarrow$)	-1	0.03	0.67	0.34	0.09	0.38	0.42	0.67	0.73	0.81	1

4   Genetic Algorithm Based Ensemble Learning

Genetic algorithm as a global randomized search technique is a powerful tool for solving optimization problems. In this section, a binary genetic algorithm based ensemble learning method (GAEN) where the proposed measure is used as the fitness function is designed and compared to Bagging and Adaboost.M1. The method starts by creating an initial population of chromosomes with each chromosome stands for a collection of based classifiers to be combined by majority vote. Each classifier occupies one bit in the chromosome. In each iteration, the fitness of the chromosomes are evaluated by the proposed measure and then the genetic operations are performed according to the fitness of the chromosomes including Roulette wheel selection, simple one-point crossover and binary mutation. The iteration continues until a stopping criterion is reached.

The experiments are conducted on six UCI benchmark datasets. Support vector machines (SVM) with radial basis function kernels are used as the base classifiers. The parameters of SVMs for Bagging and Adaboost.M1, i.e. the regularization parameter C and the kernel parameter γ, are chosen by grid search. That is, 10-fold cross-validation is conducted with different parameter combinations of C and γ, which increase exponentially in the grid, and the combination with best cross-validation accuracy is chosen. In order to enhance the diversity, the parameters of

SVMs in GAEN are obtained by injecting randomness into the parameters for Bagging and Adaboost.M1. Moreover, the training dataset for a base classifier is obtained by performing twice sequential resampling. Parameter settings for the GA portion include a selection rate of 0.1, a crossover rate of 0.9, mutation rates of 0.1, and a population size of 20. Each chromosome comprises 11 base classifiers. For each dataset, we do 10 standard 5-fold cross validation and the average classification accuracies are shown in Table 3.

Table 3. Comparison of the genetic algorithm based ensemble learning method to Bagging and Adaboost.M1.

Datasets	Bupa	Heart	Iris	Sonar	WBC	Wine
Bagging	72.75	83.63	95.73	78.56	96.76	97.58
Adaboost.M1	72.43	83.04	95.33	78.85	96.33	97.19
GAEN	72.81	83.89	96.13	78.99	96.88	97.64

As can be seen from the above table, GAEN gains highest classification accuracies for all the datasets. Since we only use the proposed measure as the fitness function, without explicitly including any other measure of classification accuracy, the experimental results show that compared to the other measures discussed in section 2, the proposed measure has a stronger relation to the accuracy.

5   Conclusion

Though there are many diversity measures which are based on the oracle outputs of base classifiers, none of them possesses enough capability to differentiate all the cases where the diversities are definitely different. Moreover, these measures should be used with some kind of accuracy measure when constructing an ensemble while it is very hard to make a good tradeoff between the accuracy and the diversity. These are the reasons why so many studies on diversity measures seldom find any valuable relation between the measures and the generalization performance of ensemble. Therefore, it is necessary to take the classification accuracy into consideration when designing a good measure. The measure proposed in this paper shows its usefulness in constructing good ensembles.

Acknowledgements. This paper is supported by National Natural Science Foundation of China (61074087), Innovation Program of Shanghai Municipal Education Commission of China (12ZZ144), and Innovation Ability Construction Project for Teachers of School of Optical-Electrical and Computer Engineering of University of Shanghai Science and Technology (GDCX-Y1111).

References

1. Hansen, L.K., Salamon, P.: Neural network ensembles. IEEE Transactions on Pattern Analysis and Machine Intelligence 12(10), 993–1001 (1990)
2. Kuncheva, L.I., Skurichina, M., Duin, R.P.W.: An experimental study on diversity for bagging and boosting with linear classifiers. Information Fusion 3(4), 245–258 (2002)
3. Dietterich, T.: An Experimental Comparison of Three Methods for Constructing Ensembles of Decision Trees: Bagging, Boosting, and Randomization. Machine Learning 40(2), 1–22 (2000)
4. Cunningham, P., Carney, J.: Diversity versus Quality in Classification Ensembles Based on Feature Selection. In: Lopez de Mantaras, R., Plaza, E. (eds.) ECML 2000. LNCS (LNAI), vol. 1810, pp. 109–116. Springer, Heidelberg (2000)
5. Breiman, L.: Bagging Predictors. Machine Learning 24(2), 123–140 (1996)
6. Freund, Y., Schapire, R.E.: A Decision-Theoretic Generalization of On-Line Learning and an Application to Boosting. Journal of Computer and System Sciences 55(1), 119–139 (1997)
7. Banfield, R., Hall, L., Bowyer, K., Kegelmeyer, W.: A new ensemble diversity measure applied to thinning ensembles. In: Proceedings of the 4th International Conference on Multiple Classifier Systems, pp. 159–159 (2003)
8. Golestani, A., Azimi, J., Analoui, M., Kangavari, M.: A New Efficient Fuzzy Diversity Measure in Classifier Fusion. In: IADIS International Conference of Applied Computing, pp. 722–726 (2007)
9. Yule, G.U.: On the association of attributes in statistics. Philosophical Transactions of the Royal Society of London, Series A 194, 257–319 (1900)
10. Ho, T.K.: The random subspace method for constructing decision forests. IEEE Transactions on Pattern Analysis and Machine Intelligence 20(8), 832–844 (1998)
11. Giacinto, G., Roli, F.: Design of effective neural network ensembles for image classification purposes. Image and Vision Computing 19(9-10), 699–707 (2001)
12. Conover, W.J.: Statistical Methods for Rates and Proportions. Technometrics 16(2), 326–327 (1974)
13. Toussaint, G.: Bibliography on estimation of misclassification. IEEE Transactions on Information Theory 20(4), 472–479 (1974)
14. Kohavi, R., Wolpert, D.: Bias Plus Variance Decomposition for Zero-One Loss Functions. In: Proc. 13th Int. Conference on Machine Learning, pp. 275–283. Morgan Kaufmann (1996)
15. Partridge, D., Krzanowski, W.: Software diversity: practical statistics for its measurement and exploitation. Information and Software Technology 39(10), 707–717 (1997)
16. Zenobi, G., Cunningham, P.: Using Diversity in Preparing Ensembles of Classifiers Based on Different Feature Subsets to Minimize Generalization Error. In: Flach, P.A., De Raedt, L. (eds.) ECML 2001. LNCS (LNAI), vol. 2167, pp. 576–587. Springer, Heidelberg (2001)
17. Kuncheva, L.I., Whitaker, C.J.: Measures of diversity in classifier ensembles and their relationship with the ensemble accuracy. Machine Learning 51(2), 181–207 (2003)
18. Tang, E.K., Suganthan, P.N., Yao, X.: An analysis of diversity measures. Machine Learning 65(1), 247–271 (2006)
19. Kapp, M.N., Sabourin, R., Maupin, P.: An empirical study on diversity measures and margin theory for ensembles of classifiers. In: 2007 10th International Conference on Information Fusion, pp. 1–8 (2007)
20. Brown, G., Kuncheva, L.I.: "Good" and "Bad" Diversity in Majority Vote Ensembles. In: El Gayar, N., Kittler, J., Roli, F. (eds.) MCS 2010. LNCS, vol. 5997, pp. 124–133. Springer, Heidelberg (2010)
21. Chung, Y.S., Hsu, D.F., Tang, C.Y.: On the relationships among various diversity measures in multiple classifier systems. In: Proceedings of 2008 International Symposium on Parallel Architectures, Algorithms, and Networks, pp. 184–190 (2008)

A Transformation Algorithm for CMMB Shadows Removal

Jun Yang and Shi-jiao Zhu

School of Computer and Information Engineering, Shanghai University of Electric Power,
Shanghai 200090, China
yangjun@shiep.edu.cn, zhusj707@hotmail.com

Abstract. Shadow is a physical phenomena observed in videos and some wireless application. This paper addresses the problem of shadow removal from videos in CMMB application. The approach proposed here uses image's properties in high-dimensional space for improve image's quality which is human-vision method. The method first uses Gabor filters to find some clues of an image and then performs produce of special kernels to generate some image-points from original image. Then through performing computing in feature space to find similar ones, we reduce the effects of shadow edges in the geometry processing. Experimental results prove the accuracy of our approach in terms of improving video quality in CMMB application.

Keywords: shadow removal, CMMB, image quality.

1 Introduction

CMMB(China Mobile Multimedia Broadcasting) application has been developed and applied in China. This paper brings an algorithm for videos blindness shadow removal in CMMB application [1]. This framework is part motivated by the task of improving end-user quality video. Toward this end we construct a system which achieves shadows removing for any video context.

It turns out to be the case that human judgment of image across different people is not uniform. User's visual effect could match well in terms of their ability to pick out interesting area, but not in term of uniform modal. For this reason, design method that can improve image quality not based on special modal remains a challenging task. For CMMB channels, videos, composed by sequence images according to time, are often disturbed from source to end. For an image shadow removal problem, algorithms can be classified as property-based, model-based and Retinex method. For model-based techniques rely on models representing a priori knowledge of the scene including geometry and objects. Property-based techniques indentify shadows by using features such as geometry, brightness or color. In some cases, Model-based approaches suits to special situations and it shows less robustness than Property-based method with dynamic changes of scene and illumination condition [2][3][4]. For method of Retinex , Ron Kimmel [5] proposed a variational model for the Retinex theory. Michael Nielsen and Claus B Madsen introduced a new concept within shadow segmentation for

F.L. Wang et al. (Eds.): CMSP 2012, CCIS 346, pp. 404–411, 2012.

usage in shadow removal and augmentation through on construction of an alpha over-lay shadow model [6]. A. Leone, C. Distante [7] presented shadow detection of mov-ing objects in visual surveillance environment by evaluating the similarity between little textured patches, since shadow regions present same textural characteristics in each frame and in the corresponding adaptive background model. The Retinex me-thod can be considered as a statistic method which exploits some statistical properties of the shadow borders after they have been enhanced through a simple edge gradient based operation [8].

In this paper, we present a solution to solve the image shadow problem in view of point calculation of images in the high dimensional space. The remainder of this pa-per is organized as follows: features and algorithm are introduced in section 2 and 3. In section 4, experimentation results are presented and the concluding remarks are given in the last section.

2   Features

Due to its biological similarity to human vision system, Gabor wavelets have been widely used in object recognition applications like fingerprint recognition, character recognition [9], etc. The Gabor filter is basically a Gaussian (with variances sx and sy along x and y axes respectively) modulated by a complex sinusoid (with centre fre-quencies U and V along x and y axes respectively) described by the following formu-las. Gabor is modulated by a complex sinusoid which can be rotated in the x-y plan by an theta. Symbolized as x' , and y' .

$$x' = x*\cos(\text{theta})+y*\sin(\text{theta}) \tag{1}$$

$$y' = x*\cos(\text{theta})-y*\sin(\text{theta}) \tag{2}$$

The even symmetric Gabor is describe as

$$G(x,y,\text{theta},f) = \exp(-\frac{1}{2}[(\frac{x'}{\text{sx}})^2 + (\frac{y'}{\text{sy}})^2])\cos(2*\text{pi}*\text{f}*x') \tag{3}$$

where s_x and s_y is variances along x and y-axes respectively, f is the frequency of the sinusoidal function. Theta gives the orientation of Gabor filter. By changing the radial frequency and the orientation, the filter makes different target features. The resulting of spatial domain by Gabor functions is shown in Fig.1 a), b), c) and d) respectively.

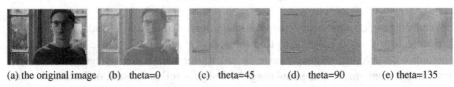

(a) the original image   (b)   theta=0   (c)   theta=45   (d)   theta=90   (e) theta=135

Fig. 1. The output filtered CAPTCHAR image where f= 6.8182

For vector in feature space, vector-valued image and its distribution is mainly due to its present in space. The definition of special exponent distribution is observed in the vector space. For Gabor space, the different channels give special distribution in high dimensional space. The distance between vectors is defined as follow.

$$d_{i,j} = \sqrt{\sum_{i=1}^{M} \sum_{j=1}^{M} \| x_i - y_j \|^2} \qquad (4)$$

where x_i is a value in vector X. Based on this measure, distribution between vectors in Gabor space is computed and filtered.

This paper use Gabor features for image representation. In this paper we focus our attention on the algorithm of removing image shadow. This algorithm requires the relative points of image in a high dimensional space. By introducing this idea to the points-based method, we present a more suitable method which has the advantage of blindness image shadow removing process.

3 Algorithm

For an image which size is M×N, we denote it with $f(x,y)$ as a point in high dimensional space, where 0<x<M,0<y<N. In order to remove the shadows in an image, we should find the points distribution of image in the high dimensional space based on original image.

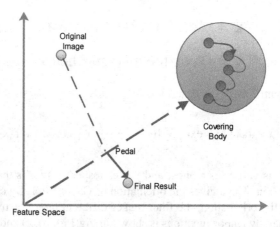

Fig. 2. Points calculation

According to Retinex theory, the brightness degree of image depends on its surface light reflecting ability. In order to find the reflect parameters, we use smooth kernel functions to convolute original image in order to generate new image points in the high dimensional space. For simulating the image's reflection and diffusion, we can define different kernel h to affect original image with operator $f*h$. The generating image points set is used to embody reflect ability. Since same class samples have same characteristic in the high dimensional space [10], points from generating $f*h$ are used to detect the image point which has the most reflecting ability of an original image. According to the theory of space geometry, the shortest distance from a point to a vector is the foot of the perpendicular. We calculate the foot of the original image point to generate image set which can represent the original image. The point transformation scheme in the high dimensional space is shown in the Fig.2. For points in the high dimensional space, we can symbolize points translate route in 2D coordinates as shown in Fig.3. Point set is generated by original image, $f\perp$ is the foot of an original image to point set, f' is the last image which is generated by the foot point and some little value adjustment. This scheme contains points calculation based on an original image. Although the kernel is not appeared in the figure, it is clearly indicated by itself and the reference points are generated along with the kernel iteration process.

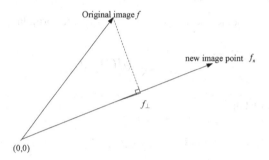

Fig. 3. Image at Pedal

The point calculation process is described as bellow.

Step 1. Operation of generating point set.
Using smooth function h_i, such as Gaussian function, to make convolution with image f, where i is number of the kernels.

$$\begin{cases} f_0 = f \\ f_{i+1} = f_i \times (1-\delta) + \delta \times [\log(f_0 + 1) - \log(f_i \times h_{i+p} + 1)] \\ \delta = 1/(1 + \exp(-i)) \\ i = 0...n \end{cases} \tag{5}$$

Formula.5 gives the generation process of new image point f_{i+1}, where δ the ith kernel coefficient weight and reflection ability is is symbolized as $\log(f_0 + 1)$-$\log(f_i * h_{i+p} + 1)$. After performing above procedure, new point is generated based on original image. In respect that the convolution operation can be performed by Gabor filter and n <10 usually, therefore, the computation complexity is about $O(N \log_2 N)$.

Step 2. Foot of original image to Point Set

The new image point f_n and its vector $\overrightarrow{f_n O}$ are obtained from the point set generated by step 1, and then the foot of original f to the vector $\overrightarrow{f_n O}$ can be calculated by Euclid distance as bellow.

$$d\,(X\,,Y\,) = \sqrt{\sum_{i=1}^{m} (x_i - y_i)^2} \qquad (6)$$

In formula 6, X , Y is the point in m dimensional space. Fig.3 gives the foot calculation.

The calculation process is described as below:

a)   Calculating the distance between f and $\overrightarrow{f_n O}$ by the formula

$$D(\overrightarrow{Of_T}) = d(f, f_n)/(d(\overrightarrow{Of_n}, \overrightarrow{Of_n})^2) \qquad (7)$$

b)   Calculate the distance $\overrightarrow{Of_n}$;

$$D(\overrightarrow{Of_n}) = d(\overrightarrow{Of_n}, \overrightarrow{Of_n}) \qquad (8)$$

c)   Get the coefficient parameter ;

$$coef = D(\overrightarrow{Of_T})/D(\overrightarrow{Of_n})^2 \qquad (9)$$

d)   Get vector f_T .

$$f_T = (f_n\text{-O})*coef \qquad (10)$$

Here f_T is the root of an original image to point set.

Step3. Further remove shadow image

In order to enhance the image, here we use the neighborhood points of $f(i, j)$ to tag some possible shadows in the image by formula 11.

$$\begin{cases} \overline{m} = 1/k \times \sum_{x=i-1}^{i+1} \sum_{y=j-1}^{j+1} f(x,y), k = 9 \\ \\ Conv(x,y) = \sqrt{\sum_{x=i-1}^{i+1} \sum_{y=j-1}^{j+1} (f(x,y) - \overline{m})^2} \end{cases} \qquad (11)$$

In formula 11, the original image is filtered, and new $Conv(x, y)$ is generated. We define two threshold value T_1, T_2 and use matrix map to tag shadow area by formula 12.

$$shadowmap(x,y) = \begin{cases} 1 & f(x,y) < T_1 \, and \, conv(x,y) < T_2 \\ 0 & others \end{cases} \qquad (12)$$

When $shadowmap(x, y)$ equals zero, it indicates shadow area in the image. For an image which gray level value range from 1 to 255, we can enlarge its value of shadows to make it clear. An image can be clearer after the process described as follows.

a)   initialize $x = 1, y = 1$;

b)   for next x,y, if shadow mapping value equals zero , execute the calculation:

$$f_{\perp}(x,y) = \alpha * |f(x,y) - f_{\perp}(x,y)|, 0 < \alpha < 1$$

if x,y is not the ending of width and height, return to b), else the process is finished.

After the process, the root image $f_{\perp}$ will be enhanced further and it is more suitable for human's view point.

4   Experiments

In this section, a prototype system is developed by MATLAB. The test video images which having shadows are collected from different video clips (encoded by H264) are performed in the same parameters $T_1=128$, $T_2=64$, $\alpha = 0.9$ f= 6.8182, theta=0.

The comparison results between the point calculation method and Retinex method are shown in Fig.4. The results indicate that the effect of shadow elimination from image based on point calculation in the high dimensional space is better than Retinex method and it is more robust for different type images. In the point calculation method, it generates some relative image points in high dimensional space which provide more information when processes blindness shadow in the image and the foot point which presents a new image in high space is the most similar one to original image. From Fig.4, we can notice Retinex result has some mosaics because Retinex method

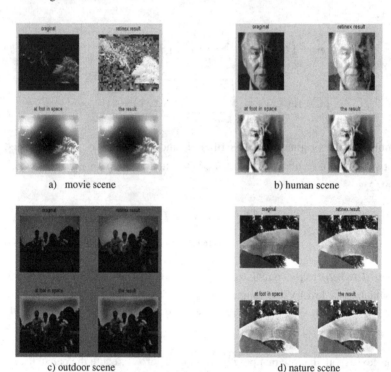

a) movie scene   b) human scene

c) outdoor scene   d) nature scene

Fig. 4. Comparative results for CMMB Videos

only uses light model to eliminate shadow area in an image which can not get more reference to some relevant information of the original image. Therefore, the result of Retinex method can not give satisfied vision effect of an image with blindness shadow.

5   Conclusions

In this paper, we present a solution for improving CMMB video's quality by removing shadow effects. The contributions of this paper can be summarized as follows:

(1) Geometry method is used to find similar features in high-dimensional space. The method is blindness with no prior knowledge. The proposed method is robust.

(2) Combined with Gabor filters, we can use multi-scale analysis which can improve speed. Unlike the previous methods, we do not make much assumption on shadows' properties.

Experimental results indicate our method is superior in terms of accuracy, robustness, and stability in shadow elimination. The novelty of this solution is the direct embedding of finding reflecting parameters of image using points in high dimensional space. More studies in the aspect of basic theory in high-dimensional space inspired by biology should be invested in future.

Acknowledgement. This work is supported by National Natural Science Fund (61073189). The authors are grateful for the anonymous reviewers who made constructive comments.

References

[1] Ren, J., Zhao, L.: Innovation in China's Mobile Multimedia Broadcasting Service. In: Service Science: Research and Innovations in the Service Economy, Part 1, pp. 33–35 (2012)

[2] Prati, A., Mikic, I., Trivedi, M., Cucchiara, R.: Detecting moving shadows: algorithms and evaluation. IEEE Transactions on Pattern Analysis and Machine Intelligence 7, 918–923 (2003)

[3] Wang, J.M., Chung, Y.C., Chang, C.L., Chen, S.W.: Shadow detection and removal for traffic images. In: Proc. IEEE Int. Conf. Networking, Sensing and Control, vol. 1(1), pp. 649–654 (2004)

[4] Bevilacqua, A.: A Novel Shadow Detection Algorithm for Real Time Visual Surveillance Applications. Image Analysis and Recognition, 906–917 (2006)

[5] Kimmel, R., Elad, M., Shaked, D., Keshet, R.: A variational framework for Retinex. International Journal of Computer Vision 52, 7–23 (2003)

[6] Nielsen, M., Madsen, C.B.: Segmentation of Soft Shadows Based on a Daylight- and Penumbra Model. In: Gagalowicz, A., Philips, W. (eds.) MIRAGE 2007. LNCS, vol. 4418, pp. 341–352. Springer, Heidelberg (2007)

[7] Leone, A., Distante, C.: Shadow detection for moving objects based on texture analysis. Pattern Recogn. 40, 1222–1233 (2007)

[8] Prati, A., Mikic, I., Trivedi, M.M., Cucchiara, R.A.C.R.: Detecting moving shadows: algorithms and evaluation. IEEE Transactions on Pattern Analysis and Machine Intelligence 25, 918–923 (2003)

[9] Bozhokin, S.V.: Continuous wavelet transform and exactly solvable model of nonstationary signals. Technical Physics 57(7), 900–906 (2012)

[10] Wang, S., Jiangliang, L.: Geometrical Learning, descriptive geometry, and biometric pattern recognition. Neuron Computing 67, 9–28 (2005)

An Implementation of Real-Time Audio Monitoring in Network Camera

Xuehao Yuan[1,2], Yumeng Zhang[1,2], and Hui Li[1,2,*]

[1] Shenzhen Key Lab of Cloud Computing & Application, Shenzhen Graduated School,
Peking University, Shenzhen, China 518055
[2] Engineering Lab of Converged Network Technology, Shenzhen Graduated School,
Peking University, Shenzhen, China 518055
yuanxuehao@sz.pku.edu.cn, zhangyumeng06@gmail.com,
lih64@pkusz.edu.cn

Abstract. Basis on the network camera, audio encoding and RTMP protocol, an audio module in network camera based on Ambarella A5s platform is designed and implemented to meet the increasing need of real-time audio in safety monitoring and live broadcast field. After audio captured by ALSA API and encoded by AAC API, audio data and video data are added timestamps to respectively for synchronization and then transmitted to web server in the form of RTMP packet. This solution can efficiently make up for the deficiency of traditional camera in audio capture, encoding and network transmission.

Keywords: network camera, audio, A5s, ALSA, AAC, RTMP.

1 Introduction

Network camera [1] is a product of new generation combining traditional camera and network video technology and a low-cost solution for remote audio and video transmission. It has obvious advantages over traditional analog camera such as high definition, high integration and low total cost of ownership. Additionally, networking, digitization and intelligence also make network camera a better choice.

Audio information is becoming of increasing importance to some applications of network camera rapidly such as audio evidence in security monitoring system and live broadcast. For analog camera, audio-supported function must be implemented only by means of extra audio wiring. However, network camera can capture audio signal through front-end audio device, synchronize digitized and compressed audio data with video data, and finally transfer audio and video data to RTMP server through network. Real-time audio and video situation can be monitored by browser or client software very conveniently, as displayed in Fig.1.

---

* Corresponding author.

F.L. Wang et al. (Eds.): CMSP 2012, CCIS 346, pp. 412–419, 2012.

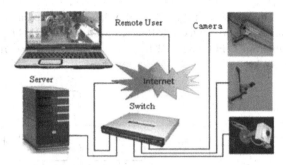

Fig. 1. Network Camera Topology

2 Solution and Principles

2.1 A Solution to Network Camera

In this paper, a network camera solution is adopted which is based on Ambarella A5s platform and embedded real-time operating system Linux. A5s is supported with a hardware reference design, SDK (software developer's kit) and full camera software application. This solution [2] realizes multimedia processing containing audio and video capture, compression and network transmission in single board by using a high-integrated chip which integrates an image sensor pipeline, a HD (High Definition) H.264 video Codec (DSP) and a 528MHz ARM11 processor. The hardware frame-work [2] of the whole system is illustrated in Fig. 2.

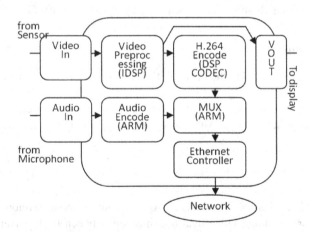

Fig. 2. Hardware Overview

As a consequence of high complexity of H.264 encoding, video encoding is im-plemented by DSP hardware, which enhances encoding efficiency greatly and guaran-tees that ARM11 processor can run application programs efficiently such as audio encoding and network transmission, both focused on in this paper. Audio subsystem framework [3] is demonstrated in Fig. 3. Audio data is captured and stored in FIFO (First In First Out) by audio device AK4642 controlled by ARM11 processor. Then audio data is read from FIFO, encoded by ARM11 processor and finally stored in buffer queue in DRAM。

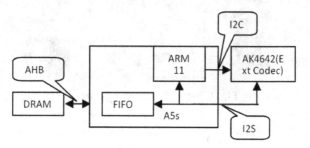

Fig. 3. Audio Subsystem

2.2   AAC

Generally, the audio information captured by audio device is PCM (Pulse Code Modulation) data with high quality but large amount, not suitable for network transmission. As a result, audio data needs to be compressed by AAC [4] encoding in order to decrease the amount of data.

AAC is an encoding method based on filter banks, exploiting masking effects of auditory system to reduce the amount of data [5], which is able to achieve much larger compression ratio than AC-3 and MP3. AAC can get the best tone quality, even matching CD, among all audio coding standards proposed by MPEG.

2.3   Timestamp

Technically, timestamp [6] is the best solution to audio and video synchronization to guarantee the correct playing. A timestamp should be added to each data block according to reference clock while creating a data stream. When played, audio and video data should be taken order with according to timestamp and current reference clock.

2.4   RTMP

RTMP (Real Time Message Protocol) [7] is a private protocol developed by Adobe Systems Inc. for audio and video data transmission between flash player and server. This protocol is established on the foundation of TCP and the default port number is 1935. For RTMP, signaling and media data are called message consisting of one or more chunks. Each chunk is a RTMP packet composed of a variable-sized packet header (1, 4, 8 or 12 bytes) and a packet body with the maximum length of 128 bytes according to reference [7]. Different types of RTMP packets are transmitted interleaved to achieve multiplexing of a single TCP connection.

3   Software Implementation

This solution mainly consists of three parts: audio module, video module and network transmission module. As demonstrated in Fig. 4, the real-time monitoring software application is implemented by creating three threads: AudioDaemon, VideoDaemon and RtmpDaemon on the basis of Linux open source library.

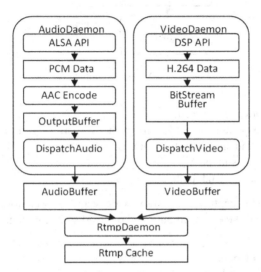

Fig. 4. Software Overview

Thread AudioDaemon and VideoDaemon capture and encode audio and video data respectively (video data encoded by DSP hardware), add timestamps to the encoded audio and video encoded frames and submit them to Thread RtmpDaemon. RtmpDaemon circularly packs data into RTMP packets and delivers them to RTMP server. Data exchange between threads is implemented by reading and writing Buffer queue AudioBuffer and VideoBuffer. With this asynchronous data exchanging mechanism, the influence of sending RTMP packets on AudioDaemon and VideoDaemon can be avoided.

3.1   Implementation of Audio Encoding

3.1.1   Audio Data Capturing

ALSA (Advanced Linux Sound Architecture) [8] used for audio capture, as shown in Fig. 5, consists of a series of kernel drivers, API (application Program Interface) and utilities for Linux audio. ALSA provides an API library called libasound to simplify audio programming.

A typical audio capturing program [9] [10] implemented by calling API functions in libasound is regularly as follows:

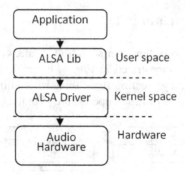

Fig. 5. ALSA Basic Architecture

(1) Open audio device: snd_pcm_open();

(2) Set hardware parameters [11]: snd_pcm_hw_params_set() assigning value to parameter variables and snd_pcm_hw_params() passing parameters to audio device;

(3) Read PCM data: snd_pcm_readi();

(4) Close audio device: snd_pcm_close().

In this way, an audio capturing program with recording function is complete. But actually step (4) won't be executed until audio thread stops running.

3.1.2   Audio Data Encoding

Audio data encoding can be realized mainly by open source software FAAC. But A5s SDK provides an optimized AAC API library called libaacenc [12] with main API functions as follows to compress audio PCM data.

(1)aacenc_setup(&au_aacenc_config): assign the AAC encode control structures "au_aacenc_config" to the internal operation variables to set the correct configurations.

(2)aacenc_open(&au_aacenc_config): allocate the related memories for the AAC before starting the AAC encode.

(3)aacenc_encode(&au_aacenc_config): start the AAC encoding and generate one frame of audio data after setting AAC encode control structure and allocating memories.

3.1.3   Audio Module Design

As illustrated in Fig. 6, audio thread AudioDaemon extracts PCM data captured by audio device from FIFO, calls AAC API functions to encode audio data block by block, adds timestamps to the encoded data and finally dispatches it to AudioBuffer. Typically, aacenc_encode function once called only encodes 1024 PCM samples. Common parameters in ALSA configuration and AAC configuration such as sample rate, channels and sample size must be set identically.

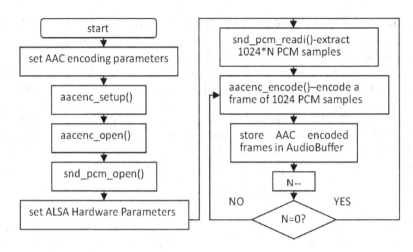

Fig. 6. Audio Module Flow Diagram

3.2   RTMP Transmission Module

When thread RtmpDaemon starts, it will make a handshake with RTMP server firstly and then can deliver RTMP packets to RTMP server. Handshake procedure is described in detail in reference [7].

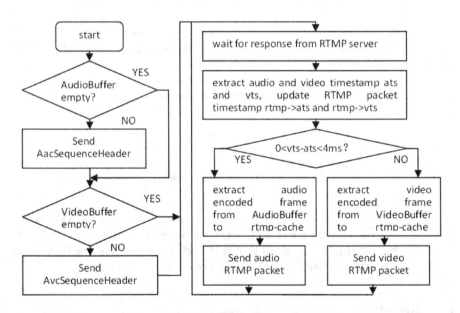

Fig. 7. RTMP Flow Diagram

RTMP transmission can be executed by two steps: firstly sends audio and video data decoding information header and then packs audio and video data into RTMP packets and deliver them interleaved to RTMP server, as illustrated in Fig. 7.

When delivering H.264 and AAC data to RTMP server, RTMP thread also needs to firstly send "AVC sequence header" and "AAC sequence header"[13], both containing important encoding information for decoding correctly. AVC sequence header loads the AVCDecoderConfigurationRecord structure in MPEG-4 AVC (or H.264) standard ISO/IEC-14496-15[14]. AAC sequence header deposits AudioSpecificConfig [5] structure, which is complicated but can be simplified as shown in Table 1 where AAC profile is set to "AAC-LC" and sample rate is set to 44.1 KHz.

Table 1. AudioSpecificConfig

Length	Field	Description
5bit	audioObjectType	Encoding pofile,2 for AAC-LC
4bit	samplingFrequencyIndex	Sample rate,4 for 44.1KHz
4bit	channelConfiguration	Channel number,2
	GASpecificConfig	Including 3 items
1bit	frameLengthFlag	IDCMT window size,0
1bit	dependsOnCoreCoder	Dependent on corecoder,0
1bit	extensionFlag	0 for AAC-LC

Then audio and video data will be packed and sent to RTMP server by RTMP thread. RTMP packet format [13] is introduced in Table 2 (not including RTMP packet header) .

Table 2. RTMP Packet Format

Video Packet

CodecFlag	AVCPacketType	Timestamp	DataStream

Audio Packet

CodecFlag	AACPacketType	Timestamp	DataStream

CodecFlag implies the codec type for audio or video. The value of AVCPacketType indicates the DataStream is AVC sequence header (the first video packet) or encoded video data. Likewise, the value of AACPacketType indicates the DataStream is AAC sequence header (the first audio packet) or encoded audio data.

4   Results

After audio and video data delivered to Adobe RTMP server Red5, client software Red5 publisher [15] is used to test the monitoring effect. The test shows:(1)When audio sample rate is typically set to 44.1 KHz at bit rate 64 kbps per channel, audio and video can be monitored normally and their synchronization performs well. (2)When audio sample rates in ALSA settings and AAC encoding settings are different, sound will be played by publisher at a lower or faster speed than normal. (3)If AAC sequence header is not sent, audio can't be played correctly by publisher. (4)Under the condition of good network status, the whole delay of capturing, encoding and transmitting data can be optimized within 3 seconds.

5   Conclusions

Fundamental principles of Network camera as well as software and hardware framework based on Ambarella A5s platform are briefly analyzed in this paper. Audio module of network camera is implemented independently. Furthermore, RTMP is used to transmit audio and video data to RTMP server Red5 for monitoring test.

Acknowledgements. This work is supported by National Basic Research Program of China 2012CB315904, NSFC (Natural Science Foundation of China) 61179028, Guangdong Natural Science Fund 2011010000923, Shenzhen Basic Research 201005260234A, 201104210120A, Shenzhen Industry 201006110044A.

References

1. Network camera, http://en.wikipedia.org/wiki/Network_camera
2. Ambarella Inc., A5s Flexible Linux Platform (September 16, 2011)
3. Ambarella Inc., A5S-IPC-054-3.1 Application Note- Use Audio (September 16, 2011)
4. Advanced Audio Coding, http://en.wikipedia.org/wiki/Advanced_Audio_Coding
5. ISO/IEC-14496-3, Information technology-Coding of audio-visual objects-Part 3: Audio
6. Timestamp, http://en.wikipedia.org/wiki/Timestamp
7. Rtmp Specification 1.0, Adobe Systems Incorporated (April 2009)
8. Advanced Linux Sound Architecture, http://www.alsaproject.org/
9. Introduction to Sound Programming with ALSA, http://www.linuxjournal.com/article/6735
10. Ambarella Inc., Allen Cao, A5S-IPC-053-0.3 ALSA Develop (Sound)
11. ALSA Hardware Parameters, http://www.alsa-project.org/alsa-doc/alsa-lib/
12. Ambarella Inc., A5S-IPC-074-3.1 AAC_Encode (September 16, 2011)
13. http://www.cnblogs.com/haibindev/archive/2011/12/29/2305712.html
14. ISO/IEC-14496-15, Information technology-Coding of audio-visual objects-Part 15: Advanced Video Coding (AVC) file format
15. http://bashell.sinaapp.com/archives/install-and-config-red5-server-1.html

High-Performance Implementation of Stream Model Based H.264 Video Coding on Parallel Processors

Nan Wu, Mei Wen, Ju Ren, Huayou Su, and Dafei Huang

Computer School, National University of Defense Technology, Changsha, Hunan,
P.R. of China, 410073
nanwu@nudt.edu.cn

Abstract. Model-based design is widely accepted in developing parallel program. Stream model, an emerging model-based programming method, shows surprisingly good efficiency in many compute-intensive domains, especially for complex media processing. On the basis, this paper illustrates how to map the stream H.264 encoder onto concrete parallel processors such as stream processor. Results show that our encoder achieves significant speedup over the original X264 encoder on various programmable architectures.

Keywords: Stream, H.264 coding, real-time, programmable, 1080P HD.

1 Introduction

The H.264 standard, developed by the Video Coding Experts Group (VCEG) and the ISO/IEC Motion Picture Experts Group (MPEG), is widely adopted in applications from high definition living room entertainment (BluRay/ HD-DVD) to Handhold terminals (DVB-H). It can save 25%-45% and 50%-70% of bitrates when compared with MPEG-4 Advanced Simple Profile (ASP) and MPEG-2, respectively. However, the H.264 coding performance comes at the price of significantly increased computational complexity. Especially, real-time encoding of high-definition H.264 video (up to 1080p) is a challenge for most existing programmable processors.

The stream model, an emerging model-based programming method, shows surprisingly good efficiency on many compute-intensive domains especially for Media/Graphic Processing and Scientific Computing [1]. This gives an alternative approach to accelerating applications on programmable processor instead of long-term and expensive dedicated ASIC design.

To meet this goal, we try to implement a streaming high-definition (HD) H.264 encoder. However, the inherent difficulty lies in constructing the initial algorithm representation in the stream model. In this paper, a set of novel streaming techniques for H.264 encoding is presented. Furthermore, we implement a streaming full HD (1080p) H.264 encoder, and evaluate it on multiple programmable processors, including CPU, emerging stream processor (STORM) and GPU. Our results show that the stream code achieves significant speedup over the original X264 code on all processors. In particular, real-time encoding of HD H.264 sequences (up to 1080p) is achieved on STORM and Nvidia GPU.

F.L. Wang et al. (Eds.): CMSP 2012, CCIS 346, pp. 420–427, 2012.
© Springer-Verlag Berlin Heidelberg 2012

2   Stream Model

In the stream model, the data primitive is a stream, an ordered set of data of an arbitrary data type. Operations in the stream model are expressed as operations on entire streams. These operations include *streamload*, *streamstore* and computation in the form of kernels, which operate on one or more input and output stream(s). Moreover, considering execution efficiency on hardware, the stream model does not allow global variables, pointers, function calls, or control-flow constructs other than loops appearing in kernels.

Transforming a regular program to a stream program, which is called streaming requires analyzing the dataflow within the desired algorithm, dividing the data in the program into streams and the computation in the program into kernels. The optimal stream program completely   decouples computation and memory accesses by boosting the memory reads before the computation, and postponing the writes of the live data to memory after the computation. It is therefore possible to effectively overlap computation and memory.

3   Implementation

This section focuses on implementation techniques for modern parallel processors including stream processors and GPUs. Introduction of streaming of X.264 encoder [9] has already been discussed by previous studies [2] in detail, which also indicate that the stream framework is general for multiple architectures.

3.1   Target Architecture

This paper chooses STORM processor [3] as a representative of stream processors for that STORM architecture is typical among architectures of emerging stream processors and data parallel processor such as Imagine, FT64, CELL, ClearSpeed et al. This paper also chooses GTX460 [4] as a representative GPU. It's a very common GPU that contains a lot of stream processor units in the SIMT (Single Instruction Multiple Threads) fashion, partially software managed memory hierarchy. Section 3.2 describes the major tasks of mapping for the Strom processor in detail. Section 3.3 describes it for the GTX460 processor in short.

3.2   Mapping onto Architectures with Modest Degree of Parallelism: Case of STORM

Parallel processing granularity of the stream H264 encoder can be classified into Macroblock level and subblock level. When mapping the encoder onto the Storm processor, Macroblock level parallelism means that each iteration of the main loop of a kernel processes a Macroblock on each lane, while subblock level parallelism means that each iteration of the main loop of a kernel processes a subblock on each lane. Since the number of arithmetic lanes of STORM is 16, kernels' DLP degree is 16.

In other word, 16 arithmetic lanes process 16 stream elements at once time, the stream elements may be a Macroblock or a subblock.

Macroblock Level Parallelism. For Inter-prediction, Transform Coding, CAVLC, Deblock filter of the stream H.264 encoder, parallel processing granularity is cat the Macroblock level.

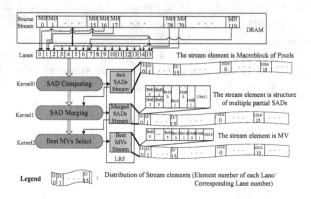

Fig. 1. Macroblock level parallelism of ME on Storm processor

We take Motion Estimate (ME) as an example to illustrate how to map kernel with Macroblock-level parallelism onto lanes with a DLP degree of 16, as shown in Figure 1. Other modules' kernels are mapped likewise. Inter Prediction is mainly implemented by three parameterized kernels: SAD Computing, SAD Merging, The best MVs Select, and the data process granularity of each kernel is up to 3MByte. The input stream of the first kernel of inter-prediction may be defined as a Macroblock stream of a 16x1920 pixel Stripe for a 1920x1080 image (stream length is also restricted by the size of on-chip memory. In Storm, all streams processed by a kernel have to be loaded on LRF previously and manually). Therefore, lanes of STORM can naturally process Macroblocks in stream in module 16 for these kernels, while all the intermediate streams are also organized by module 16 in on-chip memory-LRF.

Subblock Level Parallelism. For Intra-prediction, parallel processing granularity is 4x4 subblock level. We take kernels Predict16x16 as examples to illustrate how to map kernels with subblock level parallelism onto lanes with a DLP degree of 16.

16x16 Luma Intra-Prediction kernel's data process granularity is up to 16 subblock. Thus each lane processes a subblock of a Macroblock independently, as shown in Figure 2(a).

4x4 Luma Intra-Prediction kernel's data process granularity is 4n subblocks. These subblocks are processed in a 7-stage procedure by using 16 lanes, as shown in Figure 2(b). All lanes read stream elements (subblocks) in sequence, so that data stream can be organized conveniently. Since the DLP degree of each stage in a slice is less than 16 and all lanes have to compute in parallel, only specific lanes' results are valid at each stage. The results produced by the last stage are transferred to the next stage by

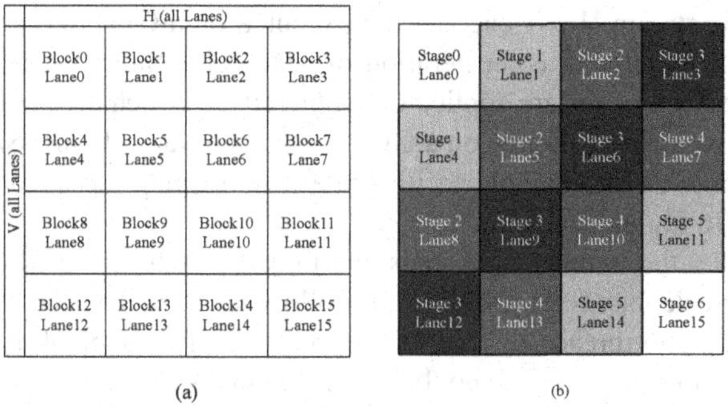

H (all Lanes)			
Block0 Lane0	Block1 Lane1	Block2 Lane2	Block3 Lane3
Block4 Lane4	Block5 Lane5	Block6 Lane6	Block7 Lane7
Block8 Lane8	Block9 Lane9	Block10 Lane10	Block11 Lane11
Block12 Lane12	Block13 Lane13	Block14 Lane14	Block15 Lane15

Stage0 Lane0	Stage 1 Lane1	Stage 2 Lane2	Stage 3 Lane3
Stage 1 Lane4	Stage 2 Lane5	Stage 3 Lane6	Stage 4 Lane7
Stage 2 Lane8	Stage 3 Lane9	Stage 4 Lane10	Stage 5 Lane11
Stage 3 Lane12	Stage 4 Lane13	Stage 5 Lane14	Stage 6 Lane15

(a)   (b)

Fig. 2. Subblock level parallelism of Intra-prediction on Storm processor

inter lane communication. If the number of slices is 4 or more, 16 lanes may work with full workload.

3.3   Mapping onto Architectures with Larger Degree of Parallelism: Case of GPU

This section will describe how the stream code is mapped onto GPU. The full stream-ing H.264 encoder is also easily implemented on GPU, which is different from many previous studies about parallelization of some key modules of the H.264 encoder on GPU [5][6]. These previous studies have to solve certain key problems caused by workload balance and data communication between CPU and GPU, which do not exist in our implementation. This section's focus is on the difference of mapping me-thods between stream processor and GPU.

In a stream processor, the number of arithmetic lanes is in the order of 10s, and the compute capability of each lane is relatively strong. It means that a stream proces-sor is suited for processing few heavy-weight kernels simultaneously. Whereas, in a GPU, the number of stream process unit is in the order of 100s, and the compute ca-pability of each SP is relatively weak. It means that GPU is suited for processing a large amount of light-weight of kernels (threads) simultaneously.

In addition, the global memory of a GPU is used for streams storage due to large capability. However, it is not on-chip memory, which results in long access latency. Thus the shared memory needs to be elaborately scheduled manually for thread blocks to improve performance. Since each SM can support multiple thread blocks simultaneously, the shared memory is not enough for storing all streams needed by all thread blocks. Furthermore, in only inter-thread communication in a GPU is imple-mented by the shared memory and synchronization operations. The overhead is far more than the thatof Storm with the inter-lane communication scheme. Therefore, the key of exploiting parallelism on a GPU is to provide sufficiently many active thread blocks to make full use of abundant SPs. In other word, we have to adjust the size of thread block with respect to   the size of on-chip memory and the number of SMs, so that there are adequate candidates that can be switched in once a thread block needs to be switched out due to stall.

Kernels of the stream H.264 encoder are executed on a GPU in the form of thread blocks. A thread is defined as an iteration of a kernel. Subblock level parallelism and slice parallel techniques are applied on all threads to match the parallel processing granularity and parallelism degree on a GPU. This paper takes kernel SAD computing of the ME module as an example to illustrate how to map the stream code onto a GPU, as shown in Figure 3.

In the example, the number of threads and thread blocks executed simultaneously on GPU can be calculated according to the following formulas (the size of a thread block is set to be 256 threads by experience, the size of a subblock is 4*4, different rows of Macroblocks in a slice cannot be processed in parallel):

$$\text{Thread\_nums} = (\text{Frame\_width}/4)*(\text{MB\_height}/4)*N*32*32 \qquad (1)$$
$$\text{ThreadBlock\_nums} = \text{Thread\_nums}/256 \qquad (2)$$

N is the number of slices of an image;
32*32 is the size of searching window.

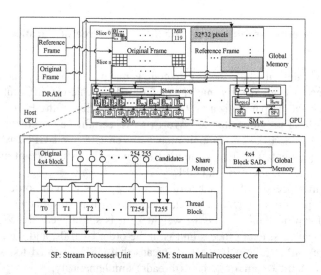

SP: Stream Processer Unit   SM: Stream MultiProcesser Core

Fig. 3. Mapping of kernel SAD computing on GPU

Obviously, the number of threads calculated by formula (1) constitutes one of sub-block which can be processed in parallel for an image. For a full high definition video sequence (resolution is 1920*1080), the number of threads and thread blocks executed simultaneously on a GPU are up to 1966080*N, 7680*N respectively. Since there are 7 SMs on GTX460, each SM can be assigned with hundreds or even thousands thread blocks. The number of active thread blocks on a SM is set as 4 at one time (the total number of active threads on a SM is 1536 at most). Thus there is abundant threads resource to be scheduled, which can efficiently hide memory access latency and make the SPs of a GPU work with full workload.

It can be seen that, data of reference frame and original frame are loaded to the global memory first. Then each original subblock and its corresponding 256 candidates are loaded to the shared memory gradually, processed by a thread block of kernel SAD computing. Each thread (Ti) performs a SAD computing of a candidate and an original subblock. It significantly reduces global memory accesses at the restriction of on-chip memory capability. Unlike LRF on Storm, the shared memory is not a pure software managed memory. As one of date providers for a large amount of threads (they also can access registers and global memory), it can be used by defining some shared memory groups, but nobody knows which thread blocks are accessing it at any time. Thus performance optimization of the H.264 encoder on a GPU is still a very hard work.

4   Results and Discussion

As shown in table 1, the evaluation is performed on five kinds of programmable processors, which are a desktop CPU, an embedded CPU, a DSP, a stream processor and a GPU.

Table 1. Experimental platforms' configurations

Platform / Parameter	Desktop CPU / IntelE8200	Embed CPU / MIPS 4KEc	DSP / TI C64	Stream Processor / STORM-G220	GPU / Nvidia GTX460
Core No.	2 Cores	1 Core	1 Core	2MIPS+ 16 Lane	336 stream processors
CPU Frequency	2.67GHz	330 MHz	600MHz	700MHz	1.3 GHz
Peak Power	~65W	<1W	1.6W	10W	260W
Main Memory	4GB DDR3	2GB DDR2	1GB DDR2	2GB DDR2	4GB DDR3
Bandwidth	10.7GB/s	8.3GB/s	4.2 GB/s	8.3GB/s	12 GB/s
On-Chip	64KBICache	16KBICache	16KBICache	256KB Stream	448KB share mem
Memory	64KB DCache	32KB DCache	32KB DCache	Register File	1.68M Contex RF

Table 2. Encoding video quality before and after streaming

Test Video Name	Blue_sky	Rush_Hour	Station2
Raw size	659138KB	1518750KB	950738KB
Encoded size of Original code	9105KB	13434KB	4708KB
Encoded size of Streaming code	9237KB	13523KB	4775KB
Compression rate of Original code	72:1	113:1	202:1
Compression rate of Streaming code	71:1	112:1	199:1
PSNR Lose	0.72db	0.56db	0.49db

Correctness and Quality. On each platform,   both X264 and the stream code of H.264 encode three high definition video sequences (only the stream code can run on GPU), meanwhile a standard H.264 decoder in VLC   media player decodes the encoded bit streams directly to verify the correctness. Comparison of the two decoded results shows that the output bit streams of our stream code is correct. Table 2 shows the detailed results.

Encoding Performance. Table 3 lists the overall frame encoding rate and speedup of both the X264 code and our stream code. It shows that the stream code achieves a significant speedup over the X264 code on all four platforms. It's quite excellent for streaming, a program level optimization technique without any special hardware support, to obtain such degree of speedup on various different architectures. The experimental results also show that our encoder is capable of real-time 1080p H.264 video encoding on a completely programmable processor—STORM. Meanwhile the stream code on GPU also gets better encode performance than other GPU implementations [5][6][7].

Table 3. Average Performances on processors for 200 frames of 1080P HD video sequences – BlueSky/Station2/Rush_hour, latency, compression rate and speedup

Platform	Original code		Stream code		
	Time	Frame/s	Time	Frame/s	Speedup
P4 E8200	35.4s	5.6fps	18.8s	10.6fps	1.9
MIPS 4KEc	1052.6s	0.2fps	256.1s	0.8fps	3.9
TI C64	503.5	0.4fps	95.9s	2.1fps	5.2
STORM-G220	39.9	5.0fps	6.3s	31.6fps	6.3
GPU GTX460	N/A	N/A	8.09s	25.1fps	N/A

Comparing with other Parallelization Techniques In essence, streaming is a model-based parallelization technique. However, there are many general parallelization techniques for accelerating H.264 encoding, such as frame/slice level parallelism, wavelet/MB pipeline and fine granularity block parallelism [8][10[11]. Compared with streaming, these techniques only focus on data dependency of some level with the risk of side-effects. For example, frame level parallelism will increase the requirement for bandwidth, while slice level parallelism will reduce the compression rate. Differently, this paper presents a completely synthesized technique based on the stream model. On modern programmable processors, single level optimization is insufficient for good performance, so multi level translation and parallelism is an inevitable trend. However, the novelty of this paper is choosing the stream model as a foundation for other optimizations, a key reason for getting such improved performance.

Further speedup of our software H.264 encoder may be achieved by less effort in algorithm level optimization beyond program level optimization. For example, K-L or wavelet transform can be used to replace the DCT transform in transform coding, CABAC can also be used to replace CAVLC in entropy coding. However, this may have a downside , because the improvement may be bound with some special algorithm, thus limiting the applicable domain of the streaming technique. Furthermore, the streaming techniques can be combined with other parallelization techniques. Our measurement on X86 shows that slice level parallelism (2 slices) accelerates HD H.264 encoding to 6.38fps for the BlueSky 1080P sequence, while the streaming approach accelerates it to 10.6fps, and the combination of these two techniques achieves 13.2fps.

5   Conclusion

In this paper, we have proposed a set of novel model-based technique called streaming for H.264 encoding, and mapped the stream encoder onto concrete processors. Our results on several programmable processors show that the stream encoder can achieve significant performance acceleration. In particular, real-time encoding of high-definition H.264 video (up to 1080p) is achieved on a typical stream processor and a desktop GPU. It makes streaming technique more attractive. To achieve performance comparable with ASIC, using programmable processors is wise with respect to both time and cost, for this type of media processing whose standards are various and often varied.

Acknowledgments. This work was supported by the National Natural Science Foundation of China, through grants No. 61033008 and No. 60903041.

References

1. Mattson, P.R.: A Programming System for the Imagine Media Processor. PhD thesis, Stanford University (2002)
2. Wu, N., et al.: Streaming HD H.264 encoder on programmable processors. In: Proc. ACM Multimedia (2009)
3. Stream Processors Inc. SPI Software Documentation (2008),
   http://www.streamprocessors.com
4. NVIDIA, GeForce_GTX_200_GPU_Technical_Brief, NVIDIA, Tech. Rep. (2008)
5. Chen, W.-N., Hang, H.-M., et al.: H.264/AVC motion estimation implmentation on Compute Unified Device Architecture (CUDA). In: IEEE International Conference on Multimedia and Expo., pp. 697–700 (2008)
6. Lin, Y., Li, P., Chang, C., Wu, C., Tsao, Y., Chien, S.: Multi-pass algorithm of motion estimation in video encoding for generic GPU. In: Proc. IEEE International Symposium of Circuits and Systems (2006)
7. Huang, Y.-L., Shen, Y.-C., et al.: Scalable computation for spatially scalable video coding using NVIDIA CUDA and multi-core CPU. In: Proc. ACM Multimedia, pp. 361–371 (2009)
8. Ahmad, I., He, Y., Liou, M.L.: Video Compression with Parallel Processing. Parallel Computing 28(7-8), 1039–1078 (2002)
9. Reference software X264-060805,
   http://www.videolan.org/developers/x264.html
10. Xun, C., et al.: A framework for stream programming on DSP. In: Proc. 4th International Conference on Embedded and Multimedia Computing (2009)
11. Cheung, N.-M., Fan, X., et al.: Video Coding On Multi-Core Graphics Processors. IEEE Signal Processing, 79–89 (March 2010)

Multimedia Telemedicine Environment: A System Design of Integrate Portable and Wearable Devices

Ming Xue, Shibao Zheng, Chongyang Zhang, and Hua Yang

Department of of Electronic Engineering,
Shanghai Jiaotong University, Shanghai, 200240, China
{silas_xue,sbzh,sunny_zhang,hyang}@sjtu.edu.cn

Abstract. This paper proposes a remote multimedia telemedicine system that is focusing on the integration of different kinds of devices. Based on the portable and wearable devices as the center, the proposed system could provide high definition video monitoring, wearable Video-and-Voice-over-IP (V2IP), physiological parameter and signal monitoring and data management based on database. Hardware and software solution of the devices in the proposed system is firstly presented. And then, main issues including HD video compression, V2IP and physiological signal processing are discussed. Finally, a hardware system prototype with software interface is demonstrated.

Keywords: telemedicine, high definition video, wearable device, V2IP, video communication.

1 Introduction

During the past years, there has been an increase in the demand for noninvasive intelligent devices that can help detect vital signs without interference of the users' daily routine. This demand was also fueled by the need that public and private health institutions have for monitoring and providing services to the dependent patients under their care [5, 7].

New technologies, especially the modern network and wearable computer techniques, based on modern signal communication protocols or standards could meet such requirements [3, 6, 8]. Accordingly, telemedicine [4] appears and are now being gradually used by doctors, hospitals, and other health care providers around the world. With the help of a video-based telemedicine system, remote monitoring, face-to-face communication and even operation could be realized.

Different with the existing works, which only one kind of video or non-video telemedicine device is mainly proposed, this paper proposes a system in another way, which makes a sub-system-level device integration and collaboration. The rest part of this paper is organized as follows. Section 2 introduces the whole system and network architecture. Section 3 describes the two core subsystem components. Section 4 discusses the main function implementation issues in video and physiological signal processing. Section 5 shows the hardware subsystem prototypes with software interfaces. Section 6 concludes the whole paper.

F.L. Wang et al. (Eds.): CMSP 2012, CCIS 346, pp. 428–435, 2012.

2   System Architecture Overview

The architecture of the proposed system is shown in Fig.1. Generally, the system is composed of six parts: portable HD-video subsystem, wearable wireless communication subsystem, software-embedded subsystem, database subsystem, server subsystem, and the network module.

The former three components are often distributedly located at the remote sites, and acquire information in the form of still image, video in different resolutions, audio, text and physiological data. The data are compressed and transmitted over the communication network based on different kinds of network topologies and protocols and reproduced to the user at the local site. It is noted that the users in our system are not limited to doctors and patients, but could also include caregiver, the patient's relatives and any other person that is related to the corresponding treatment.

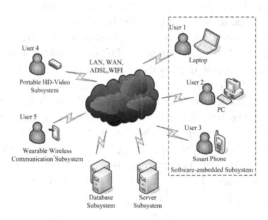

Fig. 1. General System Architecture

3   Design of Portable and Wearable Subsystems

Portable and wearable subsystems are discussed in the rest parts of this section, including the hardware and software platforms.

3.1   Portable HD-Video Subsystem

3.1.1   Hardware Platform Design

In our proposed system, a C/S architecture is applied, where the server part is a portable device, a Linux OS embedded board is designed. Standard sensors are used to collect the physiological data. RS232 interface is chosen for asynchronously physiological data transferring. As a point-to-point communication, the maximum data rate with the fastest transceivers is about 1 megabit, which is enough for our system. Considering HD video data processing, which is another major issue for this portable device, a specific encoding chip is chosen for this part, because hardware-based encoding is much faster than software-based way. Remote pan, tilt and zoom (PTZ) controlling are also included within this system. The PTZ camera could be controlled by the users at the remote site to focus on the local area where they are likely to be more interested. In implementation, RS485 interface and Pelco-D protocol are chosen for PTZ data transferring and controlling.

3.1.2   Software Platform Design

According to the hardware platform, the proposed portable software consists of two parts: the server and the client. The server software part is running on an ARM processor under a Linux OS. When the server starts, the initialization step includes hardware checking, memory allocation and other preparation. Then multi-threads are started for different tasks, including multi-media data processing, medical data processing, remote controlling and configuration. The GoAhead webserver [2] is chosen for data transmission across the network, which waits for the client's connection request and acts as a transferring module. Various kinds of data collected by different tasks are packaged to be sent out to the client.

Typically, in the proposed subsystem, the client software part is running under the Windows XP OS as an ActiveX application. The main task of the client is to receive the data from the server and to display these data accordingly. Once the connection is done, data is received through the network interface and then analyzed for further displaying. H.264 stream is decoded with the help of CoreAVC [1] project and displayed by HD screen and headphone. Audio data is collected and send out to perform full-duplex voice communication with the server. Physiological data is displayed in separate sub-windows in different formats including waveforms, images and Arabic numerals. Moreover, all receiving data could be saved on the hard disk, based on the standard DICOM formation. These data could be reviewed with the help of our specific database application anytime later.

3.2   Wearable Wireless Communication Subsystem

3.2.1   Hardware Platform Design

The hardware of wearable subsystem is an embedded board based on i.MX27 [10] by FreeScale. I.MX27 is a multimedia application chip derived from the popular i.MX21 processor and based on the ARM926EJ-S™ core, the i.MX27 processor adds an h.264 D1 hardware codec for high-resolution video processing, an Ethernet 10/100 MAC, security, plug-and-play connectivity and more power management features. This rich feature set makes it an excellent choice for video-and-voice-over-IP (V2IP) communication, mobile phones, intelligent remote controls, point-of-sale terminals and many other wireless applications. More details about the chip could refer to [11].

The proposed peripheral interface based on i.MX27 is shown in Fig.2(a), which could be further divided into central processing unit, media data processing module, peripheral interface module, power management module and storage module. The center processing unit mainly refers to the ARM kernel and Video Processing Unit (VPU) of the chip, the latter of which could provide hardware-based video encoding and decoding for high-speed application. For the video display format transformation in the media data processing module, chip TVP5190 and CH7024 are used. Thus the digital video signal could be transformed for displaying in Phase Alternating Line (PAL) or National Television System Committee (NTSC) format. Moreover, 128MB DDR SDRAM , 64MB NAND FLASH and 4GB SD card constitute the storage part, which could basically meet the video data recording and playing requirement of the proposed system. The peripheral interface module mainly consists of wireless network and Ethernet chip, serial device and interface (RS485) and Universal Serial Bus (USB) ports *et al.*

3.2.2   Software Platform Design

The Android-based software architecture is shown in Fig. 2(b). Generally, we divide it into three levels, the system and driver level, the intermediate level, and the application level. The system and driver lever provides the basic driver and Linux-based system kernel support. The intermediate level mainly consists of the run-time library, while the application level contains the independent Java-based application. We reserve some basic applications which are already included in Android system, so that the functions of wearable subsystem could be further extended.

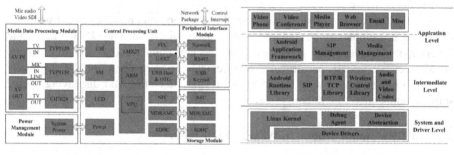

(a) Hardware platform   (b) Software platform

Fig. 2. Architecture of wearable wireless communication subsystem

4   Basic Function Analysis

Main functions of the proposed system are presented in this section, including HD video processing, V2IP communication and physiological signal processing.

4.1   HD Video Processing in Portable Subsystem

In a common video processing platform like a personal computer (PC), video data compression is often conducted by software, which means the encoding and decoding process is finished by the central processing unit (CPU) of the system, which also provides computation service for other application. The software-based encoding and decoding process has the following disadvantages: firstly, it occupies most parts of CPU resources and memory during the coding process, which could create negative influence on the parallel computation performance of the system; secondly, the cost of a CPU which could meet the real-time and HD processing requirement is often very high. In contrast, hardware-based coding process, which means that the processing is conducted by a specific application specific integrated circuit (ASIC), takes the following advantages. Firstly, it could easily provide video processing performance with a HD resolution and low time delay; secondly, a hardware-based video encoding process could be almost finished independently on the ASIC, which would seldom influence the performance of CPU; thirdly, the cost is more reasonable compared with that of a high-performance CPU.

Accordingly, hardware-based encoding is chosen for the proposed subsystem. A specific H.264 encoding chip is chosen, and performs the data stream encoding tasks on the portable board. Tests shows that system designing in this way could process HD video and other physiological data simultaneously in real time. As for decoding on the software-embedded subsystem, an ActiveX+Directshow solution is designed for the platform. It is easy and convenient to develop a multi-thread and multimedia program including video displaying, voice processing and data analysis in the form of an ActiveX plug-in application. However, there is no H.264 decoding filter available in Directshow toolboxes. So a H.264 decoding project is needed for video displaying on the clients' device.

CoreAVC decoder is an open-source and free video compression project with low development complexity. Compared with other projects such as JM86, x264 and FFmpeg, its fast decoding speed, which is the key·point for our decoding design, could meet our system performance requirement. To sum up, CoreAVC is finally chosen to be integrated with Directshow for video decoding and displaying on the software-embedded subsystem.

4.2   V2IP Communication in Wearable Subsystem

The SIP protocol [9] is an Application Layer protocol designed to be independent of the underlying Transport Layer; it can run on Transmission Control Protocol (TCP), User Datagram Protocol (UDP), or Stream Control Transmission Protocol (SCTP). It is a text-based protocol, incorporating many elements of the Hypertext Transfer Protocol (HTTP) and the Simple Mail Transfer Protocol (SMTP).The main thread of the Android-based V2IP application is shown in Fig.3. Once an SIP listening thread is created, it would first check the state of registration to SIP server, and then launch or receive the session data to update the corresponding android activity, which includes the video frame and audio data reading and playing.

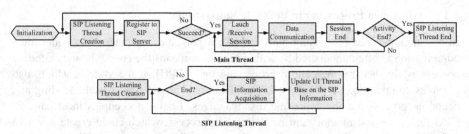

Fig. 3. Main thread of Android-based V2IP application

4.3   Physiological Signal Processing

The physiological diagnosis and treatment is one of the basic functions in a telemedicine system. In the proposed system, the recording parameters include ECG, SPO_2, temperature and blood pressure.

Compared with HD video stream, real time physiological data size is little. However the availability and accuracy of the data is extremely important. A specific package format is designed for physiological data encoding and decoding, which is shown in Fig. 4. Each block in this figure refers to one byte data size. 0x55 and 0xaa are the package head. SUM0 and SUM1 are designed as checking bits. SUM0 is defined as the check sum from STATUS0 to RESPW, and SUM1 is defined as the check sum from DATA1 to DATA4. When a new package is received, SUM0 and SUM1 are checked at the first time for package data validation.

0x55	0xaa	STATUS 0	STATUS 1	DATA 0	ECGWI 4	ECGWI 3	ECGWI 2	ECGWI 1	ECGWII 4	ECGWII 3	ECGWII 2	ECGWII 1
ECGWV 4	ECGWV 3	ECGWV 2	ECGWV 1	SATW	RESPW	SUM 0	DATA 1	DATA 2	DATA 3	DATA 4	SUM 1	

Fig. 4. Package format of physiological parameters' transferring protocol

5   Prototype and Use Cases

Photos of the hardware subsystem and screenshots of the related software are shown in this section.

5.1   Subsystem Hardware Prototype

Figure 5(a) shows the hardware prototype of our portable subsystem. It consists of a portable embedded ARM system, PTZ, physiological sensors, and headphones. The HD screen allows the medical specialist to monitor the patient and read the physiological data at the same time, while in Fig. 5(b), the prototype of wearable subsystem is shown. Currently, it consists of a mobile wearable multimedia processing board, shown in Fig. 5(c), glasses display screen, video camera, a multi-touch screen, portable battery charger, and related media cables. The users could see each other via glasses display in a video call or video conference. Moreover, PCs, HD screens are optional for database service and visualization.

 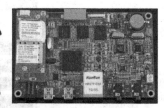

(a) Portable subsystem   (b) Wearable subsystem   (c) Multimedia processing
     prototype   prototype   board of wearable subsystem

Fig. 5. Subsystem hardware prototype

5.2   Subsystem Software Interface Prototype

5.2.1   Video Communication

We first illustrate the result of portable device for video communication. The screen-shot of real-time hardware-based video encoding and decoding is shown in Fig.6, with a digital clock used to measure the time delay. Based on multiple measurements, average time delay of the proposed system is 0.3 second. For the wearable video communication, the screenshots of corresponding android V2IP application are shown in Fig 7.

Fig. 6. Screenshot of hardware-based video coding and displaying

Fig. 7. Screenshot of Android-based V2IP application

5.2.2   Physiological Signal Diagnose

Via the GoAhead webserver, the client could have access to our system by a web browser. Figure 8 shows the diagnosing web of our system, and it could display the information and physiological data of the patient at the same time.

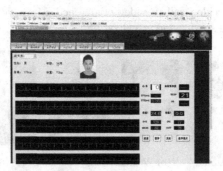

Fig. 8. Diagnosing web

6   Conclusion

In this paper, an integrate system for remote video telemedicine is proposed. The system is mainly composed of wearable and portable devices used by clients, and the related servers and database subsystems controlled by providers. We describe both the hardware and software design of the system. Photos of the system prototype are shown, while some evaluation is conducted to demonstrate the efficiency of the system.

We believe that the systems still require much work to be done. Possibly, our future work would focus on testing the system in realistic environments such as hospitals and old-age homes, and improve the proposed solution based on the corresponding feedback.

References

1. Coreavc, http://corecodec.com/products/coreavc
2. The goahead webserver, http://www.goahaed.com
3. Anliker, U., Ward, J.A., Lukowicz, P., Troster, G., Dolveck, F., Baer, M., Keita, F., Schenker, E.B., Catarsi, F., Coluccini, L., Belardinelli, A., Shklarski, D., Alon, M., Hirt, E., Schmid, R., Vuskovic, M.: Amon: a wearable multiparameter medical monitoring and alert system. IEEE Transactions on Information Technology in Biomedicine 8(4), 415–427 (2004)
4. Cabral Jr, J.E., Kim, Y.: Multimedia systems for telemedicine and their communications requirements. IEEE Communications Magazine 34(7), 20–27 (1996)
5. Figueredo, M.V.M., Dias, J.S.: Mobile telemedicine system for home care and patient monitoring. In: 26th Annual International Conference of the IEEE Engineering in Medicine and Biology Society, IEMBS 2004, vol. 2, pp. 3387–3390 (September 2004)
6. Guillen, S., Arredondo, M.T., Traver, V., Garcia, J.M., Fernandez, C.: Multimedia telehomecare system using standard tv set. IEEE Transactions on Biomedical Engineering 49(12), 1431–1437 (2002)
7. Hung, K., Zhang, Y.-T.: Implementation of a wap-based telemedicine system for patient monitoring. IEEE Transactions on Information Technology in Biomedicine 7(2), 101–107 (2003)
8. Lee, R.-G., Chen, H.-S., Lin, C.-C., Chang, K.-C., Chen, J.-H.: Home telecare system using cable television plants - an experimental field trial. Trans. Info. Tech. Biomed. 4(1), 37–44 (2000)
9. Rosenberg, J., Schulzrinne, H., Camarillo, G., Johnston, A., Peterson, J., Sparks, R., Handley, M., Schooler, E.: Sip: Session initiation protocol (2002)
10. Freescale Semiconductor, Inc., i.MX27 and i.MX27L Data Sheet, MCIMX27EC (December 2009)
11. Freescale Semiconductor, Inc., MCIMX27 Multimedia Applications Processor Reference Manual, MCIMX27RM (September 2007)

Automatic Music Generation and Machine Learning Based Evaluation

Semin Kang, Soo-Yol Ok, and Young-Min Kang*

TONGMYONG University
535, Yongdang-Dong, Nam-Gu, Busan, Korea, 608-711
{semins,ymkang,sooyol}@tu.ac.kr

Abstract. This paper describes the automatic music composition system and automatic music evaluation system . The system composes short pieces of music by choosing some factors in music, such as pitch interval. timbre, tempo, rhythm. The most important features of the composition system include using the concept of mode, and density. mode control the pitch interval and densyty control the rhythm of music. We use Neural Network algorithm for automatic evaluation system of music. especially we used Back Propagation algorithm for objectification of user's taste.

Keywords: Machine Learning, Automatic Music Composition, Automatic Music Evaluation, Backpropagation.

1 Introduction

The development of computer technologies and smart devices brought a turning point in music creation. Many individual and independent developers are in needs of their own music for their own apps, and increasing people try to express their own personalities with their own styles of ring tones. Therefore, the individual users are now trying to create their own music. However, the composition of music requires deep knowledge about music which cannot be easily obtained. The ordinary people have unfortunately little time to learn music composition techniques. Therefore, easy and automated composition of music for individual purpose will become more and more important.

There have been various efforts to automatically compose music. The general approaches are categorized into two classes: 1) rule-based automatic composition with musical grammar and 2) procedural composition with mathematical models such as fractal, cellular automata or L-system. However, the previous approaches required users to have detailed knowledge about music. Otherwise, the previous methods could not generate music with various styles. Therefore, the high level control over the automated composition of various music has not been successfully achieved.

It is obvious that the music is not the composition of random sounds. The fact that we usually predict the next tune after the current tune demonstrates

---

* Corresponding author.

F.L. Wang et al. (Eds.): CMSP 2012, CCIS 346, pp. 436–443, 2012.
© Springer-Verlag Berlin Heidelberg 2012

the music obeys certain rules such as harmonics and counterpoint. However, the variety and subjectivity of music cannot be easily expressed with simple combination of known rules. Moreover, the evaluation of music depends on complex and subjective understanding so that the quantative and objective measurement cannot be easily modeled.

The automated composition of music can be achieved anyhow with music theory, mathematical models, or randomness. However, the more important issue in the composition of desired music lies rather in controllability of the music generation. The previous research efforts usually focused on the music generation itself and often neglected the evaluation of the procedurally generated music. Therefore, the high level control over the mood or style of music has not been successfully implemented.

In this paper, we propose an automated music composition system that enables users to create their own music for their own purpose by controlling the music with high level control parameters. The system is based on the supervised machine learning approach to evaluate music to take the subjective tastes of users into account.

2 Previous Work

The earliest form of automatic music composition is to compose the fragments of melodies in accordance with randomly generated numbers. Since Mozart threw dice to select melody fragments for some minuets [2], various random number based approaches have been proposed and studies. The most common approaches to the automated music composition is to utilize mathematical models or some simple rules known in music literature.

Puente [5] used musical grammar to procedurally generate music. Boenn[1] also used musical grammars such as harmonics to implement 'Anton', an automated composition system. The system actually produced plausible music. However, the variety of the obtained music was not satisfactory enough.

Many researchers proposed various methods based on fractal, L-system, or other mathematical models. Pressing[4] employed mathematical equations to generate music, and Worth [7] utilized L-systerm. However, the mathematical models could not successfully model the actual music composition rules that is customary and has been accumulated during the long time in human history. Therefore, the previous methods were sometimes useful only when people wants to create really new and fresh styles because the generated music tends to be unfamiliar and strange. In contrast, the methods usually failed to create ordinary music peaple are comfortable with.

There exist no common rules for music so that discords sometime sound fresh and nice. In the consequence, the automatic composition of music eventually fails when the musical grammar is overstressed. The well-defined grammars can be a predefined and limited set of musical pieces.

The limitation of the previous approaches is caused by the ignorance or neglectance of the importance of evaluation.

3 Automatic Music Generator

A music piece is composed of various components such as pitch intervals, beats, and timbre. However, we usually regard different music pieces with the same melody as an identical piece even when the it is played with different instruments in different rhythms. Such experience demonstrates that the most important factor in distingushing music pieces is the melody.

The melody can be defined as time series of notes. Therefore, the music generation can be essentially reduced to the note determination at each time step. The most compelling example of such concept is 'music box'. The music box spins a cylinder with several tracks assigned to differently tuned teeth of a steel comb. The cylinder has pins placed on the surface, and the pins pluck the tuned teeth to produce sounds. The different tunes of the teeth are the states, and the time when the music box turns into each state is determined by the rotating speed. The music generated with our method is based on the model inspired by the music box.

Although the melody is the key factor in recognizing the identity of music pieces, the mood of an identical music can vary in accordance with other factors. It is often experience that an identical piece generates completely different moods when played with different instruments. In contrast, we can produce the variety of emotions with an identical instruments. Therefore, to control the mood and style of music, we took into account the 4 different factors: pitch interval, rhythm, tempo, and timbre. The variety of music was obtained by combining different instances of the four factors, and the evaluation was also performed on the domain defined by the factors. structure of the system is shown in Fig. 1.

3.1 The Automated Generation of Music

The music composition in this paper is essentially reduced to determining the tunes of 16 eighth notes respectively. We have 16 time steps where the state must be determined. Each state can be one of 13 possible tunes or a mute sound. The

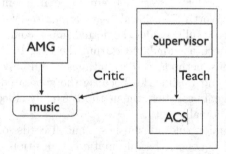

AMG: Automatic Music Generator
ACS: Automatic Classification System

Fig. 1. System structure

$$\boxed{C}\boxed{\otimes}\boxed{G}\boxed{F}\boxed{C}\boxed{\otimes}\boxed{C}\boxed{\otimes}\boxed{D}\boxed{F}\boxed{E}\boxed{\otimes}\boxed{G}\boxed{G}\boxed{C}\boxed{\otimes}$$

Fig. 2. An example sequence of decided states

note determined to be mute plays a role as a rest note. An example of decided states sequence is shown in Fig2. After the states of all the notes are determined, the timbre and tempo of the music is decided and the generated music is played with the tune color of the timbre in the speed assigned to the tempo.

The random selection from available timbres or the random determination of tempo between the pre-defined minium and the maxium do not produce weird music. However, the ramdomly selected pitch intervals sequences hardly sounds like real music. In most cases, the sequence creates awkward and unstable melody. In order to avoid such problem, we employed 'mode' in the automated music composition.

The mode restricts the availability of the tunes. Therefore, our composition system selects one of the limited set of tunes in accordance with the current mode and previous tunes. By employing the mode, the music composition based on randomness can produce more reasonable set of music pieces, and the weird music pieces are avoided in the generation process.

The rhythm of music in the proposed system is determined by the sequence of mute notes and audible notes. Once the rhythm of a music piece is set, the probability of audible notes in the melody is also computed. The different rhythms of music pieces can be essentially regarded the density of the audible notes in the piece. Therefore, we employed 'density' parameter that determines the rhythm and actually controls the probability of the appearance of audible notes.

Mode. The seven modes are known, and the mode is similar to the scale of music in that it restricts the available tunes. For instance, the mode 'C Ionian' is similar to the scale 'C Major'. In the C Ionian mode, the scale is generate as C-D-E-F-G-A-B-C where the pitch intervals between the 3rd and the 4th notes and between the 6th and the 7th notes are semitones. The different modes have different locations where the semitones intervals appear in the scale. For example, semitones appear between 2nd and 3rd and between 5th and 6th notes in Dorian mode. The interval sequence corresponding to the modes are listed in Tab 1.

If the music composition is restricted to use the scale defined in accordance with the specific mode, the discords drastically decrease and plausible and stable music pieces are usually generated. Moreover, each mode produces different mood of music. In the literature of music, the different moods by the modes are interpreted and proposed as shown in Tab. 2. The system proposed in this paper employed the mode not to produce strange and uncomfortable music pieces which are usually obtained when random selection of sounds.

Density. The 'density' parameter of our method controls the probability of the generation of audible notes. Strictly speaking, the density is not exactly the

Table 1. Seven modes and corresponding interval sequences: T represents whole tones and e represents semitones

modes	interval sequence
Ionian	T-T-e-T-T-T-e
Dorian	T-e-T-T-T-e-T
Phrygian	e-T-T-T-e-T-T
Lydian	T-T-T-e-T-T-e
Mixolydian	T-T-e-T-T-e-T
Aeolian	T-e-T-T-e-T-T
Locrian	e-T-T-e-T-T-T

Table 2. Correlation of modes and feeling

modes	D'arezzo	Fulda
Ionian	serious	any feeling
Dorian	sad	sad
Phrygian	mystic	vehement
Lydian	harmonious	tender
Mixolydian	happy	happy
Aeolian	devout	pious
Locrian	angelical	of youth

same as the rhythm. However, the model of our method is based on music box where the rhythmic effect is generated by the alternation of audible notes and mute notes. Therefore we can suppose that the density is indirectly related to the rhythm. The difference between the high density music and the low density music is shown in Fig. 3.

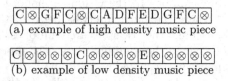

(a) example of high density music piece

(b) example of low density music piece

Fig. 3. Difference between High Density & Low Density

3.2 Automated Genration of Drum Beats

In general, famous music pieces are remixed by various musicians and the remixed versions have different feels. In order to create new mood of the music, drum beats are usually the most likely to be modified. For example, hip-hop musicians frequently use sampling, and the samples are often from classic or rock music pieces. However, the mood of the hip-hop music is usually quite different from that of the original music, and it seems the drum beats are the main reason of the difference.

Basic elements for the drum beats are hi-hat, snare and bass. The combination of those elements creates various rhythms such as bossanova, shufle, dub, and drum'n bass. The automatic generation of the drum beats in this paper is essentially reduced to determining the states of 16 sixteenth notes respectively. We have 16 time steps where the state must be determined. Each state can be 'Touched' or a mute sound.

In order to determine one drum beat, 16 sixteenth notes were generated for each element (i.e, hi-hat, snare and bass). The beat determination is performed for each adjacent two notes. Therefore, the 16 notes are grouped as 8 states variables. Each state can have one of four possible values such as 00, 01, 10 and 11. We grouped the adjacent beats to control the probability each possible values so that the generated beats are more reasonable and plausible. For example, the hi-hat beats should have more frequent beats than snare or bass. However, snare or bass should have lower probability for the states such as 11, 01 and 10. Fig. 3 shows how the shuffle rhythm can be generated with our approach.

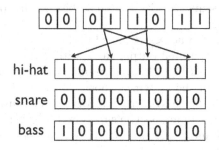

Fig. 4. Composition of shufle rhythm

3.3   Automated Classification of Generated Music

It is hard to quantify the evaluation of music because the understanding or emotional acceptance of music pieces is extremely subjective process. Therefore, it might be almost impossible to design a well-defined functions or measurement for the evaluation of music. Therefore, we employed the machine learning based evaluation system based on backpropagation neural network.

The backpropagation is an example of supervised learning system. According to the delta learning rule, the network adjusts the weights to obtain optimized connections to recognize the data set of which recoginition result is given. After the learning phase, the system can be utilized to recognize any data set based on the previous learning. Therefore, the method is proper to be quantify the subjective evaluation of music based on the user tastes, and can be utilized for the evaluation of various music pieces.

The machine learning of the backpropagation method is based on the input vector and weights of the links that connects the input to the output vector.

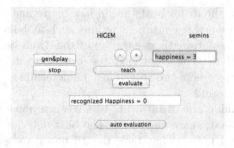

Fig. 5. System interface

Therefore, it is very important to determine what parameters involved in music generation to be selected as the part of input vector[6,3].

We selected mode, timbre, tempo and pitch interval to be used as input vector. The parameters have 7, 16, 2, and 128 possible cases respectively, and expressed with 3, 4, 1, 8, and 4 bits in the gene sequence. The melody and drum beats are also coded in the gene sequence with 60 and 48 bits, so the total size of the gene sequence is 128 bits long.

The input layer with 128 notes are linked to hidden layer with 30 nodes, and they are also linked to the final output layer with 3 nodes. The learning final output was translated back to high level meaning of the input music.

The actual interface of the system is shown in Fig. 5. Users can easily generate various music and teach system to recognize the music in terms of high level description such as happiness. The supervised learning is utilzed further to recognize or classfy the music pieces which have never been evaluated before.

4   Conclusion and Future Work

In this paper, we proposed an automated generation and evaluation of music is proposed. The composition of music is based on the randomness. However, the automated composition with pure randomness seldom produces reasonable or plausible music pieces so that a method that restrict the possible output space to be limited within the plausible set of music pieces. In order to achieve such goal, we employed the concept of 'mode' in the generation process.

The automated composition of music requires two different conflicting capabilities: 1) the generation of restricted set of plausible music pieces and 2) the generation of variety of music pieces. While the mode is employed to restrict the generation, we also employed density, tempo, and timbre to increase the variety of the generated music pieces. The controlling parameters are converted into binary code to be given to a learning system based on backpropagation. The machine learning enabled users to automatically evaluate the music pieces generated by our system.

The evaluation system made it possible to classify the huge amount of automatically generated music pieces. The automated evaluation will be succefully utilized for the customized or purpose-based music generation.

The binary sequence expression of the music can be also successfully utilized to integrate our system to any evolutionary approach to automatically generate desired music or discover the unknown music fit to user defined objectives.

Unfortunately, the proposed system is not closely interoperable with the possible services that generate and control the user created music with high level parameters. We are intensively trying to integrate our system into the high level music composition system where the quntified evaluation and evolution-based music composition is implemented.

Acknowledgments. This work was supported in part by the Ministry of Knowledge Economy (MKE), Korea, under the Information Technology Research Center (ITRC) support program supervised by the National IT Industry Promotion Agency (NIPA) (NIPA-2011-(C-1090-1021-0006)), and this work (Grants No.C0033371) was supported by Business for Cooperative R&D between Industry, Academy, and Research Institute funded Korea Small and Medium Business Administration in 2012.

References

1. Boenn, G.: Anton: Answer Set Programming in the Service of Music. In: Proceedings of the Twelfth International Workshop on Non-Monotonic Reasoning, pp. 85–93. University of New South Wales, Sydney (2008)
2. Alpern, A.: Tecnique for Algorithmic Composition of Music. Hampshire College (1995)
3. Gose, E., et al.: Pattern recognition and image analysis. Prentice Hall Press PTR (1996)
4. Pressing, A.: Nonelinear maps as generator of muscal design. Computer Music Journal (1988)
5. Puente, A., et al.: Automatic composition of music by means of grammatical evolution. In: Proceedings of the 2002 Conference on APL, pp. 148–155 (2002)
6. Tzanakou, E.: Supervised and unsupervised pattern recognition. CRC Press (2000)
7. Worth, P., Stepney, S.: Growing Music: Musical Interpretations of L-Systems. In: Rothlauf, F., Branke, J., Cagnoni, S., Corne, D.W., Drechsler, R., Jin, Y., Machado, P., Marchiori, E., Romero, J., Smith, G.D., Squillero, G. (eds.) EvoWorkshops 2005. LNCS, vol. 3449, pp. 545–550. Springer, Heidelberg (2005)

Condition and Key Issues Analysis on the Smarter Tourism Construction in China

Xian-kai Huang[1], Jia-zheng Yuan[2,3], and Mei-yu Shi[1]

[1] Tourism Institute of Beijing Union University, Beijing 100101, China
[2] Beijing Key Laboratory of Information Service Engineering, Beijing 100101, China
[3] Computer Technology Institute of Beijing Union University, Beijing 100101, China
{Xiankai,Xxtjiazheng}@buu.edu.cn

Abstract. Smart Tourism, cored in massive tourism resources data center, supported by IOT and cloud computing, focused on tourists through intelligent identification, intelligent monitoring and location based service, is a new tourism form to provide application services to government, businesses and residents. This paper firstly analyzes certain areas with ST construction pilots and summarizes the works of some well-known scholars in China, and then further elaborates the conceptual definition of ST and the existing problems. Finally, proposes a Triple-A theory model and general technical architecture of systematic design, in order to provide theoretical, methodological and operational references for the study of ST.

Keywords: ST, Define concept, Theory model, System Architecture, Resolution.

1 Introduction

"Smarter Tourism (ST)" already becomes the hottest topics currently, and also the most cutting edge research topic, catching much attention in society.

Currently, domestic researchers define ST from different viewpoints, propose different conceptual models [1,2], and several ST construction plan with different models already appear. Yet, theoretical model and systematic framework to direct ST is still weak even deficient. ST construction system framework, system standard, interest subject, operation model and expansion model, etc, needing further explanation.

Therefore, the paper opens to the deficiencies of research and application from researchers, area panel, relevant information technical service vendors, system solution vendors, etc, further analyzes the content, development model and construction plan, systematically analyzes domestic representative ST application, existing research problems, and predict the future work, to provide reference of theory, application and experiment for domestic ST.

F.L. Wang et al. (Eds.): CMSP 2012, CCIS 346, pp. 444–450, 2012.

2   Conceptual Model of ST

ST is a brand new tourism, part of smarter earth or smarter city. For the content, the real sense of ST is to focus on tourists' need, combining the information intelligent technology with casual culture, tourist innovation industry, to promote tourism service quality, improve tourism management level, and enlarge industry scale of modern engineering. ST, apart from general information system or engineering core technology, cloud computing, the Internet of things (IOT), mobile terminal communication and human intelligent, four technologies. Its concept is defined as "one center, two support, and three application", as tourist related "eat, accommodation, travel, tourist, purchase, entertainment" various information data as the data center of tourism resource, supported by IOT and cloud computing smarter technology, through various tourism related industry resource and tourism service equipment to lain for

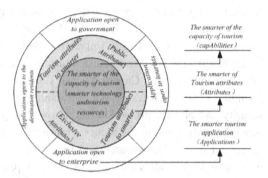

Fig. 1. The Conceptual Model of ST construction

various type sensing equipment to sense tourism resource (sight, tourist) to use cloud computing technology to integrate various sensing information to process data analysis, to realize three application of smarter identification, smarter monitor and identification service. Therefore, ST should satisfy the feature of tourist oriented, smarter sense, and smarter service. Fig.1 gives the concept model to construct ST, in which the core is tourism resource data center, supported by IOT and tourism cloud, surrounded by smarter identification, smart monitoring and location service to assist government, company and resident.

3   Construction Condition and the Key Issues Analysis

And the smarter of tourism construction related research in various fields has made many achievements, China Tourism Academy professor Wei-Xiaoan puts forward to want "intelligent" tourism concept, using the "intelligence" of the Chinese tourism industry deals with the crisis of the golden key, the tourism industry to build a intelligent estate industry [3]; the smarter of the nation tour service center director of national intelligence to YU-Jianwu puts forward to accelerate tourism service center construction is elaborated, the national tourism administration information in heart director Tang-Hongguang questions smarter of tourism should include public service platform, the application layer, infrastructure three levels [4], Capital University of Economics and Business Professor Li-Yunpeng for Smarter City tourism service system and its establishment [5], Shanxi Normal University College of tourism and environment Dr Li-Junyi create tourism information science to promote tourism development [6]; Beijing University of Posts and Telecommunications professor Du-Junping content based intelligent guide system, based on Agent and data mining for holiday tourism status, tourism information method research and safety accident forecast and early warning research has done a lot of research [7,8], Beijing Union University, Dr. Li Nao and Chinese Academy of science and technology policy [9] and management science research The professor Wu Jing Agent application in intelligent scenic tour open computer simulation to make a preliminary research in scenic spots [10]; digitizing and three-dimensional scene modeling, economics professor Yuan Jiazheng [11], Beijing Union University and Liaoning Normal University professor Wang Fangxiong [12] made outstanding contribution; based on LBS theory and applied research is more, Capital Normal University, Zhejiang University professor Li-Shanping [13]and professor Wang-Yanhui [14] in the LBS location service model, security and privacy protection has its own unique insights. These studies into fruit general mainly contains the focus on tourism, leisure and cultural tourism creative and intelligent innovation research and focus on supporting tourism intelligent information technology studies two aspects, such as promoting Chinese smarter of tourism development to make important contribution, but still a few to close the important key issues that need to be further study.

(1) Theoretical Model and System Architecture Needs to be Deeply

From the relevant scholars and industry research and development results, despite many achievements have been obtained, presenting smarter traveling different conceptual model, and there have been different ST practice patterns, but, overall, the ST is still a lack of a unified, standardized, scientific argument, guiding ST construction theoretical framework and system architecture lacks authority or missing, this lost theory foundation.

(2) The Information Technology and Tourism Creative Needs Integration

The industry in terms of definition or construction, in the information technology layer surface consider too much, emphasize IOT, cloud computing and other new technology and information system construction, these considerations is the general meaning of tourism information and category, the lack of tourism content, creativity and leisure culture, management and service of Tourism resources innovation, so it is not the true sense of the smarter of tourism, thus requires a thorough consideration of intelligent technology and tourism resources of the connotation of innovation, considering the relationship between the two, so that the integration and fusion, the formation of a new discipline.

(3) Business Norms and Industry Standards to be Formulated

The ST public basic platform and system construction should be based on the standard first. Because intelligent tourism is still at the exploratory stage, a comprehensive coverage of all construction content standards has certain difficulty, so the level of what level of business planning and industry standard, need to be deeply studied content.

(4) The Main Benefits and Operation Mode to Clear

The ST development tourism industry from the traditional "low investment, high yield goes out"" dimensions economy" to " high investment, high risk, high Output" sustainable development "system", its construction changed the tourists behavior patterns, the mode of operation of enterprises and administrative departments of management mode, also need to coordinate the government, tourists, tourism enterprises and the relationship between local residents.

(5) Evaluation System and Management Mechanism Need Improvement

From several pilot city tourism constructions in view of smarter, smarter marketing and electronic commerce has made great progress, and has achieved some success, but the smarter of the management and services still consider little or absent, but also the lack of ST construction evaluation system. Than such as system meets the interests of the main requirements, whether there is a feedback mechanism, how to manage the order of each interest principal part needs a scientific, objective evaluation system and evaluation model, as the basis for assessment and evaluation.

4   Solutions to Key Issues for ST Construction in China

ST construction generally includes development main body, application and operation of the main body, wherein the subject of the development and operation of the main body mainly comprises the government or enterprise, application subject by tourists, government, enterprises and residents in the construction purpose, involving a critical problem is how to make clear the three body and the relationship between them, make clear each interest role orientation and level.

Aiming at this key issues, put forward the ST construction 3A model, by the smarter of the capacity of tourism, ST attributes and ST application on three factors. Refers to the ability of the smarter of tourism with smarter technology and tourism, leisure culture and creative tourism resources provided by the smarter and power, such as IOT/Internet, cloud computing services platform, tourism resources data center and smarter terminal; attribute refers to the ST to provide applications and services are public or exclusive, public property refers to the applications and services by the government or third party to provide, to the public management and service for the purpose, is a non-profit, exclusive properties applications and services by exclusive service providers, to profitability for the purpose; application refers to the operation of the main body to provide a variety of application specific application functions, such as the government palace emergency management, dynamic tourism information services, the scenic spot tube of managers visitor flows management, and marketing, for tourists destination guides, navigation, navigation, guide and emergency assistance; ST construction 3A theory model as shown in fig. 2.

Subject, relationship and content of 3A theoretical model for ST development :

(1) The development of main body to provide ST capacity factors, such as the construction of grassroots network platform, the development of tourism of intelligent database, providing a variety of creative tourism resources.

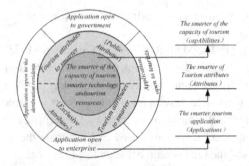

Fig. 2. The 3A Theory Model of ST Construction

(2) The operation of the main body is used to develop a public property or proprietary attributes to provide application subject with public or non-profit nature of the various specific application function.

(3) The application from the main tourist destination is clear in concept of smarter, ST oriented covers regional tourism destination, tourism city and area concept, application subject besides the general tourism covered by tourists, government, enterprise, still should be incorporated into the destination residents.

(4) In the three factors, the ability is a foundation, property is support, application is the purpose, and attribute determines development main body, operation main body and application body. Public attribute and exclusive property for a variety of applications as well as between through the ability to attribute connectivity and interoperability, avoided to the greatest extent of the information island.

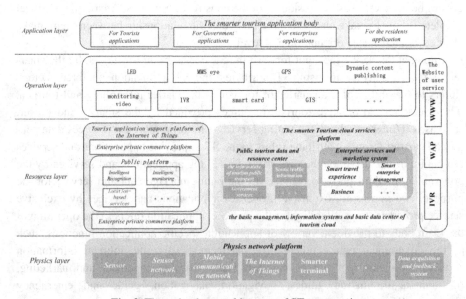

Fig. 3. The technology architecture of ST construction

Based on the above theoretical model, intelligent tourism construction system architecture could be constructed. Fig. 3 shows a kind of ST construction architecture. In Fig.3 the system framework, the whole system is divided into physical layer, data resources, the business layer and application layer, wherein the physical layer is mainly related to the construction of network / Internet, mobile communication network and intelligent terminal based network, data resources include cloud computing services platform, tourism resources data center and data resource construction, service layer contains a number of public service platform and enterprise service platform, the application layer provides various application specific subject service function. Physical layer corresponding ST capacity factors, data resources and business layer corresponding ST attribute factors, application layer. The application of intelligence factors corresponding to travel.

5   Conclusions and Prospect

Tourism is the traditional ST and information industry convergence is a new form of tourism and China's industrial upgrading a driving force, ST development and implementation, will lead the Chinese tourism industry into the future.

Since the ST concept has been proposed, the domestic scholars, government and enterprises made a lot of discussions and in-depth research, obtained more achievements, but overall still study achievement is relatively single, remain in the conceptual aspect more, and concept of public opinions are divergent, currently cannot find a unified, standard, scientific argument, this lost theory foundation; ST construction is not very successful cases, even walking in front of several regions, can only be as pilot units in exploration; in addition, our tourism information of starting point is low, instability, and the ST construction eventually do not drive off the category of information.

This paper, based on the current results, puts forward integrated intelligent tourism to build the problem of existence, puts forward construction to close bond smarter travel solutions to problems, and gives the smarter of tourism concept, theory model and designed the system framework, travel the next construction in order to draw lessons from action.

Finally, the ST research field, involving more complicated, is a complex system engineering, this paper studies the internal volume still at the theoretical level, details of which need to be further in-depth. In the following, we will settle in the intelligent recognition, intelligent monitoring and emergency management, in order to travel service demand for the LBS services in areas such as research, to promote China's tourism to contribute to the construction of ST.

Acknowledgement. This work is supported by a grant from Nation Natural Science Foundation (No.61271369), Natural Science Foundation of Beijing (No.4102060), the science-technology development plan of Education Committee of Beijing (No. KM201111417014) , and Funding Project for Academic Human Resources Development in Institutions of Higher Learning Under the Jurisdiction of Beijing Municipality (PHR201107302).

References

1. Smarter Tourism [EB/OL], http://baike.baidu.com/view/5217093.html
2. The ST show the wisdom of a city [EB/OL], 10, 11 (2011),
   http://blog.china.alibaba.com/blog/bes82668286/article/
   b0i26472207.html
3. Wei, X., Yang, J., Wei, S.: Intelligence: China tourism industry deals with the crisis of the golden key [EB/OL], 8, 24 (2009),
   http://blog.sina.com.cn/weixiaoanlaoshi
4. Wu, X.: ST: It is to achieve sustainable development of tourism industry [J/OL]. China Tourism News (Digital Edition) 12, 28 (2011)
5. Huang, C., Li, Y.-P.: An Research on The "Smart Tourism" system based on the "Smart City" during "the 12th five-year plan" period. In: Tourism Tribune China Tourism Research Annual Conference 2011, pp. 55–68 (2011)
6. Li, J.-Y.: An Evaluation of Web-based Marketing System in Tourism Destinations Based on Visitors' Demand. Tourism Tribune 25(8), 45–51 (2010)
7. Du, J.-P., Zhou, Y.-P.: Study on Data-based Tourism Management Decision Support System. Acta Automatica Sinica 35(6), 834–840 (2009)
8. Jiao, D.-L., Du, J.-P.: Intelligent Decision Support System For Tourism Accident Forecasting. Journal of Beijing Technology and Business University (Natural Science Edition) 26(2), 55–58 (2008)
9. Li, N., Du, S.-Z.: Study on the Computer Simulation System for Recreational Behaviors in Scenic Spots. Tourism Tribune 26(7), 85–94 (2011)
10. Qiu, R., Li, S., Wu, J.: A review and prospect of agentbased modeling in tourism simulation. Geography and Geoinformation Science 25(5), 102–107 (2009)
11. Yuan, J.-Z., Xu, D., Wang, Y.-J., Bao, H.: An Effective Method for SVG-Based Rendering of Real Images. Acta Electronica Sinica 36(1), 188–193 (2008)
12. Wang, F., Ma, S.: Design and Implementation of ArcEngine-based Three-Dimensional Terrain Visualization System. Geospatial Information 9(3), 38–43 (2011)
13. Lin, X., Li, S.-P., Yang, Z.-H.: Attacking Algorithms Against Continuous Queries in LBS and Anonymity Measurement. Journal of Software 20(4), 1058–1068 (2009)
14. Li, Y., Wang, Y.: SVG based representation and compression of spatial data in LBS. Journal of Image and Graphics 16(5), 903–908 (2011)

Education and Training Environments for Skill Mastery

Approach to a Simulation System Using Haptic Device for Acupuncture

Ren Kanehira[1], Weiping Yang[2], and Hideo Fujimoto[3]

[1] FUJITA Health University, 1-98 Dengakugakubo, Kutsukake-cho,
Toyoake, Aichi, 470-1192, Japan
[2] Aichi Shukutoku University, Nagoya, Japan
[3] Nagoya Institute of Technology, Nagoya, Japan
kanehira@fujita-hu.ac.jp, wpyang@asu.aasa.ac.jp,
fujimoto@vier.mech.nitech.ac.jp

Abstract. Computer-supported learning and training systems with highly advanced information and communication technology (ICT) have recently been paid more and more attention. In such a system, the skill training function by which a new kind of education and training system may be developed was paid particular attention. In this study, we proposed an education and training system for oriental acupuncture, emphasizing on how to train the use of tiny force and small movements. Research subjects were set to solve such problems as the measurement and presentation of small operation forces, and their training methods and the construction of training environment, towards the construction of an idea training system combining satisfactorily both knowledge learning and skill training. The acupuncture as one typical example of the traditional oriental medicine treatments has been more and more accepted by the world for its miraculous healing effect in recent years. It is mostly important in acupuncture to become highly skilled by training with repeated practice. However, such repeated practice can hardly be done on a real human body, which may always be accompanied with pain and misery. In this study, a computer training system for acupuncture with force feedback function was proposed. A human acu-points model with acu-point's name, position, meridians, stinging techniques and healing functions was created within the computer, and devices with force feedback functions for skill training were used in the system. A trainee gets acupuncture experience not only by visual information, but also from sensing the force information with a true-false judgment of his movement being real-timely given during the exercise.

Keywords: Training Environments for Skills, Quantification of Technique, Acupuncture, PHANTOM, Force-feedback.

1 Introduction

New possibilities of using computer in education and training arise due to the highly developing ICT. The appearance of new devices such as highly advanced sensors and

F.L. Wang et al. (Eds.): CMSP 2012, CCIS 346, pp. 451–458, 2012.

actuators makes it possible to develop new kind of education and learning systems conventionally being impossible. In our study, the training for use of tiny forces and small movement which has hardly been found in conventional training systems was paid special attention, and a training system for oriental acupuncture was proposed. Solutions for such problems as the measurement of small operation forces and their presentation, the training methods, and the construction of such a training environment were given towards the construction of an idea training system combining satisfactorily both knowledge learning and skill training.

Acupuncture is an ancient Chinese healing method in which stimulations are applied to the acupoints (defined positions on the human body), leading to an increase of the inner healing power of the human himself and the recovery of the sickness [1]. Recently, acupuncture has been paid more attention worldwide, so the Acupuncture of Chinese Medicine has been registered in the humanity national intangible cultural heritage list by UNESCO in November 2010. Although the miraculous ancient Chinese healing method has still some parts not yet being explained scientifically, it is used with increased worldwide interests, and even an Acupuncture Universities has been established in Japan [2].

It is important in acupuncture, similar as most of the oriental medical treatments, to use fully the human 5 senses, and to become skillful mainly by repeated exercises. However, there are problems in learning and training for acupuncture, such as the lack of clarity in the textbook, the difficulties for a judgment of the accuracy when stinging an acu-point, and so on. Thus, the development of an acupuncture training system using the advanced computer technology can be of great help.

We have been doing researches on the development of a computer-assisted acupuncture training system for quite a long time. In this study, we reported an improvement on such system. A human body acu-point model was created within a computer, with which the study of recognition of correct 3D acu-point position, and the sting action on them was done with a true-false judgment. When building up the system, we paid more attention to the representation, teaching and training of the tiny operation force applied in the sting action. The teaching of the insertion angle and insertion speed for a sting operation on an acu-point using a mechanical force feedback system was proposed [3]-[8].

As one of the series researches for the training system, this study reported an improvement on the system by introducing a haptic device PHANTOM. The teaching of the tiny force adjustment in sting was studied with the system, and the results were tested by repeated exercises of trainees with real-timely true- false judgments.

2   Learning and Training of Acupuncture

2.1   Point of the Skill Training

Acupuncture therapy is a medical treatment using acupuncture needle or moxibustion to stimulate the acu-points of body according to the symptoms. An acu-point is the defined point on the human body, going to receive the needle with proper stimulus. There are hundreds of such acu-points located on the important positions over the human body on the meridian. And the meridian is such an imaged flow (you may not see them) connecting the acu-points to the internal organs. Therefore, it is very important to find the correct position of the acu-points, and the proper stimulus for the highest healing effect.

That is, the acupuncture education requires both a textbook for memorizing, and repeated practice/exercises to master the skill. With the help of advanced computer technology, a better training effect can be expected using the textbook with the series of processes of basic theory, case prehension, treatment policy, acu-points combination and handling, which are systematically combined with a computer.

Acupuncture has techniques of not only holding and insertion, but also those of stinging, trail, whirl, according to different symptoms. It is further required for good healing to use different techniques such as the stinging angle, the speed, and the depth upon different acu-points for each symptom. Therefore, it is especially important to be trained by repeated practice.

2.2   Training with Force Feedback

The proposed system can be roughly divided into two parts. One is the software for teaching and explanation of the sequence of basic theory, case prehension, treatment policy, acu-points combination and handling. The software contains detailed description on the names, position, depths of meridian and meridian point, and its flow or moving, some are demonstrated by 3D expressions for a better understanding. Another, and one of the most important things in the acupuncture training, is the development of a training system with force feedback function with a precise correspondence to the acu-point model. For such a system with force feedback function, firstly, information of operation forces from well-experienced doctors are measured and stored in the computer as a training index. Then, training functions are input to the computer based on the human model and basic techniques of acupuncture.

A trainee is trained, using the system with force feedback, to master the basic techniques such as the methods of holding, stinging, and so on. He gets the correct feeling by repeated practice referring the standard from well-experienced doctors. The system has the character of real-timely response, giving a true-false judgment during the practice. The results are evaluated by the computer.

As stated above, while the former part can be found a lot in the e-learning or database fields, the latter part is quite few because of being a kind of practice training accompanied by technical difficulties. Our study has paid attention to the latter, and experiment was done for a development of a computer training system for acupuncture. In this paper, the construction of a training system using force feedback device PHANTON was done with detailed description of the construction of education environment and the functions of the system, and the problems and perspectives were addressed.

3   The Acupuncture Training System

3.1   System Construction

A 3D human acu-points model was created on a computer. A training system was constructed upon the 3D model. The schematic of the system composed of a computer

(XPS6, 30Dell) for simulation, a monitor to show the information, and a haptic device (PHANTOM Omni®. SensAble Technologies, Inc.), and the software of OpenHaptic toolkit, is shown in Figure 1.

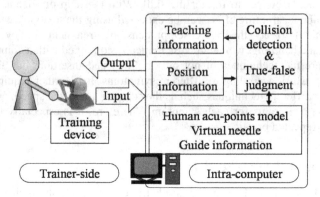

Fig. 1. The construction of the training system

3.2   Haptic Device PHANTOM

The PHANTOM is a 3D input-output haptic device capable of force interaction with high precision. The interaction between a 3D object and the operator makes it possible to present not only visual but also force information. The reaction force from the hand when touching an object, therefore, can be real-timely represented, to achieve a high operational effect with real-time response.

The PHANTOM Omni model is one of the highest cost-effective haptic devices available today. Portable design, compact footprint, and IEEE-1394 FireWire® port interface ensure quick installation and ease-of-use performance.

The PHANTOM is equipped with position sensors capable of doing precise force operations. A reactive force corresponding to the hand movement is produced by reverse rotating of inner motors to wind the wires. A 3D force vector is output on the tip of the stylus by controlling the torque of the DC motor. The maximum force output is 3.5N. A high rate of input-output change is achieved by 1 kHz high speed processing. The PHANTOM was then introduced into the system considering such characteristics. Acupuncture training with high reality, most near the practical sting, is expected with the system.

3.3   Simulation Environment Configuration

The following functions were applied to the system in the construction of computer simulation environment for acupuncture training using data base.

① Presentation and variation of information on human body acu-points model, acu-points and needle.
② Simulation for stinging operation
③ Evaluation and scoring
④ Score management and password control

⑤   Editing and supplement of information in ①
⑥   Device maintenance

Actions such as the learning of human body information, the accurate position of an acu-point, medical treatments knowledge (acu-position, therapy items, stinging angle, stinging methods, etc.), selection of needles, other acupuncture operations, real-time true-false judgment, personal score management, and repeated practices, etc., are possible with the above simulation system and functions.

System simulation environment and database configuration is shown in Figure 2.

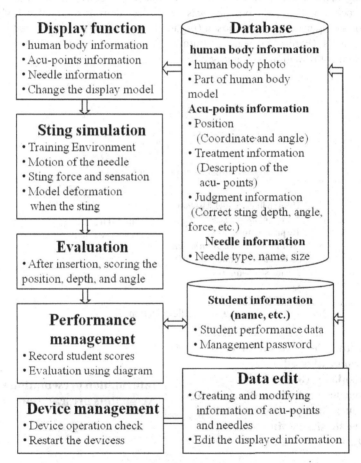

Fig. 2. Simulation environment and database configuration

4   Characteristics of the System

The characteristics and functions of the system can be that to provide information on both visual and operational at the same time, satisfying the skill training with presence.

4.1   Presentation of the Information Not Visible in the Real World

The precise positions of the acu-points, which are usually invisible on the human body with the human eyes, can be easily displayed on the 3D model on a computer. The acu-points of a human body in the ordinary textbook are described in a 2D form so it is difficult to identify the 3D information (such as the depth of the acu-points). The developed system, however, is with the ability to demonstrate 3D information because of the use of a 3D human body model, resulting in a highly improved understanding of the 3D position of acu-point including the depth and the relationship with the surrounding organs, which has not been possible in the conventional training. On a training process, the part for practice was first selected from the human body model (Figure 3), a proper needle was chosen (Figure 4), the information presentation can be selected himself (Figure 5), and the training was carried on according to personal desire, with a confirmation on training effects.

Fig. 3. Human acu-points arm model

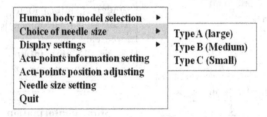

Fig. 4. Needle selection

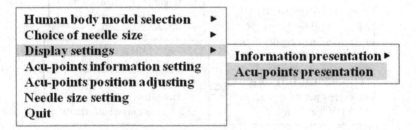

Fig. 5. Information presentation selection

4.2   Repetitive Training with Force Feedback

It is easy to use the system to carry out exercises repeatedly almost without limitation, which is very important for learning and training skills of acupuncture in contrast to the conventional training using human body. In conventional training process, a trainee usually learn technique by sting the points of himself or between the trainees each other and this may lead to a resistance or fear to continue further the acupuncture practice.

A trainee is trained, using the system with force feedback, to master the basic techniques with tiny force operations such as the methods of stinging, insertion, holding, and so on. He gets the correct feeling by repeated practice referring the standard from well-experienced doctors.   Force index was taken from experienced doctors as an index for operation force training. The results of insertion force vs. insertion time were plotted in Figure 6 for the Expert doctor. A proper value of 260gf was obtained after analyzing the experiment results. This value can then be applied as the standard insertion force as the index used in the system to judge real-timely during the practice, and the training results are evaluated by the computer.

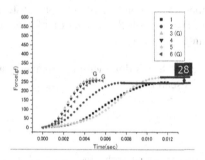

Fig. 6. Operation force results of expert

4.3   True-False Judgment in Real Time

A precise judgment of a correct stinging to the proper acu-point position with the proper force has been difficult in the conventional training method, while it can be easily and real-timely done with the developed computer system. Using the device with force feedback on hand movement promotes the training towards the most practical one. It is also possible to do reliable true-false judgment on a sting using the computer system, because a beginner is difficult to judge the correct force used to sting into an acu-point. A trainee gets acupuncture experience not only by visual information, but also from sensing the force information with a true-false judgment of his movement being real-timely given during the exercise. The teaching of the tiny force adjustment in sting was studied with the system, and the results were tested by repeated exercises of trainees.

5   Conclusions

In summary of this research, a computer training system for acupuncture with force feedback functions was proposed. An acu-point model with precise name, position, flow, sting techniques and healing function, was created on a computer. The information on each operation, especially the tiny force adjustment was obtained and made visualized on the computer. A trainee gets experience not only by visual information, but also senses the force information with a true or false judgment of his movement being real-timely given during the exercise. The system has the character of doing exercise repeatedly without pain, and the ability of reducing operation mistakes at low cost, even with more information not yet possible in reality. The system is expected to contribute to a successful training of acupuncture doctors through the realization of the series processes of study of the basic theory, case prehension, decision of the treatment policy, acu-points combine and technique training on computer.

One of the research subjects for the next step is the enrichment of the acupuncture data base and training-related environment. The quantification of operation skill has to be done in more detail using the system by more experiments and analysis. For this purpose, more operation data from the experienced doctors are to be introduced as the standard for training. Further, evaluation functions of the system are to be enhanced. Continued studies are carried on towards the realization of a simulation system capable of quantitative study, training, evaluation etc.

Acknowledgments. This research was done with the financial support from the JSPS Grant-in-Aid for Scientific Research(C).

References

1. Sugiyama, I.: Manual of acupuncture Gensosha, Inc., pp. 13–21 (2003) (in Japanese)
2. The Japan Society of Acupuncture and Moxibustion, http://www.jsam.jp//
3. Chen, L., Atsumi, H., Fujimoto, H.: A computer training system for acupuncture with force feedback. In: Proceedings of the First International Conference on Complex Medical Engineering, pp. 245–248 (2005)
4. Kanehira, R., Shoda, A., Yagihashi, M., Narita, H., Fujimoto, H.: Development of an acupuncture training system using virtual reality technology. In: Proceedings of 5th FSKD, pp. 665–668. IEEE Press (2008)
5. Kanehira, R., Yang, W., Tateishi, M., Yagihashi, M., Narita, H., Fujimoto, H.: Insertion angle teaching for an acupuncture training system. In: Proceedings of CSEDU 2009, pp. 281–284. IEEE Press (2009)
6. Kanehira, R., Yang, W., Shoda, A., Narita, H., Fujimoto, H.: Indexing of insertion speed for acupuncture training system. In: Proceedings of HCI 2009, pp. 692–696. IEEE Press (2009)
7. Kanehira, R., Yang, W., Narita, H., Fujimoto, H.: Insertion Force of Acupuncture for a Computer Training System. In: Wang, F.L., Deng, H., Gao, Y., Lei, J. (eds.) AICI 2010, Part II. LNCS, vol. 6320, pp. 64–70. Springer, Heidelberg (2010)
8. Kanehira, R., Yang, W., Narita, H., Fujimoto, H.: Acupuncture Education System with Technique-oriented Training. In: Proceedings of 2011 Eighth International Conference on Fuzzy Systems and Knowledge Discovery, pp. 2524–2528. IEEE Press (2011)

Integrate Hand Constraints with Image Features to Build an Observation Model for Hand Tracking

Bingchao Liu and Zhiquan Feng

School of Information Science and Engineering
University of Jinan
Shandong provincial Key Laboratory of Network based Intelligent Computing
Jinan, China
574833179@qq.com,
ise_fengzq@ujn.edu.cn

Abstract. 3D hand tracking in recent years has become a hot spot in Human Computer Interaction (HCI), and it also exists many difficulties. Our research roots in the observation model which is used to estimate the optimal hand state according current observation. We integrate hand constraints with skin color feature and edge feature to build an observation model. Firstly, using hand constraints to judge the hand state is whether or not a gesture. Secondly, using skin color feature and edge feature to build two similarity measurement probability functions to measure the similarity between hand image and hand state. Finally, the hand constraints and similarity measurement probability functions constitute the observation model and it is then used in particle filter for hand tracking. The observation model is used through three steps: particle revise, particle negative and particle weight calculation.

Keywords: Hand Tracking, Skin Color Feature, Gaussian Mixture Model, Edge Detection, Distance Transform, Observation Model, Particle Filter.

1 Introduction

There are two types of tracking strategy: appearance-based tracking and model-based tracking. Appearance-based methods [1,2,3] build map between image feature and hand state and then directly recovers hand state from the established map. Model-based method can accurately track hand movement, it generally compares the projection of hand model with hand image to evaluate current hand state. B.Stenger [4] builds an accurate hand model from truncated quadrics and gets hand model's 2D profiles from projective geometry. It estimates hand model by minimizing the geometry error between the profiles and edges extracted from image. B.Stenger [5] achieves a template-based shape matching using edge feature and skin color feature. O.B.Henia et al [21] proposes a dissimilarity function which combines the non-overlapping surface and the directed chamfer. Y.Wu et al [6,7] utilizes edge feature and silhouette feature to build an observation model to measure the likelihood of the hypotheses. On the other hand there are also many researches on hand constraints [8,9,10]. E.Brown

F.L. Wang et al. (Eds.): CMSP 2012, CCIS 346, pp. 459–466, 2012.
© Springer-Verlag Berlin Heidelberg 2012

and A.Vardy [8] produces a model of the human hand that would allow manipulation of model parameters in a manner consistent with the mechanics of the actual human hand. The model includes a number of constraints on model parameters. Some of these constraints are static and simply describe ranges of allowable motion, others are dynamic and introduce dependencies between joints. S.Cobos et al [9] describes dynamic constraints of human hand and apply Inter-finger and Intra-finger constraints to obtain a realistic manipulation.

We introduce hand constraints to hand state to build two probability functions, the aim is to reduce the effects of un-reasonable particles. Combining skin color feature with edge feature to build two similarity measurement probability funcutions to accurately calculate the similarity between hand state and hand image according current observation.

2   Hand Constraints

There are many researches on hand constraints [6,7,8,10,11], most are about t-he joint angle. As there exist some differences between different people, we c-hoose some universal constraints and apply them in three dimensional hand m-odel. The se constraints are divided into two types: static constraints (c_{static}) a-nd dynamic constraints($c_{dynamic}$). Static constraints mean the scope of joint an-gle without any external force and dynamic constraints mean the relationships between joint angl es when fingers move. Dynamic constraints are also divided into two types: intra dynamic constraints and inter dynamic constraints. Intra d-ynamic constraints mea n the relationships between joint angles in same finger and inter dynamic constrai nts mean the relationships between joint angles in d-ifferent fingers. According to these constraints we define two probability functi-ons: p_{static} and $p_{dynamic}$ to judge the hand state is whether or not a gesture.

3   Observation Model

Most model-based hand tracking needs an observation model to estimate hand state's probability according current observation. Here we combine hand constraints with skin color feature and edge feature to build the observation model.

3.1   Skin Color Feature-Based Similarity Measurement Function

Skin color is an important feature, it is widely used to detect hand and face [12,13,14]. We firstly model the skin color and background, and then we build a similarity measurement function according this feature.

The choice of color space is the primary step to model skin color and background. Here we choose YCrCb color space [15] where color is represented by luminance, constructed as a weighted sum of the RGB values, and two color difference values Cr and Cb that are formed by subtracting luminance from RGB red and blue components. Then we use Gaussian mixture model(GMM) to model skin color and background. GMM is a robust model that can accommodate large variation in color space, highlights and shadows [16]. GMM is defined as:

$$P(x) = \sum_{i=1}^{k} w_i p_i(x_i) = \sum_{i=1}^{k} w_i \frac{1}{(2\pi|\Sigma_i|)^{1/2}} \exp[-\frac{1}{2}(x_i - \mu_i)^T \Sigma_i^{-1}(x_i - \mu_i)] \tag{1}$$

x is a color vector representing Y, Cr, Cb; k is the number of mixture components and w_i is the contribution of the i th component; μ_i and Σ_i are the mean vector and covariance matrix respectively , and they can be estimated from training data through the following formula:

$$\mu_i = \frac{1}{n}\sum_{j=1}^{n} x_j; \Sigma_i = \frac{1}{n-1}\sum_{j=1}^{n}(x_j - \mu_i)^T(x_j - \mu_i) \tag{2}$$

Where n is the total number of training samples.

Firstly the parameter of GMM of the background can be estimated from a set of background images captured in real-time. Secondly, we estimate the parameters of GMM of skin color from a set of skin images. According the initialization method proposed in [17], the hand keeps in a relative fixed position and we only sample on the palm area because it is bigger and not easy to contain non-skin pixels, so the skin image is also captured in real-time, as displayed in Fig. 1 left. After getting the parameters of GMM of background and skin color, the pixel in the image has a probability belongs to background or skin color, and the hand region can be separated from background according a threshold which is set to the ratio of skin color probability and background probability, the separation result is display as Fig. 1 right.

Fig. 1. The left is the origin image and the pixels inside green rectangle are the skin color training data. The right is the separation result, red pixel represents the skin color.

On the other hand we can get hand model silhouette from model projection, the knuckle of each finger and palm are treated as rigid so that they can be approximately expressed as quadrilateral, the got hand model silhouette is disp-layed as Fig. 2 left. Now we define a similarity measurement function accordi-ng the non-overlap area between the separated skin region and hand model sil-houette:

$$P_{color} = \prod_{i=1}^{n} p_i^{background} \prod_{j=1}^{m} p_j^{skin} \tag{3}$$

Where $p_i^{background} \in R_{image} - R_{projection}$ and $p_j^{skin} \in R_{projection} - R_{image}$, $p_i^{background} \in R_{image} - R_{projection}$ re-pr esents the pixel that belongs to skin region but not model silhouette and its proba bility belongs to background, $p_j^{skin} \in R_{projection} - R_{image}$ represents the pixel bel-ongs to model silhouette but not skin region and its probability belongs to ski-n. As Fig. 2 right displayed. To increase computational efficiency, we calculateits log-likelih ood instead of multiplication operation.

$$\log p_{color} = \sum_{i=1}^{n} \log p_i^{non-skin} + \sum_{j=1}^{m} \log p_j^{skin} \tag{4}$$

Fig. 2. The left represents the hand model silhouette got from hand model projection. The right represents the overlap of hand model silhouette and the separated binary hand image, $R_{image} - R_{projection}$ is represented by red color, $R_{projection} - R_{image}$ is represented by blue color. The green region is the overlapping region.

3.2   Edge Feature-Based Similarity Measurement Function

Edge feature is an another important feature. As it is relatively robust to lighting change, many tracking system use it to build similarity measurement function. We also use this feature to measure the similarity between hand image and hand model. There are many edge detection operators, here we choose canndy operator because it has a smooth process to reduce the influence of image noise.

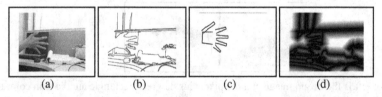

(a)   (b)   (c)   (d)

Fig. 3. (a) represent the origin image.(b) is the resulted edge image got from canndy detec-tion.(c) is the hand model contour got from hand model projection.(d) is the distance image got from edge image.

The resulted edge image is displayed in Fig. 3(b). On the other hand, we can get hand model contour from hand model projection, Fig. 3(c) displays the hand model contour. After getting the edge and contour, we measure their similarities by caculating their chamfer distance [5]. There have points set $A = \{a_i\}_{i=1}^{N_a}$ and points set $B = \{b_i\}_{i=1}^{N_b}$, the chamer distance from A to B is defined as:

$$d_{chamfer}(A, B) = \frac{1}{N}\sum_{a \in A}\min_{b \in B}\|a - b\|^2 \tag{5}$$

To effectively calculate their chamfer distance, we use the two pass algorithm [18] to get distance map from edge map, Fig. 3(d) displays the resulted distance map. After getting the distance image, we caculate the chamfer distance from contour to edge by summing up the distance of each pixel which contour is corresponded to. The defined similarity measurement function p_{edge} is:

$$p_{edge} = \exp(-d_{chamfer}(edge, contour)) \tag{6}$$

Finally we combine hand constraints probability functions with similarity probability functions to build a total observation likelihood model:

$$P_{observation} = P_{static}P_{dynamic}P_{color}P_{edge} \tag{7}$$

From this observation likelihood model we can judge the hand state is whether or not a gesture, and it also gives its similarity probability according current observation, so the optimal hand state can be estimated through this model.

4   Observation Model in Hand Tracking

We apply the established observation likelihood model to calculate particle's weight, it includes three steps: particle revise, particle negative and particle weight caculation. The details of the tracking algorithm are as follows:

(1)   Initialization: At time $t = 0$, using the initial method proposed in [19] to get initial hand states x_0, and then sample according priori probability $p(x_0)$ to get the initial particles set $\{(x_0^i, 1/N), i = 1, ...N\}$, N represents the number of particles and x_0^i represents the ith particle.

(2)   Prediction: Transfer the particles got from last time according the state transition equation $p(x_t | x_{t-1})$, then sample in the new position to get new samples set $\{x_t^i, i = 1, ...N\}$. The state transition equation [20] can be expressed as $x_t^i = \overline{x_{t-1}} + A(x_{t-1}^i - \overline{x_{t-1}}) + Bw_t$, $\overline{x_{t-1}}$ is the optimal state of last time, A is a constant controlling the moving speed, and Bw is the random noise.

(3)   Weight calculation: Using the established observation likelihood model $p_{observation}$ to caculate the weight of each particle according current observation. Firstly according p_{static} to judge whether or not the joint angles of samples beyong their maximal or minimal value, if so revise joint angle to the defined maximal or minimal value. Secondly, according $p_{dynamic}$ to deny the dissatisfied particles and then revise the dissatisfied particles to the optimal value of last time. Thirdly, give the particles after revising and denying a similarity probability according $p_{color}p_{edge}$, the

final particle's weight $w_t^i = p_{observation}(z_t \mid x_t^i)$ is equal to $p_{color}(color \mid x_t^i)p_{edge}(edge \mid x_t^i)$.
Therefore we get a set of weighted particles $\{(x_t^i, w_t^i), i = 1,...N\}$, then normalizing the

weight according $w_t^i = \dfrac{w_t^i}{\sum_{j=1}^{N} w_t^i}$, $i = 1,...N$.

(4)   Output optimal state: After getting the normalized particle the optimal state

can be represented as $\varepsilon[x_t] = \sum_{i=1}^{N} x_t^i w_t^i$, hand state updated as $\varepsilon[x_t]$.

(5) $t = t+1$, go to step(2).

5   Experiment Results

We track several different kinds of hand movements, as displayed in Fig. 4 and 5. From the tracking result we can see that our tracking system can accurately track hand movement not only the global movement but also the local movement, even their combination. From the tracking result we can also see that the hand segmentation implemented by GMM is not very good, there are many non-skin color pixels are included. The hand segmentation is implemented according a threshold which is their probability ratio of the forground and background, the setting of the ratio has an effect on the segmentation result. While the similarity measurement function based on skin color feature is not affected by the segmentation result cause it directly caculates the similarity between hand image and hand model silhouette according the probability of pixel belongs to foreground or background. The edge feature can be got even with a changing lighting because it is based gradient, and the effects of noise can be reduced with a smooth process. The chamfer distance between hand edge and hand model contour can effectively measure their similarity. For testing our tracking system's accuracy we compare the tracking result to ground data got from 5DT data glove, as showed in Fig. 6. We can see that the tracking result can approximate the ground data. As the sample is random, the estimated optimal hand state may fluctuate around the ground data.

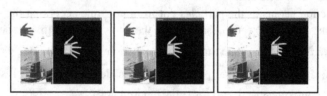

Fig. 4. Tracking fingers move

Fig. 5. Tracking fingers move while hand rotates

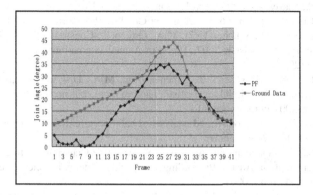

Fig. 6. The comparison between ground data and tracking result(MCP joint angle of index finger)

6   Conclusion

In this paper we combine hand constraints with image features to build an observation model which is later used in the calculation of particle weight. The observation model can effectively reduce the effects of unreasonable particles as same as raise the weight of optimal particles through three steps. Several tracking results show that our tracking system can accurately track hand movements.

Acknowledgements. This paper was supported by the National Natural Science Foundation of China (No. 61173079, No. 60973093) and Key Project of Natural Science Foundation of Shandong Province (ZR2011FZ003).

References

1. Athitsos, V., Sclaroff, S.: Estimating 3D hand pose from a cluttered image. In: Proc. Conf. Computer Vision and Pattern Recognition, Madison, pp. 432–439 (2003)
2. Rosales, R., Sclaroff, S., Athitsos, V.: 3D hand pose reconstruction using specialized mappings. In: Proc. IEEE Int'l Conf. on Computer Vision, Vancouver (2001)
3. Wu, Y., Huang, T.: View-independent recognition of hand postures. In: IEEE Computer Society Conference on Computer Vision and Pattern Recognition, vol. 2, pp. 88–94 (2000)
4. Stenger, B., Mendonça, P.R.S., Cipolla, R.: Model based 3D tracking of an articulated hand. In: Proc. Conf. Computer Vision and Pattern Recognition, Kauai, pp. 310–315 (2001)
5. Stenger, B.: Model-Based Hand Tracking Using A Hierarchical Filter. PhD thesis, University of Cambridge, Cambridge (2004)
6. Wu, Y., Lin, J.Y., Huang, T.S.: Capturing natural hand articulation. In: Proc. 8th Int. Conf. on Computer Vision, Vancouver, pp. 426–432 (2001)
7. Lin, J., Wu, Y., Huang, T.S.: Modeling the constraints of human hand motion. In: IEEE Human Motion Workshop, pp. 121–126 (2000)

8. Brown, E., Vardy, A.: Articulated Human Hand Model with Inter-Joint Dependency Constraints, Computer Science 6752, Computer Graphics Project Report (1998)
9. Cobos, S., Ferre, M., Sanchez-Urán, M.A., Ortego, J.: Constraints for Realistic Hand Manipulation. In: PRESENCE 2007, The 10th Annual International Workshop on Presence, Barcelona (2007)
10. Ferre, M., Cobos, S., Ortego, J., Sanchez-Urán, M.A.: D 4.4.1-First prototype of hand model, sufficient for mimicking realistic hand motions, but not full hand manipulation of objects yet -2007-immersence.info
11. Lee, J., Kunii, T.L.: Model-Based analysis of hand posture. IEEE Computer Graphics and Applications 15, 77–86 (1995)
12. Hassanpour, R., Shahbahrami, A., Wong, S.: Adaptive Gaussian Mixture Model for Skin Color Segmentation. Austria Proceedings of World Academy of Science, Engineering and Technology 31, 1–6 (2008)
13. Hsu, R.-L., Abdel-Mottaleb, M., Jain, A.K.: Face detection in color images. IEEE Trans. Pattern Analysis and Machine Intelligence 24, 696–706 (2002)
14. Sobottka, K., Pitas, I.: Segmentation and tracking of faces in color images. In: Proc. of the Second Intl. Conf. on Automatic Face and Gesture Recognition, pp. 236–241 (1996)
15. Vezhnevets, V., Sazonov, V., Andreeva, A.: A survey on pixel-based skin color detection techniques. Graphicon-2003, Moscow (2003)
16. Kakumanu, P., Makrogiannis, S., Bourbakis, N.G.: A survey of skin-color modeling and detection methods. Pattern Recognition 40, 1106–1122 (2007)
17. Feng, Z., Zhang, M., Pan, Z., Yang, B., Xu, T., Tang, H., Li, Y.: 3D-Freehand-Pose Initialization Based on Operator's Cognitive Behavior Models. The Visual Computer 26, 607–617 (2010)
18. DistanceTransform,
    http://www.cs.auckland.ac.nz/~rklette/Books/MK2004/
    pdfLectureNotes/08slides.pdf
19. Deutscher, J., Blake, A., Reid, I.: Articulated body motion capture by annealed particle filtering. In: International Conference on Computer Vision and Pattern Recognition, vol. 2, pp. 126–133 (2000)
20. Isard, M., Blake, A.: Condensation-Conditional density propagation for visual tracking. Intl. J. of Computer Vision 29 (1998)
21. Henia, O.B., Hariti, M., Bouakaz, S.: A two-step minimization algorithm for model-based hand tracking. In: 8th International Conference on Computer Graphics, Visualization and Computer Vision, WSCG (2010)

Smoke Simulation with Two-Scale Vorticity Confinement

Yi-Xin Xu, Shi-Guang Liu[*], and Li-Qun Wu

School of Computer Science and Technology, Tianjin University, Tianjin 300072, China
lsg@tju.edu.cn

Abstract. Enhancing the details of the smoke rendering is a major direction in virtual reality. One common solution is enhancing turbulence by adding vorticity confinement force. The traditional methods mostly add it on the global grid which would lead to expensive cost. To address this problem, we propose an adaptive two-scale vorticity confinement method. With a new scheme of computational grid, our method can determine the region with rich detail adaptively. First, the Navier-Stokes equations are solved on the coarse grid by the semi-Lagrangian method. Then, we divide the coarse grid using the defined threshold of vorticity. Finally, we obtain the velocity field of coarse grid by sampling from the fine grid, and advect density by it. In addition, we combine the helicity method which can avoid "blow up" when calculating vorticity confinement force. Various experiments validated our method.

Keywords: physically-based, smoke simulation, vorticity confinement, turbulence.

1   Introduction

Physically-based smoke simulation is always a popular research topic in computer graphics. Smoke simulation technique is not only the essential part of game engine, but also the key technology in movie special effects, such as the smoke in the popular shooting games, the mushroom cloud of an atomic bomb explosion, the fog of some natural scenes, etc.

Currently, Physically-based smoke simulation methods are dominant in computer graphics which can be divided into two types: one is Euler method based on grids, the other is Lagrangian method based on particles. Stam [1] first proposed an unconditional stable model called semi-Lagrangian iteration algorithm to solve the fluid equations. It laid a solid foundation for later fluid simulation method. It solves the Navier-Stokes equations (N-S equations) by adding external forces, advection, diffusion and projection. Because of the inherent drawbacks of difference calculation it takes, there exists numerical dissipation problem. Many solutions were proposed to solve this problem in order to enhance fluid details. One of the common methods is adding the vorticity confinement force to compensate the numerical dissipation caused in [1]. It is easy to implement and also can generate a good effect. However,

---

[*] Corresponding author.

F.L. Wang et al. (Eds.): CMSP 2012, CCIS 346, pp. 467–474, 2012.
© Springer-Verlag Berlin Heidelberg 2012

this method usually adds the vorticity confinement force uniformly to global grids, which leads to a relatively huge computation.

To overcome the above problems, we propose an adaptive grid based smoke simulation method. The adaptive grid is generated based on vorticity field, which is used to determine which grids need detail enhancement. This method compare the vorticity field value of each grid with a threshold, then find the grid which need turbulence enhancement and subdivide it. It can avoid the large computation of the simulation on the global fine grid directly. In addition, in order to avoid "blow up" phenomena, we combine the helicity method.

The rest of this paper is organized as follows: Section 2 is related work about detail enhancement of smoke simulation. Section 3 introduces the method of two-scale grid and the grid division scheme. The vorticity confinement force method which considers helicity is in Section 4. Some results of our method are in Section 5. Conclusions and the future work conclude the paper.

2   Related Work

Until now, there are many methods about smoke simulation in computer graphics. Here we mainly review some detail enhancement methods in smoke simulation.

It is a common way to enhance details by adding vorticity confinement force. Fedkiw et al. [2] first proposed this method to solve the numerical dissipation problem in [1] and enhance the details of smoke. One of the shortcomings is that the parameter of vorticity confinement force cannot be set a high value. He et al. [3] improved this method by considering the helicity of smoke movement which can overcome the problem of "blow up" when vorticity confinement force parameter value is high.

Adding noise is a popular technique to enhance the smoke details. Neyret [4] blended the velocity field and noise texture in order to enhance details. Kim et al. [5] proposed a method according to k-ε turbulence model. They first calculated the velocity on low resolution grid. Then interpolated the velocity to high resolution grid and got a fine result by adding wavelet noise. This method avoided the large computation in high resolution grid. Bridson et al. [6] proposed a method which can generate turbulent velocity field based on Perlin noise.

Another type of method about detail enhancement is using particles. Selle et al. [7] added details to the results in [2] by adding particles around obstacles and regions with large turbulence. The extra computational cost was negligible. Narain et al. [8] determined the regions which need noise by calculating the energy field, and then enhanced details in these areas by adding improved curl noise particles. This method is fast too. Based on [5], Pfaff et al. [9] added guide particles in detail-rich region to ensure anisotropic movement when the smoke encounters obstacles. But this method may cause distortion in some cases. Zhu et al. [10] proposed SPH (Smoothed Particle Hydrodynamics) to ensure the details around the obstacles. But the turbulence generated process is not strictly precise in physics.

Detail enhancement can also be achieved by irregular grid structure. In order to capture details, Losassa et al. [11] proposed a grid method using octree data structure, which lead to a good result. Dobashi et al. [12] proposed an overlapping grid method to deal with the interaction between smoke and rigid obstacles. They generated local fine grids based on global grid, and these fine grids moved along with obstacles. However, the computational cost will increase with the increase amount of the obstacles. Lentine et al. [13] accelerated the simulation by a mapping method between coarse and fine grid. Pfaff et al. [14] proposed to add artificial boundary layer around obstacles, and used a turbulence model to identify which regions of this layer will transform into actual turbulence. It is efficient but hard to be applied to obstacles which can deform like cloth. There are also other methods [15-16] to enhance fluid details using improved mathematical method or solver. [17] gave a detailed summary of the research status about fluid simulation.

3   Two-Scale Grid Method and Grid Division Scheme

In this section, we first give a brief overview about the incompressible N-S equations. Then describe the method used in the two-scale grid simulation. Finally, we propose the grid division scheme based on the vorticity field.

3.1   Incompressible Navier-Stokes Equations

Physically based fluid simulations are mostly based on the incompressible fluid N-S equations shown as follows:

$$\frac{\partial u}{\partial t} = -(u \cdot \nabla)u - \nabla p/\rho + f \tag{1}$$

$$\nabla \cdot u = 0 \tag{2}$$

Equation (1) is momentum equation, where u denotes velocity, t denotes time, p is pressure, ρ is density, and f represents external force, such as buoyancy and gravity. Equation (2) is mass equation. It ensures the conservation of the fluid mass.

3.2   Two-Scale Grid Method

In theory, the richness of details is related to the grid resolution. The higher resolution is the more details gets. As the increase of grid resolution, the computational cost becomes higher. In this paper we first calculate the velocity on coarse grid to obtain the general movement of the smoke. Then sample the velocity values to fine grid and simulate to increase smoke details. Finally, sample the fine grid velocity back to the coarse grid and obtain the final velocity. This method can avoid the large computational cost when simulate on global fine grid directly and lead to a good effect.

We use the method proposed in Stam [1] and Fedkiw et al. [2] to solve the N-S equations in coarse grid, which divided the calculation into several steps: add external forces (buoyancy, vorticity confinement force), advection, diffusion, and projection. We need additional storage for the vorticity field for the later use of grid division.

On fine grids, we adopt the following model to calculate the velocity field (refers to [18]):

$$\frac{\partial u_S}{\partial t_S} = -(u_L + u_S) \cdot \nabla u_S \tag{3}$$

where u_L and u_S is the velocity in coarse grid and fine grid respectively, t_S denotes the time step in fine grid (here we set $t_S = 0.25 \times t_L$). As there is only one advection term in the right hand side of equation (3) and there is no projection term which needs high computation cost, this method is efficient. Moreover, experiments show that it will not lead to the unstable phenomenon with our method.

3.3   Vorticity-Based Grid Division Scheme

If we adopt the global grid division scheme, i.e. treat all the coarse grids in the same way, the computation will increase sharply. Considering that not all grids contain rich detail, we proposed a new grid division scheme based on vorticity field. It can identify the grids with rich details adaptively, and divide them into fine grids. The resolution of fine grid is two times of the coarse one per dimension.

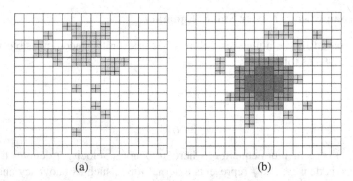

(a)   (b)

Fig. 1. The results of grid division. The coarse grid resolution of both (a) and (b) is 16×16×16, they represent a slice of the simulation at some time. The pink part represents the grids which need division. In figure (b), the blue part represents the obstacle. The green grids around the obstacle are divided.

Vorticity can be regarded as a phenomenon of local smoke rotates around a particular axis, which represents the richness of the smoke details. Therefore we use this quantity to determine whether a coarse grid is needed to be divided into fine one. We get vorticity field value through each coarse grid's curl of velocity field as follows:

$$\omega = \nabla \times u \tag{4}$$

Then, compare the modulus of each coarse grid's vorticity field value $|\omega_L|$ with the modulus of threshold $|\omega_{th}|$. If $|\omega_L| > |\omega_{th}|$, then this coarse grid need to be divided into fine one. Otherwise, it remains unchanged. Every time step, we compared these two quantities in coarse grid and reset the fine grid to ensure detail enhancement adaptive.

For the circumstance with obstacles, besides dividing some grids into fine ones by above method, we would also divide the coarse grids around obstacles directly without comparing the vorticity.

Figure 1 shows the grid division results using our method. (a) is the circumstance with no obstacle, and (b) is with obstacle.

4   Vorticity Confinement Force with Helicity

4.1   Vorticity Confinement Force

Fedkiw et al. [2] points out that, fluid details can be enhanced by adding vorticity confinement force. In incompressible fluid, we get the vorticity field through equation (4). The normalized vorticity position vector N can be calculated through the gradient of $|\omega|$ as the following:

$$N = \frac{\nabla|\omega|}{|\nabla|\omega||} \qquad (5)$$

At last, we get the vorticity confinement force form the the equation (6):

$$f_{conf} = \varepsilon h(N \times \omega) \qquad (6)$$

where ε is the user defined parameter in order to control the vorticity, and h denotes the grid size. The vorticity confinement force can be added as an external force to the fluid simulation model.

4.2   The Helicity

Through equation (6) we can see that, if we want to get more details, we can set ε larger. But it may lead to some non-realistic effects or even cause the "blow up" phenomenon if ε is too large. The main reason is that we have not considered the helicity factor when calculating the vorticity confinement force:

$$H = \int u \cdot \omega \, dV \qquad (7)$$

It measures the amount of rotation of a fluid rotating around an axis that is parallel to the main flow direction [3], where V denotes volume. According to this physical quantity, He et al. [3] improved equation (6) as follows:

$$f_{conf} = \varepsilon h|u \cdot \omega|(N \times \omega) \qquad (8)$$

where $|u \cdot \omega|$ represents for helicity. Then the vorticity confinrment force is not only determined by the value of grid size h, but also by the helicity.

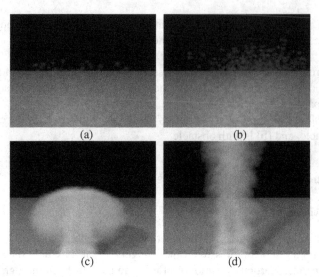

Fig. 2. A comparison between (top) the simulation without helicity and (bottom) with helicity. The resolution of all the figure is 64×64×64. In (a) and (b), $\varepsilon = 11.0$; in (c) and (d), $\varepsilon = 30.5$. (a) and (c) show the simulation result at a same time, (b) and (d) are as well. We can see the "blow up" obviously in (a) and (b).

This method has effectively solved the un-realistic problem when ε was set too large. As Fig. 2 shows, in the resolution of 64×64×64 grid space, when add vorticity confinrment force without helicity, it resulted to obvious "blow up" phenomenon with large ε. But after considering helicity, it has not led to this phenomenon even the ε is larger. The method of paper [3] simulated the smoke scenes on the uniform grid, we have extended it to non-uniform grid.

5   Results

Based on the above computational model, we simulated the smoke with hardware environment as follows: Intel Core i3 3.07GHz processor, ATI Radeon HD 5450 1GB video card, 2GB memory. Our compiler environment is Visual Studio 2008, and the rendering-environment is Pov-Ray.

Table 1. Resolution of the simulation grid and the rendering time

Figure	Target Grid Resolution	Average of coarse grids need division per frame	Time per frame (second)
3(a)	32×32×32	1002.21	0.20875
3(b)	64×64×64	13510.2	1.93825
3(c)	64×64×64	9848.65	2.00087

Figure 3 shows more results of our method. In this experiment, we set the velocity of the vertical direction **0**. The upward movement of smoke is guided by the buoyancy, as shown in Figure 3(a). 3(b) represents the movement of slant upward direction, and the initial velocity is not **0**. 3(c) denotes the smoke moves up cross a sphere. We set the direction of velocity around the sphere be opposite from its original direction.

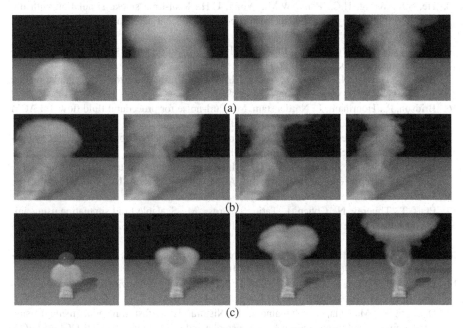

Fig. 3. Some results. Every row represents a scene of 4 different time from left to right.

6   Conclusions and Future Work

Based on the Two-scale Grid method, we have proposed a grid division scheme with vorticity to simulate smoke scenes. Our method can adaptively find the grid which is needed to add detail. At the same time, we have considered the helicity when calculating the vorticity confinement force. We can see that our method have good effects from the results.

However, there is still some work to be done. First, we will use better interpolation method when sampling from coarse grid to fine grid. Second, the advection step can simulate through some new schemes to eliminate the numerical dissipation further. We leave these issues as our future work.

Acknowledgements. The research was supported by National Science Foundation of China Nos. 61170118 and 60803047, the Specialized Research Fund for the Doctoral Program of Higher Education of China No. 200800561045, and the Open Project Program of the State Key Lab of CAD&CG, Zhejiang University No. A1210.

References

1. Stam, J.: Stable fluids. In: ACM SIGGRAPH, pp. 121–128 (1999)
2. Fedkiw, R., Stam, J., Jensen, H.W.: Visual simulation of smoke. In: ACM SIGGRAPH, pp. 15–22 (2001)
3. He, S.F., Wong, H.C., Pang, W.M., Wong, U.H.: Real-time smoke simulation with improved turbulence by spatial adaptive vorticity confinement. Computer Animation and Virtual Worlds 22(2-3), 107–114 (2011)
4. Neyret, F.: Advected textures. In: ACM SIGGRAPH/Eurographics Symposium on Computer Animation, pp. 147–153 (2003)
5. Kim, T., Thurey, N., James, D., Gross, M.: Wavelet turbulence for fluid simulation. In: ACM SIGGRAPH, vol. 27(3), pp. 50:1–50:9 (2008)
6. Bridson, R., Houriham, J., Nordenstam, M.: Curl-noise for procedural fluid flow. In: ACM SIGGRAPH, vol. 26(3), pp. 46:1–46:3 (2007)
7. Selle, A., Rasmussen, N., Fedkiw, R.: A vortex particle method for smoke, water and explosions. In: ACM SIGGRAPH, pp. 910–914 (2005)
8. Narain, R., Sewall, J., Carlson, M., Lin, M.C.: Fast animation of turbulence using energy transport and procedural synthesis. In: ACM SIGGRAPH ASIA, vol. 27(5), pp.166: 1–166:8 (2008)
9. Pfaff, T., Thuerey, N., Cohen, J., Tariq, S., Gross, M.: Scalable fluid simulation using anisotropic turbulence particles. In: ACM SIGGRAPH ASIA, vol. 29(6), pp. 174:1–174:8 (2010)
10. Zhu, B., Yang, X., Fan, Y.: Creating and preserving vortical details in SPH fluid. In: Pacific Graphics, vol. 29(7), pp. 2207–2214 (2010)
11. Losasso, F., Gibou, F., Fedkiw, R.: Simulating water and smoke with an octree data structure. In: ACM SIGGRAPH, vol. 23(3), pp. 457–462 (2004)
12. Dobashi, Y., Matsuda, Y., Yamamoto, T., Nishita, T.: A fast simulation method using overlapping grids for interactions between smoke and rigid objects. In: EUROGRAPHICS, vol. 27(2), pp. 477–486 (2008)
13. Lentine, M., Zheng, W., Fedkiw, R.: A novel algorithm for incompressible flow using only a coarse grid projection. In: ACM SIGGRAPH, vol. 29(4), pp. 114:1–114:9 (2010)
14. Pfaff, T., Thuerey, N., Selle, A., Gross, M.: Synthetic turbulence using artificial boundary layers. In: ACM SIGGRAPH ASIA, vol. 28(5), pp. 121:1–121:10 (2009)
15. McAdams, A., Sifakis, E., Teran, J.: A parallel multigrid Poisson solver for fluids simulation on large grids. In: ACM SIGGRAPH/ Eurographics Symposium on Computer Animation, pp. 65–74 (2010)
16. Mullen, P., Crane, K., Pavlov, D., Tong, Y., Desbrun, M.: Energy-preserving integrators for fluid animation. In: ACM SIGGRAPH, vol. 28(3), pp. 38:1–38:8 (2009)
17. Tan, J., Yang, X.: Physically-based fluid animation: A Survey. Science in China Series F-Information Sciences 52(5), 723–740 (2008)
18. Jang, T., Kim, H., Bae, J., Seo, J., Noh, J.: Multilevel vorticity confinement for water turbulence simulation. Visual Computer 26(6-8), 873–881 (2010)

Tree Animation Based on Hierarchical Shape Matching

Sang-Min Song, Young-Min Kang, Eung-Joo Lee, and Soo-Yol Ok*

TONGMYONG University
535, Yongdang-Dong, Nam-Gu, Busan, Korea, 608-711
{songsmir,ymkang,ejlee,sooyol}@tu.ac.kr

Abstract. In this paper, we propose a method that produces the realistic motion of L-system based virtual trees. Virtual trees generated with traditional L-system were usually animated with physically-based approaches which require complex motion equations to be solved. Therefore, realtime and plausible animation of such models has been regarded a very difficult problem, and has been rarely employed in interactive applications. The method proposed in this paper plausibly animates the virtual trees based on hierarchical shape matching (HSM) without any complex dynamic equations. The HSM is an improved version of usual shape matching. In this approach, the object is divided into small clusters, and each cluster is locally animated with the shape matching while the global shape is also adjusted in accordance with the original shape.

Keywords: Shape matching, virtual tree, L-system, hierarchical animation.

1 Introduction

In graphics literature, the tree modeling approaches based on L-system can be easily found[1]. However, those methods do not usually generate the motion of trees because the realistic animation of the complex virtual tree is not a simple problem. The animation of such model usually requires heavy computation for stably solving the motion equation.

In this paper, we propose a hierarchical shape matching(HSM) method. The method is an improved version of usual shape matching. In this approach, an object is divided into small clusters, and each cluster is locally animated with the shape matching while the global shape is also adjusted in accordance with the original shape. The proposed method was successfully employed in a realtime game environment.

2 Previous Work

In computer graphics literature, various modeling methods have been intensively studied for realistic representation of the appearance of tree [2,3,4,5]. However, those methods focus only on the geometric shapes of the trees [6].

---

* Corresponding author.

F.L. Wang et al. (Eds.): CMSP 2012, CCIS 346, pp. 475–482, 2012.

Recently, for the realism in the virtual world, the plausible animation of virtual trees is becoming more important. Therefore, various research efforts are being made for the tree animation. Some of those methods generate the behavior of a virtual tree by animating its branches [7,8,9] while some others animates the tree by taking only the leaves into account [10,11].

The method proposed in [11] models the motion of a tree based on the oscillation function of control points. The simulation can be easily performed on GPU in order to represent the forest. However, versatile control over the wind cannot be obtained in this method.

Deformation based animation was also proposed [16]. In this method, the vertices in the tree geometry are translated and rotated in accordance with the external force of the wind and the restoration based on shape matching proposed in [17]. However, this method also suffers from heavy computation when the number of the clusters increases.

3   Tree Modeling and Deformation

We employed the L-system in order to procedurally generate the shape of virtual tree. The L-system employs the rewriting system that modifies the initial string to another string in accordance with mathematical substitution rules. Fig. 1 shows the process of the tree shape modeling based on the L-system.

The deformation techniques have been intensively studied in computer graphics literature. In order to alleviate the computational burden of physical simulation, free form deformation (FFD) approaches have been proposed. However, the deformation based on the FFD cannot produce physically plausible motion. So far, physically plausible and computationally efficient method for realtime animation of complex and realistic virtual tree has not been proposed.

Shape matching method was proposed in[17]. The method focuses on the fact that deformed objects tend to return the original shapes. In the shape matching method, the restoration force can be efficiently computed by finding the optimal linear transformation between the current shape and the original one.

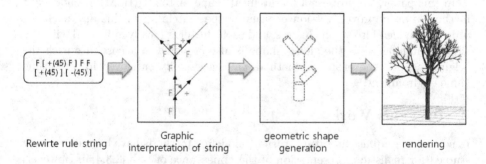

| Rewirte rule string | Graphic interpretation of string | geometric shape generation | rendering |

Fig. 1. The process of L-System based tree modeling

Let us assume, for instance, a deformable object. The set of the vertices of the object is denoted to be $\mathbf{X}$. The original center of mass can be denoted as p_0. If the deformation can be described with a linear transformation $\mathbf{A}$, then the new state $\mathbf{X}'$ can be expressed as follows:

$$\mathbf{X}' = \mathbf{A}\mathbf{X} + p_0 \tag{1}$$

If the object has the exactly the same shape as the original state, the linear transformation should involve only rotation $\mathbf{R}$ and translation $\mathbf{T}$. In this case the new state can be expressed as follows:

$$\mathbf{X}' = \mathbf{R}\mathbf{X} + (\mathbf{T}\mathbf{X} + p_0) \tag{2}$$

where $\mathbf{T}\mathbf{X} + p_0$ is the new center of mass p_1.

Eq. 2 can be considered the target shape that the deformable object should be restored to. In fact, the deformable object undergoes the deformation by the external forces. Therefore, the current state $\mathbf{X}'$ cannot be exactly obtained with $\mathbf{R}$ and $\mathbf{T}$. If we find the $\mathbf{R}$ and $\mathbf{T}$ that optimally transform the original shape close to the current shape, we can obtain the target shape $\mathbf{G}$. Each vertex x_i' should be animated to move back to the goal position g_i in the set $\mathbf{G}$.

Eq. 2 can be rewritten for each vertex x_i as follows:

$$w_i\mathbf{R}(x_i^0 - x_{cm}^0) + x_{cm} - x_i \tag{3}$$

where x_i is the location of the vertex i, and w_i is the weight of the vertex, x_{cm}^0 denotes the center of mass of the object at the initial state while x_{cm} is the current center of mass. The translation transformation $\mathbf{T}$ can be easily computed with Eq. 3. However, $\mathbf{R}$ cannot be easily obtained. Therefore, we first obtain a linear transformation $\mathbf{A}$, and approximate the $\mathbf{R}$ by removing the scaling factors in the transformation.

The optimal linear transformation can be obtained by the least square method as follows[17]:

$$\mathbf{A} = (\textstyle\sum_i m_i p_i q_i^T)(\textstyle\sum_i m_i q_i q_i^T)^{-1} = \mathbf{A}_{pq}\mathbf{A}_{qq} \tag{4}$$

where $p_i = x_i - t$, and $q_i = x_i^0 - t_0$. Since $\mathbf{A}_{qq}$ is symmetric, $\mathbf{R}$ should be is $\mathbf{A}_{pq}$[17]. The rotation matrix $\mathbf{R}$ can be obtained with polar decomposition of $\mathbf{A}_{pq}$ as follows:

$$\begin{aligned}\mathbf{A}_{pq} &= \mathbf{R}\mathbf{S} \\ \mathbf{R} &= \mathbf{A}_{pq}\mathbf{S}^{-1}\end{aligned} \tag{5}$$

We obtain $\mathbf{S}^{-1}$ by exploiting the right Cauchy-Green deformation tensor law. The goal location g_i of each vertex can then be descirbed with $\mathbf{R}$ and $\mathbf{T}$.

$$g_i = \mathbf{R}(x_i^0 - t_0) + t \tag{6}$$

The required velocity to easily compute with the goal location with the rigidity control parameter α ranging from 0 to 1 as follows:

$$\begin{aligned}v_i(t+h) &= v_i(t) + \alpha\frac{g_i(t) - x_i(t)}{h} + h\frac{F^{ext}(t)}{m_i} \\ x_i(t+h) &= x_i(t) + hv_i(t+h)\end{aligned} \tag{7}$$

4   Hierarchical Shape Matching for Realistic Animation

In order to avoid the problems of the multi-cluster approach, we propose a hierarchical shape matching. When the goal locations are computed, the hierarchical approach not only performs the local cluster-based shape matching but also employs the global shape matching for preserving the initial shape of the tree.

4.1   Global Shape Matching

The multi-cluster approach cannot maintain the original shape of the tree since the shape matching forces only considers the shape of each local cluster. In this method, each vertex is forced to move back to the original location of the vertex. The whole shape of the tree can then be easily restored by global shape matching with the adjusted velocity as follows:

$$v_i^{global} = v_i^{local} + k_d(p_i^{original} - p_i) \tag{8}$$

where v_i^{global} is the velocity of i after the global shape matching, and v_i^{local} is the velocity computed in the cluster-based local shape matching. p_i is the location of the particle determined by the local shape matching while $p_i^{original}$ denotes the original location of the vertex. k_d denotes the damping or controlling parameter for the speed of the global restoration.

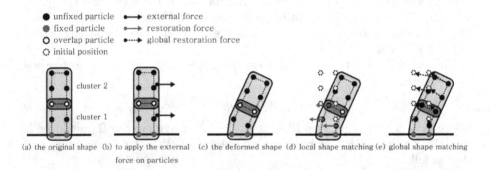

(a) the original shape (b) to apply the external   (c) the deformed shape (d) local shape matching (e) global shape matching
                         force on particles

Fig. 2. Hierarchical shape matching concept

Fig. 2 shows the concept of the hierarchical shape matching with the local and global shape matchings. Each cluster in a tree model changes its shape when an external force is applied. The local shape matching restores the original shape of each cluster with the waves and oscillations generated. The global shape matching makes the tree more plausible by removing the unrealistic waves and oscillations on the tree.

4.2 Improved Animation Based on Physical Properties

The shape matching method does not take into account the physical properties such as mass. Therefore, in some cases, unrealistic animation is generated where thick branches and thin branches are similarly bended by external forces. However, the thick branches should be less accelerated than thin ones. In order to express such behaviors, we assigned larger masses to the vertices in the thicker branches. If we model every branch with the same number of vertices, the vertices in a cluster with bigger volume can be regarded a sample of the larger area. Therefore, such vertices should be assigned larger masses. Therefore, the mass of each vertex can be computed by considering the volume of the cluster where the vertex is located. V_c, the volume of the cluster of which shape is truncated cone can be easily computed as follows:

$$V_c = \frac{\pi}{3} * (r_t^2 + r_t r_b + r_b^2) * l \tag{9}$$

where r_t and r_b are the radii of the circles at the top and the bottom respectively, and l is the length of the truncated cone. The volume-based mass assignment generates plausible branch animation. Let us assume the volume of the cluster is decreasing in accordance with the height. In that case, the cluster at top-most location will be lighter than others. When an external force is applied to the clusters, the top-most cluster will be accelerated more than any other clusters. After the reasonable animation, the hierarchical shape matching will restore the shape to a plausibly deformed state as shown in the figure.

The real world leaves can be separated from the tree by strong external forces. In our method, the leaves can be easily detached from the tree branches by invalidating the overlapping properties of the overlapping vertices in the leave clusters when the force exceeds a given threshold. The global shape matching will keep the leaves from floating away from the tree. Therefore, we turn off the initial position based matching when the overlapping property of the leave cluster is disabled.

5 Experiment

We implemented the proposed method on a system with Intel 3.47 GHz i7 CPU, 24 G DDR3 RAM, and NVidia GTX 590 GPUs running on Windows 7 OS.

The computational performance in the aspect of frame rates is shown in Table. 1. As shown in the table, even with the complex model with 211,812 vertices, the proposed method could generate an interactive animation with the performance of 32 frames per second.

Fig. 3 shows the growing of a virtual tree. The L-system based production rules can generate plausible trees as shown in the figure. By changing the rules or the initial string, we could generate various types of trees. By the nature of the exponential growth, a realistic tree could be easily obtained with a few steps of growth.

Table 1. FPS(Frame Per Second)

clusters	particles	FPS
5	300	258
15	900	200
293	13,548	79
867	38,772	62
2,230	99,816	46
4,975	211,812	32

Fig. 3. Growth of a virtual tree

The animation result is shown in Fig. 4. For the animation, 211,812 vertices and 4,975 clusters were used. As shown in the figure, the hierarchical shape matching produced a plausible animation where thin branches and leaves move more than thicker branches. The bending tendency of the branches, of course, can be easily controlled in our method.

Fig. 4. Animation with the hierarchical shape matching

The leaves could be easily detached from the tree as shown in Fig. 5. As shown in the figure, the detached leaves float in the air and generate realistic wind and tree interaction animation.

Fig. 5. Detachable tree leaves

6   Conclusion

In this paper, we proposed an efficient and effective animation techniques for virtual trees modeled with L-system. The method proposed in this paper plausibly animates the virtual trees based on hierarchical shape matching (HSM) without any complex dynamic equations. The HSM is an improved version of usual shape matching. In this approach, the object is divided into small clusters, and each cluster is locally animated with the shape matching while the global shape is also adjusted in accordance with the original shape.

The proposed method can be easily exploited to animate various virtual trees, and the computational burden of the proposed method is relatively smaller than those of the traditional approaches such as free form deformation or physically based animation techniques. Moreover, the proposed method generates plausible animation with numerical stability. The method proposed in this paper will be successfully employed in interactive applications such as game.

Acknowledgments. This work was supported in part by the Ministry of Knowledge Economy (MKE), Korea, under the Information Technology Research Center (ITRC) support program supervised by the National IT Industry Promotion Agency (NIPA) (NIPA-2011-(C-1090-1021-0006)), and this work (Grants No.C0033371) was supported by Business for Cooperative R&D between Industry, Academy, and Research Institute funded Korea Small and Medium Business Administration in 2012.

References

1. Lindenmayer, A., Rozenberg, G.: Developmental Systems and Languages. In: STOC, pp. 214–221 (1972)
2. Aono, M., Kunii, T.L.: Botanical Tree Image Generation. In: IEEE Computer Graphics and Applications, pp. 55–64 (1982)
3. Weber, J., Penn, J.: Creation and rendering of realistic trees. In: SIGGRAPH, pp. 119–128 (1995)

4. Měch, R., Prusinkiewicz, P.: Visual models of plants interacting with their environment. In: SIGGRAPH, pp. 397–410 (1996)
5. Prusinkiewicz, P., Hammel, M., Hanan, J., Měch, R.: Visual models of plant development. Springer-Verlag New York, Inc. (1997)
6. Livny, Y., Pirk, S., Cheng, Z., Yan, F., Deussen, O., Cohen-Or, D., Chen, B.: Texture-Lobes for Tree Modelling. ACM Transactions on Graphics (Proceedings of SIGGRAPH 2011), 53:1–53:10 (2011)
7. Stam, J.: Stochastic Dynamics: Simulating the Effects of Turbulence on Flexible Structures. Comput. Graph. Forum, 159–164 (1997)
8. Sakaguchi, T., Ohya, J.: Modeling and animation of botanical trees for interactive virtual environments. ACM (1999)
9. Ding, L., Chongcheng, C., Liyu, T., Qinmin, W., Wenqiang, X.: Interactive Physical Based Animation of Tree Swaying in Wind. IEEE Computer Society (2009)
10. Ota, S., Tamura, M., Fujimoto, T., Muraoka, K., Chiba, N.: Stochastic Dynamics: A hybrid method for real-time animation of trees swaying in wind fields. The Visual Computer, 613–623 (2004)
11. Diener, J., Rodriguez, M., Baboud, L., Reveret, L.: Wind Projection Basis for Real-Time Animation of Trees. Computer Graphics Forum (2009)
12. Manchester, R.-U.: Eurographics Workshop on Computer Animation and Simulation. Springer (2001)
13. Oliapuram, N.J., Kumar, S.: Proceedings of the Seventh Indian Conference on Computer Vision, Graphics and Image Processing. ACM (2010)
14. Akagi, Y., Kitajima, K.: Computer animation of swaying trees based on physical simulation. Computers and Graphics, 529–539 (2006)
15. Ota, S., Fujimoto, T., Tamura, M., Muraoka, K., Fujita, K., Chiba, N.: $1/f^\beta$ Noise-Based Real-Time Animation of Trees Swaying in Wind Fields. In: Computer Graphics International Conference, pp. 1530–1052 (2003)
16. Steinemann, D., Otaduy, M.A., Gross, M.: Proceedings of the 2008 ACM SIGGRAPH/Eurographics Symposium on Computer Animation. Eurographics Association (2008)
17. Müller, M., Heidelberger, B., Teschner, M., Gross, M.: ACM SIGGRAPH 2005 Papers. ACM (2005)

An Efficient and Stable Water Surface Animation for Interactive Applications

Sang-Min Song, Young-Min Kang, and Soo-Yol Ok*

TONGMYONG University
535, Yongdang-Dong, Nam-Gu, Busan, Korea, 608-711
{songsmir,ymkang,sooyol}@tu.ac.kr

Abstract. In this paper, we propose a realtime approach to water surface animation based on shape matching. The method proposed in this paper is based on shape matching method. The water surface is modeled as a mesh structure which is divided into multiple clusters composed of mesh vertices. The clusters are overlapped with adjacent clusters, and each cluster is animated with shape restoration forces. The shape restoration property of each cluster produces wave effect on the water surface. We exploited GPU parallelism to animate the water surface in realtime, and the water surface can plausibly interact with external objects.

Keywords: shape matching, wave equation, wave, cluster based shape matching, GPU parallelism.

1 Introduction

As the recent graphics hardware is being rapidly developed, more and more realtime applications are trying to employ realistic water representation. The previous methods can be classified into two major categories: approximation with parametric wave functions and physics animation with wave equation. Although the approximation approach can efficiently generate the water surface, the interaction between the water surface and other objects cannot be easily implemented. In contrast, the simulation based on the wave equation requires heavy computation but the interaction between water and external objects can be easily represented. In order to employ the water animation in an interactive application such as game, the interaction between the water and other object should be taken into account. In this paper, we propose an interactive water surface animation method based on shape matching. The method produces realistic water animation with plausible interaction with external objects. Moreover, the method is stable enough to be employed in interactive applications.

2 Previous Work

In the early techniques, the water surface was represented as a height map computed with continuous periodic functions[1]. The method was improved to represent more realistic water surface by considering the water depth[2]. Such methods

---

* Corresponding author.

F.L. Wang et al. (Eds.): CMSP 2012, CCIS 346, pp. 483–490, 2012.

based on approximation can efficiently produce the water surface. However, a large amount of periodic functions is required to represent a complex and realistic water surface. Chen[3] exploited GPU parallelism to efficiently process the periodic functions. The method produces a bump map to represent the water surface. LOD approach was also exploited to alleviate the computational cost[4,5,6].

The motion of water surface can be easily modeled and animated with the periodic functions. However, the periodic function cannot easily produce complex surface. In order to represent the complex surface, fast Fourier transform (FFT) was also exploited[7,8]. However, the method with FFT cannot effectively control the water surface. Therefore, the methods cannot be employed interactive application.

In order to enable the interaction with external objects, physically based approach should be employed. The major categories for physics based water simulation are grid-based Euler method [9,10] and particle-based Lagrange method[11]. However, the physics based approaches require too heavy computation to be integrated into realtime applications.

Recently, an efficiently method based on 'wave particles' were proposed[12]. However, the method cannot produce the wave valleys so that the surface is not sufficiently realistic.

3   Basic Concept of Water Surface Animation

Our method links the deformable object to generate wave effect. The physical property of each object is dominated by restoration force computed by shape matching. Therefore, each cluster element of water surface is constrained to maintain original shape. Since each element is overlapped with adjacent element, the motion of each element is transported to the adjacent elements. Therefore we can obtain the wave effect along the adjacent object chain.

The shape matching approach produces force to move deformed vertices back to the target position. The deformable objects try to maintain the original shape, but the locations of vertices in the objects are not strictly constrained. The deformable object is deformed when external force is exerted as shown in Fig.??. In this paper, V denotes the set of vertices. A vertex i is an element of the set V. The properties of i include the current position x_i, the original position x_i^0, goal position g_i, acceleration a_i, velocity v_i, and the mass m_i. If the object is rigid, the position of vertex i can be expressed with a rotation matrix $\mathbf{R}$ and a translation matrix $\mathbf{T}$. Once we know the matrix $\mathbf{R}$, the goal position can be easily computed as follows:

$$x_i^{'} = m_i R(x_i^0 - t_0) + t - x_i \tag{1}$$

where t is the current center of mass and t_0 denotes the original center of mass.

In order to compute the rotation matrix $\mathbf{R}$ in Eq.1, we employed a optimal linear transformation matrix as follows:

$$x_i^{'} = m_i A(x_i^0 - t_0) + t - x_i \tag{2}$$

Least square method is applied to compute the matrix $\mathbf{A}$ in Eq. 2. The change of vertices can be described as follows:

$$\varepsilon_i = Aq_i - p_i \tag{3}$$

We should minimize the following:

$$S = \sum_i \varepsilon_i^2 = \sum_i (Aq_i + p_i)^2 \tag{4}$$

Then the matrix $\mathbf{A}$ is obtained as follows:

$$\begin{aligned} A &= (\textstyle\sum_i m_i p_i q_i^{\mathbf{T}})(\textstyle\sum_i m_i q_i q_i^{\mathbf{T}})^{-1} \\ &= Apq\,Aqq \end{aligned} \tag{5}$$

The matrix $\mathbf{A}$ in Eq. 5 can be decomposed into $\mathbf{A}pq$ and $\mathbf{A}qq$. Since the symmetric matrix $\mathbf{A}qq$ involves no rotation, the matrix $\mathbf{A}pq$ is actually utilized. The rotation matrix $\mathbf{R}$ can be obtained as follows:

$$\begin{aligned} A_{pq} &= RS \\ R &= A_{pq}S^{-1} \end{aligned} \tag{6}$$

Each vertex in the object are forced to move to a goal position g_i, and the goal position can be obtained with the rotation matrix $\mathbf{R}$ as follows:

$$g_i = \mathbf{R}(x_i^0 - t_0) + t \tag{7}$$

4   Water Surface Model and Animation

The shape matching approach utilizes the rotation matrix $\mathbf{R}$. However, the matrix restores the original shape of each object so that the wave vanishes too rapidly. Therefore, we employed the matrix $\mathbf{A}pq$ instead of $\mathbf{R}$ to produce more realistic water surface.

Our methods represent the water surface with the collection of small geometric elements called clusters which are essentially deformable objects. The objects share some vertices with overlapping adjacent clusters as shown in Fig. 1. The shape matching process is applied to each cluster. Total n clusters are denoted as c_1, c_2, ..., and c_n respectively, and C denotes the set of the clusters.

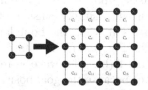

Fig. 1. Water surface structure with clusters

Fig. 2. Overlapping clusters: the cluster c_6 shares the vertices x_7, x_8, x_{12}, x_{13} with adjacent clusters $c_1, c_2, c_3, c_5, c_7, c_9, c_{10}$, and c_{11}

As shown in Fig.1, the cluster c_i is composed of 4 vertices, and Each cluster shares some vertices with adjacent clusters as shown in Fig. 2.

In this paper we employed distortion transportation between shape matching based deformable objects. The difference between the goal position of deformed cluster and undeformed cluster is transferred along the chained clusters, and the effect of the transfer produces wave motion.

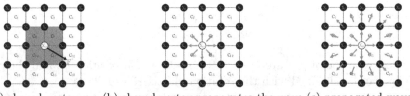

(a) shared vertex x_{13} (b) shared vertex propagates the wave (c) propagated waves

Fig. 3. Wave energy transportaion

When an external force is applied to x_{13} in Fig. 3, the clusters which share the vertex also deformed as shown in Fig. 3. The clusters are animated to restore the original shape by shape matching algorithm. The shape matching applied to each cluster produces different goal position of x_{13} such as g_{13}^6, g_{13}^7, g_{13}^{10}, and g_{13}^{11} as follows:

$$g_{13} = (g_{13}^6 + g_{13}^7 + g_{13}^{10} + g_{13}^{11})/N_{cluster} \qquad (8)$$

where $N_{clusture}$ denotes the number of clusters that share the vertex.

Water Surface Boundary. For the realistic animation of water surface, the wave should be reflected at the boundary of the water surface. However, the previous methods cannot easily produce the wave reflection. In our method, the reflection can be easily produced by simply constrain the boundary vertices. Fig. 4 shows the wave reflection result when the boundary vertices are constrained not to move. As shown in the Fig. 4 (a), the external force applied to a vertex produces wave shown in Fig. 4 (b). The wave is reflected at the constrained vertices as shown in Fig. 4 (c) because the goal positions of the vertices are constant. Our method, therefore, easily produce wave reflection and the boundary of the water surface can be easily specified.

(a) external force

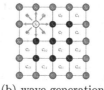
(b) wave generation

(c) wave reflection

Fig. 4. Wave reflection

Damping with Original Position. The method proposed in this paper produces wave effect by keeping each cluster maintaining the original shape. However, the simple shape matching of each cluster produces long-lasting oscillation. The actual water surfaces easily become calm when no more external forces are exerted. In order to represent such property of water surface, we employed damping with original shape. Each vertex are animated not only with the shape matching force, but also with the restoration force back to the original position. As shown in Fig. 5, the vertices are accelerated to move back to the original position x_i^0, and the result animation shows plausible damping on the water surface. Such behavior can be regarded a damping process that dissipates the wave energy to restore the global water surface back to the energy equilibrium. The restoration force is of course proportional to the deformation amount, and the resulting behavior is naturally exponential function of the opposite direction of the deformation. In our case, the deviation tendency of each particle was measured by the velocity of the particle, and the actual acceleration for each particle i is computed as $a_i = (x_i^0 - x_i) \exp(-v_i)$.

Fig. 5. Damping with original shape: the deformed vertices x_1, x_2, x_3, x_4 incur restoration force back to the original positions $x_1^0, x_2^0, x_3^0,$ and x_4^0

Wave Interference. In order to produce realistic wave surface, interference of different waves is very important. In the previous methods, the wave interference was often ignored or required additional computation. However, our method produces plausible wave interference without any additional consideration or computation. figure to the left in Fig. 6 shows single wave while the figure to the right shows the interference of two different waves. As shown in the figure, the amplitude of the wave is computed by the average goal position of adjacent clusters. This property easily enables the wavy interference.

Improved Cluster Shape. The simple rectangular clusters cannot represent various shape deformation so that the complex water surface cannot be produced.

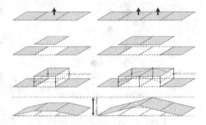

Fig. 6. Wave interference: the differences of goal positions produces plausible wave interference

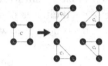

Fig. 7. The rectangular cluster C is subdivied into 4 clusters c_1, c_2, c_3, and c_4

Therefore, we improved the shape of the clusters as shown in Fig. 7 to generate various deformations within the original rectangular cluster.

5   Experiments

The proposed method was implemented on a system with intel Core i7-3960X CPU system running on Windows 7 64bit OS with 32GB RAM and three NVidia Geforce GTX 580 graphics hardwares.

Fig. 8 shows the wave reflection at the surface boundary. The waves are plausible reflected without any additional consideration or computation. Fig. 9 also shows the wave reflection. The black-colored external object is located on the surface, and the wave is reflected at the boundary when it hits the object.

Fig. 10 shows the interference effect of different waves. The proposed method plausibly and efficiently expresses the wave interference. The figures to the left show the rendering results of interfering waves, and the figure to the right shows the amplitudes of wave surface in order to highlight the interfering effect. Fig. 11 shows the water animation and rendering result with our method.

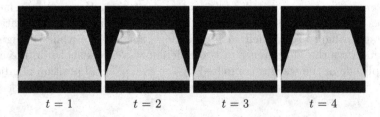

| $t = 1$ | $t = 2$ | $t = 3$ | $t = 4$ |

Fig. 8. Wave colliding with the water surface boundary

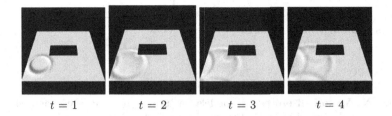

$t = 1$ $t = 2$ $t = 3$ $t = 4$

Fig. 9. Wave reflection at the external object boundary

(a) Rendering of interfering waves   (b) wave amplitude map

Fig. 10. Wave interference result

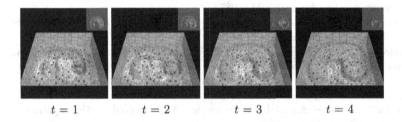

$t = 1$ $t = 2$ $t = 3$ $t = 4$

Fig. 11. Water animation result

6   Conclusion

In this paper, we proposed interactive animation techniques for water surface. The proposed method requires no special computation for water-object interaction. Moreover, the method produces stable and physically plausible animation results, and the waves are efficiently interferes each other. The water surface element objects are divided into clusters and efficiently processed with parallel GPU. The efficiency and plausibility of the method proposed in this paper make it possible to employ realistic water representation in realtime applications.

Acknowledgments. This work was supported in part by the Ministry of Knowledge Economy (MKE), Korea, under the Information Technology Research Center (ITRC) support program supervised by the National IT Industry Promotion Agency (NIPA) (NIPA-2011-(C-1090-1021-0006)), and this work (Grants No.C0033371) was supported by Business for Cooperative R&D between

Industry, Academy, and Research Institute funded Korea Small and Medium Business Administration in 2012.

References

1. Max, N.: Vectorized procedural models for natural terrain: Waves and islands in the sunset. In: ACM SIGGRAPH, pp. 517–324 (1981)
2. Peachey, D.: Modeling waves and surf. SIGGRAPH Comput., Graph., 65–74 (1986)
3. Chen, H., Li, Q., Wang, G., Zhou, F., Tang, X., Yang, K.: An Efficient Method for Real-Time Ocean Simulation. In: Hui, K.-c., Pan, Z., Chung, R.C.-K., Wang, C.C.L., Jin, X., Göbel, S., Li, E.C.-L. (eds.) Edutainment 2007. LNCS, vol. 4469, pp. 3–11. Springer, Heidelberg (2007)
4. Finch, M.: Effective Water Simulation from Physical Models, pp. 5–29. Addison-Wesley (2004)
5. Lee, H.-M., Go, C.A.L., Lee, W.-H.: An Efficient Algorithm for Rendering Large Bodies of Water. In: Harper, R., Rauterberg, M., Combetto, M. (eds.) ICEC 2006. LNCS, vol. 4161, pp. 302–305. Springer, Heidelberg (2006)
6. Lee, H.-M., Go, C., Lee, W.-H.: A frustum-based ocean rendering algorithm. Agent Computing and Multi-Agent Systems, 584–589 (2006)
7. Masting, G., Watterberg, P., Mareda, J.: Fourier synthesis of ocean scenes. IEEE Comput. Graph. Appl., 16–23 (1987)
8. Premoze, S., Ashikhmin, M.: Rendering natural waters. IEEE Computer Society, 23. 4, 7, 10, 13, 14 (2000)
9. Kass, M., Miller, G.: Rapid, stable fluid dynamics for computer graphics. In: ACM SIGGRAPH, pp. 49–57 (1990)
10. Foster, N., Metaxas, D.: Realistic Animation of Liquid. Graphical Models and Image Processing, 23–30 (1995)
11. Miller, G., Pearce, A.: Globular Dynamics: A Connected Particle System For Animating Viscous Fluids (1989)
12. Yuksel, C.: Wave Particles. In: ACM SIGGRAPH 2007 (2007)

The Application of Optimization of Gradual Steps in Blended-Fuel Power Plant

Min Chen[1], Yan Zhang[2], Yaojin Liang[2], and Daogang Peng[1]

[1] School of Electric Power and Automation Engineering, Shanghai University of Electric Power,
Shanghai, China
[2] Power Plant of Baoshan Iron &Steel Co. Ltd., Shanghai 200941, China

Abstract. With the development of science and technology, the energy and resource we need are increasing gradually. But the limitation of natural resource, human reliance on natural resource and the urgency of national environmental requirements make us to think about how to use our natural resource efficiently. In order to reduce the coal consumption rate for power supply and keep the unit running economically, the blended-fuel power plant plays an more and more important role in our country. It mainly involves the following aspects: the optimization in Automatic Gain Control, the optimization in distribution of load and fuel and the optimization in Start/Stop service. What we should do is making rational analysis and research on the mathematical model, then find a reasonable and practical simulation algorithm and optimize allocation scheduling design based on it.

Keywords: optimization of gradual steps, blended-fuel power plant, power plant integrated benefit, the optimization in Automatic Gain Control.

1 Introduction

The optimization of generating sets in blended-fuel power plant is a novel and independent way of energy scheduling, and the relevant research is also in the early stage. Because of its big difference from the conventional coal-fired power plant on scheduling and optimization, so there is no existing scheduling model and optimized dispatching method can apply.

But the economy and integrated benefit of power plant is always the focus of our attention, so in the designation of scheduling optimization problem between 5 generators is only a question of the optimization in Automatic Gain Control, but also a question of start/stop maintenance, unit aging, labor cost and maintenance expense, so we usually use power supply cost as economy index that can accurately response unit production economy. This thesis is mainly about the multi-objective decision in unit optimization scheduling, BFG/coal/electric optimization, making the maximize use of industrial waste gas, in order to improve the efficiency to achieve the objective of energy saving and emission reduction. Guarantee the power for power plant itself and

F.L. Wang et al. (Eds.): CMSP 2012, CCIS 346, pp. 491–498, 2012.
© Springer-Verlag Berlin Heidelberg 2012

the surplus power can also replenish the power system at the same time, provide enterprises with good economic benefits.

2   The Establishment of the Model of the Optimization in Automatic Gain Control

Nowadays, large-scale thermal power units are mainly composed of three parts: boilers, steam turbines and generators. Its production process is through the combustion of different fuels F and a series of intermediate energy conversion, and finally output power which we used to call P. In stable combustion process, a single unit coal consumption characteristics, which we named the progress of the relationship between the input fuel F and the output power P, generally use the two curves to approximate representation:

$$F_i = f(P_i) = a_i P_i^2 + b_i P_i + c_i \quad i=1,2,3...k \qquad (1)$$

Among them, F as the coal consumption, t/h; P as the power, MW; a, b, c as the coefficient.

The research object of this article is the mixed gas fuel combustion gases, mainly for the blast furnace gas (BFG), it must be converted to standard coal consumption, which means the consumption of the burning BFG under the power P_i is:

$$Q_i = \frac{m}{l} F_i = \frac{m}{l} f_i(P_i) = \frac{m}{l}(a_i P_i^2 + b_i P_i + c_i) \quad i=1,2,3...k \qquad (2)$$

Q_i as the BFG consumption, km^3/h; m as the standard coal value, constant 29270 kJ/kg; 1 for blast BFG value, constant 3200 kJ/m^3, and among them :

$$P_{i,min} \le P_i \le P_{i,max}, \quad Q_{i,min} \le Q_i \le Q_{i,max} \quad i=1,2,3...k \qquad (3)$$

Through the actual operation of the unit data, we can simulate the available 5 units of the respective coal consumption curve, through the analysis and the previous operation experience which shows coal consumption of mixed combustion unit, we can find the characteristic equation which can be fitted to two yuan two equations:

$$F_i = f(P_i, Q_i) = a_i P_i^2 + b_i Q_i^2 + c_i P_i + d_i Q_i + e_i + f_i$$

$$i=k+1,k+2,k+3...n \qquad (4)$$

Each unit is restricted by the power load and blast furnace gas supply constraints, so:

$$P_{i,min} \leq P_i \leq P_{i,max} , \quad Q_{i,min} \leq Q_i \leq Q_{i,max} \quad i=k+1,k+2,k+3...n \qquad (5)$$

As for the special case of mixing and combustion of each unit and fuel medium in the blended-fuel power plant, so reasonable allocation of 5 units between BEG, COG and electricity allocation, meeting the Standard of output condition and BFG zero discharge conditions, makes the coal consumption the lowest, in order to improve the power generation efficiency, make economic benefits and reduce energy consumption at the same time. The corresponding function:

$$F_{min} = \sum_{i=1}^{n} F_i = \sum_{i=1}^{k} f_i(P_i) + \sum_{i=k+1}^{n} f_i(P_i, Q_i) \qquad (6)$$

$$i=1,2,3...,k,k+1,k+2,k+3...n$$

Among them, P, Q must satisfy the following relations:

$$\begin{cases} \sum_{i=1}^{n} P_i = D \\ \sum_{i=1}^{n} Q_i = G \end{cases} , \quad P_{i,min} \leq P_i \leq P_{i,max} , \quad Q_{i,min} \leq Q_i \leq Q_{i,max} , \qquad (7)$$

$$i=1,2,3...,k,k+1,k+2,k+3...n$$

Among them, D as the total power ; G as the whole plant of BFG volume.

3   The Optimization of Gradual Steps

To solve the equation above, we should transform it into a Lagrange function extremum problem, so it is just a question to solve a function extreme value problem under certain conditions. First of all, according to the characteristics of dual variable, I structure an objective function which contains two Lagrange multipliers, as follows:

$$L = \sum_{i=1}^{k} f_i(P_i) + \sum_{i=k+1}^{n} f_i(P_i, Q_i) + \lambda_1 (\sum_{i=1}^{k} P_i - D) + \lambda_2 (\sum_{i=1}^{k} Q_i - G) \qquad (8)$$

The independent variables are:

$$P_1, P_2,..., P_k, P_{k+1}..., P_n, Q_{k+1}..., Q_n , \lambda_1 , \lambda_2.$$

As we all know that the Lagrange function extremum conditions are that on the function of each variables for partial derivative must equal to 0, so:

$$\begin{cases} \dfrac{\partial L}{\partial P_i} = 0 \quad i = 1,2,3...k \\[2mm] \dfrac{\partial L}{\partial Q_i} = 0 \quad i = k+1, k+2, k+3...n \\[2mm] \dfrac{\partial L}{\partial \lambda_1} = 0 \\[2mm] \dfrac{\partial L}{\partial \lambda_2} = 0 \end{cases} \tag{9}$$

Calculating the equation:

$$\begin{cases} P_i = \dfrac{1}{2a_i}\left(\dfrac{-\lambda_1}{1+\dfrac{m}{1}\lambda_2} - b_i\right) \\[2mm] \qquad i = 1,2,3...k & (1) \\[2mm] P_i = \dfrac{-\lambda_1 - d_i - c_i Q_i}{2a_i} \\[2mm] \qquad i = k+1, k+2, k+3...n & (2) \\[2mm] Q_i = \dfrac{-\lambda_2 - e_i - c_i P_i}{2b_i} \\[2mm] \qquad i = k+1, k+2, k+3...n & (3) \\[2mm] \displaystyle\sum_{i=1}^{n} P_i - D = 0 & (4) \\[2mm] \displaystyle\sum_{i=1}^{n} Q_i - G = 0 & (5) \end{cases} \tag{10}$$

Use the coal consumption curve which obtained by the simulation data of the power plant and the practical experience, it shows that the coefficient P, Q is very small in the actual production and without loss of generality and has no affecting to the calculation accuracy, so the influence of the coal consumption in power plant can be ignored under the this condition, so I make, (i=k+1,k+2,...,n), so The equation can be simplified to:

$$\begin{cases} \sum_{i=1}^{k} \frac{1}{2a_i} \left(\frac{-\lambda_1}{1+\frac{m}{1}\lambda_2} - b_i \right) + \sum_{i=k+1}^{n} \frac{-\lambda_1 - d_i}{2a_i} - D = 0 \\ \sum_{i=1}^{k} \frac{m}{1} \left[\frac{1}{4a_i} \left(\frac{-\lambda_1}{1+\frac{m}{1}\lambda_2} - b_i \right)^2 + \frac{b_i}{2a_i} * \left(\frac{-\lambda_1}{1+\frac{m}{1}\lambda_2} - b_i \right) + c_i \right] + \sum_{i=k+1}^{n} \frac{-\lambda_2 - e_i}{2b_i} - G = 0 \end{cases} \quad (11)$$

Take the power plant data into equations (12), and then obtain λ_1, λ_2 into equations (10-1)~(10-3), end.

So, based on the calculation process above and the constraint conditions combine with the power plant operation of the actual situation, we can draw the algorithm which shown in Fig.1 :

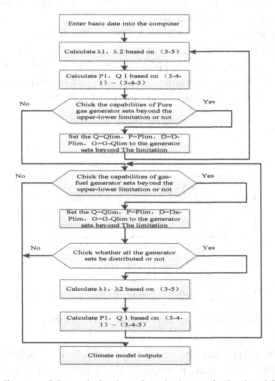

Fig. 1. Block diagram of the optimization of gradual steps for load and fuel calculation

4   Optimization of Practical Example and Its Analysis

In the power plant operation, there is many optimal scheduling methods between different units and the implementation, but each one has its advantages and disadvantages and the most optimization schemes can be only applicable to the coal fired power units. The methods we all know are the as the rate of increase curve method and the dynamic programming method.

Among them, though the as the rate of increase curve method is simple, intuitive, easy to master and has a smaller amount of calculation, But it has a large limitation such as a high request on monotonicity and convexity of the coal consumption curve, This makes it a bad job in the actual operation. While it's easy to find the objective function and constraint conditions in dynamic programming method, and its decision between upper and lower will never influence each other in order to reduce the calculation amount of the system, but when the system has a large scale, the computation is still so slow, so must use the priority sequence table to compress and search bandwidth reduction state point.

From Fig.1 we can know that the optimization of gradual steps can do a great job with a step-by-step calculation, and it has no requirement on the convexity and the monotonicity of the coal consumption curve, with a smaller amount of calculation, faster running speed and other advantages.

So in order to verify the actual operation effect of the optimization of gradual steps, I choose a set of data (the plant daily load curve and the plant daily BFG consumption curve) on July 9, 2010 to calculate the optimization of the Load distribution and the fuel distribution .In order to ensure accuracy, I   divide a day into 96 periods, each time 15 minutes, so the plant daily load curve and   the plant daily BFG consumption curve as the Fig.2 shows:

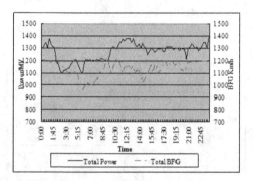

Fig. 2. Daily load and BFG date curves of the plant

We can learn from Fig.2 that the whole plant load change reached 400MW and the total volume of BFG in amplitude fluctuation. So I choose the BFG allocation strategy is: gas turbine unit No.0,4 are priority allocated of load, No.0 in full load operation. Input the data into Matlab, and calculate the curves of load optimization in each unit. Compare with the curves which calculated by the dynamic programming method, just as Fig.3~7 are showed, Power1 is the power of dynamic programming method, Power2 is the power of optimization of gradual steps; BFG1 is the BFG consumption volume of dynamic programming method, BFG2 is the BFG consumption volume of optimization of gradual steps:

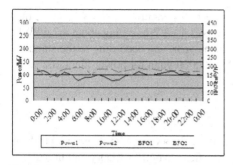

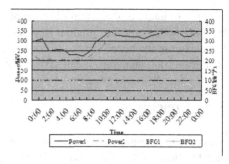

Fig. 3. Curve comparison of Unit 0 between 2 optimizations

Fig. 4. Curve comparison of Unit 1 between 2 optimizations

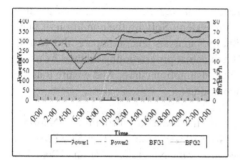

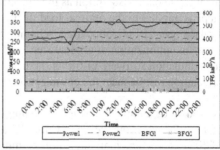

Fig. 5. Curve comparison of Unit 2 between 2 optimizations

Fig. 6. Curve comparison of Unit 3 between 2 optimizations

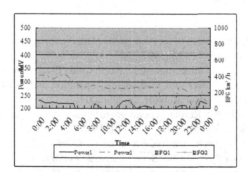

Fig. 7. Curve comparison of Unit 4 between 2 optimizations

Comparison of these 5 pictures of the coal and BFG consumption curves, we can apparently find that the average coal consumption and whole plant load are in inversely proportional relationship, in other words: the higher Plant total load, the lower average coal consumption; on the contrary, the lower Plant total load, the higher average coal consumption. So, the result by optimization of gradual steps is much better than that by dynamic programming method in this situation. The power of the average coal consumption rate of the actual plan during the period is about 332.1 g/kWh, while that by using optimization of gradual steps is about 327.4 g/kWh, saving about 4.7 g/kWh. If we extense the benefit in this accordance to one year, and according to the standard coal price 1000 yuan/ton, It can save about 25,488,000 yuan for power plant one year.

5   Conclusion

This paper is mainly research the optimization in Automatic Gain Control in blended-fuel power plant, and is of positive significance both in theory and in practice to promote mixing combustion power plant load optimal dispatch. In this paper I mainly completed the following work: optimization of multiple units under normal condition of blast furnace gas distribution under constant power of the power plant; use plant total coal consumption as the objective function, and the optimization of gradual steps is applied to the optimal load distribution system; Solving the condition of blast furnace gas (BFG) allocation scheme; Finally, analysis and compare the results between optimization of gradual steps and the dynamic programming method by using the simulation software of fitting the unit coal consumption curve, And ensure that the simulation results meet the optimization calculation.

Acknowledgment. This work was supported by the State Key Program of National Natural Science Foundation of China (Grant No. 61034004), Innovation Key Program of Shanghai Municipal Education Commission (Grant No. 12ZZ177) and Shanghai Science and Technology Key Program (Grant No. 10250502000).

References

1. Jin, X.: Economic load dispatch of thermal power plant the foreground analysis. North China Electric Power Technology, 50–52 (1997)
2. Si, R.: AGC automatic load allocation study. North China Electric Power Institute (2010)
3. Li, Z., Yi, Y.: Thermal power unit load optimal operation and real-time visual operation platform. Thermal Power Generation (4), 28–36 (2002)
4. Sheble, G.B., Britting, K.: Refine genetic galgorithm economic dispatch example. IEEE Transactions on Power Systems 10(1), 117–123 (1995)
5. Rau, N.S.: Optimal Dispatch of a System based on Offers and Bids A Mixed Integer LP Formulation. On Power Sysrem PWRS-14(1), 274–279 (1999)
6. Qiang, Z.: Comprehensive economic goal of generating unit load optimal dispatching method of Shanghai Jiao Tong University (2010)

Sensor Management for Target Search with Unknown Detection Performance

Jianbin Lu[1,2], Zemin Xi[2], Xianghui Yuan[2], Guishui Yu[2], and Mingmin Zhang[2]

[1] College of Naval Architecture and Power
[2] Electronic Engineering College
Naval University of Engineering, 430033 Wuhan, China
{lu_jian_bin,yuguisshui_66}@163.com,
{xizemin,yuanxianghui}@sohu.com, zhangmm_hg@126.com

Abstract. In the real-world applications, the detection performance of the target is unknown before the sensor captures the target. In this paper, a sensor management method for target search is presented with unknown detection performance. Firstly, a search model based on maximal information gain criterion is proposed, in which the information gain of each cell is predicted before the sensor detection, and the observation is made in the cell with the maximal information gain. Secondly, beta distribution is used to model the unknown detection performance and its posterior probability density with the sensor observation is derived based on Bayesian theory. Compared with the conventional method, simulation results show that the proposed search strategy can distinctly improve the search performance and the sensor can capture target with much less time resources.

Keywords: Sensor management, detection performance, information gain, beta distribution.

1 Introduction

The modern sensing environment is increasingly characterized by a large number of smart sensors, and each of these sensors will have different detection performance. Thus, sensor management technique is presented to provide for the autonomous operation of these sensors in such a way as to best fulfill the desired mission goals subject to available resource constrains[1].

Sensor management has been studied for a wide variety of applications, such as military sensor control, target tracking and classification, wireless network management. Mahler has studied the problem by using finite-set statistics to develop sensor management procedures[2]. Kastella proposed a sensor management method using a joint multi-target probability density for the multi-target tracking[3,4] and Kreucher extended the results of Kastella to the non-myopic optimization problems[5]. The covariance control strategy is presented by Kalandros for multi-sensor management multi-target tracking[6,7]. Based on the information theory, a sensor management strategy is proposed for multi-function radar, which search the target with the maximal

F.L. Wang et al. (Eds.): CMSP 2012, CCIS 346, pp. 499–505, 2012.

information gain[8]. But for the real-world applications, the detection performance of the target is unknown before the sensor captures the target. In this paper, a sensor management method for target search with unknown detection performance is studies, and the unknown detection performance is modeled by beta distribution which can be updated effectively with the sensor observations to approach the true value.

2   Search Strategy Based on Information Gain

Assumed that the search region with M given cells contains a static target, there are two hypotheses in each search cell, $H_k=1$ for target existing and $H_k=0$ for not. Before the sensor starts to search, the prior probability of each cell $\pi_k(0)=P(H_k=1)$, $k=1,2...,M$ is specified. For each step of the search, one cell $i(t)\in\{1,2,...,M\}$ is selected, and a detection result $z(t)$ is obtained. If one target is detected at current time, the expression of $z(t)=1$ is hold, otherwise $z(t)=0$.

Based on detection result at time t, the conditional probabilities of all cells at time $t+1$ are given by Bayesian formula[9], as

$$\pi_k(t+1)=\begin{cases} P\big(H_k=1\mid z(t)=1,k=i(t)\big) \\ P\big(H_k=1\mid z(t)=0,k=i(t)\big) \\ P\big(H_k=1\mid z(t)=1,k\neq i(t)\big) \\ P\big(H_k=1\mid z(t)=0,k\neq i(t)\big) \end{cases} \tag{1}$$

$$=\begin{cases} \dfrac{\pi_k(t)\cdot P\big(z(t)=1\mid H_k=1\big)}{\pi_k(t)\cdot P\big(z(t)=1\mid H_k=1\big)+\big(1-\pi_k(t)\big)\cdot P\big(z(t)=1\mid H_k=0\big)} \\[3mm] \dfrac{\pi_k(t)\cdot P\big(z(t)=0\mid H_k=1\big)}{\pi_k(t)\cdot P\big(z(t)=0\mid H_k=1\big)+\big(1-\pi_k(t)\big)\cdot P\big(z(t)=0\mid H_k=0\big)} \\[3mm] \dfrac{\pi_k(t)\cdot P\big(z(t)=1\mid H_k=0\big)}{\pi_{i(t)}(t)\cdot P\big(z(t)=1\mid H_k=1\big)+\big(1-\pi_{i(t)}(t)\big)\cdot P\big(z(t)=1\mid H_k=0\big)} \\[3mm] \dfrac{\pi_k(t)\cdot P\big(z(t)=0\mid H_k=0\big)}{\pi_{i(t)}(t)\cdot P\big(z(t)=0\mid H_k=1\big)+\big(1-\pi_{i(t)}(t)\big)\cdot P\big(z(t)=0\mid H_k=0\big)} \end{cases}$$

where above $P(z(t)|H_k)$ is determined by the detection probability P_d and the false alarm probability P_f. In the real application, the detection probability may be unknown, which can be assumed to be a random with the probability density function $f(P_d)$. Then, $P(z(t)|H_k=1)$ can be expressed as

$$P\big(z(t)\mid H_k=1\big)=\int P\big(z(t)\mid H_k=1,P_d\big)\cdot f(P_d)dP_d \tag{2}$$

Furthermore, (2) can be simplified as follows

$$P\big(z(t)=1\mid H_k=1\big)=1-P\big(z(t)=0\mid H_k=1\big)=E[P_d] \tag{3}$$

where $E[\cdot]$ is the expected value operator. Similarly $P(z(t)|H_k=0)$ can be derived as follows

$$P\big(z(t)=1\,|\,H_k=0\big)=1-P\big(z(t)=0\,|\,H_k=0\big)=E[P_f] \tag{4}$$

If the cell selected at time t is $i(t)$, the corresponding search result $z(t)$ can be predicted as

$$P\big(z(t)\,|\,i(t)\big)=\sum_{j=0}^{1}P\big(z(t)\,|\,H_{i(t)}=j,i(t)\big)\cdot P(H_{i(t)}=j) \tag{5}$$

Now the information gain obtained is analyzed when the cell $i(t)$ is determined for next search. The measure function of information gain is expressed as $f(p_k,q_k)$ which can be defined according to Shannon entropy, Kullback-Leibler entropy, Renyi entropy etc. The parameters q_k and p_k are the probabilities of the target existing before and after the sensor search in the cell k respectively. So the total information gain considering all cells and possible detection results is expressed as

$$\Delta D\big(t,i(t)\big)=\sum_{j=0}^{1}\sum_{k=1}^{M}f\big(P(H_k=1\,|\,z(t)=j,i(t)),\pi_k(t)\big)\cdot P\big(z(t)=j\,|\,i(t)\big) \tag{6}$$

The search process is that: first the total information gain $\Delta D(t,i(t))$ for each cell $i(t)$ is predicted, and then the cell with the maximal information gain is selected and used for next search, which can decrease uncertainty of the target furthest.

3   Cued Search with Unknown Detection Performance

When the probabilities of detection and false alarm are unknown, the mathematics of the previous section can no longer be straightforwardly applied. Rather, probability densities must be used to model unknown probabilities of detection and false alarm, which may be a random value between 0 and 1. In this paper, beta distribution is selected, and the reasons are: (1) beta distribution is the natural conjugate prior for a binomial process, and its posterior probability density is also a beta distribution; (2) beta distribution can simulate most of probability density functions such as uniform distribution, normal distribution, Rayleigh distribution, Log-normal distribution and so on.

The beta distribution used to model the probability density function of P_d is expressed as follows

$$f(P_d,a,b)=\frac{1}{B(a,b)}\cdot P_d^{a-1}\cdot(1-P_d)^{b-1},\ 0<P_d<1 \tag{7}$$

where $B(a,b)$ is the beta function. Beta distribution has two positive parameters a and b with mean $a/(a+b)$ and variance $ab/((a+b)^2(a+b+1))$. The model of the false alarm probability is the same to that of detection probability. So the modeling process for the false alarm probability is omitted.

According to the beta distribution model, (3) can be rewritten as

$$P\big(z(t)=1\,|\,H_k=1\big)=1-P\big(z(t)=0\,|\,H_k=1\big)=a/(a+b) \tag{8}$$

When a new observation $\{z(t),i(t)\}$ is obtained, the conditional probability density of P_d can be calculated by Bayesian formula

$$f\left(P_d \mid z(t)=1, H_{i(t)}=1\right)=\frac{P\left(z(t)=1\mid P_d, H_{i(t)}=1\right)\cdot f(P_d)}{\int_0^1 P\left(z(t)=1\mid P_d, H_{i(t)}=1\right)\cdot f(P_d)dP_d}=\frac{P_d^a\cdot(1-P_d)^{b-1}}{B(a+1,b)} \quad (9)$$

From the result of (9), it's shown that the posterior probability density of P_d with a new observation is still a beta distribution with the parameter $(a+1,b)$. Similar derivations for the other cases are calculated as follows

$$f\left(P_d \mid z(t)=0, H_{i(t)}=1\right)=\frac{P_d^{a-1}\cdot(1-P_d)^b}{B(a,b+1)} \quad (10)$$

$$f\left(P_d \mid z(t)=1, H_{i(t)}=0\right)=f\left(P_d \mid z(t)=0, H_{i(t)}=0\right)=\frac{P_d^{a-1}\cdot(1-P_d)^{b-1}}{B(a,b)} \quad (11)$$

Apply the total probability formula, and the conditional probability density of P_d can be written as

$$f\left(P_d \mid z(t),i(t)\right)=\sum_{j=0}^{1}\frac{P\left(z(t)\mid P_d, H_{i(t)}=j\right)\cdot f(P_d)}{\int_0^1 P\left(z(t)\mid P_d, H_{i(t)}=j\right)\cdot f(P_d)dP_d}P\left(H_{i(t)}=j\right) \quad (12)$$

For the case $z(t)=0$, (12) is the linear combination of two beta distributions, as follows

$$f\left(P_d \mid z(t)=0,i(t)\right)=\frac{P_d^{a-1}\cdot(1-P_d)^b}{B(a,b+1)}\cdot\pi_{i(t)}(t)+\frac{P_d^{a-1}\cdot(1-P_d)^{b-1}}{B(a,b)}\cdot\left(1-\pi_{i(t)}(t)\right) \quad (13)$$

Its mean μ and variance D can be calculated according to (13) as follows

$$\mu=\frac{a(a+b+1)-a\pi_{i(t)}(t)}{(a+b)(a+b+1)} \quad (14)$$

$$D=\frac{ab}{(a+b)^2(a+b+1)}+\frac{2a(a-b)\pi_{i(t)}(t)}{(a+b)^2(a+b+1)(a+b+2)}-\frac{a^2\pi_{i(t)}^2(t)}{(a+b)^2(a+b+1)^2} \quad (15)$$

Then, a new beta distribution updated by the new observation can be constructed for the next search, and its parameters (a',b') are calculated as follows

$$a'=\frac{(1-\mu)\mu^2-\mu D}{D}, \quad b'=\frac{(1-\mu)^2\mu^2-\mu(1-\mu)D}{\mu D} \quad (16)$$

Similar results can be obtained for the case $z(t)=1$. Above process shows that for each new observation a new beta distribution is produced and approaches to the real probability density function of P_d, which makes the estimation $\pi_k(t)$ of each cell more precise for current observations.

Assumed the search time is T, the sensor search can be realized as follows:

Step 1: Get the probability distribution $\pi_k(t)$ and the initial probability density of P_d and P_f at time t;

Step 2: Predict the detection result of each cell using (5), and calculate the corresponding information gain using (6);

Step 3: Select the cell $i(t)$ with the maximal information gain to make the observation, and get the detection result $\{z(t),i(t)\}$;

Step 4: Produce a new beta distribution using (16) to update the probability densities of P_d and P_f;

Step 5: Let $t = t+1$. If $t > T$, then the algorithm ends, otherwise return to **Step 1**.

4   Simulation Result and Analysis

In the simulation, the sensor searches a static target within a 3×3 cell grid. The true value of the detection probability and the false alarm probability are 0.8 and 0.2 which both are unknown. The prior target distribution probability of each cell is[8]

$$\pi(0) = \{\pi_k(0), k = 1, 2, ..., 9\} = \{0.065, 0.11, 0.065, 0.11, 0.30, 0.11, 0.065, 0.11, 0.065\}$$

Without loss of generality, assume that the true position of the target is in the center cell of the search region, the fifth cell. Now two kind of search method are selected. For the first algorithm, the sequence search method is adopted in which the sensor searches each cell uniformly while the probabilities of detection and false alarm are selected artificially as 0.7 and 0.3 which denote the pessimistic estimation of detection performance. The second algorithm is based on the maximal information gain with Shannon entropy and the beta distribution is used to model the detection performance, and the

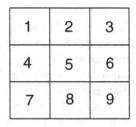

Fig. 1. search region with 9 cells

model parameters (a=14, b=6) and (a=6, b=14) are selected for the probabilities of detection and false alarm, which average values are 0.7 and 0.3 respectively.

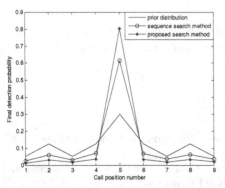

Fig. 2. Search results for two algorithms

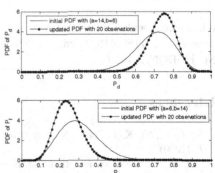

Fig. 3. PDF of P_d and P_f

The search region is shown in fig.1. The results with 1000 times simulations are shown in fig.2 for the above two algorithms in which 20-steps searching process (corresponding search time is 2s with 0.1s detection time for each beam dwell) is executed for each simulation. From fig.2 we can draw some valuable conclusions: (1) Both algorithms can point out the right target position, i.e. the probability of the fifth cell is distinctly larger than the others; (2) Compared with the sequence search method, the algorithm proposed in this paper can get better performance. The simulation results validate the efficiency of the proposed search method based on maximal information gain.

Furthermore, the probability density function of P_d after 20-steps updates is shown in fig.3 for some one trial. From fig.3, though there is obvious error between the initial detection probability and the true value 0.8, the beta distribution model can be modified using the observation and the error gradually decreases. The similar result can be obtained for the probability of false alarm.

5   Conclusions

The target search is one main function of the sensor systems for the surveillance applications, and the key technique of the sensor management is to improve its search performance and decrease sensor resources. In this paper, a search strategy with sensor management is presented to allow the incorporation of unknown probabilities of detection and false alarm such as are likely to be found in a realistic scenario. The sensor searches the detection cell with the maximal information gain which can decrease uncertainty of the target furthest. And the beta distribution is used to model unknown detection performance effectively which can be modified by the sensor observation real time. Comparing with the conventional search method, the proposed method can achieve better search performance with the same search time. But in this paper, only beta distribution is used to model the unknown detection performance, and more distribution functions need an in-depth study and should be considered in the future research.

Acknowledgment. This work was supported by the Postdoctoral Science Foundation of China (No. 201150M1546) and the Youth Found of Naval University of Engineering (No. HGDQNJJ11029).

References

1. Ng, G.W., Ng, K.H.: Sensor Management - Wat, Why and How. Information Fusion 1, 67–75 (2000)
2. Mahler, R.: Objective Functions for Bayesian Control-theoretic Sensor Management, I: Multitarget First-moment Approximation. In: IEEE Aerospace Conference, pp. 1905–1923. IEEE Press, New York (2002)
3. Kastella, K.: Joint Multitarget Probabilities for Detection and Tracking. In: SPIE, pp. 122–128. SPIE Press, New York (1997)

4. Kastella, K.: Discrimination Gain to Optimize Detection and Classification. IEEE Trans. on Systems, Man, and Cybernetics-Part A: Systems and Humans. 27, 112–116 (1997)
5. Kreucher, C., Hero, A.O.: Non-myopic Approaches to Scheduling Agile Sensors for Multistage Detection, Tracking and Identification. In: IEEE International Conference on Acoustics, Speech, Signal Processing, pp. 885–888. IEEE Press, New York (2005)
6. Kalandros, M., Pao, L.Y.: Covariance Control for Multisensor Systems. IEEE Trans. on AES 38, 1138–1157 (2002)
7. Kalandros, M., Pao, L.Y.: Multisensor Covariance Control Strategies for Reducing Bias Effects in Interacting Target Scenarios. IEEE Trans. on AES 41, 153–173 (2005)
8. Lu, J.B., Hu, W.D., Xiao, H.: Novel Cued Search Strategy based on Information Gain for Phased Array Radar. Journal of Systems Engineering and Electronics 19, 292–297 (2008)
9. Berger, J.O.: Statistical Decision Theory and Bayesian Analysis. Springer, New York (2004)

Improved KL (K-means-Laplacian) Clustering with Sparse Graphs

Lai Wei[1] and Feifei Xu[2]

[1] Department of Computer Science, Shanghai Maritime University, Haigang Avenue 1550,
Shanghai, China
weilai@shmtu.edu.cn
[2] Department of Computer Science and Technology, Shanghai University of Electric Power,
Pingliang Road 2103, Shanghai, China
xufeifei1983@hotmail.com

Abstract. KL (K-means-Laplacian) clustering combines K-means and spectral clustering algorithm together to use both of the attribute values of data and the pairwise relations between the data points. However, a full connected graph used in KL clustering may not be appropriate to indicate the similarity relations between the data points. This paper has improved the KL clustering with sparse graphs constructed by b-matching method and sparse representation. The b-matching graph, in which each node has strictly b neighbors, is more regular than KNN (K nearest neighbors) graph. Graph constructed by sparse representation (l1 graph) also has many merits such as sparsity and datum-adaptive neighborhoods. Hence the improved KL clustering with the constructed graphs has more attractive properties than the classic KL clustering. The experiments on the benchmark datasets (COIL-20 and MNIST) show the effectiveness of the improved KL clustering with promising results.

Keywords: B-matching, Sparse representation, K-means, Spectral clustering.

1 Introduction

Clustering has been among the most active research topics in machine learning and pattern recognition communities [1-2]. Intuitively, clustering finds a partition of the data points into clusters such that the points within a cluster are more similar to each other. Many clustering algorithms have been developed over the past few decades [3], including spatial clustering [4-5], sub-space clustering [6-7], density-based clustering [8], and so on. Among them, K-means clustering [9] is one of the most popular and efficient clustering methods, it aims to minimize the sum of the squared distance between the data points and their corresponding cluster centers. However, researches also indicate that there are some problems existing in the K-means algorithm [10]. Firstly, the predefined criterion is usually non-convex which causes many local optimal solutions; secondly, the iterative procedure for optimizing the criterion usually makes the final solutions heavily depend on the initializations. Therefore, a kind of effective methods using spectral relaxation technique have been proposed to alleviate the problems [11-12].

F.L. Wang et al. (Eds.): CMSP 2012, CCIS 346, pp. 506–513, 2012.

However, there is still a drawback existing in these improved K-means algorithms which is that they group examples just based on their attribute values. It is shown that relation information of data sets provides the hidden structure information of data sets and is very useful for clustering [13-14]. Hence, it is reasonable to combine the attribute values and relation information of data sets together for handling clustering tasks. Wang. et al recently proposed an integrated KL (K-means - Laplacian) cluster-ing algorithm to use both of the attribute values and pairwise relations of data sets [15]. In the applications, this approach seems an effective way to make use of mul-tiple information sources of data sets. However, it should be pointed that a full con-nected graph is used in KL clustering algorithm. A full connected graph may not be appropriate to represent the similarity relation between data points, and the pairwise similarity of distant points is not reliable [16-17]. In addition, the abundant super-fluous edges in the graph will cause algorithms based on it less efficient. Hence, graph sparsification is certainly required in KL clustering.

The most frequently used graph sparsification method is K-nearest neighbor. However, as many reports claimed [18-19], KNN adjacency graph may not be a finer approach for approximating the structure of data sets. So this paper will improve the KL clustering algorithm with graphs constructed by other graph sparsification tech-niques such as b-matching and sparse representation. B-matching algorithm ensures the graph is exactly regular, namely every node has b neighbors at termination. Graphs constructed by sparse representation (l_1 graph) also have many merits such as sparsity and datum-adaptive neighborhoods. Therefore, based on the new constructed graphs, the integrated KL clustering will get great improvements.

2   Background

2.1   Integrated KL Clustering

Given a data matrix $(\mathbf{x}_1, \mathbf{x}_2, \cdots, \mathbf{x}_n) = \mathbf{X} \in \mathbf{R}_{d \times n}$ and their pairwise relationship matrix $\mathbf{W} \in \mathbf{R}_{n \times n}$ such that w_{ij} represents the similarity between $\mathbf{x}_i$ and $\mathbf{x}_j$. Sup-pose the data set has C classes. The objective function of integrated KL algorithm is [15]

$$J = \min(\alpha J_k + (1 - \alpha) J_s) \qquad (1)$$

where $0 < \alpha < 1$ is a tradeoff parameter, J_k and J_s are the objective functions of K-means clustering and spectral clustering respectively. The inputs of the spectral clustering method is the relationship matrix $\mathbf{W}$. For free the tradeoff parameter, a trace quotient formulation of the objective function has been proposed, namely

$$J = \min(\frac{J_s}{J_k}) \qquad (2)$$

Based on [11-12], the objective function of K-means can be deduced into the following form

$$J_k = \max Tr(\mathbf{H}^T \mathbf{X}^T \mathbf{X} \mathbf{H}) \tag{3}$$

where $\mathbf{H} \in \mathbf{R}^{n \times K}$ is a nonnegative indicator matrix and

$$h_{ij} = \begin{cases} 1/\sqrt{n_j} & x_i \in C_j \\ 0 & otherwise \end{cases} \tag{4}$$

Clearly, $\mathbf{H}^T \mathbf{H} = \mathbf{I}, Tr(\bullet)$ is the trace of corresponding matrix and n_j is the number of points in C_j. Meanwhile, the objective function of spectral clustering can be expressed as $J_s = \min Tr(\mathbf{H}^T \mathbf{L} \mathbf{H})$ [13-14], where $\mathbf{L} = \mathbf{I} - \mathbf{D}^{-1/2} \mathbf{W} \mathbf{D}^{-1/2}$, $w_{ij} = \exp(-\|\mathbf{x}_i - \mathbf{x}_j\|^2 / 2\sigma^2)$, $\sigma \in R$ is a manually defined scale parameter. D is a diagonal matrix whose entries are column sums of $\mathbf{W}$, namely $d_{ii} = \sum_j w_{ij}$. Hence, Eq. (2) is equivalent to solve the following optimization problem

$$\max_H \quad Tr\left(\left(\mathbf{H}^T \mathbf{L} \mathbf{H} \right)^{-1} \left(\mathbf{H}^T \mathbf{X}^T \mathbf{X} \mathbf{H} \right) \right) \tag{5}$$

$$s.t. \quad \mathbf{H}^T \mathbf{H} = \mathbf{I}$$

Hence, $\mathbf{H}$ is composed by the largest C eigenvectors of the matrix $\mathbf{L}^+ \mathbf{X}^T \mathbf{X}$, and $\mathbf{L}^+$ is the pseudo-inverse of $\mathbf{L}$.

As we mentioned above, the full connected graph is used in the algorithm, then the similarity between data pints is defined on it. Moreover, the frequently used KNN graph is not an excellent approach to represent the relationship between all data points. Hence, b-matching and sparse representation, the new two sparse graph construction methods, will be used in this article to improve the KL clustering algorithm.

2.2   Sparse Graphs

2.2.1   B-Matching
Every node in an adjacency graph constructed by b-matching algorithm has b neighbors. Construct an affinity graph for data sets by b-matching contains two steps: graph sparsification and graph edge re-weighted.

Graph Sparsification: The objective of b-matching is to find a binary matrix to minimize the following optimization problem:

$$\min_{P \in B} \quad \sum_{ij} P_{ij} S_{ij}$$

$$s.t. \quad \sum_j P_{ij} = b, P_{ii} = 0, P_{ij} = P_{ji} \tag{6}$$

where $\mathbf{P}$ is a binary matrix, $\mathbf{S}$ is the distance matrix obtained from $\mathbf{X}$ as $S_{ij} = \|x_i - x_j\|^2$. $P_{ij} = 1$ indicates that an edge is existed between points $\mathbf{x}_i$ and $\mathbf{x}_j$, otherwise the edge is absent. By enforcing the additional constraints $P_{ij} = P_{ji}$, an undirected sub-graph which the degree of every node is strictly b can be obtained. This advantage plays a key role when conducting label propagation on data sets which are unevenly and non-uniformly distributed.   If relax the constraint $P_{ij} \in \{0,1\}$ to $P_{ij} \in [0,1]$, this optimal problem can be solved by linear programming. In [20], an algorithm in polynomial time $O(bn^3)$ via loopy belief propagation is presented.

Graph Edge Re-weighted: Once the binary matrix $\mathbf{P}$ is available, the weight of the graph edgecould be computed by several approaches, such as Gauss kernel [16], 0-1 way, l_1-norm, locally linear reconstruction weights [10] etc. Based on the definition of b-matching graph, it can be seen that the new graph is sparser than KNN graph. Figure 1 is the visualization of the neighborhood relation on a synthetic data set.

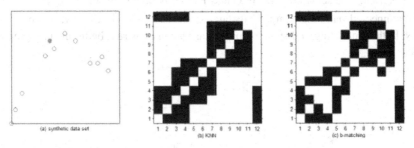

Fig. 1. (a) the synthetic dataset. (b) adjacency matrix constructed by KNN method; (c) adjacency matrix constructed by b-matching method. Notice: The green point in (a), denoted as point No.4, has 7 neighbors in KNN graph and 4 neighbors in b-matching graph.

2.2.2   Graph Construction by Sparse Representation

The goal of SR (Sparse Representation) is to represent $\mathbf{x} \in \mathbf{X}$ using as few elements of $\mathbf{X}$ as possible. This can be formally expressed as solving the following optimization problem:

$$\min_w \quad \|\mathbf{w}\|_0$$
$$s.t. \quad \mathbf{x} = \mathbf{X}\mathbf{w}$$
(7)

where $\mathbf{w} \in \mathbf{R}_n$ is the coefficient vector, $\|\bullet\|_0$ denotes the l_0-norm which counts the number of nonzero entries in a vector. However, finding the sparsest solution of Eq. (6) is NP-hard. Fortunately, recent reports [21] reveals that if the solution $\mathbf{w}_0$ is sparse enough, the solution of the above l_0 minimization problem can be bypassed by convexizing the following l_1 minimization problem:

$$\min_W \quad \|\mathbf{w}\|_1$$
$$s.t. \quad \mathbf{x} = \mathbf{Xw} \tag{8}$$

Eq. (7) can be solved by standard linear programming. Hence, for each $\mathbf{x}_i \in \mathbf{X}$, a sparse reconstructive weight vector $\mathbf{w}_i = \left[w_{i1}, ..., w_{ii-1}, 0, w_{ii+1}, ..., w_{in} \right]^T$ can be found. Therefore, a weighted affinity graph $\mathbf{W} = \left[\mathbf{w}_1, \mathbf{w}_2, ..., \mathbf{w}_n \right]^T$ can be composed by the solutions of n standard linear programming problems. The weight matrix $\mathbf{W}$ reflects some intrinsic geometric properties of the data. Figure 2(c) shows affinity matrix of the partial ORL face dataset constructed by sparse representation technique. It can be found most of the non-zero adjacency weights link the samples from the same class. Besides, affinity matrixes constructed by KNN and b-matching are also illustrated as Figure 2(a) and Figure 2(b). Here, graph edge is re-weighted by Gauss Kernel. The scale size σ in Gauss Kernel is manually set as the medium value of connected pairwise samples' distances, and $b = k = 3$. Clearly, compare with KNN, both b-matching and sparse representation can construct better affinity graphs.

(a) KNN   (b) b-matching   (c) L1-minimization

Fig. 2. Affinity matrix constructed by KNN, b-matching and l_1-minimization

3   The Algorithm

The algorithmic procedure of the improved KL clustering is summarized as follows.

STEP 1: Suppose a data set $\mathbf{X} \in \mathbf{R}_{d \times n}$,

    (a) Constructed weighted matrix $\mathbf{W}$ graph using b-matching method, namely using Eq. (6) and graph edge re-weighted methods;

    (b) Constructed weighted matrix $\mathbf{W}$ graph using sparse representation method, namely using Eq. (8);

STEP 2: Constructed the normalized Laplacian matrix $\mathbf{L} = \mathbf{I} - \mathbf{D}^{-\frac{1}{2}}\mathbf{W}\mathbf{D}^{-\frac{1}{2}}$, where $\mathbf{D}$ is a diagonal matrix whose entries are column sums of $\mathbf{W}$;

STEP 3: Find eigenvectors of the matrix $\mathbf{L}^{+}\mathbf{X}^{T}\mathbf{X}$ corresponding to its largest C eigenvalues, form the matrix $\mathbf{H} = [\mathbf{h}_1, \mathbf{h}_2, ..., \mathbf{h}_C]$, $\mathbf{L}^{+}$ is the pseudo-inverse matrix of $\mathbf{L}$;

STEP 4: Treating each row of $\mathbf{H}$ as a point in $\mathbf{R}_C$, cluster them into C clusters via K-means, assign the original point $\mathbf{x}_i$ to cluster j if and only if row i of the matrix $\mathbf{H}$ was assign to cluster j.

4   The Experiments

To test and verify the efficiency of improved KL clustering with sparse graphs, experiments on handwritten digits from the well-known MNIST database, objects from COIL20 database are conducted in this subsection. Cluster accuracy is used to evaluate the algorithms performance. The evaluated algorithms including K-means, spectral clustering, KL algorithm, KL+KNN, KL+BM(b-matching), KL+L1(l_1 graph).

A. MNIST Data

MNIST database has a training set of 60,000 examples and a testing set of 10,000 examples about 10 handwritten digits. The digits in the database have been size normalized and centered to 28×28 gray-level images, so the dimensionality of the digit space is 784. One hundred images for each digit in $\{1, 4, 7\}$ and $\{6, 8, 9\}$ are chosen from the MNIST test sets. Then clustering algorithms are evaluated on the two sub-datasets respectively. The neighbor parameter k and b are set at the best value searched in [3,20]. The clustering results are showed as Figure 3. Clearly, the improved KL clustering algorithms with sparse graphs outperform all of the other algorithms.

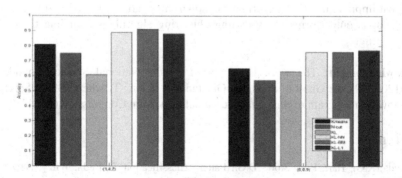

Fig. 3. Clustering results on the two subsets of MNIST database. (a) clustering results on $\{1, 4, 7\}$, $k = b = 7$; (b) clustering results on $\{6, 8, 9\}$, $k = b = 6$

B. COIL20 Dataset

COIL20 database contains 20 objects. The images of each object were taken 5 degrees apart as the object is rotated on a turntable and each object has 72 images. The size of each image is 32×32 pixels, with 256 grey levels per pixel. Thus, each image is represented by a 1024-dimensional vector. Three objects are randomly chosen from the database. The algorithms are evaluated on them. The neighbor parameter k and b are set at the best value searched in [3, 20]. The experiments are repeated 3 times, performances of clustering algorithms are shown in Figure 6. It can be found that KL clustering based on l_1 graph shows the prominent performance due to the particularity of the database.

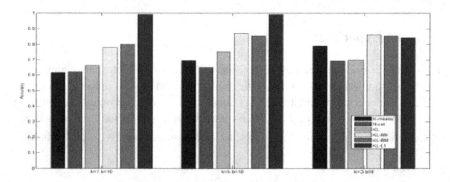

Fig. 4. Clustering results on subsets of COIL20

5   The Conclusions

This paper improves the classic KL clustering with sparse graphs constructed by b-matching and sparse representation. Graph construction plays a key role on learning algorithms based on graph Laplacian, and sparse graph can ensure the algorithm based on it remain efficient and robust. Incorporate the sparse graphs, KL clustering gets great improvement. As experiments shown in the article, the KL clustering with sparse graphs outperforms many exiting clustering algorithms including the classic KL clustering.

Acknowledgement. The work is supported by the National Science Foundation (No.61203240), the Grant of Shanghai Outstanding Young Teachers (B211058K) and the Innovation Program of Shanghai Municipal Education Commission (Z2011-080).

References

1. Duda, R.O., Hart, P.E., Stork, D.G.: Pattern Classification, 2nd edn. Wiley, New York (2000)
2. Jain, A.K.: Data clustering: 50 years beyond K-means. Pattern Recognition Letters 8(31), 651–666 (2010)

3. Jain, A.K., Dubes, R.: Algorithms for clustering data. Prentice Hall, New Jersey (1988)
4. Indulska, M., Orlowska, M.E.: Gravity based spatial clustering. In: 10th ACM International Symposium on Advances in Geographic Information Systems, vol. 22 (2002)
5. Ng, R.T., Han, J.: Clarans: a method for clustering objects for spatial data mining. IEEE Transactions on Knowledge and Data Engineering 14(5), 1003–1016 (2002)
6. Baumgartner, C., Plant, C., Kailing, K., Kriegel, H.P., Kroer, P.: Subspace selection for clustering high-dimensional data. In: 4th IEEE International Conference on Data Mining, ICDM (2004)
7. Agrawal, R., Gehrke, J., Gunopulos, D., Raghavan, P.: Automatic sub space clustering of high dimensional data for data mining applications. In: ACM SIGMOD International Conference on Management of Data (1998)
8. Palmer, C.R., Faloutsos, C.: Density biased sampling: an improved method for data mining and clustering. In: ACM SIGMOD International Conference on Management of Data (2000)
9. Hartigan, J., Wang, M.: A K-means clustering algorithm. Applied Statistics 28, 100–108 (1979)
10. Wang, F., Zhang, C.S., Li, T.: Clustering with Local and Global Regularizations. IEEE Transactions on Knowledge and Data Engineering (TKDE) 12, 1665–1678 (2009)
11. Zha, H., He, X., Ding, C., Gu, M., Simon, H.: Spectral Relaxation for Kmeans Clustering. In: Advances in Neural Information Processing Systems (2001)
12. Ding, C., He, X.: K-means clustering and principal component analysis. In: Proceedings of the 21st International Conference on Machine Learning, Banff, Canada, vol. 69, pp. 29–38 (2004)
13. Ng, A., Jordan, M., Weiss, Y.: On spectral clustering: Analysis and an algorithm. In: Proc. Neural Info. Processing Systems (2001)
14. Shi, J., Malik, J.: Normalized Cuts and Image Segmentation. IEEE Trans. on Pattern Analysis and Machine Intelligence 22(8), 888–905 (2000)
15. Wang, F., Ding, C., Li, T.: Integrated, K.L. (K-means – Laplacian) Clustering: A New Clustering Approach by Combining Attribute Data and Pairwise Relations. In: The 9th SIAM Conference on Data Mining, SDM (2009)
16. Belkin, M., Niyogi, P.: Laplacian Eigenmaps for Dimensionality Reduction and Data Representation. Neural Computation 15(6), 1373–1396 (2003)
17. Roweis, S.T., Saul, L.K.: Nonlinear dimensionality reduction by locally linear embedding. Science 290(5500), 2323–2326 (2000)
18. Zhu, X.: Semi-Supervised Learning Literature Survey, Computer Sciences Technical Report 1530, University of Wisconsin-Madison (2008)
19. Jebara, T., Shchogolev, V.: B-Matching for Spectral Clustering. In: Fürnkranz, J., Scheffer, T., Spiliopoulou, M. (eds.) ECML 2006. LNCS (LNAI), vol. 4212, pp. 679–686. Springer, Heidelberg (2006)
20. Huang, B., Jebara, T.: Loopy belief propagation for bipartite maximum weight b-matching. In: Artificial Intelligence and Statistics, AISTATS (2007)
21. Donoho, D.: For most large underdetermined systems of linear equations the minimal l1-norm solution is also the sparsest solution. Comm. on Pure and Applied Math. 59(6), 797–829 (2006)

Sub-optimal Multiuser Detector Using a Wavelet Chaotic Simulated Annealing Neural Network

Yunxiao Jiang

Key Laboratory of Electronic Restriction of AnHui Province,
Electronic Engineering Institute,
Hefei 230037, China
j_yunxiao@sohu.com

Abstract. This paper proposes a sub-optimal multiuser detector (MUD) algorithm for CDMA system based on the neural network with a novel Wavelet Chaotic Simulated Annealing Neural Network (WCSANN), and gives a concrete model of the MUD after appropriate transformations and mappings. The WCSANN makes use of the wavelet and chaotic simulated annealing parameters of the recurrent neural network to control the network evolving behavior so that the network has richer and more flexible dynamics rather than conventional neural networks, so that it can be expected to have much powerful ability to search for globally optimal or sub-optimal solutions, and can refrain from the serious local optimal problem of Hopfield-type neural networks. Simulation experiments have been performed to show the effectiveness and validation of the proposed method for MUD problem.

Keywords: MUD, Wavelet, Chaotic Simulated Annealing Neural Network.

1 Introduction

MUD came to the focus in CDMA systems as traditional single user receivers have shown poor performance due to uncorrelation produced by multipath propagation. In Verdu's opinion[1], minimizing the objective function of the Optimal multisuer Detector (OMD) is a NP-complete problem, however the OMD has been shown to have the exponential computation complexity in the number of users, and cannot satisfy the real time demand. Consequently, many authors proposed different sub-optimal solutions. The first Hopfield type of receiver was introduced by Varanasi and Aazhang [2], They defined a multi-stage detector. However, due to local optimization, this structure does not provide optimal detector. Lots of articles have discussed modified recurrent neural network structures for multiuser detector to achieve performance improvement. Yoon,Chen, et al.[3] proposed an annealed neural network multiuser receiver. Kechriotis and Manolakos introduced another modified structure which was named as hybrid detector[4]. Wang, et al. considered a transiently chaotic neural network based multiuser receiver scheme[5] which originates from chaos theory. In [6], a Hopfield neural network with transient chaos and time-varying gain (NNTCTG) was proposed. However, the optimality of all the previously listed techniques has not yet

F.L. Wang et al. (Eds.): CMSP 2012, CCIS 346, pp. 514–522, 2012.

been proven theoretically, but rather tested by simulations. Therefore, developing optimal detector for MUD still remains an open question.

In this paper, on the basis of NNTCTG, WCSANN was proposed and used to deal with MUD. The WCSANN makes use of the wavelet and chaotic simulated annealing parameters of the recurrent neural network to control the evolving behavior of the network so that it has richer and more flexible dynamics. Unlike the conventional networks detectors, the detector based on WCSANN has richer and far-from equilibrium dynamics with various coexisting attractors, not only of fixed points and periodic points but also of strange attractors, to avoid getting stuck in local minima.

The paper is organized as following: The proposed neural model of WCSANN and its neural dynamics analysis are presented in Section 2, the proposed WCSANN based MUD in CDMA system is given in Section 3. In Section 4, some simulation experiments are performed for the comparison of our model with the existing detector models. Finally, conclusion remarks are given in Section 5.

2   Chaotic Neural Network Models

It is well known that Hopfield network with continuous-time or asynchronously discrete-time state transitions guarantee convergence to a stable equilibrium solution but suffer from local minimum problems. Since the chaotic neural network has richer and more flexible neural dynamics, therefore, it can be used to efficiently escape from local minima problem in chaotically. In this section, two chaotic neural network models are given. The first NNTCTG is presented by Y.tan[6], the second is the proposed WCSANN which makes use of the wavelet and chaotic simulated annealing parameters of the recurrent neural network to control the evolving behavior of the network.

2.1   Neural Network with Transient Chaos and Time-Varying Gain (NNTCTG)

In order to obtain a global optimal or sub-optimal convergent solution for nonlinear optimization, Y.tan, et al.[6] proposed a neural network with transient chaos and time-varying gain(NNTCTG), as defined below:

$$x_i(t) = \frac{1}{1 + e^{-y_i(t)/(\varepsilon_i(t)+1)}} \tag{1}$$

$$y_i(t+1) = ky_i(t) + \alpha(\sum_{j=1, j\neq i}^{n} w_{ij}x_j(t) + I_i) - z_i(t)(x_i(t) - I_0) \tag{2}$$

$$z_i(t+1) = (1-\beta)z_i(t) \tag{3}$$

$$\varepsilon_i(t+1) = (1-\gamma)\varepsilon_i(t) \tag{4}$$

where x_i is output of neuron i, y_i is internal state of neuron i, w_{ij} is connection weight from neuron j to neuron i, I_i is input bias of neuron i, I_0 is a positive parameter, α is positive scaling parameter for inputs, k is damping factor of nerve membrane ($0 \leq k \leq 1$), $z_i(t)$ is self-feedback connection weight($z_i(t) \geq 0$), β is damping factor of the time-dependent $z_i(t)$,($0 \leq \beta \leq 1$), $\varepsilon_i(t)$ is gain parameter of the output function ($\varepsilon_i(t) \geq 0$), γ is damping factor of the time-dependent $\varepsilon_i(t)$,($0 \leq \gamma \leq 1$).

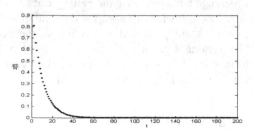

Fig. 1. The time evolutions of $z_i(t)$ of NNTCTG

The term $z_i(t)(x_i(t) - I_0)$ in (2) is related to inhibitory self-feedback or refractoriness and is the main factor generating chaotic phenomenon. NNTCTG actually has transiently chaotic dynamics which eventually converges to a stable equilibrium point through successive bifurcations with the temporal evolution of $z_i(t)$ and $\varepsilon_i(t)$ in (3). The time evolutions of self-feedback connection weight $z_i(t)$ is shown in **Fig.1** with respect to damping parameter β .

2.2 The Proposed Wavelet Chaotic Simulated Annealing Neural Network (WCSANN)

In order to prevent the chaotic dynamics of NNTCTG from vanishing so quickly to realize sufficient chaotic searching, this paper proposed the Morlet-Sigmoid chaotic simulated neural network, described as follows:

$$x_i(t) = f(y_i(t)) \tag{5}$$

$$y_i(t+1) = ky_i(t) + \alpha(\sum_{j=1, j \neq i}^{n} w_{ij} x_j(t) + I_i) - z_i(t)(x_i(t) - I_0) \tag{6}$$

$$z_i(t+1) = (1-\beta)z_i(t) \tag{7}$$

$$\varepsilon_i(t+1) = (1-\gamma)\varepsilon_i(t) \tag{8}$$

$$\eta_i(t+1) = \frac{\eta_i(t)}{\ln(e + \lambda(1-\eta_i(t)))} \tag{9}$$

$$f(y_i(t)) = e^{-\frac{(u_1 y_i(t)(1+\eta_i(t)))^2}{2}} \cos(5u_1 y_i(t)(1+\eta_i(t))) + \frac{1}{1+e^{-u_0 y_i(t)(1+\eta_i(t))}} \tag{10}$$

where x_i, y_i, w_{ij}, I_i, α, k, $z_i(t)$, β, $\varepsilon_i(t)$, γ are the same with the above. $\eta_i(t)$ is the simulated annealing factor, and $\eta_i(t) > 0$;λ is a positive parameter, which controls the speed of this annealing process. u_0 and u_1 are important parameters of activation function which should be varied with kinds of special optimization problems.

2.3   Application to Traveling Salesman Problem (TSP)

The coordinates of 10-city is as follows:

(0.4, 0.4439), (0.2439, 0.1463), (0.1707, 0.2293), (0.2293, 0.716), (0.5171, 0.9414), (0.8732, 0.6536), (0.6878, 0.5219), (0.8488, 0.3609), (0.6683, 0.2536), (0.6195, 0.2634). The shortest distance of the 10-city is 2.6776.

Here are the results of the test about Y.tan's NNTCTG model and WCSANN. The objective function we adopt is that provided in the reference [7]. The parameters of the objective function are set as follows: A=2.5, D=1.
The parameters of NNTCTG are set as follows :

$$\alpha = 0.5, k = 1, I_0 = 0.5, \varepsilon(0) = [0.5, 0.5], \gamma = 0.3, z(0) = [0.5, 0.5].$$

The parameters of WCSANN are set as follows :

$$\alpha = 0.5, k = 1, I_0 = 0.5, \varepsilon(0) = [0.5, 0.5], \gamma = 0.3, z(0) = [0.5, 0.5]$$
$$u_0 = 10, u_1 = 0.8, \lambda = 0.001, \eta(0) = [0.8, 0.8]$$

We make the test for 1000 iterations in different β, as is shown in table 1. (VN=valid number; GN=global number; VP=valid percent; GP=global percent.)

Table 1. Test result of two chaotic neural network

β	Reference	VN	GN	VP	GP
0.035	WCSNN	951	948	95.1%	94.8%
	NNTCTG	891	823	89.1%	82.3%
0.011	WCSNN	955	950	95.5%	95%
	NNTCTG	893	830	89.3%	83%
0.008	WCSNN	988	983	98.8%	98.3%
	NNTCTG	911	903	91.1%	90.3%

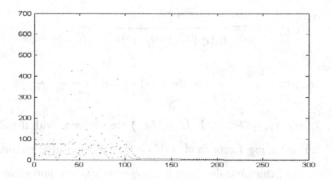

Fig. 2. Energy time evolution figure of WCSANN

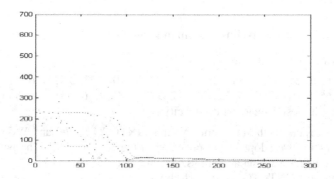

Fig. 3. Energy time evolution figure of NNTCTG

The time evolution figures of the energy function of WCSANN and NNTCTG in solving TSP are respectively given in Fig.2 and Fig.3 when β =0.008.

By comparison, it is concluded that WCSANN is superior to NNTCTG model. From the Fig.2, Fig.3, one can see that the velocity of convergence of WCSANN is much faster than that of NNTCTG in solving TSP.

The superiority of WCSANN contributes to several factors: First, because of the quality of Morlet wavelet function, the activation function of WCSANN has a further performance in solving combinatorial optimization problems than NNTCTG . Second, it is easier to produce chaotic phenomenon [8] in that the activation function is non-monotonic. Third, η is varied with time, which denotes steepness parameter of WCSANN.

3   WCSANN-Based Multiuser Detector in CDMA System

Let us assume that K users are transmitting (2M+1) symbol long packets on the same channel in CDMA system. Applying the complex baseband equivalent model, the transmitted signal of the kth user can be written in the following form:

$$q_k(t) = \sqrt{E_k} \sum_{i=-M}^{M} b_k(i) s_k(t - iT) \qquad (11)$$

where T denotes the symbol length, $s_k(t)$ denote the signature waveform related to the kth user, $b_k(i)$ be the ith symbol of the kth user and $\sqrt{E_k}$ is the symbol energy of the kth user.

In[1],Verdu derive the optimal MUD as a maximum likelihood sequence estimation(MLSE) problem which can then be obtained in the following fashion:

$$\hat{b}^{opt} = agr \min_{x \in \{-1,+1\}^k} [x^T Rx - 2x^T b] \qquad (12)$$

where R is the signature waveform cross-correlation matrix, b is the symbol of the user. The optimal solution can be found, for example, by exhaustive search using (12), however, it implies exponentially increasing computational complexity as the number of users grows. We cannot afford to use such a time wasting mechanism in real life implementation, thus many sub-optimal MUD algorithms have been researched in the recent past.

In [2][3][4], Hopfield neural network(HNN) is used for the purpose of MUD. The energy function of HNN can be written as:

$$E = -\frac{1}{2} x^T Wx - x^T I \qquad (13)$$

where x is the output of HNN, and W is neural weight matrix. I is the input biases. It is apparent from (12) that the objective function of the MLSE is very similar to the HNN energy function (13). With the replacement $W \sim R$ and $x \sim x$, and mapping the HNN parameters to (5)-(9),then we can get the WCSANN-based Multiuser detector.

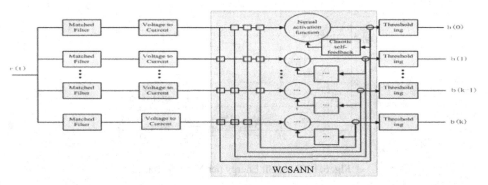

Fig. 4. WCSANN -based multiuser detector

The structure of the WCSANN-based MUD receiver is shown in Fig.4. WCSANN-based MUD has richer and far-from equilibrium dynamics with various coexisting attractors to avoid getting stuck in local minima, especially when the number of the users or the packet length becomes very large(in the order of hundreds of users) .

4   Experimental Results

The simulations were performed in a $K = 33$ user environment with 31 length Gold codes, which entails that the channel were overloaded. The number of symbols in one block was chosen to be $2M + 1 = 51$, chip level synchronization was assumed, and samples were taken in the middle of chip intervals. For all users a $L_k = 5$ path propagation model was used, where the attenuation was generated subjected to Rayleigh distribution. The delay parameters of each path were chosen to be uniformly distributed over one symbol length.

Since the quality of digital communication link can be measured by Bit Error Ratio (BER) in all the figures on the vertical axis the simulated BER is depicted. The performance of the optimal detector based on MLSE cannot be simulated due to its computational complexity (there are $2^{(2M+1)K} = 2^{1683}$ possible sequences), thus the theoretical BPSK AWGN bound is depicted in the figures, which is expected to be close to the curve of optimal detector[9].It is given as the function of bit energy per noise variance ratio(E_b / N_o)in the following form:

$$ BER = Q(-\sqrt{\frac{E_b}{N_o/2}}) = \int_{-\infty}^{-\sqrt{\frac{E_b}{N_o/2}}} \frac{1}{\sqrt{2\pi}} e^{-\frac{x^2}{2}} dx \qquad (14) $$

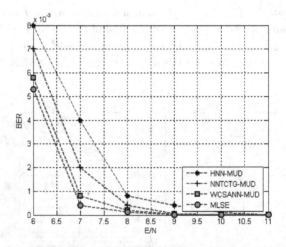

Fig. 5. BER vs. Bit Energy per Noise Variance

In Fig.5 the performance versus bit energy per noise variance ratio E_b / N_o is depicted. WCSANN-based MUD detector shows satisfactory performance, which is very close to the optimal detector. WCSANN-based MUD detector results in better performance than NNTCTG-based MUD detector, namely 1...2dB gain in performance can be achieved.

Table 2. Number of Iterations needed by NNTCTG-MUD and WCSANN-MUD

E_b / N_o	Average Iterations		BER(10^{-3})
	NNTCTG	WCSANN	
6 dB	14.997	21.663	5.9
7 dB	11.5	19.6	2.1
8 dB	10.1	18.8	0.71
9 dB	9.9	16.9	0.25
10 dB	9.7	16.0	0.17
11 dB	9.2	15.5	0.06

Although we have seen that WCSANN-based MUD detector outperforms the NNTCTG-based MUD detector, but it is still a question how much additional iteration is needed in exchange for better performance. It is worth comparing this in **Table 2**, where the number of iterations need to reach the steady state by NNTCTG and WCSANN are shown from $E_b / N_o = 6$ to 11dB. It is very clear that WCSANN needs 7~8 additional iterations to exchange for her better performance.

5   Conclusions

In this paper we have proposed a novel multi-user detection scheme, which makes use of WCSANN optimization algorithm in MUD. The new method resulted in better performance than NNTCTG detector algorithms, namely 1..2dB gain in performance can be achieved, only 7..8 additional iteration is needed. In the future, we would like to develop a more sophisticated, adaptive version of the algorithm.

Acknowledgments. This paper is supported by Natural Science Fund of Anhui Province of China (050420101).

References

1. Verdu, S.: Minimum probability of error for asynchronous Gaussian multiple-access channels. IEEE Trans. Inform.Theory IT-32, 85–96 (1986)
2. Varanasi, M.K., Azhang, B.: Multistage Detection in Asynchronous Code-Division Multiple Access Communications. IEEE Trans. on Comm. 38, 509–519 (1990)
3. Yoon, S.H., Rao, S.: Multiuser detection in CDMA based on the annealed neural network. In: IEEE Int. Conf. Neural Networks, vol. 4, pp. 2124–2129 (1996)
4. Kechriotis, G., Manolakos, E.S.: A Hybrid Digital Signal Processing-Neural Network CDMA Mulituser Detector Scheme. IEEE Trans. Cicuits and Systems 43(2), 96–104 (1996)
5. Wang, B., He, Z., Nie, J.: To Implement the CDMA Multiuser Detector by Using Transiently Chaotic Neural Network. IEEE Trans. Aerospace and Elec. Sys. 33, 1068–1071 (1997)
6. Tan, Y., Deng, C., Wang, B., He, Z.: A Neural Network with Transient Chaos and Time-Varying Gain and its Application to Optimization Calculation. Acta Electronica Sinica 26(7), 123–127 (2005)

7. Sun, S., Zheng, J.: A Kind of Improved Algorithm and Theory Testify of Solving TSP in Hopfield Neural Network. Acta Electronica Sinca 1(23), 73–78 (1995)
8. Potapove, A., Kali, M.: Robust Chaos in Neural Networks. Physics Letters A 277(6), 310–322 (2000)
9. Teich, W.G., Seidl, M.: Code Division Multiple Access Communications: Multi-user Detection based on a Recurrent Neural Network Structure. IEEE Trans. Veh. Technol. 46, 979–984 (1996)

Easier Encoding-Decoding Distributed Arithmetic Coding for Slepian-Wolf Coding

Yuye Pang

School of Computer and Information Engineering
Shanghai University of Electric Power
Shanghai, 200090, China
pangyuye@163.com

Abstract. Distributed Arithmetic Coding (DAC) is an effective implementation of Slepian-Wolf problem. In this paper, the coding theory of DAC is introduced including two implements for asymmetric Slepian-Wolf problem, Distributed Overlap Arithmetic Coding (DOAC) and Distributed Quasi-Arithmetic Coding (DQAC). Both of the implementation schemes are analyzed. The advantages and disadvantages of them are compared and discussed. Then an improved scheme with easier encoding and decoding is proposed. Simulation results show that the proposed scheme is better than DOAC and DQAC.

Keywords: distributed Arithmetic coding; distributed source coding; arithmetic coding.

1   Introduction

Distributed Source Coding (DSC) considers a situation where two or more statistically dependent data sources must be encoded separately. DSC is mainly used in wireless sensor network and multi-view video coding. DSC is based on the theory of Slepian-Wolf [1], which proves that if two statistically dependent sources X and Y are encoded separately by rate R_x and R_y respectively, satisfy $R_x + R_y \geq H(X,Y)$, $R_x \geq H(X/Y)$, $R_y \geq H(X/Y)$, and are decoded jointly, then the source X and Y can be compressed lossless even they do not communicate with each other. Here, the source X and Y is encoded with conditional entropy symmetrically. So the phenomena is also called symmetric Slepian-Wolf problem. However, if the source Y is encoded by its entropy, and the source X is encoded by the corresponding conditional entropy, then at the decoder, the sequence X is reconstructed by compressed X and side information Y. This is called asymmetric Slepian-Wolf problem. Slepian-Wolf problem only considers lossless compression of correlated sources. Later, based on the theory of Slepian-Wolf, Wyner and Ziv extend its coding field to loss compression of continuous source and set up rate-distortion theory of loss distributed source coding. Wyner-Ziv theory [2] proves that the optimum rate-distortion performance of loss compression can be reached by separate encoding and joint decoding. Thus, the theory DSC system is established.

F.L. Wang et al. (Eds.): CMSP 2012, CCIS 346, pp. 523–530, 2012.

Slepian-Wolf coding can be implemented by source coding and channel coding. However, many existing schemes use channel coding, e.g. the DISCUS scheme, which transmits the syndromes of channel codes to compress. Now, many new schemes use channel codes with performance approaching channel capacity , e.g. Turbo code [4] and LDPC code [5]. The good performance of these codes can approach channel capacity only for very long source sequences with at least 10^4 source symbols. Moreover, these channel codes cannot use the statistical characteristic of sources. Therefore, how to use entropy coding to solve the problem of Slepian-Wolf becomes a new research direction. DAC [6~7] is just one of a hotspot. Preliminary studies have shown that, compared to channel coding, DAC can not only obtain excellent performance for short source sequence but also can make use of the prior probabilities of information sources and the relevance of their owns. DAC encoding complexity is linear with the block size, and generally smaller than turbo codes, while decoding complexity is higher; hence, it is suitable for DSC applications. Moreover, since the encoding is a simple extension of the arithmetic coding process, it is straightforward to extend an existing compression scheme in order to provide DSC functionalities.

The existing two schemes of DAC in literatures are DOAC and DQAC. The encoding process of DOAC is more easier than DQAC, but the decoding of DOAC is more complicated than DQAC. Moreover, the performance of DOAC depends on the memories of system excessively. So, in this paper, a new scheme of DAC is proposed to make the encoding more easier and the decoding performance better and decoding complexity more lower.

The rest of this paper is organized as follows. Firstly, the coding theories of DOAC and DQAC are introduced. Secondly, the advantages and disadvantages of these two schemes are analyzed, compared and discussed,. Then an improved DAC scheme is proposed. The simulation results show that the performance of the proposed scheme is better than existing schemes . The conclusions are given at last.

2   Distributed Arithmetic Coding

2.1   Arithmetic Coding

Let $X = [X_0, X_1, ..., X_i, ..., X_{N-1}]$ be a length-N binary source sequence with probability $p_0 = P(X_i = 0)$ and $p_1 = P(X_i = 1) = 1 - p_0$ and the side information Y .The basic idea of AC is to map the input source sequence into disjoint sub-intervals of a given initial interval $[0,1)$ according to p_0 and p_1. This procedure is repeated by a recursive partition of the interval driven by the source sequence. Let $[l^k, h^k)$ denote, respectively, the lower limit and the upper limit of the interval after encoding the k-th symbol. The recursive partition process can be described as follows,

$$l^k = l^{k-1} + (h^{k-1} - l^{k-1}) \cdot F_X((X(s_k) - 1) \mid X(s_{k-1})), \tag{1}$$

$$h^k = l^{k-1} + (h^{k-1} - l^{k-1}) \cdot F_X(X(s_k) \mid X(s_{k-1})). \tag{2}$$

where, X is a random variable, and $F_X(\cdot)$ is the cumulative probability. After all source symbols have been processed, the source sequence is represented by the final interval I. The codeword C_X can be any binary number in I. Usually, the smallest number of bits is used to represent a value in the interval. The minimum number of bits required for representing the interval is $\lceil -\log_2 I \rceil$, where $\lceil x \rceil$ represents the smallest integer greater than or equal to x. The decoding is a dual process of the encoding, given the received sequence C, iteratively selecting the decoding interval $[l^k, h^k)$.

2.2   Distributed Overlap Arithmetic Coding

The scheme of DOAC is first proposed by Grangetto et al. in [6], which is based on the principle of inserting an ambiguity in the encoding process. This is obtained using a modified interval subdivision strategy, where the interval length is proportional to the modified probabilities $\tilde{p}_0$ and $\tilde{p}_1$, such that $\tilde{p}_0 > p_0$ and $\tilde{p}_1 > p_1$. In order to fit the enlarged sub-intervals $\tilde{p}_i$ into interval $[0,1)$, the sub-intervals are allowed to partially overlap. This leads to overlapped subintervals, then the decoder can not decode the source unambiguously without knowledge of the side information. At the same time, the overlapping leads to larger final interval, and hence a shorter codeword.

Let $\tilde{p}_i = \alpha_i p_i, \alpha_i \geq 1$, then $\tilde{p}_0 + \tilde{p}_1 \geq 1$. The average coding rate of DOAC is expressed as

$$R_X = -\sum_{i=0}^{1} p_i (\log_2 p_i + \log_2 a_i) = \sum_{i=0}^{1} p_i (r_i - \delta r_i). \tag{3}$$

Where δr_i represents saved number of bits of the i-th source symbol. If let $\delta r_i / r_i = k, 0 \leq k \leq 1$, and k be a constant. Then the ambiguity will be uniformly distributed over all input bits and $\alpha_i = p_i^{-k}$, and the modified probabilities are $\tilde{p}_i = p_i^{1-k}$. For the DOAC, the average coding rate can be further expressed as

$$R_X = -(1-k)\sum_{i-0}^{1} p_i \log_2 p_i = (1-k)H. \tag{4}$$

Equation (4) indicates that the expected average coding rate can be obtained by setting any constant k.

Figure 1 shows the encoding process of DOAC. Supposing the symbol sequence to be encoded is $\{0,1,0,\cdots\}$ with probability $p = P(X_i = 0)$. According to (3), initial interval $[0,1)$ is divided in $[0, p^{1-k})$ and $[1-(1-p)^{1-k},1)$, where the overlapped interval is $[(1-p)^{1-k}, p^{1-k})$ and the first encoding interval $[0, p^{1-k})$ is chosen. To encode the second source symbol, the subinterval $[p^{1-k} - [p(1-p)]^{1-k}, p^{1-k})$ is chosen. For the third input symbol "0", the chosen encoding interval is $[p^{1-k} - [p(1-p)]^{1-k}, p^{2(1-k)})$. The encoding process is repeated driven by the input source symbols until the end of the source sequence.

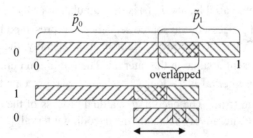

Fig. 1. Encoding process of DOAC

The decoding of DOAC is almost the same as the decoding of AC except the decoding interval belongs to the overlapped region between two intervals. For the ambiguous decoding, M-algorithm is used.

2.3   Distributed Quasi-Arithmetic Coding

DQAC [7] is based on quasi-arithmetic coding and uses Finite State Machine (FSM) to generate different variable length codes. DQAC can implement asymmetric Slepian-Wolf coding by puncturing the encoded codeword. DQAC represents the coding interval using integrals, confining the number of following bits to a constant. The coding state of DQAC can be expressed as $\{0, U, f, s\}$, where U represents the maximum of the initial interval, which decides the coding precision, f represents the maximum number of following bits, s represents the prior encoding symbol in the source sequence.

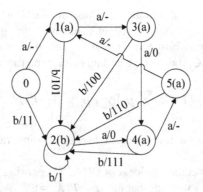

Fig. 2. FSM representation of DQAC

A FSM representation of DQAC for a first order markov binary source sequence with source symbol a and b is shown in Figure 2 as in [7], where $a/-$ represents inputting symbol a but no output.

The probability of symbol a is $p_a = 0.8$, the source correlation coefficient is $\rho_m = 0.3$, $U = 8$, $f = 1$. The encoding process can be expressed as follows.

Step1: Initialize the coding interval to $\{0, 8, 0, Null\}$.

Step2: Partition the current coding interval Ic according to source probability and correlation coefficient, $I_c^a = [l^a, u^a]$, and $I_c^b = [l^b, u^b]$.

Step3: Normalize I_c^a and I_c^b as need as necessary.

Step4: Two states $\{l^a, u^a, f, s\}$ and $\{l^b, u^b, f, s\}$ are obtained. If they have been never appeared before, add them as new states, otherwise go to step 5.

Step5: Repeat step 2,3 and 4 until there is no new state to appear.

In order to obtain the expected distributed rate, puncturing is used in DQAC. The puncturing segment is decided by theoretical rate Rq, expected rate Rt, the length of source sequence Lx and the length of encoded codeword Ls. Since there are $\lceil (Rq - Rt) \times Ls \rceil$ bits to be punctured, so the factual puncturing segment is $\lfloor (Rq - Rt) \times Ls / Lx - 1 \rfloor$ bits. However, if $(Rq - Rt) \times Ls > Lx / 2$, the above segment should be bit position not to be punctured.

The decoding of DQAC can use improved Viterbi algorithm or BCJR algorithm, along with side information and the knowledge of source correlation.

2.4   Proposed Distributed Arithmetic Coding

The encoding of DOAC is easier than that of DQAC, especially the expected coding rate can be obtained conveniently by adjusting a parameter without changing the encoding strategy, let alone puncturing. However, using M-algorithm to decode DOAC needs more memories and more computational complexity to get better decoding performance. To the contrary, decoding DQAC becomes easier because of the FSM representation. For the above reasons, a new DAC scheme is proposed.

The proposed DAC implements the encoding process using overlapped interval as that in DOAC to produce wanted coding rate, but during encoding process record the FSM representation as DQAC. Thus, the proposed DAC does not need puncturing to get the expected coding rate, and can softly and jointly decode with lower complexity to obtain better performance. Here, List-Viterbi algorithm [8].

3   Simulation Results

The DAC schemes described above are applied in the following experiment, assuming that the side information Y is available at the decoder. Two situations are considered in the experiment, the source length and probability, to observe and study how they affect the performance of DAC. Two different length binary uncorrelated source sequences with symmetric probability $p_0 = p_1 = 0.5$ and asymmetric probability $p_0 = 0.9$ and $p_1 = 0.1$ are encoded respectively. The same source sequence is encoded with length $N=200$, and $N=1000$. For proposed DAC and DQAC, the FSM representation of the proposed DAC for the simulation use $U=256$, $f=1$, and both decoders use List-Viterbi algorithm with the length of List 32. For DOAC, when decoding codeword falls in ambiguous interval, at most 1024 best paths are preserved. The BER at the output of the decoder is averaged over 10^5 realizations.

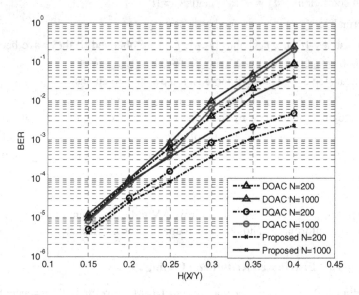

Fig. 3. BER vs. $H(X/Y)$ for $p_0=p_1=0.5$

The simulation results in Figure 3 for the symmetric source in the same format as in [6], the abscissa $H(X/Y)$ is such that the less correlated the sources are, hence the higher $H(X/Y)$ is. The performance is measured by the residual Bit Error Rate (BER) after decoding. As can be seen from the figure, the performance of DAC is a little affected by the length of source sequence. The shorter the source sequence is, the better performance is obtained. Moreover, the performance of proposed DAC is a little better than that of DOAC and DQAC. Though in the experiment, the list number of List-Viterbi algorithm is only 1/32. of the number of preserved best paths in M-algorithm. The reason is that for decoding of DOAC, its performance greatly depends on the number of preserved most likely paths. Especially for less correlated sources using M-algorithm in DOAC, the side information Y cannot provide sufficient information to confine the decoding tree increasing along with the proper decoding path. However, using List-Viterbi algorithm, each list decoding using Viterbi algorithm will preserve a most likely path corresponding to the source. At last, the most likely path is selected from the 32 preserved paths. Furthermore, the results show that the performance of DOAC decreases more quickly than that of DQAC and proposed DAC, when the conditional entropy $H(X/Y)$ increases. The reason is that when decoding using M-algorithm in DOAC, the number of preserved paths confined to M and less side information make the decoding tree to have to prune branches temporary with little Maximum A Posteriori Probability. Maybe, the pruned branches are just in the proper path in the long run.

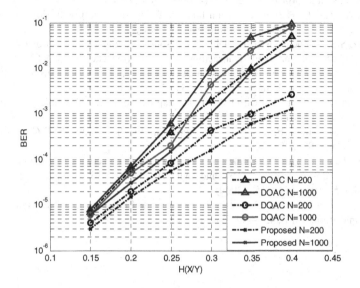

Fig. 4. BER vs. H(X/Y) for $p_0=0.9$ and $p_1=0.1$

Comparing Figure 3 and Figure 4, one can find, whatever length of the source sequence is, and whatever the implement scheme is, the decoding performance for asymmetric source sequence is better than that of symmetric source sequence. The results show that DAC is more suited for asymmetric source sequences. This is an advantage inheriting from the characteristic of AC.

4   Conclusions

DAC is an effective implementation of Slepian-Wolf coding, especially for shorter source sequence with asymmetric statistical characteristics. Two implementation schemes of DAC in existing literatures is discussed. Then based on the advantage and disadvantage of them, a new scheme of DAC is proposed. The proposed DAC implements the encoding process using overlapped interval as that in DOAC to produce FSM representation. Consequently, the decoding is implemented using optimized List-Viterbi algorithm. The simulation results show that the proposed DAC not only has consistent performance trend but is better than the two existing schemes.

Acknowledgement. This work is acknowledged to Excellent Young Fund of Shanghai Education Commission (sdl10003) and Shanghai Science and Technology Commission Research Programs (10dz1501000).

References

1. Slepian, D., Wolf, J.K.: Noiseless coding of correlated information sources. IEEE Transactions on Information Theory 19(4), 471–480 (1973)
2. Wyner, A., Ziv, J.: The rate-distortion function for source coding with side information at the decoder. IEEE Transactions on Information Theory 22(1), 1–10 (1976)
3. Pradhan, S.S., Ramchandran, K.: Distributed source coding using syndromes (DISCUS): Design and construction. IEEE Transactions on Information Theory 49(3), 626–643 (2003)
4. Garcia-Frias, J., Zhao, Y.: Compression of correlated binary sources using turbo codes. IEEE Communications Letters 5(10), 417–419 (2001)
5. Varodayan, D., Aaron, A., Girod, B.: Rate adaptive codes for distributed source coding. Signal Processing 86(11), 3123–3130 (2006)
6. Grangetto, M., Magli, E., Olmo, G.: Distributed arithmetic coding. IEEE Communications Letters 11(11), 883–885 (2007)
7. Malinowski, S., Artigas, X., Guillemot, C., et al.: Distributed coding using punctured quasi-arithmetic codes with memoryless and memory sources. IEEE Transactions on Signal Processing 57(10), 4154–4158 (2009)
8. Roder, M., Hamzaoui, R.: Fast tree-Trellis list viterbi decoding. IEEE Transactions on Communicaltions 54(3), 453–461 (2006)

A Perceptual Weighted Trellis-Coded Quantization Algorithm

Wei Jiang, Junjie Yang, and Jason Gao

School of Computer and Information Engineering,
Shanghai University of Electric Power, Shanghai 200090, China
zzm7406@sina.com

Abstract. The rate-distortion optimization algorithm (RDOTCQ) was proposed to improve the coding performance efficiently in our former work. However, human visual characteristics are not considered. In this paper, a perceptual weighted rate-distortion optimization TCQ (PRDOTCQ) algorithm is proposed. By introducing the vision model that takes into account various masking effects of human visual perception and a perceptual distortion metric, the proposed algorithm obtains better subjective quality. The experiment shows that PRDOTCQ algorithm provides better performance compared to SPIHT with the maximum gain 0.6dB. Though it behaves a little PSNR loss compared with RDOTCQ, it results in better subjective quality with the same rate.

Keywords: Rate-distortion, JND, TCQ.

1 Introduction

Trellis-Coded Quantization (TCQ) stems from trellis-coded modulation. By using the expanded signal set and set partitioning ideas it can be thought of being a type of vector quantization [1]. Because of its excellent MSE performance and moderate complexity, TCQ-based schemes have been widely applied to image compression [2]-[4]. The entropy-constrained TCQ (ECTCQ) is introduced in [5]-[6]. Though these ECTCQ systems achieve good performance, it is difficult to be implemented because separate TCQ codebooks must be precomputed for each encoding rate. Based on rate-distortion criterion, a rate-distortion optimized Trellis-Coded Quantization (RDOTCQ) algorithm is presented [7]. By introducing the rate-distortion cost into the trellis path selection it can improves the performance with a little computational complexity increase. These algorithms aim at improvement of coding efficiency in information theory. Since most images will be perceived by human consumers, encoding and transmission of the unaware data is a waste of bitrates. Therefore, there is a large room for coding efficiency improvement by reducing the perceptual data redundancy according to human visual theory.

In this paper, a perceptual weighted rate-distortion optimization trellis-coded quantization algorithm (PRDOTCQ) is proposed. The human visual theory is applied to get rid of the unaware data. Moreover, it optimizes the decisions on how to map input

F.L. Wang et al. (Eds.): CMSP 2012, CCIS 346, pp. 531–538, 2012.
© Springer-Verlag Berlin Heidelberg 2012

coefficients into quantization indices according to perceptually weighted rate-distortion cost.

The remaining part of this paper is organized as follows. Section 2 provides intro-duction to RDOTCQ. Section 3 describes PRDOTCQ algorithm in detail. The expe-rimental results are shown in section 4. Finally, this paper is concluded in section 5.

2   RDOTCQ Algorithm

In TCQ the Viterbi algorithm is used to choose the sequence of codewords that mini-mizes the cumulative distortion D for a given data sequence. Since the rate is not considered in trellis path selection in TCQ, it is not optimal. According to Shannon's rate-distortion theory, RDOTCQ algorithm introduces the rate-distortion cost in trellis path selection. Then the optimal quantization performance can be acquired by mini-mizing D subject to a bit budget constraint $R \leq R_c$. It is known that the distribution of wavelet coefficients (except the coefficients in low frequent subband) is closely ap-proximated by Laplacian law, which is steep in small signal zone and flat in large signal zone [8]. RDOTCQ algorithm emphasizes on processing the small signals near zero. Suppose the narrowed signal space is S, the corresponding quantization level set is I and the quantization level set corresponding to the subsets is $Z_G = \{ z_{D_i} \mid z_{D_i} \in I, \; 0 \leq i \leq M - 1 \}$. Then the optimal quantization level of the signal $x \in S$ allowed by the trellis can be determined as follows:

$$z^* = arg \min_{0 \leq i \leq M-1, z_{D_i} \in Z_D} \{ J_\lambda(x', z_{D_i}) \} \tag{1-a}$$

$$J_\lambda(x, z_{D_i}) = D_e(x, z_{D_i}) + \lambda \times R(z_{D_i}) \tag{1-b}$$

where λ is the Lagrange parameter. It can be determined by the fast convex search, e.g., the bisection method [9], golden-ratio search[10].

Therefore the proposed algorithm is to find the point on convex-hull by solving

$$\overset{(b)}{\underset{\lambda \geq 0}{max}} \; \overset{(a)}{\underset{z_{D_i} \in Z_D, 0 \leq i \leq M-1}{min}} \{ D_e(x, z_{D_i}) + \lambda \times R(z_{D_i}) \} \tag{2}$$

where the innermost minimization (a) involves the search for the best quantization level for signals in S and the outermost optimization (b) is the convex search for the optimal value of λ that satisfies the desired rate constraint. Accordingly, the final solution (λ^*, z^*) is obtained in two sequential optimization steps.

An example is shown in Fig.1 to explain the idea clearly. In the Figure 1 the dotted line curves are the trellis path selected by the original TCQ quantizer. It can be seen that though only x_3 belongs to the defined signal space S, rate-distortion measure influences the trellis path selection of all the input samples.

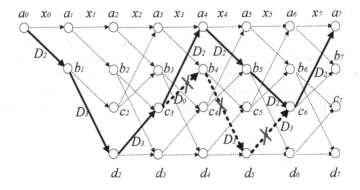

Fig. 1. An example of the trellis path selection

RDOTCQ algorithm has no extra parameters and completely complies with the original decoder. It is implemented on the platform of the quadtree classified and trellis coded quantized (QTCQ) wavelet image compression system [11].

3   Perceptual Based Trellis-Coded Quantization Algorithm

Since the human observer is the end user of most image information, it is more appropriate to consider the human vision characteristics in image compression. To maximize compression efficiency, both visually lossy algorithms must exploit properties of the HVS. Thus the human vision characteristics are introduced in RDOTCQ algorithm. Just Noticeable Difference (JND) threshold and a perceptual weighted-distortion metric are defined in the proposed algorithm. Given the wavelet transformed coefficients, JND threshold $t_{JND}(\xi,\theta,i,j)$ is calculated for each DWT transformed coefficient at location (i,j) within subband (ξ,θ) , where ξ is the transform level and θ is the orientation. Three visual factors are considered to compute the JND thresholds: contrast sensitivity, luminance masking and contrast masking. JND threshold is computed as follows[12]

$$t_{JND}(\xi,\theta,i,j) = JND_{\xi,\theta} \cdot a_l(\xi,\theta,i,j) \cdot a_c(\xi,\theta,i,j) \qquad (3)$$

where $JND_{\xi,\theta}$ is the base detection threshold for a subband (ξ,θ) , $a_l(\xi,\theta,i,j)$ is the luminance masking adjustment and $a_c(\xi,\theta,i,j)$ is the contrast masking adjustment. $JND_{\xi,\theta}$ is a measure of the smallest contrast that yields a visible signal over a background of uniform intensity. It is related to the amplitude of the DWT basis function, the viewing distance and the display resolution. The luminance masking $a_l(\xi,\theta,i,j)$ is computed according to the highest level of the DWT decomposition, the mean luminance of the display and the value of the DWT coefficient corresponding to location (ξ,θ,i,j) . The contrast masking effect $a_l(\xi,\theta,i,j)$ is related to the self contrast masking adjustment factor and the neighborhood contrast masking adjustment factor.

According to the above visual model, JND threshold should be calculated for each coefficient. In HL subband block coefficients greater than their corresponding JND are visible and are chosen. In LH and HH subband coefficients greater than their corresponding JND multiply by 1.2 are selected [13]. In this way it can allocate more bits to the area that human eyes are sensitive and do not allocate bit to the invisible area.

Moreover the perceptual distortion metric between the original coefficient and the recovered coefficient is introduced in the proposed algorithm. It can be defined as

$$D_{F(n_1,n_2)} = \left(\sum_{(\xi,\theta,i,j)\in F} \left| \frac{e(\xi,\theta,i,j)}{t_{JND}(\xi,\theta,i,j)} \right|^{\beta} \right)^{\frac{1}{\beta}} \tag{4}$$

Where $F(n_1,n_2)$ denotes the area in the spatial domain that is centered at location (n_1,n_2), $e(\xi,\theta,i,j)$ is the quantization error at location (ξ,θ,i,j) and F is the set of DWT coefficients whose values affect the $F(n_1,n_2)$ reconstruction.

Then the perceptual rate-distortion cost J_p is

$$J_p = D_{F(n_1,n_2)} + \lambda \times R \tag{5}$$

where the output rate R can be approximated by the theoretical first-order entropy.

$$H(X \mid A) = -\sum_{i=0}^{1} P(A_i) \sum_{x \in A_i} P(x \mid A_i) \log_2 P(x \mid A_i) \tag{6}$$

where A is the superset[1]. From Eqn.(5), it can be seen that the human vision characteristics is considered in the rate distortion optimization. Then the PRDOTCQ algorithm can allocate more bits to the area that human eyes are more sensitive and allocate less bits to the area that human eyes are less sensitive.

With the above discussion, the PRDOTCQ algorithm can be divided into two parts. Firstly, the transformed coefficients are classified according to JND threshold. Only the coefficients greater than the threshold are retained. Then the perceptual weighted rate-distortion cost is used to optimize the trellis path selection. For a fixed λ PRDOTCQ algorithm takes the following main steps:

1. Calculate JND threshold for each DWT transformed coefficient.
2. For all of the transformed coefficients detect if the coefficient is retained by comparing the transformed coefficient with the JND threshold.

   If the coefficient in HL subband block is less than the JND, the coefficient is not selected.

   If the coefficient in LH and HH subband is less than the corresponding JND multiply by 1.2 , the coefficient is not selected.
3. Suppose the total state number is N_s and Initialize the N_s total cost $J_{tot}(i)$ to 0, $0 \leq i \leq N_s-1$.
4. Estimate the rate for the signals falling into the predefined window.
5. Examine if the current sample located in the predefined window. If no, calculate the distortion cost as the original quantization method; else compute the perceptual weighted rate-distortion cost for all the subsets according to Eqn.(5).

6. Add the cost calculated in step 4 up to the total cost J_{tot} (i) respectively.

7. Go to the next sample and repeat step 4 and step 5 until all samples are processed.

8. Find out the minimum total cost in J_{tot} (i) , $0 \leq i \leq N_s$-1, and then the corresponding trellis path is optimal in rate-distortion sense.

The PRDOTCQ algorithm has been designed for optimally quantizing the input signals by adaptively optimizing trellis path. Moreover it introduces JND threshold and the perceptual weighted rate-distortion cost to acquire better subjective image quality. This algorithm has no extra parameters and completely complies with the original decoder. In addition, it can be applied to the TCQ-based image compression system.

4   Experimental Results

The PRDOTCQ algorithm has been verified on the platform of QTCQ system. Experiments are performed on standard 512×512 greyscale, Peppers and baboon images at several bit rates. In our experiment the processed window is defined as zone including the first and second quantization cell. Since the first-order entropy is the good estimate of the real coding bits with long input sequence, the average bit rate is estimated by the first-order entropy [7].

The performance curves of PRDOTCQ, RDOTCQ and SPIHT algorithm are shown in Fig.2-3. It can be seen that PRDOTCQ algorithm outperforms SPIHT algorithm for all test sequences and all rates considered. A maximum gain up to 0.6 dB can be achieved respectively with the same rate compared with SPIHT. Moreover, the performance of RDOTCQ algorithm is better than the purposed algorithm. It is reasonable since the purposed algorithm considers the human visual characteristic in the rate distortion optimization.

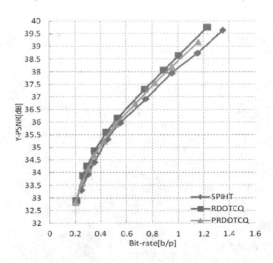

Fig. 2. Comparison of RD performance for SPIHT, RDOTCQ and PRDOTCQ for "peppers" 512×512 format

Although the PSNR numbers indicates inferior objective performance for PRDOTCQ algorithm, the coded image reveals the better subjective quality with the same rate. The subjective evaluation complying with Recommendation ITU-R BT.500-11[14] is conducted. Two decoded images with the same rate are displayed synchronously on the screen side by side; one is from the RDOTCQ algorithm, the other is from the proposed algorithm. Audiences do not know which one is original. After one compare, the locations of the two sequences on the screen were exchanged. The average subjective quality score of the PRDOTCQ algorithm is better. Thus although the PSNR numbers indicates inferior objective performance for PRDOTCQ algorithm, the coded image reveals the same or better subjective quality. It is also can be seen from Fig.4

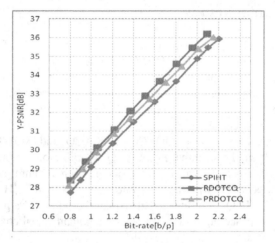

Fig. 3. Comparison of RD performance for SPIHT, RDOTCQ and PRDOTCQ for "baboon" 512×512 format

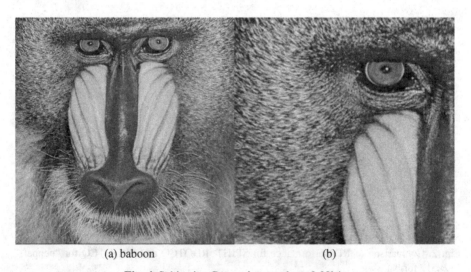

(a) baboon   (b)

Fig. 4. Subjective Comparison at about 0.09b/p

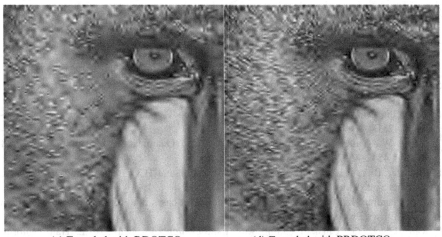

(c) Encoded with RDOTCQ   (d) Encoded with PRDOTCQ

Fig. 4. (*continued*)

5   Conclusion

The perceptual weighted rate-distortion optimization TCQ algorithm is presented with the goal to achieve consistent reconstructed image quality and the lowest possible bit rate for the desired perceptual distortion. A vision model that takes into account various masking effects of human visual perception and a perceptual distortion metric are incorporated in rate-distortion optimization. This algorithm has no overhead and completely complies with the decoder. The experiment shows that PRDOTCQ algorithm provides better performance at all rates considered compared to SPIHT. The max gain is about 0.6dB. Compared with RDOQTCQ, it behaves acceptable PSNR loss. However, Subjective viewing tests have shown that PRDOTCQ algorithm results in better performance in picture quality assessment applications.

Acknowledgment. This work is supported by Shanghai Technology Innovation Project (09160501700, 10110502200, 11510500900), Innovation Program of Shanghai Municipal Education Commission (09ZZ185,12ZZ176), Project of Science and Technology Commission of Shanghai Municipality (10PJ1404500) and Leading Academic Discipline Project of Shanghai Municipal Education Commission(J51303)

References

1. Marcellin, M.W., Fischer, T.R.: Trellis coded quantization of memoryless and Gaussian-Markov sources. IEEE Trans. Commun. 38, 82–93 (1990)
2. Joshi, R.L., Crump, V.J., Fischer, T.R.: Image subband coding using arithmetic and trellis coded quantization. IEEE Trans. Circuits Syst. Video Technol. 5, 515–523 (1995)

3. Marcellin, M.W., Sriram, P., Tong, K.: Transform coding of monochrome and color images using trellis coded quantization. IEEE Trans. Circuits Syst. Video Technol. 3, 270–276 (1993)
4. Sriram, P., Marcellin, M.W.: Image coding using wavelet transforms and entropy-constrained trellis-coded quantization. IEEE Trans. Image Processing 4, 725–733 (1995)
5. Fischer, T.R., Wang, M.: Entropy-constrained trellis-coded quantization. IEEE Trans. Inform. Theory IT-8, 415–426 (1992)
6. Marcellin, M.W.: On entropy-constrained trellis-coded quantization. IEEE Trans. Commun. 42, 14–16 (1994)
7. Jiang, W., Yang, J.: An Improved Trellis-Coded Quantization Algorithm. Journal of JCIS 6, 4542–4552 (2010)
8. Banister, B.A., Fischer, T.R.: Quadtree classification and TCQ image coding. IEEE Trans. Circuits Syst. Video Technol. 11, 3–8 (2001)
9. Ramchandran, K., Vetterli, M.: Best wavelet packet bases in a rate distortion sense. IEEE Trans. Image Processing 2, 160–175 (1993)
10. Ungerboeck, G.: Channel coding with multilevel/phase signals. IEEE Trans. Inform. Theory 28, 55–67 (1982)
11. Jiang, W., Wang, J., Yang, J.: A novel algorithm of solving the optimal slope on rate-distortion curve for the given rate budget. Journal of Donghua University, 259–263 (2009)
12. Liu, Z., Karam, L.J.: JPEG2000 Encoding With Perceptual Distortion Control. IEEE Transactions on Image Processing 15(7), 1763–1778 (2006)
13. Jan, Z., Jaffar, A.: Watermarking Scheme Based on Wavelet Transform. In: Genetic Programming and Watson Perceptual Distortion Control Model for JPEG 2000. ICET, pp. 128–133 (2010)
14. ITU-R: Methodology for the Subjective Assessment of the Quality of Television Pictures. Recommendation ITU-R BT.500-11 (2002)

Computer Aided Measuring the Viscosity of Castor Oil

Dong Sheng Chen, Bin Wu,Yao Chang Liu, and Wan Lin Liu

College of Mathematics and Physics,
Shanghai University of Electric Power, Shanghai 200090, China
cds78@shiep.edu.cn

Abstract. A new data acquisitions method to measure the viscosity of caster oil is proposed. Compared with the traditional ones, an automated system----a web camera connected to a personal computer, is used in the new method to precisely measure distance and time. Meanwhile, the relationship of the viscosity of caster oil (η) and temperature (T) is described by fitting the curve based on the software Matlab.

Keywords: digital camera, castor oil, personal PC.

1   Introduction

In the teaching area, the measurement of the liquid viscosity has long been of great scientific interest to the educators. There are a variety of ways to measure the liquid viscosity in the undergraduate physics laboratory such as rotating cylinder method、 capillary tube method and falling sphere method [1].

The falling sphere method based on the Stokes's law is to drop a sphere into the liquid, and measure the time and distance which the sphere falls. In traditional experiment, the measurements of time and distance are usually carried out by using stopwatch and ruler. However, a difficult with this approach is that the time and distance of starting and ending is extremely affected by the personal error. To reduce the error, A simple and cheap data acquisition method—by using a web camera connected to personal PC have been designed.

The new approach proposed requires a web camera and a personal PC with a resolution of $800{\times}600$ or higher. Most web cameras can record not only digital images but also digital videos. Recently, Salvador Gil [2] and Martı́n Eduardo Saleta [3] discussed the technique of using visual digital images to analyze elementary topics in mechanics、 the ray theory and Bernoulli's equation with losses. S Nedev and V Ch Ivanova discussed the utilization of the web camera in undergraduate physics teaching laboratories for measuring the positions and the brightness of objects [4]. However, in present work, another useful feature of web camera is not discussed which can measure the moving time of the objects, which is particularly useful for studying the kinematics of objects such as pendulum damped oscillations and coupled oscillations[5].

This paper illustrates and describes in detail the use of digital techniques to measure and analyze data. One of the purposes of the manuscript is to follow the trend to use new technologies in experiment. Through which one can obtain knowledge as well as keep in contact with what is available in the market.

F.L. Wang et al. (Eds.): CMSP 2012, CCIS 346, pp. 539–545, 2012.

2   Defining the Equation in Order to Obtain the Value of Viscosity Coefficent

The viscosity coefficient η at room temperature is determined by Stokes's law

$$F = 3\pi\eta vd \tag{1}$$

where d is the sphere's diameter, v is the constant velocity of falling after equilibrium among the gravitational, buoyancy and viscous force are established. F is the viscosity force in liquid , determined by.

$$F = mg - \rho'gV = \frac{1}{6}\pi d^3 g(\rho - \rho') \tag{2}$$

Where ρ, V and m are the sphere's density, volume, and mass in air, respectively, and ρ' the density of liquid[1].

By replacing F with $3\pi\eta vd$ in the equation (2), Let v be l/t, one one obtains.

$$\eta = \frac{(\rho - \rho')gd^2t}{18l} \tag{3}$$

Stokes's law requires the sphere to fall in the liquid with infinite width and extensive, but the diameter and the depth of the vessel are always finite, so the actual velocity should multiply an amending coefficient $1+2.1\frac{d}{D}$ (D is the inner diameter of the vessel). Thus, the expression of calculating the coefficient of the viscosity can be written as.

$$\eta = \frac{(\rho - \rho')gd^2t}{18l(1+2.1\frac{d}{D})} \tag{4}$$

Where l and t are the distance and time of sphere falling after equilibrium among the gravitational , buoyancy and viscous force are established.

3   Computer Software

Flash is a popular software, and can be downloaded freely from the Internet [6]. Compared with the programs written in Delphi or C++, Flash has the advantages of easy-using, freely cost and work under Windows operating system which is in common use.

Flash has the function of editing *.avi format digital video, which can help to measure the time and distance.

3.1   (a)The Transformation from Pixel Coordinates to Object Coordinates

Let Δh_1 be the distance of two scale lines in pixel coórdinates (yellow circle in Figure 1), which is measured by the Flash software, Δh_2 be the actual distance of the two scale lines in object coordinates, and P be the coordinate transforming coefficient, one can obtains.

$$p = \frac{\Delta h_2}{\Delta h_1} \tag{5}$$

3.2   (b)The Measurement of the Falling Time of the Sphere

After inputted into the Flash scene, the digital video was cut into 10 frames per second videos which can present the motion of the falling sphere in the castor oil. So per frame corresponds to 0.1 second time interval in the flash scene. By mouse, we can reappear and control the motion of the falling sphere. Figure 1 shows the 15th frame to the 165th frames, which makes it easy to calculate the falling time $t = 16.4 - 1.4 = 15s$.

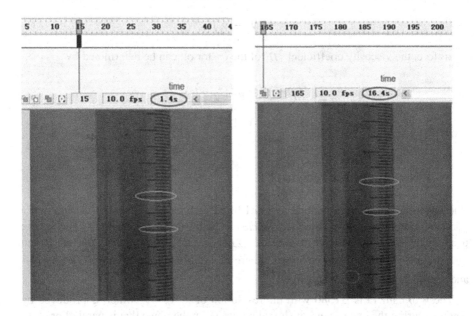

Fig. 1. Two different frames for determining the falling time of the sphere

3.3   (c)The Measurement of Falling Distance of the Sphere

By reading the mouse position coordinates which are provided automatically by Flash software (see Figure 2), it is convenient to determine the falling distance of the sphere.

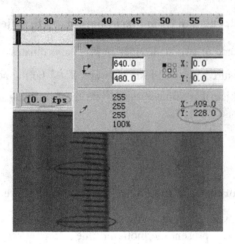

Fig. 2. Reading mouse position to obtain the pixel coordinates of the sphere

Define y_1, y_2 as pixel coordinates corresponding to different time t_1 and t_2 in Flash scene, the falling distance l in object coordinate can be expressed as

$$l = p(y_2 - y_1) \tag{6}$$

Therefore, the viscosity coefficient η of the castor oil can be determined by

$$\eta = \frac{(\rho - \rho')gd^2(t_2 - t_1)}{18p(y_2 - y_1)(1 + 2.1\dfrac{d}{D})} \tag{7}$$

4   Experimental Procedure

The experimental devices include a vessel filled with castor oil, a web camera and a personal computer. The vessel is $6.72cm$ in diameter and $50cm$ high. The sphere used in the experiment have two sizes, $2.00mm$ and $1.59mm$ in diameter. Room temperature is $17.5°c$. The density of sphere and castor oil are $\rho = 7.90 \times 10^3 \, Kg/m^3$ and $\rho' = 0.966 \times 10^3 \, Kg/m^3$ respectively.

The web camera is ET380 with the resolution of 800×600 which is produced by lenovo. During the experiment, it should be placed in the plane that is parallel or close to the vessel filled with the castor oil, the distance is about 1 meter from the vessel meanwhile, the focal length is adjusted so that the falling ball can be clearly seen. The diagrammatic layout is presented in Figure 3.

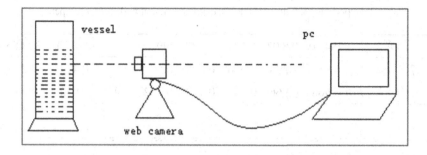

Fig. 3. Diagrammatic layout for the measurement

Release the sphere into the castor oil; and record the motion of the falling sphere for 4~5 mins by web camera and then analyze the video by the Flash software to gain some important data(see Table 1).

Table 1. The data to determine the viscosity of castor oil

$d(mm)$	$\Delta h_1(px)$	$\Delta h_2(cm)$	$y_1(px)$	$y_2(px)$	$\Delta t = (t_2-t_1)(s)$
2.00±0.02	60±1	2.9±0.1	65±1	402±1	13.0±0.1
2.00±0.02	60±1	2.9±0.1	40±1	404±1	14.0±0.1
2.00±0.02	53±1	2.9±0.1	34±1	378±1	15.0±0.1
1.59±0.02	60±1	2.9±0.1	37±1	328±1	17.6±0.1
1.59±0.02	64±1	2.9±0.1	35±1	368±1	19.0±0.1
1.59±0.02	60±1	2.9±0.1	40±1	385±1	21.0±0.1

where d is the sphere's diameter, $\Delta h_1, \Delta h_2$ is the distance of two scale lines on the vessel in pixel coordinates and object coordinates, y_1, y_2 is the pixel coordinates in the flash scene, and Δt is the sphere's falling time .

Based on Equation (8) and the above data in Table 1,the value.

$$\eta = 1.154 \pm 0.002 (Pa \cdot s) \tag{8}$$

The measured value of the coefficient of viscosity agrees to within 3% with the value given in the Hand of Chemistry and Physics.

The measurement of the viscosity coefficient as a function of temperature can also be a suitable experiment in an undergraduate laboratory. To explore the relationship between temperature and viscosity coefficient, a heating and a temperature control device are fixed on the vessel. Record the moving videos of the sphere at different temperatures, and calculate the viscosity coefficient η. Table 2 shows the experiment result, and meanwhile the relationship is described by $\eta \sim T$ curve in Figure 4. The experimental results $\eta = 6.379 \times 10^9 e^{-0.07716T}$ is obtained using the software Matlab.

Table 2. Experimental values of the viscosity coefficient at different temperature

$T(K)$	284.30	288.02	292.26	296.95	299.35	301.65	304.50	308.85
$\eta(Pa{\cdot}s)$	1.915	1.393	1.026	0.695	0.589	0.513	0.414	0.298
$\rho\times10^{3}(Kg/m$	0.968	0.966	0.962	0.959	0.952	0.955	0.952	0.947

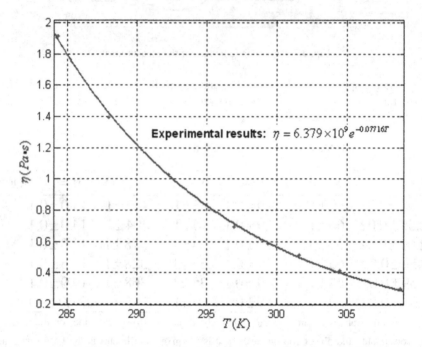

Experimental results: $\eta = 6.379\times10^{9}e^{-0.07716T}$

Fig. 4. The Curve describing the relationship between η and T.

With the increasing of temperature, intermolecular distance rises so that the interaction force decreases. So, the viscosity coefficient will decrease when the temperature increases. From the fig.4, we can know that temperature dependence of the viscosity is exponential, which is consistent to the theory.

5   Summary

The software—Flash provides an alternative approach in the time and distance measurement, while Web camera is not only used to capture interesting physical phenomena but also used for data acquisitions in many cases. The utilization of a web camera connected to PC allows us to record the motion of the objects which is very helpful to solve many kinematics problems.

References

1. Nahshol, D.: Measuring Viscosity by Stokes's law. Am. J. Phys. 33, 657–658 (1965)
2. Gil, S., Reisin, H.D., Rodriguez, E.E.: Using a digital camera as a measuring device. Am. J. Phys. 74, 43–45 (2006)
3. Saleta, M.E., Tobia, D., Gil, S.: Experimental study of Bernoulli' equation with losses. Am. J. Phys. 73, 598–602 (2005)
4. Nedev, S., Lvanova, V.C.: Web camera as a measuring tool in the undergraduate physics laboratory. Eur. J. Phys. 27, 1213–1219 (2006)
5. Greczylo, T., Debowska, E.: Using a digital video camera to examine coupled oscillations. Eur. J. Phys. 23, 441–447 (2002)
6. Flash, http://www.onlinedown.net/soft/9866.htm

V_σ-Test for Determining the Degree
of Nonlinearity of Time Series

Ye Yuan and Zhi Qiang Huang

College of Engineering, Shantou University,
Shantou 515063, China
yuanye@stu.edu.cn

Abstract. This paper presents a new method named V_σ-test for analyzing nonlinearity in time series. The degree of nonlinearity of the tested time series is determined through the statistical results of comparing the variances of phase space reconstruction vectors of the tested time series to those of its surrogate time series, and a simple procedure based on V_σ-test for determining the nonlinearity of the tested time series with known information about embedding dimension is also given. V_σ-test proposed in this paper can not only determine whether the tested time series is linear or nonlinear, but also show the degree of nonlinearity of the tested time series. The results of numerical simulations on three artificial and one real-world time series indicate the effectiveness and applicableness of the proposed V_σ-test method.

Keywords: V_σ-test, degree of nonlinearity, time series.

1   Introduction

In recent years, analyzing the property of time series has received more and more attention[1-5], the properties of time series include linearity, nonlinearity, deterministic and randomness. Most signals in practice contain both linear and nonlinear components, it is necessary to determining the linear or nonlinear property of a signal before applying practical methods to deal with it. In practice, the presence of linearity or nonlinearity, or the change of degree of nonlinearity of biomedical time series can indicate the health status of the monitored subject[6,7].

Up to now, the methods for determining the nonlinearity of a time series can be divided into two categories: the first one, different models such as linear or nonlinear models are employed to match the tested time series[6,8,9], and the matching accuracy of the selected models are evaluated; the second one, some nonlinearity criterion is calculated for the tested signal and the results are compared to those for the linearized surrogate data, this kind of methods is called surrogate data test. The first category of methods are affected considerably by the accuracy of the selection of models, the flexibility and expandability are not strong; comparatively, the second category of methods are more flexible and not restricted by the selection of models. Surrogate

F.L. Wang et al. (Eds.): CMSP 2012, CCIS 346, pp. 546–553, 2012.

data is the non-parametric linear representation of the tested time series (namely the tested time series), that is, the tested time series is supposed to be linear. There are several methods for generating surrogate time series, the method called iterative amplitude adjust Fourier transform (iAAFT) proposed by Schreiber and Schmitz is used in this paper. Surrogate time series generated by iAAFT can reserve the characteristic of distribution and amplitude spectrum of the original time series.

V_σ-test is proposed in this paper to determine the degree of nonlinearity of time series using the variances of phase space reconstruction vectors as nonlinearity measure. Firstly, the tested time series is supposed to be linear, and then the corresponding surrogate time series is generated by iAAFT. The null hypothesis that the tested time series is linear can be verified by the statistical results of comparing the variances of phase space reconstruction vectors of the tested time series to those of its surrogate time series. Further the degree of nonlinearity of the tested time series can be judged out as well based on the statistical results of comparison. The method proposed in this paper can not only determine whether the tested time series is linear or nonlinear, but also show the degree of nonlinearity of the tested time series (the degree of nonlinearity of a linear time series is zero).

2 V_σ-Test

V_σ-test proposed in this paper determines the linear or nonlinearity property of a time series through the statistical results of comparing the variances of phase space reconstruction vectors of the tested time series to those of its surrogate time series, and gives the numerical representation of degree of nonlinearity of the original time series. To determine the linear or nonlinear property, or degree of nonlinearity of a time series by V_σ-test, we can follow the steps below:

(A). Based on Takens theorem, the tested time series can be reconstructed as a set of vectors of the embedding dimension m, i.e. $x(k) = [x_{k-m\tau},...,x_{k-\tau}]$, where τ is delay time.

(B). Compute the mean β and standard derivation σ over every two vectors, then take Euclidean distance value r which satisfies $\beta - n\sigma < r < \beta + n\sigma$, where n is the control parameter to make delay vector variance to converge to 1.

(C). Find the subset $\Omega_k(r)$ of the vector set $x(k)$ within the Euclidean distance r, namely $\Omega_k(r) = \{x(i)\| \|x(k) - x(i)\| \le r\}$.

(D). Compute the variance $\sigma_k^2(r)$ corresponding to each set $\Omega_k(r)$, then the variances of phase space reconstruction vectors of the tested time series $O(t)$ can be denoted as:

$$\sigma^{*2}(r) = (1/K)\sum_{k=1}^{K} \sigma_k^2(r)/\sigma_x^2 \tag{1}$$

where σ_x^2 is the variance of $O(t)$, K is the number of sets of vectors. Then the obtained variance of the tested time series $O(t)$ is $\sigma_o^{*2}(r)$.

(E).   Estimate the surrogate time series $S(t)$ of the tested time series $O(t)$ by iAAFT, and then repeat the steps (A-D) to compute the variances of phase space reconstruction vectors $\sigma_s^{*2}(r_d)$ of the surrogate time series $S(t)$.

(F).   Compute the difference between the variances of phase space reconstruction vectors of the tested and those of its surrogate time series, i.e. the difference between $\sigma_o^{*2}(r)$ and $\sigma_s^{*2}(r)$:

$$\sigma_{diff}^{*2}(r) = \sigma_o^{*2}(r) - \frac{\sum_{i=1}^{N} \sigma_{si}^{*2}(r)}{N} \tag{2}$$

where σ_O^2 and σ_S^2 are the variances of the tested time series $O(t)$ and the surrogate time series $S(t)$, respectively; N is the number of surrogate time series, at a significance level of $\alpha = 0.1$, 19 surrogate time series are generated.

(G).   Finally, estimate the relative standard error $\sigma_{diff}^{*2}(r)$, which is denoted by V_σ in this paper, of the difference between the variances of phase space reconstruction vectors of the tested and those of its surrogate time series. V_σ value is employed in this paper to indicate the degree of nonlinearity of the original time series $O(t)$.

3   Experiments

Three kinds of artificial time series for verifying V_σ-test are generated by the models below. The first one is Hénon map, given by:

$$\begin{cases} x_k = 1 - ax_{k-1}^2 + by_{k-1} \\ y_k = x_{k-1} \end{cases} \tag{3}$$

where $a = 1.4$ and $b = 0.3$, here Hénon map outputs chaotic time series. The second one is Logistic map shown below:

$$x_{n+1} = kx_n(1 - x_n), \quad x \in (0, 1), k \in [1, 4] \tag{4}$$

where $k = 4$, here Logistic map is in completely chaotic state. The remaining one is the fourth-order AR model (a linear stochastic model), described below:

$$x_k = 1.79x_{k-1} - 1.85x_{k-2} + 1.27x_{k-3} - 0.41x_{k-4} \tag{5}$$

here AR model outputs linear time series.

To verify the V_σ-test method by artificial time series, firstly, the embedding dimension of the output time series of Hénon map, Logistic map and AR model are determined by Cao's method, the obtained embedding dimension values corresponding to the output time series of Hénon map, Logistic map and AR model are 2, 2 and 4, respectively.

Then, the proposed V_σ-test is applied to analyze the nonlinearity of the output time series of Hénon map, Logistic map and AR model. 1000 sampling points are taken for each kind of time series to compute V_σ value. The obtained V_σ values corresponding to the time series generated by Hénon map, Logistic map and AR model are 0.2635, 0.2512 and 0.0038, respectively.

4   Analysis of Results

4.1   Influence of Length of Data on the Results of V_σ-Test

To discuss the influence of the sampling point number n_p of the tested time series on the results of V_σ-test, we take $\Delta n = 100$ as an interval to generate time series with 500-2900 sampling points by Hénon map, Logistic map and AR model

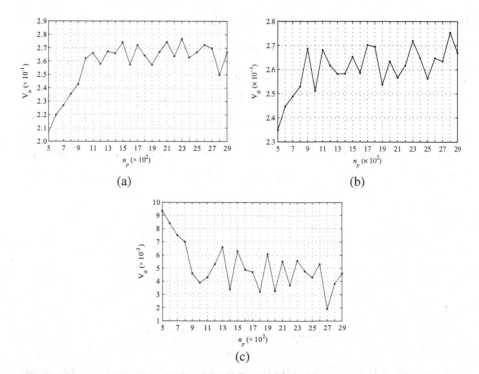

(a)   (b)

(c)

Fig. 1. Results of V_σ values of tested time series with different numbers of sampling points. (a) Hénon map (b) Logistic model (c) AR model

respectively, and then the V_σ values for the time series with different number of sampling points are computed. As shown in Figs. 1 (a), (b) and (c), when $n_p < 1000$, V_σ values increase rapidly as n_p increases for the time series generated by Hénon map and Logistic map, whereas V_σ value descends rapidly as n_p increases for the time series generated by AR model; when $n_p \geq 1000$, V_σ values tend to be stable and fluctuate in a small interval for all three kinds of time series, the fluctuation intervals for Hénon map, Logistic map and AR model are 0.25~0.28, 0.25~0.28 and 0.002~0.007, respectively. Apparently, V_σ-test has no high requirement on the number of sampling points of the tested time series, and stable results can be obtained only if the number of sampling points of the tested time series is more than 1000. Moreover, for the time series generated by AR model, V_σ values are smaller than 0.01 for all n_p values, therefore, it is considered to set 0.01 as a threshold value, i.e., if $V_\sigma < 0.01$, the tested time series is linear ; conversely, the tested time series is nonlinear if $V_\sigma > 0.01$.

4.2   Influence of Noise on the Results of V_σ-Test

Different levels of Gaussian white noise are added to the tested time series, and then V_σ values are computed. The level of noise is measured by $lon = \dfrac{Power_n}{Power_{tts}}$, where $Power_n$ is the power of the added noise, and $Power_{tts}$ is the power of the tested time series. Figure 2 shows the results of V_σ values of the tested time series with different level of noise. With the power of the added noise increasing, the V_σ values descend for both kinds of tested time series. When lon is equal to 1, i.e., the power of the added noise is equal to that of the tested time series, the corresponding V_σ values for both Hénon map and Logistic map are close to 0.01, at this time V_σ-test may

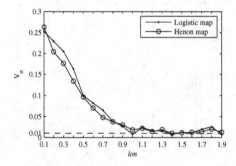

Fig. 2. Results of V_σ values of tested time series with different level of noise. (*lon* stands for the level of noise)

misjudge the nonlinearity of the tested time series. This phenomenon, we think, is reasonable. The signal constituted by the tested time series and the added noise can be considered as a whole, when $lon < 1$, i.e., $Power_n < Power_{tts}$, the tested time series is dominant, and the property of the tested time series determines the property of the whole signal, thus the property of the whole signal is nonlinear at this time.

4.3   Influence of the Embedding Dimension of the Tested Time Series on the Results of V_σ -Test

Figures 3 (a), (b) and (c) show the V_σ values corresponding to the time series generated by Hénon map, Logistic map and AR model with the embedding dimension values from 1 to 10, respectively. For the time series generated by Hénon map and Logistic map, the largest V_σ value appears when the embedding dimension is the optimal value $m = 2$ (the optimal embedding dimensions for Hénon map and Logistic map are both equal to 2), and the further the taken embedding dimension value is away from the optimal embedding dimension value, the smaller the corresponding V_σ value is; for the time series generated by AR model, the V_σ value is the smallest one when the embedding dimension is taken as the optimal value $m = 4$, and the further the taken embedding dimension value is away from the optimal embedding dimension value is, the larger the corresponding V_σ value is basically (except when $m = 2, 9$ and 10 , but these V_σ values are still larger than that obtained with the optimal embedding dimension value $m = 4$).

By observing Figs. 3 (a), (b) and (c), it can be found that for the time series generated by Hénon map, Logistic map and AR model, V_σ curves show extreme point when the embedding dimension is taken as the optimal one, the only difference is that the V_σ curves corresponding to the time series generated by Hénon map and Logistic map have maximum values, whereas the V_σ curve corresponding to the time series generated by AR model has minimum value. Therefore, we summarize that for a nonlinear time series, the corresponding embedding dimension-V_σ curve shows maximum value, whereas for a linear time series, the corresponding embedding dimen-sion- V_σ curve shows minimum value. According to the results above, we propose a simple procedure based on V_σ -test for determining whether a time series with known information about embedding dimension is linear or nonlinear: if the range of embed-ding dimension values of the tested time series is known, it is not needed to calculate its optimal embedding dimension, whereas it is only needed to pick up an embedding dimension within the known range randomly to compute the corresponding temporary $V_{\sigma-temp}$. If the obtained $V_{\sigma-temp} > 0.01$, the tested time series must be nonlinear, since for a nonlinear time series, the $V_{\sigma-optimal}$ value obtained with the optimal em-bedding dimension value is larger than other $V_{\sigma-temp}$ values obtained with non-optimal embedding dimension values, namely $V_{\sigma-optimal} > V_{\sigma-temp} > 0.01$, and in general we make use of the $V_{\sigma-optimal}$ value obtained with the optimal embedding dimension for determining whether a tested time series is linear or nonlinear. Similarly, if the obtained $V_{\sigma-temp} < 0.01$, the corresponding tested time series must be linear, since for a linear time series, the $V_{\sigma-optimal}$ obtained with the optimal embedding dimension value is smaller than other $V_{\sigma-temp}$ values obtained with non-optimal embedding dimension values, namely $V_{\sigma-optimal} < V_{\sigma-temp} < 0.01$. We call this "simple V_σ-test" for determining the degree of nonlinearity of time series with known information about embedding dimension.

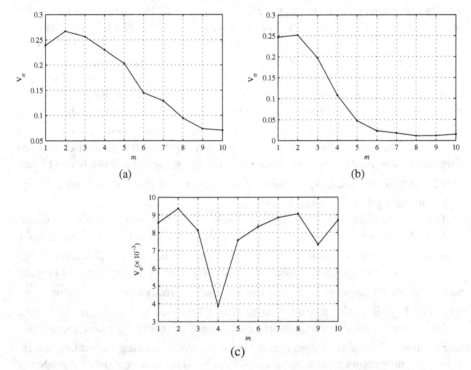

Fig. 3. Results of V_σ values computed based on different embedding dimension values. (a) corresponds to Hénon map (b) corresponds to Logistic model (c) corresponds to AR model

5   Conclusions

This paper presents V_σ-test for analyzing nonlinearity of a time series, numerical results of V_σ-test could show the degree of nonlinearity of the tested time series, which is favorable for analyzing the change of property of a time series. The proposed V_σ-test has no high requirement on the number of sampling points of the tested series, and is robust to noise. A simple V_σ -test for determining the nonlinearity of time series with known information about embedding dimension is also given, which could shorten the time for computation and reduce workload. The results of numerical experiments on EEG time series show the effectiveness of the proposed simple V_σ - test.

Acknowledgement. This work is supported by the National Natural Science Foundation of China (Grant No. 61002047) and Foundation for Distinguished Young Talents in Higher Education of Guangdong, China (Grant No. LYM09076).

References

1. Blume, W.T., Lüders, H.O., Mizrahi, E., Tassinari, C., Boas, W.E., Engel, J.: Glossary of Descriptive Terminology for Ictal Semiology: Report of the ILAE Task Force on Classification and Terminology. Epilepsia, 1212–1218 (2001)
2. Iasemidis, L.D., Principe, J.C., Sackellares, J.C.: Measurement and quantification of spatio-temporal dynamics of human epileptic seizures. In: Akay, M. (ed.) Nonlinear Signal Processing in Medicine, pp. 1–27. IEEE Press (1999)
3. Saito, K., Suzukis, H., Kawakami, Y.: Power Spectrum Density of EEGs of Sleeping Epilepsy-Prone El Mice and Their Non-epileptic Mother Strain. J. Physiol. Sci. 56, 313–316 (2006)
4. Proposal for revised clinical and electroencephalographic classification of epileptic seizures. Epilepsia, 489–501 (1981)
5. Babloyantz, A., Destexhe, A.: Low-Dimensional Chaos in an Instance of Epilepsy. Proc. Nat. Acad. Sci. 83, 3513–3517 (1986)
6. Iasemidis, L.D., Sackellares, J.C., Zaveri, H.P., Williams, W.J.: Phase space topography and the Lyapunov exponent of electrocorticograms in partial seizures. Brain Topogr. 2, 187–201 (1990)
7. Iasemidis, L.D., Barreto, A., Uthman, B.M., Roper, S., Sackellares, I.C.: Spatio temporal evolution of dynamical measures precedes onset of mesial temporal lobe seizures. Epilepsia 129:133 (1995)
8. Iasemidis, L.D., Shiau, D.S., Chaovalitwongse, W., Sackellares, J.C., Pardalos, P.M., Principe, J.C., Carney, P.R., Prasad, A., Veeramani, B., Tsakalis, K.: Adaptive Epileptic Seizure Prediction System. IEEE Trans. Biomed. Eng. 50, 616–627 (2003)
9. Elger, C.E., Lehnertz, K.: Seizure prediction by nonlinear time series analysis of brain electrical activity. Eur. J. Neurosci. 10, 786–789 (2003)

Performance Evaluation for Radar Signal Recognition Based on AHP

Huan Wang, Ming-hao He, Jing Xu, and Duan Xu

Wuhan Electronic Information Institute,
Wuhan 430019, China
whatwh@163.com

Abstract. The recognition of radar emitter signals (RES) is one of the key technologies in electronic countermeasure intelligence system. It's a brand new subject to evaluate the recognition performance scientifically. Formerly most scholars evaluated radar signals recognition methods based on the recognition rate. Aiming at the problem that the evaluation index of recognition effect evaluation of radar signals is single, the paper proposes new evaluation indices. In this paper Analytic Hierarchy Process (AHP) is used to determine the weight of each index, and relevant evaluation model is established for performance evaluation. Simulation result validates that the evaluation model is effective and has certain application prospect.

Keywords: radar signal recognition, evaluation index, measurement of recognition rate, Analytic Hierarchy Process, comprehensive evaluation.

1 Introduction

As the key technology in the electronic intelligence (ELINT), electronic support measures (ESM) and radar warning receiver (RWR) system, Radar signals recognition is the prerequisite and foundation of electronic attack. The recognition level is the important symbol of the advanced degree of radar countermeasure equipment. Scientific assessment of radar signal recognition performance can be effective for subsequent processing to provide an objective and scientific reference. Previously, radar signals recognition performance evaluation is based on the recognition rate [1-5] this single index, with more and more complex electromagnetic environment as well as operational requirements of diversified development. It is obviously unscientific to use a single indicator to evaluate the quality of the evaluation result. Therefore, this paper will apply mathematical statistics knowledge and put forward the new evaluation indices. The indices values are selected as the system input in performance evaluation, while evaluation results are the output of the system. Being applied to radar signals recognition performance evaluation, AHP builds corresponding evaluation model and implements the mapping from the evaluation indices to the evaluation results, which thereby provides the basis for the performance evaluation results for radar signals recognition.

F.L. Wang et al. (Eds.): CMSP 2012, CCIS 346, pp. 554–561, 2012.

2   Indices for the Recognition Performance Evaluation

Evaluation indices selection is determined by the demand of performance evaluation, based on the focus concerned performance, form indices that can be quantified.

2.1   Meaning and Calculation of the Recognition Rate

The comparison of radar signals recognition performance is generally based on the recognition rate, namely in the recognition test. The pulse number of correct recognition divided by the total number of pulses is the signal recognition rate of the condition, which can also be interpreted as the recognition ability of the method to the target signal in the condition. This understanding is correctly identified as "1" on the premise that it is falsely or not identified as "0". Supposing the true value of the recognition rate of the method is p, thus the correct probability of the i th recognition is p. The correct probability of the i th recognition is as the law of $0-1$ distribution. Do Bernoulli (Bernoulli) experiment of signal recognition, then the number of correct recognition obeys the distribution of $B(n, p)$, n is the number of experiments.

2.2   Measurement of Recognition Rate

For the general sense, solving the recognition rate is the result of limited experiments, which can only be infinitely close to the true value and can not achieve the true value. If for different tests, it can be found that the recognition rate is fluctuant variable, and the variation range as well as the number of great changes of the recognition rate reflects the recognition performance.

The paper introduces the concept of measurement of recognition rate [6] (MRR), dividing n test results into m subgroups, which can separately acquire the mean value of each group of n/m test results, then we get m MRR samples. For radar signals recognition, it is supposed that there are l radar radiating sources which will eventually generate $l \times m$ MRR samples. Because of the consistency of the algorithm and solution, it is only needed to research MRR samples of a single radar radiation source, namely m MRR samples. Because MRR is a variable which has distribution, mean and variance, together with the independence of external conditions, by using its characters, we can strictly obtain accurate estimation of radar signals recognition results.

2.3   Acquirement of MRR Samples

Every MRR sample, which contains n/m recognition results obeys $0-1$ distribution from the above analysis. Based on independence and identical distribution as well as the central limit theorem, MRR obeys normal distribution which can be proven[7].

Literature [8] thinks that M is bigger than 50 meets the large sample capacity of using the central limit theorem of independence and same distribution. When

$M > 50$ satisfied, MRR is approximately normal distributed. Power function [9-10] is used to calculate the number of original tests required to generate a MRR. With the calculation process being simplified, the calculation result M is more than 95. $M = 100$ is selected here.

For the generation of MRR samples, the number of MRR needs to be determined. With the demand to meet different testing requirements, the minimum value of m can be calculated. Generate MRR in accordance with the following methods:

$$MRR_m = \frac{1}{100} \sum_{k=100(m-1)+1}^{100m} x_k \tag{1}$$

Where, x_k is the result of every test, $k = 1, 2, \cdots, 100m$.

2.4   Selection and Calculation of Evaluation Indices

1)   Index with respect to correct recognition
The mean value of MRR of the recognition results, directly reflecting the recognition ability of recognition method, is written as MRR mean.

2)   Index with respect to robustness

(a).Whether MRR is normally distributed reflects the robustness shown in the processes of recognition results, which it's called distribution index (Index of Distribution), represented by the symbol I_{dis}. Calculated as: mark the threshold of distribution hypothesis test μ, the test statistic calculated from experiment is w, normalize the index, using following linear utility function:

$$I_{dis} = \begin{cases} \dfrac{\mu - w}{\mu} & , w \le \mu \\ 0, & w > \mu \end{cases} \tag{2}$$

(b). The variance of MRR can reflect the dynamic range of the recognition performance under specific condition, which can be also used as an important index of recognition robustness. Let the variance of MRR be D, the bigger D is; the poorer the stability is, so it belongs to the cost index. Use the following linear utility function:

$$I_{var} = \begin{cases} 1 - D \times 10^3, & D \le 10^{-3} \\ 0, & D > 10^{-3} \end{cases} \tag{3}$$

3)   Index with respect to independence of recognition
In certain range of external condition, independence of recognition method for generating MRR samples can be measured through independent hypothesis testing, which can reflect the influence degree that dynamic changes of external conditions have on the MRR change. It's called Index of MRR Independence, written as I_{ind} .Calculated

as: supposing the threshold of independence hypothesis testing is θ, the test statistic calculated is χ^2. Similarly index is gotten as:

$$I_{ind} = \begin{cases} \left(\dfrac{\theta}{\chi^2}\right)^{1/5}, & \chi^2 > \theta \\ 1, & \chi^2 \le \theta \end{cases} \quad (4)$$

4)   Index with respect to the cost

The cost recognition system for signal processing requires for is also an important index to study. Here we select recognition time as a cost index. Mark recognition control time t_{th}, recognition time in the experiments is t .Its decreasing trend belongs to the convex decreasing function .Convex decreasing function refers to a score value that decreases with the actual value increases, and the decreasing trend gradually grows faster. We can get:

$$I_{cos} = \begin{cases} \cos(\dfrac{t}{t_{th}} \cdot \dfrac{\pi}{2}), & t \le t_{th} \\ 0, & t > t_{th} \end{cases} \quad (5)$$

3   Performance Evaluation Model Based on AHP

3.1   System Model of Recognition Performance Evaluation

Firstly, the analytic hierarchy process is applied, according to the recognition result assessment of the nature of the problem and the overall target, besides various factors between the interrelated effects and subordinating relation to determine the weights of performance indices. Establish a multi-level analysis structure model, including the target layer, rule layer and index layer, as shown in figure 1.

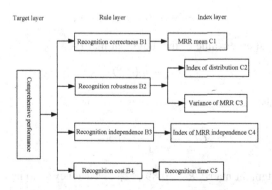

Fig. 1. Hierarchy diagram of recognition performance

3.2   Weight Vectors

With the calculation method of AHP, we can construct the judgment matrix of corresponding levels and the hierarchy ordering of the evaluation system, then calculate the corresponding weights, and finally carry on stochastic consistency test. Since rule layers having only one or two indices lays which are completely consistent, so there is no need to construct judgment matrixes between the rule layers and the indices layers.

This paper uses $9/9 \sim 9/1$ scale method [11] to construct the judgment matrix between target layer and rule layers.

Based on the experts' judgments on the relative importance between the rule layers B1, B2, B3 and B4, the corresponding judgment matrix can be established:

$$A = \begin{bmatrix} 9/9 & 9/7 & 9/5 & 9/2 \\ 7/9 & 9/9 & 9/7 & 9/3 \\ 5/9 & 7/9 & 9/9 & 9/5 \\ 2/9 & 3/9 & 5/9 & 9/9 \end{bmatrix} \tag{6}$$

The weight vector can be gotten by normalizing the eigenvector of the largest eigenvalue of the judgment matrix. Use the square root method to obtain the eigenvector:

$$\varpi_i = \left(\prod_{j=1}^{4} a_{ij} \right)^{1/4} \quad i = 1, 2, 3, 4 \tag{7}$$

where, a_{ij} is the element of the judgment matrix A . Normalizing $\overline{\varpi}$ is the weigh vector:

$$\omega_i = \frac{\varpi_i}{\sum_{j=1}^{4} \varpi_j} \quad i = 1, 2, 3, 4 \tag{8}$$

So, the weight vector between the target layer and the rule layers is obtained as:

$$\omega = (0.399, 0.2924, 0.2086, 0.1) \tag{9}$$

Calculate the largest eigenvalue of the judgment matrix:

$$\lambda_{\max} = 4.0129 \tag{10}$$

Carry on the consistency test, the consistency index is:

$$CI = \frac{\lambda_{\max} - n}{n - 1} = 0.0043 \tag{11}$$

For four order judgment matrix $RI = 0.89$ [12], consistency ratio is:

$$CR = \frac{CI}{RI} = 0.0048 \ll 0.1 \tag{12}$$

Thus, the judgment matrix is satisfactorily consistent.

Calculate the weight vector from the rule layer B2 to the indices layers C2 and C3, namely $\left(\dfrac{9}{9+7}, \dfrac{7}{9+7}\right)$. Determine the weight of each index as shown in table1:

Table 1. Weights of performance evaluation indices

Recognition performance	Performance index	Weight
Recognition correctness B1	MRR mean C1	0.399
Recognition robustness B2	Index of distribution C2	0.1645
	Variance of MRR C3	0.1279
Recognition independence B3	Index of MRR independence C4	0.2086
Recognition cost B4	Recognition time C5	0.1

3.3   Evaluation Simulation

Use six typical radar emitter signals for simulation experimentation, signal type and working parameters are shown in table 2.

Table 2. Type and working parameter of radar signal

Sequence number	Signal type	RF/MHz	PW/ μs	PRI/ μs
1	CW			
2	LFM			
3	NLFM	400~2300	2~13	40~800
4	FSK			
5	BPSK			
6	QPSK			

Among them, the central frequency of the signal is 30MHz, pulse width is $10\,\mu s$, the sampling frequency is 120MHz. The bandwidth of LFM signal is 5MHz; NLFM is a sinusoidal modulation signal; the coded rule of FSK signal is [122112]; the phase coded rule of BPSK signal is [11100010010]; the phase coded rule of QPSK signal is [01230312223300112012].Each type of signal is generated in a sample of 300, 100 for training, the remaining 200 used for testing.

Now three recognition methods can be adopted to carry on the evaluation experiment. The first recognition method uses carrier frequency, pulse width and pulse repetition interval of five conventional parameters as a three-dimensional characteristic vector $[f_{RF}, \tau, PRI]$, in which classifier is selected as probability neural network (PNN); the second method decomposes six kinds of signals with wavelet packet into three layers respectively , selects carrier frequency and W_{pt6} 、 W_{pt7} [13] as the characteristic parameters to constitute the three-dimensional characteristic vector $[f_{RF}, W_{pt6}, W_{pt7}]$, in which classifier is selected as probability neural network (PNN); the third method chooses the same characteristic vector $[f_{RF}, W_{pt6}, W_{pt7}]$, in which classifier is selected as support vector machine SVM, kernel function selects RBF kernel.

In order to test the independence between three kinds of recognition methods and SNR, 100×30 primitive recognition experiments are done respectively in the SNR of 5dB, 10dB, 15dB and 20dB. The numbers of right recognition and wrong recognition are respectively as shown in table 3.

Table 3. Measurement of independence for recognition performance

Y		SNR			
		5dB	*10dB*	*15dB*	*20dB*
Method 1	right	2163	2375	2489	2550
	wrong	837	625	511	450
Method 2	right	2577	2843	2902	2971
	wrong	423	157	98	29
Method 3	right	2703	2876	2941	2991
	wrong	297	124	59	9

Skewness and kurtosis test method is used for distribution hypothesis testing, significant level $\alpha = 0.01$, thus threshold μ is $z_{\alpha/4} = 1.96$; the significant level of independence testing $\alpha = 0.01$,threshold θ is $\chi^2(4-1)(2-1) = 11.345$; recognition control time is 1s.

The final evaluation results of three recognition methods are shown in table 4:

Table 4. Recognition evaluation results

	MRR mean	Index of distribution	Variance of MRR	Index of MRR independence	Recognition time	Comprehensive result
Method 1	0.784	0.2694	0.8317	0.5753	0.8018	0.6637
Method 2	0.9374	0.2990	0.8442	0.4627	0.9158	0.7193
Method 3	0.9877	0.3420	0.9021	0.4895	0	0.6678

4   Conclusion

Based on the analytic hierarchy process, this paper establishes a hierarchical structure model of evaluation indices, determines the weight of each index, and does simulation experiment at last. The experimental results demonstrate the effectiveness of the model, which can be used in performance comprehensive evaluation for radar signal recognition and has certain reference value.

References

1. Han, J., He, M.-H., Mao, Y., Ren, M.-Q.: A New Method for Recognizing Radar Radiating-source. In: ICWAPR 2007, vol. 4, pp. 1665–1668 (2007)
2. Zhang, G.-X., Hu, L.-Z., Jin, W.-D.: Quantum Computing Based Machine Learning Method and Its Application in Radar Emitter Signal Recognition. In: Torra, V., Narukawa, Y. (eds.) MDAI 2004. LNCS (LNAI), vol. 3131, pp. 92–103. Springer, Heidelberg (2004)
3. Zhang, G.-Z.: Radar Emitter Recognition technology research, pp. 103–106. National University of Defense Technology, Changsha (2005)
4. Zhang, G.-X.: Intelligence Recognition Methods for Radar Emitter Signals, pp. 80–82. Southwest Jiaotong University, Chengdu (2005)
5. Liu, H.-J.: Researches on Identification Key Technology for Radar Emitter, pp. 101–105. National University of Defense Technology, Changsha (2010)
6. Zhuang, Z.-W., Li, X., Li, Y.-P., et al.: Performance Evaluation Technology for Automatic Target Recognition, pp. 61–62. National Defense Industry Press, Beijing (2006)
7. Li, Y.-P., Li, X., Wang, H.-Q., et al.: Performance Evaluation in Automatic Target Recognition Based on Fuzzy Comprehensive Evaluation and Statistics. Engineering Science 3(7), 64–68 (2005)
8. Sheng, Z., Xie, S.-Q., Pan, C.-Y.: Probability Theory and Mathematical Statistics, pp. 134–138. Higher Education Press, Beijing (1989)
9. Wu, Y., Li, Y.-L., Hu, Q.-J.: Applied Mathematical Statistics. National University of Defense Technology Press, Changsha (1995)
10. Yu, Y.: Advanced Engineering Mathematics. Huazhong University of Science and Technology Press, Wuhan (1995)
11. Chen, Y., Chen, X.-K., Lin, Y.: Application of improved radar chart evaluation method on evaluation of automobile comprehensive performances. Journal of Jilin University (Engineering and Technology Edition) 41(6), 1522–1526 (2011)
12. Lei, B., Zhang, L., Xia, T.-T., et al.: Eco-environmental Quality Evaluation Model of the New Rural in Chongqing Based on AHP. Journal of Beijing University of Technology 39(9), 1393–1398 (2011)
13. Zhang, G.-X.: Intelligence Recognition Methods for Radar Emitter Signals, pp. 42–44. Southwest Jiaotong University, Chengdu (2005)

Target Number Recognition for Low-Resolution Radar Based on Hilbert-Huang Transform

Fengchen Huang[1,2], Guobing Hu[1,3,*], Mingwei Shen[1], and Jian Li[1,2]

[1] Computer and Information College, Hohai University, Nanjing 211100, China
[2] Institute of Communication and Information System Engineering
[3] School of Electronic and Information Engineering,
Nanjing College of Information Technology, Nanjing 210046
hugb@njcit.cn

Abstract. An estimation algorithm of formation target number for low-resolution radar based on Hilbert-Huang Transform (HHT) was proposed in this article. The radar echo signals were processed by HHT to extract Hilbert spectrum at first and then to find the peaks by Hough transform and the number of peaks was the estimator of formation target number. In this paper, the improved methods were proposed to suppress the end effect of HHT and the noises. The simulation results showed that the proposed method not only has nicer noise immunity and multi-target resolution capability but also can recognize the number of targets in formation effectively in the moderate SNR.

Keywords: Radar target recognition, Target number recognition, Hilbert-Huang Transform.

1 Introduction

In modern war, the fighters in formation attacking the enemy targets in the air has become the major way of the war, however, the normal radar cannot conduct effective target number recognition in both distance and azimuth because of its low resolution. Therefore, the research about the method of the target number recognition is helpful to understand the warfare environment and it is also of great military significance in terms of the taking initiative in the war, making the study of which a classical task in the field of electronic reconnaissance[1-3].

At present, referring to the target number recognition of low-resolution radar, the relatively effective way is taking advantage of the differences of Doppler frequency caused by the distances of the fighters. As the radar echo signals of the fighters are typical non-stationary signals, the traditional Fourier transform is not suitable. The commonly time-frequency analysis method of the target number recognition is Wigner-Ville Distribution(WVD)[4-6] method has better aggregation in time-frequency concentrate, but for the multi-component signal, theirs WVD has serious cross-term interference that will affect the accuracy of the recognition of the number

---

* Corresponding author.

F.L. Wang et al. (Eds.): CMSP 2012, CCIS 346, pp. 562–569, 2012.

of fighters. Thought there are various ways to suppress the cross-term, it will make the algorithm more complicated and it cannot completely remove the effect of the cross-term because of the uncertainty principle.

In 1998, Norden E. Huang [7] posed the theory of Hilbert-Huang Transform based on the concept of IF(instantaneous frequency), which not only gives a reasonable definition for it, but also lays out specific procedures to calculate it. In this article, the HHT is applied to the analysis of the target number recognition of the radar echo signal by solving the Hilbert spectrum of the signal to recognize the number of the fighters. Simulation results show that proposed method not only has nicer noise immunity and multi-target resolution capability but also can recognize the number of targets effectively in the moderate SNR.

2   Signal Model

In the relevant processing time, the echo signal of   target could be regarded as linear combination of several LFM signals which has similar frequencies and same range, and the signal model is given by

$$s(t) = \sum_{i=1}^{M} a_i \exp\left\{ j[2\pi(f_{0i}t + \frac{1}{2}\mu_i t^2) + \varphi_i]\right\}, 0 \le t \le L \qquad (1)$$

where M is the number of the fighters, a_i, f_{0i}, μ_i and φ_i are the range of the signal, initial frequency, the coefficient of frequency and initial phase, respectively ,L is the time of observation.

3   Hilbert-Huang Transform[7]

3.1   The IMF and the EMD

The IMF must satisfy two conditions below:

(1) In the entire wavelength of a signal, the number of the extreme values (including the maximum and minimum values) and the number of zero-crossing points should be same or the difference value of them is 1.
(2) For the arbitrary time point, the average value of the upper envelope line defined by the local maximum value and the lower envelope line defined by the local minimum value is 0.

According to the two conditions of IMF, the steps of the EMD of arbitrary signal are as follows:

1) Find out all the local maximum values and minimum values of the initial signal $x(t)$, then the upper envelope $x_{max}(t)$ and lower envelope $x_{min}(t)$ could be ascertained by respectively connecting the local maximum and minimum values with smooth interpolating curve.

2) Calculate the average value $m(t)$ of the upper envelope and lower envelope, that is

$$m(t) = \frac{1}{2}\left[x_{max}(t) + x_{min}(t)\right] \tag{2}$$

And minus the $m(t)$ from the initial signal $x(t)$, that is

$$h_1(t) = x(t) - m(t) \tag{3}$$

Test whether $h_1(t)$ could satisfy the two conditions of IMF. If not, take $h_1(t)$ as the new initial signal and repeat the steps above until $h_1(t)$ satisfy the two conditions, then the first IMF can be written as

$$c_1(t) = h_1(t) \tag{4}$$

3) Minus $c_1(t)$ from signal $x(t)$, the result is written as $r_1(t)$

$$r_1(t) = x(t) - c_1(t) \tag{5}$$

And then take $r_1(t)$ as the new signal and repeat steps 1), 2), 3) until $r_n(t)$ becomes monotone function or constant.

By the decomposition above, the arbitrary signal $x(t)$ could be decomposed as the linear combination of IMFs below

$$x(t) = \sum_{i=1}^{n} c_i(t) + r_n(t) \tag{6}$$

3.2   The IF and Hilbert Spectrum

As for a real signal $x(t)$, its analytic signal is given by

$$X(t) = x(t) + j\hat{x}(t) \tag{7}$$

where $\hat{x}(t)$ means the Hilbert transform of the real signal $x(t)$, that is

$$\hat{x}(t) = \frac{1}{\pi} \int_{-\infty}^{\infty} \frac{x(\tau)}{t - \tau} d\tau \tag{8}$$

The formula (7) could be rewritten in the polar coordinate form

$$X(t) = a(t)e^{j\phi(t)} \tag{9}$$

where

$$\begin{cases} a(t) = \sqrt{x^2(t) + \hat{x}^2(t)} \\ \phi(t) = \arctan\left[\dfrac{\hat{x}(t)}{x(t)}\right] \end{cases} \tag{10}$$

$a(t)$ and $\phi(t)$ are the instantaneous range and instantaneous phase of the real signal $x(t)$. The IF is defined as the derivative of instantaneous phase to time t, the formula is

$$\omega(t) = \frac{d\phi}{dt} = \frac{d}{dt}\left\{\arctan\left[\frac{\hat{x}(t)}{x(t)}\right]\right\} \tag{11}$$

Reference [7] points that in order to make the IF meaningful in practice, the signal should satisfy the following conditions: (1) Narrowband signal. (2) The average value of the signal should be 0; (3) the signal should be symmetrical locally. It's found that, every IMF of the signals satisfies the three conditions above; therefore, by formula (11), we can calculate the IF of every IMF, and then estimate the Hilbert spectrum of entire signal.

4   Target Number Recognition Based on HHT

Since the radar echo signal of target could be regarded as linear combination of several LFM signals which has similar frequencies and same range, we could see a couple of parallel lines with slope in the Hilbert spectrum of the signal. The number of the lines in the spectrum is the number of the targets. Fighters are taken as an example to illustrate the algorithm in this paper.

Without the interference of noise, through the discrete equidistance sampling, the formula can be written as

$$s(n) = \sum_{i=1}^{2} a_i \exp\left\{ j[2\pi(f_{0i}nT + \frac{1}{2}\mu_i(nT)^2) + \varphi_i] \right\}, n = 0, 1, \cdots, N-1 \tag{12}$$

Where T is sample interval, N is the number of the samples. In the relevant processing time, suppose the signal amplitude a_i of the two fighters is a constant 1, the initial phase φ_i is 0, the coefficients of linear-frequency modulation of two LFM signals is the same, and the change of the normalization frequency of them are 0.05~0.2 and 0.2~0.35 respectively, N is 512. As in Fig.1, (a) and (b) are the waves of the two LFM signals above, (c) is the linear combination of (a) and (b).

1) Signal decomposition

Use the EMD of the HHT to decompose the echo signals of the formation target, and get a set of IMF, as in Fig.2. Fig.2 shows that the EMD decompose the signal from high frequency to low frequency. While, imf1 and imf2 are the LFM signals contained in the formation target, and imf3~imf8 are the component generated by the errors caused by EMD.

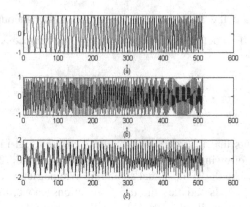

Fig. 1. The waves of the two LFM signals and the wave after they added together

2) Calculating the Hilbert spectrum of the signal

Conduct Hilbert Transform on the IMFs, and get the Hilbert spectrum of the signal, as shown in Fig.3. As shown in Fig.3, the two diagonals are the IF curves of imf1 and imf2, due to the range of IF of imf3~imf8 are very low that it's not clear in this figure. Because there are errors and end effect, jitter appears at the end of the IF curves of imf1 and imf2; the problem can be solved by smoothing filter with appropriate bandwidth. The Fig.4 shows the Hilbert spectrum after smooth processing.

Consider the noises, the observed signal could be expressed as $r(n) = s(n) + w(n)$,where $w(n)$ is an additive white Gaussian noise with variance σ^2 and zero mean, which is independent of the signal $s(n)$.

Fig.5 shows Hilbert spectrum of the signal when signal-to-noise ratio (SNR) is 10dB. It can be seen that the jitter of the IF curves of imf1 and imf2 is enhanced because of the interference of noise, even some outlier value. In order to eliminate the effect of noise, 1/3 values of the IF should be selected to fit a straight line, if some value of the IF exceed the corresponding value of the line by 1.5 times, it should be regarded as a outlier value. Then the fitted value is taken as the estimated value. At last smooth processing is taken on the correcting value of the IF and the result is as shown in Fig.6.

3)Target number estimation

Conduct Hough Transform on the Hilbert spectrum of Fig.6 to transform the lines into corresponding peaks as shown in Fig.7., and get the number of peaks by setting a specific threshold value. The number of the peaks is the estimator of the target number.

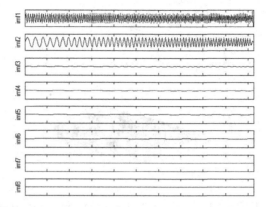

Fig. 2. The decomposition of the signals containing two LFM signals

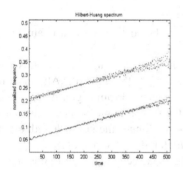

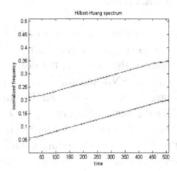

Fig. 3. The Hilbert spectrum of the signal   **Fig. 4.** The Hilbert spectrum after smooth

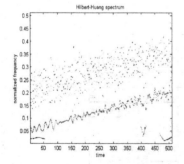

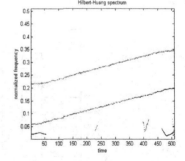

Fig. 5. The Hilbert spectrum with noise   **Fig. 6.** The Hilbert spectrum after processing

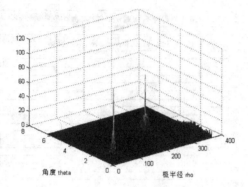

Fig. 7. Hough Transform on the Hilbert spectrum of the signal

5   Simulation

Still take the radar echo signal of two fighters in the section 4 as an example, and keep the same simulation conditions.

Fig.8 shows the curve of the correct rate of the proposed algorithm in this paper under different SNR and the sample numbers (64, 128, 256 and 512).All simulation results have been averaged over 100 independence runs . From Fig.9, it can be seen that, under the same SNR condition, the longer the samples are, the better the correct rate of the target number recognition is. Because the longer the signal length are, the richer the information of the target number is, which reduce the risk of misjudge.

Given SNR=10dB and N=512 to simulate the radar echo signals of consisting of 1,2,3,4 fighters respectively. Then use the proposed algorithm to recognize the target number by 100 simulation times. The results are shown in Table 1, the vertical axis means the actual number of the fighters and the lateral axis means the number of fighters got from the algorithm.

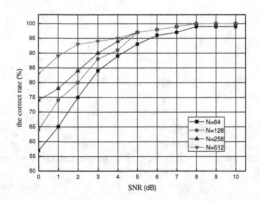

Fig. 8. The correct rate of recognition under different SNR

Table 1. The correct rate of recognition under different fighters number

Target number	1	2	3	4	correct rate
1	100	0	0	0	100%
2	0	100	0	0	100%
3	0	6	91	3	91%
4	0	6	11	81	81%

Table 1 shows that when $SNR = 10dB$ and the formation target is 1 or 2 fighters, the correct rate of recognition is 100%; when the formation target is 4 fighters, the correct rate falls, which is caused by the complexity of the signal structure of the target. But even so, the correct rate has reached more than 80%. It indicates that the proposed algorithm based on HHT not only have a good recognition for the formation target that contains less fighters, but also is adaptable for the formation target that contains more fighters.

6   Conclusions

A target number recognition method for low-resolution radar based on Hilbert-Huang transform is proposed in the paper. The simulation test shows that the method has better anti-noise performance and multi-target recognition ability, which has applicable value in engineering project.

Acknowledgments. This paper was supported by Province Science Foundation of Jiangsu (No. BK2011837).

References

1. Lizhong: Wireless Network and Communication Signal Processing. Intelligent Automation and Soft Computing 1, 1019–1021 (2011)
2. Huibin, W.: An approach for target detection and extraction based on biological vision. Intelligent Automation and Soft Computing 17, 909–921 (2011)
3. Ding Xiaofeng, X.L.: Robust Visual Object Tracking Using Covariance Features in Quasi-Monte Carlo Filter. Intelligent Automation and Soft Computing 17, 571–582 (2011)
4. Jiang, Z.: A new method of resolving multiple targets of low resolution radar. Presented at National Aerospace and Electronics Conference, NAECON 2000. Proceedings of the IEEE 2000, Dayton, OH (2000)
5. Wood, J.C., Barry, D.T.: Linear signal synthesis using the Radon-Wigner transform. IEEE Transactions on Signal Processing 42, 2105–2111 (1994)
6. Wang, M., Chan, A.K., Chui, C.K.: Linear frequency-modulated signal detection using Radon-ambiguity transform. IEEE Transactions on Signal Processing 46, 571–586 (1998)
7. Huang, N.E., Shen, Z., Long, S.R., Wu, M.C., Shih, H.H., Zheng, Q., Yen, N.C., Tung, C.C., Liu, H.H.: The empirical mode decomposition and the Hilbert spectrum for nonlinear and non-stationary time series analysis. Proceedings of the Royal Society of London. Series A: Mathematical, Physical and Engineering Sciences 454, 903–995 (1998)

The Application of Wavelet-Based Contourlet Transform on Compressed Sensing

Mei Du[1,2,3,4,*], Huaici Zhao[1,3,4], Chunyang Zhao[1,2,3,4], and Bo Li[1,2,3,4]

[1] Department of Optical-Electronics and Information Processing,
Shenyang Institute of Automation, Chinese Academy of Science,
Shenyang 110016, China
[2] Graduate School of Chinese Academy of Science,
Beijing 100049, China
[3] Key Laboratory of Optical-Electronics Information Processing,
Chinese Academy of Science,
Shenyang 110016, China
[4] Key Laboratory of Image Understanding and Computer Vision,
Liaoning Province, Shenyang 110016, China
dumei@sia.cn

Abstract. Reasonable sparse representation of signals are one of the key factors to ensure the quality of compressed sampling, so a proper sparse representing methods should be selected to make the signals sparse to the greatest extent in the applications of compressed sensing. In this paper we adopted the framework of block compressed sensing to sample the images, used the iterative hard thresholding(IHT) algorithm to reconstruct the original images, and employed the wavelet-based contourlet transform, an improved contourlet transform, to decompose 2D images in IHT reconstruction process. Numerical experiments indicated that the runtime of the reconstruction algorithm adopting wavelet-based contourlet transform is the shortest compared to that adopting contourlet transform and that adopting wavelet transform; under low compression ratios, the quality of the reconstructed images using wavelet-based contourlet transform is superior to that using contourlet transform and that using traditional wavelet transform.

Keywords: Sparse Representation, Wavelet-Based Contourlet Transform, Block Compressed Sensing, Iterative Hard Thresholding Algorithm.

1 Introduction

Recently an innovative idea named Compressed Sensing appeared in signal processing area[1,2]. The central idea of compressed sensing(CS) is that, when dealing with signals which are highly compressible in some transform domain, one can take much less samples than traditional ones which are contributing of the whole data stream. There are some key factors in CS and selecting a proper sparse basis is one

---

* Corresponding author.

F.L. Wang et al. (Eds.): CMSP 2012, CCIS 346, pp. 570–577, 2012.

of these factors.   These factors have no exceptions when CS is applied to 2D signals, so in this paper we lay stress on the sparse representation of 2D images.

Recent years multiscale geometric analysis(MGA) technologies[3,4] suitable to 2D images have developed rapidly.   These MGA transforms feature a highly directional decomposition and have brought hope to overcome deficiencies of traditional wavelet transforms in several application areas.   One of the MGA transforms, contourlet[5,6], has shown high performance in nonlinear approximation of 2D images.   The contourlet has a property of non-redundancy, which attracts many researchers to make various improvements based on contourlet.   In this paper we apply these reformative contourlet transforms to CS in order to improve the quality of the reconstructed images.

2   The WBCT Construction

Contourlet transform, a recently introduced directional transform, is referred to as a 'true' two dimensional image-representing method.   Contourlet transform breakdowns the transform task into two parts — multiscale analysis and directional decomposition. Multiscale analysis is first obtained by employing Laplacian pyramid (LP) which can capture the discontinuous points.   Directional decomposition is then acquired by applying a directional filter bank(DFB) to the result of multiscale analysis. Thus LP and DFB together compose the Contourlet transform structure.   This structure can decompose an image into many directional subbands at differential scales. Fig.1(a) illustrates a schematic plot of the contourlet transform using 3 LP levels and 8-4-4directional levels (8 directions at the finest level).

From Fig.1(a) and (b) we can see that, Laplacian pyramid has not down-sampled at parts of high frequency, which results in an additional 1/3 size compared to mallat pyramid decomposition of wavelet.   Although representing an image by contourlet transform can preserve better details and contours in comparison to a wavelet transform, it may not be the most excellent choice.   This observation motivated researchers to investigate for a new multiresolution decomposition mechanism to replace Laplacian pyramid.   As for multiresolution analysis, the most famous one is mallat pyramid decomposition of wavelet.   Compared to Laplacian pyramid decomposition, the mallat pyramid decomposition has the feature of non-redundancy in addition to the feature of multiresolution.   Consequently, we introduced the wavelet-based contourlet transform (WBCT) [7-10] that is a non-redundant version of the contourlet transform.

The basic idea of WBCT is that first to substitute mallat pyramid decomposition for Laplacian pyramid, then to convolute the data of each high frequency subbands of mallat decomposition by a directional filter bank.   The principle of WBCT is illustrated in Fig. 1(b) in which a 3-level wavelet decomposition was used, 16 directions were set in each high frequency subbands of the first wavelet level, and both 8 directions was set in the second and the third wavelet levels.   Because of the non-redundancy, WBCT shows promise over contourlet decomposition on image compression.

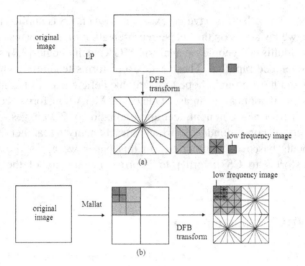

Fig. 1. schematic plots of contourlet transform and WBCT (a) a schematic plot of the contourlet transform using 3 LP levels and 4-3-3directional levels. (b) A schematic plot of the WBCT using 3 dyadic wavelet levels and 4-3-3directional levels.

3   The Reconstruction Method of Block Compressed Sensing Using WBCT

As applied to 2D images, CS faces two main difficulties: one is enormous computation encountered in reconstruction procedure; the other is huge storage requirement in order to store the random sampling operator. In this paper, we adopt the framework of block compressed sensing(BCS)[11]. In this framework, the original image is divided into a certain number of blocks depending on rows and columns of the image and each block is sampled independently using the same measurement operator matching the size of the blocks. This method provides comparable performances compared to existing CS strategies with much lower implementation cost and makes the real time image processing possible.

In BCS scheme first an image with $N = I_r \times I_c$ pixels is divided into blocks of size B×B each. We can assign B to 16 or 32. Suppose that x_i is a vector representing block i. Sample x_i with the same measurement operator $\mathbf{\Phi}_B$. Then the corresponding y_i is $y_i = \mathbf{\Phi}_B x_i$ where $\mathbf{\Phi}_B$ is an $M_B \times B^2$ orthonormal measurement matrix with $M_B = \lfloor \dfrac{M}{N} B^2 \rfloor$. Here M is the times of CS measurement and the size of M should meet the principle of Restricted Isometry Property[1,2]. We get M CS values after BCS operation.

Because of the low efficiency of the traditional reconstruction approaches such as basis pursuit, Orthogonal Matching Pursuit, we employ the iterative hard thresholding (IHT) algorithm in reconstruction process[12]. In addition wiener filtering is incorporated into IHT in order to eliminate the blocking artifacts inducted by BCS. Finally, as illustrated above, our schema can be represented as Fig.2.

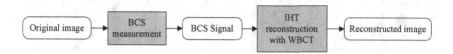

Fig. 2. BCS reconstruction process based on WBCT

4   Numerical Experiments

We now present several experiments employing BCS sampling scheme and IHT reconstruction algorithm by WBCT, contourlet transform and 2-D discrete wavelet transform(DWT), and compare the results by WBCT with the ones by the other two transforms. First, Fig. 3. presents an example of WBCT decomposition on Barbara image which uses 4 decomposition levels and 1,1,1,2,3 DFB decomposition levels — 3 at the finest scale. The following experiments use 4 decomposition levels and the number of DFB decomposition levels is 3,3,3,3 at each scale. In these experiments, for a given value R, we select R percent of the most significant coefficients in each transform domain, and then evaluate the reconstructed images from these sets of R percent of the coefficients. Fig. 4 shows the reconstruction results of 10 or 20 percent of total coefficients of a part of the Barbara,Baboon,Boat, Goldhill, Lena and Peppers images by WBCT, contourlet and DWT. The detailed imges and the PSNR values show that WBCT capture finer contours than contourlet and DWT do.

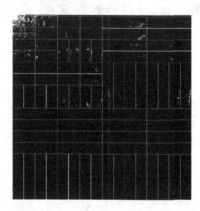

Fig. 3. An example of WBCT decomposition

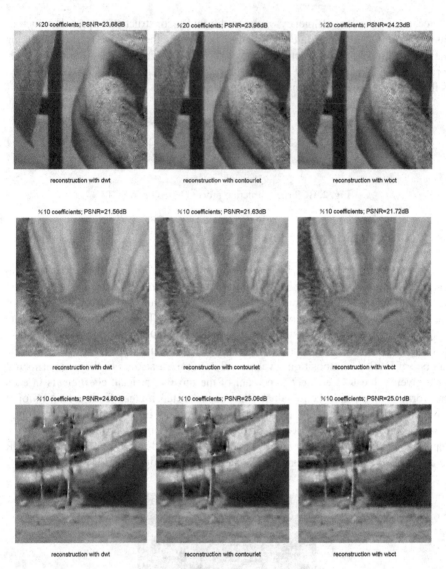

Fig. 4. Reconstructed results by WBCT, contourlet and DWT of different percent of coefficients. (a) Reconstructed results of dwts. (b) Reconstructed results of contourlets. (c) Reconstructed results of WBCTs.

(a)   (b)   (c)

Fig. 4. (*continued*)

Fig. 5. and Fig. 6. present some curves obtained by selecting different transform domain coefficients from 10 percent to 90 percent when reconstructing Barbara. Fig. 5. shows that the PSNR values of WBCTs are comparable to contourlets and are larger than DWTs when the coefficients are under 50 percent. From Fig. 6. we can see that the reconstruction time of WBCTs is a bit shorter than that of contourlets and much shorter than that of DWTs at different percent of coefficients. These experiments prove that WBCT is a bit superior compared with contourlet and DWT in capturing better contours. The similar comparison results are obtained when reconstructing other images. We truncates a part of performance comparison values obtained from reconstructed images using 10 percent of transform domain coefficients and show them in Table 1.. The PSNR and time values in Tab. 1. indicates the trend that on the whole, WBCT is more excellent than the other two transforms.

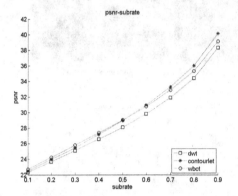 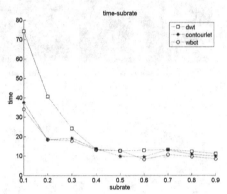

Fig. 5. The PSNR-coefficient curves for the reconstructed results

Fig. 6. The time-subrate curves for the reconstructed results

Table 1. Performance comparison (coefficient ratio=10%)

Item\Image	PSNR(dB)			Time(sec)		
	WBCT	Contourlet	DWT	WBCT	Contourlet	DWT
barbara	22.69	22.46	22.33	34.10	37.53	74.33
baboon	21.72	21.63	21.56	25.58	38.93	89.23
boat	25.01	25.06	24.80	32.49	35.52	59.65
goldhill	26.77	23.48	26.83	56.84	42.99	60.59
lena	28.05	27.46	27.59	46.03	52.20	60.28
peppers	27.03	26.25	27.20	108.58	106.12	130.81

5   Conclusion

This paper has proposed a scheme of compressed sensing employing the sparse representation of WBCT. Sparse representation is one of the key elements of CS, so we should select proper basis to preserve details and contours of images. Having the advantage of non-redundancy and being capable of capturing finer contours, WBCT is relatively a perfect sparse transform. In our experiments we have adopted the general paradigm of BCS coupled with an IHT reconstruction using WBCT sparse basis promoting not only sparsity but also smoothness of the reconstruction.

References

1. Candès, E.: Compressive Sampling. In: Int. Congress of Mathematics, Madrid, Spain, vol. 3, pp. 1433–1452 (2006)
2. Candès, E., Wakin, M.: An introduction to compressive sampling. IEEE Signal Processing Magazine 25(2), 21–30 (2008)
3. Gao, X., Lu, W., Tao, D., et al.: Image Quality Assessment Based on Multiscale Geometric Analysis. IEEE Transactions on Image Processing 18(7), 1409–1423 (2009)
4. Jiao, L., Hou, B., Wang, S., et al.: Image Multiscale Geometric Analysis: Theory and Applications, pp. 1–24, 280–335. Press of Xidian University, Xi'an (2008)
5. Do, M.N., Vetterli, M.: The contourlet transform: an efficient directional multiresolution image representation. IEEE Transactions on Image Processing 14, 2091–2106 (2005)
6. Do, M.N.: Contourlets and sparse image representations. In: SPIE Conference on Wavelet Applications in Signal and Image Processing X, San Diego, USA (August 2003)
7. Eslami, R., Radha, H.: Wavelet-based Contourlet Transform and Its Application to Image Coding. In: Proc. of IEEE International Conference on Image Processing (ICIP), Singapore, vol. 5, pp. 3189–3192 (October 2004)
8. Owjimehr, M., Yazdi, M., Zolghadr Asli, A.: A new scheme of face image encoding through wireless fading channels using WBCT and Block thresholding. Machine Vision and Image Processing, 1–4 (October 2010)
9. Kun, L., Lei, G.: Image fusion algorithm using dependencies among coefficients of wavelet-based Contourlet transform. Control and Decision 26(5), 695–699 (2011)
10. Eslami, R., Radha, H.: Wavelet-based Contourlet Packet Image Coding. In: Proc. of Conference on Information Sciences and Systems (CISS), Baltimore, MD (March 2005)
11. Mun, S., Fowler, J.E.: Block Compressed Sensing of Images Using Directional Transforms. In: Proceedings of the International Conference on Image Processing, Cairo, Egypt, pp. 3021–3024 (November 2009)
12. Blumensath, T., Davies, M.E.: Iterative hard thresholding for compressed sensing. Applied and Computational Harmonic Analysis 27(3), 265–274 (2009)

The Simulation and Analysis of Temperature Field Distribution of Core in Dry-Type Power Transformer

Haoyang Cui[*], Jundong Zeng, Naiyun Tang, Jie Zhu, and Zhong Tang

School of Computer and Information Engineering,
Shanghai University of Electric Power, Shanghai 200090, China
cuihy@shiep.edu.cn

Abstract. The temperature elevate of transformer core is one of the most important parameter must be considered in the transformers design and manufacturing. It is also a key factor affecting the transformer operating performance. The error of traditional method based on empirical formula estimate is large. In this paper, the dry-type power transformer core temperature field distribution of 1000 kVA rated capacity has been systematically studied using the sequential coupling method of ANSYS software based on finite element theory. The electromagnetic field distribution of the transformer has been extracted first, and then the analysis result of electromagnetic field can be as the load of the heat generation rate to obtain the core temperature field distribution. This method can be applied to the transformer design process in order to reduce the cost of the transformers design. Also, it can be used to the run equipment electromagnetic field and thermal field distribution analysis in order to improve the operational reliability of the transformer.

Keywords: transformer; finite element; magnetic field; temperature field.

1   Introduction

The power transformer core is a key component to achieve the energy conversion, and the loss is one of the main heat sources [1]. With the rapid increase of the operating frequency as well as the capacity and voltage level, the leakage flux in the transformer core is growing. If the transformer design structure is unreasonable, the overheating problems caused by the core and other component heat source will inevitably lead to the lifetime of transformer reduction and the operational failure increasing. It can reduce the cost of design, improve the reliability of operation and extend the lifetime of the transformer by simulating and analyzing the thermal field distribution of core in the transformer design process [2,3]. Therefore, using an appropriate theoretical model to predict the temperature distribution field of the transformer core is necessary in the condition of a given design parameters.

There are two types of traditional analytical methods for the core of the electromagnetic behavior and hest transfer behavior, the first is a section of analytical

---

[*] Corresponding author.

F.L. Wang et al. (Eds.): CMSP 2012, CCIS 346, pp. 578–584, 2012.
© Springer-Verlag Berlin Heidelberg 2012

methods, the other one is empirical data recognized[1] . As the increase of the transformer capacity and size, however, the simple physical simulation and empirical data has been unable to meet the core thermal field analysis. In recent years, computational electromagnetic is becoming mature, such as the finite element method, finite difference methods and integral equation method, etc.[4]。 Among them, the finite element method is an effective tool in the field of electrical engineering electromagnetic problems. This algorithm can get the approximate numerical solution of the overall discrete, the calculation is more accurate, and the results of its analysis with the microscopic meaning, intuitive, short period, thus it has been widely used. But the core loss caused by the fever related to the coupling between the electromagnetic field and thermal field two physical, this makes the finite element method to calculate the core process of the temperature field relatively more complicated. ANSYS is common engineering analysis software based on finite element theory, it has a variety of model library and can solve the problem of multi-field coupling; this provides the possibility of thermal field simulation for the transformer core. For these reasons, the thermal field distribution of SC8-1000/10 power transformers core was simulated and analyzed by using ANSYS software.

2   The Core Thermal Simulation Solve Process Using ANSYS Software

Core loss and winding loss are the main source of heat transformer [5], the main heating mechanism is induction heating, related to two physical field including the

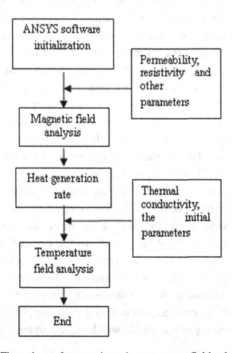

Fig. 1. Flow chart of magnetic and temperature field calculation

electromagnetic field and thermal field. For electromagnetic field and thermal field analysis, we use the sequential coupling method of ANSYS software, which is to analyze the magnetic field of the transformer, and then the magnetic field analysis of results are as the load of the heat generation rate thermal analysis, the analysis process shown in Figure 1 [6].

3   The Analysis of Electromagnetic-Thermal Coupling in Core

The analysis of the transformer electromagnetic field and temperature field using ANSYS finite element software include the following basic steps: build the model, mesh, applied load and solving.

3.1   Thermal Simulation Model

The studied transformer consist three parts, core, low-voltage windings, and high-voltage windings. To the SC8-1000/10 dry-type transformers, fore example, we simulated the thermal field distribution. The SC8-1000/10 type transformer is three phase dry type transformer, the rated capacity of 1000 kVA, no-load loss is 2 kW, short-circuit loss of 8.9 kW, its structure cross-section is shown in Fig 2. A_2, A_1, A_3 are the core, low-voltage windings, high-voltage windings, respectively. The transformer is three-phase symmetrical in the structure, thus, it can be appropriate assumptions to simplify the model in the calculations. The high and low voltage windings suits in the same column for the same phase, core is formed by Z10 cold-rolled silicon steel sheet stacking, the diameter of core is 22.5 cm, and the distribution of the electromagnetic field r=0 is symmetrical. The rest boundary conditions can be written as: convective heat transfer boundary; fever caused by hysteretic eddy current, that is, load loss of transformer. Let us assuming that the silicon steel thermal conductivity coefficient λ=23 W/mK, the magnetic flux density of the silicon steel sheet B=10000 Gs, resistivity of the silicon steel sheet ρ=50 $\mu\Omega\cdot$cm. The current density of the winding part is 2.5 A/mm^2, the rated frequency is 50 Hz, and the winding flux density is 1 Gs. As the winding part of the actual model is relatively complex, in order to avoid the complicated and unnecessary calculation, the model will be simplified. Assuming that the 45 cm low and high voltage winding are building located next to the core central region. In addition, due to the heat exchange boundary conditions do not exist much difference for the same height of the winding, one can ignore the small temperature changes in the circumferential direction, i.e., there is no gradient among the circumferential direction φ for the distribution of winding temperature field T=T(r,z,φ) the windings. Thus the 3-D temperature field distribution can be simplified to the 2-D temperature field distribution for calculation process. The complexity of computation can by greatly simplified by this assumption, and the calculation accuracy of the results will have less impact. In order to obtain the electromagnetic field distribution and the influence of the thermal convection on the core temperature field, a physical model adding air convection must be established, moreover, the air district must completely cover the part of the whole winding, and adjacent to the core. The flux density of the air is 1 Gs, the air convection coefficient is 12.5 W/(m^2·K).

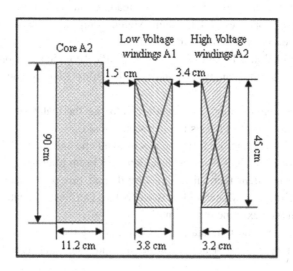

Fig. 2. The schematic structure of the transformer cross-section

3.2   Division of the Grid

The finite element mesh plays a vital role in the numerical simulation process, which directly affects the subsequent numerical calculation accuracy and precision of the analysis results. The number of grid number will also affect the efficiency and the size of the computational calculations. In general, calculation accuracy will be increased with the number of grid, but the calculate amount will also increase at the same time, thus, the two factors should be taken into account when determine the number of cells. To ensure the difference of the cell size is not large, and to obtain a satisfied simulation result in large temperature gradient, we divided the entire model into uniform grid automatically, thus the simulation process can be conducted normally.

3.3   Voltage Loads Imposed and Results of Solving

The applied load is voltage drop in the magnetic field analysis. A DO loop program was used to cycle back and forth between the harmonic electromagnetic and transient thermal analysis. The voltage value at different time is written to a number of load steps, then the SOLVE command was used to perform each load step. The magnetic flux density map of dry-type transformer core will be obtained using the ANSYS software simulation, which is shown in Fig3. The specific steps and mode of operation is as follows:

(1) Electromagnetic physical parameters were read into the software to solve and analyze: GUI: Main Menu>Solution>Current LS;

(2) The temperature and volume force were reading into the software to assignment the material properties: GUI: Main Menu> Preprocessor> -Loads-> Apply> Temperature> From Thermal Ana.

(3) Re-point ESAV and EMAT files using ASSIGN command in order to prepare the transient thermal analysis restart: GUI: Utility Menu> File> ANSYS File Options;

(4) The physical environment was reading into the thermal analysis: GUI: Main Menu> Preprocessor> Physics Environment> Read;

(5) Joule heat was reading out from the electromagnetic analysis: GUI: Main Menu> Preprocessor> -Loads-> Apply> Heat Generat> From Mag Ana;

(6) Solving the transient thermal analysis by default time increment; Re-default to the file: GUI:Utility Menu> File> ANSYS File Options; Repeating the previous time step in the next time increment.

(7) One can achieve the temperature field solution if the results of magnetic field analysis obtained by the heat generation rate had been taken as a reading file.

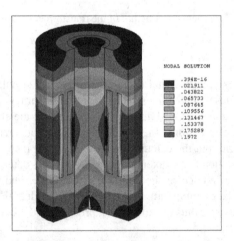

Fig. 3. Node equivalent magnetic current density profile

The temperature field simulation process is iterative process, the result of the thermal analysis shown in Figure 4. In Fig 3 and Fig 4, if the magnetic field and temperature field at each location are separated in groups depending on the value, then given color where the highest value are red and the lowest blue.

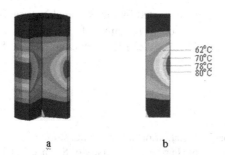

a   b

Fig. 4. 3-D temperature field of the core part and their profile

3.4   Results and Analysis

Fig3 and Fig4 present magnetic field of the transformer core and windings and the temperature field distribution respectively. It can be seen from Fig 3: the distribution of the magnetic field in the core is not uniform; the magnetic flux density at the middle region of core and the high voltage windings is relatively large. The maximum of the magnetic flux density is at the middle of the core surface and minimum at the top and bottom of the core. From Fig 4 one can know that the highest temperature region is at the middle surface of the core, which is 80 °C, while the lowest temperature region is at the top and bottom of the core, which is 40 °C. This is similar to the simulation results of magnetic flux density shown in Fig3. This can be attributed to the flux density in the core middle region is relatively large, leading to the loss increase in the high frequency case, therefore, the temperature reached the highest value; on the other hand, the heat dissipation effect is better at top and bottom of the core column, thus the temperature are lower.

4   Conclusions

The internal temperature rise of the transformer will affect the operation of the equipment directly. In this paper, the ANSYS finite element software was used to simulate the magnetic field and temperature field distribution of the SC8-1000/10 power transformer. The simulation results show that: (1) the magnetic flux density at the middle region of core and the high voltage windings is relatively large; (2) the highest temperature region is at the middle surface of the core, while the lowest temperature region is at the top and bottom of the core; (3) the flux density in the core middle region leading to the loss increase in the high frequency case, therefore, the temperature reached the highest value; the heat dissipation effect is better at top and bottom of the core column, thus the temperature are lower. Moreover, it can be used for the magnetic field and thermal field distribution analysis of equipment which has been running in order to improve the transformer's operational reliability and to extend the service lifetime. Also, the analysis method can locate the transformer's hot spots so as to provide a theoretical basis to determine the fiber or thermocouple sensor embedded point.

Acknowledgement. Project supported by the National Natural Science Foundation of China (61107081), Innovation Program of Shanghai Municipal Education Commission of China (10YZ158, 12ZZ176), Shanghai Natural Science Foundation of China (10ZR1412300).

References

[1] Gu, C.L.: Theory and calculation of the power transformer core magnetic field, loss and temperature field, pp. 4–6. Huazhong University of Science and Technology Press, China (1993)

[2] Zhang, Q., Yao, S.G., Ma, S.Z.: Numerical calculation and analysis of temperature field of winding in dry-type transformer. Journal of East China Shipbuilding Institute 19(3), 80–83 (2005)

[3] Chen, Y.Q., Cai, B.: The finite element analysis of leakage magnetic field of large-Scale electric transformer. Journal of Electric Power 23(6), 442–445 (2008)

[4] Li, J., Lou, L.F., Xu, J.Z., Li, Y.: 3D Thermal-magnetic field calculation of transformer using FEM. In: Proceeding of the CSU-EPSA, vol. 19(1), pp. 96–99 (2007)

[5] Liu, X.B., Li, M.D., Wang, J.Y.: Use of finite element method in the field of transformer magnetic field calculation. Science Technology and Engineering 8(24), 6603–6606 (2008)

[6] Yan, X.Q., Du, Y., Liang, L.Z.: Study on simulation of the core magnetic field and leakage field in power transformer based on Ansys. Journal of Xinjiang University 22(3), 361–364 (2005)

The Implementation and Application of Energy Consumption Monitoring and Management System[*]

Dandan Liu[1,2], Xingyu Ma[1], Jia Liu[1], and Qijun Chen[1]

[1] School of Electronics and Information, Tongji University, Shanghai 201804, China
qjchen@tongji.edu.cn
[2] School of Computer and Information Engineering,
Shanghai University of Electric Power, Shanghai 200090, China
2009lddlala@tongji.edu.cn

Abstract. An energy consumption monitoring and management system was established in the wind tunnel center of Tongji University. The hardware of the system included electronic measuring instrument, programmable logic controller (PLC) and an energy-saving data collection server, EcoWebServer II. The electronic measuring instrument collected electric parameters of each circuit node and EcoWebServer II monitored and stored the energy consumption data. The software of the system included project management module, system configuration module, system maintenance module and data monitoring and analysis module. In the data analysis module, an energy consumption model was developed with the decision tree algorithm. The model can predict the hourly electricity consumption of the office building in wind tunnel center. The equipment energy consumption also can be analyzed and the warm-up time can be predicted using collected data. The users can reduce the warm-up time to save energy consumption.

Keywords: Energy consumption monitoring and management, programmable logic controller, decision tree algorithm.

1   Introduction

Statistics show that the building energy consumption accounts for 28% of social total energy consumption in China. Large public buildings account for 5% of civil buildings. However, they consume more than 30% electricity of civil buildings [1]. An effective building energy consumption management system can provide the specific data on building energy consumption. It is a foundation for building energy conservation [2].

A number of scholars have made studies on establishing building energy monitoring and management system. Reference [3] developed a large public building energy monitoring and management system, and the system has been run in the control center

---

[*] This work was supported by Strategic International Cooperative Program, Ministry of Science and Technology (MOST) (No.2009DFA12520).

F.L. Wang et al. (Eds.): CMSP 2012, CCIS 346, pp. 585–592, 2012.

of Construction Department in Jiangsu Province, China. Reference [4] has designed an energy consumption monitoring system according to the technical guidelines made by national authorities. Reference [5] studied the design and composition of energy consumption monitoring platform. Reference [6] studied the measuring technique and management system of energy consumption for large public buildings. Thus it is demonstrated that Chinese government, universities and research institutes have done lots of effective work on energy investigation and conservation of the buildings. However, these jobs mainly focus on real-time collection and management of the energy consumption data, rather than the data analysis. Also it didn't study the rela-tionship between building energy consumption and its effect factors (energy activities, energy structure, climate, energy efficiency).

The wind tunnel center of Tongji University is a high energy consumption building and it includes an office area and an experiment area to test the performance of automobiles. In the wind tunnel center, an energy consumption monitoring and man-agement system was established. And based on the collected data, energy-saving potential of buildings can be found.

2   The Structure of Energy Consumption Monitoring and Management System

The energy consumption monitoring and management system is an online monitoring and dynamic analysis system. It includes two sections: hardware system and software system. The hardware structure is shown in Fig.1.

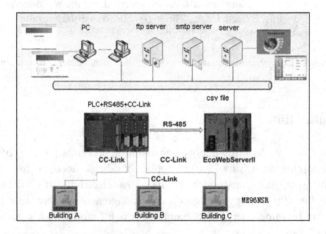

Fig. 1. The schematic diagram of the system was shown in this figure.

First, electronic measuring instrument ME96NSR collects voltage, current, power, reactive power, apparent power, power factor, frequency and other electric parameters of each circuit node. Then the data is transferred to the PLC (Programmable logic

Controller) via CC-Link (Control&Communication Link), and PLC transports the collected data to EcoWebServe II by RS-485 communication module. EcoWebServer II is an energy-saving data collection server and is produced by Mitsubishi. It is the core of the whole system. Users can view real-time data on the EcoWebServer II server through a web browser, also they can analyze and manage the data online.

2.1 Data Acquisition

Valuable data can be obtained by sub-metering and real-time measurement. In this program, ME96NSR electronic measuring instruments accomplished real-time measurement and sub-metering for electric parameters. These instruments meter and display multiple electrical parameters automatically.

2.2 Data Transmission

The data is transmited from the electronic measuring instruments to PLC by CC-Link bus. And the RS-485 bus sends the data from PLC to EcoWebServer II. The function of PLC is to convert the communication mode.

CC-Link is the open fieldbus launched by Mitsubishi Electric in 1996, which is a complex, open, adaptable network based on the device layer. The system uses three CC-Link bus modules QJ61BT11N as the three main stations. They constitute three CC-Link networks and transmit the data between the three buildings and servers.

2.3 Data Monitoring and Storage

As the core of the whole system, EcoWebServe II embodies kinds of functions such as sending information to web and display, data storage and on-line analysis .Meanwhile it has the HTTP server function, with which data collected from the measurement and control layer can be delivered to the internet by Ethernet, allowing users to monitor the use of energy in real-time.

EcoWebServer II module can store data. It can read data and save it every minute. The collected data will be stored and written into CSV files. Finally three kinds of CSV files (records per 5 minutes, records per hour, and daily records)will be produced. Users can download the data files through a Web browser.

EcoWebServer II can show the measured data in charts through the Web browser. And users will be able to monitor the energy consumption data. For example, comparison will be made between data of the same type on different dates and data in different types on the same date by switching display mode. This function allows users to catch outliers of energy, and find the energy consumption differences before and after energy-saving measures are applied. Also voltage or current and some other values will be displayed according to users' needs. Fig.2 shows the comparison of lighting data between two stations.

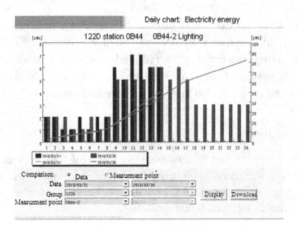

Fig. 2. The comparison of measurement data

3   Software of Energy Consumption Monitoring and Management System

Using the B/S mode, the software not only provides comprehensive and reliable data management platform for managers to monitor and manage different projects, but also enables common users to view data and download the data files through the web browser. The system software includes four modules: project management, system configuration, system maintenance and data monitoring and analysis. In addition to the function of routine maintenance, the system also includes two main functions.

The first function is visualization of energy consumption data. Data visualization is carried out by the data monitoring module. Comparison and analysis on the collected data can be achieved visually by graphics such as curves, cylindrical and round cake. Users will be reminded to play the role of energy conservation at any time while viewing the comparison diagram via Web browser.

The other function is prediction and diagnosis of energy. It is implemented by data analysis module. The aim of energy consumption monitoring is to make reasonable energy-saving methods for buildings. Energy consumption data is used to help establish an appropriate model, the energy consumption and energy saving potential are predicted and analyzed. Finally a reasonable energy-saving method will be chosen.

4   Application

Energy monitoring and management system has laid a foundation for realizing building energy efficiency. On the basis of real-time data, building energy consumption model is established, and energy consumption under different circumstances will be forecasted.

The energy consumption in buildings is generally related to time, climate, and the number of people. For example, the energy consumption in office buildings is concerned with the working hours, climate and number of people. While in commercial buildings, it is related to the running hours, weather and passengers. The wind tunnel center contains an office area and an experimental area. In it there are many high-power devices. So it needs detailed data to analyze its energy consumption.

4.1   Application of Data Mining in Office Building

Energy consumption of office buildings can be divided into three categories: lighting energy consumption, office equipment energy consumption and air conditioning energy consumption. The energy monitoring and management system is used for wind tunnel center to meter energy and then the measurement data is processed in minutes, hours and days. Take the lighting electricity consumption as an example. Fig.3 shows the daily energy consumption in a month, and Fig.4 shows the hourly energy consumption in a day.

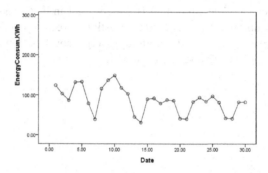

Fig. 3. Daily lighting electricity energy consumption data in office

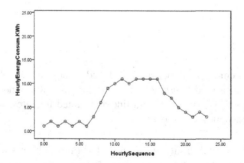

Fig. 4. Hourly lighting electricity energy consumption data in office

From the figures we can see that there are some obvious rules on time. Fig.3 shows that the energy consumption during 5 working days is much larger than that on rest days which is almost constant but not zero. In Fig.4, energy consumption is generally coincident with the working hours.

Several characteristics are concluded as follows: (1) The energy consumption isn't zero when nobody works in the office; (2) Hourly data has a gradual rising and declining process in working time. These two features also show that the energy consumption data has certain connection with the external environment and the number of people. For example, in the morning, the number of people in offices is gradually increasing while the solar radiation gradually turns stronger. After 16 o'clock, the number of people gradually turns fewer and the solar radiation intensity also turns weaker. It can be inferred that the more persons and the weaker solar radiation intensity will increase the lighting energy consumption.

According to the data analysis, the decision tree algorithm can be applied to forecast hourly energy consumption. It can be seen that the lighting energy consumption has two effect factors: solar radiation intensity and number of people in offices and the relationship is nonlinear. Classification and regression tree (CART) algorithm was chosen to develop the model of energy consumption data and to forecast hourly data.

Decision tree algorithm calculates the information gain of each attribute, of which those with the highest gain are selected for test attributes in a given set S. Create a node, tag it with this attribute, build branches for each value, and divide the sample accordingly[7]. Decision Tree Algorithm is widely used in data classification[8], and has been gradually applied to power load forecasting in recent years[9,10]. This algorithm is used to classify and predict lighting energy consumption data. The whole classification tree contains 27 nodes, 14 end nodes.

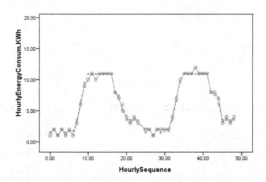

Fig. 5. This figure is a comparision between predicted values and actual values. The circular symbols represent the measured hourly energy consumption values and the five-pointed star symbols are predicted values. Then the solid line and dotted line are curves of the measured values and the predicted values respectively.

Fig.5 compares the actual values with predicted ones. The results show that the algorithm can meet the needs of forecasting the office lighting power consumption data. Differences between the predicted and actual values can be used to analyze the abnormal phenomena, to choose the optimal building management method and hit the target of saving energy.

4.2   Equipment Energy Consumption Analysis

The wind tunnel center owns a large number of experiment equipment. They are big fans, small fans and a variety of environmental simulation equipment. All of them have large electricity consumption. The energy monitoring and management system has measured and counted the power consumption of equipment. Taking the big fan as an example, the hourly consumption in a day is shown in Fig.6.

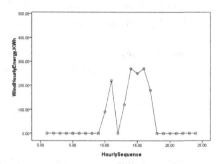

Fig. 6. Experimental equipment hourly electricity energy consumption

From the Fig.6, it can be seen that the energy consumption of experiment equipment is much higher than that of the office building. And the energy consumption is generated only in running time. Consequently, the equipment energy consumption is only affected by the time and experiment parameters (wind speed etc.).

Apart from energy consumption data collected by the system, prediction of the equipment energy needs other data such as equipment parameters, experimental conditions. The users can compare the predicted data with the measured data and analyze energy-saving potential. Fig.7. shows the operational process. The horizontal axis is running time and vertical axis is electricity. It may cause unnecessary power consumption when the equipment is in the duration of opening and closing process. According to the experimental program the best warm-up time can be predicted. The users can reduce the warm-up time to save energy consumption.

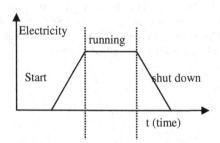

Fig. 7. The process of equipment operation

5   Conclusions

To ensure effective energy saving, it is important that every person is aware of how energy is being used. So an energy monitoring and management system was established. The users can monitor the energy consumption in real-time. According to the reliable energy consumption data provided by the system, the energy consumption model was developed. The model can predict the energy consumption. The users also can compare the differences between the predicted and actual values to analyze the abnormal phenomena, choosing the optimal building management method and meeting the need of saving energy.

Meanwhile the data mining algorithms should be study deeply to enhance the anti-noise ability of the model. When data noise increases abruptly, the model is inaccurate.

References

1. Yi, J.: Current building energy consumption in China and effective energy efficiency measures. Heating Ventilating & Air Conditioning 35, 30–40 (2005)
2. Zheng, M., Chen, S.: Research on Building Energy Consumption Monitoring Platform. Construction Conserves Energy 37, 65–67 (2009)
3. Tang, G., Zhang, G.: Study on Key Technologies for Energy Consumption Monitoring and Management System for Public Buildings. Building Science 25, 27–31 (2009)
4. Chen, M., Zhang, Y., Niu, Q.: Study on Energy Consumption Monitoring System of Public Buildings. Journal of Electronic Measurement and Instrument 23, 167–170 (2009)
5. Zheng, M., Chen, S.: Research on Building Energy Consumption Monitoring Platform. Construction Conserves Energy 37, 65–67 (2009)
6. Huang, B., Du, Y., Cao, X.: Design and Application of Energy-consuming Supervising System in Large Public Buildings Based on Acrel-5000. Electrical Technology of Buildings 3, 46–50 (2009)
7. Han, J., Kamber, M.: Data Mining: Concepts and Techniques, 2nd edn. China Machine Press, Beijing (2006)
8. Timofeev, R.: Classification and Regression Trees (CART) Theory and Applications, Master Thesis, Humboldt University, Berlin (2004)
9. Li, R., Liu, Y., Li, J.: Study on the daily characteristic load forecasting based on the optimizied algorithm of decision tree. Proceedings of the CSEE 25, 36–44 (2005)
10. Zhu, L.: Short-term Electric Load Forecasting with Combined Data Mining Algorithm. Automation of Electric Power Systems 30, 82–86 (2006)

Frequency and Angle Measurement System Based on Monobit Receiver

Xiuqing Zhang[1], Zhiyong Meng[2], and Guochen An[3]

Institute of Information Science & Engineering
Hebei University of Science & Technology
Shijiazhuang, China
Zhangxiuqing@hebust.edu.cn

Abstract. Receiver based on single-bit multi-target frequency measurement, the finding algorithm frequency measurement performance in different circumstances (such as the number of data bits, the number of samples, etc.), by constructing a simulation system, a large number of simulation and performance analysis. The different measured to the accuracy of the system and finding a large number of simulation and performance analysis. The final single-bit receiver by studying the practical application of the project is given reasonable suggestions given to improve the measurement accuracy improvement measures.

Keywords: Single-bit, Receiver, Frequency Measurement, Simulation System, multi-target.

1   Introduction

Matlab simulink to build the receiver simulation system of single-bit, compare single-bit receiver frequency measurement of the difference in performance of the receiver, seeking single-bit receiver frequency receiver in combination with other measurements to compensate for their own lack of possibility also need construction of the other frequency measurement receiver simulink simulation module, such as building wideband digital channelized receiver, digital channel received orders bit receiver frequency measurement system. To build simulink platform for simulation analysis, simulation conditions: AD sampling frequency the 5GHz, instantaneous bandwidth of 2GHz. ADC can adjust the number of output bits (e.g. 1bit, 2BIT and 3BIT), the DFT kernel functions of quantization bits, DFT conversion points, the number of the input signal, the input signal to noise ratio, the threshold detector to the threshold size, etc., in order to adopt a large number of simulation trials single-bit receiver frequency measurement sensitivity and dynamic range, multi-target frequency measurement processing and analysis, and by changing these parameters, the analysis of the impact of the changes in these parameters on a single-bit frequency measurement performance to optimize these parameters to identify improve

F.L. Wang et al. (Eds.): CMSP 2012, CCIS 346, pp. 593–600, 2012.

the measurement the precision improvement measures. By FFT operation due to single-bit receiver, the signal amplitude information is lost, it can not directly measure the direction of arrival of the signal using amplitude comparison method, but it can take advantage of multi-element digital beam former technology than amplitude measurement by improving transform FFT points of the direction of arrival of the target signal, digital channel phase comparator is placed after the receiver of the single-bit, and find other single bit DFT transform kernel function in order to improve the accuracy of frequency measurement of the single-bit receiver.

1.1   Construction of Simulation System Based on Simulink

The use of the Matlab simulink building single-bit receiver simulation system, such as the composition diagram of the system according to Fig. 1 single bit receiver measurement frequency to build simulink simulation system. In order to compare single-bit receiver and the other measured frequency receiver performance differences, seeking single-bit receiver frequency receiver combined with other measurements to compensate for their own lack of possibility, and also need to build a frequency measurement receiver simulink simulation modulesuch as building the broadband digital signal channelized receiver, digital channelized receiver orders bit the receiver frequency measurement system[1].

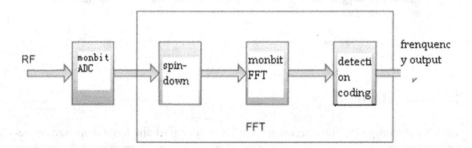

Fig. 1. Construction of single-bit receiver frequency measurement system block diagram simulink simulation system

1.2   Algorithm Principle

The single-bit receiver by multiplication, in the discrete Fourier transform is not only for addition and subtraction, so that the hardware design to simplify DFT operation becomes very simple. AS formulas(1)showed, Simplify the operation, there are two: one is the use of one of the ADC, its output is only +1 and -1, i.e., the DFT of input data only two situations; second is the DFT computation kernel function in the number of bits reduced to 1, about the kernel function is set to 1, -1, j, -j.

$$e^{-j2\pi kn/N} = \begin{cases} 1 & -\pi/4 \le -2\pi kn/N \le \pi/4 \\ j & \pi/4 \le -2\pi kn/N \le 3\pi/4 \\ -1 & 3\pi/4 \le -2\pi kn/N \le 5\pi/4 \\ -j & -3\pi/4 \le -2\pi kn/N \le -\pi/4 \end{cases} \tag{1}$$

The main advantages of the single-bit receiver is a simple structure, and this receiver is non-linear, so its RF part of the design is also very simple, RF channel, and the ADC that can be integrated into a single chip, the entire single-bit receiver cana chip to achieve, that is, the entire design in a single chip, giving rise to a new trend in ASIC design[2].

1.3   Performance Analysis

Single-bit input of the receiver frequency range from 1.375 to 2.375GHz, FFT with 256 points, is fixed at 102. 4 ns time resolution, each A channel bandwidth of about 9. 77 MHz (1/102. 4), the frequency resolution of approximately 10 MHz. He has a better sensitivity (about - 70 dBm), and can be processed Single maximum signal level of 10 dBm, and that is a single signal dynamic range can be reached to 80 dB. Single-bit dual signal receiver spurious-free dynamic range than pass the system's receiver is much higher, because he can only handle two simultaneous letter Number, can not be detected to determine the lower limit of the third letter of the spurious-free dynamic range Number. In addition, since the nonlinear limiter amplifier will result in the capture effect (i.e.Strong signal suppression weak signals), which greatly limits the instantaneous dynamic range, therefore, Receiver transient single-bit dynamic range is generally not more than 5 dB. Let ADC 8 b, the sampling frequency of 3 GHz showed in Table 1.

Table 1. Traditional digital receiver and the single-bit comparison of the performance of the receiver

Heading level	Traditional digital receiver	Single-bit receiver
Input bandwidth/GHz	1	1
FFT points	32	256
Single signal dynamic range/dB	55	80
Dual signal instantaneous dynamic range/dB	50	5
Narrowest pulse width/ns	*100*	100

2   Frequency Measurement

Currently, there are a lot of mature finite data length measured frequency technology, can be divided into two broad categories. The most simple class frequency measurement algorithms are based on FFT technique, this is because of the frequency measurement algorithm based on FFT is relatively fast, easy to hard Pieces to achieve, but because of the impact of noise and short data, frequency measurement accuracy is not high. In order to improve the accuracy of the frequency measurement, Lee using the spectrum interpolation technique to approximate the original continuous spectrum of the signal. FFT-based interpolation method was first used by Singhal and Vlach .Fraser made a series of analysis test. Sinusoidal signal of frequency estimates The meter often requires computational complexity of the nonlinear optimization, and only when the respective frequency components is sufficiently large interval can be simplified algorithm. Multiple iterative frequency estimation cancellation of more than , each frequency component as a single signal into Line frequency estimates. Another frequency estimation algorithm parameter estimation algorithm, similar to the linear likelihood estimation parameters frequency estimation algorithm, able to distinguish between frequency interval small signal, high precision. In addition, Different from the estimated non-parametric frequency FFT-based algorithm is no need to assume that the signal within the observation time period . However, such algorithm is not easy to hardware implementation, a large amount of computation.

FFT frequency measurement-based techniques to study a fast, simple double solid sinusoidal frequency estimation operator method. Frequency components in the signal amplitude than simply a one-dimensional the squared signal spectrum peak search, you can get the signal and the sum and difference frequencies of the estimated value of the component, and interpolation techniques to improve the accuracy of the frequency measurement. The algorithm able to accurately estimate the frequency interval of the small double signal frequency, and easy to extend to the multiplexing signal, FPGA hardware implementation simple[3].

2.1   Frequency Measurement Algorithm

First consider the noiseless double solid sinusoidal signal observation sequence.

$$x(n) = a_1 \sin(\omega_1 n) + a_2 \sin(\omega_2 n) \qquad\qquad n = 0, 1, \cdots, N-1 \qquad (2)$$

A1 and a2 is the certainty of the signal frequency component amplitude, the angular frequency $\omega_1 = 2\pi f_1 / f_s$, $\omega_2 = 2\pi f_2 / f_s$,fs is mining sampling frequency, N is the FFT length. It should be noted that the phase of a signal does not affect the derivation of the algorithm and the frequency estimation Performance. Apparent according to the above derivation, is very small when the two frequencies of the signal interval, the new algorithm is still able to accurately distinguish, this is because the frequency interval has been relatively increased to 2f2. In other words, the new algorithm can prep area Sub interval small signal frequency. Moreover, the algorithm with a single one-dimensional spectrum peak search, The linear transformation can be obtained an estimated value of the signal frequency. When the signal and noise is not relevant, the above derivation completely Applicable to additive white Gaussian noise in the double solid sinusoidal frequency estimation, this is because the large N (Average N> 64), when the noise spectrum is independent and identically distributed with zero mean, even if the non-Gaussian distribution of the noise can be approximated by a Gaussian distribution. In particular, since the real sinusoidal signal can be regarded as two complex exponential function. And by processing the real part of the complex exponential signal, the new algorithm can be easily estimated that the frequency of the complex signal[4].

2.2   Simulation

Computer simulation of zero mean Gaussian white noise of double sine signal frequency estimator method, wherein by adjusting the noise sequence to obtain a different signal-to-noise ratio. In the simulation shown in Fig. 2 Signal-to-noise ratio is set to 5dB, the sampling frequency is set to 400MHz.   The other parameters are set as follows: $f_1=90MHz, f_2=60MHz, a1=0.8, a2=1, N=256$.

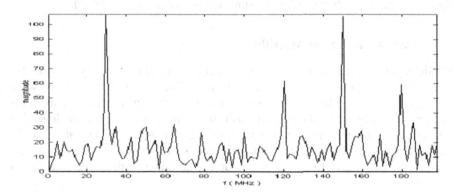

Fig. 2. The square sequence s (n) the spectrum

Table 2. The simulation results(N=128)

SNR(dB)	r	(f_1,f_2)MHz	(f_1,f_2)MHz
0	0.6	(16, 30)	(16.0233,29.8585)
	1	(31, 34)	(31.0349,33.8542)
	1.5	(49, 43)	(48.9899,42.9226)
3	0.6	(16, 30)	(16.0675, 30.0110)
	1	(31, 34)	(31.1078,33.8065)
	1.5	(49, 43)	(42.9697 ,49.0933)
5	0.6	(16, 30)	(15.9591,29.9209)
	1	(31, 34)	(30.9445,33.8804)
	1.5	(49, 43)	(50.0034,43.0943)

The emulation also considered different amplitude ratio, SNR, and the signal frequency of the frequency estimation .Among them,200s f = MHz, N = 128,50 times independent test results as shown in Table 2.

3   Angle Measurement

If signal spatial spectrum can be got, signal Direction-of-Arrival (DOA) can be also got. Therefore, spatial spectrum estimation technology has differentiation capability of spatial signal, it can break through and more improve differentiation capability of signal coming from different direction within a beam forming width. Linear array and circular array are the two commonest types in adaptive antenna arrays. Based on the linear array this thesis has analyzed application area and performance of several spatial spectrum estimation algorithms. Simulation and analysis have been performed on these algorithms application in linear array .In this thesis The applications of the classical MUSIC algorithm, the extract MUSIC algorithm, based on beam forming space MUSIC algorithm and based on concerned dispel MUSIC algorithm in linear array have been separately discussed。 it can be concluded the MUSIC algorithm has more better differentiation capability, estimation precision and stability[5].

3.1   Angle Measurement Algorithm

MUSIC algorithm has good performance under ideal conditions became so bad, but the performance of the algorithm in the coherence of the source. This is because when the signal source is coherent, the rank of the data covariance matrix of the array receiver is reduced to 1, and obviously this will lead to the signal subspace dimension is less than the number of signal sources. That signal subspace "proliferation" to the noise subspace, which will lead to some coherent source boot vector and noise subspace is not completely orthogonal, thus unable to accurately estimate the direction of the signal source.

Correctly estimated the core issue of the direction of the signal in the case of coherent signal source is to be effectively restored the rank of the signal covariance matrix through a series of processing or transformation, to correctly estimate the direction of the signal source.

The spatial smoothing algorithm principle for the case of a narrowband uniform linear array, the L array element data is

$$x_1(t) = \sum_{i=1}^{N} a_1(\theta_i)s_i(t) + n_1(t) \quad l = 1, 2\cdots, M \tag{3}$$

In formula(3), $a_l(\theta_i) = e^{-j\omega_0\tau_{li}}$, $\tau_{li} = (l-1)d\sin\theta_i/c$, M is the number of array elements, N is the number of sources. Wherein, d is the spacing of the uniform linear array, c is the velocity of signal propagation.In addition, for the uniform linear array $\beta_i = 2\pi d/\lambda \sin\theta_i$, $i = 1, 2, \cdots, N$.

Smoothing method with backward divided sub-array, the i-th array data vector is

$$x_i^b(t) = \begin{bmatrix} x_{M-i+1} & x_{M-i} & \cdots & x_{M-m-i+2} \end{bmatrix}^* \tag{4}$$

So the backward spatial smoothing correction of the data matrix is

$$R^b = \frac{1}{p}\sum_{i=1}^{p} R_{p-i+1}^b$$

$$= A(\frac{1}{p}\sum_{i=1}^{p} D^{-(m+i-2)} R_s^* D^{(m+i-2)})A^H + \sigma^2 I$$

$$= AR_s^b A^H + \sigma^2 I \tag{5}$$

3.2   3.2   Simulation

Two sources, the number of array elements N = 8, the array element spacing d = 0.5, the signal-to-noise ratio is equal to zero, before and after the use of space smoothing MUSIC algorithm can effectively estimate the two coherent signals to wave direction, and the accuracy of high in Fig.3..

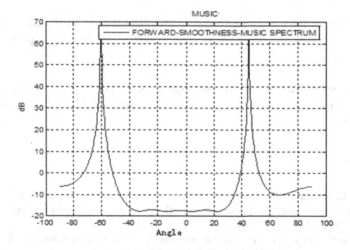

Fig. 3. The forward spatial smoothing MUSIC algorithm simulation Figure

4   System Simulation

Under the same conditions, in order to improve the accuracy of the frequency measurement, the only way is to increase the length of the FFT, because frequency point can not be just at discrete points. However, the spectrum around the peak amplitude of a partial response in real frequency of position information. Frequency estimates reflect exactly the peak in the spectrum and neighboring spectral lines interpolation showed in Fig.4. The majority of the sinusoidal signal spectral energy is concentrated in the three spectral lines. Even in the worst case (frequency Point Offset = 0.5), the peak and adjacent spectral lines also contains 85% of the total energy. A meter count simple and can be the root mean square error $N^{3/2}$ order interpolation estimation algorithm simply calculate the peak and the adjacent spectrum line value.

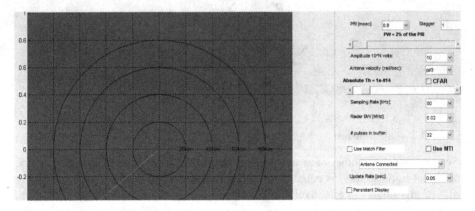

Fig. 4. The system simulation of frequency and angle measurement based on monobit receiver

To ensure that the reproduction of your illustrations is of a reasonable quality, we advise against the use of shading. The contrast should be as pronounced as possible[6].

Acknowledgements. The present research was supported by the department of education of Hebei Province(Project No:2011116),and Hebei University of Science & Technology (Project No:XL201068).

References

1. Grajal, J., Blazquez, R., Lopez-Risueno, G., et al.: Analysis and characterization of a monobit receiver for electronic warfare. IEEE Trans. on Aerospace and Electronic Systems 39(1), 244–258 (2003)
2. Tsui, J.B.Y., Stephens, J.P.: Digital microwave receiver technology. IEEE Trans. on Microwave Theory and Techniques 50(3), 699–705 (2002)
3. Tsui, J.B.Y., Schamus, J.J., Kaneshiro, D.H.: Monobit receiver. In: MTT-S International Microwave Symposium Digest, pp. 469–471 (1997)
4. Pok, D., Chen, C.I.H., Montgomery, et al.: ASIC design for monobit receiver. In: Proceedings Tenth Annual IEEE International ASIC Conference and Exhibit, pp. 142–146 (1997)
5. Pok, D.S.K., Chen, C.I.H., Schamus, J.J., et al.: Chip design for monobit receiver. IEEE Trans. on Microwave Theory and Techniques 45(12), 2283–2295 (1997)
6. Tsui, J.B.Y.: Digital Techniques for Wideband Receivers. Artech House, Norwood (1995)

Design of an Active Adjustable Band-Pass Filter

Huanhong Yang[1,*], Menghan Chen[2], Jianming Zhou[3], Keqin Bao[1], and Jiong Chen[1]

[1] Shanghai University Of Electric Power, Shanghai 200090, China
[2] University Of Washington , Seattle, WA 98105, USA
[3] Data Center of Industrial and Commercial Bank of China, Shanghai 200131, China
yanghuanhong@gmail.com

Abstract. In this paper we design, simulate, build an active adjustable band-pass filter that is connected to a portable audio device such as an mp3 player or laptop. The low pass filter has an adjustable bass, the high-pass filter has an adjustable treble, and the overall system has a volume control. By combining with a low-pass filter, a high-pass filter, a band- pass filter and a summing amplifier the system achieves adjustable pass band, volume and both treble and bass control.

Keywords: active filter, adjustable band-pass , treble and bass , audio amplifier.

1   Introduction

A filter is a circuit that is designed to pass signals with desired frequencies and reject or attenuate others. As a frequency-selective device, a filter can be used to limit the frequency spectrum of a signal to some specified band of frequencies.

A passive filter consists of only passive elements R, L, and C. However, active filters consist of combinations of resistors, capacitors, and op amps. They offer some advantages over passive RLC filters. First, they are often smaller and less expensive, because they do not require inductors. This makes feasible the integrated circuit realizations of filters. Second, they can provide amplifier gain in addition to providing the same frequency response as RLC filters. Third, active filters can be combined with buffer amplifiers (voltage followers) to isolate each stage of the filter from source and load impedance effects. This isolation allows designing the stages independently and then cascading them to realize the desired transfer function.

There are four types of filters whether passive or active[1,6].

(a)   A low-pass filter passes low frequencies and stops high frequencies;
(b)   A high-pass filter passes high frequencies and rejects low frequencies;
(c)   A band-pass filter passes frequencies within a frequency band and blocks or attenuates frequencies outside the band;
(d)   A band-stop filter passes frequencies outside a frequency band and blocks or attenuates frequencies within the band.

---

* Corresponding author.

F.L. Wang et al. (Eds.): CMSP 2012, CCIS 346, pp. 601–608, 2012.
© Springer-Verlag Berlin Heidelberg 2012

2   Design of an Adjustable Band-Pass Filter

We build 3 separate filters (low-pass, high-pass, and band-pass) then combine them with a summing operational amplifier. The low-pass filter blocks any frequencies greater than 200Hz. The high-pass filter blocks any frequencies lower than 800Hz. The band-pass filter allows any frequencies between 200Hz and 800Hz. The summing filter controls the volume of all three filters [4,5].

2.1   The Low-Pass Filter

A low-pass filter is designed to pass only frequencies from dc up to the cutoff frequency. Fig. 1 shows a typical active low-pass filter.

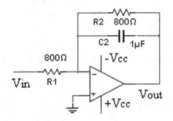
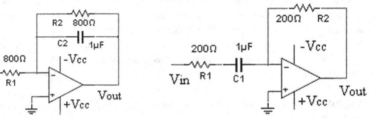

Fig. 1. Active low-pass filter   **Fig. 2.** Active high-pass Filter

For this filter, the transfer function is

$$H(s) = -\frac{\dfrac{1}{R_1}}{SC_2 + \dfrac{1}{R_2}} = -\frac{R_2}{R_1}\frac{1}{SR_2C_2 + 1}$$

The magnitude of frequency response is

$$|H(j\omega)| = \left|-\frac{R_2}{R_1}\frac{1}{j\omega R_2 C_2 + 1}\right| = \frac{R_2}{R_1}\frac{1}{\sqrt{(\omega R_2 C_2)^2 + 1}}$$

If $R_1 = R_2$, then the gain is $A = \dfrac{R_2}{R_1} = 1$, we design the low-pass filter to have a cutoff frequency of $f_C = 200\,\text{Hz}$ and the capacitor $C_2 = 1\mu\text{F}$, the magnitude is :

$$|H(0)| = 1, \quad |H(j\omega_c)| = \frac{1}{\sqrt{2}} \quad \text{and} \quad |H(\infty)| = 0,$$

Because of $\omega_C = \dfrac{1}{R_2 C_2}$, then we calculate

$$R_1 = R_2 = \frac{1}{\omega_C C_2} = \frac{1}{(2\pi \times 200) \times 10^{-6}} = 795.775\Omega$$

We choose the closest value resistor $R_1 = R_2 = 800\Omega$

Table 1. Low-pass filter components

Resistor 1 (R1)	Resistor 2 (R2)	Capacitor (C2)	Operational Amplifiers
800Ω	800Ω	1 μ F	LT1013ACH

2.2   The High-Pass Filter

A high-pass filter is designed to pass all frequencies above its cutoff frequency. Fig. 2 shows a typical active high-pass filter. For this filter, the transfer function is

$$H(s) = -\frac{R_2}{\dfrac{1}{sC_1} + R_1} = -\frac{SR_2 C_1}{SR_1 C_1 + 1}$$

The magnitude of frequency response is

$$|H(j\omega)| = \left| -\frac{j\omega R_2 C_1}{j\omega R_1 C_1 + 1} \right| = \frac{\omega R_2 C_1}{\sqrt{(\omega R_1 C_1)^2 + 1}}$$

If $R_1 = R_2$, the cutoff angle frequency $\omega_C = \dfrac{1}{R_1 C_1}$, the magnitude of frequency

response: $|H(0)| = 0$, $|H(j\omega_C)| = \dfrac{1}{\sqrt{2}}$ and $|H(\infty)| = 1$, we design the high pass

to have a cutoff frequency of $f_C = 800$ Hz and the capacitor $C_1 = 1\mu F$,

We can calculate $R_1 = R_2 = \dfrac{1}{\omega_C C_1} = \dfrac{1}{(2\pi \times 800) \times 10^{-6}} = 198.944\Omega$

We choose the closest value resistor $R_1 = R_2 = 200\Omega$

Table 2. High-pass filter components

Resistor 1 (R1)	Resistor 2 (R2)	Capacitor (C1)	Operational Amplifiers
200Ω	200Ω	1 μ F	LT1013ACH

2.3   The Band-Pass Filter

By cascading a unity-gain low-pass filter, a unity-gain high-pass filter, and an inverter, we can design a band-pass filter. The actual construction of the band-pass filter is shown in Fig. 3.

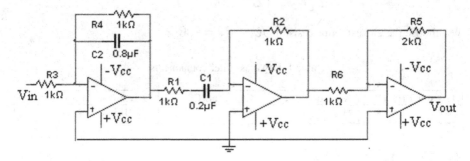

Fig. 3. Active Band-pass Filter

If $R_1 = R_2 = R_3 = R_4 = R$ then $H(s) = (-\dfrac{1}{SRC_2 + 1})(-\dfrac{SRC_1}{SRC_1 + 1})(-\dfrac{R_5}{R_6})$

and $H(j\omega) = -\dfrac{R_5}{R_6}(\dfrac{1}{j\omega RC_2 + 1})(\dfrac{j\omega RC_1}{j\omega RC_1 + 1})$

The high-pass section sets the lower corner frequency as $\omega_1 = \dfrac{1}{RC_1}$

The low-pass section sets the upper corner frequency as $\omega_2 = \dfrac{1}{RC_2}$

With these values of ω_1 and ω_2, the center frequency and bandwidth are found as follows: $\omega_0 = \sqrt{\omega_1 \omega_2}$ and $B = \omega_1 - \omega_2$

We rewrite

$$H(j\omega) = -K(\dfrac{1}{1 + j\dfrac{\omega}{\omega_2}})(\dfrac{j\dfrac{\omega}{\omega_1}}{1 + j\dfrac{\omega}{\omega_1}}) = -K(\dfrac{1}{\omega_2 + j\omega})(\dfrac{j\omega \omega_2}{\omega_1 + j\omega})$$

and $|H(j\omega_0)| = \dfrac{K\omega_2}{\omega_1 + \omega_2}$,

We set this equal to the gain of the inverting amplifier as

$\dfrac{K\omega_2}{\omega_1 + \omega_2} = \dfrac{R_5}{R_6}$ from which the gain K can be determined.

We design a band-pass filter in the form of Fig. 3 to pass frequencies between 200 Hz and 800 Hz and with $K = 10$. Select $R = 1 \text{ k}\Omega$, then we obtain

$$C_1 = \frac{1}{R\omega_1} = \frac{1}{2\pi f_1 R} = \frac{1}{2\pi \times 800 \times 10^3} = 0.19894\mu\text{F}$$

$$C_2 = \frac{1}{R\omega_2} = \frac{1}{2\pi f_2 R} = \frac{1}{2\pi \times 200 \times 10^3} = 0.79577\mu\text{F}$$

We choose the closest value capacitor $C_1 = 0.2\mu\text{F}$ and $C_2 = 0.8\mu\text{F}$

$$\frac{R_5}{R_6} = \frac{K\omega_2}{\omega_1 + \omega_2} = \frac{Kf_2}{f_1 + f_2} = \frac{10 \times 200}{800 + 200} = 2$$

If we select $R_6 = 1k\Omega$ then $R_5 = 2k\Omega$.

Table 3. Band-pass filter components

R1=R2=R3=R4=R6	R5	C1	C2	Operational Amplifiers
1kΩ	2kΩ	0.2 μ F	0.8 μ F	LT1013ACH

2.4   The Summing Amplifier

In order to test the adjustable band-pass system, we use a summing amplifier to add three other filters (low, high, band-pass) together and give the final signal to the speaker[2,3]. The input is an audio signal from a portable audio device such as an mp3 player. The diagram of the amplified speaker system is shown as Fig. 4. The summing amplifier is shown as Fig. 5.

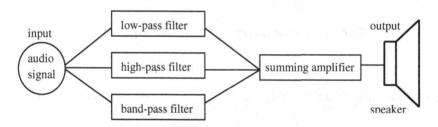

Fig. 4. Diagram of the amplified speaker system

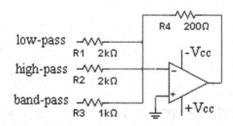

Fig. 5. Summing Amplifier

We use the potentiometers for R1 and R2, so we can control the bass and treble. We also use the potentiometer for R3 to control the volume of the system.

Table 4. Summing filter components

Potentiometer 1 (R1)	Potentiometer 2 (R2)	Potentiometer 3 (R3)	Resistor (R4)	Operational Amplifiers
2k Ω	2k Ω	1k Ω	200 Ω	LT1013ACH

3   Test Results of the Active Band-Pass Filter System

We use Multisim to simulate and test the filter system. Their magnitude frequency responses are shown as Fig. 6, 7, 8 and 9.

In the low-pass filter, at cutoff frequency of $f_C = 200$ Hz, shown as Fig. 6, the magnitude is $20\lg|H(j\omega_C)| = 20\lg\dfrac{1}{\sqrt{2}} = -3$ dB. This low-pass filter will block any frequency which is greater than 200Hz.

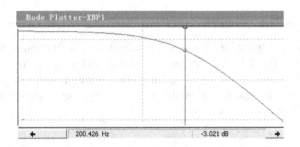

Fig. 6. Magnitude frequency response of the low-pass filter

In the high-pass filter, at cutoff frequency of $f_C = 800$ Hz, shown as Fig. 7, the magnitude is $20\lg|H(j\omega_C)| = 20\lg\dfrac{1}{\sqrt{2}} = -3$ dB, so frequencies above 800Hz can pass.

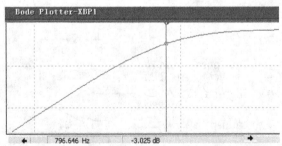

Fig. 7. Magnitude frequency response of the high-pass filter

In the band-pass filter, shown as Fig. 8, it blocks any frequency below 200Hz and above 800Hz. It only passes any frequency between 200Hz and 800Hz.

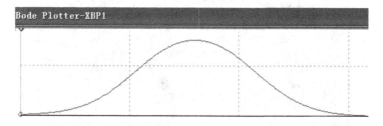

Fig. 8. Magnitude frequency response of the band-pass filter

In summing amplifier, we use the low-pass and high-pass potentiometers to control the bass and treble. We also use the summing to control the volume of the system. When we adjust the values of these resistors, we can control bass, treble and volume of audio signal.

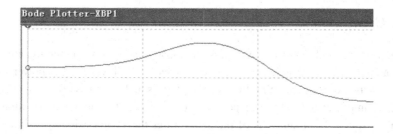

Fig. 9. Output with low-pass potentiometer at 2kΩ, high-pass potentiometer at 1.5kΩ

4   Building the Audio Amplifier

After doing various simulations with various variable resistor values and all of them coming out with acceptable outputs, we build the overall circuit construction on the breadboard. The input is connected to audio signal and the output is connected speaker. The bass, the treble and the volume work perfectly. When we adjust some potentiometers we can hear the bass or the treble being adjusted better. The final picture of the audio amplifier with treble, bass, and volume control is below:

Fig. 10. Amplified speaker system which has adjustable treble, bass and volume

5 Conclusion

This adjustable band-pass filter system needs capacitors, resistors, potentiometers, op-amps, a input jack, a portable audio device , a speaker, lead wires, a DC power supply and a breadboard. By combining low-pass, high-pass and band-pass filter signals with summing amplifier and adjusting potentiometers values the output is an adjustable band-pass signal. From analysis of the active filter theory to designing , simulating, building and testing the whole circuit, the filter system achieves the satisfying results.

References

1. Alexander, C.K., Sadiku, M.N.O.: Fundamentals of Electric Circuits. McGraw-Hill (2006)
2. Zhu, L., Sun, S., Menze, W.: Ultra-Wideband bandpass filters using multiple-mode resonator. IEEE Microwave and Wireless Components Letters, 1–3 (2005)
3. Peng, F.Z.: Application issues of active power filter. IEEE Industry Application Magazine (1998)
4. Szentirmai, G.: Synthesis of multiple-feedback active filters. BSTJ, 527–555 (April 1974)
5. Fleischer, P.E., Tow, J.: Design formulas for biquad active filters using three operational amplifiers. Proc. IEEE 61(5), 662–663 (1973)
6. Franko, S.: Design with Operational Amplifiers and Analog Integrated Circuits. McGraw–Hill (1988)

Covering Method for Short Voice Language Identification Based on PONN

Shi-jiao Zhu

School of Computer and Information Engineering,
Shanghai University of Electric Power,
Shanghai 200090,
China
zhusj707@hotmail.com

Abstract. Abstract voices verify is an important step for some applications of research related to computer. However, most of these methods suffer from accuracy and reliability problems when they are applied to a variety of voice under different conditions. Besides these issues, some methods require long training times and significant amount of parameter tuning and can not be suitable for portable platform. In this paper, it presents an architecture model for automatic language identification analysis based on human cognition but not statistical method. Firstly, voice samples are mapped into high-dimensional space. Second, it makes neurons to cover these samples. Finial, it makes measurement between trained samples and new samples. The comparison between proposed method and SVN are made, and the expected result is obtained in specter of performance and complexities.

Keywords: high-dimension space, language identification, PONN.

1 Introduction

In order to simulate man's learning, neural network are proposed to process problems and have success applied into different fields [1]. In most cases, neural networks are defined architectures. We also notice that the early links between neural network and psychology have been largely weakened. This shift was accompanied by the increasing emphasis on statistical methods, such as SVM[2] method that require a large amount of data and learn far more slowly than human beings. The mathematical orientation of researchers is closely associated with an emphasis on approaches that find the best solution to problems, while human's solution is based on heuristics which usually produce acceptable results with little effort. One of human features is forgetting brain which evaluates data with different interest according to time [3].

Automatic Language Identification has been studied using different methods, such as HMM, ANN, etc. Among these methods, there are two weakness, one is very complex, such as HMM. Anther one is black-box and very difficult to analysis, such as

F.L. Wang et al. (Eds.): CMSP 2012, CCIS 346, pp. 609–614, 2012.
© Springer-Verlag Berlin Heidelberg 2012

ANN. Feed-forward neural networks have been successfully applied to problems in pattern classification, function approximation, optimization, pattern matching [1]. Multilayer feed-forward networks which are trained by using prior fixed architecture are limited to search weight space parameters. It is known that fixed architecture network for applications are NP hard [2]. Although SVM has been used wildly, it adopts statistical theory instead of modeling the nature of human's learning. Human knowledge is always updating with time, such as old knowledge is partially replaced by newer counterpart. Knowledge has priority order. Therefore a new architecture of neural networks named Priority Ordered neural Network [3] has been introduced. In this framework, the network is constructed dynamically and the outputs of neurons are nets with different priorities. Net with a mount of neurons can proximate any function. Neurons are of different types, such as hyper-plane, RBF and so on. Each type has its own ability and formula expression. Multi-weighted neuron is the extension version of hyper-plane and RBF[1]. It is possible to use different types of neurons in one network. Since PONN can generate neural network with small prediction error in practice, we have recently investigated its abilities with different single type neuron, such as RBF function, hyper-sausage type [3]. In addition, we proposed a new general algorithm for PONN with multi-weighted neurons [4] where different type neurons with different priorities are used to cover distributions of samples in feature space.

The paper is organized as follows. Section 2 presents basic definitions and description of PONN with multi-weighted neurons. Section 3 gives a model of voice language identification. Section 4 shows its application in language identification and comparison with SVM method [5]. Finally, section 5 concludes the paper.

2   Multi-Weighted Neurons

Suppose that in PONNs, neurons or neural modules with higher property is labeled with smaller number. Special algorithm is used to construct a neural network with different priorities. The whole architecture is shown in figure 1.

Let's consider the binary classification problem. The input space is X, which is an arbitrary subset of $\mathbb{R}^n$, and the output is $Y=\{0,1\}$ which is a binary classification problem. Therefore a pair of input and output can be symbolized as $z \equiv \{x,y\}$, $x \in X, y \in Y$. The output sequence of the PONN can be written as $O = \{o_1, o_2, ..., o_p\}$ where $p(p \in Z_+)$ is the priority number which is determined in the process of network construction. The final output of PONN is Y_i where i class denotation is $Y_i = \min\{i \mid Q(o_i) = 1\}$ Where Q is a function mapping $y_i \rightarrow \{0,1\}$.

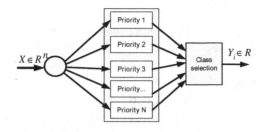

Fig. 1. The architecture of PONN

For multi-weighted neuron, formula is described as

$$\psi = f\left[\sum_{i=1}^{n} \left(\frac{w_j}{\mid w_j \mid} \right)^s \mid w_j(x_j - w_j') \mid^P - \theta \right]$$

Where θ is threshold, S is sign symbol, P is shape symbol, w' is center vector and w is direction vector. For RBF neuron, the parameters are given by $P = 2$, $w_j = 1$, $S = 1$. w_j' is center vector. For hyper-plane neuron, the parameters are given by $P = 1$, $w_j = 1$, $S = 1$. With different parameters, ψ gives different covering shapes in high dimensional space in geometric viewpoint.

For constructive algorithm, let's consider hype-ball neurons in hidden layers where high priority level is characterized by small priority number. The general algorithm can be described as follows:

Input: Feature space data set $X = \{X_1, X_2, ..., X_m\} \subset \mathbb{R}^n$, and the target is $Y \in R$ .Priority number k=1 neuron sets $\{\psi\}$, $D' = \Phi$

Output: Priority Ordered Neural Network

```
Algorithm Produrce•
While X ≠ ∅ do
For each Xᵢ in X
→get max sub set (Xᵢ,ₛᵤᵦ) of Xᵢ and its min Euclid dis-
tance•d•of Xⱼ,ᵢ≠ⱼ
→use hype-ball neuron(ψ,d) to cover Xᵢ,ₛᵤᵦ,and set
priority k to neuronψ
→add Xᵢ,ₛᵤᵦ to temp setD'
End of for
→set X-D' to X,D'=Φ
k = k + 1
```

End while
For new coming data, PONN will update the priority number
of neuron or add new neuron with a special priority. Here
is the algorithm:
Input: new feature training

set $X'=\{X'_1,X'_2,...,X'_m\}\subset \mathbb{R}^n$, $Y\in R$.

Output: Updated Priority Ordered Neural Network
Algorithm Produrce•
While $X'\neq\phi$ *do*

For each X'_i *in* X'

$\rightarrow$*Get a consistent subset* $X'_{i,sub}$ *of* X_i *randomly,* and then
do the following produce:
If covered($X'_{i,sub}$ *)*

do nothing
else
  if(misclassified($X'_{i,sub}$ *))*
  adjust covering space range of hyper-ball neuron ψ *and*
adjust its priority number to lower one.
else
  add new neuron with higher priority number k.
end if
end if
$\rightarrow$*add* $X'_{i,sub}$ *to temp set* D

End of for
$\rightarrow$*set* $X-D$ *to* X', $D=\Phi$
End while

When new samples input into PONN, the priority level of hidden neurons is strengthened or weaken. Using this method method , the old information is not destroyed
(forgot) after new data learning, but can be partly fetched at any latest priority. This
produrce is similar to man's learning procedure. As this updating and learning method
is only to adjust the special priority level of neurons, therefore, it can process large
data set with more effective heuristic algorithm. Next we will give an example of the
methods.

3   Algorithm

Let's consider distributions of languages in high-dimensional space X. Assuming that
the distributions are skewed but can be separated by neurons ψ mapping in PONN
with different priority number. Then the ALI model can be written as

$$\psi_{priority} \longrightarrow X$$

$$O_{AVLI} = \{o_1, o_2, ..., o_p\}$$

Where $\psi_{priority}$ is neurons with different priority number, X is ALI samples. O_{AVLI} is the output of PONN. o_p is the output of neural network for special language p.

For a period Voice, we will split it into some little pieces voice and transform it into eigenvector in feature space. The ultimate identify formula is written as

$$O_{AVLI} = \{O_{AVLI(1)}, O_{AVLI(2)}, ..., O_{AVLI(k)}\}$$

Where $O_{AVLI(i)}$ is the i piece time quantum. The last result is written as

$$\max\{count(i) \mid O_{AVLI(i)} = O_{AVLI(j)}, i \neq j\}$$

Where $count(i)$ is a function of taking sum number of same class in distinguished sequence.

4   Experience Results

Our experiment uses data of Chinese, English and Japanese language voice. The voice is partitioned into same time pieces and been translated into MFCC features [7]. The experiment is performed using methods of PONN and SVM in different dimension feature space [8]. The samples number is 223, 474, and 107 respectively in Table 1. Table 2 is the comparative results.

Table 1. Training Number of different language

		Training1	Training2	Training3	Training4	Training5
	Time	0.512s	1.008s	1.504s	2.000s	2.496s
Training	Chinese	5301	2323	1325	827	567
Number	English	9452	4254	2449	1611	1119
of sam-	Japanese	2126	1007	623	427	315
ples	Total	16879	7584	4397	2865	2001

Table 2. Comparative results of using PONN and SVM models

Dimension Size		496	992	1488	1984	2480
	Chinese	94.170	91.031	91.928	89.238	77.130
PONN	English	88.608	84.177	84.177	76.160	86.709
	Japanese	98.131	95.327	88.785	80.374	83.178
	AVG	91.418	87.562	86.940	80.348	83.831

Table 2. (*continued*)

	Chinese	92.562	89.256	92.562	90.083	81.818
SVM	English	88.104	84.758	82.156	75.836	90.706
	Japanese	93.443	93.443	95.082	86.885	80.328
	AVG	90.244	87.140	86.696	81.153	87.140

Table2 shows the generalization of PONN is more competitive than SVM in low dimension. Therefore, PONN is another method of solution based on human's reorganization with simple implementation which is a core issue in real application fields.

5   Conclusions

This paper reports a method of Automatic Language Identification Analysis using PONN which is biologically based on human's dynamic neurons. The primitive test gives satisfactory result. More studies in the aspect of basic theory inspired by biology should be invested in future.

References

[1] Galushkin, A.I.: Neural Network Theory. Springer, New York (2007)
[2] Judd, J.S.: Learning in networks is hards. In: Proceedings of the First International Conference on Neural Networks, SanDiego, CA, vol. 2, pp. 585–692 (1987)
[3] Wang, S.: Priority Ordered Neural Networks with Better Similarity to Human Knowledge Representation. Chinese Jounal of Electronics 8(1), 1–4 (1999)
[4] Wang, S.J.: Bionic (topological) pattern recognition − A new model of pattern recognition theory and its applications. Acta Electron. Sinica 30(10), 1–4 (2002)
[5] Chen, G.Y., Xie, W.F.: Pattern recognition with SVM and dual-tree complex wavelets. Image and Vision Computing 25(1), 960–966 (2007)
[6] Langford, J.: Tutorial on practical prediction theory for classification. Journal of Machine Learning Research 3, 273–306 (2005)
[7] Kim, H.K., Rose, R.C.: Cepstrum-domain acoustic feature compensation based on decomposition of speech and noise for ASR in noisy environments. IEEE Trans. Speech Audio Process. 11(5), 435–446 (2003)
[8] Chang, C., Lin, C.-J.: LIBSVM: - A Library for Support Vector Machines [EB/OL] (2006), http://www.csie.ntu.edu.tw/~cjlin/libsvm

Automatic Phonetic Segmentation
Using HMM Model in Uyghur Language

Gulnar Eli[1] and Askar Hamdulla[2]

[1] Institute of Information Science and Engineering of Xinjiang University,
Urumqi 830046
[2] Institute of Software of Xinjiang University,
Urumqi 830046
askar@xju.edu.cn

Abstract. Correct segmentation of phonetic unit is important to the performance of TTS system. This paper evaluated automatic segmentation of phonetic unit separately based on monophone HMM and context dependent tri-phone HMM. First, training data for HMM models was prepared, then, monophone HMM and context dependent tri-phone HMM was trained using the training data, finally, phoneme unit boundary was segmented based on these HMM models and the result of auto segmentation was analyzed. According to syllable rule and word rule in Uyghur language, syllable boundary and word boundary was obtained based on the phoneme boundary segmented. The experiments shows that the accuracy of segmentation based on phoneme based HMM and context dependent tri-phone HMM is 73.36% and 85.74%. Automatic segmentation of phonetic unit was significant to improve the efficiency and accuracy of Uyghur speech database construction.

Keywords: phonetic unit, Automatic segmentation, HMM, Uyghur language.

1 Introduction

In waveform concatenation speech synthesis system, speech units were chosen from a pre-recorded sound library by using direct waveform concatenation method. It is possible to concatenate any sentences even has the potential to retain the characteristics of the original pronunciation if only the sound library includes speech units in a variety of context. Speech unit segmentation and the accuracy of the labels directly affect the quality of synthesized speech; segmentation includes both manual and automatic method. Although the artificial segmentation can guarantee certain accuracy, however, due to its need for a very experienced person, very time-consuming and also limited by the physiological factors and attention of the person, moreover, consistency between people is not ideal, so, it takes long time to construct the library. The results of manual segmentation require repeated proofreading to ensure consistency. At present, in most of the voice systems, speech unit segmentation and labeling process is finished manually. In contrast, automatic segmentation methods in these areas

F.L. Wang et al. (Eds.): CMSP 2012, CCIS 346, pp. 615–623, 2012.

with predominance do not require manual labeling, and have a good segmentation consistency.

There are two kinds of automatic segmentation methods: 1) based on the template 2) based on the model, Hidden Markov Model (HMM) as the representative.

Basic principle of the first method is to align the template with the given voice observations by using dynamic programming approach; the second method used the state model while align, did not use a template, other principles are same to the first method. It can be seen from the research result of reference [1], HMM-based approach has better results than a template-based method. Thus, this paper used HMM-based method to segment the voice unit of Uyghur. First, mapped speech unit text to a string of hidden Markov state model then by Viterbi algorithm searched out the best match transfer path, and obtained the boundary of each voice unit.

In recent years, Uyghur speech synthesis technology has made great progress as a core technology in information process of Uyghur minority. In which, speech unit segmentation is always tagged by manually. due to manual tagging has drawbacks mentioned above, studying the automatic segmentation method which is suitable for the Uyghur can help to save the time and effort, and improve the efficiency and accuracy of Uyghur speech corpus construction work. In this paper, mono-phone and context-sensitive HMM models are used to implement the automatic segmentation of Uyghur voice unit boundary.

2   Grammar Introduction of Uyghur Language

Xinjiang Uyghur Autonomous region is located the northwest part of china. The Uyghur language is the main language in this region and belongs to the Altaic Turkic west Hungarian language branch. In structure grammar, Uyghur is an adhesive and alphabetic language based on Arabic.

The structure of Uyghur language can be divided into five levels which are sentences, words, syllables and phonemes. In which there has 32 phonemes including eight vowels and 24 consonants. Phonemes make up syllables, syllables make up words, words make up sentences, and the space is a word delimiter.

In Uyghur, words are composed of syllables, such as word "كەسكىنلىك" can be divided into "كەس","كىن" and "لىك" three syllables. Syllables can be divided into phonemes, such as syllable "كەس" composed of "ئە"، "ك" and"س"

3   Preparatory Works

Preparatory works before training the model include sample selection, manual segmentation and data preparation.

3.1   Training Sample Selection

Training sample selection is to select the samples which can cover the natural language phenomenon from the mass samples, selection method used greedy algorithm [2].

Uighur language has 32 phonemes, plus short pause and silence pause, a total of 34 phoneme units, table 1 is the Uyghur phoneme automatic segmentation list used in this paper. We should take tri-phones into consideration to the HMM automatic segmentation sample (former phoneme-current phoneme-next phoneme), i.e. m-a-n. the number of possible phoneme combination in Uyghur is 37984, in which ,some tri-phones are not included in Uyghur or not appear frequently。 Considering the widest coverage of the tri-phones, we chose 1025 sentence by using the optimal text selection algorithm presented in reference [2] from the corpus (includes 708,322 sentences and 13,607,507 words) which is developed by the Xinjiang University Intelligent information processing laboratory.

Table 1. Phoneme list in Uyghur

Phoneme	English form	Phoneme	English form
ئا	a	ل	l
ب	b	م	m
د	d	ن	n
ئې	e	ڭ	ng
ئە	ea	ئۆ	ou
ف	f	ئو	o
گ	g	پ	p
غ	gi	ج	q
خ	h	ر	r
ھ	hi	س	s
ئى	i	ت	t
ج	j	ئۇ	u
ك	k	ئۈ	v
ق	ki	ۋ	w
ش	x	ژ	zi
ي	y	Short pause	sp
ز	z	Long silence	sil

3.2   Manual Segmentation

For selected training samples conduct recording and manual segmentation. Considering the context-based tri-phone model, the manual segmentation not only segment the phoneme boundary, but also have to segment the boundaries of syllable, word, prosodic word, prosodic phrase, clause and sentence, segment using Praat tool by laboratory personnel with a certain label experience, Praat tool by laboratory personnel with a certain label experience, segmentation, segmentation results are used to generate the training required for HMM model of the lab files.

This paper manually cut the level of phoneme syllables, words, prosodic word, prosodic phrase, clause and sentence, 1025 sentences for selected training samples conducted Praat manual segmentation get the corresponding label file (the TextGrid file).

3.3   Data Preparation

Model training needs the speech files and corresponding lab files. The speech files generated by the recording of the training sample, the lab file conduct final treatment for manually segmented voice file generated after annotation file (the TextGrid file). There are three kinds of lab files:

1) Single phoneme listing lab files
Listing lab, Automatic segmentation need to use such documents, the following format:

    n
    a
    h
    x
    a

Lab files with time–dimension label (monolab), this file is only used in the training of HMM model.

2) Segmentation does not require this file. Each line of this file contains a phoneme start time, end time and phoneme name, the format is as follows:

    15922788   17302350   n
    17302350   17962141   a
    17962141   18771884   h
    18771884   20361379   x
    20361379   20991179   a

3)Context-correlated label lab files(full lab), this file will be used in training and segmentation.

Each line in this file contains a three-phoneme and its context features. HMM model training required that context attributes set and questions set need to be designed before the file is ready [3], Each line details are longer, the format is omitted here, specifically refer to [3].Corresponding with the two models,Each training speech file corresponding with a time dimension lab files and a context-correlated label lab files. Each test speech file corresponding to a single phoneme listing lab file and context-correlated label lab files.

4   HMM Model Training

When the data preparation end, need to be defined the HMM prototype before training the HMM model, design the HMM topology, the number of states, Gaussian mixture number, dimensions of spectral parameters etc. traditional training used maximum likelihood (ML) estimation method, which can train the data which is not tagged manually, however, in order to guarantee the high accuracy rate of segmentation, it is necessary to train certain amount of manual tagged data.

In this paper estimated the mono-phone HMM model and tri-phone HMM model parameters which are related with context using EM algorithm while training HMM model. In this paper, by using HInit and Hrest tool in HTK toolkit realized the HMM training. HMM training process includes the following eight steps:

1) Initializing the mono-phone HMM model
2) Through EM (Expectation maximization) algorithm find out the maximum likelihood estimation of mono-phone model parameters.
3) Extent the mono-phone HMM model into context-based triphone HMM model.
4) Find out the maximum likelihood estimation of tri-phone model parameters via EM algorithm.
5) make a state clustering by classification and recession tree to the states of tri-phone model
6) gradually increase the number of Gaussian mixture components in each state of the tri-phone HMM model
7) Find out the maximum likelihood estimation of the model parameters by through iteration
8) Repeat the step (6) and (7) several times.

In this paper, we achieved two kind of models after HMM training based on the training data, The first model is monophone HMM model(monophone.mmf),this model includes different mono-phone models which appear in training corpus; The second model is context-sensitive tri-phone model after clustering(clustered.mmf).

5   Automatic Phoneme Segmentation

In this paper, we realized the segmentation process by using Hvite in HTK tool, below is the segmentation process:

1)   Calculate the spectrum parameters and basic frequencies through wave which need to be segmented.
2)   Create the lab file through tagged file.
3)   Make model predictions through HHEd.
4)   Achieve the segmented file after Hvite segmenting

Figure 1 shows the automatic segmentation process. the two segmentation methods used in this paper are basically same, the difference is that in the mono-phone automatic segmentation, provides the corresponding mono-phone list file and mono-phone HMM model of every sentence which need to be segmented , but in context-sensitive HMM model segmentation ,provides context-sensitive tagged lab file and tri-phone HMM model; Another difference is that in mono-phone HMM model segmentation, do not need to model prediction(segmentation step 3), but in context-sensitive HMM model automatic segmentation it requires model prediction.

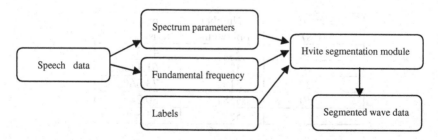

Fig. 1. Automatic segmentation processes

6   Experiments and Analysis

After eliminating the sentences which have problems during recording from the collected1025 sentences, the final 1000 sentences used as the experimental data by manually tagging, and prepared the mono-phone list lab file, time tagged lab file, context-sensitive tagged lab file. After preparing the data, training the mono-phone HMM model and context-sensitive HMM model and realized the automatic segmentation of these two models.

We carried the segmentation by choosing 900 sentences as training data and the rest 100 sentences as test data. Finally compared and analyzed the result of two kinds of segmentation and manually segmentation, make a comparison to the time period of every phoneme, and find out the error range.

6.1   Performance Evaluation Method of Automatic Segmentation

While evaluating the automatic segmentation performance, a method is used which believe that manually tagged boundary as the correct boundary and when the boundary points of automatic segmentation and the time deviation between correct boundaries is $\pm T$, that the segmentation boundary is right boundary, otherwise is wrong boundary, T called fault-tolerant threshold.

Fault-tolerant threshold is the percentage of the number of boundaries which are correctly and automatically segmented to the total number of segmented boundaries. In speech synthesis, usually fault-tolerant threshold for the automatic segmentation is 20ms.

6.2   Mono-Phones Based HMM Automatic Segmentation

100 sentences include 6955 phonemes. After calculating the fundamental frequency and spectral parameters of these 100 sentences, based on the mono-phone list of each sentence correspond with (one phoneme per line) and the trained mono-phone HMM implemented the segmentation, automatic and manually segmentation results were compared and analyzed, Table 2 shows the time period statistical result of error range of each phoneme

Table 2. Automatic segmentation accuracy of mono-phone based HMM model

error range (ms)	Number of phoneme	proportions
5	3225	46.37%
10	4250	61.11%
20	5102	73.36%
30	5581	80.24%
40	5877	84.50%

In which, $\overline{W}$ represents the average error range,

$$\overline{W} = \frac{1}{6995} \sum_{i=1}^{6995} w_i = 24.45\text{ms}$$

w_i is the error range of one phoneme.

6.3   Automatic Segmentation of Context-Sensitive Tri-Phone HMM

After calculating the fundamental frequency and spectral parameters of 100 sentences, and according to the time tagged file and context-sensitive tagged file which corresponding to each sentence, make segmentation on the basis of trained context-sensitive HMM, compared the result to the manually segmentation result and make an analysis on it, Table 3 shows the time period statistical result of error range of each phoneme

Table 3. Automatic segmentation accuracy of tri-phone based HMM model

Error range(ms)	Number of phonemes	proportion
5	5704	82.01%
10	5797	83.35%
20	5963	85.74%
30	6144	88.34%
40	6231	89.59%

In which, $\overline{W}$ still represents the average error range,

$$\overline{W} = \frac{1}{6995} \sum_{i=1}^{6995} w_i = 13.14\text{ms}$$

w_i is the error range of one phoneme.

After achieving the phoneme boundaries, also can be achieved the syllable boundary and word boundary according to the rules of syllable and words in Uyghur.

7   Comparative Analyses

Same with general speech synthesis system, in large corpus based Uyghur speech synthesis system, We examine the fault-tolerant threshold is 20ms, The comparative analysis of these two kinds of segmentation shows that the performance of context-sensitive tri-phone based HMM segmentation is higher than   the mono-phone based HMM automatic segmentation method, Shown in Figure 2.

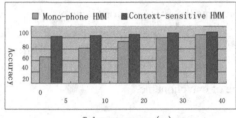

Fig. 2. Automatic segmentation accuracy rate comparison charts

8   Conclusions

In this paper, presents the automatic segmentation of Uyghur speech unit through mono-phone HMM model and context-sensitive HMM model, Experiments show that the performance of context-sensitive HMM segmentation is higher than the mono-phone based HMM automatic segmentation method. But, segmentation method of mono-phone HMM model is simple, we can use this method while can' not automatically generate context-sensitive tagged lab file.

Automatic segmentation method presents in this paper segmented the speech unit boundary accurately and consistently, through segmenting the boundary of phoneme, combining with the rules of syllables and words in Uyghur achieved the boundaries of syllables and words, can further achieved the boundary of prosodic word, prosodic phrase , intonation phrase and sentence. Thus can be saved a lot of time and effort, eliminated the mechanical steps to reduce the workload of sound library construction, Improve the accuracy of the speech corpus annotation.

Acknowledgements. This work is supported by Program for New Century Excellent Talents in University (NCET-10-0969), and Natural Science Foundation of China (No. 61062008, 61065005), and Key Technologies R&D Program of China (2009BAH41B03).

References

[1] Paulo, S., Oliveira, L.C.: DTW-based phonetic alignment using multiple acoustic features. In: Proceeding of Euro Speech, Geneva, Switzerland, pp. 309–312 (2003)
[2] Mamateli, G., Ruzi, A., Hamdulla, A.: Uyghur sentence selection algorithm of thriphone model. Computer Engineering and Applications 45(18), 242–244 (2009)
[3] Ruzi, A.: Research and Implementation of HMM Based Uyghur Speech Synthesis System. Xinjiang University (2008)
[4] Memeteli, G.: Research and Implementation of key Technologies in UTTS Based on two-level Speech Units and Prosodic Parameters, pp. 9–14. School of information science and engineering, Urumqi (2009)
[5] Huang, X.D., Acero, A., Hon, H.W.: Spoken language processing, pp. 304–316. Prentice Hall PTR, Upper Saddle River (2001)

[6] Wang, L.-J., Cao, Z.-G.: Automatic Phonetic Segmentation Using HMM Model. Journal of Data Acquisition & Processing 20(4), 381–384 (2005)
[7] Chen, K., Chai, P.Q.: Improving the Accuracy of English Automatic Seg-mentation. Microelectronics & Computer 21(5), 118–120 (2004)
[8] Ghopur, A.: Research and Implementation of Algorithms for Automatic Segmentation of Phonemes in Uyghur Continuous Speech, pp. 43–48. Institute of information science and engineering, Xinjiang University, Urumqi, Xinjiang (2011)

Design and Implementation of Voice Conversion System Based on GMM and ANN

Man Yang, Dashun Que, and Bei Li

Wuhan University of Technology,
Information Engineering College,
Wuhan 430063, P.R. China
pipayang0503@163.com

Abstract. Voice conversion has become one current researching hotspot in speech signal processing. The article designs and establishes a voice conversion system based on Gaussian mixture model (GMM) and Artificial Neural Network (ANN) after researching the existing voice conversion algorithms. The core is to obtain respectively three mapping rules by training spectral envelope and its residual with GMM, and pitch contrail with BP network. And the voice is transformed according to the three mapping rules above. Finally, the algorithm simulation, the system implementation and algorithm performance evaluating of voice conversion is completed. The theoretic analysis and simulating results reveal that the algorithm and the system of voice conversion are effective.

Keywords: Voice conversion, GMM, ANN, residual, pitch.

1 Introduction

Voice conversion is a technique that modifies a source speaker's speech to make it sound like uttered by another (the target) speaker without changing the speech content [1]. Voice conversion has become one of current researching hotspots in speech signal processing, which has been widely applied to many domains such front-end of speaker recognition, text to speech, human-computer interaction, voice restoration, film dubbing, and speech camouflage and secure communication.

There are various researches about voice conversion algorithms of the speech spectrum at home and abroad. For example, codebook mapping algorithm[2], Dynamic Time Warping[3], Artificial Neural Network[4], Gaussian mixture model[4], Hidden Markov Model[5]. These algorithms play a positive role for spectral envelope conversion; however, it still has difference between the converted speech spectral envelope and the target. Therefore, further research about efficient conversion algorithms of the spectral envelope is needed. The treatment of the excitation signal and residual signal enhance the characteristic of target in voice conversion in some degree. But there are still some distortions between converted incentive and objective encouragement. Prosodic features especially pitch has played a major role in confirming speaker's identity, which contains a great deal of speaker's identity

F.L. Wang et al. (Eds.): CMSP 2012, CCIS 346, pp. 624–631, 2012.

information. However, there are few researches about rhythm conversion at present. And its research focuses generally on the transformation of pitch.

This article tries to train the spectral envelope and its residual using GMM and simulates the prosodic features of target speech using a BP network. Then, transforming spectrum characteristics and prosodic features of source speaker's speech according to the mapping rules, and speech synthesis has target characteristics. The algorithm simulation and the system performance evaluating of voice conversion is completed. The theoretic analysis and computer simulation results reveal that the method and the system of voice conversion are effective.

2   System Design of Voice Conversion

Generally, the procedure of voice conversion mainly contains training stage and conversion stage. In the training stage, the source speaker's speech and the target speaker's speech are trained respectively in order to estimate mapping rules. The relationship between source and target of model parameter can also be obtained. In the conversion stage, source speech is transformed by the mapping rules.

Based on the LPC algorithm, the converted voice tends to target voice by adjusting suprasegmental features. The paper divides the algorithm into three modules. Transforming the spectral envelope and its residual is introduced in the first and second module. Module 3 describes the conversion of suprasegmental features. In the conversion of spectral envelope and its residual signal, the GMM based methods is more succeed in preventing the spectral envelope from over-smoothing than another methods to some extent. The conversion of residual completely keeps target speaker's information of spectra excitation. The BP algorithm is performed for pitch frequencies transformation. We could convert most personality of source speaker to target speaker. Because of unvoiced sound contains less speaker's information, the voice conversion system copies the voiceless sound directly and transforms frames of voiced sound.

Figure 1 and Figure 2 separately show the diagram of training and conversion combined with GMM and ANN. To test the validity of the algorithms, the tests of Chinese speaker's speech are given. The experiments are divided into four groups: male to male, female to female, male to female and female to male. The order of LPC is 12 and the number of GMM is 64.

3   Principle and Implementation of Voice Conversion Algorithm

3.1   Spectral Envelope Conversion

LSF has better interpolation property compare to LPC, which can transform each other. Therefore, we can achieve the conversion of speech spectral envelope by transforming LSF.

In the training stage, the article tries to find conversion functions by dealing with source and target speech, such as preemphasis, removing background noise, getting frames of speech, obtaining LPC by autocorrelation function. And LPC is transformed into LSF. At last, LSF parameters are trained by GMM.

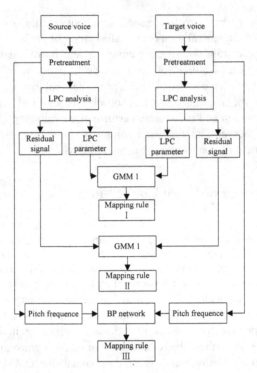

Fig. 1. Training diagram of voice conversion

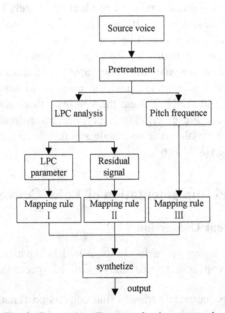

Fig. 2. Conversion diagram of voice conversion

The GMM with the number of Q assumes that the probability distribution of the observed parameters takes the followings parametric form [2][3]:

$$P(X) = \sum_{q=1}^{Q} \alpha_q N\left(x, \mu_q, \Sigma_q\right), \quad \sum_{q=1}^{Q} \alpha_q = 1, \alpha_q \geq 1 \tag{1}$$

Where α_q is the weighted coefficient of the number q and $N\left(x, \mu_q, \Sigma_q\right)$ denotes the p-dimensional normal distribution with mean vector μ_q and covariance matrix Σ_q defined by:

$$N(x; \mu, \Sigma) = \frac{1}{(2\pi)^{p/2}\sqrt{|\Sigma|}} \exp(-\frac{1}{2}(x-\mu)^T \Sigma^{-1}(x-\mu)) \tag{2}$$

The parameters of the GMM such as $\alpha_q, \mu_q, \Sigma_q$ can be estimated with the expectation-maximization (EM) algorithm.

In the conversion stage, the parameters of the conversion function are estimated by the joint density of source and target features. A joint vector $Z = [X^T Y^T]^T$, where X and Y are the aligned source and target feature, is used to estimate GMM parameters. The following form is assumed for the conversion function:

$$F(x) = \sum_{q=1}^{Q} (\mu_q^Y + \Sigma_q^{YX} (\Sigma_q^{XX})^{-1}(x-\mu_q^X)) \cdot p(c_q \mid x) \tag{3}$$

Where $p(c_q \mid x)$ is the conditional probability that a given observation vector x belongs to the acoustic class c_q of the GMM.

$$p(c_q \mid x) = \frac{\alpha_q N(x; \mu_q^X, \Sigma_q^{XX})}{\sum_{q=1}^{Q} \alpha_q N(x; \mu_q^X, \Sigma_q^{XX})} \tag{4}$$

$$\mu_q = \begin{bmatrix} \mu_q^X \\ \mu_q^Y \end{bmatrix}; \Sigma_q = \begin{bmatrix} \Sigma_q^{XX} & \Sigma_q^{XY} \\ \Sigma_q^{YX} & \Sigma_q^{YY} \end{bmatrix} \tag{5}$$

Experiments of above-mentioned algorithms are simulated. Choose one group of male voices and one group of female voices as experimental data to show and analyze. Figure 3 shows the converted envelope by GMM.

From Figure 3, we can see that the converted LPC is like the target LPC; it shows that the spectral envelope conversion with GMM is feasible.

3.2   Residual Conversion

The excitation source of speech contains a large number of speaker identification information, which can reflect speaker features. Transforming excitation source can improve quality of converted voice. Residual signal of target speaker is mainly used in residual prediction. The conversion system adopt LPC synthesis model [3][4].

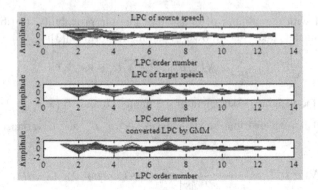

Fig. 3. The spectral envelope before and after conversion

The linear predictive residual signal $r_{n \times N}$ is obtained by sending target LPC and speech signal through inverse filter. Where n is the number of sampling points of each frame residual signal and N is frame. Then, LSF of target voiced sound is classified as $(C_1, C_2 \ldots C_Q)$ with GMM after voiced and unvoiced decision. According to the posterior probability, $p(c_q \mid y)$ is defined as follows:

$$p(c_q \mid y) = \frac{\alpha_q N(y; \mu_q, \Sigma_q)}{\sum\limits_{q=1}^{Q} \alpha_q N(y; \mu_q, \Sigma_q)} (\alpha_q, \mu_q, \Sigma_q) \tag{6}$$

$$N(y; \mu, \Sigma) = \frac{1}{(2\pi)^{p/2} \sqrt{|\Sigma|}} \exp(-\frac{1}{2}(y-\mu)^T \Sigma^{-1}(y-\mu)) \tag{7}$$

Where each component of posterior probability $p(c_q \mid y)$ is taken as weight of residual codebooks. The number of codebook Q can be determined by GMM. The least mean square error to calculate residual codebooks is $R = \left[R_1, R_2, \cdots, R_Q \right]$.

$$R = (\sum_{i=1}^{N} r_i p(c_q \mid y))(\sum_{i=1}^{N} p(c_q \mid y)'p(c_q \mid y))^{-1} \tag{8}$$

Where r_i is the linear predictive residual signal of voiced sound. According to the formula $\hat{r}_i = R p(\hat{y})$, target residual signal $\hat{r}_i$ is estimated at the conversion stage.

Experiments of above-mentioned algorithms are simulated. Choose one group of male voices and one group of female voices as experimental data to show and analyze. Figure 4 shows the converted residual with GMM.

From Figure 4, we can see that the converted residual signal is like the target residual no matter time domain waveform or energy; it shows that the residual conversion by GMM is feasible.

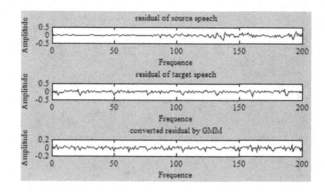

Fig. 4. The residual before and after conversion

3.3 Pitch Frequency Conversion

Firstly, pitch frequency of source and target is extracted with autocorrelation method. Secondly, size is necessary in normalization processing which are normalized to 30. Lastly, we can respectively deserve relatively pitch frequency of source and target by deducting the mean values of basic frequency.

A three-layer structure BP network is used in this work to obtain the mapping function about the rhythm of source and target speech in the training stage. The relatively pitch frequency of source speech is inputted while the relatively pitch frequency of target is outputted. Among them, linear function is used in the hidden layer. The formula is defined as $y = x$. We use one hundred training samples. Weight W_{ij} from the input layer to the hidden layer and weight W_{jk} from the hidden layer to the input layer are obtained [4].

In the conversion stage, the relatively pitch frequency of source speech is inputted into BP network. We can calculate the output of the hidden layer with the formula of $h_j = \sum_{i=1}^{30} W_{ij} x_i$. The converted relatively pitch frequency is obtained with the formula of $h_k = \sum_{j=1}^{30} W_{jk} h_j$. The converted relatively pitch frequency is added to the mean values of basic frequency. Then, the size of converted pitch frequency is adjusted to same frames of source speech.

Experiments of above-mentioned algorithms are simulated. Choose one group of male voices and one group of female voices as experimental data to show and analyze. Figure 5 shows the converted pitch frequency with BP network.

From Figure 5, we can see that the converted pitch frequency is more like the target pitch frequency. It shows that BP network can better realize nonlinear mapping between the pitch frequencies.

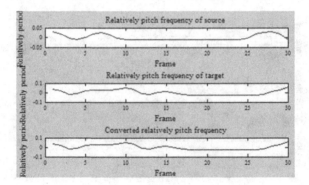

Fig. 5. Pitch before and after conversion

4   Experiments and Evaluation of Voice Conversion System

In order to evaluate the voice conversion system, we choose 15 different sentences to test and analyze one group of experimental result. The experiment includes male-male, female-female, male-female and female-male.

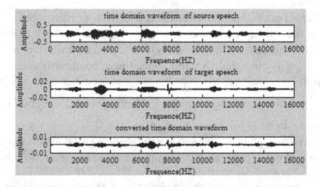

Fig. 6. The time domain waveform before and after conversion

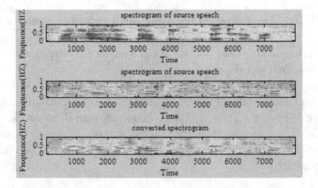

Fig. 7. Spectrogram before and after conversion

Figure 6 shows that the converted time domain waveform is more like the target. Figure 7 show that there has little difference between the converted spectrogram and the target in energy and pitch. But the converted speech has personality characteristics of target. It shows that the voice conversion system is effective.

Experiments results are analyzed with one way of subjective evaluation ABX [3] [4]. Every listener listen the converted voice. The listener give either A or B as being most similar to X. The correct rate increase when X is the right speaker. Table 1 shows ABX test results of the fifteen sub experiments under four different experimental conditions. In ABX test, the value "0" indicates entirely difference, "1" indicates different, "2" indicates difficult to be judged, "3" indicates the same, "4" indicates completely identical.

Table 1. ABX test results

speaker	Source to target	Converted to target
male-male	1.8	3.2
female-female	1.6	3.5
male-female	0.9	3.8
female-male	0.9	3.5

Table 1 show that the converted speech is more similar to target than source. The similarity of the same sex is higher than the different sex after voice conversation. This is mainly because pitch and spectral envelop of the same sex is nearer than the different sex. So the conversion error is small.

5   Conclusions

This paper adopts a voice conversion algorithm based on GMM and ANN and designs a voice conversion system. Jointly the two algorithms are performed for envelope and pitch frequencies transformation. The theoretic analysis and simulating results reveal that the algorithm and the system of voice conversion are effective.

References

1. Percybrooks, W.S., Moore, E.: Voice conversion with linerar prediction residual estimation. In: ICASSP 2008 IEEE, pp. 4673–4676 (2008)
2. Xie, W.-C., Zhang, L.-H.: Research on Voice Conversion based Codebook and GMM. In: 2010 IEEE, pp. 1403–1406 (2010)
3. Song, P., Zhao, L.: Improving the Performance of GMM Based Voice Conversion Method. In: 2008 IEEE, pp. 456–460 (2008)
4. Peng, D., Zhang, X., Sun, J.: Voice Conversion Based on GMM and Artificial Neural Network. In: ICASSP 2010 IEEE, pp. 1121–1124 (2010)
5. Wu, C.-H., Hsia, C.-C., Liu, T.-H., Wang, J.-F.: Voice Conversion Using Duration-Embedded Bi-HMMs for Expressive Speech Synthesis. IEEE Transactions on Audio, Speech, and Language Processing 14, 1109–1116 (2006)

Author Index